# Semantic Web Services:
## Theory, Tools, and Applications

Jorge Cardoso
*University of Madeira, Portugal*

**Information Science REFERENCE**

**INFORMATION SCIENCE REFERENCE**

Hershey • New York

Acquisitions Editor:          Kristin Klinger
Development Editor:           Kristin Roth
Senior Managing Editor:       Jennifer Neidig
Managing Editor:              Sara Reed
Assistant Managing Editor:    Sharon Berger
Copy Editor:                  Julie LeBlanc
Typesetter:                   Elizabeth Duke
Cover Design:                 Lisa Tosheff
Printed at:                   Yurchak Printing Inc.

Published in the United States of America by
    Information Science Reference (an imprint of IGI Global)
    701 E. Chocolate Avenue, Suite 200
    Hershey PA 17033
    Tel: 717-533-8845
    Fax:  717-533-8661
    E-mail: cust@idea-group.com
    Web site: http://www.idea-group-ref.com

and in the United Kingdom by
    Information Science Reference (an imprint of IGI Global)
    3 Henrietta Street
    Covent Garden
    London WC2E 8LU
    Tel: 44 20 7240 0856
    Fax:  44 20 7379 0609
    Web site: http://www.eurospanonline.com

Library of Congress Cataloging-in-Publication Data

Semantic Web services : theory, tools and applications / Jorge Cardoso, editor.

    p. cm.

 Summary: "This book brings together researchers, scientists, and representatives from different communities to study, understand, and explore the theory, tools, and applications of the semantic Web. It joins the semantic Web, ontologies, knowledge management, Web services, and Web processes into one fully comprehensive resource, serving as the platform for exchange of both practical technologies and research"--Provided by publisher.

 Includes bibliographical references and index.

 ISBN 978-1-59904-045-5 (hardcover) -- ISBN 978-1-59904-047-9 (ebook)

 1. Semantic Web. 2. Web services. I. Cardoso, Jorge, 1970-

 TK5105.88815.S45 2006

 025.04--dc22

                              2006033762

British Cataloguing in Publication Data
A Cataloguing in Publication record for this book is available from the British Library.

# Table of Contents

# Detailed Table of Contents

**Chapter I**

This chapter gives an overview of the evolution of the Web. Initially, Web pages were specified syntactically and were intended only for human consumption. New Internet business models, such as B2B and B2C, require information on the Web to be defined semantically in a way that it can be used by computers, not only for display purposes, but also for interoperability and integration. To achieve this new type of Web, called Semantic Web, several technologies are being developed, such as the resource description framework and the Web Ontology Language.

**Chapter II**

This chapter introduces several formal logical languages which form the backbone of the Semantic Web. The basis for all these languages is the classical first-order logic. Some of the languages presented include description logics, frame logic and RuleML.

**Chapter III**

The term "ontological engineering" defines the set of activities that concern the ontology development process, the ontology life cycle, the principles, methods and methodologies for building ontologies, and the tool suites and languages that support them. In this chapter we provide an overview of ontological engineering, describing the current trends, issues and problems.

The activities associated with Ontological Engineering require dedicated tools. One of the first activities is to find a suitable ontology editor. In this chapter we give an overview of the editing tools we consider more relevant for ontology construction.

This chapter gives a general introduction to some of the ontology languages that play an important role on the Semantic Web. The languages presented include RDFS and OWL.

In this chapter we remember the reader the fundamental of description logic and the OWL ontology language and explain how reasoning can be achieved on the Semantic Web. A real example using routers is given to explain how ontologies and reasoning can help in determining the location of resources.

This chapter reviews the history out of which Web services evolved. We will see that Web services are the result of the evolution of several distributed systems technologies. One of the concepts introduced along Web services is service-oriented architecture (SOA). Since SOA is to be used by organizations, we address important issues such as the specification of policies and security.

The Business Process Execution Language for Web Services (BPEL) is an emerging standard for specifying a business process made of Web services. In this chapter, we review some limitations of BPEL and discuss solutions to address them. We also consider the possibility of applying formal methods and Semantic Web technologies to support the development of a next generation of BPEL processes.

Several researchers have recognized that Web services standards lack of semantics. To address this limitation, the Semantic Web community has introduced the concept of Semantic Web service. When the requirements and capabilities of Web services are described using semantics it becomes possible to carry out a considerable number of automated tasks, such as automatic discovery, composition and integration of software components.

## Chapter X

This chapter explains how Web services can be annotated and described with semantics. Semantic descriptions allow Web services to be understood and correctly interpreted by machines. The focus lies in analyzing the process of semantic annotation, i.e., the process of deriving semantic descriptions from lower level specifications, implementations and contextual descriptions of Web services.

## Chapter XI

This chapter surveys existing approaches to Semantic Web service discovery. Semantic discovery will probably substitute existing keyword-based solutions in order to overcome several limitations of the latter.

## Chapter XII

This chapter presents how the Web service modeling ontology (WSMO) can be applied for service discovery. WSMO is a specification that provides a conceptual framework for semantically describing Web services and their specific properties. This chapter is closely related to Chapter XI.

## Chapter XIII

Syntactic search engines, such as Google and Yahoo!, are common tools for every user of the Internet. But since the search is based only on the syntax of keywords, the accuracy of the engines is often poor and inadequate. One solution to improve these engines is to add semantics to the search process. This chapter presents the concept of semantic search engines which fundamentally augment and improve traditional Web search engines by using not just words, but concepts and logical relationships.

# Foreword

Semantic Web is here to stay! This is not really a marketing campaign logo, but it is a truth that every year is becoming more and more relevant to the daily life of business world, industry and society.

I do not know how it happened, but the last years, through our activities in the Special Interest Group on Semantic Web and Information Systems in the Association for Information Systems (http://www.sigsemis.org), I had the opportunity to contact and collaborate with several key people for the evolution of the SW as well as many leaders in different domains trying to understand their attitude for Semantic Web[1]. I feel many times my background in Informatics and Management Science helps me to go beyond the traditional exhaustive technical discussions on Semantic Web and to see the Forest. This is full of fertile grounds, fruits for the people who will put the required tough efforts for the cultivation of the fields and many more, and of course much more value for the early adopters.

A couple years ago I had an interview with Robert Zmud, professor, and Michael F. Price, chair in MIS, University of Oklahoma. Given his legendary work in the adoption of technologies in business/organizational contexts, I asked him in a way how can we promote Semantic Web to business world. His answer influenced all of my Semantic Web activities until then. I am copying here:

*As with all adoption situations, this is an information and communication problem. One needs to segment the base of potential adopters (both in the IS community and in the business community) and then develop communication programs to inform each distinct segment of, first, the existence of the innovation (know-what), then the nature of the innovation (know-how), and finally why this innovation would be useful to them (know-why). These adopter segments are likely to be very different from each other. Each will have a different likelihood of adoption and will likely require that a somewhat unique communication strategy be devised and directed toward the segment*

So this is why Jorge's current edition, as well as planned editions, give an answer to the problem of many people. Semantic Web is discussed in the triptych know-what, know-how, and know-why and the editing strategy of the book boosts the excellent quality of well known contributors. It is really amazing how Jorge made it and so many academics and practitioners collaboratively worked for this edition.

Robert Zmud concluded his answer with one more statement which is worthy to mention.

*My advice thus, is to segment the adopter population, identify those communities with the highest potential for adoption, develop a targeted communication strategy, and then develop the relationships necessary to deliver the communication strategy. Hope this helps.*

This answer really justifies why you are fortunate to read this book. Semantics are evident everywhere in every aspect of business, life, and society (Sheth, 2005)[1]. In this sense, "Semantic Web Services: Theory, Tools, and Applications" provides a critical step forward in the understanding of the state of the art of the Semantic Web.

I am convinced that the next years Semantic Web will drive a new era of real world applications. With its transparent capacity to support every business domain, the milestone of the knowledge society will be for sure a Semantic Web primer. Within this context, computer science and information systems experts have to reconsider their role. They must be able to transform business requirements to systems and solutions that go beyond traditional analysis and design. This is why a lot of effort must be paid to the introduction of Semantic Web in computer science and information systems curricula. "Semantic Web: Theory, Tools, and Applications" can be used as an excellent text book for the relevant themes.

As a concluding remark I would like just to share with you some thoughts. There is always a questioning for the pace of the change, and the current stage in the evolution of the SW. I do believe that there is no need to make predictions for the future. The only thing we need is strategy and hard work. Educating people in Semantic Web in computer science departments and in business schools means making them realize that semantics, logic, reasoning, and trust are just our mankind characteristics that we must bring to our "electronic words." If we do not support them our virtual information world looks like a giant with glass legs. This is why I like the engineering approach of Jorge in this edition. We must be able to support the giant with concrete computer engineering in order to make sustainable solutions for real world problems. The fine grain of strategy and computer science will lead Semantic Web to a maturity level for unforeseen value diffusion.

My invitation is to be part of this exciting new journey and to keep in mind that the people who dedicate their lives in the promotion of disciplines for the common wealth from time to time need encouragement and support because their intellectual work is not valued in financial terms. This is why I want to express my deepest appreciation and respect for Jorge Cardoso as scientist and man, and to wish him to keep rocking in Semantic Web.

Dear Jorge, you did once again great job. And dear Readers, from all over the world you did the best choice. Let us open together the Semantic Web to the society. And why not let us put together the new milestones towards a better world for all through the adoption of leading edge technologies in humanistic visions.

*Miltiadis D. Lytras, University of Patras, Greece*

## ENDNOTES

[1]  Sheth, A., Ramakrishnan C., & Thomas, C. (2005). Semantics for the Semantic Web: The implicit, the formal and the powerful. *International Journal on Semantic Web and Information Systems, Inaugural Issue, 1*(1), 1-18.

[2]  Lytras, M. (2005). Semantic Web and information systems: An agenda based on discourse with community leaders. *International Journal on Semantic Web and Information Systems, Inaugural Issue, 1*(1), i-xii.

# Preface

## What is This Book About?

The current World Wide Web is syntactic and the content itself is only readable by humans. The Semantic Web proposes the mark-up of content on the Web using formal ontologies that structure underlying data for the purpose of comprehensive machine understanding. Currently most Web resources can only be found and queried by syntactical search engines. One of the goals of the Semantic Web is to enable reasoning about data entities on different Web pages or Web resources. The Semantic Web is an extension of the current Web in which information is given well-defined meaning, enabling computers and people to work in co-operation.

Along with the Semantic Web, systems and infrastructures are currently being developed to support Web services. The main idea is to encapsulate an organization's functionality within an appropriate interface and advertise it as Web services. While in some cases Web services may be utilized in an isolated form, it is normal to expect Web services to be integrated as part of Web processes. There is a growing consensus that Web services alone will not be sufficient to develop valuable Web processes due the degree of heterogeneity, autonomy, and distribution of the Web. Several researchers agree that it is essential for Web services to be machine understandable in order to support all the phases of the lifecycle of Web processes.

It is therefore indispensable to interrelate and associate two of the hottest R&D and technology areas currently associated with the Web—Web services and the Semantic Web. The study of the application of semantics to each of the steps in the Semantic Web process lifecycle can help address critical issues in reuse, integration and scalability.

## Why Did I Put a Lot of Effort in Creating This Book?

I started using Semantic Web technologies in 2001 right after Tim Berners-Lee, James Hendler, and Ora Lassila published their article entitled "The Semantic Web" in the May issue of *Scientific American*. This seminal article described some of the future potential of what was called the Semantic Web, the impact of computers understanding and interpreting semantic information, and how searches could be dramatically improved when using semantic metadata. In 2004, I started planning to teach a course on Semantic Web at the University of Madeira (Portugal). When looking for material and textbooks on the topic for my students, I realized that there was only a hand full of good books discussing the concepts associated with the Semantic Web. But none aggregated in one place the theory, the tools, and the applications of the Semantic Web. So, I decided to write this comprehensive and handy book for students, teachers, and researchers.

The major goal of this book is to bring contributions from researchers, scientists from both industry and academics, and representatives from different communities together to study, understand, and explore the theory, tools and applications of the Semantic Web. It brings together computing that deal with the design and integration, bio-informatics, education, and so forth ontological engineering is defined as the set of activities that concern the ontology development process, the ontology life cycle, the principles, methods and methodologies for building ontologies, and the tool suites and languages that support them. In Chapter III we provide an overview of all these activities, describing the current trends, issues and problems. More specifically, we cover the following aspects of ontological engineering: (a) Methods and methodologies for ontology development. We cover both comprehensive methodologies that give support to a large number of tasks of the ontology development process and methods and techniques that focus on specific activities of this process, focusing on: ontology learning, ontology alignment and merge, ontology evolution and versioning, and ontology evaluation; (b) Tools for ontology development. We describe the most relevant ontology development tools, which give support to most of the ontology development tasks (especially formalization and implementation) and tools that have been created for specific tasks, such as the ones identified before: learning, alignment and merge, evolution and versioning and evaluation, and (c) finally, we describe the languages that can be used in the context of the Semantic Web. This includes W3C recommendations, such as RDF, RDF schema and OWL, and emerging languages, such as WSML.

Chapter IV gives an overview of editing tools for building ontologies. The construction of an ontology demands the use of specialized software tools. Therefore, we give a synopsis of the tools that we consider more relevant. The tools we have selected were Protégé, OntoEdit, DOE, IsaViz, Ontolingua, Altova Semantic Works, OilEd, WebODE, pOWL and SWOOP. We started by describing each tool and identifying which tools supported a methodology or other important features for ontology construction. It is possible to identify some general distinctive features for each software tool. Protégé is used for domain modeling and for building knowledge-base systems and promotes interoperability. DOE allows users to build ontologies according to the methodology proposed by Bruno Bachimont. Ontolingua was built to ease the development of ontologies with a form-based Web interface. Altova SemanticWorks is a commercial visual editor that has an intuitive visual interface and drag-and-drop functionalities. OilEd's interface was strongly influenced by Stanford's Protégé toolkit. This editor does not provide a full ontology development environment. However, it allows users to build ontologies and to check ontologies for consistency by using the FaCT reasoner. WebODE is a Web application. This editor supports ontology edition, navigation, documentation, merge, reasoning and other activities involved in the ontology development process. pOWL is capable of supporting parsing, storing, querying, manipulation, versioning and serialization of RDFS and OWL knowledge bases in a collaborative Web enabled environment. SWOOP is a Web-based OWL ontology editor and browser. SWOOP contains OWL validation and offers various OWL presentation syntax views. It has reasoning support and provides a multiple ontology environment.

The aim of Chapter V is to give a general introduction to some of the ontology languages that play a prominent role on the Semantic Web. In particular, it will explain the role of ontologies on the Web, review the current standards of RDFS and OWL, and discuss open issues for further developments. In the context of the Web, ontologies can be used to formulate a shared understanding of a domain in order deal with differences in terminology of users, communities, disciplines and languages as it appears in texts. One of the goals of the Semantic Web initiative is to advance the state of the current Web through the use of semantics. More specifically, it proposes to use semantic annotations to describe the meaning of certain parts of Web information and, increasingly, the meaning of message elements employed by Web services. For example, the Web site of a hotel could be suitably annotated to distinguish between the hotel name, location, category, number of rooms, available services and so forth Such meta-data could facilitate the automated processing of the information on the Web site, thus making it accessible to machines and not primarily to human users, as it is the case today. The current and most prominent Web standard for semantic annotations is RDF and RDF schema, and its extension OWL.

Semantic Web, ontologies, knowledge management and engineering, Web services, and Web processes. It serves as the platform for exchange of both practical technologies and far reaching research.

## Organization of the Book

This book is divided into 13 chapters and it is organized in a manner that allows a gradual progression of the main subject toward more advanced topics. The first five chapters cover the logic and engineering approaches needed to develop ontologies and bring into play semantics. Chapters VII and VIII introduce two technological areas, Web services and Web processes, which have received a considerable amount of attention and focus from the Semantic Web community. The remaining chapters, Chapters IX, X, XI, XII, and XIII, describe in detail how semantics are being used to annotate Web services, discover Web services, and deploy semantic search engines.

Chapter I introduces the concepts of syntactic and Semantic Web. The World Wide Web composed of HTML documents can be characterized as a syntactic or visual Web since documents are meant only to be displayed by Web browsers. In the visual Web, machines cannot understand the meaning of the information present in HTML pages, since they are mainly made up of ASCII codes and images. The visual Web prevents computers from automating information processing, integration, and interoperability. Currently the Web is undergoing an evolution and different approaches are being sought for adding semantics to Web pages and resources in general. Due to the widespread importance of integration and interoperability for intra- and inter-business processes, the research community has already developed several semantic standards such as the resource description framework (RDF), RDF schema (RDFS) and the Web Ontology Language (OWL). RDF, RDFS and OWL standards enable the Web to be a global infrastructure for sharing both documents and data, which make searching and reusing information easier and more reliable as well. RDF is a standard for creating descriptions of information, especially information available on the World Wide Web. What XML is for syntax, RDF is for semantics. The latter provides a clear set of rules for providing simple descriptive information. OWL provides a language for defining structured Web-based ontologies which allows a richer integration and interoperability of data among communities and domains. Even though the Semantic Web is still in its infancy, there are already applications and tools that use this conceptual approach to build Semantic Web-based systems. Therefore, in this chapter, we present the state of the art of the applications that use semantics and ontologies. We describe various applications ranging from the use of Semantic Web services, semantic integration of tourism information sources, and semantic digital libraries to the development of bioinformatics ontologies.

Chapter II introduces a number of formal logical languages which form the backbone of the Semantic Web. They are used for the representation of both ontologies and rules. The basis for all languages presented in this chapter is the classical first-order logic. Description logics is a family of languages which represent subsets of first-order logic. Expressive description logic languages form the basis for popular ontology languages on the Semantic Web. Logic programming is based on a subset of first-order logic, namely Horn logic, but uses a slightly different semantics and can be extended with non-monotonic negation. Many Semantic Web reasoners are based on logic programming principles and rule languages for the Semantic Web based on logic programming are an ongoing discussion. Frame logic allows object-oriented style (frame-based) modeling in a logical language. RuleML is an XML-based syntax consisting of different sub-languages for the exchange of specifications in different logical languages over the Web.

In computer science, ontologies are defined as formal, explicit specifications of shared conceptualizations. Their origin in this discipline can be referred back to 1991, in the context of the DARPA knowledge sharing effort. Since then, considerable progress has been made and ontologies are now considered as a commodity that can be used for the development of a large number of applications in different fields, such as knowledge management, natural language processing, e-commerce, intelligent integration information, information retrieval, database

In Chapter VI we describe and explain how reasoning can be carried out in on the Semantic Web. Reasoning is the process needed for using logic. Efficiently performing this process is a prerequisite for using logic to present information in a declarative way and to construct models of reality. In this chapter we describe both what the reasoning over the formal semantics of description logic amounts to and to, and illustrate how formal reasoning can (and cannot!) be used for understanding real world semantics given a good formal model of the situation. We first describe how the formal semantics of description logic can be understood in terms of completing oriented labeled graphs. In other words we interpret the formal semantics of description logic as rules for inferring implied arrows in a dots and arrows diagram. We give an essentially complete "graphical" overview of OWL that may be used as an introduction to the semantics of this language. We then touch on the algorithmic complexity of this graph completion problem giving a simple version of the tableau algorithm, and give pointers to existing implementations of OWL reasoners. The second part deals with semantics as the relation between a formal model and reality. We give an extended example building up a small toy ontology of concepts useful for describing buildings, their physical layout and physical objects such as wireless routers and printers in the turtle notation for OWL. We then describe a (imaginary) building with routers in these terms. We explain how such a model can help in determining the location of resources given an idealized wireless device that is in or out of range of a router. We emphasize how different assumptions on the way routers and buildings work are formalized and made explicit in the formal semantics of the logical model. In particular we explain the sharp distinction between knowing some facts and knowing all facts (open, versus closed world assumption). The example also illustrates the fact that reasoning is no magical substitute for insufficient data. This section should be helpful when using ontologies and incomplete real world knowledge in applications.

Chapter VII gives an introduction to Web service technology. Web services are emerging technologies that allow programmatic access to resources on the Internet. Web services provide a means to create distributed systems which are loosely couple, meaning that the interaction between the client and service is not dependent on one having any knowledge of the other. This type of interaction between components is defined formally by the service-oriented architecture (SOA). The backbone of Web services is XML. Extensible Markup Language (XML) is a platform independent data representation which allows the flexibility that Web services need to fulfill their promise. Simple object access protocol, or SOAP, is the XML-based protocol that governs the communication between a service and the client. It provides a platform and programming language independent way for Web services to exchange messages. Web Service Description Language (WSDL) is an XML-based language for describing a service. It describes all the information needed to advertise and invoke a Web service. UDDI is a standard for storing WSDL files as a registry so that they can be discovered by clients. There are other standards for describing policy, security, reliability, and transactions of Web services that are described in the chapter. With all this power and flexibility, Web services are fairly easy to build. Standard software engineering practices are still valid with this new technology though tool support is making some of the steps trivial. Initially, we design the service as a UML class diagram. This diagram can then be translated (either by hand or by tools like Posiden) to a Java interface. This class can become a Web service by adding some annotations to the Java code that will be used to create the WSDL file for the service. At this point, we need only to implement the business logic of the service to have a system that is capable of performing the needed tasks. Next, the service is deployed on an application server, tested for access and logic correctness, and published to a registry so that it can be discovered by clients.

In Chapter VIII we introduce and provide an overview of the Business Process Execution Language for Web services (known as BPEL4WS or BPEL for short), an emerging standard for specifying the behavior of Web services at different levels of details using business process modeling constructs. BPEL represents a convergence between Web services and business process technology. It defines a model and a grammar for describing the behavior of a business process based on interactions between the process and its partners. Being supported by vendors such as IBM and Microsoft, BPEL is positioned as the "process language of the Internet." The chapter firstly introduces BPEL by illustrating its key concepts and the usage of its constructs to define service-oriented processes and to model business protocols between interacting Web services. A BPEL process is composed of activities that can be combined through structured operators and related through control links. In addition to the main process flow, BPEL provides event handling, fault handling and compensation capabilities. In the long-running business processes, BPEL applies correlation mechanism to route messages to the correct process instance. On the other hand, BPEL is layered on top of several XML specifications such as WSDL, XML schema and XPath. WSDL message types and XML schema type definitions provide the data model used in BPEL processes, and XPath provides support for data manipulation. All external resources and partners are represented as WSDL services. Next, to further illustrate the BPEL constructs introduced above, a comprehensive working example of a BPEL process is given, which covers the process definition, XML schema definition, WSDL document definition, and the process execution over a popular BPEL-compliant engine. Since the BPEL specification defines only the kernel of BPEL, extensions are allowed to be made in separate documentations. The chapter reviews some perceived limitations of BPEL and extensions that have been proposed by industry vendors to address these limitations. Finally, for an advanced discussion, the chapter considers the possibility of applying formal methods and Semantic Web technology to support the rigorous development of service-oriented processes using BPEL.

Web services show promise to address the needs of application integration by providing a standards-based framework for exchanging information dynamically between applications. Industry efforts to standardize Web service description, discovery and invocation have led to standards such as WSDL, UDDI, and SOAP respectively. These industry standards, in their current form, are designed to represent information about the interfaces of services, how they are deployed, and how to invoke them, but are limited in their ability to express the capabilities and requirements of services. This lack of semantic representation capabilities leaves the promise of automatic integration of applications written to Web services standards unfulfilled. To address this, the Semantic Web community has introduced Semantic Web services. Semantic Web services are the main topic of Chapter IX. By encoding the requirements and capabilities of Web services in an unambiguous and machine-interpretable form semantics make the automatic discovery, composition and integration of software components possible. This chapter introduces Semantic Web services as a means to achieve this vision. It presents an overview of Semantic Web services, their representation mechanisms, related work and use cases. Specifically, the chapter contrasts various Semantic Web service representation mechanisms such as OWL-S, WSMO and WSDL-S and presents an overview of the research work in the area of Web service discovery, and composition that use these representation mechanisms.

Web services are software components that are accessible as Web resources in order to be reused by other Web services or software. Hence, they function as middleware connecting different parties such as companies or organizations distributed over the Web. In Chapter X, we consider the process of provisioning data about a Web service to constitute a specification of the Web service. At this point, the question arises how a machine may attribute machine-understandable meaning to this metadata. Therefore, we argue for the use of ontologies for giving a formal semantics to Web service annotations, that is, we argue in favor of Semantic Web service annotations. A Web service ontology defines general concepts such as service or operation as well as relations that exist between such concepts. The metadata describing a Web service can instantiate concepts of the ontology. This connection supports Web service developers to understand and compare the metadata of different services described by the same or a similar ontology. Consequently, ontology-based Web service annotation leverages the use, reuse and verification of Web services. The process of Semantic Web service annotation in general requires input from multiple sources, that is legacy descriptions, as well as a labor-intensive modeling effort. Information about a Web service can be gathered for example from the source code of a service (if annotation is done by a service provider), from the API documentation and description, from the overall textual documentation of a Web service or from descriptions in WS* standards. Depending on the structuredness of these sources, semantic annotations may (have to) be provided manually (e.g., if full text is the input), semi-automatically (e.g. for some WS* descriptions) or fully automatically (e.g., if Java interfaces constitute the input). Hence, a semantic description of the signature of a Web service may be provided by automatic means, while the functionality of Web service operations or pre- and post-conditions of a Web service operation may only be modeled manually. Benefits of semantic specifications of Web services include a common framework that integrates semantic descriptions of many relevant Web service properties. It is the purpose of this chapter to explain the conceptual gap between legacy descriptions and semantic specifications and to indicate how this gap is to be bridged.

Chapter XI deals with methods, algorithms and tools for Semantic Web service discovery. Semantic Web has revolutionized, among other things, the implementation of Web services lifecycle. The core phases of this lifecycle, such as service discovery and composition can be performed more effectively through the exploitation of the semantics that annotate the service descriptions. This chapter focuses on the phase of discovery due to its central role in every, service-oriented architecture. Hence, it surveys existing approaches to Semantic Web service (SWS) discovery. Such discovery process is expected to substitute existing keyword-based solutions (e.g., UDDI) in the near future, in order to overcome their limitations. First, the architectural components of a SWS discovery ecosystem, along with potential deployment scenarios, are discussed. Subsequently, a wide range of algorithms and tools that have been proposed for the realization of SWS discovery are presented. The presentation of the various approaches aims at outlining the key characteristics of each proposed solution, without delving into technology-dependent details (e.g., service description languages). The descriptions of the tools included in this chapter provide a starting point for further experimentation by the reader. In this respect, a brief tutorial for a certain tool is provided as an appendix. Finally, key challenges and open issues, not addressed by current systems, are identified (e.g., evaluation of service retrieval, mediation and interoperability issues). The ultimate purpose of this chapter is to update the reader on the recent developments in this area of the distributed systems domain and provide the required background knowledge and stimuli for further research and experimentation in semantics-based service discovery.

Taking an abstract perspective, Web services can be considered as complex resources on the Web, that is, resources that might have more complex structure and properties than conventional data that is shared on the Web. Recently, the Web service modeling ontology (WSMO) has been developed to provide a conceptual framework for semantically describing Web services and their specific properties in detail. WSMO represents a promising and rather general framework for Semantic Web service description and is currently applied in various European projects in the area of Semantic Web services and Grid computing. In Chapter XII, we discuss how Web service discovery can be achieved within the WSMO Framework. First, we motivate Semantic Web services and the idea of applying semantics to Web services. We give a brief high-level overview of the Web service modeling ontology and present the main underlying principles. We discuss the distinction between two notions that are often intermixed when talking about Semantic Web services and thus provide a proper conceptual grounding for our framework, namely we strictly distinguish between services and Web services. Consequently, we distinguish between service discovery and web service discovery, whereas only the latter is then considered in detail in the chapter. Since in open environments like the Web, the assumption of homogeneous vocabularies and descriptions breaks, we briefly consider mediation and discuss its role in service and Web service Discovery. Hereby, we try to identify requirements on the discovery process and respective semantic descriptions which allow facing heterogeneity and scalability at the same time. We then present a layered model of successively more detailed and precise perspectives on Web services and consider Web service descriptions on each of them. For the two most fine-grained levels, we then discuss how to detect semantic matches between requested and provided functionalities. Based on our model, we are able to integrate and extend matching notions that have been known in the area already. First, we consider Web services essentially as concepts in an ontology, where required inputs and the condition under which a requested service actually can be delivered is neglected. Then, we move forward to a more detailed level of description, where inputs and respective preconditions for service delivery are no longer ignored. We show how to adapt and extend the simpler model and matching notions from before to adequately address richer semantic descriptions on this level. The various levels of descriptions are meant to support a wide range of scenarios that can appear in practical applications, requiring different levels of details in the description of Web services and client requests, as well as different precision and performance.

Chapter XIII focuses on semantic search engines and data integration systems. As the use of the World Wide Web has become increasingly widespread, the business of commercial search engines has become a vital and lucrative part of the Web. Search engines are common place tools for virtually every user of the Internet; and companies, such as Google and Yahoo!, have become household names. Semantic search engines try to augment and improve traditional Web search engines by using not just words, but concepts and logical relationships. We believe that data integration systems, domain ontologies and schema based peer-to-peer architectures are good ingredients for developing semantic search engines with good performance. Data integration is the problem of combining data residing at different autonomous sources, and providing the user with a unified view of these data; the problem of designing data integration systems is important in current real world applications, and is characterized by a number of issues that are interesting from a theoretical point of view. Schema-based peer-to-peer networks are a new class of peer-to-peer networks, combining approaches from peer-to-peer as well as from the data integration and Semantic Web research areas. Such networks build upon peers that use metadata (ontologies) to describe their contents and semantic mappings among concepts of different peers' ontologies. In this chapter, we will provide empirical evidence for our hypothesis. More precisely, we will describe two projects, SEWASIE and WISDOM, which rely on these architectural features and developed key semantic search functionalities; they both exploit the MOMIS (www.dbgroup.unimo.it/Momis/) data integration system. The first, SEWASIE (www.sewasie.org), rely on a two-level ontology architecture: the low level, called the peer level contains a data integration system; the second one, called super-peer level integrates peers with semantically related content (i.e., related to the same domain). The second, WISDOM (www.dbgroup.unimo.it/wisdom/), is based on an overlay network of semantic peers: each peer contains a data integration system. The cardinal idea of the project is to develop a framework that supports a flexible yet efficient integration of the semantic content.

# Acknowledgments

This book describes the most recent advances in Semantic Web and results of a collaborative effort towards the development of a comprehensive manuscript that exposes the major issues related to this new area of research. I wish to express my gratitude to everyone who contributed to making this book a reality. This project is the accumulation of months of work by many dedicated researchers. Some of the most well-know researcher in the world have dedicated their precious time to share their experience and knowledge with you. It would not have been possible for me to produce this work without their help.

# Chapter I
# The Syntactic and the Semantic Web

**Jorge Cardoso**
*University of Madeira, Portugal*

## ABSTRACT

*This chapter gives an overview of the evolution of the Web. Initially, Web pages were intended only for human consumption and were usually displayed on a Web browser. New Internet business models, such as B2B and B2C, required organizations to search for solutions to enable a deep interoperability and integration between their systems and applications. One emergent solution was to define the information on the Web using semantics and ontologies in a way that it could be used by computers not only for display purposes, but also for interoperability and integration. The research community developed standards to semantically describe Web information such as the resource description framework and the Web Ontology Language. Ontologies can assist in communication between human beings, achieve interoperability among software systems, and improve the design and the quality of software systems. These evolving Semantic Web technologies are already being used to build semantic Web based systems such as semantic Web services, semantic integration of tourism information sources, and semantic digital libraries to the development of bioinformatics ontologies.*

## MOTIVATION FOR THE SEMANTIC WEB

The World Wide Web (WWW) was developed in 1989 at the European Laboratory for Particle Physics (CERN) in Geneva, Switzerland. It was Tim Berners-Lee who developed the first prototype of the World Wide Web intended to serve as an information system for physicists.

By the end of 1990, Tim Berners-Lee had written the first browser to retrieve and view hypertext documents and wrote the first Web server—the software, which stores Web pages on a computer for others to access. The system was originally developed to allow information sharing within internationally dispersed working groups. The original WWW consisted of documents (i.e., Web pages) and links between documents.

Browsers and Web server users grew. They became more and more attractive as an information sharing infrastructure. The Web became even more interesting as the amount of available information of every sort increased. A Web page can be accessed by a URL (uniform resource locator) through the hypertext transfer protocol (HTTP) using a Web browser (e.g., Internet Explorer, Netscape, Mozilla, Safari).

Currently, the World Wide Web is primarily composed of documents written in HTML (Hyper Text Markup Language), a language that is useful for visual presentation. HTML is a set of "markup" symbols contained in a Web page intended for display on a Web browser. Most of the information on the Web is designed only for human consumption. Humans can read Web pages and understand them, but their inherent meaning is not shown in a way that allows their interpretation by computers.

The information on the Web can be defined in a way that can be used by computers not only for display purposes, but also for interoperability and integration between systems and applications. One way to enable machine-to-machine exchange and automated processing is to provide the information in such a way that computers can understand it. This is precisely the objective of the semantic Web—to make possible the processing of Web information by computers.

*The Semantic Web is not a separate Web but an extension of the current one, in which information is given well-defined meaning, better enabling computers and people to work in cooperation.* (Berners-Lee, Hendler, et al., 2001)

The next generation of the Web will combine existing Web technologies with knowledge representation formalisms (Grau, 2004).

The Semantic Web was made through incremental changes, by bringing machine-readable descriptions to the data and documents already on the Web. Figure 1 illustrates the various developed technologies that made the concept of the Semantic Web possible. As already stated, the Web was originally a vast set of static Web pages linked together. Many organizations still use static HTML files to deliver their information on the Web. However, to answer to the inherent dynamic nature of businesses, organizations are using dynamic publishing methods which offer great advantages over Web sites constructed from static HTML pages. Instead of a Web site comprising a collection of manually constructed HTML pages, server-side applications and database access techniques are used to dynamically

*Figure 1. Evolution of the Web*

| | Static | Dynamic | Syntax | Semantic |
|---|---|---|---|---|
| Encoding | HTML | + RDBMS | + XML | + RDF/OWL |
| Creation | Manually | Generated by server-side applications | Generated by applications based on schema | Generated by applications based on models |
| Users | Humans | Humans | Humans and applications | Humans and applications |
| Paradigm | Browse | Create/Query/ Update | Integrate | Interoperate |
| Applications | Browsers | Browsers | Process Integration, EAI, BPMS, Workflows | Intelligent agents, Semantic engines |

1995        2000        2005

create Web pages directly in response to requests from user browsers. This technique offers the opportunity to deliver Web content that is highly customized to the needs of individual users.

Nevertheless, the technologies available to dynamically create Web pages based on database information were insufficient for the requirements of organizations looking for application integration solutions. Businesses required their heterogeneous systems and applications to communicate in a transactional manner. The Extensible Markup Language (XML, 2005) was one of most successful solutions developed to provide business-to-business integration. XML became a means of transmitting unstructured, semi-structured, and even structured data between systems, enhancing the integration of applications and businesses.

Unfortunately, XML-based solutions for applications and systems integration were not sufficient, since the data exchanged lacked an explicit description of its meaning. The integration of applications must also include a semantic integration. Semantic integration and interoperability is concerned with the use of explicit semantic descriptions to facilitate integration.

Currently the Web is undergoing evolution (as illustrated in Figure 2) and different approaches are being sought for solutions to adding semantics to Web resources. On the left side of Figure 2, a graph representation of the syntactic Web is given.

Resources are linked together forming the Web. There is no distinction between resources or the links that connect resources. To give meaning to resources and links, new standards and languages are being investigated and developed. The rules and descriptive information made available by these languages allow the type of resources on the Web and the relationships between resources to be characterized individually and precisely, as illustrated on the right side of Figure 2.

Due to the widespread importance of integration and interoperability for intra- and inter-business processes, the research community has tackled this problem and developed semantic standards such as the resource description framework (RDF) (RDF, 2002) and the Web Ontology Language (OWL) (OWL, 2004). RDF and OWL standards enable the Web to be a global infrastructure for sharing both documents and data, which make searching and reusing information easier and more reliable as well. RDF is a standard for creating descriptions of information, especially information available on the World Wide Web. What XML is for syntax, RDF is for semantics. The latter provides a clear set of rules for providing simple descriptive information. OWL provides a language for defining structured Web-based ontologies which allows a richer integration and interoperability of data among communities and domains.

*Figure 2. Evolution of the Web*

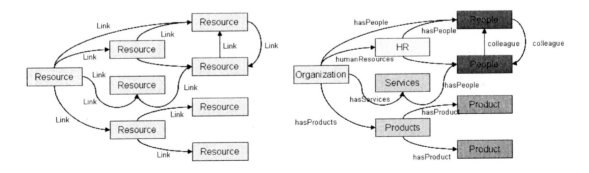

## THE VISUAL AND SYNTACTIC WEB

The World Wide Web composed of HTML documents can be characterized as a visual Web since documents are meant only to be displayed by Web browsers. In the visual Web, machines cannot understand the meaning of the information present in HTML pages, since they are mainly made up of ASCII codes and images. The visual Web prevents computers from automating information processing, integration, and interoperability.

With HTML documents, presentational metadata is used to assign information to the content and affect its presentation. Metadata is data about data and can be used to describe information about a resource. A resource can, for example, be a Web page, a document, an image, or a file. Examples of metadata that can be associated with a file include its title, subject, author, and size. Metadata mostly consists of a set of attribute value pairs that gives information about characteristics of a document. For example,

```
title = Semantic Web: Technologies and Applications
subject = Semantic Web
author = Jorge Cardoso
size = 336 Kbytes
```

In HTML pages, the content is marked-up with metadata. Specific tags are used to indicate the beginning and end of each element. For example, to specify that the title of the Web page is "Semantic Web: Technologies and Applications," the text is marked-up using the tag <Title>. To inform the Web browser that "Motivation for the Semantic Web" is a heading, the text is marked-up as a heading element, using level-one <h1> heading tag such as:

```
<Title> Semantic Web: Technologies and Applications
    </Title>
<h1> Motivation for the Semantic Web </h1>
```

One restriction of HTML is that it is semantically limited. There is a lack of rich vocabulary of element types capable of capturing the meaning behind every piece of text. For example, Google search engine reads a significant number of the world's Web pages and allows users to type in keywords to find pages containing those keywords. There is no meaning associated to the keywords. Google only carries out simple matches between the keywords and the words in its database. The metadata of HTML is not considered when searching for a particular set of keywords. Even if Google would use HTML metadata to answer queries, the lack of semantics of HTML tags would most likely not improve the search.

On the other hand, the Syntactic Web is the collection of documents in the World Wide Web that contain data not just meant to be rendered by Web browsers, but also to be used for data integration and interoperability purposes. To be able to "understand" data, a computer needs metadata which will be provided by some kind of markup language. A widespread markup language is XML. With HTML the set of tags available to users is predefined and new tags cannot be added to the language. In contrast, XML is an extremely versatile markup language allowing users to be capable of creating new tags to add syntactic meaning to information.

In order to allow data integration, the meaning of XML document content is determined by agreements reached between the businesses that will be exchanging data. Agreements are usually defined using a standardized document, such as the document type definition (DTD) (XML, 2005) or the XML schema definition (XSD) (XMLschema, 2005) that specifies the structure and data elements of the messages exchanged. These agreements can then be used by applications to act on the data.

In a typical organization, business data is stored in many formats and across many systems and databases throughout the organization and with partner organizations. To partially solve integration problems, organizations have been using solutions such as XML to exchange or move business data between information systems. Prior to XML, an organization had to hardcode modules to retrieve data from data sources and construct a message to send to other applications. The adoption of XML accelerates the construction of systems that integrate distributed, heterogeneous data. The XML language allows the flexible coding and display of data, by using metadata to describe the structure of data (e.g., DTD or XSD).

The first step necessary to accomplish data integration using XML technologies consists of taking the raw data sources (text, spreadsheets, relational tables, etc) and converting them into well-formed XML documents. The next step is to analyze and document its structure by creating a DTD or XSD for each of the data sources.

One limitation of XML is that it can only define the *syntax* of documents. XML data does not include information which can be used to describe the meaning of the tags used. The following example illustrates an XML instance.

```
<student>
 <name> John Hall </name>
 <id> 669-33-2555 </id>
 <major> Philosophy </major>
</student>
```

In this example, the XML instance indicates there is a student named "John Hall." His <id> is "669-33-2555," but no information is provided about the meaning of an <id> or the meaning of the different fields that compose an <id>. Finally, the student's <major> is "Philosophy." No information is provided concerning the relationship of this <major> with the other majors that are given at the University John attends.

## UNSTRUCTURED, SEMISTRUCTURED, AND STRUCTURED DATA

Data breaks down into three broad categories (Figure 3): unstructured, semistructured, and structured. Highly unstructured data comprises free-form documents or objects of arbitrary sizes and types. At the other end of the spectrum, structured data is what is typically found in databases. Every element of data has an assigned format and significance.

### Unstructured Data

Unstructured data is what we find in text, files, video, e-mails, reports, PowerPoint presentations,

*Figure 3. Unstructured, semistructured, and structured data*

| Unstructured data | Semi-structured data | Structured data |
|---|---|---|

Unstructured data:
```
The university has 5600
students.
John s ID is number 1, he is
18 years old and already
holds a B.Sc. degree.
David s ID is number 2, he is
31 years old and holds a
Ph.D. degree. Robert s ID is
number 3, he is 51 years old
and also holds the same
degree as David, a Ph.D.
degree.
```

Semi-structured data:
```
<University>
 <Student ID= 1">
  <Name>John</Name>
  <Age>18</Age>
  <Degree>B.Sc.</Degree>
 </Student>
 <Student ID= 2">
  <Name>David</Name>
  <Age>31</Age>
  <Degree>Ph.D. </Degree>
 </Student>

</University>
```

Structured data:

| ID | Name | Age | Degree |
|---|---|---|---|
| 1 | John | 18 | B.Sc. |
| 2 | David | 31 | Ph.D. |
| 3 | Robert | 51 | Ph.D. |
| 4 | Rick | 26 | M.Sc. |
| 5 | Michael | 19 | B.Sc. |

voice mail, office memos, and images. Data can be of any type and does not necessarily follow any format, rules, or sequence. For example, the data present on HTML Web pages is unstructured and irregular.

Unstructured data does not readily fit into structured databases except as binary large objects (BLOBs-binary large objects). Although unstructured data can have some structure—for example, e-mails have addressees, subjects, bodies, and so forth, and HTML Web pages have a set of predefined tags—the information is not stored in such a way that it will allow for easy classification, as the data are entered in electronic form.

## Semistructured Data

Semistructured data lie somewhere in between unstructured and structured data. *Semistructured data are data that have some structure, but are not rigidly structured.* This type of data includes unstructured components arranged according to some predetermined structure. Semistructured data can be specified in such a way that it can be queried using general-purpose mechanisms.

Semistructured data are organized into entities. Similar entities are grouped together, but entities in the same group may not have the same attributes. The order of attributes is not necessarily important and not all attributes may be required. The size and type of same attributes in a group may differ.

*An example of semistructured data is a Curriculum Vitae. One person may have a section of previous employments, another person may have a section on research experience, and another may have a section on teaching experience. We can also find a CV that contains two or more of these sections.*

A very good example of a semistructured formalism is XML which is a de facto standard for describing documents that is becoming the universal data exchange model on the Web and

is being used for business-to-business transactions. XML supports the development of semistructured documents that contain both metadata and formatted text. Metadata is specified using XML tags and defines the structure of documents. Without metadata, applications would not be able to understand and parse the content of XML documents. Compared to HTML, XML provides explicit data structuring. XML uses DTD or XSD as schema definitions for the semistructured data present in XML documents. Figure 3 shows the (semi) structure of an XML document containing students' records at a university.

## Structured Data

In contrast, structured data *are very rigid* and describe objects using strongly typed attributes, which are organized as records or tuples. *All records have the same fields.* Data are organized in entities and similar entities are grouped together using relations or classes. Entities in the same group have the same attributes. The descriptions for all the entities in a schema have the same defined format, predefined length, and follow the same order.

Structured data have been very popular since the early days of computing and many organizations rely on relational databases to maintain very large structured repositories. Recent systems, such as CRM (customer relationship management), ERP (enterprise resource planning), and CMS (content management systems) use structured data for their underlying data model.

## LEVELS OF SEMANTICS

As we have seen previously, semantics is the study of the meaning of signs, such as terms or words. Depending on the approaches, models, or methods used to add semantics to terms, different degrees of semantics can be achieved. In this section we identify and describe four representations that can be used to model and organize concepts to semantically describe terms, that is, controlled vocabularies, taxonomies, thesaurus, and ontologies. These four model representations are illustrated in Figure 4.

## Controlled Vocabularies

Controlled vocabularies are at the weaker end of the semantic spectrum. A controlled vocabulary is a list of terms (e.g., words, phrases, or notations) that have been enumerated explicitly. All terms in a controlled vocabulary should have an unambiguous, non-redundant definition. A controlled

vocabulary is the simplest of all metadata methods and has been extensively used for classification. For example, Amazon.com has the following (Table 1) controlled vocabulary which can be selected by the user to search for products.

Controlled vocabularies limit choices to an agreed upon unambiguous set of terms. In cataloguing applications, users can be presented with list of terms from which they can pick the term to describe an item for cataloguing. The main objective of a controlling vocabulary is to prevent users from defining their own terms which can be ambiguous, meaningless, or misspelled.

*Figure 4. Levels of semantics*

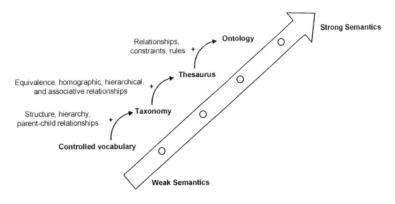

*Table 1. Controlled vocabulary used by Amazon.com*

| Books | Electronics | Travel |
|---|---|---|
| Popular Music | Camera & Photo | Cell Phones & Service |
| Music Downloads | Software | Outlet |
| Classical Music | Tools & Hardware | Auctions |
| DVD | Office Products | zShops |
| VHS | Magazines | Everything Else |
| Apparel | Sports & Outdoors | Scientific Supplies |
| Yellow Pages | Outdoor Living | Medical Supplies |
| Restaurants | Kitchen | Indust. Supplies |
| Movie Showtimes | Jewelry & Watches | Automotive |
| Toys | Beauty | Home Furnishings |
| Baby | Gourmet Food Beta | Lifestyle |
| Computers | Musical Instruments | Pet Toys |
| Video Games | Health/Personal Care | Arts & Hobbies |

## Taxonomies

A *taxonomy* is a subject-based classification that arranges the terms in a controlled vocabulary into a hierarchy without doing anything further. The first users of taxonomies were biologists in the classification of organisms. They have employed this method to classify plants and animals according to a set of natural relationships. A taxonomy classifies terms in the shape of a hierarchy or tree. It describes a word by making explicit its relationship with other words. Figure 5 shows a taxonomy of merchandise that can be bought for a home.

The hierarchy of a taxonomy contains parent-child relationships, such as "is subclass of" or "is superclass of." A user or computer can comprehend the semantics of a word by analyzing the existing relationship between the word and the words around it in the hierarchy.

## Thesaurus

A thesaurus is a networked collection of controlled vocabulary terms with conceptual relationships between terms. A thesaurus is an extension of a taxonomy by allowing terms to be arranged in a hierarchy and also allowing other statements and relationships to be made about the terms. A thesaurus can easily be converted into a taxonomy or controlled vocabulary. Of course, in such conversion, expressiveness and semantics are lost. Table 2 shows an example[1] of a thesaurus listing for the term *academic achievement*.

According to the National Information Standards Organization (NISO, 2005), there are four different types of relationships that are used in a thesaurus: equivalence, homographic, hierarchical, and associative.

- **Equivalence:** An equivalence relation says that a term $t_1$ has the same or nearly the same meaning as a term $t_2$.
- **Homographic:** Two terms, $t_1$ and $t_2$, are called homographic if term $t_1$ is spelled the same way as a term $t_2$, but has a different meaning.
- **Hierarchical:** This relationship is based on the degrees or levels of "is subclass of" and "is superclass of" relationships. The former represents a class or a whole, and the latter refers to its members or parts.
- **Associative:** This relationship is used to link terms that are closely related in meaning semantically but not hierarchically. An example of an associative relationship can be as simple as "is related to" as in term $t_1$ "is related to" term $t_2$.

## Ontologies

Ontologies are similar to taxonomies but use richer semantic relationships among terms and attributes, as well as strict rules about how to specify terms and relationships. In computer science, ontologies have emerged from the area of artificial intelligence. Ontologies have generally been associated with logical inferencing and recently have begun to be applied to the semantic Web.

*Figure 5. Example of a taxonomy*

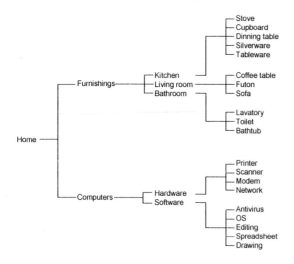

*Table 2. Example of a thesaurus listing for the term academic achievement*

| Relationship | Term |
|---|---|
| Used for | Grade point Average<br>Scholastic Achievement<br>School Achievement |
| Narrower than | Academic Overachievement<br>Academic Underachievement<br>College Academic Achievement<br>Mathematics Achievement<br>Reading Achievement<br>Science Achievement |
| Broader than | Achievement |
| Related to | Academic Achievement Motivation<br>Academic Achievement Prediction<br>Academic Aptitude<br>Academic Failure<br>Academic Self Concept<br>Education<br>Educational Attainment Level<br>School Graduation<br>School Learning<br>School Transition |

An ontology is a shared conceptualization of the world. Ontologies consist of definitional aspects such as high-level schemas and assertional aspects such as entities, attributes, interrelationships between entities, domain vocabulary and factual knowledge—all connected in a semantic manner (Sheth, 2003). Ontologies provide a common understanding of a particular domain. They allow the domain to be communicated between people, organizations, and application systems. Ontologies provide the specific tools to organize and provide a useful description of heterogeneous content.

In addition to the hierarchical relationship structure of typical taxonomies, ontologies enable cross-node horizontal relationships between entities, thus enabling easy modeling of real-world information requirements. Jasper and Uschold (1999) identify three major uses of ontologies:

1. To assist in communication between human beings

2. To achieve interoperability among software systems

3. To improve the design and the quality of software systems

An ontology is technically a model which looks very much like an ordinary object model in object-oriented programming. It consists of classes, inheritance, and properties (Fensel, 2001). In many situations, ontologies are thought of as knowledge representation.

## SEMANTIC WEB ARCHITECTURE

The Semantic Web identifies a set of technologies, tools, and standards which form the basic building blocks of an infrastructure to support the vision of the Web associated with meaning. The semantic Web architecture is composed of a series of standards organized into a certain structure that is an expression of their interrelationships. This architecture is often represented using a diagram first proposed by Tim Berners-Lee (Berners-Lee, Hendler et al., 2001). Figure 6 illustrates the different parts of the semantic Web architecture. It starts with the foundation of URIs and Unicode. On top of that we can find the syntactic interoperability layer in the form of XML, which in turn underlies RDF and RDF schema (RDFS). Web ontology languages are built on top of RDF(S). The three last layers are the logic, proof, and trust, which have not been significantly explored. Some of the layers rely on the digital signature component to ensure security.

In the following sections we will briefly describe these layers. While the notions presented have been simplified, they provide a reasonable conceptualization of the various components of the semantic Web.

## URI and Unicode

A universal resource identifier (URI) is a formatted string that serves as a means of identifying abstract or physical resource. A URI can be further classified as a locator, a name, or both. Uniform resource locator (URL) refers to the subset of URI that identifies resources via a representation of their primary access mechanism. An uniform resource name (URN) refers to the subset of URI that is required to remain globally unique and persistent even when the resource ceases to exist or becomes unavailable. For example:

- The URL http://dme.uma.pt/jcardoso/index.htm identifies the location from where a Web page can be retrieved
- The URN urn:isbn:3-540-24328-3 identifies a book using its ISBN

Unicode provides a unique number for every character, independently of the underlying platform, program, or language. Before the creation of unicode, there were various different encoding systems. The diverse encoding made the manipulation of data complex. Any given computer needed to support many different encodings. There was always the risk of encoding conflict, since two encodings could use the same number for two different characters, or use different numbers for the same character. Examples of older and well known encoding systems include ASCII and EBCDIC.

*Figure 6. Semantic Web layered architecture (Berners-Lee, Hendler, et al., 2001)*

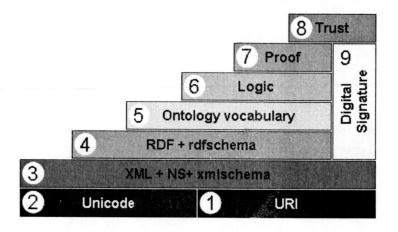

## XML

XML is accepted as a standard for data interchange on the Web allowing the structuring of data on the Web but without communicating the meaning of the data. It is a language for semistructured data and has been proposed as a solution for data integration problems, because it allows a flexible coding and display of data, by using metadata to describe the structure of data (using DTD or XSD).

In contrast to HTML, with XML it is possible to create new markup tags, such as <first_name>, which carry some semantics. However, from a computational perspective, a tag like <first_name> is very similar to the HTML tag <h1>. While XML is highly helpful for a syntactic interoperability and integration, it carries as much semantics as HTML. Nevertheless, XML solved many problems which have earlier been impossible to solve using HTML, that is, data exchange and integration.

A well-formed XML document creates a balanced tree of nested sets of open and closed tags, each of which can include several attribute-value pairs. The following structure shows an example of an XML document identifying a "Contact" resource. The document includes various metadata markup tags, such as <first_name>, <last_name>, and <email>, which provide various details about a contact.

```
<Contact contact_id="1234">
      <first_name> Jorge </first_name>
      <last_name> Cardoso </last_name>
      <organization> University of Madeira </organiza-
      tion>
      <email> jcardoso@uma.pt </email>
      <phone> +351 291 705 156 </phone>
</Contact>
```

While XML has gained much of the world's attention it is important to recognize that XML is simply a way of standardizing data formats. But from the point of view of semantic interoperability, XML has limitations. One significant aspect is that there is no way to recognize the semantics of a particular domain because XML aims at document structure and imposes no common interpretation of the data (Decker, Melnik et al., 2000). Another problem is that XML has a weak data model incapable of capturing semantics, relationships, or constraints. While it is possible to extend XML to incorporate rich metadata, XML does not allow for supporting automated interoperability of system without human involvement. Even though XML is simply a data-format standard, it is part of the set of technologies that constitute the foundations of the semantic Web.

## RDF

At the top of XML, the World Wide Web Consortium (W3C) has developed the Resource Description Framework (RDF) (RDF, 2002) language to standardize the definition and use of metadata. Therefore, XML and RDF each have their merits as a foundation for the semantic Web, but RDF provides more suitable mechanisms for developing ontology representation languages like OIL (Connolly, van Harmelen, et al., 2001).

RDF uses XML and it is at the base of the semantic Web, so that all the other languages corresponding to the upper layers are built on top of it. RDF is a formal data model for machine understandable metadata used to provide standard descriptions of Web resources. By providing a standard way of referring to metadata elements, specific metadata element names, and actual metadata content, RDF builds standards for XML applications so that they can interoperate and intercommunicate more easily, facilitating data and system integration and interoperability. At first glance it may seem that RDF is very similar to XML, but a closer analysis reveals that they are conceptually different. If we model the information present in a RDF model using XML, human readers would probably be able to infer the underlying semantic structure, but general purpose applications would not.

RDF is a simple general-purpose metadata language for representing information in the Web and provides a model for describing and creating relationships between resources. A resource can be a thing such as a person, a song, or a Web page. With RDF it is possible to add predefined modeling primitives for expressing semantics of data to a document without making any assumptions about the structure of the document. RDF defines a resource as any object that is uniquely identifiable by a Uniform Resource Identifier (URI). Resources have properties associated to them. Properties are identified by property-types, and property-types have corresponding values. Property-types express the relationships of values associated with resources. The basic structure of RDF is very simple and basically uses RDF triples in the form of subject, predicate, object.

- **Subject:** A thing identified by its URL
- **Predicate:** The type of metadata, also identified by a URL (also called the property)
- **Object:** The value of this type of metadata

RDF has a very limited set of syntactic constructs, no other constructs except for triples is allowed. Every RDF document is equivalent to an unordered set of triples. The example from Figure 7 describes the following statement using a RDF triple:

*Jorge Cardoso created the Jorge Cardoso Home Page.*

The Jorge Cardoso Home Page is a resource. This resource has a URI of http://dme.uma.pt/jcardoso/, and it has a property, "creator," with the value "Jorge Cardoso."

The graphic representation of Figure 7 is expressed in RDF with the following statements:

```
<? xml version="1.0" ?>
<RDF xmlns = "http://w3.org/TR/1999/PR-rdf-syntax-
19990105#"
        xmlns:DC = "http://dublincore.org/2003/03/24/
        dces#">

    <Description about = "http://dme.uma.pt/jcar-
    doso/">
        <DC:Creator> Jorge Cardoso </DC:Creator>
    </Description>
</RDF>
```

The first lines of this example use namespaces to explicitly define the meaning of the notions that are used. The first namespace xmlns:rdf="http://w3.org/TR/1999/PR-rdf-syntax-19990105#" refers to the document describing the syntax of RDF. The second namespace http://dublincore.org/2003/03/24/dces# refers to the description of the Dublin Core (DC), a basic ontology about authors and publications.

The Dublin Core (DC, 2005) is a fifteen element metadata set that was originally developed

*Figure 7. Graphic representation of a RDF statement*

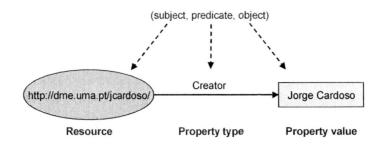

to improve resource discovery on the Web. To this end, the DC elements were primarily intended to describe Web-based documents. Examples of the Dublin Core metadata include:

- **Title:** The title of the resource
- **Subject:** Simple keywords or terms taken from a list of subject headings
- **Description:** A description or abstract
- **Creator:** The person or organization primarily responsible for the intellectual content of the resource
- **Publisher:** The publisher
- **Contributor:** A secondary contributor to the intellectual content of the resource

The following example shows a more real and complete scenario using the DC metadata. It can be observed that more than one predicate-value pair can be indicated for a resource. Basically, it expresses that the resource "http://dme.uma.pt/jcardoso" has the title "Jorge Cardoso Web Page," its subject is "Home Page," and was created by "Jorge Cardoso."

The graphic representation of Figure 8 is expressed in RDF using the DC namespace with the following statements:

```
<? xml version="1.0" ?>
<RDF xmlns = "http://w3.org/TR/1999/PR-rdf-syntax-
    19990105#"
    xmlns:DC = " http://dublincore.org/2003/03/24/
```

```
dces#">

<Description about = "http://dme.uma.pt/jcardoso/" >
    <DC:Title> Jorge Cardoso Home Page </DC:
    Title>
    <DC:Creator> Jorge Cardoso </DC:Creator>
    <DC:Date> 2005-07-23 </DC:Date>
</Description>
</RDF>
```

Very good examples of real world systems that use RDF are the applications developed under the Mozilla project (Mozilla, 2005). Mozilla software applications use various different pieces of structured data, such as bookmarks, file systems, documents, and sitemaps. The creation, access, query, and manipulation code for these resources is completely independent. While the code is completely independent, there is considerable overlap in the data model used by all these different structures. Therefore, Mozilla uses RDF to build a common data model shared by various applications, such as viewers, editors, and query mechanisms.

## RDF Schema

The RDF schema (RDFS, 2004) provides a type system for RDF. The RDFS is technologically advanced compared to RDF since it provides a way of building an object model from which the actual data is referenced and which tells us what things really mean.

*Figure 8. Graphic representation of a RDF statement*

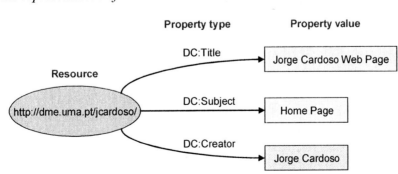

Briefly, the RDF schema (RDFS) allows users to define resources with classes, properties, and values. The concept of RDF class is similar to the concept of class in object-oriented programming languages such as Java and C++. A class is a structure of similar things and inheritance is allowed. This allows resources to be defined as instances of classes, and subclasses of classes. For example, the RDF schema allows resources to be defined as instances of one or more classes. In addition, it allows classes to be organized in a hierarchical fashion. For example the class First_Line_Manager might be defined as a subclass of Manager which is a subclass of Staff, meaning that any resource which is in class Staff is also implicitly in class First_Line_Manager as well.

An RDFS property can be viewed as an attribute of a class. RDFS properties may inherit from other properties, and domain and range constraints can be applied to focus their use. For example, a domain constraint is used to limit what class or classes a specific property may have and a range constraint is used to limit its possible values. With these extensions, RDFS comes closer to existing ontology languages. RDFS is used to declare vocabularies, the sets of semantics property-types defined by a particular community. As with RDF, the XML namespace mechanism serves to identify RDFS. The statements in Box 1 illustrate a very simple example of RDFS where classes and inheritance are used.

The rdfs:Class is similar to the notion of a class in object-oriented programming languages. When a schema defines a new class, the resource representing that class must have an rdf:type property whose value is the resource rdfs:Class. Anything described by RDF expressions is called a resource and is considered to be an instance of the class rdfs:Resource. Other elements of RDFS are illustrated in Figure 9 and described below.

- rdfs:Datatype is the class of data types and defines the allowed data types.

*Box 1.*

```
<?xml version="1.0"?>
<rdf:RDF
  xmlns:rdf= "http://www.w3.org/1999/02/22-rdf-syn-tax-ns#"
  xmlns:rdfs="http://www.w3.org/2000/01/rdf-sche-ma#"
  xml:base= „http://www.hr.com/humanresources#">
                                    class
  <rdf:Description rdf ID="staff">
  <rdf:type
rdf:resource="http://www.w3.org/2000/01/rdf-schema#Class"/>
  </rdf:Description>                  subclass of
                                       class
  <rdf:Description rdf ID="manager">
  <rdf:type
rdf:resource="http://www.w3.org/2000/01/rdf-schema#Class"/>
  <rdfs:subClassOf rdf:resource="#staff"/>
  </rdf:Description>

</rdf:RDF>
```

- rdfs:Literal is the class of literal values such as strings and integers.
- rdfs:subClassOf is a transitive property that specifies a subset-superset relation between classes.
- rdfs:subPropertyOf is an instance of rdf:Property used to specify that one property is a specialization of another.
- rdfs:comment is a human-readable description of a resource.
- rdfs:label is a human-readable version of a resource name and it can only be a string literal.
- rdfs:seeAlso specifies a resource that might provide additional information about the subject resource.
- rdfs:isDefinedBy is a subproperty of rdfs:seeAlso and indicates the resource defining the subject resource.
- rdfs:member is a super-property of all the container membership properties
- rdfs:range indicates the classes that the values of a property must be members of.

*Figure 9. Relationships between the concepts of RDF schema*

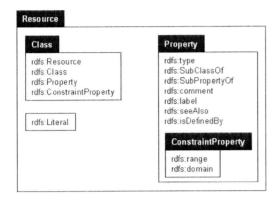

- rdfs:domain indicates the classes on whose member a property can be used.
- rdfs:Container is a collection of resources.
- rdfs:ContainerMemberShipProperty is a class that is used to state that a resource is a member of a container.

## Ontologies

An ontology is an agreed vocabulary that provides a set of well-founded constructs to build meaningful higher level knowledge for specifying the semantics of terminology systems in a well defined and unambiguous manner. For a particular domain, an ontology represents a richer language for providing more complex constraints on the types of resources and their properties. Compared to a taxonomy, ontologies enhance the semantics of terms by providing richer relationships between the terms of a vocabulary. Ontologies are usually expressed in a logic-based language, so that detailed and meaningful distinctions can be made among the classes, properties, and relations.

Ontologies can be used to increase communication either between humans and computers. The three major uses of ontologies (Jasper & Uschold, 1999) are:

- To assist in communication between humans.
- To achieve interoperability and communication among software systems.
- To improve the design and the quality of software systems.

In the previous sections, we have established that RDF/S was one of the base models and syntax for the semantic Web. On the top of the RDF/S layer it is possible to define more powerful languages to describe semantics. The most prominent markup language for publishing and sharing data using ontologies on the Internet is the Web Ontology Language (OWL, 2004). Web Ontology Language (OWL) is a vocabulary extension of RDF and is derived from the DAML+OIL language (DAML, 2001), with the objective of facilitating a better machine interpretability of Web content than that supported by XML and RDF. OWL adds a layer of expressive power to RDF/S, providing powerful mechanisms for defining complex conceptual structures, and formally describes the semantics of classes and properties used in Web resources using, most commonly, a logical formalism known as description logic (DL, 2005).

Let's analyze some of the limitations of RDF/S to identify the extensions that are needed:

1. RDF/S cannot express equivalence between properties. This is important to be able to express the equivalence of ontological concepts developed by separate working groups.
2. RDF/S does not have the capability of expressing the uniqueness and the cardinality of properties. In some cases, it may be necessary to express that a particular property value may have only one value in a particular class instance.
3. RDF/S can express the values of a particular property but cannot express that this is a closed set. For example, an enumeration for

the values for the gender of a person should have only two values: male and female.

4. RDF/S cannot express disjointedness. For example, the gender of a person can be male or female. While it is possible in RDF/S to express that John is a male and Julie a female, there is no way of saying that John is not a female and Julie is not a male.

5. RDF/S cannot express the concept of unions and intersections of classes. This allows the creation of new classes that are composed of other classes. For example, the class "staff" might be the union of the classes "CEO," "manager," and "clerk." The class "staff" may also be described as the intersection of the classes "person" and "organization employee."

Let us see a more detailed example of RDF/S limitations. Consider the sentence:

*There are three people responsible for the Web resource 'Jorge Cardoso Home Page' created in 23 July 2005: Web designer, editor, and graphic designer. Each has distinct roles and responsibilities.*

Using RDF/S we could try to model this statement in the following way:

```
<? xml version="1.0" ?>
<RDF xmlns = "http://w3.org/TR/1999/PR-rdf-syntax-
19990105#"
   xmlns:DC = " http://dublincore.org/2003/03/24/
dces#">
 xmlns:S = " http://hr.org/2005/01/14/hr#">

<Description about = "http://dme.uma.pt/jcardoso/" >
 <DC:Title> Jorge Cardoso Home Page </DC:Title>
 <DC:Creator> Jorge Cardoso </DC:Creator>
 <DC:Date> 2005-07-23 </DC:Date>
 <S:Administrator>
  <rdf:Bag>
   <rdf:li resource="Web designer"/>
   <rdf:li resource="Editor"/>
   <rdf:li resource="Graphic designer"/>
  </rdf:Bag>
 </S:Administrator>
 </Description>
</RDF>
```

In this example we have used the bag container model. In RDF, the container model is restricted to three components: bags, sequence, and alternative. Bags are an unordered list of resources or literals. A sequence is an ordered list of resources or literals. Finally, alternative is a list of resources or literals that represent alternatives for the (single) value of a property.

Using any of the three different relationships in RDF, we are only able to explain the information about the resources, but we cannot explain the second part of our statement, that is, "Each has distinct roles and responsibilities."

Using OWL, we can represent the knowledge associated with the second part of our statement as shown below.

```
<owl:AllDifferent>
 <owl:distinctMembers rdf:parse Type="Collection">
 <admin:Administrator rdf:about="#Web designer"/>
 <admin:Administrator rdf:about="#Editor"/>
 <admin:Administrator rdf:about="#Graphic designer"/>
</owl:distinctMembers>
</owl:AllDifferent>
```

The owl:AllDifferent element is a built-in OWL class, for which the property owl:distinct-Members is defined, which links an instance of owl:AllDifferent to a list of individuals. The intended meaning of such a statement is that the individuals in the list are all different from each other. This OWL representation can express that the three administrators (Web designer, Editor, and Graphic designer) have distinct roles. Such semantics cannot be expressed using RDF, RDFS, or XML.

## Logic, Proof, and Trust

The purpose of this layer is to provide similar features to the ones that can be found in first order logic (FOL). The idea is to state any logical principle and allow the computer to reason by inference using these principles. For example, a university may decide that if a student has a GPA higher than 3.8, then he will receive a merit scholarship. A logic program can use this rule to make a simple deduction: "David has a GPA of 3.9, therefore he will be a recipient of a merit scholarship."

Inference engines, also called reasoners, are software applications that derive new facts or associations from existing information. Inference and inference rules allow for deriving new data from data that is already known. Thus, new pieces of knowledge can be added based on previous ones. By creating a model of the information and relationships, we enable reasoners to draw logical conclusions based on the model. The use of inference engines in the semantic Web allows applications to inquire why a particular conclusion has been reached, that is, semantic applications can give proof of their conclusions. Proof traces or explains the steps involved in logical reasoning.

For example, with OWL it is possible to make inferences based on the associations represented in the models, which primarily means inferring transitive relationships. Nowadays, many inference engines are available. For instance:

- **Jena Reasoner:** Jena includes a generic rule based inference engine together with configured rule sets for RDFS and for OWL. It is an open source Java framework for writing semantic Web applications developed by HP Labs (Jena, 2005).
- **Jess:** Using Jess (Gandon & Sadeh, 2003) it is possible to build Java software that has the capacity to "reason" using knowledge supplied in the form of declarative rules. Jess has a small footprint and it is one of the fastest rule engines available. It was developed at Carnegie Melon University.
- **SWI-Prolog Semantic Web Library:** Prolog is a natural language for working with RDF and OWL. The developers of SWI-Prolog have created a toolkit for creating and editing RDF and OWL applications, as well as a reasoning package (Wielemaker, 2005).

- **FaCT++ :** This system is a description logic reasoner, which is a re-implementation of the FaCT reasoner. It allows reasoning with the OWL language (FaCT, 2005).

Trust is the top layer of the Semantic Web architecture. This layer provides authentication of identity and evidence of the trustworthiness of data and services. While the other layers of the semantic Web stack have received a fair amount of attention, no significant research has been carried out in the context of this layer. The idea is to allow people to ask questions concerning the trustworthiness of the information on the Web. Possible scenarios for the trust layer include the possibility to make statements such as "I trust all information from http://dme.uma.pt/jcardoso, but I don't trust anything from http://www.internetsite.com."

## APPLICATIONS OF THE SEMANTIC WEB

Even though the Semantic Web is still in its infancy, there are already applications and tools that use this conceptual approach to build semantic Web based systems. The intention of this section is to present the state of the art of the applications that use semantics and ontologies. We describe various applications ranging from the use of semantic Web services, semantic integration of tourism information sources, and semantic digital libraries to the development of bioinformatics ontologies.

### Semantic Web Services

Web services are modular, self-describing, self-contained applications that are accessible over the Internet (Curbera, Nagy, et al., 2001). Currently, Web services are described using the Web Services Description Language (Chinnici, Moreau, et al., 2006), which provide operational information. Although the Web Services Description Language (WSDL) does not contain semantic descriptions, it specifies the structure of message components using XML schema constructs. One solution to create semantic Web services is by mapping concepts in a Web service description (WSDL specification) to ontological concepts (LSDIS, 2004). The WSDL elements that can be marked up with metadata are operations, messages, and preconditions and effects, since all the elements are explicitly declared in a WSDL description. Approaches and initiatives which goal is to specify Web Services using semantics and ontologies include OWL-S (OWL-S, 2004), SWSI (SWSI, 2004), SWWS (SWWS, 2004), WSML (WSML, 2004), WSMO (WSMO, 2004), WSMX (WSMX, 2004), and WSDL-S (Akkiraju, Farrell, et al., 2006)

## Semantic Tourism Information Systems

Dynamic packaging technology helps online travel customers to build and book vacations. It can be described as the ability for a customer to put together elements of a (vacation) trip including flights, hotels, car rentals, local tours and tickets to theatre and sporting events. The package that is created is handled seamlessly as one transaction and requires only one payment from the consumer, hiding the pricing of individual components. So far, the travel industry has concentrated its efforts on developing open specification messages, based on XML, to ensure that messages can flow between industry segments as easily as within. For example, the OpenTravel Alliance (OTA, 2004) is an organization pioneering the development and use of specifications that support e-business among all segments of the travel industry. It has produced more than 140 XML-based specifications for the travel industry.

The development of open specification messages based on XML, such as OTA schema, to ensure the interoperability between trading partners and working groups is not sufficiently expressive to guarantee an automatic exchange and processing of information to develop dynamic applications. A more appropriate solution is to use technologies from the semantic Web, such as ontologies, to deploy common language for tourism-related terminology and a mechanism for promoting the seamless exchange of information across all travel industry segments. Ontologies are the key elements enabling the shift from a purely syntactic to a semantic interoperability. An ontology can be defined as the explicit, formal descriptions of concepts and their relationships that exist in a certain universe of discourse, together with a shared vocabulary to refer to these concepts. With respect to an ontology a particular user group commits to, the semantics of data provided by the data sources to be integrated can be made explicit. Ontologies can be applied to the area of dynamic packaging to explicitly connect data and information from tourism information systems to its definition and context in machine-processable form.

## Semantic Digital Libraries

Libraries are a key component of the information infrastructure indispensable for education. They provide an essential resource for students and researchers for reference and for research. Metadata has been used in libraries for centuries. For example, the two most common general classification systems, which use metadata, are the Dewey Decimal Classification (DDC) system and the Library of Congress Classification (LCC) system. The DDC system has 10 major subjects, each with 10 secondary subjects (DDC, 2005). The LCC system uses letters instead of numbers to organize materials into 21 general branches of knowledge. The 21 subject categories are further divided into more specific subject areas by adding one or two additional letters and numbers (LCCS, 2005).

As traditional libraries are increasingly converting to digital libraries, a new set of requirements has emerged. One important feature of digital libraries is the ability to efficiently browse electronic catalogues browsed. This requires the use of common metadata to describe the records of the catalogue (such as author, title, and publisher) and common controlled vocabularies to allow subject identifiers to be assigned to publications. The use of a common *controlled vocabulary, thesauri, and taxonomy* (Smrz, Sinopalnikova et al., 2003) *a*llows search engines to ensure that the most relevant items of information are returned. Semantically annotating the contents of a digital library's database goes beyond the use of a *controlled vocabulary, thesauri, or taxonomy. It* allows retrieving books' records using meaningful information to the existing full text and bibliographic descriptions.

Semantic Web technologies, such as RDF and OWL, can be used as a common interchange format for catalogue metadata and shared vocabulary, which can be used by all libraries and search engines (Shum, Motta et al., 2000) across the Web. This is important since it is not uncommon to find *library systems based on various metadata formats and built by different persons for their special purposes.* By publishing ontologies, which can then be accessed by all users across the Web, library catalogues can use the same vocabularies for cataloguing, marking up items with the most relevant terms for the domain of interest. RDF and OWL provide a single and consistent encoding system so that implementers of digital library metadata systems will have their task simplified when interoperating with other digital library systems.

## Semantic Grid

The concept of Grid (Foster & Kesselman, 1999) has been proposed as a fundamental computing infrastructure to support the vision of e-Science. The Grid is a service for sharing computer power and data storage capacity over the Internet and goes well beyond simple communication providing functionalities that enable the rapid assembly and disassembly of services into temporary groups.

Recently, the Grid has been evolving towards the Semantic Grid to yield an intelligent platform which allows process automation, knowledge sharing and reuse, and collaboration within a community (Roure, Jennings, et al., 2001). The Semantic Grid is about the use of semantic Web technologies in Grid computing; it is an extension of the current Grid. The objective is to describe information, computing resources, and services in standard ways that can be processed by computers. Resources and services are represented using the technologies of the semantic Web, such as RDF. The use of semantics to locate data has important implications for integrating computing resources. It implies a two-step access to resources. In step one, a search of metadata catalogues is used to find the resources containing the data or service required by an application. In the second step, the data or service is accessed or invoked.

## Semantic Web Search

Swoogle (Swoogle, 2005) is a crawler-based indexing and retrieval system for the semantic Web built on top of the Google API. It was developed in the context of a research project of the Ebiquity research group at the Computer Science and Electrical Engineering Department of the University of Maryland, USA. In contrast to Google (Google, 2005), Swoogle discovers, analyzes, and indexes Semantic Web Documents (SWD) written in RDF and OWL, rather than plain HTML documents. Documents are indexed using metadata about classes, properties, and individuals, as well as the relationships among them. Unlike traditional search engines, Swoogle aims to take advantage of the semantic metadata available in semantic Web documents. Metadata is extracted for each discovered document and relations (e.g., similarities) among documents are computed. Swoogle also defines an ontology ranking property for SWD which is similar to the pageRank (Brin & Page, 1998) approach from Google and uses this information to sort search results. Swoogle provides query interfaces and services to Web users. It supports software agents, programs via service interfaces, and researchers working in the semantic Web area via the Web interface.

## Semantic Bioinformatic Systems

The integration of information sources in the life sciences is one of the most challenging goals of bioinformatics (Kumar & Smith, 2004). In this area, the Gene Ontology (GO) is one of the most significant accomplishments. The objective of GO is to supply a mechanism to guarantee the consistent descriptions of gene products in different databases. GO is rapidly acquiring the status of a *de facto* standard in the field of gene and gene product annotations (Kumar & Smith, 2004). The GO effort includes the development of controlled vocabularies that describe gene products, establishing associations between the ontologies, the genes, and the gene products in the databases, and develop tools to create, maintain, and use ontologies (see http://www.geneontology.org/). GO has over 17,000 terms and it is organized in three hierarchies for molecular functions, cellular components, and biological processes (Bodenreider, Aubry, et al., 2005).

Another well-known life science ontology is the microarray gene expression data (MGED) ontology. MGED provides standard terms in the form of an ontology organized into classes with properties for the annotation of microarray experiments (MGED, 2005). These terms provide an unambiguous description of how experiments were performed and enable structured queries of elements of the experiments. The comparison between different experiments is only feasible if there is standardization in the terminology for describing experimental setup, mathematical

post-processing of raw measurements, genes, tissues, and samples. The adoption of common standards by the research community for describing data makes it possible to develop systems for the management, storage, transfer, mining, and sharing of microarray data (Stoeckert, Causton, et al., 2002). If data from every microarray experiment carried out by different research groups were stored with the same structure, in the same type of database, the manipulation of data would be relatively easy. Unfortunately, in practice, different research groups have very different requirements and, therefore, applications need mappings and translations between the different existing formats (Stoeckert, Causton, et al., 2002).

## CONCLUSION

Since its creation, the World Wide Web has allowed computers only to understand Web page layout for display purposes without having access to their intended meaning. The semantic Web aims to enrich the existing Web with a layer of machine-understandable metadata to enable the automatic processing of information by computer programs. The semantic Web is not a separate Web but an extension of the current one, in which information is given well-defined meaning, better enabling computers and people to work in cooperation. To make possible the creation of the semantic Web the W3C (World Wide Web Consortium) has been actively working on the definition of open standards, such as the RDF and OWL, and incentivate their use by both industry and academia. These standards are also important for the integration and interoperability for intra- and inter-business processes that have become widespread due to the development of business-to-business and business-to-customer infrastructures.

The Semantic Web does not restrict itself to the formal semantic description of Web resources for machine-to-machine exchange and automated integration and processing. One important feature of formally describing resources is to allow computers to reason by inference. Once resources are described using facts, associations, and relationships, inference engines, also called reasoners, can derive new knowledge and draw logical conclusions from existing information. The use of inference engines in the semantic Web allows applications to inquire why a particular logical conclusion has been reached, that is, semantic applications can give proof of their conclusions by explaining the steps involved in logical reasoning.

Even though the semantic Web is still in its infancy, there are already applications and tools that use this conceptual approach to build semantic Web based systems, ranging from the use of semantic Web services, semantic integration of tourism information sources, and semantic digital libraries to the development of bioinformatics ontologies.

## REFERENCES

Akkiraju, R., Farrell, J., Miller, J., Nagarajan, M., Schmidt M., Sheth, A., & Verma, K., (2006) *Web service semantics: WSDL-S.* Retrieved February 20, 2007 from http://www.w3.org/Submission/WSDL-S

Berners-Lee, T., Hendler, J., & Lassila, O. (2001, May). The Semantic Web. *Scientific American,* 34-43.

Bodenreider, O., Aubry, M., & Burgun, A. (2005). *Non-lexical approaches to identifying associative relations in the gene ontology.* Paper presented at the Pacific Symposium on Biocomputing, Hawaii. World Scientific.

BPEL4WS (2002). *Web services.* IBM.

Brin, S., & Page, L. (1998). *The anatomy of a large-scale hypertextual Web search engine.*
Paper presented at the Seventh World Wide Web Conference, Brisbane, Australia.

Chinnici, R., Moreau, J., Ryman, A., & Weerawarana, S. (2003) *Web services description language (WSDL) version 2.0 prt 1: Core language: W3C candidate recommendation 27 March 2006.* Retrieved February, 20, 2007 from http://www.w3.org/TR/wsdl20/

Curbera, F., Nagy, W., & Weerawarana, S. (2001). *Web services: Why and how.* Paper presented at the Workshop on Object-Oriented Web Services (OOPSLA 2001), Tampa, Florida. Retrieved February 20, 2007 from http://www.research.ibm.com/people/b/bth/OOWS2001/nagy.pdf

Connolly, D. F., van Harmelen, F., Horrocks, I., McGuinness, D. L., Patel-Schneider, P. F., & Stein, L. A., (2001 March). *DAML+OIL reference description.* Retrieved February 20, 2007 from http://www.w3.org/TR/2001/NOTE-daml+oil-reference-20011218

DC (2005). *The Dublin core metadata initiative.* Retrieved October 24, 2006, from http://dublincore.org/

DDC (2005). Dewey decimal classification. OCLC Online Computer Library Center. Retrieved October 24, 2006, from http://www.oclc.org/dewey/

Decker, S., Melnik, S., van Harmelen, F., Fensel, D., Klein, M., Broekstra, J., Erdmann, M., & Horrocks, I. (2000). The Semantic Web: The roles of XML and RDF. *Internet Computing, 4*(5), 63-74.

DERI (2004). *Digital Enterprise Research Institute (DERI).*

DL (2005). *Description logics.* Retrieved October 24, 2006, from http://www.dl.kr.org/

FaCT (2005). *FaCT++.* Retrieved October 24, 2006, from http://owl.man.ac.uk/factplusplus/

Fensel, D. (2001). *Ontologies: Silver bullet for knowledge management and electronic commerce.* Berlin: Springer-Verlag. Retrieved October 24, 2006, from http://www.cs.vu.nl/~dieter/ftp/paper/silverbullet.pdf

Foster, I., & Kesselman, C. (1999). *The grid: Blueprint for a new computing infrastructure.* San Fransisco: Morgan Kaufmann.

Gandon, F.L., & Sadeh, N.M. (2003). *OWL inference engine using XSLT and JESS.* Retrieved October 24, 2006, from http://www-2.cs.cmu.edu/~sadeh/MyCampusMirror/OWLEngine.html

Google (2005). *Google search engine.* Retrieved October 24, 2006, from http://www.google.com

Grau, B.C. (2004). *A possible simplification of the Semantic Web architecture.* Paper presented at WWW 2004, New York.

Horrocks, I., v. Harmelen, F., et al. (2001). *DAML+OIL, DAML.*

Jasper, R., & Uschold, M. (1999). *A framework for understanding and classifying ontology applications.* Paper presented at the IJCAI99 Workshop on Ontologies and Problem-Solving Methods.

Jena (2005). *Jena: A Semantic Web framework for Java.* Retrieved October 24, 2006, from http://jena.sourceforge.net/

Kumar, A., & Smith, B. (2004). On controlled vocabularies in bioinformatics: A case study in gene ontology. *Drug Discovery Today: BIO-SILICO, 2,* 246-252.

LCCS. (2005). *The Library of Congress, Library of Congress classification system.* Retrieved October 24, 2006, from http://www.loc.gov/catdir/cpso/lcco/lcco.html

LSDIS. (2004). *METEOR-S: Semantic Web services and processes.* Retrieved February 20, 2007 from http://lsdis.cs.uga.edu/projects/meteor-s/

MGED. (2005). *Microarray gene expression data society.* Retrieved October 24, 2006, from http://www.mged.org/

Mozilla. (2005). *The Mozilla Project.* Retrieved October 24, 2006, from http://www.mozilla.org/

NISO (2005). *Guidelines for the construction, format, and management of Monolingual Thesauri.* National Information Standards Organization. Retrieved October 24, 2006, from http://www.niso.org/standards/resources/z39-19a.pdf

OTA. (2004). *OpenTravel Alliance.*

OWL. (2004). *OWL Web ontology language reference*, W3C Recommendation, World Wide Web Consortium. Retrieved October 24, 2006, from http://www.w3.org/TR/owl-ref/. 2004

OWL-S. (2004). *OWL-based Web service ontology.* Retrieved February 20, 2007 from http://www.daml.org/services/owl-s/

RDF. (2002). *Resource description framework (RDF).* Retrieved October 24, 2006, from http://www.w3.org/RDF/

RDFS. (2004). *RDF vocabulary description language 1.0: RDF schema,* W3C. Retrieved October 24, 2006, from http://www.w3.org/TR/rdf-schema/

Roure, D., Jennings, N., & Shadbolt, N. (2001). *Research agenda for the future semantic grid: A future e-science infrastructure.* Retrieved October 24, 2006, from http://www.semanticgrid.org/v1.9/semgrid.pdf

Sheth, A. (2003, July). Semantic meta data for enterprise information integration. *DM Review Magazine.* Retrieved from http://www.dmreview.com/article_subcfm?articleId=6962

Shum, S.B., Motta, E., & Domingue, J. (2000). ScholOnto: An ontology-based digital library server for research documents and discourse.

*International Journal on Digital Libraries, 3*(3), 237-248.

Smrz, P., Sinopalnikova, A., & Povolny, M. (2003). Thesauri and ontologies for digital libraries. In *Digital Libraries: Advanced Methods and Technologies, Digital Collections. Proceedings of the 5ᵗʰ Russian Conference on Digital Libraries (RCDL2003)* (pp. 14-17). Saint-Petersburg, Russia. Saint-Petersburg State University Published Press

SOAP. (2002). *Simple object access protocol 1.1.* Retrieved February 20, 2007 from http://www.w3.org/TR/soap/

Stoeckert, C.J., Causton, H.C., & Ball, C. A. (2002). Microarray databases: Standards and ontologies. *Nature Genetics, 32*, 469-473.

Swoogle (2005). *Search and metadata for the Semantic Web.* Retrieved October 24, 2006, from http://swoogle.umbc.edu/

SWSI (2004). *Semantic Web services initiative (SWSI).* Retrieved February 20, 2007 from http://www.swsi.org/

SWWS (2004). *Semantic Web enabled Web service.* Digital Enterprise Research Institute (DERI).

UDDI (2002). *Universal description, discovery, and integration.* Retrieved February 20, 2007 from http://www.uddi.org/

Wielemaker, J. (2005). *SWI-prolog semantic Web library.* Retrieved October 24, 2006, from http://www.swi-prolog.org/packages/semweb.html

WSML. (2004). *Web service modeling language (WSML).* Retrieved February 20, 2007 from http://www.wsmo.org/wsml/

WSMO. (2004). *Web services modeling ontology (WSMO).* Retrieved February 20, 2007 from http://www.wsmo.org

WSMX. (2004). *Web services execution environment (WSMX).* Retrieved February 20, 2007 from http://www.wsmx.org

XML. (2005, February 4). *Extensible markup language (XML) 1.0* (3ʳᵈ ed.). W3C recommendation. Retrieved October 24, 2006, from http://www.w3.org/TR/REC-xml/

XML schema. (2005). *XML schema.* Retrieved October 24, 2006, from http://www.w3.org/XML/Schema

## ENDNOTE

[1]    http://fwrlibrary.troy.edu/1/dbhelp/dbhelp-psychology.htm

# Chapter II
# Logics for the Semantic Web

**Jos de Bruijn**
*University of Innsbruck, Austria*

## ABSTRACT

*This chapter introduces a number of formal logical languages which form the backbone of the Semantic Web. They are used for the representation of both ontologies and rules. The basis for all languages presented in this chapter is the classical first-order logic. Description logics is a family of languages which represent subsets of first-order logic. Expressive description logic languages form the basis for popular ontology languages on the Semantic Web. Logic programming is based on a subset of first-order logic, namely Horn logic, but uses a slightly different semantics and can be extended with non-monotonic negation. Many Semantic Web reasoners are based on logic programming principles and rule languages for the Semantic Web based on logic programming are an ongoing discussion. Frame Logic allows object-oriented style (frame-based) modeling in a logical language. RuleML is an XML-based syntax consisting of different sublanguages for the exchange of specifications in different logical languages over the Web.*

## INTRODUCTION

An important property of the Semantic Web is that the information contained in it is specified using a formal language in order to enable machine-processability and the derivation of new knowledge from existing knowledge. Logical languages are such formal languages.

Using logical languages for knowledge representation allows one to derive new knowledge which is implicit in existing descriptions. Additionally, the use of formal languages allows one to write unambiguous statements and allows machines to derived implicit information using formal rules of deduction associated with the language. Finally, logical languages have been extensively studied in the research areas of databases and artificial intelligence. It is for these reasons that logical languages form the backbone of the Semantic Web.

Logical languages can be used for the representation of different kinds of knowledge, most notably ontologies and rules. In this chapter we describe a number of logical languages which are being used for the representation of knowledge on the Semantic Web.

*Classical first-order logic* (Fitting, 1996) is the basis for all the languages we survey in this chapter. Full first-order logic by itself is a very expressive language. In fact, the language is so expressive that reasoning with the language is in general very hard and the most interesting problems are undecidable. The answer to a question such as "Does sentence $\phi$ follow from theory $\Phi$?" cannot always be found. For these reasons, several subsets of first-order logic have been investigated and form the basis for several languages which are used on the Semantic Web, most notably description logics and logic programming. Nonetheless, full first-order logic has been proposed as a language for the Semantic Web (Battle, Bernstein, Boley, Grosof, Gruninger, & Hull, 2005; Horrocks, Patel-Schneider, Boley, Tabet, Grosof, & Dean, 2004; Patel-Schneider, 2005).

*Description logics* (Baader, Calvanese, McGuinness, Nardi, & Patel-Schneider, 2003) are a family of languages which generally represent strict subsets of first-order logic. Description logics were originally devised to formalize frame-based knowledge representation systems. Languages in this family typically allow the definition of concepts, concept hierarchies, roles and certain restrictions on roles. Description logics receive a lot of attention as a basis for ontology languages on the Semantic Web; most notably, the W3C recommendation OWL is based on an expressive description logic (Horrocks, Patel-Schneider, & Harmelen, 2003).

*Logic programming* (Lloyd, 1987) is based on the Horn logic subset of first-order logic, which allows one to write rules of the form "if $A$ then $B$". In order to allow for efficient reasoning, the semantics of logic programming is built around Herbrand interpretation, rather than first-order

interpretations. Logic programming is being used as an implementation platform for the Semantic Web, but has also been proposed as the basis for rule and ontology languages on the Semantic Web (Angele, Boley, Bruijn, Fensel, Hitzler, & Kifer, 2005; Battle et al., 2005).

*Frame logic* (Kifer, Lausen, & Wu, 1995) is an extension of first-order logic which allows an object-oriented (frame-based) style of modeling. Frame logic does not increase the theoretical expressiveness of first-order logic, but allows a more convenient style of modeling. F-Logic programming is a subset of Frame Logic which extends logic programming with frame-based modeling primitives; in this chapter, we will restrict ourselves to this subset. F-Logic programming has been proposed as a basis for ontology and rule languages for the Semantic Web (Kifer, 2005).

In this chapter we describe each of these languages from the point-of-view of knowledge representation; that is, we describe which kind of knowledge can be described using the language. We also mention certain complexity results for reasoning with these languages, but do not describe the reasoning procedures in detail. Additionally, we describe the RuleML XML syntax for exchange of rules and logical specification in general over the Web.

## FIRST-ORDER LOGIC

The basic building blocks of first-order logic (FOL) are *constants, function symbols* and *predicates.* Constants are interpreted as *objects* in some abstract *domain.* Function symbols are interpreted as *functions* and predicates are interpreted as *relations* over the domain. The domain may consist of objects representing such things as numbers, persons, cars, and so forth. The relations may be such things as "greater-than," "marriage," "top speed," and so forth. Constants, predicates and function symbols are combined with variables and logical connectives to obtain formulas. We want to interpret such formulas as assertions. Whether such an assertion is true of false depends on the context, that is, on the choice of the domain.

In this section we will first define how *formulas* and *theories* in a first-order language are created from terms, predicates and a number of logical connectives. We will then define *interpretations* of first-order formulas and theories, and define when an interpretation is a *model* of a given formula or theory. The set of models defines the actual meaning, or *semantics*, of a theory. Using the definition of a model, we define entailment, that is, the question whether a formula logically follows from a theory. For a more detailed treatment of first-order logic, included methods for automated theorem proving, see (Fitting, 1996).

## Formulas and Theories

The signature $\Sigma$ of a first-order language $L$, also referred to as first-order signature, consists of countable sets $C$, $F$, $P$ and $V$ of *constant, function, predicate* and *variable* symbols, respectively. Each function symbol $f \in F$ and each predicate symbol $p \in P$ has an associated *arity n*, which is a non-negative integer.

*Definition 1 (Terms) We define the set of terms of the language L as follows:*

- *every constant $c \in C$ is a term in L,*
- *every variable $x \in V$ is a term in L,*
- *if $f \in F$ is an n-ary function symbol and $(t_1,...,t_n)$ are terms in L, then $f(t_1,...,t_n)$ is a term in L.*

A *ground term* is a term with no variables.

*Example 1* Given the signature $S=C,F,P,V$ with the constants $C=\{a,b\}$, function symbols $F=\{f,g\}$, both with arity 1, predicate symbols $P=\{p,q,r\}$, where $p$ and $q$ have arity 2 and $r$ has the arity 1, and variables $V=\{x,y,z\}$, then the following are examples of terms: $x,b,f(a),g(f(a)),g(y)$. Fur-

thermore, $b,f(a),g(f(a))$ are examples of ground terms.

An *atomic formula* is either a predicate expression of the form $p(t_1,...,t_n)$ where $p$ is an *n*-ary predicate symbol in $L$ and $(t_1,...,t_n)$ are terms in $L$, one of the propositional constants $\bot$, T or $t_1 = t_2$, where $t_1,t_2$ are terms in $L$. A *ground* atomic formula is an atomic formula with no variables.

*Example 2* Give the signature S as in the previous example, then the following are atomic formulas:

$$p(a,b),p(x,f(g(y))),q(f(a),b),r(g(f(a))),r(z),a{=}f(b),$$
$$f(x){=}f(g(y)), \bot$$

Of these,

$$p(a,b),q(f(a),b),r(g(f(a))),a{=}f(b), \bot$$

are ground atomic formulas.

*Definition 2 (Formulas) Given the formulas $\phi, \psi \in L$, we define the set of formulas in L as follows:*

- *every atomic formula is a formula in L,*
- *$\neg\phi$ is a formula in L,*
- *$(\phi \wedge \psi)$ is a formula in L,*
- *$(\phi \vee \psi)$ is a formula in L,*
- *$(\phi \rightarrow \psi)$ is a formula in L,*
- *given a variable $x \in V$, $\exists x.(\phi)$ is a formula in L,*
- *given a variable $x \in V$, $\forall x.(\phi)$ is a formula in L.*

A variable occurrence is called *free* if it does not occur in the scope of a quantifier $(\exists, \forall)$. A formula is *open* if it has free variable occurrences. A formula is *closed* if it is not open. A closed formula is also called a *sentence* of $L$.

*Example 3* Give the signature $\Sigma$ as before, then the following are sentences of $L$:

- $\exists x.(\forall y.(p(x,y)\wedge q(f(a),x)\rightarrow r(y)))$
- $(p(a,b)\vee\neg r(f(b)))\vee\exists z.(q(z,f(z))$

The following is an example of an open formula:

$$\exists x.(p(x,y))\rightarrow r(y)))$$

*Example 4* Let's consider the sentences:

- All humans are mortal
- Socrates is a human

This can be written in first-order logic as follows:

$$\forall x.(human(x)\rightarrow mortal(x))$$
$$human(Socrates)$$

Intuitively, these sentences can be read as:

- "For all objects it is the case that if they have the property 'human', they have the property 'mortal'."
- "The object 'socrates' has the property 'human'."

A first-order language $L$ consists of all the formulas which can be written using its signature $\Sigma$ according to Definition 2. A first-order *theory* $\Phi$ of a first-order language $L$ is a set of formulas such that $\Phi \subseteq L$.

## Interpretations, Models, and Entailment

The semantics (or meaning) of a first-order theory is defined by a set of interpretations. In particular, by all interpretations in which the theory is true. Thus, in a sense, the meaning of a theory is *constrained* by all the interpretations which make the theory true. It follows that a first-order theory does not say what is true in a particular world, or interpretation, but rather limits the number of

possible worlds which may be considered. We now give a formal definition.

*Definition 3 (Interpretation) An* interpretation *for a language L is a tuple $w=\langle U,I\rangle$, where U is a nonempty set, called the* domain *of the interpretation and I is a mapping which assigns:*

- an element $c^I\in U$ to every constant symbol $c\in C$,
- a function $f^I:U^n\rightarrow U$ to every n-ary function symbol $f\in F$, and
- a relation $p^I\subseteq U^n$, to every n-ary predicate symbol $p\in P$.

A variable assignment $B$ is a mapping which assigns an element $x^B\in U$ to every variable symbol $x\in V$. A variable assignment $B'$ is an *x-variant* of $B$ if for every variable $y\in V$ such that $y\neq x$.

We are now ready to define the interpretation of terms.

*Definition 4 Given interpretation $w=\langle U,I\rangle$, variable assignment B, and a term t of L, we define $t^{w,B}$ as follows:*

- for every constant symbol $c\in C$, $c^{w,B}=c^I$,
- for every variable symbol $x\in V$, $x^{w,B}=x^B$,
- if $t=f(t_1,...,t_n)$, $t^{w,B}=f^I(t_1^{w,B},...,t_n^{w,B})$.

We can see from Definition 4 that, given an interpretation and a variable assignment, each term is interpreted as one object in the domain. We can now define satisfaction (truth) of first-order formulas.

*Definition 5 (Satisfaction) Let $w=\langle U,I\rangle$ be an interpretation for L, B a variable assignment, and $\phi\in L$ a formula. We denote* satisfaction *of $\phi$ in w ($\phi$ is true in w), given the variable assignment B, with $w\models_B\phi$. Satisfaction is recursively defined as follows, with $\psi$, $\psi_1$, $\psi_2$ formulas, p an n-ary predicate symbol and $t_1,...,t_n$ terms:*

- $w \models_B p(t_1,...,t_n)$ iff $(t_1^{w,B},...,t_n^{w,B}) \in p^I$,
- $w \models_B \bot$ and $w \models_B T$,
- $w \models_B t_1 = t_2$ iff $t_1^{w,B} = t_2^{w,B}$,
- $w \models_B \neg\psi$ iff $w \not\models_B \psi$,
- $w \models_B \psi_1 \wedge \psi_2$ iff $w \models_B \psi_1$ and $w \models_B \psi_2$,
- $w \models_B \psi_1 \vee \psi_2$ iff $w \models_B \psi_1$ or $w \models_B \psi_2$,
- $w \models_B \psi_1 \rightarrow \psi_2$ iff whenever $w \models_B \psi_1$, $w \models_B \psi_2$,
- $w \models_B \forall x.(\psi)$ iff for every x-variant B' of B, $w \models_{B'} \psi$,
- $w \models_B \exists x.(\psi)$ iff for some x-variant B' of B, $w \models_{B'} \psi$.

A formula $\phi$ is *satisfied* by an interpretation $w$, or $\phi$ is *true* in $w$, written as $w \models \phi$, if $w \models_B \phi$ for all variable assignments $B$. We that say $w$ is a *model* of $\phi$ if $w \models \phi$.

If a formula has at least one model, we call the formula *satisfiable*; conversely, if a formula has no models, it is *unsatisfiable*. We say that a formula $\phi$ is *valid* if $\phi$ is true in every interpretation $w$ of $L$. An interpretation $w$ is a model of a theory $\Phi \subseteq L$ if $w \models \phi$ for every formula $\phi \in \Phi$.

*Example 5* Consider the first-order language $L$ with the constant symbol $a$, the unary function symbol $f$, the binary function symbol $g$, and the binary predicate $p$. Now consider the following theory:

$\forall x.(g(a,x) = x)$
$\forall x.\forall y.(g(x,y) = g(y,x))$
$\forall x.\forall y.\forall z.(g(x,g(y,z)) = g(g(x,y),z))$
$\forall x.(p(x,x))$
$\forall x.(p(x,f(x)))$
$\forall x.\forall y.\forall z.(p(x,y) \wedge p(y,z) \rightarrow p(x,z))$

Now consider the interpretation $w = \langle N, I \rangle$, with the domain of the natural numbers $N$ (including 0) and $I$ assigns to $a$ the number 0 (zero), to $f$ the successor function, that is, for every natural number $x$, $f^I(x) = x+1$, and to $g$ the addition operator, that is, for every pair of natural numbers $x,y$,

$g^I(x,y) = x+y$. Finally, $I$ assigns to the predicate $p$ the relation $\leq$ (smaller-or-equal).

Now, the first formula is interpreted as "$0+x=x$", the second formula as "$x+y=y+x$" and the third formula as "$x+(y+z)=(x+y)+z$". The fourth formula is interpreted as "$x \leq x$" (reflexivity of $\leq$), the fifth as "$x \leq x+1$" and the sixth as "if $x \leq y$ and $y \leq z$ then $x \leq z$" (transitivity of $\leq$). All these statements are obviously true for the domain of natural numbers, thus the theory is true in $w$ and $w$ is a model for this theory.

The theory of the previous example is satisfiable; the interpretation constructed in the example is a model. It is not valid; one can easily construct an interpretation which is not a model, for example, any interpretation which assigns to $p$ an antireflexive relation.

An example of a valid formula is:

$\forall x.(p(x) \vee \neg p(x))$.

It is easy to verify that in every interpretation $p(x)$ must either be true or false for every $x$, and thus the formula is true in every possible interpretation. The following formula is unsatisfiable:

$\exists x.(p(x) \wedge \neg p(x))$.

It is easy to verify that in every interpretation $p(x)$ must either be true or false for every $x$; it cannot be both. Therefore, $p(x) \wedge \neg p(x)$ cannot be true for any $x$ in any interpretation.

*Definition 6 We say that a theory $\Phi \subseteq L$ entails a formula $\phi \in L$, denoted $\Phi \models \phi$, iff for all models $w$ of $\Phi$, $w \models \phi$.*

We can reformulate this definition of entailment using sets of models. Let $Mod(\Phi)$ denote the set of models of some first-order theory $\Phi$, then we can reformulate entailment as set inclusion: $Mod(\Phi) \subseteq Mod(\phi)$ iff $\Phi \models \phi$. In a sense, the *entailing* theory is *more specific*, that is, allows fewer models, than the *entailed* theory.

We have characterized a first-order theory $\Phi$ using its set of models $Mod(\Phi)$. Another way of characterizing a first-order theory $\Phi$ is using its set of entailments $Ent(\Phi)$. The set of entailments of $\Phi$ is the set of all formulas which are entailed by $\Phi$: $\phi \in Ent(\Phi)$ *iff* $\Phi \models \phi$. Now, the less specific a theory is, the more models it has, but the fewer entailments it has. We can observe that a theory $\Phi$ entails a theory $\Psi$, that the set of entailments of $\Phi$ is a *superset* of the entailments of $\Psi$: $Ent(\Phi) \supseteq Ent(\Psi)$ *iff* $\Phi \models \Psi$.

*Example 6* Given the sentences $p \wedge q$ and $q$, where $p,q$ are null-ary predicate symbols, then clearly:

$$p \wedge q \models q$$

because in all models where both $p$ and $q$ are true, $q$ must be true.

But not the other way around:

$$q \not\models p \wedge q$$

because there are models of $q$ in which $p$ is not true.

In the example, $p \wedge q$ presents a more *constrained* view of the world than $q$, namely both $p$ and $q$ must be true, whereas $q$ only mandates that $q$ must be true, but does not say anything about $p$. Thus, the set of models of $p \wedge q$, $Mod(p \wedge q)$, is a subset of the set of models of $q$: $Mod(p \wedge q) \subseteq Mod(q)$, because every model of $p \wedge q$ is a model of $q$. It is also easy to see that the set of entailments of $p \wedge q$, $Ent(p \wedge q)$, is larger than the set of entailments of $q$: $Ent(p \wedge q) \supset Ent(p)$. For example, $p \wedge q$ entails $p \wedge q$, whereas $q$ does not.

It turns out that checking entailment in first-order logic can be reduced to checking satisfiability. In order to check whether some formula $\phi$ is entailed by some theory $\Phi$:

$$\Phi \models \phi$$

we can simply add the negation of $\phi$ to $\Phi$ and check whether this combination, $\Phi \cup \neg(\phi)$ is satisfiable, that is, has a model. If $\Phi \cup \neg(\phi)$ is not satisfiable, then the entailment holds.

*Example 7* Consider the entailment question from the previous example:

$$p \wedge q \models q.$$

We have concluded earlier that this entailment must hold, because every model of $p \wedge q$ must be a model of $q$. Now, let's rewrite this entailment problem to an unsatisfiability problem, that is, we want to check whether:

$$\{p \wedge q, \neg q\}$$

has a model. Clearly, this formula cannot have a model, because both $q$ and $\neg q$ would have to be true in this model and this is not possible. Therefore, we can conclude that $p \wedge q$ entails $q$.

We can now try to explain intuitively why we can use unsatisfiability of $\Phi \cup \neg(\phi)$ to check entailment $\Phi \models \phi$. We have seen earlier that $\Phi \models \phi$ if and only if $Mod(\Phi) \subseteq Mod(\phi)$. We know that the sets of models of $\phi$ and $\neg \phi$ are disjoint, because there can be no model in which both $\phi$ and $\neg \phi$ are true.

Now, if $\Phi \cup \neg(\phi)$ would be satisfiable, then there would be one interpretation in which both $\Phi$ and $\neg \phi$ are true. This means, by disjointness of $Mod(\phi)$ and $Mod(\neg(\phi))$, that $\Phi$ has a model which is not a model of $Mod(\phi)$, which means that $Mod(\Phi)$ is not a subset of $Mod(\phi)$ and thus $\Phi$ *does not* entail $\phi$.

The satisfiability problem for first-order logic is the problem to decide whether there is a model for a given first-order theory $\Phi$. In other words: "Does $\Phi$ have a model?"

It turns out that this question is not so easily answered and in some cases it is even impossible to find an answer. This makes the satisfiability problem for first-order logic undecidable, that is, the question of satisfiability cannot always be answered in a finite amount of time. However, it does turn out that if the answer to the satisfiability question is "yes", the answer can always be found in a finite amount of time. Therefore, first-order logic is actually *semi-decidable*. It is possible to enumerate all sentences which are entailed by a first-order theory.

## DESCRIPTION LOGICS

Description logics (Baader et al., 2003) (formerly called *Terminological Logics*) are a family of knowledge representation languages, which revolve mainly around concepts, roles (which denote relationships between concepts), and role restrictions. Description logics are actually based on first-order logic. Therefore, concepts can be seen as unary predicates, whereas roles can be seen as binary predicates. Although there are also Description Logic languages which allow n-ary roles, we will not discuss these here.

In this section we will illustrate description logics through the relatively simple description logic *Attributive Language with Complement (ALC)* which allows concepts, concept hierarchies, role restrictions and the boolean combination of concept descriptions. The currently popular expressive description logics, such as *SHIQ* and *SHOIQ*, are all extensions of *ALC*.

### The Basic Description Logic *ALC*

An *ALC* knowledge base has two parts: the TBox, with terminological knowledge, which consists of a number of class definitions, and the ABox, which consists of assertions about actual individuals.

Concept axioms in the *TBox* are of the form $C \subseteq D$ (meaning the extension of $C$ is a subset of the extension of $D$; $D$ is more general than $C$) or $C \equiv D$ (where $C \equiv D$ is interpreted as $C \subseteq D$ and $D \subseteq C$) with $C$ and $D$ (possibly complex) descriptions. Descriptions can be built from named concepts

*Box 1.*

| C,D | $\longrightarrow$ | A | (named class) |
|---|---|---|---|
| | | T | (universal concept) |
| | | $\bot$ | (bottom concept) |
| | | $C \cap D$ | (intersection) |
| | | $C \cup D$ | (union) |
| | | $\neg C$ | (negation) |
| | | $\exists R.C$ | (existential restriction) |
| | | $\forall R.C$ | (universal restriction) |

(e.g., $A$) and role restrictions (e.g., $\forall R.C$ denotes a universal value restriction), connected with negation ($\neg$), union ($\cup$) and intersection ($\cap$) (see Box 1).

Traditionally, descriptions are interpreted as sets, where the different parts of a description constrain the set. Take, for example, the description $A \cap \neg B \cap \exists R.C$. This can be read as "all elements which are member of the set $A$, but not of the set $B$ ($\neg B$); additionally, each member must be related to some member of the set $C$ via the relation $R$ ($\exists R.C$)".

Descriptions can also be understood as formulas of first-order logic with one free variable. For example, the description $A \cap \neg B \cap \exists R.C$ corresponds to the formula $A(x) \wedge \neg B(x) \wedge \exists y.(R(x,y) \wedge C(y))$. The correspondence between descriptions and first-order formulas is given in Table 1. In the table, $\pi$ is a function which takes as parameters a description and a variable and returns a first-order formula.

The TBox of a description logic knowledge base consists of a number of axioms of the forms $C \subseteq D$ and $C \equiv D$, where $C$ and $D$ are descriptions. In the set-based interpretation, $C \subseteq D$ means that $C$ is interpreted as a subset of $D$ and $C \equiv D$ means that $C$ and $D$ are interpreted as the same set. We give the translation to first-order logic in Table 2.

Description logics have been devised to formally model terminologies. The two major benefits of the formal modeling of a terminology

*Table 1. Correspondence between descriptions and first-order formulas*

| Description | First-Order Formula |
|---|---|
| $\pi(A,X)$ | $A(X)$ |
| $\pi(\top,X)$ | $\top$ |
| $\pi(\bot,X)$ | $\bot$ |
| $\pi(C\cap D,X)$ | $\pi(C,X)\wedge\pi(D,X)$ |
| $\pi(C\cup D,X)$ | $\pi(C,X)\vee\pi(D,X)$ |
| $\pi(\neg C,X)$ | $\neg(\pi(C,X))$ |
| $\pi(\exists R.C,X)$ | $\exists y.(R(X,y)\wedge\pi(C,y))$ |
| $\pi(\forall R.C,X)$ | $\forall y.(R(X,y)\rightarrow\pi(C,y))$ |

*Table 2. Correspondence between TBox axioms and first-order formulas*

| Description | First-Order Formula |
|---|---|
| $\pi(C\subseteq D)$ | $\forall x.(\pi(C,x)\rightarrow\pi(D,x))$ |
| $\pi(C\equiv D)$ | $\forall x.(\pi(C,x)\rightarrow\pi(D,x) \wedge(\pi(D,x)\rightarrow\pi(C,x))$ |

are that (1) it is possible to verify the consistency of the specification and (2) it is possible to automatically infer information which is hidden in the terminology. We illustrate both in the following example.

*Example 8* Consider the following TBox *T*:

*Person* $\equiv$ $\forall hasChild.Person\cap\exists hasFather.$
    *Father*$\cap\exists hasMother.Mother*
*Person* $\equiv$ *Man*$\cup$*Woman*
*Parent* $\equiv$ $\exists hasChild.\top$
*Mother* $\equiv$ *Woman*$\cap$*Parent*
*Father* $\equiv$ *Man*$\cap$*Parent*

*T* has two alternative definitions of the concept *Person*: (1) everyone who has a father which is a father, has a mother which is a mother and has only children which are persons (notice that this

does not require a person to have children) and (2) the union of the sets of all men and women; note that both definitions must be valid. A parent is a person who has a child. A mother is a woman who is also parent and a father is a man who is also a parent.

The TBox *T* does not contain any inconsistencies. We can infer some information from *T*. For example: *Man* is subsumed by (is a more specific concept than) *Person*: *Man*$\subseteq$*Person*.

We can see from *T* that every *Man* must be a *Person*. Therefore, it would be inconsistent to state that there is any *Man* who is not a *Person*. We can add the following axiom to *T*:

*ManNotPerson*$\equiv$*Man*$\cap\neg$*Person*

A concept in a TBox is inconsistent if it is impossible for this concept to have any instances, that is, the concept can only be interpreted as the empty set. In order to verify this, we translate the second and the last axiom of *T* to first-order logic to obtain the theory $\pi(T)$:

$\forall x.(Person(x)\rightarrow(Man(x)\vee Woman(x)))$
$\forall x.((Man(x)\vee Woman(x))\rightarrow Person(x))$
$\forall x.(ManNotPerson(x)\rightarrow(Man(x)\wedge\neg Person(x)))$
$\forall x.((Man(x)\wedge\neg Person(x))\rightarrow ManNotPerson(x))$

The second formula says that every man is a person, whereas the third formula says that every *ManNotPerson* is a man and *not* a person. This would be impossible, because by the second formula every man is necessarily a person. What follows is that every model of this theory interprets *ManNotPerson* as the empty set.

If we were to add the formula *ManNotPerson*(a) to $\pi(T)$, for some constant $a$, then the theory no longer has any model and is thus inconsistent.

Besides the concepts and role descriptions, which comprise the TBox, a Description Logic Knowledge base typically also contains individuals (instances) and relations between individuals and, in the case of OWL, equality and inequality assertions between individuals. These assertions about individuals comprise the *ABox*.

The assertions in the ABox are of the form $i \in C$, where $i$ is an individual and $A$ is an atomic concept, or of the form $(i_1, i_2) \in R$, where $i_1, i_2$ are individuals and $R$ is a (binary) role. Assertions of the form $i \in A$ are interpreted as set membership and assertions of the form $(i_1, i_2) \in R$ are interpreted as tuples in a relation. The translation to first-order logic can be found in Table 3.

*Example 9* The following ABox $A$ is an ABox for the TBox $T$ of Example 8:

*john* $\in$ *Person*
(john,mary) $\in$ R
*john* $\in$ *Man*

From this ABox $A$, together with the TBox $T$, we can derive a number of facts: *mary* is a person, since *john* is a person, *mary* is a child of *john*, and all children of persons are persons; *john* is a parent, since he has a child; finally, *john* is a father, because he is both a parent and a man.

## Reasoning in Description Logics

We are here only concerned with reasoning with description logic TBoxes; note, however, that reasoning with ABoxes can generally be reduced to TBox-reasoning (Baader et al., 2003,

*Table 3. Correspondence between ABox assertions and first-order formulas*

| Assertion | First-order Formula |
|---|---|
| $\pi(i \in A)$ | $A(i)$ |
| $\pi((i_1, i_2) \in R)$ | $R(i_1, i_2)$ |

Section 2.3). As mentioned above, there are two main motivations for using description logics: (1) detecting inconsistencies in descriptions and (2) deriving implicit information from descriptions. Both detecting inconsistency *and* deriving implicit information require reasoning over the terminology. (1) and (2) can be reduced to the following reasoning tasks:

- **Satisfiability:** A concept $C$ is satisfiable with respect to a TBox $T$ if there exists at least one model of $T$ where the interpretation of $C$, $C^I$, is non-empty.
- **Subsumption:** A concept $C$ is subsumed by a concept $D$ with respect to $T$ iff $C^I \subseteq D^I$ for every model of $T$. This can also be written as $C \sqsubseteq_T D$.

Both reasoning tasks can be reduced to reasoning problems in first-order logic. A concept $C$ is satisfiable with respect to a TBox $T$ if and only if $\pi(T) \cup \{C(a)\}$ is satisfiable. Essentially, we translate the TBox to first-order logic and add an instance $a$ of the concept $C$ and check whether the resulting theory is consistent, that is, satisfiable. Notice that we have already applied this technique in Example 8.

Subsumption can be reduced to entailment in first-order logic: $C \sqsubseteq_T D$ if and only if $\pi(T) \models \pi(C \sqsubseteq D)$. Thus, we translate the TBox to a first-order theory and translate the subsumption axiom which we want to check for a first-order sentence and check whether the one entails the other. We have already seen that entailment in first-order logic can be reduced to satisfiability checking. Similarly, subsumption can be reduced to satisfiability, namely, *C is subsumed by D* with respect to TBox $T$ if and only if $C \sqcap \neg D$ is not satisfiable with respect to $T$.

Reasoning in most description logics is decidable and there exist optimized algorithms for reasoning with certain description logics.

## LOGIC PROGRAMMING

Logic programming is based on a subset of first-order logic, called *Horn logic*. However, the semantics of Logic Programming is slightly different from first-order logic. The semantics of logic programs is based on *minimal Herbrand models* (Lloyd, 1987), rather than first-order models.

A logic program consists of rules of the form "if $A$ then $B$". Intuitively, if $A$ is true, then $B$ must be true. Logic programming plays two major roles on the Semantic Web. On the one hand, it is used to reason with RDF (Klyne & Carroll, 2004), RDF Schema (Brickley & Guha, 2004) and parts of OWL (Dean & Schreiber, 2004). On the other hand, it used is to represent knowledge on the Semantic Web in the form of *rules*.

Euler[1] and CWM[2] are examples of reasoners for the Semantic Web, based on logic programming. Euler and CWM both work directly with RDF data and can be used to derive new RDF data using rules.

Rules can be seen as a knowledge representation paradigm complementary to Description logics. Description logics are very convenient for defining classes, class hierarchies, properties and the relationships between them. More specifically, compared with logic programming, description logics have the following expressive power: existential quantification, disjunction and classical negation. Logic programs, on the other hand, have the following additional expressive power: predicates with arbitrary arities, chaining variables over predicates (there are no restrictions on the use of variables), and the use of nonmonotonic negation. An often quoted example which illustrates the expressive power of rules compared with ontologies is: "if $x$ is the brother of a parent of $y$, then $x$ is an uncle of $y$". This example cannot be expressed using description logics, because the variables $x$ and $y$ are both used on both sides of the implication, which is not possible in description logics.

In this section we will first explain the general syntax of logic programs. After that, we will the semantics of logic programs, based on minimal Herbrand models. An important result in the area of logic programming is the equivalence of both semantics. We then introduce default negation in logic programs and show how it differs from negation in classical first-order logic.

### Logic Programs

Classical logic programming makes use of the Horn logic fragment of first-order logic. A First-order formula is in the Horn fragment, if it is a disjunction of literals with at most one positive literal, in which all variables are universally quantified:

$$(\forall)\ h \vee \neg b_1 \vee ... \vee \neg b_n \qquad (1)$$

This formula can be rewritten to the following form:

$$(\forall)\ h \leftarrow b_1 \wedge ... \wedge b_n \qquad (2)$$

Such a formula is also called a *Horn formula*. A Horn formula with one positive literal, and at least one negative literal is called a *rule*. The positive literal $h$ is called the *head* of the rule. The conjunction of negative literals is called the *body* of the rule. A rule without a body is called a *fact* and a rule without a head is called a *query*. A *logic program* consists of a set of horn clauses.

In this section we use a slightly different notation for rules, which diverges from the usual first-order syntax. A rule is written as follows:

h1 :- b1,...,bn.

A fact is written as:

h1.

A query is written as:

?- b1,...,bn.

A *positive logic program* **P** is a collection of rules and facts.

## Minimal Herbrand Model Semantics

We will first define the minimal Herbrand model semantics for positive logic programs **P**.

*Definition 7 (Herbrand universe) The Herbrand universe HU of **P** is the set of all ground terms which can be formed using the constant and function symbols in the signature $\Sigma$ of **P** (in case **P** has no constants, we add some constant c).*

*Definition 8 (Herbrand base and Herbrand interpretation) The Herbrand base HB of **P** is the set of all ground atomic formulas which can be formed with the predicate symbols in $\Sigma$ of **P** and the terms in HU, that is, all formulas of the form:*

p(t1,...,tn)

*with p an n-ary predicate symbol and t1,...,tn $\in$ HU. A Herbrand interpretation of **P** is a subset of HB.*

*Example 10* Consider the logic program  P :

p(a).
q(b).
p(X) :- q(X).
p(X) :- p(f(X)).

This Herbrand universe *HU* of **P** consists of all ground terms which can be constructed out of the constant and function symbols which occur in **P**. Therefore, $HU$ = {a, b, f(a), f(b), f(f(a)), f(f(b)), f(f(f(a))), f(f(f(b))), ...}.

The Herbrand base of **P**, *HB*, consists of all ground atomic formulas which can be formed using the predicate symbols of **P** combined with the Herbrand universe *HU*: *HB* = {p(a), p(b), q(a), q(b), p(f(a)), q(f(a)), p(f(b)), q(f(b)), p(f(f(a))),...}.

Examples of Herbrand interpretations are $w_1$ = {p(f(a)), q(b), q(f(b))}, $w_2$ = {p(a), p(b), q(b)}, and $w_3$ = {p(a), p(b), q(a), q(b), p(f(a))}.

In this example, the Herbrand universe is infinite. In fact, as soon as function symbols are used in the logic program, the Herbrand universe becomes infinite. An infinite Herbrand universe means also an infinite Herbrand base.

Note that a Herbrand interpretation $w^H$ of **P** corresponds to a first-order interpretation $w=\langle HU, I \rangle$ where *HU* is the Herbrand universe, and *I* satisfies the following conditions:

1.  $c^I = c$ for every constant symbol $c \in C$,
2.  $(f(t_1,...,t_n))^w = f(t_1,...,t_n)$ for every *n*-ary function symbol $f \in F$ and ground terms $t_1,...,t_n$,
3.  $(p(t_1,...,t_n))^w$ for $p(t_1,...,t_n) \in w^H$.

The grounding of a logic program **P**, denoted *Ground*(**P**), is the union of all possible ground instantiations of **P**. A ground instantiation of a logic program is obtained by, for each rule $r \in$ **P**, replacing each variable with a term in the Herbrand Universe *HU*.

The definition of Herbrand models is as follows:

*Definition 9 (Herbrand model) Let **P** be a positive logic program. A Herbrand interpretation w of **P** is a model of **P** if for every rule $r \in Ground($**P**$)$ the following condition holds:*

*   *If* b1,...,bn $\in w$ *then* h $\in w$

The intersection of all Herbrand models of **P** is also a model of **P** and is called the *minimal Herbrand model*. Therefore, each logic program has a minimal Herbrand model and this model is *unique*.

*Example 11* Among the three interpretations in the previous example, $w_1$, $w_2$, $w_3$, only $w_2$ and $w_3$ are Herbrand models of **P**. Furthermore, $w_2$ is the minimal model of **P**.

*Definition 10 (Ground entailment) A logic program* **P** *entails a ground atomic formula* A, *denoted* **P**|=A, *if and only if A is included in the minimal Herbrand model of* **P**.

We say a conjunction of ground formulas $A_1 \wedge ... \wedge A_n$ is entailed by a program **P**, denoted **P** $|=A_1 \wedge ... \wedge A_n$, if and only if each of the ground formulas in the conjunction is entailed by **P**: **P** $|=A_i$ for $1 \leq i \leq n$.

By this definition of entailment it is only possible to check whether particular facts follow from a logic program, but not whether some rule or formula follows from the program. However, it turns out that this definition of entailment is sufficient for the most prominent reasoning task in logic programming: query answering.

A *query* q is a rule without a body, that is, a conjunction of atomic formulas, with a number of free variables. We write a query as:

?- A1,...,An.

A variable substitution is an assignment of objects in the Herbrand universe to variables. A variable substitution is written as $[x_1/a_1,...,x_n/a_n]$ and applying a variable substitution to a formula yields a new formula in which variables are replaced with terms as specified in the substitution.

*Example 12 A number of variable substitutions:*

- $p(x)[x/a]=p(a)$
- $(p(x,y) \wedge q(x) \wedge q(z))[x/f(a),y/a]=p(f(a),a) \wedge q(f(a)) \wedge q(z)$
- $(q(y) \wedge r(z,f(y)))[y/g(b),z/a]=q(g(b)) \wedge r(a,f(g(b)))$

An *answer* to a query q for a program **P** is a variable substitution $[x_1/a_1,...,x_n/a_n]$ for all variables in q such that is entailed by **P**.

*Example 13 Recall the program* **P** *from Example 10. Now, consider the query* q:

?- p(Y).

Now, [Y/a] and [Y/b] are answers to this query. In fact these are the only answers to the query. This can be easily verified by considering the minimal Herbrand model of **P**.

## Recursion in Logic Programs

Interest in the use of logic for databases has given rise to the field of *deductive databases*. Datalog (Ullman, 1988) is the most prominent language for deductive databases. Datalog can be seen as an expressive query language for relational databases, based on logic programming. Compared with the relational query language SQL, Datalog allows to specify recursive queries[3]. Datalog can be seen as a logic programming without the use of function symbols.

*Example 14 Given the following logic program:*

```
parent(john,mary).
brother(mary,jack).

uncle(X,Z) :- parent(X,Y), brother(Y,Z).
```

This logic program consists of two parts, namely (a) the facts that mary is a parent of john and jack is a brother of mary and (b) the "uncle" rule which states that the brother of someones parent is that person's uncle.

In order to test whether there is recursion in a logic program, one can build the *dependency graph* of the logic program. The dependency graph is a directed graph where the predicates in the logic program are represented by nodes in the graph. There is an arc from some predicate *p* to some predicate *q* if they occur in a rule with *p* in the body and *q* in the head. A logic program is *recursive* if and only if there is a cycle in the dependency graph.

*Example 15 Given the following logic program* **P**:

```
mother(mary,jill).
father(john,jill).
parent(jack,john).
parent(X,Y) :- mother(X,Y).
parent(X,Y) :- father(X,Y).
ancestor(X,Y) :- parent(X,Y).

ancestor(X,Z) :- ancestor(X,Y), ancestor(Y,Z).
```

The ancestor relation is defined as the transitive closure of the parent relation. From this, we can already see that the logic program is recursive, because ancestor depends on itself. We can also verify this in the dependency graph of **P**, depicted in Figure 1.

## Negation in Logic Programs

An often used extension of logic programs is *negation*. In this section we explain the basics of negation in logic programming. As the treatment is rather involved, the reader may skip this section on first reading.

A *normal logic program* **P** consists of a number of *rules*. Each rule is of the form:

```
h :- b1,...,bk,not n1,...,not nl.
```

where h is an atomic formula (as defined in the previous section), also called the *head* of the rule, and b1,...,bn,n1,...,nl are atomic formulas, also called *atoms*, and b1,...,bk,not n1,...,not nl is called the *body* of the rule. b1,...,bk are said to occur *positively* and n1,...,nl are said to occur *negatively* in the body

of the rule; b1,...,bk are *positive literals* and not n1,...,not nl are *negative literals*. A positive rule is a rule which has no negative literals in the body. A positive program is a program which consists only of positive rules. The signature of a logic program **P** is the first-order signature where the constant, function, predicate, and variable symbols are exactly those which occur in **P**.

The difference with the logic programs we have discussed above is that normal logic programs allow negation in the body of a rule. Note that the negation in logic programs, denoted with not differs from negation in classical first-order logic, which is denoted with $\neg$. The negation in logic programs is also called *default negation* because all facts are assumed to be false, unless we can infer otherwise. The default negation of some atomic formula $\alpha$, denoted not $\alpha$ is true, if $\alpha$ cannot be derived, whereas in first-order logic, the classical negation of $\alpha$, denoted $\neg\alpha$, is only true if it can be explicitly derived[4].

We can straightforwardly extend the Herbrand semantics to programs with negation. However, it turns out that there may be several minimal models.

*Definition 11 (Herbrand model) Let **P** be a normal logic program. A Herbrand interpretation w of **P** is a model of **P** if for every rule r∈Ground(**P**), h∈w:*

*Figure 1. Dependency graph of the ancestor program*

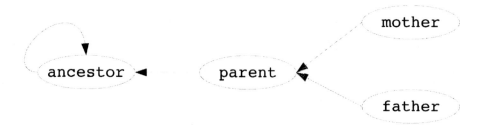

- *if all positive body literals* b1,...,bk *are in w and*
- *all negative body literals* n1,...,nl ∈*w are not in.*

*Example 16* Consider the logic program **P**:

```
p(a) :- not p(b).
p(b) :- not p(a).
```

This program has two minimal models: $\{p(a)\}$ and $\{p(b)\}$.

The existence of multiple minimal models increases the complexity of finding a minimal model. A class of logic programs with negations which have a single minimal model which can be straightforwardly computed is the class of *stratified* logic programs. The predicates in a stratified program can be divided into a number of strata such that there is no negative dependency between predicates in the same stratum. A stratification has to fulfill two conditions:

1. if some predicate $q$ is at stratum $i$ and depends positively on some predicate $p$, then $p$ must be in a stratum $j$ such that $j \le i$, and
2. if some predicate $q$ is at stratum $i$ and depends negatively on some predicate $p$, then $p$ must be in a stratum $j$ such that $j < i$.

In order to check whether a program is stratifiable, we can check the dependency graph. This graph is build in a similar way as discussed above, with the addition that if there is a rule with head $q$ and with a negative body literal not $p$, then there is an arc between $p$ and $q$ and this arc is marked with "not". If there are cycles in the graph which include a negative arc, then the program is not stratifiable.

*Example 17* Consider the logic program:

```
p :- q.
q :- not r, p.
r :- q.
```

This program is not stratifiable; this can be easily seen by constructing the dependency graph. Clearly, the second rule requires r to be in a lower stratum then q, whereas the third rule requires r to be in a higher (or the same) stratum than q.

Now consider the following logic program:

```
p :- q.
p :- r.
q :- not r.
```

This program is stratifiable with the following stratification:

- stratum 0: $\{r\}$
- stratum 1: $\{p,q\}$

Now consider the following logic program:

```
p :- q.
q :- not r.
p :- not s.
r :- s.
t :- not q.
```

This program has the following stratification:

- stratum 0: $\{r,s\}$
- stratum 1: $\{p,q\}$
- stratum 2: $\{t\}$

It is now straightforward to evaluate a stratified logic program by first computing the predicates in the lowest stratum and then working up stratum-by-stratum until the highest stratum is reached and the minimal model is computed. It turns out that each stratified program has a single minimal Herbrand model which is the intersection of all Herbrand models of the program.

There are different semantics for logic programs which are not stratifiable. The most popular ones are the Stable Model Semantics (Gelfond & Lifschitz, 1988) and the Well-Founded Semantics (Gelder et al., 1991). These semantics are beyond the scope of this chapter.

# FRAME LOGIC

Frame logic (Kifer et al., 1995) (F-Logic) is an extension of first-order logic which adds explicit support for object-oriented modeling. It is possible to explicitly specify methods, as well as generalization/specialization and instantiation relationships. The syntax of F-Logic has some seemingly higher-order features, for example, the same identifier can be used for both a class and an instance. However, the semantics of F-Logic is strictly first-order.

Although F-Logic was originally defined as an extension to full First-Order Logic, the original paper (Kifer et al., 1995) already defined a Logic Programming-style semantics for the subset of F-Logic based on Horn logic. Intuitively, the Horn subset is obtained in the usual way with the addition that, beside predicate symbols with arguments, F-Logic molecules can also be seen as atomic formulas. In the remainder, we will refer to the Horn subset of F-Logic with logic programming semantics as F-Logic programming. There exist several implementations of F-Logic programming, most notably (Decker, Erdmann, Fensel, & Studer, 1999; Yang, Kifer, & Zhao, 2003). Since most attention around F-Logic is around F-Logic programming, we will restrict ourselves to the logic programming semantics for F-Logic and disregard the FOL semantics.

## F-Logic Programs

To simplify matters, we focus only on a subset of F-Logic. We do not consider parametrised methods, functional (single-valued) methods and we consider only non-inheritable methods. We also do not consider compound molecules.

Formally, an F-Logic theory is a set of formulas constructed from atomic formulas, as defined for first-order logic, and so called *molecules*. Let $\Sigma$ be a first-order signature, as defined before and let $T$ be the set of terms which can be constructed

from the constants, function symbols, and variables in $\Sigma$.

*Definition 12 (Molecule) A molecule in F-Logic is one of the following statements:*

1.  *An is-a assertion of the form* C:D *where* $C, D \in T$,
2.  *A subclass-of assertion of the form* C::D *where* $C, D \in T$,
3.  *A data molecule of the form* C[D -» E] *where* $C, D, E \in T$, *or*
4.  *A signature molecule of the form* C[D =» E] *where* $C, D, E \in T$.

An F-Logic molecule is called ground, if it contains no variables.

An is-a assertion C:D states that C is an instance of the class D; a subclass assertion C::D states that C is a subclass of D. Data molecules of the form C[D -» E] have the meaning that the attribute D of the individual C has the value E. Signature molecules of the form C[D =» E] indicate that the class C has an attribute D and that all values associated with this attribute are of type E.

An important concept in F-Logic is *object identity* (Khoshafian & Copeland, 1986). Each object (e.g., class, instance, method) has a unique object identifier, where an object identifier is in fact a term. In F-Logic, classes and methods are interpreted *intentionally*, which means that class identifiers and method identifiers are interpreted by themselves and not directly as sets or as binary relations, as is the case with concepts and roles in description logics. Classes and methods are first interpreted as objects in the domain and these objects are then related to sets of objects and sets of binary tuples, respectively.

An F-Logic rule is similar to a logic programming rule as defined in the previous section, with the distinction that besides atomic formulas, F-Logic rules *also* allow molecules in place of atomic formulas.

*Example 18 We will now model the description logic knowledge base of Example 8 using F-Logic programming.*

We first define the attributes of the class `Person`. That can be done using a number of ground facts:

```
person[child =>> person].
person[father =>> father].
person[mother =>> mother].
```

We now define Man and Woman as subclasses of Person. It is not possible to say that every person is either a man and a woman, because disjunction is not allowed in the head of rules. We can also capture the facts that Mother is a subclass of both Woman and Parent and that Father is a subclass of both Man and Parent. These subclass assertions are all facts in F-Logic programming:

```
man::person.
woman::person.

mother::woman.
mother::parent.
father::man.
father::parent.
```

Finally, we use a number of rules to capture the facts that anybody who has a child is a parent and that every woman who is also a parent is a mother; similar for father:

```
X:parent :- X[child ->> Y].
X:mother :- X:woman, X:parent.
X:father :- X:man, X:parent.
```

As we can see from the example, there are, on the one hand, several things which can be expressed in basic description logics, but which cannot be expressed in F-Logic programming. Essentially, the two things which could not be expressed are: (1) every person is either a man or a woman and (2) every parent has a child. This is not surprising, since (1) would require disjunction in the head of a rule and (2) would require

existentially quantified variables in the head of a rule. Both are not allowed in (F-)logic programming. On the other hand, there are certain kinds of knowledge which can be expressed using (F-)logic programming which cannot be expressed using basic description logics, for example, the uncle rule of Example .

Note that in F-Logic there is no distinction between classes and instances. An *object identifier* can denote a class, an instance, or an attribute, but there is no separation in the signature $\Sigma$ for the identifiers denoting either. The advantage of such an overloading object notion is that objects denote classes, instances and attributes depending on the syntactic context, which allows certain kinds of meta-statements. For example, in the example above, we might define an attribute parent which is not related to the class parent:

```
person[parent =>> person].
```

We will now make a few brief remarks about the semantics of F-Logic programming. A full treatment (see Kifer et al., 1995) of the F-Logic semantics is beyond the scope of this chapter.

In F-Logic programming, molecules are similar to atomic formulas. In fact, is-a and subclass-of molecules can be seen as binary atomic formulas and data and signature molecules can be seen as ternary atomic formulas. F-Logic does mandate that some additional restrictions hold in the face of is-a and subclass-of molecules. Namely, the subclass-of relation is transitive and an instance of a class is also an instance of all super-classes. However, F-Logic does not prescribe any dependency between data molecules and signature molecules. The definition of type-correctness, that is, what it means for values of attributes to be correct with respect to the attribute definition, is up to the user of the language.

An *F-program* (a collection of F-Logic rules) is said to be well-typed if all data atoms implied by the program comply with the signatures implied by the program (Kifer, Lausen, & WuKifer et al., 1995). The notion of type-correctness is not built into the logical language, but can be defined using a logical meta-theory, which can be typically captured using rules. This has two main advantages: (1) it is possible to use different theories for type-correctness for programs in the same language and (2) it enables checking where in the program typing errors occur, instead of just saying that the entire program (or Knowledge Base) is unsatisfiable.

Frame logic and description logics (DL) both have constructs for modeling classes, class hierarchies, and attributes. The main difference in the way classes and attributes are modeled in F-Logic and DL is that in F-Logic classes and attributes are modeled *intentionally*, whereas in DL they are modeled *extensionally*. This means that, where in F-Logic classes and attributes are interpreted as objects in the domain, which are then associated to sets of objects and sets of (binary) tuples, in description logics classes are directly interpreted as subsets of the domain of interpretation and attributes are directly interpreted as binary relations over the domain. An advantage of the intentional interpretation of classes and attributes is that it is possible to make statements about classes and properties while staying in a first-order framework, whereas making statements about classes and attributes in description logics would require a higher-order logic.

## RULEML

RuleML (Boley, Dean, Grosof, Kifer, Tabet, & Wagner, 2005; Hirtle, Boley, Grosof, Kifer, Sintek, & Tabet, 2005) provides an XML-based exchange syntax for different rule languages, as well as for first-order logic.

RuleML can be seen as an exchange format for most of the languages which have been mentioned in this chapter. In order to capture different logical languages, RuleML defines a number of so-called sublanguages. A sublanguage is defined using an XML Schema which comprises a number of modules representing the features which are present in the sublanguage. Using the XML Schema modules, a user may compose his/her own sublanguage. We illustrate a number of sublanguages which correspond to the languages we have surveyed in this chapter:

- **fologeq:** First-order logic with equality is captured using the sublanguage fologeq. http://www.ruleml.org/0.9/xsd/fologeq.xsd
- **nafhornlog:** Logic programming with default negation is captured using the sublanguage nafhornlog. http://www.ruleml.org/0.9/xsd/nafhornlog.xsd
- **nafdatalog:** Function-free logic programming (Datalog) with default negation is captured using the sublanguage nafdatalog. http://www.ruleml.org/0.9/xsd/nafdatalog.xsd
- **datalog:** Function-free logic programming (Datalog) without negation is captured using the sublanguage datalog. http://www.ruleml.org/0.9/xsd/datalog.xsd

As an illustration of how the schema's for the sublanguages are composed of modules, we show part of the schema for the sublanguage nafdatalog in Figure 2. At the top of the schema we see the usual XML namespace declarations, as part of the top-level element xs:schema. This is followed by documentation for the human reader. After this we see that the module for the negation is imported using the xs:include element. Finally, the original schema datalog.xsd is refined to include the possibility of adding negation in the body of rules. For reasons of space we do not show this refinement.

Figure 3 shows the simple program from Example 14 in the datalog sublanguage of RuleML.

## CONCLUSION

Logical languages allow one to infer information which is implicit in descriptions one creates in these languages. The ability to infer new information from existing information is seen as an important feature for languages on the Semantic Web. Therefore, many Semantic Web languages, described in the other chapters of this book, are based on formal languages such as the ones we have seen in this chapter.

As we have seen in this chapter, there are many differences between these formal languages, but also in terms of modeling in the language.

We summarize the most important traits of the surveyed languages:

*First-order logic.* A very expressive language. Reasoning with first-order logic (FOL) is in general undecidable.

*Description logics* (DL) are, in general, based on a decidable subset of first-order logic. An important property of Description Logic languages is that they allow, to some extent, frame-based modelling. The most important reasoning task in DL is subsumption reasoning, that is, checking whether one description is more general than another.

*Figure 2. XML schema for nafdatalog*

```
<?xml version="1.0" encoding="UTF-8"?>
<xs:schema
targetNamespace="http://www.ruleml.org/0.9/xsd"
xmlns="http://www.ruleml.org/0.9/xsd"
xmlns:xs="http://www.w3.org/2001/XMLSchema">

 <xs:annotation>
  <xs:documentation xml:lang="en">
  XML Schema for a Datalog RuleML sublanguage,
   including negation as failure (NAF)
  File: nafdatalog.xsd
  Version: 0.9
  Last Modification: 2005-11-09
  </xs:documentation>
 </xs:annotation>

 <!-- nafdatalog includes the 'naf' module -->
 <xs:include schemaLocation="modules/naf_module.
xsd"/>

 <xs:redefine schemaLocation="datalog.xsd">
 .......
 </xs:redefine>
 </xs:schema>
```

*Figure 3. Datalog RuleML example*

```
<?xml version="1.0" encoding="UTF-8"?>
<RuleML xmlns="http://www.ruleml.org/0.9/xsd"
xmlns:xsi="http://www.w3.org/2001/XMLSchema-
instance"
xsi:schemaLocation="http://www.ruleml.org/0.9/xsd
http://www.ruleml.org/0.9/xsd/datalog.xsd">

<Implies>
 <head>
 <Atom>
  <op><Rel>uncle</Rel></op>
  <Var>x</Var>
  <Var>z</Var>
 </Atom>
 </head>
 <body>
 <And>
  <Atom>
  <op><Rel>parent</Rel></op>
  <Var>x</Var>
  <Var>y</Var>
  </Atom>
  <Atom>
  <op><Rel>brother</Rel></op>
  <Var>y</Var>
  <Var>z</Var>
  </Atom>
 </And>
 </body>
</Implies>

<Atom>
 <op><Rel>parent</Rel></op>
 <Ind>John</Ind>
 <Ind>Mary</Ind>
</Atom>

<Atom>
 <op><Rel>brother</Rel></op>
 <Ind>Mary</Ind>
 <Ind>Jack</Ind>
</Atom>

</RuleML>
```

*Logic programming* is based on the Horn logic subset of FOL, but with extension of default negation in the body. In general reasoning with logic programs is undecidable, but when restricting to the datalog subset, that is, disallowing function symbols, reasoning becomes decidable and for programs under the well-founded semantics even tractable.

*Frame logic.* First-order logic does not have explicit constructs for modeling classes and attributes. Frame logic overcomes this limitation by introducing a number of constructs for object-oriented modeling which do not increase the complexity of reasoning in the language.

We have seen that RuleML provides an XML-based syntax for exchange of these languages over the Web.

Many of the formal languages described in this chapter have found their way to language recommendations and proposals for the Semantic Web. The language proposals SWSL-FOL (Battle et al., 2005) and SWRL-FOL (Patel-Schneider, 2005) are based on full FOL. The W3C recommendation OWL (Dean & Schreiber, 2004) is based on description logics (Horrocks et al., 2003). Finally, the rule language proposals WRL (Angele et al., 2005) and SWSL-Rules (Battle et al., 2005) are based on (F-)Logic programming.

## REFERENCES

Angele, J., Boley, H., Bruijn, J. de, Fensel, D., Hitzler, P., & Kifer, M. (2005). *Web rule language (WRL)*. W3C Member Submission 09 September 2005.

Baader, F., Calvanese, D., McGuinness, D.L., Nardi, D., & Patel-Schneider, P.F. (Eds.). (2003). *The description logic handbook*. Cambridge University Press.

Battle, S., Bernstein, A., Boley, H., Grosof, B.,

Gruninger, M., & Hull, R. (2005). *Semantic Web services language (SWSL)*. W3C Member Submission 09 September 2005.

Boley, H., Dean, M., Grosof, B., Kifer, M., Tabet, S., & Wagner, G. (2005, April). RuleML position statement. In *Proceedings of the W3C Workshop on Rule Languages for Interoperability,* Washington, DC. Retrieved October 23, 2006, from http://www.w3.org/2004/12/rules-ws/paper/96

Brickley, D., & Guha, R.V. (2004). *RDF vocabulary description language 1.0: RDF schema* (Recommendation No. 10 February 2004). W3C. Retrieved October 23, 2006, from http://www.w3.org/TR/rdf-schema/

Dean, M., & Schreiber, G. (Eds.). (2004). *OWL web ontology language reference* (W3C Recommendation 10 February 2004).

Decker, S., Erdmann, M., Fensel, D., & Studer, R. (1999). Ontobroker: Ontology based access to distributed and semi-structured information. R.M. et al. (Ed.), *Semantic issues in multimedia systems.* Kluwer Academic.

Fitting, M. (1996). *First order logic and automated theorem proving* (2nd ed.). Springer-Verlag.

Gelder, A.V., Ross, K., & Schlipf, J.S. (1991). The well-founded semantics for general logic programs. *Journal of the ACM, 38*(3), 620-650.

Gelfond, M., & Lifschitz, V. (1988). The stable model semantics for logic programming. In R.A. Kowalski & K. Bowen (Eds.), *Proceedings of the Fifth International Conference on Logic Programming* (pp. 1070-1080). Cambridge, MA: The MIT Press.

Gelfond, M., & Lifschitz, V. (1991). Classical negation in logic programs and disjunctive databases. *New Generation Computing, 9*(3/4), 365-386.

Hirtle, D., Boley, H., Grosof, B., Kifer, M., Sintek, M., & Tabet, S. (2005). *Schema specification of*

*RuleML 0.9*. Retrieved October 23, 2006, from http://www.ruleml.org/0.9/

Horrocks, I., Patel-Schneider, P.F., Boley, H., Tabet, S., Grosof, B., & Dean, M. (2004). *SWRL: A Semantic Web rule language combining OWL and RuleML* (Member Submission 21 May 2004). W3C. Retrieved October 23, 2006, from http://www.w3.org/Submission/SWRL/

Horrocks, I., Patel-Schneider, P.F., & van Harmelen, F. (2003). From SHIQ and RDF to OWL: The making of a Web ontology language. *Journal of Web Semantics, 1*(1), 7-26.

Khoshafian, S. & Copeland, G. (1986). Object identity. In *Proceedings of the ACM Conference on Object-Oriented Programming, Systems, Languages, and Applications (OOPSLA'86)* (pp. 406-416).

Kifer, M. (2005, July). Rules and ontologies in f-logic. In *Proceedings of Reasoning Web, First International Summer School, Tutorial Lectures* (pp. 22-34). Msida, Malta.

Kifer, M., Lausen, G., & Wu, J. (1995). Logical foundations of object-oriented and frame-based languages. *JACM, 42*(4), 741-843.

Klyne, G., & Carroll, J.J. (2004). *Resource description framework (RDF): Concepts and abstract syntax* (Recommendation No. 10 February 2004). W3C.

Lloyd, J.W. (1987). *Foundations of logic programming* (2nd ed.). Springer-Verlag.

Patel-Schneider, P.F. (2005). *A proposal for a swrl extension towards first-order logic* (W3C Member Submission 11 April 2005).

Ullman, J.D. (1988). *Principles of database and knowledge-base systems* (Vol. i). Computer Science Press.

Yang, G., Kifer, M., & Zhao, C. (2003). FLORA-2: A rule-based knowledge representation and inference infrastructure for the Semantic Web. In *Proceedings of the Second International Conference on Ontologies, Databases and Applications of Semantics (odbase)*, Catania, Sicily, Italy.

## FURTHER READING

**First-order logic** (Fitting, 1996)

**Logic programming** (Lloyd, 1987)

**Description logics** (Baader, Calvanese, McGuinness, Nardi, & Patel-Schneider, 2003)

**Frame logic** (Kifer, Lausen, & Wu, 1995)

**RuleML** (Hirtle et al, 2005; Boley et al, 2005)

## ENDNOTES

[1] http://www.agfa.com/w3c/euler/

[2] http://www.w3.org/2000/10/swap/doc/cwm.html

[3] Note that a recent version of SQL, namely SQL:99, allows a limited form of recursion in queries.

[4] Note that there are extensions of logic programming which deal with classical negation (Gelfond & Lifschitz, 1991), but we will not discuss these here.

# Chapter III
# Ontological Engineering:
## What are Ontologies and How Can We Build Them?

**Oscar Corcho**
*University of Manchester, UK*

**Mariano Fernández-López**
*Universidad San Pablo CEU and Universidad Politécnica de Madrid, Spain*

**Asunción Gómez-Pérez**
*Universidad Politécnica de Madrid, Spain*

## ABSTRACT

*Ontologies are formal, explicit specifications of shared conceptualizations. There is much literature on what they are, how they can be engineered and where they can be used inside applications. All these literature can be grouped under the term "ontological engineering," which is defined as the set of activities that concern the ontology development process, the ontology lifecycle, the principles, methods and methodologies for building ontologies, and the tool suites and languages that support them. In this chapter we provide an overview of ontological engineering, describing the current trends, issues and problems.*

## INTRODUCTION

The origin of ontologies in computer science can be referred back to 1991, in the context of the DARPA Knowledge Sharing Effort (Neches, Fikes, Finin, Gruber, Senator, & Swartout, 1991). The aim of this project was to devise new ways of constructing knowledge-based systems, so that the knowledge bases upon which they are based did not have to be constructed from scratch, but by assembling reusable components. This reuse applies both to static knowledge, which is modeled by means of ontologies, and dynamic problem-solving knowledge, which is modeled by means of problem solving methods.

Since then, considerable progress has been made in this area. Ontologies are now considered as a commodity that can be used for the development of a large number of applications in different fields, such as knowledge management, natural language processing, e-commerce, intelligent integration information, information retrieval, database design and integration, bio-informatics, education, and so forth.

The emergence of the Semantic Web (Berners-Lee, 1999) has caused a growing need for knowledge reuse, and has strenghtened its potential at the same time. Therefore, ontologies and problem-solving methods (which in some cases are considered as the precursors of Semantic Web Services) are playing an important role in this context.

As described in the chapter title, we will present the *what* and *how* of ontologies, describing the activities that should be carried out during the ontology development process, the principles to be followed in ontology design, and the methods, methodologies, software tools and languages that give support to each one of these activities. The second section defines the word "ontology" and explains which are the main components that can be used to model ontologies. The third section focuses on methods and methodologies for the development of ontologies, either used for the whole ontology development process or only for specific activities. The fourth section focuses on ontology tools, which normally give support to the previous methodological approaches. The fifth section describes ontology languages that can be used to implement ontologies. All these sections are structured in a similar way: first we give a brief overview of their evolution, then we describe the current trends, and finally we pay attention to the open issues and practical aspects. Finally, conclusions and future lines of work are presented in the last section.

## WHAT IS AN ONTOLOGY AND WHICH ARE ITS COMPONENTS?

There are two different views about the use of the term "ontology," considering whether the person who uses that term is interested in its philosophical roots or in its application to computer science.

For philosophers, the term *Ontology* (normally typed with uppercase) refers to the "the essence of things through the changes." Greek philosophers, from Parmenides of Elea to Aristotle, were interested in these aspects. In the 18th century, Kant worked also on these ideas. More recently, people working in the area of formal ontologies are also interested in these philosophical ideas and its application in the context of computer science.

On the other side, ontology engineers in the context of computer science are more interested in how ontologies (typed with lowercase) can be used to represent reusable and sharable pieces of domain knowledge and how they can be used in applications. In this context, ontologies are reusable and sharable artifacts that have to be developed in a machine interpretable language (Gruber, 1993; Studer, Benjamins, & Fensel, 1998). This point of view is clearly addressed in the definition given by Studer and colleagues (1998): *An ontology is a formal, explicit specification of a shared conceptualization.* We consider that this definition is one of the most complete ones from those available in the literature.

Once we have analysed these different definitions of the term "ontology," we will focus on the second use of this term, that is, on what is normally known as ontological engineering (Gómez-Pérez, Fernández-López, & Corcho, 2003). First we will discuss about the components that are used to create an ontology.

Different knowledge representation formalisms (and corresponding languages) exist for the fomalisation (and implementation) of ontologies.

Each of them provides different components that can be used for these tasks. However, they share the following minimal set of components.[1]

*Classes* represent concepts, which are taken in a broad sense. For instance, in the traveling domain, concepts are: locations (cities, villages, etc.), lodgings (hotels, camping, etc.) and means of transport (planes, trains, cars, ferries, motorbikes and ships). Classes in the ontology are usually organised in taxonomies through which inheritance mechanisms can be applied. We can represent a taxonomy of entertainment places (theater, cinema, concert, etc.) or travel packages (economy travel, business travel, etc.). In the frame-based KR paradigm, metaclasses can also be defined. Metaclasses are classes whose instances are classes. They usually allow for gradations of meaning, since they establish different layers of classes in the ontology where they are defined.

*Relations* represent a type of association between concepts of the domain. They are formally defined as any subset of a product of n sets, that is: $R \subset C1 \times C2 \times ... \times Cn$. Ontologies usually contain binary relations. The first argument is known as the domain of the relation, and the second argument is the range. For instance, the binary relation arrivalPlace has the concept Travel as its domain and the concept Location as its range. Relations can be instantiated with knowledge from the domain. For example, to express that the flight AA7462-Feb-08-2002 arrives in Seattle we must write: (arrivalPlace AA7462-Feb-08-2002 Seattle).

Binary relations are sometimes used to express concept attributes (i.e., slots). Attributes are usually distinguished from relations because their range is a datatype, such as *string, number,* and so forth, while the range of relations is a concept. The following code defines the attribute flightNumber, which is a *string*. We can also express relations of higher arity, such as "a road connects two different cities."

According to Gruber (1993), *formal axioms* serve to model sentences that are always true. They are normally used to represent knowledge that cannot be formally defined by the other components. In addition, formal axioms are used to verify the consistency of the ontology itself or the consistency of the knowledge stored in a knowledge base. Formal axioms are very useful to infer new knowledge. An axiom in the traveling domain would be that it is not possible to travel from the America to Europe by train.

*Instances* are used to represent elements or individuals in an ontology. An example of instance of the concept AA7462 is the flight AA7462 that arrives at Seattle on February 8, 2006 and costs 300 (US Dollars, Euros, or any other currency).

Besides formalisms and languages specifically designed for representing knowledge, ontologies can be formalised with other approaches coming from the areas of software engineering, such as the Unified Modeling Language (UML) (Rumbaugh, Jacobson, & Booch, 1998) or entity-relationship (ER) diagrams (Chen, 1976).

In this context, the Object Management Group (OMG)[2] is working on a specification to define the meta-models of some of the diagram types and languages used in ontology representation. This specification is known as ontology description model (ODM, 2005), and uses a common formal notation to describe the metamodels. Such metamodels (defined for UML, entity-relationship, OWL, RDF(S), etc.) can be considered formalisations of knowledge representation ontologies. All these correspondences are formally described in the ODM document (ODM, 2005).

The purpose of ODM documents is to allow software engineers to model ontologies with familiar notations for them, for example, UML and ER, and to transform their conceptual models into formal ontologies represented in ontology languages.

## METHODS AND METHODOLOGIES FOR THE DEVELOPMENT OF ONTOLOGIES

Several proposals for ontology development have been reported in the literature. In 1990, Lenat and Guha published the general steps (Lenat & Guha, 1990) and some interesting points about the Cyc development. Some years later, in 1995, on the basis of the experience gathered in developing the Enterprise Ontology (Uschold & King, 1995) and the TOVE (TOronto Virtual Enterprise) project ontology (Grüninger & Fox, 1995) (both in the domain of enterprise modeling), the first guidelines were proposed and later refined in (Uschold, 1996; Uschold & Grüninger, 1996). At the 12th European Conference for Artificial Intelligence (ECAI'96), Bernaras and colleagues (Bernaras, Laresgoiti, & Corera, 1996) presented a method used to build an ontology in the domain of electrical networks as part of the Esprit KACTUS (Schreiber, Wielinga, & Jansweijer, 1995) project. The methodology methontology (Gómez-Pérez, Fernández-López, & de Vicente, 1996) appeared at the same time and was extended in later papers (Fernández-López, Gómez-Pérez, & Juristo, 1997; Fernández-López, Gómez-Pérez, Pazos, & Pazos, 1999). In 1997, a new method was proposed for building ontologies based on the SENSUS ontology (Swartout, Ramesh, Knight, & Russ, 1997). Some years later, the on-to-knowledge methodology appeared as a result of the project with the same name (Staab, Schnurr, Studer, & Sure, 2001). A comparative and detailed study of these methods and methodologies can be found in (Fernández-López & Gómez-Pérez, 2002a).

All the previous methods and methodologies were proposed for building ontologies. However, many other methods have been proposed for specific tasks of the ontology development process, such as ontology reengineering (Gómez-Pérez & Rojas, 1999), ontology learning (Aussenac-Gilles, Biébow, Szulman, 2000a; Kietz, Maedche, & Volz, 2000), ontology evaluation (Gómez-Pérez, 1994, 1996, 2001, 2004; Guarino, 2004; Gua-

rino & Welty, 2002; Kalfoglou & Robertson, 1999a, 1999b; Welty & Guarino, 2001), ontology evolution (Klein & Fensel, 2001; Klein, Fensel, Kiryakov, & Ognyanov, 2002; Noy & Klein, 2002; Noy & Musen, 2004a, 2004b; Noy, Kunnatur, Klein, & Musen, 2004; Stojanovic, 2004), ontology alignment (Benebentano et al., 2000; Castano, De Antonellis, & De Capitani diVemercati, 2001; Ehring & Staab, 2004; Euzenat, 2004; Madhavan, Bernstein, & Rahm, 2001; Melnik, García-Molina, & Rahm, 2002; Noy & Musen, 2001; Pan, Ding, Yu, & Peng, 2005; Shvaiko, Giunchiglia, & Yatskevich, 2004), and ontology merging (Gangemi, Pisanelli, & Steve, 1999; Steve, Gangemi, & Pisanelli, 1998) (Noy & Musen, 2000; Stumme & Maedche, 2001), among others.

In the following subsections we will describe what we understand by ontology development process and ontology lifecycle. Then we will describe the methods and methodologies used for the whole ontology development process. And finally we will focus on ontology learning, ontology merging, ontology alignment, ontology evolution and versioning, and ontology evaluation.

### Ontology Development Process and Lifecycle

The ontology development process and the ontology lifecycle were identified by Fernández-López and colleagues (1997) in the framework of methontology. These proposals were based on the IEEE standard for software development (IEEE, 1996).

The ontology development process refers to the activities that have to be performed when building ontologies. They can be classified in three categories (Figure 1):

*Ontology management activities* include scheduling, control and quality assurance. The *scheduling* activity identifies the tasks to be performed, their arrangement, and the time and resources needed for their completion. This activity is essential for ontologies that use ontologies stored in ontology libraries or for ontologies that require a high level of abstraction and generality. The *control* activity guarantees that scheduled tasks are completed in the manner intended to be performed. Finally, the *quality assurance* activity assures that the quality of each and every product output (ontology, software and documentation) is satisfactory.

*Ontology development oriented activities* are grouped, as presented in Figure 1, into predevelopment, development and postdevelopment activities. During the predevelopment, an *environment study* identifies the problem to be solved with the ontology, the applications where the ontology will be integrated, and so forth. Also during the predevelopment, the *feasibility study* answers questions like: is it possible to build the ontology?; is it suitable to build the ontology?; and so forth.

Once in the development, the *specification* activity[3] states why the ontology is being built, what its intended uses are and who the end-users are. The *conceptualisation* activity structures the domain knowledge as meaningful models

either from scratch or reusing existing models. In this last case, related activities like pruning branches of the existing taxonomies, extending the coverage of ontologies with the addition of new concepts in the higher levels of their taxonomies, or specialising branches that require more granularity. Given that the conceptualisation activity is implementation-language independent, it allows modeling ontologies according to the minimal encoding bias design criterion. The *formalisation* activity transforms the conceptual model into a formal or semi-computable model. The *implementation* activity builds computable models in an ontology language.

During the postdevelopment, the *maintenance* activity updates and corrects the ontology if needed. Also during the postdevelopment, the ontology is *(re)used* by other ontologies or applications. The evolution activity consists in managing ontology changes and their effects by creating and maintaining different variants of the ontology, taking into account that they can be used in different ontologies and applications (Noy et al., 2004).

Finally, *ontology support activities* include a series of activities that can be performed dur-

*Figure 1. Ontology development process (adapted from Fernández-López et al., 1997)*

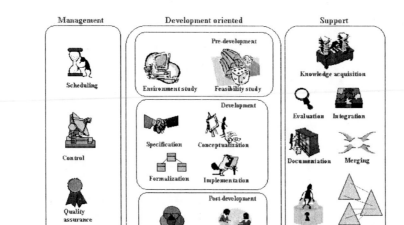

ing the development-oriented activities, without which the ontology could not be built. They include knowledge acquisition, evaluation, integration, merging, alignment, documentation, and configuration management. The goal of the *knowledge acquisition* activity is to acquire knowledge from experts of a given domain or through some kind of (semi)automatic process, which is called ontology learning (Kietz et al., 2000). The *evaluation* activity (Gómez-Pérez, 1994) makes a technical judgment of the ontologies, of their associated software environments, and of the documentation. This judgment is made with respect to a frame of reference during each stage and between stages of the ontology's lifecycle. The *integration* activity is required when building a new ontology by reusing other ontologies already available. Another support activity is *merging* (Gangemi et al., 1999; Noy & Musen, 2000; Steve et al., 1998; Stumme & Maedche, 2001), which consists in obtaining a new ontology starting from several ontologies on the same domain. The resulting ontology is able to unify concepts, terminology, definitions, constraints, and so forth, from all the source ontologies. The merge of two or more ontologies can be carried out either in run-time or design time. The *alignment* activity establishes different kinds of mappings (or links) between the involved ontologies. Hence this option preserves the original ontologies and does not merge them. The *documentation* activity details, clearly and exhaustively, each and every one of the completed stages and products generated. The *configuration management* activity records all the versions of the documentation and of the ontology code to control the changes. The *multilingualism activity* consists in mapping ontologies onto formal descriptions of linguistic knowledge (Declerck & Uszkoreit, 2003). It has not usually been considered as an ontology support activity, but has become more relevant in the context of networked ontologies available in the Semantic Web.

The ontology development process does not identify the order in which the activities should be performed. This is the role of the *ontology lifecycle*, which identifies *when* the activities should be carried out, that is, it identifies the *set of stages* through which the ontology moves during its life time, describes what activities are to be performed in each stage and how the stages are related (relation of precedence, return, etc.).

The initial version of the lifecycle process model of methontology (see Figure 2) proposes to start with a scheduling of the activities to be

*Figure 2. Ontology lifecycle in methontology*

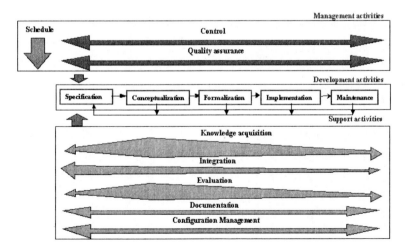

performed. Then, the specification activity begins, showing why the ontology will be built, which its possible uses will be, and who its users. When the specification finishes, the conceptualisation begins. The objective of the conceptualisation is to organise and structure the acquired knowledge in the knowledge acquisition activity, using a set of representations easy to manipulate for the experts on the domain. Once the conceptual model has been built, it has to be formalised and implemented (although if the conceptual model is formal enough then it will not be necessary to go through these two stages but just directly to the implementation). More details can be found in Gómez-Pérez et al. (2003).

The original ontology lifecycle of methontology has been modified recently to take into account the fact that more ontologies are available in ontology libraries or spread over the Internet, so that their reuse by other ontologies and applications has increased. Domain ontologies can be reused to build others of more granularity and coverage, or can be merged with others to create new ones. Using an analogy with an underground map, it can be noted that there exists a main line (in the middle of the Figure 3), which proposes the main development activities already identified in the early versions of methontology. Others lines start from the main one or finish in it, and others go in parallel ways and fork in a point. Thus, *interdependence relationships* (Gómez-Pérez & Rojas, 1999) arise between the lifecycle of several ontologies, and actions of evaluation, pruning and merging can be carried out on such ontologies. That is, the lifecycles of the different ontologies intersect, producing different scenarios with different technological requirements. Corcho and colleagues (2007) describe some of the most common scenarios that appear in this new context.

## Methods and Methodologies Used for the Whole Ontology Development Lifecycle

Several methods and methodologies have been proposed in the literature as a guide for the main phases of the ontology development lifecycle. The

*Figure 3. The ontology development process of networked ontologies*

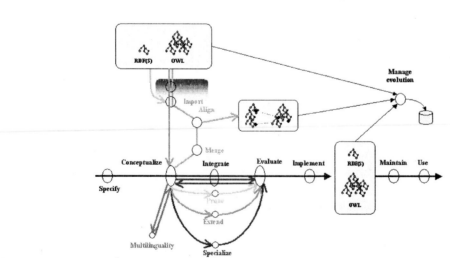

selection of one or another will mainly depend on the characteristics of the ontology to be developed, including the context where they are being developed and the experience of the ontology engineers with the each approach. At the end of this section we provide a comparison of the approaches according to several factors that can be considered for ontology development.

The **Cyc** method (Lenat & Guha, 1990), which is given this name because it was used for the development of the Cyc knowledge base, is mainly oriented to support the knowledge acquisition activity, and is structured in three phases. In all of them, the objective is to derive common sense knowledge that is implicit in different sources. The difference between them is the degree of automation of the knowledge acquisition process (from manual to automatic). Once knowledge has been acquired, it is divided into microtheories (or contexts), which are bundles of assertions in the same domain.

The *Uschold and King's* method (Uschold & King, 1995) covers more aspects of the ontology development lifecycle. It proposes four phases: (1) to identify the purpose of the ontology, (2) to build it, integrating other ontologies inside the current one if necessary, (3) to evaluate it, and (4) to document it. The authors propose three strategies for identifying the main concepts in the ontology: a top-down approach, in which the most abstract concepts are identified first, and then, specialised into more specific concepts; a bottom-up approach, in which the most specific concepts are identified first and then generalised into more abstract concepts; and a middle-out approach, in which the most important concepts are identified first and then generalised and specialised into other concepts. Depending on the characteristics of the ontology to be developed, different strategies will be considered.

*Grüninger and Fox* (1995) propose a methodology that is inspired on the development of knowledge-based systems using first order logic. They propose first to identify intuitively the possible applications where the ontology will be used, and determine the scope of the ontology using a set of natural language questions, called competency questions. These questions and their answers are used both to extract the main ontology components (expressed in first order logic). This methodology is very formal and can be used as a guide to transform informal scenarios in computable models.

In the method proposed in the *KACTUS* project (Bernaras et al., 1996) the ontology is built on the basis of an application knowledge base (KB), by means of a process of abstraction (that is, following a bottom-up strategy). The more applications are built, the more reusable and sharable the ontology becomes.

The method based on *Sensus* (Swartout et al., 1997) aims at promoting the sharability of knowledge, since it proposes to use the same base ontology to develop ontologies in particular domains. It is a top-down approach where the authors propose to identify a set of "seed" terms that are relevant to a particular domain. These terms are linked manually to a broad-coverage ontology (in this case, the Sensus ontology, which contains more than 50,000 concepts). Then, all the concepts in the path from the seed terms to the ontology root are included. For those nodes that have a large number of paths through them, the entire subtree under the node is sometimes added, based on the idea that if many of the nodes in a subtree have been found to be relevant, then, the other nodes in the subtree are likely to be relevant as well.

*Methontology* (Fernández-López et al., 1999) is a methodology that can be used to create domain ontologies that are independent of the application where they will be used. The ontology development process and lifecycle presented in the previous section are derived from this methodology. Besides, the methodology proposes specific techniques to carry out each of the activities identified there. The main phase in the ontology development process is the conceptualisation phase.

The *on-to-knowledge* methodology (Staab et al., 2001) is based on an analysis of usage scenarios. The steps proposed by the methodology are: *kick-off*, where ontology requirements are captured and specified, competency questions are identified, potentially reusable ontologies are studied and a first draft version of the ontology is built; *refinement*, where a mature and application-oriented ontology is produced; *evaluation*, where the requirements and competency questions are checked, and the ontology is tested in the application environment; and *ontology maintenance*.

If we analyse the approaches according to the part of the ontology development process that they describe, we can conclude (Fernández-López & Gómez-Pérez, 2002a):

1. None of the approaches covers all the processes involved in ontology building. Most of the methods and methodologies for building ontologies are focused on the development activities, specially on the ontology conceptualisation and ontology implementation, and they do not pay too much attention to other important aspects related to management, learning, merge, integration, evolution and evaluation of ontologies. Therefore, such types of methods should be added to the methodologies for ontology construction from scratch (Fernández-López & Gómez-Pérez, 2002b).

2. Most of the approaches are focused on development activities, especially on the ontology implementation, and they do not pay too much attention to other important aspects related to the management, evolution and evaluation of ontologies. This is due to the fact that the ontological engineering field is relatively new. However, a low compliance with the criteria formerly established does not mean a low quality of the methodology or method. As de Hoog (1998) states, a not very specified method can be very useful for an experienced group.

3. Most of the approaches present some drawbacks in their use. Some of them have not been used by external groups and, in some cases they have been used in a single domain.

4. Most of the approaches do not have a specific tool that gives them technology support. Besides, none of the available tools covers all the activities necessary in ontology building.

## Methods and Techniques Aimed at Specific Activities of the Ontology Development Process

Now we will provide an overview of some of the most important methods and techniques that are proposed to give support to specific activities of the ontology development process, such as those for ontology learning (which support the knowledge acquisition activity), ontology alignment and merge (which support the integration, merge and alignment activities), ontology evolution and versioning (which support the maintenance activity), and ontology evaluation.

## Methods and Techniques for Ontology Learning

*Ontology learning* is defined as the set of methods and techniques used for building an ontology from scratch, enriching, or adapting an existing ontology in a semi-automatic fashion using distributed and heterogeneous knowledge and information sources, allowing to reduce the time and effort needed in the ontology development process. Though the fully automatic acquisition of knowledge remains far to be reached, the overall process is considered as semi-automatic, meaning that the human intervention is necessary in some parts of the learning process.

Several approaches have appeared during the last decade for the partial automatisation of the knowledge acquisition process, applied to different types of unstructured, semistructured, and fully structured data (Maedche & Staab, 2000). Most of these approaches are based on linguistic patterns, which are used to extract linguistic relations that reflect ontological relations (taxonomic and nontaxonomic relations as well as possible attributes or their values, depending on the pattern's type). In the same sense, these patterns are also used for detecting attribute-value pairs. All the presented methods require the participation of an ontologist to evaluate the final ontology and the accuracy of the learning process. There are not methods or techniques for evaluating the accuracy of the learning process either.

Regarding *ontology learning methods*, some of the most known ones are due to Maedche and colleagues (Kietz et al., 2000), Aussenac-Gilles and colleagues (2000a, 2000b), and Khan and Luo (2002). *Maedche and colleagues' method* (Kietz et al., 2000) proposes to learn the ontology using as a base a core ontology (SENSUS, WordNet, etc.), which is enriched with the learnt concepts. New concepts are identified using natural language analysis techniques over the resources previously identified by the user. The resulting ontology is pruned and then focused on a specific domain by means of several approaches based on statistics. Finally, relations between concepts are established applying learning methods.

*Aussenac-Gilles and colleagues' method* (Aussenac-Gilles et al., 2000a, 2000b) combines knowledge acquisition tools based on linguistics with modeling techniques to keep links between models and texts. After selecting a corpus, the method proposes to obtain linguistic knowledge (terms, lexical relations, and groups of synonyms) at the linguistic level. This linguistic knowledge is then transformed into a semantic network, which includes concepts, relations and attributes.

*Khan and Luo's method* (Khan & Luo, 2002) aims to build a domain ontology from text documents using clustering techniques and WordNet (Miller, 1995). The user provides a selection of documents, which are clustered using the SOAT

algorithm (Wu & Hsu, 2002). After building a hierarchy of clusters, a concept is assigned to each cluster in the hierarchy using a bottom-up fashion and a predefined set of topic categories. For this purpose, a topic tracking algorithm (Joachims, 1998) is used. Then, each topic is associated with an appropriate concept in WordNet, and other nodes in the hierarchy are assigned according to the concepts in the descendent nodes and their hyperyms in WordNet. Relations between concepts are ignored.

## Methods and Techniques for Ontology Alignment and Merge

Ontologies aim to capture consensual knowledge of a given domain in a generic and formal way, to be reused and shared across applications and by groups of people. From this definition we could wrongly infer that there is only one ontology for modeling each domain (or even a single universal ontology). Though this can be the case in specific domains, commonly several ontologies model the same domain knowledge in different ways.

Noy and Musen (2000) defined ontology alignment and merging as follows: (1) *ontology alignment* consists in establishing different kinds of mappings (or links) between two ontologies, hence preserving the original ontologies (see Figure 4); and (2) *ontology merging* proposes to generate a unique ontology from the original ontologies. In this chapter we will assume that a *mapping* between ontologies is a set of rewriting rules that associates terms and expressions defined in a source ontology with terms and expressions of a target ontology (inspired from Mitra, Wiederhold, & Kersten, 2000). Table 1 shows the mappings that can be established between the two ontologies of Figure 4. The symbol ":=" means "is transformed into," and "λ" is the empty word. Therefore, date := λ means that the attribute date has no correspondence with terms of the ontology 2.

Given that a reusable and machine interpretable database schema can be considered as an ontology (see second section), the galaxy of ontology alignment methods is huge. Some examples of these methods are: *S-Match* (Shvaiko et al., 2004), *QOM* (Ehring & Staab, 2004), *Pan and colleagues proposal* (2005), *Artemis* (Benebentano et al., 2000; Castano et al., 2001), *Cupid* (Madhavan et al., 2001), *AnchorPrompt* (Noy & Musen, 2001), *Similarity Flooding* (Melnik et al., 2002), and so forth.

In the context of the workshop on Evaluation of Ontology Tools EON2004, an experiment was performed about the quality of the mappings provided by different methods and tools. This will be continued in other efforts. To know more on ontology alignment and merging we recommend to access to the Ontology Matching Web page.[4]

With regard to *ontology merging methods and methodologies*, one of the most elaborated proposals for ontology merging is *ONIONS* (Gangemi et al., 1999; Steve et al., 1998), developed by the Conceptual Modeling Group of the CNR in Rome, Italy. With this method we can create a library of ontologies originated from different sources. The main underlying ideas of this method are: (1) to link the ontologies taking into account lexical relations between their terms (polysemy, synonymy, etc.); and (2) to use generic theories (part-whole or connectedness theories, for example) as common upper ontologies of the library ontologies, that is, to use generic theories as the glue to integrate the different ontologies.

*Table 1. Mappings for the two ontologies of Figure 4*

| Description of the mapping in natural language | Rewriting rule |
|---|---|
| The concept travel (in ontology 1) is equivalent to the concept traveling (in ontology 2). | Travel := Traveling |
| The concept travel by plane (in ontology 1) is equivalent to the concept such as it is subclass of traveling (in ontology 2) and its transport mean is a plane (in ontology 2). | TravelByPlane := C such as subclassOf(C, Traveling) $\wedge$ C.hasTransporMean = Plane |
| The concept such as it is subclass of travel (in ontology 1) and its transport mean is a bus (in ontology 2) is equivalent to the concept traveling by bus (in ontology 2). | C such as subclassOf(C, Travel) $\wedge$ C.hasTransporMean = Bus := TravelingByBus |
| The attribute origin (in ontology 1) is equivalent to the attribute origin place (in ontology 2). | Origin := OriginPlace |
| The attribute destination (in ontology 1) is equivalent to the attribute destination place (in ontology 2). | Destination := DestinationPlace |
| The value New York of attributes origin and destination (in ontology 2) is equivalent to the value NY of origin place and destination place (in ontology 2). | "New York" := "NY" |
| The attribute date (in ontology 1) does not have correspondence in ontology 2. | Date := $\lambda$ |
| The attribute price (in ontology 1) is equivalent to a combination of the attributes price and tax in ontology 2. | Price := Price * (1 + Tax/100) |
| The attribute has transport mean (in ontology 1) is equivalent to the attribute has transport mean in ontology 2. | HasTransportMean := HasTransportMean |

*Figure 4. Example of ontology alignment*

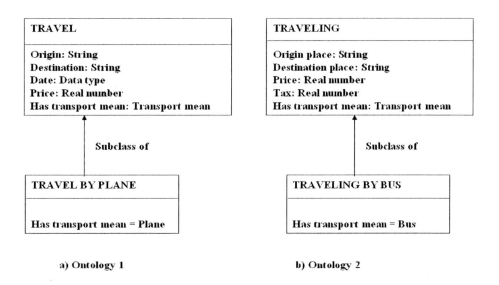

a) Ontology 1          b) Ontology 2

*FCA-Merge* (Stumme & Maedche, 2001) was developed at the Institute AIFB of the University of Karlsruhe, Germany. This approach is very different from the other approaches presented in this section. FCA-Merge takes as input the two ontologies to be merged and a set of documents on the domains of the ontologies. The appearances of instances of the concepts in the different documents guides the merging such concepts.

The *PROMPT* method (Noy & Musen, 2000) has been elaborated by the Stanford Medical Informatics group at Stanford University. The main assumption of PROMPT is that the ontologies to be merged are formalised with a common knowledge model based on frames. This method proposes first to elaborate a list with the candidate operations to be performed to merge the two ontologies (e.g., merge two classes, merge two slots, etc.). Afterwards, a cyclic process starts. In each cycle the ontologist selects an operation of the list and executes it.

*PromptDiff* is a component of Prompt (Noy & Musen, 2004b) that allows maintaining ontology views or mappings between ontologies. PromptDiff provides an ontology-comparison API

that other applications can use to determine, for example, the mapping needs to be updated when new versions of mapped ontologies appear (Noy et al., 2004).

## Methods and Techniques for Ontology Evolution and Versioning

Ontologies are often developed by several groups of people and may evolve over time. Therefore, they cannot be understood as static entities, but rather as dynamic ones. As a consequence, ontology versioning becomes necessary and essential.

Ontology engineers working in parallel on the same ontology need to maintain and compare different versions, to examine the changes that others have performed, and to accept or reject the changes. Ontology-based application developers should easily see the changes between ontology versions, determine which definitions were added or deleted, and accept or reject the changes. Let's note that, for ontologies, we must compare the semantics of the ontologies and not their serialisations, since two ontologies that are exactly the same conceptually may have very different text representations when implemented in some ontology languages.

The most relevant methods (and corresponding tools) for ontology evolution and versioning are the *change management KAON plug-in* (Stojanovic, 2004) and the *PromptDiff algorithm* (Noy et al., 2004).

The *change management KAON plug-in* allows establishing the effects of changes through *evolution strategies* (Stojanovic, 2004). A particular evolution strategy allows establishing, for example, what happens with its subclasses when a concept $C$ is deleted: if they can be also deleted, or they can become subclasses of the superclasses of $C$.

The *PromptDiff algorithm*, which is integrated in the PROMPT plug-in of the Protégé tool, compares ontologies producing an initial set of mappings between two versions of the same ontology (Noy et al., 2004). For instance, if a term $t_1$ of the version $v_1$ has the same type as the term $t_2$ of the version $v_2$ (both of them are concepts, both of them are properties, etc.) and $t_1$ has a similar name to $t_2$, it is assumed that the semantics of $t_1$ and $t_2$ are similar. Therefore, $t_1$ and $t_2$ are mapped as similar terms. This initial set of mappings is propagated using a fixed-point algorithm that combines the results of the previous step. Thus, for example, if all the siblings of the concept $c_1$ of $v_1$ are mapped with siblings of the concept $c_2$ of $v_2$, $c_1$ and $c_2$ are candidates to be mapped through a change operation (e.g., the addition of a new subclass).

## Methods and Techniques for Ontology Evaluation

Work on ontology content evaluation was started by Gómez-Pérez (1994). A survey on evaluation methods and tools can be found in (Gómez-Pérez et al., 2003). These evaluation efforts can be examined under the following four perspectives:

From a *content perspective*, many libraries exist where ontologies are published and publicly available (SWOOGLE[5], Oyster[6], DAML[7], Protégé[8], etc.). No documentation is available about how ontologies available in libraries or well-known and large ontologies (e.g., Cyc (Lenat & Guha 1990), or Sensus (Swartout et al., 1997)) were evaluated. However they have been used to build many successful applications.

From a *methodology perspective*, the main efforts to evaluate ontology content were made by Gómez-Pérez (1996, 2001) in the framework of methontology, and by Guarino and colleagues (Welty & Guarino, 2001) with the OntoClean method.

*Gómez-Pérez* has identified and classified different kinds of errors in taxonomies. Such identification can be used as a checklist for taxonomy evaluation. Such a list presents a set of possible errors that can be made by ontology engineers when modeling taxonomic knowledge in an ontology under a frame-based approach. They are classified in: inconsistency, incompleteness, and redundancy errors. The ontology engineer should not postpone the evaluation until the taxonomy is finished; the control mechanisms should be performed during the construction of the taxonomy.

*OntoClean* is a method elaborated by the Ontology Group of the CNR in Padova (Italy). Its goal is to remove wrong *Subclass-Of* relations in taxonomies according to some philosophical notions such as *rigidity, identity* and *unity*. According to this method, the ontology engineer, first, assigns some meta-properties to each concept of the taxonomy (for example, if each instance of the concept is a whole), then it applies a set of rules that establish the possible incompatibilities of values in the taxonomy. Such rules allow pruning wrong *subclass of* links if the values assigned to a concept are incompatible with the values assigned to its children.

Recently, some researchers have published a synthesis of their experience in ontology evaluation (Daelemans & Reinberger, 2004; Gómez-Pérez, 2004; Guarino, 2004; Noy, 2004). According to their conclusions, although good ideas have been provided in this area, there are still important lacks. Other interesting works are (Guo, Pan, & Heflin, 2004) and the aforementioned EON2004 experiment.

## ONTOLOGY TOOLS

Ontology tools appeared in the mid-1990s with the objective of giving support to the development of ontologies, either following a specific set of methods or a methodology or not. Taking into account the characteristics of their knowledge models, ontology tools can be classified in the following two groups:

- Tools whose knowledge model maps directly to an ontology language, hence developed as ontology editors for that specific language. This groups includes: the Ontolingua Server (Farquhar, Fikes, & Rice, 1997), which supports ontology construction with Ontolingua and KIF; OntoSaurus (Swartout et al., 1997) with Loom; WebOnto (Domingue, 1998) with OCML; OilEd (Bechhofer, Horrocks, Goble, & Stevens, 2001) with OIL first, later with DAML+OIL, and finally with OWL; and SWOOP (Kalyanpur, Parsia, & Hendler, 2005) and KAON2 (Hustadt, Motik, & Sattler, 2004) with OWL.
- Integrated tool suites whose main characteristic is that they have an extensible architecture, and whose knowledge model is usually independent of ontology languages. These tools provide a core set of ontology related services and are easily extended with other modules to provide more functions. In this group we have included Protégé (Noy, Fergerson, & Musen, 2000), WebODE (Arpírez, Corcho, Fernández-López, Gómez-Pérez, 2003; Corcho, Fernández-López,

Gómez-Pérez, & Vicente, 2002), OntoEdit (Sure, Erdmann, Angele, Staab, Studer, & Wenke, 2002), and KAON1 (Maedche, Motik, Stojanovic, Studer, & Volz, 2003).

## Tools that Give Support to Most of the Activities of the Ontology Development Process

In this section we will focus on those tools that give an integrated support to the ontology development process, and consequently cover most of the activities needed to develop ontologies. From all of them we will only describe those that belong to the new generation of ontology-engineering environments, in particular, in Protégé, WebODE, OntoEdit and KAON1.[9]

These tools have been created to integrate ontology technology in actual information systems. As a matter of fact, they are built as robust integrated environments or suites that provide technological support to most of the ontology lifecycle activities. They have extensible, component-based architectures, where new modules can easily be added to provide more functionality to the environment. Besides, the knowledge models underlying these environments are language independent.

*Protégé* (Noy et al., 2000) has been developed by the Stanford Medical Informatics (SMI) at Stanford University. It is an open source, standalone application with an extensible architecture. The core of this environment is the ontology editor, and it holds a library of plugins that add more functionality to the environment. Currently, plugins are available for ontology language import/export (FLogic, Jess, XML, Prolog), ontology language design (Knublauch, Fergerson, Noy, & Musen, 2004), OKBC access, constraints creation and execution (PAL), ontology merge (Prompt (Noy & Musen, 2000)), and so forth.

*WebODE* (Arpírez et al., 2003; Corcho et al., 2002) has been developed by the Ontological

Engineering Group of the Technical University of Madrid (UPM). It is also an ontology-engineering suite created with an extensible architecture. WebODE is not used as a standalone application, but as a Web server with several frontends. The core of this environment is the ontology access service, which is used by all the services and applications plugged into the server, especially by the WebODE's Ontology Editor. There are several services for ontology language import/export (XML, RDF(S), OWL, CARIN, FLogic, Jess, Prolog), axiom edition, ontology documentation, ontology evaluation and ontology merge. WebODE's ontologies are stored in a relational database. Finally, WebODE covers and gives support to most of the activities involved in the ontology development process proposed by methontology, although this does not prevent it from being used with other methodologies or without following any methodology.

*OntoEdit* (Sure et al., 2002) has been developed by AIFB in Karlsruhe University, and is commercialised by Ontoprise. It is similar to the previous tools: it is an extensible and flexible environment, based on a plugin architecture, which provides functionality to browse and edit ontologies. It includes plugins that are in charge of inferring using Ontobroker, of exporting and importing ontologies in different formats (FLogic, XML, RDF(S) and OWL), and so forth. Two versions of OntoEdit are available: OntoEdit Free and OntoEdit Professional.

The *KAON1* tool suite (Maedche et al., 2003) is an open source extensible ontology engineering environment. The core of this tool suite is the ontology API, which defines its underlying knowledge model based on an extension of RDF(S). The OI-modeler is the ontology editor of the tool suite that provides capabilities for ontology evolution, ontology mapping, ontology generation from databases, and so forth.

An interesting aspect of tools is that only OntoEdit and WebODE give *support to ontology*

*building methodologies* (on-to-knowledge and methontology respectively), though this does not prevent them from being used with other methodologies or with no methodology at all.

From the *KR paradigm* point of view, KAON is based on semantic networks plus frames, and the rest of tools allow representing knowledge following a hybrid approach based on frames and first order logic. *Expressiveness of the underlying tool knowledge model* is also important. All the tools allow representing classes, relations, attributes, and instances. Only KAON1, and Protégé provide flexible modeling components like metaclasses. Before selecting a tool for developing an ontology, it is also important to know the *inference services* attached to the tool, which includes: constraint and consistency checking mechanisms, type of inheritance (single, multiple, monotonic, non-monotonic), automatic classifications, exception handling and execution of procedures. KAON1 does not have an inference engine. OntoEdit uses FLogic (Kifer, Lausen, & Wu, 1995) as its inference engine, WebODE uses Ciao Prolog (Hermenegildo, Bueno, Cabeza, Carro, García, López, & Puebla, 2000), and Protégé uses an internal PAL engine. Besides, Protégé and WebODE provide ontology evaluation facilities. WebODE and Protégé include a module that performs ontology evaluation according to the OntoClean method (Guarino & Welty, 2002; Welty & Guarino, 2001). Finally, Protégé (with the OWL plug-in) performs automatic classifications by means of connecting to a description logic reasoner.

Another important aspect to take into account in ontology tools is the *software architecture and tool evolution*, which considers which hardware and software platforms are necessary to use the tool, its architecture (standalone, client/server, n-tier application), extensibility, storage of the ontologies (databases, ASCII files, etc.), failure tolerance, backup management, stability and tool versioning policies. From that perspective, all these tools are based on Java platforms and provides database storage support. Backup management functionality is just provided by WebODE, and extensibility facilities are allowed in KAON, OntoEdit, Protégé and WebODE.

Related to the *cooperative and collaborative construction of ontologies*, Protégé incorporates some synchronisation functionalities. In general, more features are required in existing tools to ensure a successful collaborative building of ontologies.

## Tools that Give Support to Specific Activities of the Ontology Development Process

Here we will only cover tools for ontology learning and ontology merge and alignment, since the ones for evolution and evaluation are very close to each of the methods described previously and consequently there is not much more that can be described about them.

## Tools that Give Support to Ontology Learning

We will describe Caméléon (Aussenac-Gilles & Seguela, 2000), LTG Text Processing Workbench (Mikheev & Finch, 1997), Prométhée (Morin, 1998, 1999), SOAT tool (Wu & Hsu, 2002) and Text-To-Onto (Maedche & Staab, 2000).

*Caméléon* (Aussenac-Gilles & Seguela, 2000) assists in learning conceptual relations to enrich conceptual models. Caméléon relies on linguistic principles for relation identification: lexico-syntactic patterns are good indicators of semantic relations. Some patterns may be regular enough to indicate the same kind of relation from one domain to another. Other patterns are domain specific and may reveal domain specific relations. This tool gives technological support to some steps of the Aussenac-Gilles and colleagues' method.

Language Technology Group (*LTG*) *Text Processing Workbench* (Mikheev & Finch, 1997) is a set of computational tools for uncovering internal structure in natural language texts written in English. The main idea behind the workbench is the independence of the text representation and text analysis. In LTG, ontology learning is performed in two sequential steps: representation and analysis. At the representation step, the text is converted from a sequence of characters to features of interest by means of annotation tools. At the analysis step, those features are used by tools of statistics-gathering and inference to find significant correlations in the texts. The workbench is being used both for lexicographic purposes and for statistical language modeling.

*Prométhée* (Morin, 1998, 1999) is a machine learning based tool for extracting and refining lexical-syntactic patterns related to conceptual specific relations from technical corpora. It uses pattern bases, which are enriched with the ones extracted in the learning. To refine patterns, the authors propose the Eagle (Guarino, Masolo, & Vetere, 1999) learning system. This system is based on the inductive paradigm *learning from examples*, which consists in the extraction of intentional descriptions of target concepts from their extensional descriptions, and previous knowledge on the given domain. This fact specifies general information, like the object characteristics and their relations. The tool extracts *intentional* descriptions of concepts from their *extensional* descriptions. The learned definitions are later used in recognition and classification tasks.

*SOAT* (Wu & Hsu, 2002) allows a semi-automatic domain ontology acquisition from a domain corpus. The main objective of the tool is to extract relationships from parsed sentences based on applying phrase-rules to identify keywords with strong semantic links like hyperonyms or synonyms. The acquisition process integrates linguistic, commonsense, and domain knowledge. The restrictions of SOAT involve that the quality of the corpus must be very high, in the sense that the sentences must be accurate and enough to include most of the important relationships to be extracted.

*Text-To-Onto* (Maedche & Staab, 2000) integrates an environment for building domain ontologies from an initial core ontology. It also discovers conceptual structures from different German sources using knowledge acquisition and machine learning techniques. Text-To-Onto has implemented some techniques for ontology learning from free and semistructured text. The result of the learning process is a domain ontology that contains domain-specific and domain-independent concepts. Domain-independent concepts are withdrawn to better adjust the vocabulary of the domain ontology. The result of this process is a domain ontology that only contains domain concepts learnt from the input sources related before. The ontologist supervises the whole process. This is a cyclic process, in the sense that it is possible to refine and complete the ontology if we repeat the process.

An important conclusion that we can obtain in the revision of ontology learning tools is that it does not exist a fully automatic tool that carries out the learning process. Some tools are focused on helping in the acquisition of lexico-semantic knowledge, others help to elicit concepts or relations from a pre-processed corpus with the help of the user, and so forth. A deeper description of methods and tools can be found in (Gómez-Pérez & Manzano, 2003).

## Tools that Give Support to Ontology Alignment and Merge

With regard to ontology alignment tools, we will describe the QOM toolset, S-Match, Pan and colleagues tool and OLA.

The *QOM toolset* (Ehring & Staab, 2004) gives support to the QOM method. It is implemented in Java using the KAON framework. It has been basically used to make experiments with the method and compare it with other methods.

*S-Match* tool translates and preprocesses the input ontologies. Then, it orders the transformation of prefixes, the expansions of abbreviations, and so forth. Later, using resources like Wordnet, it generates a first mapping base. Finally, using the SAT solvers, new mappings are generated.

*Pan and colleagues* (2005) apply their method combining the Google search engine and text classifiers (such as Rainbow[10] or cbacl[11]) to calculate the prior probabilities of the Bayesian network. Then, the subsequent probability is calculated using any Bayesian network tool.

*OLA*[12] (Euzenat, 2004) is an API for manipulating alignments between ontologies in OWL. It allows applying and combining different algorithms, and even adding others new. Currently, this API has been mainly used with mapping methods based on lexical similarity measures. OLA implements a format for expressing alignments in RDF.

With regard to ontology merge tools, we will describe OGSERVER, Chimaera, the Prompt plug-in, the FCA-Merge toolset and GLUE.

*OBSERVER* (Mena, Kashyap, Sheth, & Illarramendi, 1996) merges automatically ontologies of the same domain to access heterogeneous information sources. However, the merge process is carried out by an internal module and, therefore, it is invisible to the user.

*Chimaera* (McGuinness, Fikes, Rice, & Wilder, 2000) was built by the Knowledge Systems Laboratory (KSL) to aid in the process of ontology merge, and the *Prompt plug-in* (Noy & Musen, 2000), integrated in Protégé, was built by the Stanford Medical Informatics (SMI). The added value of the latter was that it provided support to the ontology merge method Prompt.

Approximately at the same time, the Institute AIFB of the University of Karlsruhe developed the *FCA-Merge toolset* (Stumme & Maedche, 2001) to support the FCA-Merge method.

Finally, in 2002, *GLUE* (Doan, Madhavan, Domingos, & Halevy, 2002) was developed at the University of Washington. GLUE is a system that semi-automatically finds mappings between concepts from two different ontologies.

The current ontology merging approaches have the following lacks: (1) mappings to perform the merging are usually established by hand; (2) all the tools need the participation of the user to obtain the definitive result of the merging process; and (3) no tool allows merging axioms and rules. The natural evolution of merging tools should lead to increase the use of knowledge and to decrease the participation of the people in the process. This could improve the possibilities of the merging at run-time.

## ONTOLOGY LANGUAGES

*Ontology languages* started to be created at the beginning of the 1990s, normally as the evolution of existing knowledge representation (KR) languages. Basically, the KR paradigms underlying such ontology languages were based on first order logic (e.g., KIF (Genesereth & Fikes, 1992)), on frames combined with first order logic (e.g., Ontolingua (Farquhar et al., 1997) (Gruber, 1992), OCML (Motta, 1999) and FLogic (Kifer et al., 1995)), and on description logics (e.g., Loom (MacGregor, 1991)). In 1997, OKBC (Chaudri et al., 1998) was created as a unifying frame-based protocol to access ontologies implemented in different languages (Ontolingua, Loom and CycL, among others). However it was only used in a small number of applications.

The boom of the Internet led to the creation of ontology languages for exploiting the characteristics of the Web. Such languages are usually called *Web-based ontology languages* or *ontology markup languages*. Their syntax is based on existing markup languages such as HTML (Raggett, Le Hors, & Jacobs, 1999) and XML (Bray, Paoli, Sperberg-McQueen, & Maler, 2000), whose purpose is not ontology development but data presentation and data exchange respectively. The most important examples of these markup languages are: SHOE (Luke & Helfin, 2000), XOL (Karp, Chaudhri, & Thomere, 1999), RDF (Las-

sila & Swick, 1999), RDF Schema (Brickley & Guha, 2004), OIL (Horrocks, Fensel, Harmelen, Decker, Erdmann, & Klein, 2000), DAML+OIL (Horrocks & van Harmelen, 2001), and OWL (Dean & Schreiber, 2004). From all of them, the ones that are being actively supported are now RDF, RDF Schema and OWL. Finally, in the context of the work on Semantic Web Services and more specifically in the context of the WSMO framework, a new ontology language is being developed, named WSML.

We will describe the most relevant ontology mark-up languages, since they are the most useful for the work on Semantic Web Services.

RDF (Lassila & Swick, 1999) was developed by the W3C (the World Wide Web Consortium) as a semantic-network based language to describe Web resources. Finally, the RDF Schema (Brickley & Guha, 2004) language was also built by the W3C as an extension to RDF with frame-based primitives. The combination of both RDF and RDF Schema is normally known as RDF(S). RDF(S) only allows the representation of concepts, taxonomies of concepts and binary relations. Some inference engines and query languages have been created for this language.

*Ontology Web Language* (OWL) was proposed as a W3C recommendation in February 2004. OWL is built on top of RDF(S), extending its expressiveness with more primitives that allow representing complex expressions to describe concepts and relations. OWL is divided into three layers (OWL Lite, OWL DL and OWL Full), each of them providing different levels of expressiveness that can be used depending on the representation and inference needs of an ontology. OWL is based on the description logic language $SHOIN(D+)$ and has several inference engines that can be used for constraint checking of concepts, properties and instances, and for automatic classification of concepts into hierarchies.

For instance, using OWL we can describe a flight as a kind of travel where the means of transport used is a plane. If we specify this condition as necessary and sufficient and then we define a travel where a light aircraft is used as the means of transport (and we assume that light aircraft is a specialisation of a plane) then a reasoner will be able to derive that this travel is a specialisation of a flight. Similarly, this same principle can be used for checking the consistency of the definitions provided in an ontology.

Finally, *Web Service Modeling Language* (WSML) (de Bruijn, 2006) is being developed in the context of the WSMO framework.[13] This language is aimed to be used not only for representing ontologies, but also for representing Semantic Web Services; hence it contains many additional features that are not present in the languages aforementioned. Like OWL, it is divided in several layers. Each of these layers is based on different KR formalisms: description logic, logic programming and first order logic.

## CONCLUSION

In the beginning of the 1990s ontology development was similar to an art: ontology developers did not have clear guidelines on how to build ontologies but only some design criteria to be followed. Work on principles, methods and methodologies, together with supporting technology, made ontology development become an engineering. This migration process was mainly due to the definition of the ontology development process and the ontology lifecycle, which described the steps to be performed in order to build ontologies and the interdependencies among all those steps.

In this chapter we have reviewed existing ontology principles, methods and methodologies, tools, and languages. The following is a summary of the chapter:

Ontology engineers have available methodologies that guide them along the ontology development process. Methontology is the methodology that provides the most detailed descriptions of the processes to be performed; On-To-Knowledge

is the one that covers most activities, although with very short descriptions of processes; and Grüninger and Fox methodology is the most formal one. All of them consider the reuse of existing ontologies during the development process, but only methontology has recently adapted its proposal for a lifecycle to the environment of networked ontologies. In any case, the development activities are the most detailed in all of them, mainly the specification, conceptualisation and implementation. There is still a lack of proposals for ontology management activities (scheduling, control and quality assurance), and for some pre-development (e.g., environment study) and post-development activities (e.g., (re)use).

Concerning support activities, some interesting contributions have been done in ontology learning, ontology merging and alignment, ontology evolution, and ontology evaluation. Nevertheless, important work has to be done in all of these activities. For example, the time in which activities like ontology learning or ontology merging are applied to heavyweight ontologies is far away.

One of the problems that the ontology engineer can find when (s)he has to build an ontology is that (s)he has to use different methods that are not integrated. For example, ontology learning methods are not integrated in methodologies that cover the whole development process (e.g., in methontology or On-To-Knowledge). Some experiences exist in the integration of methods in methodologies. For example, the OntoClean method has been integrated in methontology (Fernández-López & Gómez-Pérez, 2002b).

A similar problem appears in the use of ontology tools, given that there is a lack of integrated environments for ontology development. Tools are usually created as isolated modules that solve one type of problems, but neither are fully integrated nor do they interoperate with other tools that implement other activities of the ontology lifecycle.

Finally, work on ontology languages has been in constant evolution since the first languages that were made available for ontology implementation, most of them based on existing knowledge representation languages. The existence of heterogeneous networked ontologies has been mainly considered in the recent language developments created in the context of the Semantic Web (RDF, RDF Schema and OWL) and of Semantic Web Services (WSML), with the addition of namespaces that allow referring to ontology components that have been defined elsewhere and with the use of import primitives to include an existing model in an ontology.

## ACKNOWLEDGMENTS

This work has been partially supported by the IST project Knowledgeweb (FP6-507482) and by the Spanish project Semantic Services (TIN 2004-02660).

## REFERENCES

Arpírez, J.C., Corcho, O., Fernández-López, M., & Gómez-Pérez, A. (2003). WebODE in a nutshell. *AI Magazine*.

Aussenac-Gilles, N., Biébow, B., & Szulman, S. (2000a). Revisiting ontology design: A methodology based on corpus analysis. In R. Dieng & O. Corby (Eds.), *Proceedings of the 12th International Conference in Knowledge Engineering and Knowledge Management (EKAW'00)*, Juan-Les-Pins, France, (LNAI, 1937, pp. 172-188). Berlin: Springer-Verlag.

Aussenac-Gilles, N., Biébow, B., & Szulman, S. (2000b). Corpus analysis for conceptual modelling. In N. Aussenac-Gilles, B. Biébow & S. Szulman (Eds.), *Proceedings 51 of EKAW'00 Workshop on Ontologies and Texts*, Juan-Les-Pins, France (pp. 1.1-1.8), CEUR Workshop. Amsterdam, The Netherlands. Retrieved October 23, 2006, from http://CEUR-WS.org/Vol-51/

Aussenac-Gilles, N. & Seguela, P. (2000). Les relations sémantiques: du linguistique au formel. In A. Condamines (Ed.), *Cahiers de grammaire, N° spécial sur la linguistique de corpus* (Presse de l'UTM, Vol 25, pp. 175-198). Toulouse.

Bechhofer, S., Horrocks, I., Goble, C., & Stevens, R. (2001). OilEd: A reasonable ontology editor for the Semantic Web. In F. Baader, G. Brewka, & T. Eiter (Eds.), *Joint German/Austrian Conference on Artificial Intelligence (KI'01)* (pp. 396-408). Vienna, Austria. Lecture Notes in Artificial Intelligence 2174. Berlin: Springer-Verlag.

Beneventano, D., Bergamaschi, S., Castano, S., Corni, A., Guidetti, R., Malvezzi, G., Melchiori, M., & Vincini, M. (2000). Information integration: The MOMIS project demonstration. In A. El Abbadi, M.L. Brodie, S. Chakravarthy, U. Dayal, N. Kamel, G. Schlageter, & K.Y. Whang (Eds.), *26th International Conference On Very Large Data Bases*, El Cairo, Egypt (pp. 611-614). San Francisco: Morgan Kaufmann Publishers.

Bernaras, A., Laresgoiti, I., & Corera, J. (1996). Building and reusing ontologies for electrical network applications. In W. Wahlster (Ed.), *European Conference on Artificial Intelligence (ECAI'96)*, Budapest, Hungary (pp. 298-302). Chichester, UK: John Wiley & Sons.

Berners-Lee, T. (1999). *Weaving the Web: The original design and ultimate destiny of the World Wide Web by itsiInventor*. New York: HarperCollins Publishers.

Bray, T., Paoli, J., Sperberg-McQueen, C.M., & Maler, E. (2000). Extensible markup language (XML) 1.0. W3C Recommendation. Retrieved October 23, 2006, from http://www.w3.org/TR/REC-xml

Brickley, D., & Guha, R.V. (2004). *RDF vocabulary description language 1.0: RDF schema*. W3C

Recommendation. Retrieved October 23, 2006, from http://www.w3.org/TR/PR-rdf-schema

Castano, S., De Antonellis, V., & De Capitani diVemercati, S. (2001). *Global viewing of heterogeneous data sources. IEEE Transactions on Data Knowledge Engineering, 13*(2), 277-297.

Corcho, O., Fernández-López, M., Gómez-Pérez, A., & Vicente, O. (2002). WebODE: An integrated workbench for ontology representation, reasoning and exchange. In A. Gómez-Pérez & V.R. Benjamins (Eds.), *13th International Conference on Knowledge Engineering and Knowledge Management (EKAW'02)* Sigüenza, Spain, (pp. 138-153). Lecture Notes in Artificial Intelligence 2473. Berlin: Springer-Verlag.

Corcho, O., Fernández-López, M., & Gómez-Pérez, A. (2007). Ontological engineering: Principles, methods, tools and languages. In C. Calero, F. Ruiz, & M. Piattini (Eds.), *Ontologies for software engineering and technology*. Springer-Verlag.

Chaudhri, V.K., Farquhar, A., Fikes, R., Karp, P.D., & Rice, J.P. (1998). *Open knowledge base connectivity 2.0.3* (Tech. Rep.). Retrieved October 23, 2006, from http://www.ai.sri.com/~okbc/okbc-2-0-3.pdf

Chen, P.P. (1976). The entity-relationship model: Toward a unified view of data. *ACM Transactions on Database Systems, 1*(1), 9-36.

Daelemans, W. & Reinberger, M.L. (2004). Shallow text understanding for ontology content evaluation. *IEEE Intelligence Systems, 19*(4), 76-78.

De Bruijn, J. (2006). *The Web service modeling language WSML* (Deliverable D16.1v0.21). Retrieved October 23, 2006, from http://www.wsmo.org/TR/d16/d16.1/v0.21/

de Hoog, R. (1998). Methodologies for building knowledge based systems: Achievements and prospects. In J. Liebowitz (Ed.), *Handbook of expert systems (Chapter 1)*. Boca Raton, FL: CRC Press.

Dean, M. & Schreiber, G. (2004). *OWL Web ontology language reference*. W3C Recommendation. Retrieved October 23, 2006, from http://www.w3.org/TR/owl-ref/

Declerck, T. & Uszkoreit, H. (2003). State of the art on multilinguality for ontologies, annotation services and user interfaces. Esperonto deliverable D1.5. Retrieved October 22, 2006, from http://www.esperonto.net

Doan, A., Madhavan, J., Domingos, P., & Halevy, A. (2002). Learning to map between ontologies on the Semantic Web. In D. Lassner (Ed.), *Proceedings of the 11th International World Wide Web Conference (WWW 2002)*, Honolulu, Hawaii. Retrieved October 23, 2006, from http://www2002.org/refereedtrack.html

Domingue, J. (1998). Tadzebao and webOnto: Discussing, browsing, and editing ontologies on the Web. In B.R. Gaines & M.A. Musen (Eds.), *11th International Workshop on Knowledge Acquisition, Modeling and Management (KAW'98)* (KM4, pp. 1-20). Banff, Canada.

Ehring, M., & Staab, S. (2004). QOM – quick ontology mapping. In S.A. McIlraith & D. Plexousakis (Eds.), *3rd International Semantic Web Conference (ISWC'04)*, Hiroshima, Japan. (LNCS 3298, pp. 683-697). Berlin: Springer-Verlag.

Euzenat, J. (2004). An API for ontology alignment. In S.A. McIlraith & D. Plexousakis (Eds.), *3rd International Semantic Web Conference (ISWC'04)*, Hiroshima, Japan. (LNCS 3298, pp. 698-712). Berlin: Springer-Verlag.

Farquhar, A., Fikes, R., & Rice, J. (1997). The ontolingua server: A tool for collaborative ontology construction. *International Journal of Human Computer Studies, 46*(6), 707-727.

Fernández-López, M., & Gómez-Pérez, A. (2002a). Overview and analysis of methodologies for building ontologies. *The Knowledge Engineering Review, 17*(2), 129-156.

Fernández-López, M. & Gómez-Pérez, A. (2002b). The integration of ontoClean in webODE. In J. Angele & Y. Sure (Eds.), *Proceedings 62 of CEUR Workshop EKAW'02 Workshop on Evaluation of Ontology-based Tools (EON2002),* Sigüenza, Spain. (pp. 38-52). Amsterdam, The Netherlands. Retrieved October 23, 2006, from http://CEUR-WS.org/Vol-62/

Fernández-López, M., Gómez-Pérez, A., & Juristo, N. (1997). *Methontology: From ontological art towards ontological engineering.* Paper presented at the Spring Symposium on Ontological Engineering of AAAI (pp. 33-40). Stanford University.

Fernández-López, M., Gómez-Pérez, A., Pazos, A., & Pazos, J. (1999). Building a chemical ontology using methontology and the ontology design environment. *IEEE Intelligent Systems & Their Applications, 4*(1), 37-46.

Gangemi, A., Pisanelli, D.M., & Steve, G. (1999). An overview of the ONIONS project: Applying ontologies to the integration of medical terminologies. *Data & Knowledge Engineering, 31*(2), 183-220.

Genesereth, M.R. & Fikes, R.E. (1992). *Knowledge interchange format. Version 3.0. Reference Manual* (Tech. Rep. Logic-92-1). Stanford University, Computer Science Department. Retrieved October 23, 2006, from http://meta2.stanford.edu/kif/Hypertext/kif-manual.html

Gómez-Pérez, A. (2004). Evaluating ontology evaluation. *IEEE Intelligence Systems, 19*(4), 74-76.

Gómez-Pérez, A. (1994). *Some ideas and examples to evaluate ontologies.* Stanford University, Knowledge Systems Laboratory. Retrieved October 23, 2006, from http://www-ksl.stanford.edu/KSL_Abstracts/

KSL-94-65.html

Gómez-Pérez, A. (1996). A framework to verify knowledge sharing technology. *Expert Systems with Application, 11*(4), 519-529.

Gómez-Pérez, A. (2001). Evaluation of ontologies. *International Journal of Intelligent Systems, 16*(3), 391-409.

Gómez-Pérez, A., Fernández-López, M., & Corcho, O. (2003). *Ontological engineering.* London: Springer.

Gómez-Pérez, A., Fernández-López, M., & de Vicente, A. (1996). *Towards a method to conceptualize domain ontologies.* In P. van der Vet (Ed.), *ECAI'96 Workshop on Ontological Engineering* (pp. 41-52). Budapest, Hungary.

Gómez-Pérez, A., & Manzano, D. (2003). A survey of ontology learning methods and techniques. OntoWeb deliverable D.1.5. Retrieved October 23, 2006, from http://www.ontoweb.org

Gómez-Pérez, A. & Rojas, M.D. (1999). Ontological reengineering and reuse. In D. Fensel & R. Studer (Eds.), *11th European Workshop on Knowledge Acquisition, Modeling and Management (EKAW'99),* Dagstuhl Castle, Germany. (LNAI 1621, pp. 139-156). Berlin: Springer-Verlag.

Gruber, T.R. (1992). *Ontolingua: A mechanism to support portable ontologies* (Tech. Rep. No. KSL-91-66). Stanford University, Knowledge Systems Laboratory, Stanford, California. Retrieved October 23, 2006, from ftp://ftp.ksl.stanford.edu/pub/KSL_Reports/KSL-91-66.ps

Gruber, T.R. (1993). A translation approach to portable ontology specification. *Knowledge Acquisition, 5*(2), 199-220.

Grüninger, M. & Fox, M.S. (1995). Methodology for the design and evaluation of ontologies. In D. Skuce (Ed.), *IJCAI95 Workshop on Basic Ontological Issues in Knowledge Sharing* (pp. 6.1–6.10).

Guarino, N. (2004). Toward formal evaluation of ontology quality. *IEEE Intelligence Systems, 19*(4), 78-79.

Guarino, N., Masolo, C., & Vetere, G. (1999). OntoSeek: Content-based access to the Web. *IEEE Intelligent Systems & Their Applications, 14*(3), 70-80.

Guarino, N., & Welty, C. (2002). Evaluating ontological decisions with ontoClean. *Communications of the ACM, 45*(2), 61-65.

Guo, Y., Pan, Z., & Heflin, J. (2004). An evaluation of knowledge base systems for large OWL datasets. In S.A. McIlraith & D. Plexousakis (Eds.), *3rd International Semantic Web Conference (ISWC'04),* Hiroshima, Japan. (LNCS 3298, pp. 274-288). Berlin: Springer-Verlag.

Hermenegildo, M., Bueno, F., Cabeza, D., Carro, M., García, M., López, P., & Puebla, G. (2000). The ciao logic programming environment. In J.W. Lloyd, V. Dahl, U. Furbach, M. Kerber, K. Lau, C. Palamidessi, L.M. Pereira, Y. Sagiv, & P.J. Stuckey (Eds.), *International Conference on Computational Logic (CL'00),* London. (LNCS 1861). Berlin: Springer-Verlag.

Horrocks, I., Fensel, D., Harmelen, F., Decker, S., Erdmann, M., & Klein, M. (2000). OIL in a nutshell. In R. Dieng & O. Corby (Eds.), *12th International Conference in Knowledge Engineering and Knowledge Management (EKAW'00),* Juan-Les-Pins, France. (LNAI 1937, pp. 1-16). Berlin: Springer-Verlag.

Horrocks, I., & van Harmelen, F. (Eds). (2001). *Reference description of the DAML+OIL (March 2001) ontology markup language* (Tech. Rep.). Retrieved October 23, 2006, from http://www.daml.org/2001/03/reference.html

Hustadt, U., Motik, B., & Sattler, U. (2004). Reducing SHIQ descrption logic to disjunctive datalog programs. In M.A. Williams (Ed.), *9th International Conference on the Principles of Knowledge Representation and Reasoning (KRR'04)* (pp. 152-162). Whistler, Canada.

IEEE. (1996). *IEEE standard for developing software life cycle processes* (Std 1074-1995). New York: IEEE Computer Society.

Joachims, T. (1998). A probabilistic analysis of the Rocchio Algorithm with TFIDF for text categorization. In D.H. Fisher (Ed.), *14th International Conference on Machine Learning (ICML'97),* Nashville, Tennessee. (pp. 143-151). San Francisco: Morgan Kaufmann Publishers.

Kalfoglou, Y., & Robertson, D. (1999a). Use of formal ontologies to support error checking in specifications. In D. Fensel & R. Studer (Eds.), *11th European Workshop on Knowledge Acquisition, Modelling and Management (EKAW'99),* Dagsthul, Germany. (LNAI 1621, pp. 207-224). Berlin: Springer-Verlag.

Kalfoglou, Y., & Robertson, D. (1999b). Managing ontological constraints. In V.R. Benjamins, A. Chandrasekaran, A. Gómez-Pérez, N. Guarino, & M. Uschold (Eds.), *Proceedings 18 of CEUR Workshop IJCAI99 Workshop on Ontologies and Problem-Solving Methods (KRR-5),* Stockholm, Sweden (pp. 5.1-5.13). Amsterdam, The Netherlands. Retrieved October 23, 2006, from http://CEUR-WS.org/Vol-18/

Kalyanpur, A., Parsia, B., & Hendler, J. (2005). A tool for working with Web ontologies. *International Journal of Semantic Web and Information Systems, 1*(1), 36-49.

Karp, P.D., Chaudhri, V., & Thomere, J. (1999). *XOL: An XML-based ontology exchange language. Version 0.3* (Tech. Rep.). Retrieved October 23, 2006, from http://www.ai.sri.com/~pkarp/xol/xol.html

Khan, L., & Luo, F. (2002). Ontology construction for information selection. In C.V. Ramamoorthy (Ed.), *CV 14th IEEE International Conference on*

*Tools with Artificial Intelligence* (pp. 122-127). Washington, DC.

Kietz, J.U., Maedche, A., & Volz, R. (2000). A method for semi-automatic ontology acquisition from a corporate intranet. In N. Aussenac-Gilles, B. Biébow, & S. Szulman (Eds.), *Proceedings 51 of EKAW'00 Workshop on Ontologies and Texts, CEUR Workshop*, Juan-Les-Pins, France, (pp. 4.1-4.14). Amsterdam, The Netherlands. Retrieved October 23, 2006, from http://CEUR-WS.org/Vol-51/

Kifer, M., Lausen, G., & Wu, J. (1995). Logical foundations of object-oriented and frame-based languages. *Journal of the ACM, 42*(4), 741-843.

Klein, M. & Fensel, D. (2001). Ontology versioning on the Semantic Web. In I.F. Cruz, S. Decker, J. Euzenat, & D.L. McGuinness (Eds.), *First International Semantic Web Workshop (SWWS'01)*, Stanford, California.

Klein, M., Fensel, D., Kiryakov, A., & Ognyanov, D. (2002). Ontology versioning and change detection on the Web. In A. Gómez-Pérez & V.R. Benjamins (Eds.), *13th International Conference on Knowledge Engineering and Knowledge Management (EKAW'02)*, Sigüenza, Spain (LNAI 2473, pp. 197-212). Berlin: Springer-Verlag.

Knublauch, H., Fergerson, R., Noy, N.F., & Musen, M.A. (2004). The protege OWL plugin: An open development environment for Semantic Web applications. In S.A. McIlraith & D. Plexousakis (Eds.), *3rd International Semantic Web Conference (ISWC'04)* (pp. 229-243), Hiroshima, Japan. Lecture Notes in Computer Science 3298. Berlin: Springer-Verlag.

Lassila, O., & Swick, R. (1999). *Resource description framework (RDF) model and syntax specification.* W3C Recommendation. Retrieved October 23, 2006, from http://www.w3.org/TR/REC-rdf-syntax/

Lenat, D.B., & Guha, R.V. (1990). *Building large knowledge-based systems: Representation and inference in the cyc project.* Boston: Addison-Wesley.

Luke, S., & Heflin, J.D. (2000). *SHOE 1.01. Proposed specification* (Tech. Rep.). University of Maryland, Parallel Understanding Systems Group, Department of Computer Science. Retrieved October 23, 2006, from http://www.cs.umd.edu/projects/plus/SHOE/spec1.01.htm

MacGregor, R. (1991). Inside the LOOM classifier. *SIGART Bulletin, 2*(3), 70-76.

Madhavan, J., Bernstein, P.A., & Rahm, E. (2001). Generis schema matching with Cupid. In P.M.G. Apers, P. Atzeni, S. Ceri, S. Paraboschi, K. Ramamohanarao, & R.T. Snodgrass (Eds.), *27th International Conference on Very Large Data Bases* (pp. 49-58), Roma, Italy. San Francisco: Morgan Kaufmann Publishers.

Maedche, A., Motik, B., Stojanovic, L., Studer, R., & Volz, R. (2003). Ontologies for enterprise knowledge management. *IEEE Intelligent Systems, 18*(2), 26-33.

Maedche, A., & Staab, S. (2000). Semi-automatic engineering of ontologies from text. In S.K. Chang & W.R. Obozinski (Eds.), *12th International Conference on Software Engineering and Knowledge Engineering (SEKE 2000)*, Chicago.

McGuinness, D., Fikes, R., Rice, J., & Wilder, S. (2000). The chimaera ontology environment. In P. Rosenbloom, H.A. Kautz, B. Porter, R. Dechter, R. Sutton, & V. Mittal (Eds.), *17th National Conference on Artificial Intelligence (AAAI'00)* (pp. 1123-1124). Austin, Texas.

Melnik, S., García-Molina, H., & Rahm, E. (2002). Similarity flooding: A versatile graph matching algorithm and its application to schema matching. In D. Georgakopoulos (Ed.), *18th International Conference on Data Engineering ICDE'2002* (pp. 117-128). San José, California.

Mena, E., Kashyap, V., Sheth, A.P., & Illarra-mendi, A. (1996). OBSERVER: An approach for query processing in global information systems based on interoperation across pre-existing ontologies. In W. Litwin (Ed.), *First IFCIS International Conference on Cooperative Information Systems (CoopIS'96)* (pp. 14-25). Brussels, Belgium.

Mikheev, A., & Finch, A. (1997). A workbench for finding structure in texts. In R. Grishman (Ed.), *5th Applied Natural Language Processing Conference (ANLP'97)*. Washington, DC.

Miller, G.A. (1995). WordNet: A lexical database for English. *Communications of the ACM, 38*(11), 39-41.

Mitra, P., Wiederhold, G., & Kersten. (2000). A graph-oriented model for articulation of ontology interdependencies. In P.C. Lockemann (Eds.), *7th International Conference on Extending Database Technology, EDBT 2000* (pp. 1777-1786).

Morin, E. (1998). Prométhée un outil d'aide a l'acquisition de relations semantiques entre temes. In P. Zweigenbaum (Ed.), *5ème National Conference on Traitement Automatique des Langues Naturelles (TALN'98)* (pp. 172-181). Paris, France.

Morin, E. (1999). Acquisition de patrons lexico-syntaxiques caractéristiques dúne relation sémantique: *TAL (Traitement Automatique des Langues), 40*(1), 143-166.

Motta, E. (1999). *Reusable components for knowledge modelling: Principles and case studies in parametric design.* Amsterdam, The Netherlands: IOS Press.

Neches, R., Fikes, R.E., Finin, T., Gruber, T.R., Senator, T., & Swartout, W.R. (1991). Enabling technology for knowledge sharing. *AI Magazine, 12*(3), 36-56.

Noy, N.F. (2004). Evaluation by ontology consumers. *IEEE Intelligence Systems, 19*(4), 80-81.

Noy, N.F., Fergerson, R.W., & Musen, M.A. (2000). The knowledge model of Protege-2000: Combining interoperability and flexibility. In R. Dieng & O. Corby (Eds.), *12th International Conference in Knowledge Engineering and Knowledge Management (EKAW'00)*, Juan-Les-Pins, France. (LNAI 1937, pp. 17-32). Berlin: Springer-Verlag.

Noy, N.F., & Klein, M. (2002). *Ontology evolution: Not the same as schema evolution* (Tech. Rep. No. SMI-2002-0926). Stanford, California. Retrieved October 23, 2006, from http://smi-web.stanford.edu/pubs/SMI_Abstracts/SMI-2002-0926.html

Noy, N.F., Kunnatur, S., Klein, M., & Musen, M.A. (2004). Tracking changes during ontology evolution. In S.A. McIlraith & D. Plexousakis (Eds.), *3rd International Semantic Web Conference (ISWC'04)*, Hiroshima, Japan. (LNCS 3298, pp. 259-273). Berlin: Springer-Verlag.

Noy, N.F., & Musen, M.A. (2000). PROMPT: Algorithm and tool for automated ontology merging and alignment. In P. Rosenbloom, H.A. Kautz, B. Porter, R. Dechter, R. Sutton, & V. Mittal (Eds.), *17th National Conference on Artificial Intelligence (AAAI'00)* (pp. 450-455). Austin, Texas.

Noy, N.F. & Musen, M.A. (2001). Anchor-PROMPT: Using non-local context for semantic matching. In A. Gómez-Pérez, M. Grüninger, H. Stuckenschmidt, & M. Uschold (Eds.), *IJCAI'01 Workshop on Ontologies and Information Sharing* (pp. 63-70), Seattle, Washington.

Noy, N.F. & Musen, M.A. (2004a). Specifying ontology views by traversal. In S.A. McIlraith & D. Plexousakis (Eds.), *3rd International Semantic Web Conference (ISWC'04)*, Hiroshima, Japan. (LNCS 3298, pp. 713-725). Berlin: Springer-Verlag.

Noy, N.F. & Musen, M.A. (2004b). Ontology versioning in an ontology-management framework. *IEEE Intelligent Systems, 19*(4), 6-13.

ODM. (2005). *Ontology definition metamodel.* Third Revised Submission to OMG/RFP ad/2003-

03-40. Retrieved October 23, 2006, from http://www.omg.org/docs/ad/05-08-01.pdf

Pan, R., Ding, Z., Yu, Y., & Peng, Y. (2005). A bayesian network approach to ontology mapping. In *Proceedings of the 4th International Semantic Web Conference (ISWC'05)*, Galway, Ireland. (LNCS 3729, pp. 563-577). Berlin: Springer-Verlag.

Raggett, D., Le Hors, A., & Jacobs, I. (1999). *HTML 4.01 specification. W3C Recommendation.* Retrieved October 23, 2006, from http://www.w3.org/TR/html401/

Rumbaugh, J., Jacobson, I., & Booch, G. (1998). *The unified modeling language reference manual.* Boston: Addison-Wesley.

Schreiber, A.Th., Wielinga, B.J., & Jansweijer, W. (1995). The KACTUS view on the "O" world. In D. Skuce (Ed.), *IJCAI95 Workshop on Basic Ontological Issues in Knowledge Sharing* (pp. 15.1–15.10).

Shvaiko, P., Giunchiglia, F., & Yatskevich, M. (2004). S-Match: An algorithm and an implementation of semantic matching. In D. Fensel & R. Studer (Eds.), *1st European Semantic Web Symposium (ESWS'04)*, Heraklion, Greece. (LNCS 3053, pp. 61-75). Berlin: Springer-Verlag.

Staab, S., Schnurr, H.P., Studer, R., & Sure, Y. (2001). Knowledge processes and ontologies. *IEEE Intelligent Systems, 16*(1), 26-34.

Steve, G., Gangemi, A., & Pisanelli, D.M. (1998). Integrating medical terminologies with ONIONS methodology. In H. Kangassalo & J.P. Charrel (Eds.), *Information Modeling and Knowledge Bases VIII.* Amsterdam, The Netherlands: IOS Press. Retrieved October 23, 2006, from http://ontology.ip.rm.cnr.it/Papers/onions97.pdf

Stojanovic, L. (2004). *Methods and tools for ontology evolution.* Doctoral Thesis, FZI, Karlsrhue, Germany.

Studer, R., Benjamins, V.R., & Fensel, D. (1998). Knowledge engineering: Principles and methods. *IEEE Transactions on Data and Knowledge Engineering, 25*(1-2), 161-197.

Stumme, G., & Maedche, A. (2001). FCA-MERGE: Bottom-up merging of ontologies. In B. Nebel (Ed.), *Proceedings of the Seventeenth International Joint Conference on Artificial Intelligence (IJCAI 2001)*, Seattle, Washington, (pp. 225-234). San Francisco: Morgan Kaufmann Publishers.

Sure, Y., Erdmann, M., Angele, J., Staab, S., Studer, R., & Wenke, D. (2002). OntoEdit: Collaborative ontology engineering for the Semantic Web. In I. Horrocks & J.A. Hendler (Eds.), *First International Semantic Web Conference (ISWC'02)*, Sardinia, Italy. (LNCS 2342, pp. 221-235). Berlin: Springer-Verlag.

Swartout, B., Ramesh, P., Knight, K., & Russ, T. (1997). Toward distributed use of large-scale ontologies. In A. Farquhar, M. Gruninger, A. Gómez-Pérez, M. Uschold, & P. van der Vet (Eds.), *AAAI'97 Spring Symposium on Ontological Engineering* (pp. 138-148). Stanford University.

Uschold, M. (1996). Building ontologies: Towards a unified methodology. In I. Watson (Ed.), *16th Annual Conference of the British Computer Society Specialist Group on Expert Systems*, Cambridge, UK. Retrieved October 23, 2006, from http://citeseer.nj.nec.com/uschold96building.html

Uschold, M., & Grüninger, M. (1996). Ontologies: Principles, methods and applications. *Knowledge Engineering Review, 11*(2), 93-155.

Uschold, M., & King, M. (1995). Towards a methodology for building ontologies. In D. Skuce (Ed.), *IJCAI'95 Workshop on Basic Ontological Issues in Knowledge Sharing* (pp. 6.1-6.10), Montreal, Canada.

Welty, C., & Guarino, N. (2001). Supporting onto-logical analysis of taxonomic relationships. *Data and Knowledge Engineering, 39*(1), 51-74.

Wu, S.H., & Hsu, W.L. (2002). SOAT: A semi-automatic domain ontology acquisition tool from chinese corpus. In W. Lenders (Ed.), *19th International Conference on Computational Linguistics (COLING'02)*, Taipei, Taiwan.

## ENDNOTES

[1]  Component names depend on the formal-ism. For example, classes are also known as concepts, entities and sets; relations are also known as roles and properties; and so forth.

[2]  http://www.omg.org/

[3]  In (28) *specification* is considered as a pre-development activity. However, following more strictly the IEEE standard for software development, the specification activity was considered part of the proper development process. In fact, the result of this activity is an ontology description (usually in natural language) that will be transformed into a conceptual model by the *conceptualization* activity.

[4]  http://www.ontologymatching.org/

[5]  http://swoogle.umbc.edu/

[6]  http://oyster.ontoware.org/

[7]  http://www.daml.org/ontologies/

[8]  http://protege.stanford.edu/

[9]  Other tools (Ontolingua Server, OntoSaurus, WebOnto, etc.) are described in (Gómez-Pérez et al., 2003).

[10]  http://www-2-cs-cmu.edu/~mccallum/bow/rainbow

[11]  http://www.lbreyer.com/

[12]  http://co4.inrialpes.fr/align

[13]  http://www.wsmo.org/

# Chapter IV
# Editing Tools for Ontology Creation

**Ana Lisete Nunes Escórcio**
*Escola Básica e Secundária do Carmo, Portugal*

**Jorge Cardoso**
*University of Madeira, Portugal*

## ABSTRACT

*This chapter gives an overview of some editing tools for ontology construction. At the present time, the development of a project like the one of building an ontology demands the use of a software tool. Therefore, it is given a synopsis of the tools that the authors consider more relevant. This way, if you are starting out on an ontology project, the first reaction is to find a suitable ontology editor. Furthermore, the authors hope that by reading this chapter, it will be possible to choose an editing tool for ontology construction according to the project goals. The tools have been described following a list of features. The authors believe that the following features are pertinent: collaborative ontology edition, versioning, graphical tree view, OWL editor and many others (see Appendix 2).*

## INTRODUCTION

The World Wide Web is mainly composed of documents written in HTML (Hypertext Markup Language). This language is useful for visual presentation since it is a set of "markup" symbols contained in a Web page intended for display on a Web browser. Humans can read Web pages and understand them, but their inherent meaning is not shown in a way that allows their interpretation by computers. The information on the Web can

be defined in a way that can be used by computers not only for display purposes, but also for interoperability and integration between systems and applications (Cardoso, 2005).

"The Semantic Web is not a separate Web but an extension of the current one, in which information is given a well-defined meaning, better enabling computers and people to work in cooperation" (Berners-Lee, Hendler, & Lassila, 2001). The Semantic Web was made through incremental changes by bringing machine readable descriptions to the data and documents already on the Web. In recent times, instead of a Web site comprising a collection of manually constructed HTML pages, server-side applications and database access techniques are used to dynamically create Web pages directly in response to requests from user's browsers. The technologies available to dynamically create Web pages based on databases information were insufficient for requirements of organizations looking for application integration solutions. Business required their heterogeneous systems and applications to communicate in a transactional manner.

Ontologies can be used to increase communication either between humans and computers. An ontology is a shared conceptualization of the world. Ontologies consist of definitional aspects such as high-level schemas and assertional aspects, entities, attributes, interrelationships between entities, domain vocabulary and factual knowledge, all connected in a Semantic manner (Sheth, 2003). They have generally been associated with logical inferencing and recently have begun to be applied to the Semantic Web. Ontologies provide specific tools to organize and provide a useful description of heterogeneous content. The three major uses of ontologies are:

- To assist in communication between humans
- To achieve interoperability and communication among software systems
- To improve the design and the quality of software systems

The most prominent markup language for publishing and sharing data using ontologies on the internet is the Web Ontology Language (OWL, 2004). There are several ontology development tools for domain modeling, for building knowledge base systems, for ontology visualization, for project management or other modeling tasks. Many of the tools are research prototypes that have been built for a particular project or for an Institute/University. There has been a significant growth in the number of ontology technologies products.

After studying Michael Deny's *Survey on Ontology Tools* and reading the paper *The Hitchhiker's Guide to Ontology Editors* of Loredana Laera and Valentina Tamma we decided to do an updated study of the tools that are available. Some of the tools described in the Michael Deny's Survey either were no longer available (the project has finished) or have been improved. There are also new tools and new languages since there are new projects that demand so. In composing the list shown on Table 1, we have selected the tools that comprise some of the following features: are robust and ready to be used; free and open source; provide support to most of the activities involved in the ontology development process and ontology practice; support resource description framework (RDF), resource description framework schema (RDFS) and Web Ontology Language (OWL); offer collaborative environment; provide multiple ontology environment; offer server-based environment with support for consistency checking; offer easy-to-use functionality for visual creation and editing; offer a query builder; support a methodology; support editing formal axioms and rules; support the growth of large scale ontologies; support versioning; promote interoperability; has a reasoner; has a graphical view; promotes easy and fast navigation between concepts; has tutorial support; and offers Plug-ins.

We have chosen the following tools: Protégé; OntoEdit; differential ontology editor (DOE); IsaViz; Ontolingua; Altova SemanticWorks 2006; OilEd; WebODE; pOWL and SWOOP.

Protégé is one of the most widely used ontology development tool. It is free and open source. It is an intuitive editor for ontologies and there are plug-ins available to carry out some of the tasks for building an ontology. OntoEdit is an ontology editor that integrates numerous aspects of ontology engineering. OntoEdit environment supports collaborative development of ontologies.

DOE is a simple prototype developed with Java that allows users to build ontologies according to the Bruno Bachimont proposed methodology. IsaViz is a visual environment for browsing and authoring RDF models as graphs. Ontolingua was built to ease the development of ontologies with a form-based Webinterface.

Altova Semantic Works is a commercial visual Semantic Web editor that offers easy-to-use functionality for visual creation and editing. It can be downloaded for 30 days free evaluation period. OilEd is an editor that allows the user to construct and manipulate DAML+OIL (DAML- DARPA Agent Markup Language; OIL-Ontology Inference Layer) and OWL ontologies and which uses a reasoner to classify and check consistency of ontologies. It is provided free of charge. WebODE is the Web counterpart for ODE (Ontology Design Environment). It has support for multiple-users. This editor gives support to the methodology Methontology. pOWL is an open source ontology management tool in a collaborative Web enabled environment. SWOOP is a Web-based OWL ontology editor and browser. This editor has default plug-ins for different presentation syntax for rendering ontologies.

The main purpose of this chapter is to give an overview of some of the ontology tools available at the present time. This way, if you are starting out on an ontology project, the initial step is to find a suitable ontology editor.

## PROTÉGÉ

Protégé (Noy, Sintek, Decker, Crubezy, Fergerson, & Musen, 2001) is one of the most widely used ontology development tool that was developed at Stanford University. Since Protégé is free and open source, it is supported by a large community of active users. It has been used by experts in domains such as medicine and manufacturing for domain modeling and for building knowledge-base systems. Protégé provides an intuitive editor for ontologies and has extensions for ontology visualization, project management, software engineering and other modeling tasks.

In early versions, Protégé only enabled users to build and populate frame-based ontologies in accordance with the open knowledge base connectivity protocol (OKBC). In this model, an ontology consisted of a set of classes organized in a subsumption hierarchy, a set of slots associated to classes to describe their properties and relationships, and a set of instances of those classes. Protégé editor included support for classes and

*Figure 1. Protégé editor*

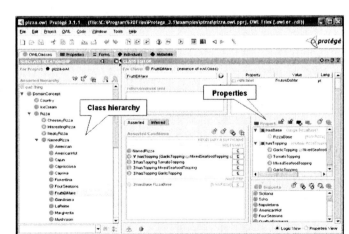

class hierarchies with multiple inheritance; templates and slots; predefined and arbitrary facets for slots, which included permitted values, cardinality restrictions, default values, and inverse slots; metaclasses and metaclass hierarchy.

While the first architecture of Protégé was based on frames, in 2003 it has been extended to support OWL. This extension has attracted many users captivated by the Semantic Web vision. The OWL plug-in extends the Protégé platform into an ontology editor for the OWL enabling users to build ontologies for the Semantic Web. The OWL plug-in allows users to load, save, edit and visualize ontologies in OWL and RDF. It also provides interfaces for description logic reasoners such as racer.

Protégé ontologies can be exported into a variety of formats including RDF(S), OWL, and Extended Mark-up Language (XML) schema. The current Protégé version can be used to edit classes and their characteristics, to access reasoning engines, to edit and execute queries and rules, to compare ontology versions, to visualize relationships between concepts, and to acquire instances using a configurable graphical user interface. Protégé is a tool installed locally in a computer and does not allow collaborative editing of ontologies by groups of users.

Protégé can be extended by way of a plug-in architecture and a Java-based Application Programming Interface (API) for building knowledge-base tools and applications. Protégé is based on Java and provides an open-source API to develop Semantic Web and knowledge-base stand-alone applications. External Semantic Web applications can use the API to directly access Protégé knowledge bases without running the Protégé application. An OWL API is also available to provide access to OWL ontologies. Its extensible architecture makes it suitable as a base platform for ontology-based research and development projects. Protégé also includes a Programming Development Kit (PDK), an important resource for programmers that describe how to work directly with Protégé APIs and illustrates how to program plug-in extensions for Protégé.

Several plug-ins are available. For example, JSave (http://protege.stanford.edu/plug-ins/jsave/) is an application plug-in to generate Java class definition stubs for Protégé classes and Protégé Web Browser is a Java-based Web application that allows users to share Protégé ontologies over the Internet. The WordNet plug-in (http://protege.stanford.edu/plug-ins/wordnettab/wordnet_tab.html) provides Protégé users an interface to WordNet knowledge base. Users can easily annotate a Protégé knowledge base using information from WordNet database. The information in WordNet can be searched by name and then be used to annotate ontologies with terms, concept IDs, synonyms, and relations.

The XML schema (http://faculty.washington.edu/gennari/Protege-plug-ins/XMLBackend/XMLBackend.html) is a backend plug-in that transforms a Protégé knowledge base into XML. The plug-in generates an XML schema file describing the Protégé knowledge model and an XML file where the classes and instances are stored. The UML plug-in (http://protege.stanford.edu/plug-ins/uml/) is also a backend plug-in which provides an import and export mechanism between the Protégé knowledge model and the object-oriented modeling language UML. To enables the exchange of ontologies and UML class diagrams, the UML plug-in uses the standard format for UML diagram exchange, XMI, which is supported by major CASE tools. The use of the XMI standard enables users to work with Protégé in combination with Software Engineering tools and Integrated Development Environments.

The DataGenie (http://faculty.washington.edu/gennari/Protege-plug-ins/DataGenie/index.html) is an import/export plug-in that allows reading and creating a knowledge model from relational databases using JDBC. Users can select a proper subset of a relational database to be converted into Protégé classes. Typically, during the conversion, tables become classes and attributes becomes slots.

The Docgen (http://protege-docgen.sourceforge. net/) is also an import/export plug-in that allow users to create reports describing Protégé knowledge bases or ontologies. Classes, instances and documentation can be exported to various output formats such as HTML, Dynamic Hypertext Markup Language (DHTML), PDF, and XML.

Plug-ins are also available to carry out rule-based programming using the information stored in a Protégé frame-based knowledge base. Two worth mentioning examples are JessTab (http://www.ida.liu.se/~her/JessTab/) and Algernon (http://algernon-j.sourceforge.net/doc/algernon-protege.html). JessTab is a plug-in that provides a Jess console window where it is possible to interact with Jess while running Protégé. This plug-in extends Jess with supplementary features that map Protégé knowledge bases to Jess facts. Users can deploy applications that handle Protégé knowledge bases and react when patterns in the knowledge base are found. Algernon is a system implemented in Java that performs forward and backward inference of frame-based knowledge bases. Compared to Jess, Algernon operates directly on Protégé knowledge bases rather than requiring a mapping operation to and from a separate memory space.

The PROMPT plug-in (Noy & Musen, 2003) allows to manage multiple ontologies within Protégé, mainly compare versions of the same ontology, merge ontologies into one, and extract parts of an ontology.

The OWL-S Editor plug-in (http://owleditor.semwebcentral.org/) is an easy-to-use editor which allows loading, creating, managing, and visualizing OWL-S services. OWL-S (formerly DAML-S) is emerging as a Web service description language that semantically describes Web Services using OWL ontologies. OWL-S consists of three parts expressed with OWL ontologies: the service profile, the service model, and the service grounding. The profile is used to describe "what a service does," with advertisement and discovery as its objective. The service model describes "how a service works," to enable invocation, enactment, composition, monitoring and recovery. Finally, the grounding maps the constructs of the process model onto detailed specifications of message formats and protocols. The OWL-S Editor plug-in provides an excellent overview of the relations between the different OWL-S ontologies which are shown in an intuitive way in the graphic user interface (GUI) and can also be shown as a graph

## OntoEdit

OntoEdit (Sure, Angele, & Staab, 2002) was developed by the Knowledge Management Group of the AIFB Institute at the University of Karlsruhe. It is an ontology engineering environment which allows creating, browsing, maintaining and managing ontologies. The environment supports the collaborative development of ontologies (Sure, Erdmann, Angele, et al., 2002). This is archived through its client/server architecture where ontologies are managed in a central server and various clients can access and modify these ontologies. Currently, the successor of OntoEdit is OntoStudio (Figure 2) which is a commercial product based on IBM's development environment Eclipse. It can be downloaded for three months free evaluation period.

OntoEdit was developed having two major goals in mind. On the one hand, the editor was designed to be as much as possible independent and neutral of a concrete representation language. On the other hand, it was planned to provide a powerful graphical user interface to represent concept hierarchies, relations, domains, ranges, instances and axioms. OntoEdit supports F–Logic (fuzzy logic), RDF schema and OIL. The tool is multilingual. Each concept or relation name can be specified in several languages. This is particularly useful for the collaborative development of ontologies by teams of researchers spread across several countries and speaking different languages. From the technical perspective, this

*Figure 2. OntoStudio editor*

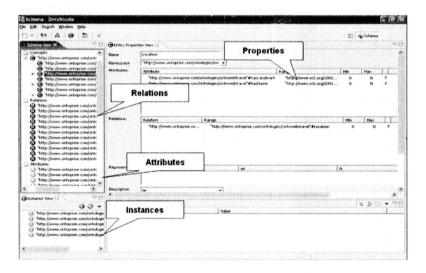

feature is achieved by using unique identifiers so that each ontological statement remains clearly defined. The names selected by users work merely as an external representation.

OntoEdit is built on top of an internal data representation model. The data model of OntoEdit is OXML 2.0 which is frame based. OXML is defined in XML using XML-schema. Besides concepts, relations and instances, the model can represent predicates, predicate instances, and axioms. Predicates are n-ary associations and are very similar to predicates defined in first order logic (FOL). Several types of relationships can be established between concepts, such as symmetric, reflexive, transitive, antisymmetric, asymmetric, irreflexive, or intransitive.

The internal representation data model can be exported to DAML+OIL, F-Logic, RDF(S), and OXML. Additionally, ontologies can be exported to relational databases via JDBC. OntoEdit can import external data representation in DAML+OIL, Excel, F-Logic, RDF(S), and OXML.

OntoSudio can also import and export OWL files. OntoEdit provides an API for accessing ontologies in an object-oriented fashion. The default API implementation stores ontologies in main-memory, but an additional API exists for persistent storage.

The inference engine that OntoEdit uses is OntoBroker (Decker, Erdmann, Fensel, & Studer, 1999). Using this engine, OntoEdit exploits the strength of F-Logic in that it can represent expressive rules. OntoBroker is the result of several years of research and it is now a commercial product. Like Protégé, OntoEdit is based on a plug-in architecture. The architecture consists of three layers (Figure 3): GUI, OntoEdit core and Parser.

Using a plug-in architecture enables users to extend OntoEdit with specific functionalities. Since the plug-in interface is open to third parties, anyone with special requirements can deploy a component to satisfy specific needs. Several plug-ins are available. For example, the Sesame plug-in (Broekstra, Kampman, & Van Harmelen, 2002) is a generic application for storing and querying RDF and RDF schema. Sesame allows persistent storage of RDF data and schema information. It supplies a useful query engine which supports RQL, an OQL-style query language.

*Figure 3. OntoEdit architecture*

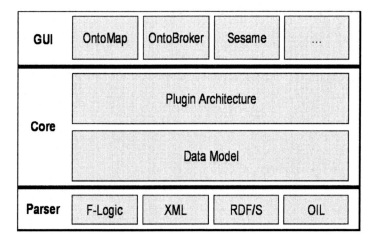

## DOE

DOE is a simple ontology editor and was developed by the INA (Institut National de l'Audiovisuel - France). DOE allows users to build ontologies according to the methodology proposed by Bruno Bachimont (Bachimont et al., 2002).

DOE has a classical formal specification process. DOE only allows the specification part of the process of structuring ontology. DOE is rather a complement of others editors (DOE, 2006). It is not intended to be a direct competitor with other existing environments (like Protégé, OilEd, OntoEdit or WebODE), instead it was developed to coexist with other editors in a complementary way. This editor offers linguistics-inspired techniques which attach a lexical definition to the concepts and relations used, and justify their hierarchies from a theoretical, human-understandable point of view (DOE, 2006). Therefore, DOE should be used in combination with another editor. For instance, an editor that has advanced formal specification, for example Protégé.

DOE is a simple prototype developed in Java that supports the three steps of the Bruno Bachimont methodology (Isaac et al., 2002). The Bruno Bachimont methodology can be described in the following three steps. In the first step, the user builds taxonomies of concepts and relations. The user has to unambiguously justify the position for each notion in the hierarchy. The user builds a definition, following four principles which come from the *Differential Semantics* theory (Isaac et al., 2002), that is, (1) Similarity with Parent, (2) Similarity with Siblings, (3) Difference with Sibling and (4) Difference with Parent. For each notion, a meaning and a description has to be given.

Consequently, the user has to explicit state why a notion is similar but more specific than its parent (i.e., Similarity with Parent and Similarity with Siblings), and why this notion is similar but different from its siblings (i.e., Difference with Sibling and Difference with Parent). Hence, every concept is located in a justified and convinced position. It is possible, for the user, to add synonyms and an encyclopedic definition in a few languages for all notions in the Differential Ontology view. The main goal of this step is to reach a semantic agreement about the meaning of the labels used for naming concepts (Isaac et al., 2002).

In the second step, the ontological tree obtained in the first step allows to disambiguate the notions. Consequently, the meaning is clarified for a

*Figure 4. The differential principles bound to the notion addressed in the DOE tool (differential ontology view)*

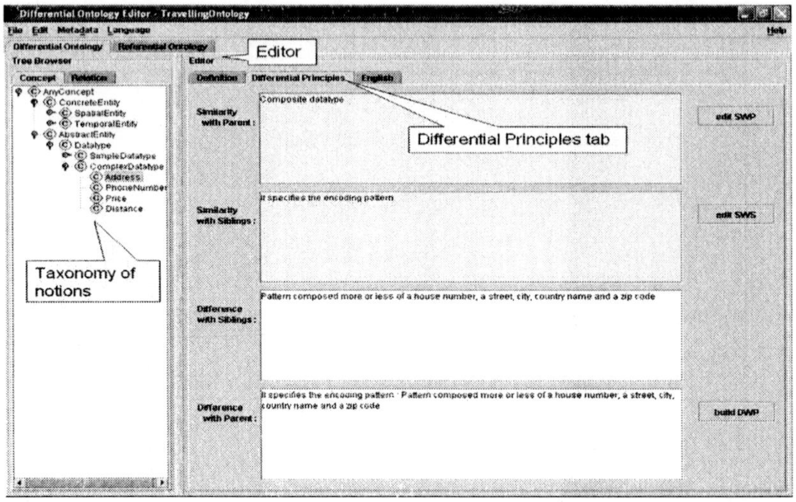

domain-specific application. The notions become concepts behaving as formal primitives. In the referential ontology each concept refers to a set of objects in the domain (its extension) (Isaac et al., 2002). The taxonomies are considered from an extensional semantic point of view. The user can expand them with new entities (defined) or add constraints onto the domains of the relations. In this step, the user ought to do consistency checking in order to look for propagation of the arity all along the hierarchy- if specified - and inheritance of domains. As we said before, DOE main goal is to guide the user during the first steps of the process of building an ontology. It is not possible to write axioms in DOE since there is not an axiom editor.

Finally, on the third step, the ontology can be translated into a knowledge representation language. The referential concepts are compared with the possible computational operations available in the application Knowledge Based Systems (KBS). As a result, it is possible to use it in an appropriate ontology-based system or to import it into another ontology-building tool to specify it further. An export mechanism was implemented in order to translate the taxonomies into convenient exchange languages (for example, OWL). This mechanism can also be used to complete the third step

DOE allows building a *differential ontology* and a *referential ontology*, corresponding to the first two steps of the methodology proposed by Bruno Bachimont. The Differential Ontology view is divided in two frames. On the left side there is a tree browser and on the right side there is an editor. The tree browser shows hierarchically the concepts and the relations (there is a tab for concepts and a tab for relations too, like in the Referential Ontology view). The editor has three tabs: a definition tab, a different principles tab and an English tab (or other language that the user wishes to translate the ontology to). If the definition tab is selected, it will show the "properties" of the items illustrated in the tree browser. The different principles tab is used to justify the taxonomy of notions that was build. In other words, the sense of a node is specified by the gathering of all similarities and differences attached to the notions found on the way from the root notion (the more generic) to the node that is selected on the tree browser (on the left)

*Figure 5. The referential ontology view with a concept tree of the traveling ontology*

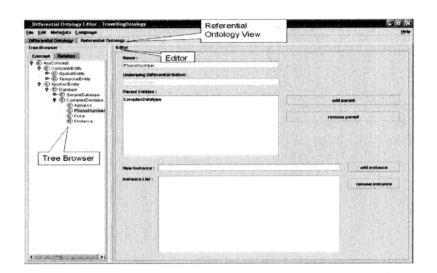

(Isaac et al., 2002). In the referential ontology view, the tree browser has the same features as in the Differential Ontology view (there are two tabs concept tab and relation tab).

While DOE does not have a graph view of the ontology, it includes a tree view that can show separately the concepts and the relations between the concepts. It is possible to view an ontology in two different ways: a differential ontology view and referential ontology view.

DOE can import RDFS and (OWL) formats. It is possible to export to CGXML, DAML+OIL, OIL (Ontology Inference Language) Plain Text, OIL XML, RDFS, RDF/XML, and OWL. The RDFS import/export feature is very helpful when "exchanging" files between editors, for instance OilEd, Protégé and OntoEdit and vice-versa.

DOE uses XSLT to promote interoperability (Isaac et al., 2003). XSLT is a language for transforming XML documents into other XML documents. All the exchange facilities are done with XSLT transformations. The DOE project does not have a mailing list available to the users. The installation instructions are very simple. There are no plug-ins for this editor and no user manual too.

In DOE Web page (http://opales.ina.fr/public/) there is a self-contained installer of the complete product for Windows. The user has to fill out a form in order to access the download page. The installation is fast. After downloading the product, the user has to run the Setup-DOE-v1.51.exe file and follow the instructions. To run DOE in another platform, it is required to have a Java 2 (TM) Platform, Standard Edition Version 1.3 or later (recommended v1.4.1).

## IsaViz

IsaViz is a visual environment for browsing and authoring RDF models as graphs. This tool is offered by W3C Consortium. IsaViz (2006) was developed by Emmanuel Pietriga. The first version was developed in collaboration with Xerox Research Centre Europe which also contributed with XVTM, the ancestor of ZVTM (Zoomable Visual Transformation Machine) upon which IsaViz is built. As of October 2004, further developments are handled by INRIA Futurs project In Situ. IsaViz also includes software developed by HP

Labs (Jena 2 Semantic Web Toolkit), the Apache Software Foundation (Xerces Java 2), and makes use of the GraphViz library developed by AT&T Research. IsaViz does not follow or include any methodology for building an ontology.

IsaViz imports RDF/XML and N-Triples, and exports RDF/XML, N-Triples, portable network graphics (PNG) and scalable vector graphics (SVG). Therefore, it is possible to import ontologies to other editors, for instance, Protégé or OilEd. The IsaViz environment is composed of four main windows: the IsaViz RDF Editor window, the Graph window, the Definition window and the Attribute window.

The IsaViz RDF Editor window contains the main menus and a palette of tools. The Graph window is a ZVTM view in which is displayed the RDF model represented as a 2D graph. ZVTM views display an area of an endless space as seen through a camera. This camera can be moved in the virtual space and its altitude can be changed, resulting in a 2.5D Graphical User Interface with smooth zooming capabilities. IsaViz has a user friendly interface. IsaViz has three different ways of viewing a graph. This can be a distinguishing feature when evaluating this tool with others tools. There are 3 different ways of viewing a graph: graph view; radar view and property browser. IsaViz is also recognized by its zoomable user interface (ZUI). This interface allows rapid navigation of the graphs used to represent the RDF models. The Definitions window is composed of five tabs:

1. The tab Namespaces is a table containing namespace definitions (with their optional prefix bindings).
2. The tab Property Types is a table containing property type definitions.
3. The tab Property Browser is a text browser in which is exhibit all the properties associated with the currently selected resource.
4. The tab Stylesheets (since version 2.0) is a table containing all Graph Stylesheets (GSS)

that should be applied to the model.
5. The tab Quick Input (since version 2.0) is a text area used for pasting statements expressed in RDF/XML, N-Triples or Notation3.

The Attribute window shows the attributes of a selected item of the graph. All the attributes shown in this window can be edited.

IsaViz can render RDF graphs using GSS, a stylesheet language derived from cascade style sheet (CSS) and scalable vector graphics (SVG) for styling RDF models represented as node-link diagrams. Resources and literals are the nodes of the graph (ellipses and rectangles respectively), with properties represented as the edges linking these nodes.

This editor has a user manual and a Web page with installation instructions. It also has a mailing list and a list of the most common problems. For that reason, it is really simple to start using this tool. The user can easily solve the problems that can emerge during installation or usage, by using the mailing list of IsaViz.

The current stable version is 2.1 (October 2004) and it is being developed an alpha version 3.0 (December 2005). IsaViz is implemented in Java and requires a JVM 1.3.x or later to run (1.4.0 or later is strongly recommended), Jena 1.2 (or later), GraphViz 1.8.x, Xerces 1.4.x, as well as GraphViz for some features. Installation instructions are available at the editor's Web page (IsaViz, 2006).

## Ontolingua

The Ontolingua server was the first ontology tool created by the Knowledge Systems Laboratory at Stanford University. Ontolingua was built to ease the development of ontologies with a form-based Web interface. Initially the main application inside the Ontolingua Server was an ontology editor. The Ontology Editor is a tool that supports distributed, collaborative editing, brows-

*Figure 6. IsaViz window view with a node selected*

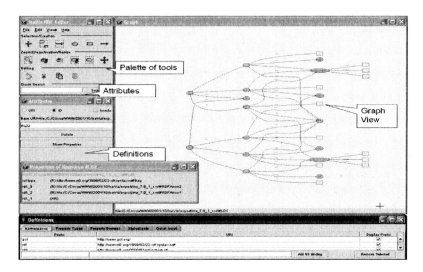

ing and creation of Ontolingua ontologies. Other systems were included in the environment, such as Webster, Open Knowledge Base Connectivity (OKBC) Server and Ontology merge tool. The Ontolingua Server ontology editor is also known as the Ontolingua Server frame-editor or even as the Ontolingua Server.

It is possible to export or import to the following formats: DAML+OIL, Knowledge Interchange Format (KIF), Open Knowledge Base Connectivity (OKBC), LOOM, Prolog, Ontolingua, C Language Integrated Production System (CLIPS). It is also possible to import Classic Ocelot and Protégé knowledge bases, but it is not possible to export to these formats.

If an ontology is available in the Ontolingua Server, there are two ways of using it from an external application: connecting to the OKBC Server from a remote client or using the ontology editor to translate the ontology into an implementation language.

The Ontolingua Server is organized as a set of ontology related Web applications, which are built on top of the Ontolingua Knowledge Representation (KR) System. Ontolingua uses an OKBC model with full KIF axioms. The base language is Ontolingua. This language consists of the combi-

nation of frames and first order logic, and allows representing classes. Classes are organized in taxonomies, relations, functions, formal axioms, and instances. The ontology editor is divided in two frames. The frame at the top shows the menu with the editing options available to users. The other frame shows the form to create the new class, where the user must specify the class name, and optionally the natural language documentation and superclasses of the concept. After the form is filled, the user must send its description to the server to store the definition in Ontolingua.

A session can be accessed at http://www.ksl. stanford.edu/software/ontolingua/ by any user in the group that owns the session. The other users connected to the session will be notified of the side-effects that are performed. To establish a new group, the user should use the comment button to e-mail the group name that the user wishes to use along with an initial list of members. The Ontolingua Server ontology editor permits to manage users and user groups who can share their ontologies. Users can work in different sessions and with different groups for each session, and then decide which ontologies can be shared with the members of each group (Farquhar, Fickas, & Rice, 1995).These multi-user sessions

*Figure 7. Ontolingua editor view*

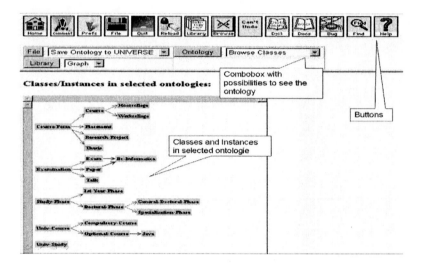

encourage collaborative ontology development. Nevertheless, since no locking mechanisms for ontology terms or version management functions exist in the editor, collaboration may sometimes be somewhat limited. The user can export an ontology (or a set of ontologies) as static HTML files to a local site. It is possible to compare ontologies. The contents of an ontology can be compared with any other loaded ontology. Users often want to split an ontology into a set of more easily understood, more tightly focused modules. The server provides direct support for splitting a large ontology into several smaller ontologies that may include each other. The Ontolingua Server allows assembling Ontolingua Ontologies, so that ontologies can be built in a modular way. Users can reuse existing ontologies from a modular structured library. Ontologies can be reused by inclusion, polymorphic refinement, and restriction. The primary mechanism for supporting ontology reuse is through the library of ontologies. This library acts as a central repository for reusable ontologies (Farquhar et al., 1995 ).

The main difference from other editors is the fact that users must have some notions of KIF and of the Ontolingua language in order to fill in the forms. Hence, if the user does not have any knowledge of KIF and of the Ontolingua language, the user will not be able to create an ontology since there is no help menu to build the KIF expression of an Ontolingua axiom. The interface is not very user friendly since the buttons are large and primitive and the drawings inside the buttons can sometimes be ambiguous.

There is no need for an installation since this editor has Web access. The user has to be registered in order to use the system. After being registered the following services are available: Chimaera, the Ontology Editor and Webster. Chimaera helps users to reorganize taxonomies and resolve name conflicts in a knowledge-base. It is especially useful when merging KBs, but also useful as an ontology browser and ontological sketchpad. The Ontology Editor allows users to browse, create and edit ontologies using a Web browser. Webster is an online version of the Webster Dictionary, that is, a searchable hypertext dictionary.

## Altova SemanticWorks™ 2006

Altova SemanticWorks 2006 is a commercial visual Semantic Web editor which provides powerful,

*Figure 8. Semantic works 2006 view bound to the e-tourism ontology*

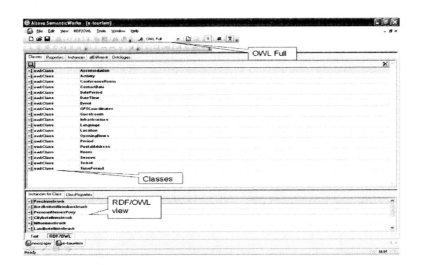

easy-to-use functionality for a visual creation and editing of RDF, RDF schema (RDFS), OWL Lite, OWL DL, and OWL Full documents. This editor has an intuitive visual interface and drag-and-drop functionalities. It allows users to visually design Semantic Web instance documents, vocabularies, and ontologies. There is no evident orientation or methodology associated to this tool.

This editor has the ability to manage the following files: N-triples, XML, OWL, RDF and RDFS. This tool provides powerful features for working with RDF in RDFS vocabularies and OWL ontologies. Users are capable of printing the graphical RDF and OWL representations to create documentation for Semantic Web implementations. The user can switch from the graphical RDF/OWL view to the text view to see how documents are being built in RDF/XML, OWL or N-triples format. The RDF/XML, OWL or N-triples code is automatically generated based on the user's design. Therefore, users can learn and try out with the concepts of the Semantic Web without having to write complicated code.

The graphical display is highly configurable. The user has the possibility to adjust the width of the items in the graph, exhibit them with a verti-cal or horizontal orientation, adjust the distances between parent and child nodes, and change the font styles and colors used.

An intelligent right menu and context sensitive entry helpers give support to change or add details to the RDF resource according to the user choices. The entry helpers and menus only offer the choices permitted based on the RDF specification, so that users can be certain to create valid documents. Any conflicts are listed in the error window. The errors are written as links so that the user can find and repair them promptly and easily.

A full version of this editor can be installed using a self-contained installer. It is easy and fast to install. The user has to request a free evaluation key, by giving the following information: Name, Company name and e-mail. Users can test this editor for a period of 30 days after receiving the key password by e-mail.

## OilEd

OilEd is a graphical ontology editor developed by the University of Manchester for description logic ontologies (Gómes-Pérez et al., 2004). The main purpose of OilEd is to provide a tool for ontologies or schemas editing, as opposed to knowledge acquisition, or the construction of large knowledge base of instances (Laera & Tamma, 2005). OilEd's interface was strongly influenced by Stanford's Protégé toolkit. The initial intention behind OilEd was to provide a simple editor that demonstrated the use of, and stimulated interest in, the Ontology Inference Layer (OIL) language.

The current version of OilEd does not provide a full ontology development environment. OilEd is not capable of supporting the growth of large-scale ontologies, the migration and integration of ontologies, versioning, argumentation and many other activities that are involved in ontology construction. Rather, it is the "Notepad" of the ontology editors, offering enough functionality to allow users to build ontologies and to demonstrate how the Fast Classification of Terminologies (FaCT) reasoner checks ontologies for consistency (Laera & Tamma, 2005). OilEd does not follow any methodology.

OilEd's internal data format is DAML+OIL (DAML- DARPA Agent Markup Language; OIL-Ontology Inference Layer). It is possible to import from DAML+OIL and export ontologies as RDFS, DAML OWL, RDF/XML and others formats.

Figure 7 shows OilEd Editor. The tabs on the main window give access to classes, properties, individuals and axioms. In each tab, a list on the left sides illustrates all the items. On the right panel there is the editor. This editor is used to see or to change the information concerning the entry selected in the item list on the left. The editor was reimplementated reasoner interface so that it was possible to use the DIG (DL Implementation Group) protocol. OilEd includes a DAML+OIL checker. Given the location of an ontology the application checks the syntax of DAML+OIL ontologies and returns a report of the model.

OilEd is provided free of charge, but the user has to provide some information before downloading this editor. Registration is a simple process requiring a valid e-mail address. The user has to be registered, in order to receive a password to revisit the main Web page to download patches and extensions when necessary.

In order to use OWL ontologies, the user must download the sesame-oil.jar library, place it in the /lib directory of the user's installation and remove the existing oil.jar. Sesame is a repository for OWL ontologies. This will add new options to the menus

*Figure 9. OilEd ontology editor view bounded with the class anomaly detection*

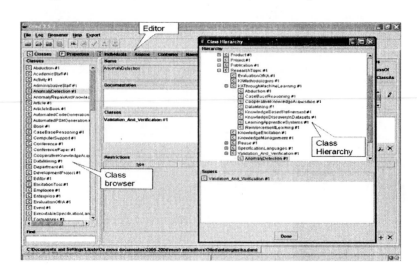

to open and save to Sesame repositories. **OilEd** expects that these Sesame repositories contain OWL files (rather than, say, DAML+OIL). This only happens since the ontologies are stored in Sesame repositories

The OilEd user manual is included in the distribution which is available as an open-source project under the GPL license. The latest version of OilEd (version 3.5) can be download at http://OilEd.man.ac.uk/. Additionally, Angus Roberts has produced a brief tutorial introduction to OilEd. The following sample ontologies produced using OilEd are available:

- **Knowledge Acquisition:** The (KA)2 demo ontology from the Ontobroker project.
- **Wines:** Deborah McGuinness' DAML+OIL wines ontology.
- **Diving:** An ontology of terms from scuba diving.
- **Mad Cows:** An ontology demonstrating the use of the reasoner to spot inconsistent concepts.

There are several possible packages for installation. OilEd comes packaged with the FaCT reasoner, although alternative reasoners can be used. OilEd 3.5.7 (Windows)+reasoner. This archive contains a FaCT reasoner for Windows. OilEd 3.5.7 (Linux)+reasoner. This updated version supports export information knowledge base models to OWL-RDF. This archive also contains the FaCT reasoner. OilEd 3.5.7 (no reasoner). This archive does not contain a reasoner. Use this distribution only if you are not interested in using a reasoner or wish to use OilEd with an alternative DIG reasoner.

## WebODE

WebODE has been developed by the Ontological Engineering Group (OEG) from the Artificial Intelligence Department of the Computer Science Faculty (FI) from the Technical University

of Madrid (UPM). WebODE is an ontological engineering workbench that provides various ontology related services (Laera and Tamma, 2005). It provides support to most of the activities involved in the ontology development process and ontology practice such as ontology edition, navigation, documentation, merge, reasoning, and so forth

The WebODE ontology editor is a Web application. It was build on top of the ontology access service (ODE API).

The WebODE platform has been built using a three-tier model (illustrated in Figure 10) which include:

1. Presentation Tier;
2. Middle Tier;
3. Database Tier.

The first tier (or presentation tier) provides the user interface. This interface is provided by means of a Web browser and uses standard Web technologies. The presentation tier was implemented using HTML (Hyper Text Markup Language), CSS (cascading style sheets) and XML (Extended Mark-up Language), because these technologies permit a simple interoperability between applications. Technologies like JavaScript and Java were used in order to ease the server of the weight of user validations. JavaScript provides easy and quick form validation. Java allows more complex presentation and logic schemas like graphical design or formula validation.

The second tier, the middle tier, provides the business logic. This tier is the result of the combination of two other subtiers: presentation subtier and logic subtier. The presentation subtier is in charge of generating the content to be presented in the user's browser. It is also aimed at handling user requests from the client (such as form and query handling) and forwards them to the ODE service as appropriate. Technologies such as servlets or JSPs (Java Server Pages) were used for this purpose. The logic subtier provides

*Figure 10. Architecture of the WebODE platform*

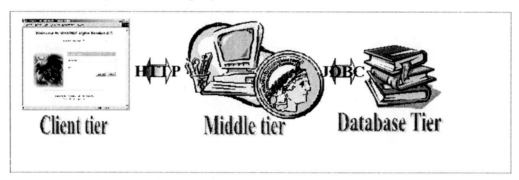

direct access to ontologies. This direct access is made by means of a well-defined API supplied through an application server (Minerva Application Server). This server provides access to services through RMI (Remote Method Invocation) thus making application development and integration very easy.

The third tier, the database tier, contains the data. Ontologies in WebODE can be stored in any relational database. The database is accessed by means of the JDBC (Java Database Connectivity) standard.

Ontologies in WebODE are conceptualized with a very expressive knowledge model. This knowledge model is based on the reference set of intermediate representations of the Methontology methodology (Laera & Tamma, 2005). The following ontology components are included in the WebODE's knowledge model: concepts and their local attributes (both instance and class attributes), whose type can be any XML schema type; concept groups, which represent sets of disjoint concepts; concept taxonomies, and disjoint and exhaustive class partitions; ad hoc binary relations between concepts, which may be characterized by relation properties (symmetry, transitiveness, etc.); constants; formal axioms, expressed in first order logic; rules; and instances of concepts and relations.

WebODE contains an ontology editor, an ontology-based knowledge management system (ODEKM), an automatic Semantic Web portal generator (ODESeW), a Web resource annotation tool (ODEAnnotate), and a Semantic Web service tool (ODESWS). The ontology editor has three user interfaces: an HTML form-based editor for editing all ontology terms except axioms and rules, a graphical user interface (OntoDesigner) and a WAB (WebODE Axiom Builder) for editing formal axioms and rules. This editor has the following ontology building services: documentation service, OKBC-based Prolog Inference engine, and ODEClean. WebODE has automatic exportation and importation services from and into XML. WebODE has translation services to other languages and systems or to and from diverse ontology specification languages. Therefore, WebODE presents vast potential capabilities for interoperability.

Ontology export services allow generating WebODE ontologies in XML and in several other ontology languages, such as RDF(S), OIL, DAML+OIL, OWL, and F-Logic. Ontologies can be transformed and used with the Protégé ontology editor or use the interoperability capabilities provided by this tool. There are several ways of using WebODE ontologies inside ontology-based applications: by its Java API via a local service or application running on the same computer where the ontology server is installed, by generating WebODE ontologies in XML and in several other ontology languages, by transforming ontologies into Protégé-2000 or into Java.

The Java API avoids accessing directly the

relational database. WebODE ontologies can be accessed not only from inside the local server but also remotely with RMI and Web services (Gómes-Pérez et al., 2001). It is possible to generate We-bODE ontologies into: RDF(S), OIL, DAML+OIL and OWL. The WebODE ontologies can be used inside Protégé-2000 ontology editor.

During this process of transforming ontologies into Java, concepts are transformed into Java beans, attributes into class variables, ad hoc relations into associations between classes. This Java code can then be used to create other Java applications and uploaded in rule systems like Jess.

WebODE has support for multiple-users. User groups can be created to collaborate in the edition of ontologies. Several users can edit the same ontology without errors by means of synchronization mechanisms. One important advantage of using this application server is that we can decide which users or user groups may access each of the services of the workbench. This editor provides Web access and therefore, there is no need for any installation activity (http://kw.dia.fi.upm.es/wpbs/#download).

## pOWL

pOWL (Auer, 2005) is a PHP-based open source ontology management tool. pOWL is capable of supporting parsing, storing, querying, manipulation, versioning, serving and serialization of RDFS and OWL knowledge bases in a collaborative Web enabled environment.

pOWL does not follow any specific methodology for developing ontologies. It supports heterogeneous data and its formal description. pOWL tries to follow the W3C Semantic Web Standards. pOWL can import and export model data in different serialization formats such as RDF/XML, and N-Triple.

pOWL is designed to work with ontologies of arbitrary size. This action is limited by the disk space. Therefore, only some parts of the ontology are loaded into main memory. The parts loaded are the ones required to display the information requested by the user on the screen. It offers an RDQL (RDF Data Query language) query builder. pOWL has a tab that correspond to the RDQL query builder. This RDQL is an implementation of an SQL-like query language for RDF. It is possible to query the knowledge base as well as a

*Figure 11. WebODE view bounded to the divider concept*

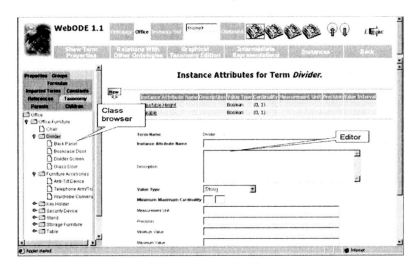

full-text search for literals and resources. pOWL has an object oriented API. This means that all functionalities are accessed with a clean application programming interface. Models are stored in database tables. It is possible to edit and view models from different points of view.

pOWL's architecture is formed by four tiers:

1. **pOWL store:** pOWL store stores its data in a relational database. This database is used to store all the information concerning ontologies and their history.

2. **RDFAPI, RDFSAPI, OWLAPI:** In order to handle RDF, RDFS and OWL there are three different APIs: RDFAPI, RDFSAPI and OWLAPI. All classes of RDFSAPI are extended with methods for handling OWL predefined properties, description logic axioms and restrictions, as well as basic subsumption inference as Lassila and Swick (1999) stated.

3. **pOWLAPI:** The pOWLAPI includes classes and functions to build Web applications. These Web applications are built on top of the APIs already described (Auer, 2005).

4. **The user interface:** The API that permits accessing, browsing, viewing and editing data models in the pOWL store is the user interface. This interface is based on PHP pages. It is possible to have three different viewpoints of an OWL knowledge base: triple view, database view and a description logic axiom view.

The RDF statements can be viewed on the "triple" view. These statements are written following this principle: subject/predicate/object. The knowledge base can be checked as if it was an object-relational database. OWL classes are represented as tables. The columns of the table represent the properties and the rows represent the instances. On the description logic (DL) axiom view, the DL axioms are detected and represented using DL. pOWL does not have a graph view but a tree view is shown on the left side panel (see Figure 9). It has multi language support and has versioning control.

pOWL has the following available documentation: user documentation, installation and administration documentation, developer documentation and application and usage scenarios. pOWL Website has six public areas: an area for

*Figure 12. View of the pOWL ontology editor showing the property elements of the coCondition*

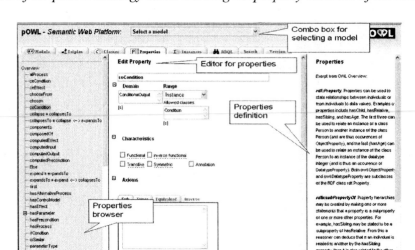

bugs, an area for support requests, an area for feature requests, a public forum, a mailing list and a CVS (concurrent version system) repository. All edits of a knowledge base may be logged and rolled back. This will only depend on time, user and edit action.

pOWL requires a PHP enabled Web server and a database backend for storing data models. pOWL is available under GNU Public license. The complete source code is also available at http://sourceforge.net/projects/pOWL/.

## SWOOP

SWOOP is a Web-based OWL ontology editor and browser. SWOOP contains OWL validation and offers various OWL presentation syntax views. It has reasoning support and provides a multiple ontology environment. Ontologies can be compared, edited and merged. Different ontologies can be compared against their description logic-based definitions, associated properties and instances. SWOOP's interface has hyperlinked capabilities so that navigation can be simple and easy. SWOOP does not follow a methodology for ontology construction.

Users can reuse external ontological data (Kalyanpur, Parsia, & Hendler, 2005). This is possible either by purely linking to the external entity, or importing the entire external ontology. It is not possible to do partial imports of OWL. There are several ways to achieve this, such as a brute-force syntactic scheme to copy/paste relevant parts (axioms) of the external ontology, or a more elegant solution that involves partitioning the external ontology while preserving its semantics and then reusing (importing) only the specific partition as desired.

It is possible to search concepts across multiple ontologies. SWOOP makes use of an ontology search algorithm, that combines keywords with DL-based in order to find related concepts. This search is made along all the ontologies stored in the SWOOP knowledge base.

With SWOOP it is possible to have collaborative annotation using the Annotea plug-in. This plug-in presents a useful and efficient Web ontology development. Users may also download annotated changes for a given ontology. The plug-in is used by the users to write and share annotations on any ontological entity. Different SWOOP users can subscribe to the server. Users can maintain different version of the same ontology since mechanisms exist to maintain versioning information using a public server.

SWOOP takes the standard Web browser as the User Interface paradigm. This Web ontology browser has a layout that is well known by most of the users. There is a navigation side bar on the left (Figure 13). The sidebar contains a multiple ontology list and a class/property hierarchy of the ontology. The center pane works like an editor. There is a range of ontology/entity renders for presenting the core content.

This editor provides support for ontology partitioning. OWL ontologies can be automatic portioned into distinct modules each describing a separate domain. There is also support for ontology debugging/repair. SWOOP has the ability to identify the precise axioms that causes errors in an ontology and there are also natural language explanation of the error. An automatic generation of repair plans to resolve all errors are provided. To better understand the class hierarchy, a "Crop-Circles" visualization format was implemented.

SWOOP is based on the conventional Model-View Controller (MVC) paradigm. The SWOOP Model component stores all ontology-centric information pertaining to the SWOOP workspace and defines key parameters used by the SWOOP UI objects. A SWOOP ModelListener is used to reflect changes in the UI based on changes in the SWOOP Model (Kalyanpur et al., 2005). Control is managed through a plug-in based system. This system loads new Renders and Reasoners dynamically. Therefore, it is possible to guarantee modularity of the code, and encourage external

*Figure 13. SWOOP view bounded to the e-tourism ontology*

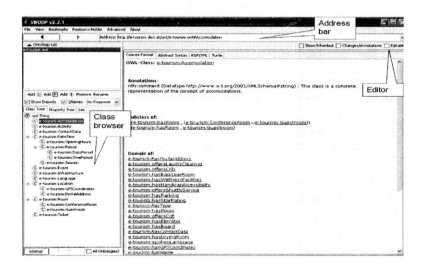

developers to contribute to the SWOOP project easily.

SWOOP uses the Wonder Web OWL API. This API provides programmatic access to data representing OWL ontologies. This API is used as the underlying OWL representation model. It has Ontology Renderers that display statistical information about the ontology, the annotations, the DL expressivity and the OWL species level. There are default plug-ins for different presentation syntax for rendering ontologies. For instance, there are the following presentations syntax RDF/XML, OWL and N3. It is easy to install and has two public mailing lists available: General SWOOP (for users) and Technical SWOOP (for developers). A SWOOP application can be downloaded from http://www.mindswap.org/. After downloading the package, the user has only to run the "runme" batch file.

SWOOP is developed as a separate Java application that attempts to provide the look and feel of a browser-based application. Its architecture was designed to optimize OWL browsing and to be extensible via a plug-in architecture.

## CONCLUSION

Software tools are available to achieve most of the activities of ontology development. Projects often involve solutions using numerous ontologies from external sources. Sometimes there is also the need to use existing and newly developed in-house ontologies. By this reason it is important that the editing tools for ontology construction promote interoperability. As we have stated, Protégé is used for domain modeling and for building knowledge-base systems. Protégé provides an intuitive editor for ontologies and has extensions for ontology visualization, project management, software engineering and other modeling tasks. It also provides interfaces for description logic reasoners such as Racer. Protégé ontologies can be exported into a variety of formats including RDF(S), OWL, and XML schema. It is a tool installed locally in a computer and does not allow collaborative editing of ontologies by groups of users. There are several plug-ins available for this tool. OntoEdit offers an ontology engineering environment which allows creating, browsing, maintaining and managing ontologies. This editor supports collaborative development of ontologies. The successor of OntoEdit is OntoStudio. OntoEdit supports F–Logic, RDF schema and OIL. The tool is multilingual. The internal representation data model can be exported to DAML+OIL, F-Logic, RDF(S), and OXML. The inference engine that OntoEdit uses is OntoBroker. OntoEdit is based on a plug-in architecture as Protégé.

DOE allows users to build ontologies according to the methodology proposed by Bruno Bachimont. This editor only permits the specification part of the process of structuring ontology. It should be used in combination with another editor. A *differential ontology* and a *referential ontology* can be built. It is possible to import RDFS and OWL formats and it is possible to export to CGXML, DAML+OIL, OIL Plain Text, OIL XML, RDFS, RDF/XML, and OWL. DOE uses XSLT to promote interoperability.IsaViz is a visual environment for browsing and authoring RDF models as graphs. IsaViz has a user friendly interface and has three different ways of viewing a graph. IsaViz is also recognized by its ZUI. This interface allows rapid navigation of the graphs used to represent the RDF models. IsaViz imports RDF/XML and N-Triples, and exports RDF/XML, N-Triples, PNG and SVG.

Ontolingua was built to ease the development of ontologies with a form-based Web interface. It is a tool that supports distributed, collaborative editing, browsing and creation of Ontolingua ontologies. Ontolingua uses an OKBC model with full KIF axioms. The base language is Ontolingua. It is possible to compare ontologies. Users can reuse existing ontologies from a modular structured library. It is important that users have some notions of KIF and of the Ontolingua language. The interface is not very user friendly. It is possible to export or import to the following formats: DAML+OIL, KIF, OKBC, LOOM, Prolog, Ontolingua, CLIPS.

Altova SemanticWorks is a commercial visual editor that has an intuitive visual interface and drag-and-drop functionalities. Users are capable of printing the graphical RDF and OWL representations to create documentation for Semantic Web implementations. It is possible to switch from the graphical RDF/OWL view to the text view to see how documents are being built in RDF/XML, OWL or N-triples format. The code is automatically generated based on the user's design. This editor has the ability to manage the following files: N-triples, XML, OWL, RDF and RDFS.

OilEd's interface was strongly influenced by Stanford's Protégé toolkit. This editor does not provide a full ontology development environment. However, allows users to build ontologies and to check ontologies for consistency by using FaCT reasoner. OilEd's internal data format is DAML+OIL. It is possible to import from DAML+OIL and export ontologies as RDFS, DAML OWL, RDF/XML and others formats.

WebODE is a Web application. This editor supports ontology edition, navigation, documentation, merge, reasoning and other activities involved in the ontology development process. User groups can be created to collaborate in the edition of ontologies. WebODE has automatic exportation and importation services from and into XML.

pOWL (Auer, 2005) is a PHP-based open source ontology management tool. pOWL is capable of supporting parsing, storing, querying, manipulation, versioning, serving and serialization of RDFS and OWL knowledge bases in a collaborative Web enabled environment. This editor was designed to work with ontologies of arbitrary size. pOWL offers an RDQL query builder. pOWL has versioning control. pOWL supports heterogeneous data and its formal description.

SWOOP is a Web-based OWL ontology editor and browser. SWOOP contains OWL validation and offers various OWL presentation syntax views. It has reasoning support and provides a multiple ontology environment. Ontologies can be compared, edited and merged. It is possible to have collaborative annotation with the Annotea plug-in. Users can reuse external ontological data.

To sum up, there are commercial ontology tools (Semantic Works and OntoStudio), there are ontology tools that demand learning/knowing a specific language (Ontolingua and OilEd) and there are ontology tools that are more graphic (IsaViz and Semantic Works). Other tools are Web-based application (WebODE, pOWL and SWOOP) or follow a methodology (DOE and WebODE).

There are several available ontology tools that can help to build an ontology. Some tools only support common edition and browsing functionalities. Other tools provide ontology documentation, ontology import/export for different formats, graphical view of ontologies, ontology libraries and attached inference engines.

In this chapter, we compared a selection of some of the available ontologies tool and environments that can be used for ontology construction, either from scratch or by reusing other existing ontologies. As we have shown, there are many ontology development tools for ontology construction

## REFERENCES

Auer, S. (2005, May 30). pOWL – A Web based platform for collaborative Semantic Web development. In *Proceedings of the Workshop on Scripting for the Semantic Web*, Heraklion, Greece.

Bachimont, B., Isaac, A., & Troncy, R. (2002, October 1-4). Semantic commitment for designing ontologies: A proposal. In A. Gomez-Pérez & V.R. Benjamins (Eds.), *13th International conference on knowledge engineering and knowledge management, (EKAW 2002),* Sigüenza, Spain. (LNAI 2473, pp. 114-121). Springer-Verlag.

Bechhofer, S., Horrocks, I., Goble, C., & Stevens, R. (2001). OilEd: A reason-able ontology editor for the Semantic Web. In *Proceedings of KI2001, Joint German/Austrian Conference on Artificial Intelligence* (Vol. 2174, pp. 396-408)

Berners-Lee, T.J., Hendler, & Lassila, O. (2001, May). The Semantic Web. *Scientific American,* 35-43.

Broekstra, J., Kampman, A., & Van Harmelen, F. (2002). Sesame: A generic architecture for storing and querying RDF and RDF schema. In I. Horrocks & J. Hendler, (Eds.), *Proceedings of the 1st Int. Semantic Web Conf. (ISWC 2002),* Sardinia, Italy (LNCS 2342, pp. 54-68). Springer-Verlag.

Cardoso, J. (2005, March) Semantic web processes and ontologies for the travel industry. *AIS SIG-SEMIS Bulletin, 2*(1), 8.

Cardoso, J., & Sheth, A.P. (2006). The Semantic Web and its applications. In *Semantic Web Services, Processes and Applications* (pp. 7-38). Springer.

Decker, S., Erdmann, M., Fensel, D., & Studer, R. (1999). Ontobroker: Ontology-based access to distributed and semi-structured information. In R. Meersman et al. (Eds.), Database semantics: Semantic issues in multimedia systems. In *Proceedings of TC2/WG 2.6 8th Working Conference on Database Semantics (DS-8),* Rotorua, New Zealand, (pp. 351-369). Boston: Kluwer Academic Publishers.

DOE (2006). The differential ontology editor. Retrieved October 22, 2006, from http://opales.ina.fr/public/index.html

Farquhar, A., Fickas, F., & Rice, J. (1995). *The ontolingua server: A tool for collaborative ontology construction* (Tech Rep No. KSL 96-26, 1996). Stanford.

Gómez-Pérez, A., Fernández-López, M., & Corcho, O. (2004). *Ontological engineering: With examples from the areas of knowledge management, e-Commerce and the semantic web,* 293-362, 2004.

Gómez-Pérez, A., Fernández-López, M., Corcho, O., & Aspiréz, J. (2001). *WebODE: A scalable ontological engineering workbench*. Paper presented at the First International Conference on Knowledge Capture (K-CAP 2001), Canada.

IsaViz (2006). IsaViz: A visual authoring tool for RDF. Retrieved October 22, 2006, from http://www.w3.org/2001/11/IsaViz/Overview.html

Kalyanpur, A., Parsia, B., & Hendler, J. (2005, January-March). A tool for working with Web ontologies. In *Proceedings of the International Journal on Semantic Web and Information Systems, 1*(1). Retrieved October 22, 2006, from http://www.mindswap.org/papers/Swoop-Journal.pdf

Laera, L. & Tamma, V. (2005). *The hitchhhiker's guide to ontology editors*. Retrieved October 22, 2006, from http://ontoweb.aifb.uni-karlsruhe.de/About/Deliverables/D13\_v1-0.zip

Lassila, O. & Swick, R.R. (1999, February). *Resource description framework (RDF) model and syntax specification*. Recommendation, W3C. Retrieved October 22, 2006, from http://www.w3.org/TR/1999/RECrdf-syntax-19990222

Noy, N.F., Sintek, M., Decker, S., Crubezy, M., Fergerson, R.W., & Musen, M.A. (2001). Creating semantic Web contents with protege-2000. *IEEE Intelligent Systems, 16*, 60-71.

Noy, N.F. & Musen, M.A. (2003). The PROMPT suite: Interactive tools for ontology merging and mapping. *International Journal of Human-Computer Studies, 59*(6) 983-1024.

Oldakowski, R. & Bizer, C. (2004). *RAP: RDF API for PHP*. Paper presented at the First International Workshop on Interpreted Languages.

OWL (2004, February 10) *OWL Web ontology language overview, W3C recommendation*. Retrieved February 20, 2007 from www.w3.org/TR/2004/REC-owl-features-20040210/

Sheth, A. (2003, July). Semantic metadata for enterprise information integration. *DM Review.*

Sure, Y., Angele, J., & Staab, S. (2002, October 28-November 1). OntoEdit: Guiding ontology development by methodology and inferencing. In *Proceedings of the International Conference on Ontologies, Databases and Applications of Semantics ODBASE 2002* (LNCS 2519, pp. 1205-1222), University of California, Irvine.

Sure, Y., Erdmann, M., Angele, J., Staab, S., Studer R., & Wenke, D. (2002, June 9-12). OntoEdit: Collaborative ontology development for the semantic. In *Proceedings of the International Semantic Web Conference*, Sardinia, Italy (LNCS 2342, pp. 221-235). Springer.

Troncy, R. & Isaac, A. (2002, June 9-12). *Semantic commitment for designing ontologies: A tool proposal*. Poster Session at the 1st International Conference on the Semantic Web, ISWC'2002, Sardinia, Italia.

## APPENDIX 1

*Table 1. List of some of the representative ontology tools*

| Tool | Product or Project Web Page |
|---|---|
| Apollo | http://apollo.open.ac.uk/index.html |
| CoGITaNT | http://cogitant.sourceforge.net/ |
| DAMLImp (API) | http://codip.grci.com/Tools/Components.html |
| Differential Ontology Editor (DOE) | http://opales.ina.fr/public/ |

*Table 1. continued*

| Tool | Product or Project Web Page |
|------|------------------------------|
| Disciple Learning Agent Shell | http://lalab.gmu.edu/ |
| DUET | http://codip.grci.com/Tools/Tools.html |
| Enterprise Semantic Platform (ESP) including Knowledge Toolkit | http://www.semagix.com/ |
| GALEN Case Environment (GCE) | http://www.kermanog.com/ |
| ICOM | http://www.cs.man.ac.uk/~franconi/icom/ |
| Integrated Ontology Development Environment | http://www.ontologyworks.com/ |
| IsaViz | http://www.w3.org/2001/11/IsaViz/ |
| JOE | http://www.cse.sc.edu/research/cit/demos/java/joe/ |
| KAON (including OIModeller) | http://kaon.semanticweb.org/ |
| KBE – Knowledge Base Editor (for Zeus AgentBuilding Toolkit) | http://www.isis.vanderbilt.edu/Projects/micants/Tech/Demos/KBE/ |
| LegendBurster Ontology Editor | http://www.georeferenceonline.com/ |
| LinKFactory Workbench | http://www.landc.be/ |
| Medius Visual Ontology Modeler | http://www.sandsoft.com/products.html |
| NeoClassic | http://www-out.bell-labs.com/project/classic/ |
| OilEd | http://oiled.man.ac.uk/ |
| Onto-Builder | http://ontology.univ-savoie.fr/ |
| OntoEdit | http://www.ontoprise.de/com/ontoedit.htm |
| Ontolingua with Chimaera | http://www.ksl.stanford.edu/software/ontolingua/ |
| Ontopia Knowledge Suite | http://www.ontopia.net/solutions/products.html |
| Ontosaurus | http://www.isi.edu/isd/ontosaurus.html |
| OntoTerm | http://www.ontoterm.com/ |
| OpenCyc Knowledge Server | http://www.opencyc.org/ |
| OpenKnoMe | http://www.topthing.com/ |
| PC Pack 4 | http://www.epistemics.co.uk/ |
| Protégé-2000 | http://protege.stanford.edu/index.html |
| RDFAuthor | http://rdfweb.org/people/damian/RDFAuthor/ |
| RDFedt | http://www.jan-winkler.de/dev/e_rdfe.htm |
| SemTalk | http://www.semtalk.com/ |
| Specware | http://www.specware.org/ |
| Taxonomy Builder | http://www.semansys.com/about_composer.html |
| TOPKAT | http://www.aiai.ed.ac.uk/~jkk/topkat.html |
| WebKB | http://meganesia.int.gu.edu.au/~phmartin/WebKB/doc/generalDoc.html |
| WebODE | http://delicias.dia.fi.upm.es/webODE/ |
| WebOnto | http://kmi.open.ac.uk/projects/webonto/ |

## APPENDIX 2

The following table (Table 2) lists the features that we considered more important when deciding which ontology tool to use: versioning; collaborative ontology edition; graphical class/properties taxonomy; graphical tree view; support the growth of large scale ontologies; querying; friendly user interface; consistency check and OWL editor. The feature versioning keeps track of the version evolution that the ontology suffers. The collaborative ontology edition is a very useful feature since it allows users to edit ontologies in a collaborative manner. The graphical class/properties taxonomy provides an interesting view of the classes and of the properties of the ontology. This feature permits viewing classes and properties with graphically. The graphical tree view shows a generic graph view of the ontology. It is possible to have an overview of the structure of the ontology. If the ontology editor supports the growth of large scale ontologies, then the user can be sure that it is possible to build an ontology by using only one editor. The feature concerning querying allows querying the knowledge base. It is important that the user interface is friendly and similar to others interface. As a result, the user does not need to spend too much time getting to know the tool. Consistency checking is important in order to look for propagation of the arity all along the hierarchy and inheritance of domains.

*Table 2. Most representative features*

| Features | DOE | IsaViz | Ontolingua | Semantic Works 2006 | OilED | SWOOP | pOWL | WebODE |
|---|---|---|---|---|---|---|---|---|
| Versioning | × | × | × | × | × | ✓ | × | × |
| Collaborative ontology edition | × | × | ✓ | × | × | ✓ | ✓ | ✓ |
| Graphical class/ properties taxonomy | ✓ | × | ✓ | ✓ | ✓ | ✓ | ✓ | ✓ |
| Graphical tree view | × | ✓ | ✓ | ✓ | ✓ | × | × | ✓ |
| Support growth of large scale ontologies | × | ✓ | ✓ | ✓ | × | ✓ | ✓ | ✓ |
| Querying | × | × | × | × | × | × | ✓ | × |
| User Interface (multi-language, intuitive) | × | ✓ | × | ✓ | ✓ | ✓ | ✓ | ✓ |
| Consistency Check | × | × | × | × (Syntax) | ✓ | × | | ✓ |
| OWL Editor | ✓ | × | ✓ | ✓ | ✓ | ✓ | ✓ | ✓ |

# Chapter V
# Web Ontology Languages

**Grigoris Antoniou**
*FORTH-ICS, Greece*

**Martin Doerr**
*FORTH-ICS, Greece*

## ABSTRACT

*Web ontology languages will be the main carriers of the information that we will want to share and integrate. The aim of this chapter is to give a general introduction to some of the ontology languages that play a prominent role on the Semantic Web. In particular, it will explain the role of ontologies on the Web and in ICT, review the current standards of RDFS and OWL, and discuss open issues for further developments.*

## THE ROLE OF WEB ONTOLOGIES

### The Role of Ontologies in ICT

The term *ontology* originates from philosophy. In that context, it is used as the name of a subfield of philosophy, namely, the study of the nature of existence (the literal translation of the Greek word Οντολογία, the branch of metaphysics concerned with identifying), in the most general terms, the kinds of things that actually exist, and how to describe them. For example, the observation that the world is made up of specific objects that can be grouped into abstract classes based on shared properties is a typical ontological statement.

In the early 1990s, a series of large-scale experiments took place in order to integrate multiple, heterogeneous databases (Bayardo et al., 1996; Chawathe, Garcia-Molina, Hammer, Ireland, Papakonstantinou, Ullman, & Widom, 1994; Wiederhold, 1992). These experiments revealed that database integration must ultimately be based on explicit, formal knowledge representation of the underlying common meaning of the involved data structures rather than on formal schema manipulation only. With the work of Thomas Gruber (1994) and others (Guarino, 1998; Sowa, 2000; Uschold & Gruninger, 1996) the extraordinary importance of formal ontology for the design and operation of information systems was widely recognized towards 1998, and scientists started to see a series of previously disparate fields in this new light, such as automated Natural Language translation and semantic networks, conceptual modeling and subject indexing in information science. The word formal ontology, with the new plural ontologies, also became the term for the product of an ontology engineering process, that is, the process of identifying a set of concepts and their relationships that formalize a domain of interest.

For our purposes, we will use Nicola Guarino's definition:

*An ontology is a logical theory accounting for the intended meaning of a formal vocabulary, that is, its ontological commitment to a particular conceptualization of the world. The intended models of a logical language using such a vocabulary are constrained by its ontological commitment. An ontology indirectly reflects this commitment (and the underlying conceptualization) by approximating these intended models.* (Guarino, 1998)

Implicit in this definition is the fact that a conceptualization resides in the human mind, and its precise formal structure is not directly accessible. On the one side, we have good reasons to believe (Fauconnier & Turner, 2002; Lakoff, 1987) that our real mental structure is richer than the logics we apply in computer science. On the other side, any formalization has practical value only, if it is computationally tractable, and practice shows that even relatively simple reasoning forms can yield valuable results.

The challenge of designing ontology languages can therefore be described as a compromise between the expressive power needed to approximate human conceptualization, and the minimal complexity needed to achieve a practical result in the target application area. In general, an ontology describes formally a domain of discourse. In the simplest form, an ontology consists of a finite list of terms and the relationships between

these terms. The *terms* denote important *concepts* (*classes* of objects) of the domain. For example, in a university setting, staff members, students, courses, lecture theaters, and disciplines are some important concepts.

The *relationships* typically include hierarchies of classes. A hierarchy specifies a class C to be a subclass of another class C' if every object in C is also included in C'. For example, all faculty are staff members.

Apart from subclass relationships, ontologies may include information such as

- Properties (X teaches Y)
- Value restrictions (only faculty members can teach courses)
- Disjointness statements (faculty and general staff are disjoint)
- Specification of logical relationships between objects (every department must include at least ten faculty members)

## The Role of Ontologies on the Web

In the context of the Web, ontologies can be used to formulate *a shared understanding of a domain* in order deal with differences in terminology of users, communities, disciplines and languages as it appears in texts. For instance, "car" in English means the same as "voiture" in French. "Wissenschaft" in German implies the meanings of both "science" and "humanities" in English. Even more, two applications may use the same term with different meanings: In one context, "school" refers to a place in a city, in another to a social institution, in a third to an artistic style. Such differences can be overcome by mapping the particular terminology to a shared ontology or by defining direct mappings between the ontologies (Kalfoglou & Schorlemmer, 2003). These cases demonstrate that ontologies support semantic interoperability.

Since the Web does not impose any discipline on content, a predominant application is free text search. Ontology mappings allow for relating keywords and thus widening the recall of the search. In addition, Web searches can exploit generalization/specialization information. If a query fails to find any relevant documents under a certain term, it may try to find documents pertaining to specializations of the term. Otherwise, the search engine may suggest to the user a more general query. It is even conceivable for the engine to run such queries proactively to reduce the reaction time in case the user adopts a suggestion. Or if too many answers are retrieved, the search engine may suggest to the user some specializations. In this way, differences in terminology between Web pages and the queries can be overcome.

Also, ontologies are useful for the organization of content and navigation of Web sites in the manner of library classification systems. Many Web sites today expose on the left-hand side of the page the top levels of a concept hierarchy of terms. The user may click on one of them to expand the subcategories. Ontologies may better represent and relate concepts the user is looking for than traditional library classification.

## The Role of Ontologies on the Semantic Web

The aim of the Semantic Web initiative is to advance the state of the current Web through the use of semantics. More specifically, it proposes to use semantic annotations to describe the meaning of certain parts of Web information and, increasingly, the meaning of message elements employed by Web Services. For example, the Web site of a hotel could be suitably annotated to distinguish between the hotel name, location, category, number of rooms, available services and so forth Such meta-data could facilitate the automated processing of the information on the Web site, thus making it accessible to machines and not primarily to human users, as it is the case today. The current web standard for semantic annotations is RDF and RDF Schema, and its extension OWL.

Suitable annotations are useful for improving the accuracy of Web searches. The search engines can look for pages in which precise *concepts* from an ontology are marked instead of collecting all pages in which certain, generally ambiguous, keywords occur.

But the vision of the Semantic Web cannot be achieved solely by disambiguating and relating individual concepts. At least equally important is the integration or transformation of data structure elements. Besides some platform specific parts, data structures reflect in a contracted and simplified way how the designer perceives the possible states of affairs of the respective application (Guarino, 1998). Ontologies allow for the formal specification of an application domain that can be shared by different systems. For instance, one system may distinguish hotels from guest houses. Another only refers to accommodation in general. Location may be given in coordinates, in metric distances or in walking distances to relevant fix points. Ontologies allow intelligent systems for mediating between these different forms to organize information. This ability constitutes a major prerequisite for the global access to Web services. A particularly interesting application of ontologies is the seamless integration of services, information systems and databases containing general knowledge. For instance, an ontology combining kinds of geographic units, kinds of tourist services and their relationships could be used to determine that Crete is an island in Greece, and therefore a Greek island and Heraklion a city on Crete. It would further describe that accommodations are immobile, and that hotels are kinds of accommodation. Such information would be crucial to establish a connection between a requester looking for accommodation on a Greek island, and a hotel advertisement specifying Heraklion as the hotel location.

## BASICS OF ONTOLOGY LANGUAGES

### Basic Ingredients of Ontology Languages

How do we describe a particular domain? Let us consider the domain of courses and lecturers at a university. First we have to specify the "things" we want to talk about. Here we will make a first, fundamental distinction. On one hand we want to talk about particular lecturers, such as David Billington, and particular courses, such as Discrete Mathematics. But we also want to talk about courses, first year courses, lecturers, professors and so forth In the first case we talk about *individual objects* (*resources*), in the second we talk about *classes* which define types of objects. A class can be thought of as a set of elements. Individual objects that belong to a class are referred to as *instances* of that class.

An important use of classes is to *impose restrictions* on what can be stated. In programming languages, typing is used to prevent nonsense from being written (such as A+1, where A is an array; we lay down that the arguments of + must be numbers). Similarly, in knowledge systems we would like to disallow statements such as:

- Discrete mathematics is taught by object-oriented programming.
- Room G228 is taught by David Billington.

The first statement is undesired because we want courses to be taught by lecturers only. This imposes a restriction on the values of the property "is taught by." In mathematical terms, we restrict the *range* of the property.

The second statement is undesired because only courses can be taught. This imposes a restriction on the objects to which the property can be applied. In mathematical terms, we restrict the *domain* of the property.

### Class Hierarchies and Inheritance

Once we have classes we would also like to establish relationships between them. For example, every professor is an academic staff member. We say that professor is a *subclass* of academic staff member, or equivalently, that academic staff member is a *superclass* of professor. The subclass relationship defines a hierarchy of classes. In general, if A is a subclass of B then every instance of A is also an instance of B.

A hierarchical organization of classes has a very important practical significance, which we outline now. Consider the range restriction

Courses must be taught by academic staff members only.

Suppose Michael Maher was defined as a professor. Then, according to the restriction above, he is not allowed to teach courses. The reason is that there is no statement which specifies that Michael Maher is also an academic staff member. Obviously, this difficulty could be overcome by adding that statement to our description. However, this solution adds redundancy to the representation, with the usual negative effects on maintainability. Instead we would like Michael Maher to *inherit* the ability to teach from the class of academic staff members.

### Property Hierarchies

We saw that hierarchical relationships between classes can be defined. The same can be done for properties. For example, "is taught by" is a *subproperty* of "involves". If a course c is taught by an academic staff member a, then c also involves a. The converse is not necessarily true. For example, a may be the convenor of the course, or a tutor who marks student homework, but does not teach c. In general, if P is a subproperty of Q then Q(x,y) whenever P(x,y).

- **Summary:** As a consequence of the discussion above, (Web) ontology languages consist of:

    - the important concepts (classes) of a domain
    - important relationships between these concepts. These can be hierarchical (subclass relationships), other predefined relationships contained in the ontology language, or user defined (properties).
    - further constraints on what can be expressed (e.g. domain and range restrictions, cardinality constraints etc).

## Design Issues for Ontology Languages

### Requirements for Ontology Languages

Ontology languages allow users to write explicit, formal conceptualizations of domains models. The main requirements are (Antoniou & van Harmelen, 2004):

1. well-defined syntax;
2. well-defined semantics;
3. efficient reasoning support;
4. sufficient expressive power;
5. convenience of expression.

The importance of a *well-defined syntax* is clear and known from the area of programming languages; it is a necessary condition for machine-processing of information. Web ontology languages have a syntax based on XML, though they may also have other kinds of syntaxes.

Of course it is questionable whether the XML-based syntax is very user-friendly; there are alternatives better suitable for humans. However this drawback is not very significant, because ultimately users will be developing their ontologies using authoring tools, or more generally ontology development tools, instead of writing them directly in the Web ontology language.

*Formal semantics* describes precisely the meaning of knowledge. "Precisely" here means that the semantics does not refer to subjective intuitions, nor is it open to different interpretations by different persons (or machines). The importance of formal semantics is well-established in the domain of mathematical logic, among others.

## The Role of Reasoning

One use of formal semantics is to allow humans and systems to reason about the knowledge. For ontological knowledge we may reason about:

- **Class Membership:** If x is an instance of a class C, and C is a subclass of D, then we can infer that x is an instance of D.
- **Equivalence of classes:** If class A is equivalent to class B, and class B equivalent to class C, then A is equivalent to C, too.
- **Consistency:** Suppose we have declared x to be an instance of the classes A and B, and that A and B are disjointed. Then we have an inconsistency, which points to a possible error in the ontology.
- **Classification:** If we have declared that certain property-value pairs are sufficient condition for membership of a class A, then if an individual x satisfies such conditions, we can conclude that x must be an instance of A.

Semantics is a prerequisite for *reasoning support*: Derivations such as the above can be made mechanically, instead of being made by hand. Reasoning support is important because it allows one to:

- Check the consistency of the ontology and the knowledge

- Check for unintended relationships between classes
- Automatically classify instances in classes.

Automated reasoning support allows one to check many more cases than what can be done manually. Checks like the above are valuable (a) for designing large ontologies, where multiple authors are involved; and (b) for integrating and sharing ontologies from various sources.

Formal semantics and reasoning support is usually provided by mapping an ontology language to a known logical formalism, and by using automated reasoners that already exist for those formalisms.

## Trade-Off Between Requirements

In designing an ontology language one should be aware of the trade-off between expressive power and efficient reasoning support. Generally speaking, the richer the language is, the more inefficient

the reasoning support becomes, often crossing the border of noncomputability. Thus we need a compromise, a language that can be supported by reasonably efficient reasoners, while being sufficiently expressive to express large classes of ontologies and knowledge.

## THE KEY SEMANTIC WEB ONTOLOGY LANGUAGES

We now turn to a discussion of specific ontology languages that are based on the abstract view from the previous version: RDF Schema and OWL. Quite a few other sources already exist that give general introductions to these languages. Some parts of the RDF and OWL specifications are intended as such introductions (such as Manola & Miller, 2004; McGuiness & van Harmelen,

2004; Smith, Welty, & McGuiness, 2004), and also didactic material such as Antoniou and van Harmelen (2003, 2004).

Our presentation is structured along the layering of OWL: OWL Lite, OWL DL and OWL Full. This layering is motivated by different requirements that different users have for a Web ontology language:

- RDFS is intended for those users primarily needing a classification hierarchy
- OWL Lite adds the possibility to express (in)equalities and simple constraints on such hierarchies
- OWL DL supports those users who want the maximum expressiveness while retaining computational completeness (all conclusions are guaranteed to be computable) and decidability (all computations will finish in finite time).
- OWL Full is meant for users who want maximum expressiveness, syntactic freedom, and full compatibility with RDF Schema, with no computational guarantees.

We use the normative abstract syntax for OWL as defined in (Patel-Schneider, Horrocks & van Harmelen, 2002). While this syntax in only meant for OWL itself, we use the same syntax for introducing RDFS in order to clarify the relation between the languages (note that the semantics of the same constructs in RDFS and OWL can differ). We will use symbols $c_i$ for classes, $e_i$ for instances of classes, $p_i$ for properties between $e_i$ and $o_i$ for ontologies. Whenever useful, we will prefix classes and instances with pseudo-namespaces to indicate the ontology in which these symbols occur, for example, $o_1{:}e_1$ and $o_2{:}e_1$ are two different instances, the first occurring in ontology $o_1$, and the second in ontology $o_2$.

Note that the XML-based syntax is far better known, but arguably not as readable. In fact, the XML-syntax is clearly geared towards machine processing, while the abstract syntax is tailored to human reading, thus our choice in this section. The reader should understand that the characteristics of the ontology languages are independent of the syntax used.

## RDF Schema

In RDF, every object (on the Web) is called a *resource* and comes along with a unique identifier, called URI. Special kinds of resources are classes and properties.

The most elementary building block of RDFS is a *class*, which defines a group of individuals that belong together because they share some characteristics. In the university domain, professors, students, courses, lecture theatres and so forth would form classes. A class is defined as follows:

Class(c)

There is the obvious distinction between individual objects and classes which are collections of objects. The following states that an individual e belongs to (is an instance of) a class c:

Individual(e type(c)) ("e is of type c").

The second elementary statement of RDFS is the subsumption relation between classes, subClassOf, which allows to organize classes in class hierarchies:

subClassOf($c_i$ $c_j$)

In RDF, instances are related to other instances through properties:

Individual($e_i$ value(p $e_j$))

In the university domain, properties might be teaching, studying, age and so forth Properties are declared as follows:

Property(p)

Just as with classes, properties are organized in a subsumption hierarchy:

SubPropertyOf($p_i$ $p_j$)

Finally, we may associate domain and range restrictions with properties:

ObjectProperty(p domain($c_i$) range($c_j$))

Given a statement

Individual($e_i$ value(p $e_j$))

The domain and range restrictions have the following effect:

Individual($e_i$ type($c_i$))
Individual($e_j$ type($c_j$))

It is worth noting that there is no negation in RDFS. As a consequence, domain and range restrictions never lead to some kind of inconsistency. Instead, they can always be fulfilled by adding instances to classes.

In summary, the basic building blocks offered by RDF Schema are:

- Classes and their instances
- Binary properties between classes
- Organisation of classes and properties in hierarchies
- Domain and range restrictions

## Limitations of the Expressive Power of RDF Schema

RDF and RDFS allow the representation of *some* ontological knowledge, but a number of other features are missing. Here we list a few:

- **Local Scope of Properties:** rdfs:range defines the range of a property, say eats, for all classes. Thus in RDF Schema we cannot declare range restrictions that apply to some classes only. For example, the fathers of elephants are elephants, while the fathers of mice are mice.

- **Disjointness of Classes:** Sometimes we wish to say that classes are disjoint. For example, male and female are disjoint. But in RDF Schema we can only state subclass relationships, for example, female is a subclass of person.
- **Boolean Combinations of Classes:** Sometimes we wish to build new classes by combining other classes using union, intersection and complement. For example, we may wish to define the class person to be the disjoint union of the classes male and female. RDF Schema does not allow such definitions.
- **Cardinality Restrictions:** Sometimes we wish to place restrictions on how many distinct values a property may or must take. For example, we would like to say that a person has exactly two parents, and that a course is taught by at least one lecturer. Again such restrictions are impossible to express in RDF Schema.
- **Special Characteristics of Properties:** Sometimes it is useful to say that a property is *transitive* (like "greater than"), *unique* (like "has mother"), or the *inverse* of another property (like "eats" and "is eaten by").

## WEB ONTOLOGY LANGUAGE OWL

OWL is a W3C standard. Developed from its predecessors OIL (Fensel, Horrocks, van Harmelen, McGuinness, & Patel-Schneider, 2001) and DAML+OIL (Patel-Schneider, Horrocks, & van Harmelen, 2002), it is at present the standard ontology language on the Web.

## OWL Lite

One of the significant limitations of RDF Schema is the inability to make equality claims between individuals. Such equality claims are possible in OWL Lite:

SameIndividual($e_i$ $e_j$)

Besides equality between instances, OWL Lite also introduces constructions to state equality between classes and between properties. Although such equalities could already be expressed in an indirect way in RDFS through a pair of mutual Subclassof or SubPropertyOf statements, this can be done directly in OWL Lite:

EquivalentClasses($c_i$ $c_j$)
EquivalentProperties($p_i$ $p_j$)

Just as importantly as making positive claims about equality or subsumption relationships, is stating negative information about inequalities. A significant limitation of RDFS, but motivated by a deliberate design decision concerning the computational and conceptual complexity of the language, is the inability to state such inequalities. Since OWL does not make the unique name assumption, two instances $e_i$ and $e_j$ are not automatically regarded as different. Such an inequality must be explicitly stated, as:

DifferentIndividuals($e_i$ $e_j$)

Whereas the above constructions are aimed at instances and classes, OWL Lite also has constructs specifically aimed at properties. An often occurring phenomenon is that two a property can be modeled in two directions. Examples are ownerOf vs. ownedBy, contains vs. isContainedIn, childOf vs. parentOf. The relationship between such pairs of properties is established by stating

ObjectProperty($p_i$ inverseOf($p_j$))

In addition, OWL Lite allows to specify characteristics of properties:

ObjectProperty($p_i$ Transitive)
ObjectProperty($p_i$ Symmetric)

Another significant limitation of RDFS is the inability to state whether a property is optional or required (in other words: should it have at least one value or not), and whether it is single- or multi-valued (in other words: is it allowed to have more than one value or not). Technically, these restrictions constitute 0/1-cardinality constraints on the property. The case where a property is allowed to have at most one value for a given instance (i.e., a max-cardinality of 1) has a special name: FunctionalProperty. The case where the value of a property uniquely identifies the instance of which it is a value (i.e. the inverse property has a max-cardinality of 1) is called InverseFunctional-Property. These two constructions allow for some interesting derivations under the OWL semantics: If an ontology models that any object can only have a single "age":

(ObjectProperty age Functional)

then different age-values for two instances $e_i$ and $e_j$ allow us to infer that

DifferentIndividuals($e_i$ $e_j$)

(if two objects have a different age, they must be different objects).

Another important feature of OWL Lite is that it allows it to impose domain and range restrictions, depending on the class to which a property is applied.

Class($c_i$ restriction($p_i$ allValuesFrom ($c_j$)))

says that all $p_i$ values *for members of* $c_i$ must be members of $c_j$. This differs from the RDFS range restriction

ObjectProperty($p_i$ range($c_j$))

which says that all $p_i$-values must be members of $c_j$, irrespective of whether they are members of $c_i$ or not. This allows us to use the same property name with different range restrictions depending on the class to which the property is applied. For example, we can specify that the parents of cats are cats, while the parents of dogs are dogs. An RDFS range restriction would not be able to capture this.

Similarly, although in RDFS we can define the range of a property, we cannot enforce that properties actually do have a value: we can state the authors write books:

ObjectProperty(write domain(author) range(book))

but we cannot enforce in RDFS that every author must have written at least one book. This is possible in OWL Lite:

Class(author restriction(write someValuesFrom (book)))

Technically speaking, these are just special cases of the general cardinality constraints allowed in OWL DL. The someValuesFrom corresponds to a min-cardinality constraint with value 1, and the functional property constraint mentioned above corresponds to a max-cardinality constraint with value 1. These can also be stated directly:

Class(author restriction(write minCardinality(1)))
Class(object restriction(age maxCardinality(1)))

When a property has a minCardinality and max-Cardinality constraints with the same value, these can be summarised by a single exact Cardinality constraint.

## OWL DL

With the step from OWL Lite to OWL DL, we obtain a number of additional language constructs. It is often useful to say that two classes are disjoint (which is much stronger than saying they are merely not equal):

DisjointClasses($c_i$ $c_j$)

OWL DL allows arbitrary Boolean algebraic expressions on either side of an equality of subsumption relation. For example we can write

SubClassOf($c_i$ unionOf($c_j$ $c_k$))

which says that $c_i$ is subsumed by the union of $c_j$ and $c_k$, though it may not be subsumed by either $c_j$ or $c_k$. Similarly we can write

EquivalentClasses($c_i$ intersectionOf($c_j$ $c_k$))

Of course, the unionOf and intersectionOf may be taken over more than two classes, and may occur in arbitrary Boolean combinations.

Besides disjunction (union) and conjunction (intersection), OWL DL completes the Boolean algebra by providing a construct for negation:

complementOf($e_i$ $e_j$)

In fact, arbitrary class expressions can be used on either side of subsumption or equivalence axioms.

There are cases where it is not possible to define a class in terms of such algebraic expressions. This can be either impossible in principle. In such cases it is sometimes useful to simply enumerate sets of individuals to define a class. This is done in OWL DL with the oneOf construct:

EquivalentClasses($c_j$ oneOf($e_1$ ... $e_n$))

Similar to defining a class by enumeration, we can define a property to have a specific value by stating the value:

Class($c_i$ restriction($p_j$ hasValue $e_k$))

The extension from OWL Lite to OWL DL also lifts the restriction on cardinality constraints to have only 0/1 values.

## OWL Full

OWL Lite and OWL DL are based on a strict segmentation of the vocabulary: no term can be both an instance and a class, or a class and a property, and so forth A somewhat less strict proposal is RDFS(FA) (Pan & Horrocks, 2003), which does allow a class to be an instance of another class, as long as this is done in a stratified fashion. Full RDFS is much more liberal still: a class $c_1$ can have both a type and a subClassOf relation to a class $c_2$, and a class can even be an instance of itself. In fact, the class Class is a member of itself. OWL Full inherits from RDFS this liberal approach.

Schreiber (2002) argues that this is exactly what is needed in many cases of practical ontology integration. When integrating two ontologies, opposite commitments have often been made in the two ontologies on whether something is modeled as a class or an instance. This is less unlikely than it may sound: is "747" an *instance* of the class of all airplane-types made by Boeing or is "747" a *subclass* of the class of all airplanes made by Boeing? And, are particular jet planes instances of this subclass? Both points of view are defensible. In OWL Full, it is possible to have equality statements between a class and an instance.

In fact, just as in RDF Schema, OWL Full allows us even to apply the constructions of the language to themselves. It is perfectly legal to (say) apply a max-cardinality constraint of 2 on the subclass relationship. Of course, building any efficient reasoning tools that support this very liberal self-application of the language is out of the question.

## ALTERNATIVES AND EXTENSIONS

### Potential Extensions of OWL

In the following we list some important features not captured by the current version(s) of OWL. Future extensions may address some of these issues.

### Modules and Imports

The importing facility of OWL is very trivial: It only allows importing of an entire ontology, not parts of it. Modules in programming languages based on information hiding; they state functionality and hide implementation details. It is an open question how to define appropriate module mechanism for Web ontology languages.

### Defaults

Many practical knowledge representation systems allow inherited values to be overridden by more specific classes in the hierarchy. Thus they treat inherited values as defaults. No consensus has been reached on the right formalization for the nonmonotonic behaviour of default values.

### Closed World Assumption

OWL currently adopts the open-world assumption: A statement cannot be assumed true on the basis of a failure to prove it. On the huge and only partially knowable WWW, this is a correct assumption. An alternative approach is the closed-world assumption (CWA), under which a statement is true when its negation cannot be proved. CWA is tied to the notion of defaults, leading to nonmonotonic behaviour. One idea championed

is to extend OWL in a way that it still adopts open world assumption, but allows one to declare parts for which CWA should be adopted.

### Unique Names Assumption

Typical database applications assume that individuals with different names are indeed different individuals. OWL follows the usual logical paradigm where this is not the case. This design decision is plausible on the WWW. Future extensions may allow one to indicate portions of the ontology for which the assumption does or does not hold.

### Procedural Attachments

A common concept in knowledge representation is to define the meaning of a term by attaching a piece of code to be executed for computing the meaning of the term. Although widely used, this concept does not lend itself very well to integration in a system with a formal semantics, and it has not been included in OWL.

### Rule-Based Languages

A current trend is to study rule-based languages for the Semantic Web. These languages have been thoroughly studied in the knowledge representation community, are generally well understood and can be implemented efficiently. Moreover, rules are far better known and used in mainstream IT, compared to other logical systems; thus they may be of interest to a broader range of persons, and may be integrated more easily with other ICT systems.

One of the simplest kinds of rule systems is Horn logic. It is interesting to note that description logics and Horn logic are orthogonal in the sense that neither of them is a subset of the other. For example, it is impossible to assert that persons who study and live in the same city are "home students" in OWL, whereas this can be done easily using rules:

studies(X,Y), lives(X,Z), loc(Y,U), loc(Z,U) → homeStudent(X)

On the other hand, simple rules in Horn logic cannot assert information that can be expressed in OWL. Such cases include:

• Existential quantification, for example, that all persons must have a father.
• Disjunction and union, for example, that persons are men or women.
• Negation/complement, for example, that a person is either a man or a woman.

The first idea for combining OWL with Horn logic essentially considered the intersection of the two logics, that is, knowledge that can be expressed both in OWL and in Horn logic. This led to the language of Description Logic Programs (Grosof, Horrocks, Volz, & Decker, 2003). It provides compatibility with the language of OWL, but allows implementation using rule technology.

More recent work tries to combine OWL and rules in richer ways. One proposal is SWRL (Horrocks, Patel-Schneider, Boley, Tabet, Grosof, & Dean, 2004) which enhances OWL with Datalog rules, at the expense of decidability. It is still an open research problem to find the balance between expressive power including some form of rules, and computational computability and efficiency. The challenge is to identify sublanguages of SWRL that maintain at least decidability; (e.g., Horrocks, Patel-Schneider, Bechhofer, & Tsarkov, 2005; Motik, Sattler & Studer, 2005; Rosatti, 2005).

Other approaches to combining rules with ontologies include work on F-Logic (Kifer, 2005) and answer set programming (Eiter, Lukasiewicz, Schindlauer, & Tompits, 2004).

## CONCLUSION

The aim of this chapter was to give a general introduction to some of the ontology languages that play a prominent role on the Semantic Web. In particular, it explained the role of ontologies on the web and in ICT, reviewed the current standards of RDFS and OWL, and discussed open issues for further developments. Important open research questions include:

• Finding the right balance between expressive power and efficiency, especially when combining description logic based with rule based languages.
• Adding nonmonotonic features, such as closed world assumption, default knowledge and inconsistency tolerance, to ontology languages.

## REFERENCES

Antoniou, G. & van Harmelen, F. (2003). Web ontology language: OWL. In S. Staab & R. Studer (Eds), *Handbook on ontologies in information systems*. Springer.

Antoniou, G., & van Harmelen, F. (2004). *A Semantic Web primer*. MIT Press.

Bayardo, R.J., et *al*. (1996). *InfoSleuth: Agent-based semantic integration of information in open and dynamic environments* (MCC Tech. Rep. No. MCC-INSL-088-96).

Chawathe, S., Garcia-Molina, H., Hammer, J., Ireland, K., Papakonstantinou, Y., Ullman, J., & Widom, J. (1994). The TSIMMIS project: Integration of heterogeneous information sources. In *Proceedings of IPSI Conference* (pp. 7-18).

Eiter, T., Lukasiewicz, T., Schindlauer, R., & Tompits, H. (2004). Combining answer set programming with description logics for the Semantic

Web. In *Proceedings of KR'04* (pp. 141-151). MIT Press.

Fauconnier, G. & Turner, M. (2002). *The way we think: Conceptual blending and the mind's complexities*. New York: Basic Books.

Fensel, D., Horrocks, I., van Harmelen, F., McGuinness, D.L., & Patel-Schneider, P.F. (2001). OIL: An ontology infrastructure for the Semantic Web. *IEEE Intelligent Systems, 16*(2), 38-44.

Grosof, B., Horrocks, I., Volz, R., & Decker, S. (2003). Description logic programs: Combining logic programs with description logic. In *Proceedings of WWW'2003 Conference* (pp. 48-57). ACM Press.

Gruber, T. (1994). Toward principles for the design of ontologies used for knowledge sharing. In N. Guarino & R. Poli (Eds), *Formal ontology in conceptual analysis and knowledge representation*. Kluwer.

Guarino, N. (1998). Formal ontology and information systems. In N. Guarino (Ed.), Formal ontology in information systems. In *Proceedings of the 1st International Conference*. IOS Press.

McGuinness, D.L., & van Harmelen, F. (2004). OWL Web ontology language overview. Retrieved October 22, 2006, from http://www.w3.org/TR/owl-features/

van Harmelen, F., & Fensel, D. (1999). Practical knowledge representation for the Web. In *Proceedings of IJCAI'99 Workshop on Intelligent Information Integration*.

Horrocks, I., Patel-Schneider, P., Bechhofer, S., & Tsarkov, D. (2005). OWL rules: A proposal and prototype implementation. *Journal of Web Semantics, 3*(1).

Horrocks, I., Patel-Schneider, P., Boley, H., Tabet, S., Grosof, B., & Dean, M. (2004). *SWRL: A Semantic Web rule language combining OWL and ruleML*. Retrieved October 22, 2006, from http://www.w3.org/Submission/SWRL

Kalfoglou, Y. & Schorlemmer, M. (2003). Ontology mapping: The state of the art. *The Knowledge Engineering Review, 18*(1), 1-31.

Kifer, M. (2005). Rules and ontologies in f-Logic. In N. Eisinger & Maluszynski (Eds), *Reasoning Web* (*LNCS* 2564 pp. 22-34). Springer.

Lakoff, G. (1987). *Women, fire, and dangerous things: What categories reveal about the mind*. Chicago: University of Chicago Press.

Manola, F. & Miller, E. (2004). RDF primer. Retrieved October 22, 2006, from http://www.w3.org/TR/rdf-primer/

Motik, B., Sattler, U., & Studer, R. (2005). Query answering for OWL-DL with rules. *Journal of Web Semantics, 3*(1).

Pan, J. & Horrocks, I. (2003). RDFS(FA) and RDF MT: Two semantics for RDFS. In *Proceedings of International Semantic Web Conference (ISWC 2003)* (LNCS 2870, pp. 30-46). Springer.

Patel-Schneider, P., Horrocks, I., & van Harmelen, F. (2002). Reviewing the design of DAML+OIL: An ontology language for the semantic web. In *Proceedings of the Eighteenth National Conference on Artificial Intelligence*. AAAI Press.

Patel-Schneider, P., Hayes, P., & Horrocks, I. (2004). OWL Web ontology language semantics and abstract syntax. Retrieved October 22, 2006, from http://www.w3.org/TR/owl-semantics/

RDF. *Resource Description Framework*. Retrieved October 22, 2006, from http://www.w3.org/RDF/

Rosatti, R. (2005). On the decidability and complexity of integrating ontologies with rules. *Journal of Web Semantics, 3*(1).

Schreiber, G. (2002). The Web is not well-formed. *IEEE Intelligent Systems, 17*(2).

Smith, M.K., Welty, C., & McGuinness, D.L. (2004). OWL Web ontology language guide. Retrieved October 22, 2006, from http://www.w3.org/TR/owl-guide/

Soergel, D., Lauser, B., Liang, A., Fisseha, F., Keizer, J., & Katz, S. (2004). Reengineering thesauri for new applications: The AGROVOC example. *Journal of Digital Information, 4*(4).

Sowa, J. (2000). *Knowledge representation: Logical, philosophical, and computational foundations.* Brooks/Cole.

Uschold, M. & Gruninger, M. (1996). Ontologies: Principles, methods and applications. *The Knowledge Engineering Review, 11*(2), 93-136.

Wiederhold, G. (1992). Mediators in the architecture of future information systems. *IEEE Computer, 25*(3), 38-49.

# Chapter VI
# Reasoning on the Semantic Web

**Rogier Brussee**
*Telematica Instituut, The Netherlands*

**Stanislav Pokraev**
*Telematica Instituut, The Netherlands*

## ABSTRACT

*We describe reasoning as the process needed for using logic. Efficiently performing this process is a prerequisite for using logic to present information in a declarative way and to construct models of reality. In particular we describe description logic and the owl ontology language and explain that in this case reasoning amounts to graph completion operations that can be performed by a computer program. We give an extended example, modeling a building with wireless routers and explain how such a model can help in determining the location of resources. We emphasize how different assumptions on the way routers and buildings work are formalized and made explicit in our logical modeling, and explain the sharp distinction between knowing some facts and knowing all facts (open vs. closed world assumption). This should be helpful when using ontologies in applications needing incomplete real world knowledge.*

## WHAT DO WE MEAN BY REASONING AND WHAT IS IT GOOD FOR?

Any reader of this text is equipped with the most capable reasoner found on this planet: the human brain. Thus, it is not surprising that we have come to take reasoning for granted. That sound reasoning follows a restricted set of formal rules is a relatively recent invention. Long after people learned to grow food, rule empires and measure land, the Greek philosophers formalized the rules of logic and set standards for mathematical proof. They also realized the importance of sound reasoning for rhetoric and decision making. Formal axiomatic logic is much younger, dating to the late nineteenth and twentieth century, with applications to computer science going back to the 1930s, predating computers themselves. Historically speaking, we need to define what we actually mean by reasoning.

In this chapter we will take the viewpoint that reasoning is a tool for formulating concise models of "real world" phenomena such as people, mobile phones, transactions, services or databases. Roughly speaking, we want to model the world in terms of dots and arrow (subject predicate object) diagrams, that model how "things" relate to each other, and define classes to group "things." In fact, interpreting dots and arrows in a sufficiently general way using different dots for "things" and for "classes" the latter can be considered a special case of the former. We want to impose logic rules that force the existence (or non existence) of *implied* arrows. In practice, this means that we can specify model concepts in terms of fewer primitive properties, that our model can be more accurate and that we need not specify all the properties that logically follow from possessing primitive properties. It also means that we can query a model in terms of the implied property arrows in addition to the stated ones. On the downside, it means that we need a computer program to compute these implied arrows, at least at query time, and that we want to control the time it takes the computer to do this.

This viewpoint naturally fits with an orientation towards ontologies as a consensual vocabulary for "real world" phenomena. In its most restricted form, a vocabulary is merely a collection of words, and a description of the real world amounts to naming: associating the word with something. Such a vocabulary has just points and no arrows. In a more liberal interpretation of vocabulary we not only have symbols to name real world phenomena, but we also have names for the relations that exist between them such as groupings, and attribute values. There are many computer applications where we define attributes and values. Such a model has both points and arrows, but each arrow must be explicitly mentioned. Finally the real world relations may naturally satisfy constraints. These relations are often used in programs and, if you are lucky, they are documented. For example, we have abstract constraints such as "the member of a group is a member of any larger group" or concrete ones such as "a database record has exactly one primary key." Such a model is often specified with only a generating set of arrows, for example, by only explicitly stating subclass relations. Making use of such implied constraints, and making them an explicit part of information model has the advantage that models can often be simpler and is a primary motivation for using semantic techniques. Reasoning is computing the implied relations and constructing the missing arrows.

## LOGICAL IMPLICATIONS IN DESCRIPTION LOGIC

The reasoning we do here deals with organizing *Classes, Individuals* and *Properties*. The associated logic is called description logic (DL) (Calvanese, McGuinness, Nardi & Patel-Schneider, 2003) which has become popular as the basis for the Web Ontology Language (OWL) (Dean, Schreiber, Bechhofer, van Harmelen, Hendler, Horrocks, et al., 2004) which for our purposes can be considered as an extension of RDF.[1] Difficult papers have been written about the subject but since we want to draw practical conclusions we give as mundane a description as possible. A similarly practical approach is present in the Protégé OWL-manual (Horridge, Knublauch, Rector, Stevens, & Wroe, 2004). A list of further reading material was collected by Franconi (2002).[2]

### Individuals and Classes

Individuals represent entities or phenomena in a domain of interest, for example, *John, TopTechCompany* or *London* (Figure 1). Logically an individual is an assertion of existence for example, by naming *JohnSmith* we assert the existence of John. Two individuals can be equal to each other but known under a different name for example, *John* and *JSmith*. Existence can already be interesting, but usually we want to assert the existence of individuals with certain properties.

*Classes* provide an abstraction mechanism for grouping individuals with similar properties, for example, ***Human***, ***Company*** or ***all things that have a red color*** (Figure 2). A class has an *intentional* meaning, that is, it is a *membership criterion* or equivalently a *unary predicate*. For example, the two special classes ***Thing*** and ***Nothing*** are defined by the membership condition always *true* respectively always *false*.

The membership criterion point of view allows us to identify a class with a unary predicate. For some classes this membership criterion is explicit (like *having a red color*), but often that membership criterion is axiomatic, like a club for which you are a member if and only if you own a membership card. Every class is also associated with a set of individuals, called the *class extension*. For these individuals it is asserted explicitly that they satisfy the membership criterion, that is, they are "handed out a membership card." In particular such an assertion claims the existence of such an individual. Two classes may have the same class extension, but still be different classes. For example, we often use classes for which we know no members at all, but that still have a different intentional meaning. We denote class membership like

*John* ∈ ***Man*** or as *John a **Man*** or as ***Man*** (*John*)

As the notation suggests it is often convenient to think of a class as a set with some known, but potentially many more individuals characterized by some property. Be warned however that this is technically not 100% correct. See below for the technically correct interpretation.

A *Property* is a binary relationship (i.e., a binary predicate) from one class to another or from a class to a data type. We can assert that two individuals or an individual and a data value are related through a property for example, ***worksFor***(*John, TopTechCompany)* or ***hasAge***(*John, 35)*. Because it reads more intuitively we often write the property relationship in infix notation

*John **worksFor** TopTechCompany*

We call such a "sentence" a *subject predicate object* triple, or just a triple. We also say that *TopTechCompany* is a value of ***worksFor*** on *John* (a value and not the value because there could be more than one). The triple can be graphically represented as two points connected by an arrow (Figure 3).

*Figure 2. Classes with some known members*

*Figure 1. Some individuals*

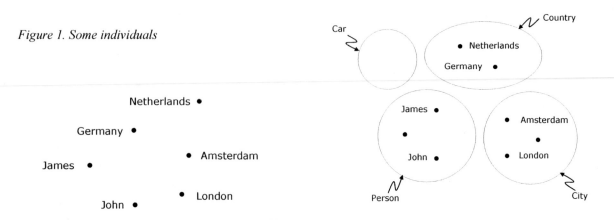

*Figure 3. A triple assertion*

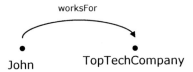

A property goes from a *domain* class to a *range* class. If not defined explicitly, a property can always be thought of as having domain and range ***Thing***. A useful way to think about the domain and range is that *P* is a multi-valued function defined on its domain with values in its range. If class *A* is the domain of a property *P*, and class *B* is the range of *P*, then every time we assert a triple *x P y* we assert in particular that *x* ∈ *A* and *y* ∈ *B.* For example if the class ***Person*** is the domain, and ***Organisation*** the range of property ***worksFor,*** we conclude from the existence of the triple above that *John*∈ ***Person,*** and *TopTechCompany* ∈ ***Organisation.*** Note that this is a conclusion, not an assumption used as a constraint for "applying" the property ***worksFor*** on the individual *John.* However, in practice, this is how we often use it. For example, tools like the ontology editor Protégé[3] or Triple20[4] effectively enforce the usage in this way.

Be aware that properties are defined independent of the triples, just like classes are defined independent of their members. A property (binary predicate) has an intentional meaning just like a class (unary predicate). A triple is an assertion that the (subject, object) pair satisfies the binary property predicate corresponding to that property. Likewise, the assertion that an individual is a member of a class is the assertion that the individual satisfies the unary predicate corresponding to that class. Thus, the set of all triples with a given property as predicate is completely analogous to the extension of the class.

## Technical Interpretation of Classes and Predicates: Models

The technically correct interpretation of classes and properties is to study *all possible* interpretations of the logical formulas in set theory, so called models. This means that one studies all the ways that the membership predicate for classes in the sense of logical formulas can be interpreted as predicates on a set Δ, that is, as a function Δ → {True, False} or equivalently as a subset of Δ, and we study all the ways properties as logical formulas can be interpreted as a binary predicates on Δ, that is as a function Δ×Δ → {True, False} or equivalently as a subset of Δ×Δ. The upshot is, that if we interpret classes as subsets of "things" in some particular context we are cheating a bit, because we have fixed the set Δ, and it clearly makes a difference what the "things" are. We often have such a context in mind, but we can only reason about our stated axioms and nothing more. As far as the logic is concerned, the set Δ is "variable," and the axioms are "equations" restricting the possibilities. Thinking about classes as having a few known and potentially many other individuals with a few known and potentially many other properties unless stated or proved otherwise, is an effective way to deal with this mostly psychological problem, and forces us to only reason with known(!) properties.

## The Open vs. Closed World Assumption

If we state the existence of individuals, properties or classes we do *not* make a claim that these individuals, properties or classes are the only ones that exist or could exist. We merely state that these are *known* and have to be given their place in any concrete realization where we can interpret individuals as elements, classes as (sub)sets and properties as binary predicates. Such an assumption is particularly well suited for an environment like the Web where we have to assume incomplete knowledge and cannot assume full control. It also fits with the idea that different sources contain different pieces of a more complete description. However, in many applications the situation is opposite. For example, if we have a database, then the database records are *all* the individuals in the database, and the columns define *all* (the values of) its properties. Moreover, the result of a query is supposed to be an authorative answer in that the records returned *do*, and the others *do not* satisfy the query. These different points of view are complementary. A database often contains incomplete information, and the answer of a query is merely authorative for information about whatever people have put in the database. Conversely, we can state that a class consists exactly of a number of instances and no others. It merely points out to us that we have to be careful about the distinction. We will later give an example that illustrates the difference later in this chapter.

## More on Classes

Classes can be defined in different ways:

- axiomatically, by stating that the class exists, for example, **Human**
- extensionally, by enumerating all individuals that belong to the class, for example, {*Belgium, Netherlands, Luxembourg*}
- intentionally, by defining the membership criteria of the class, for example, **having a red color.**
- as the *intersection* of two or more classes, for example, **Human ∩ Male**. In terms of membership criteria this is the conjunction of the criteria, for example, **Human and Male.**
- as the *union* of two or more classes, for example, **American ∪ Canadian**. In terms of membership criteria this is disjunction of the criteria, for example, **American or Canadian.**

- as the *complement* of another class, for example, **¬Vegetarian**. In terms of membership criterion this is negation of the original criterion, for example, **not Vegetarian.**

Classes can be organised into a subclass-superclass hierarchy (also known as *taxonomy*). In terms of the membership criterion, a class *C* is a subclass of a class *D* if the membership criterion for *C* implies the membership criterion for *D*. For example, **Nothing** is a subclass of all classes and no individual is a member of **Nothing**. Likewise, Thing is a superclass of all classes and all individuals are member of **Thing.**

We usually just assert that one class is a subclass of another. For example, we can define **Father** as a subclass of **Man** and **Man** as a subclass of **Human**. An individual which is a member of a class, is also a member of all its superclasses. For example, if *John* is a **Father**, then *John* is also a **Man** and a **Human**:

$$(John \in Father) \wedge (Father \subseteq Man) \wedge (Man \subseteq Human) \Rightarrow (John \in Man) \wedge (John \in Human)$$

Two classes are *equivalent* (i.e., synonyms) if they are subclasses of each other. Thus a necessary and sufficient condition to belong to a class is to belong to an equivalent class. For example, **Person** can be defined as an equivalent of the class **Human**. Then

$$(Person \equiv Human) \Rightarrow$$
$$(John \in Person \Leftrightarrow John \in Human)$$

Classes can be asserted to be *disjoint*. This means that the conjunction (logical and) of the corresponding membership criteria is always *false*, so that the classes cannot have common members. For example, if we define **Man** and **Woman** to be disjoint, no individual can be member of **Man** and **Woman** at the same time. The definition implies in particularly that the members of the two disjoint classes are distinct:

$$(John \in \textbf{Man}) \wedge (Mary \in \textbf{Woman}) \Rightarrow$$
$$John \neq Mary$$

## Restrictions as Special Classes

A class can also be defined by a restriction on property values. An *existential restriction* (from the existential quantifier ∃, which reads as *"for some," "there exists,"* or *"for at least one"*) has as membership criterion that for some give property **P** there exists a value instance in some given class **C**. For example, the class **ParentOfGirl** can be defined as someone that **has** at least one **Child** that is a **Girl** (Figure 4).

**ParentOfGirl** ≡ ∃ **hasChild.Girl**

Thus, a necessary and sufficient condition to be member of **ParentOfGirl** is to have *at least one hasChild* relation to a member of class **Girl**

John ∈ **ParentOfGirl** ⇔
$$(\exists y \in \textbf{Girl}) \wedge (John \textbf{ hasChild } y)$$

There are useful variations of the existential restriction. The simplest is the *hasValue* (∋) restriction which asserts the existence of a specific property value. For example, **Londoner** is someone who **livesIn** the city *London:*

*Figure 4. ParentOfGirl as defined by a restriction on the hasChild property*

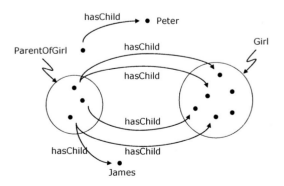

**Londoner** ≡ ∋ **livesIn.London** ⇒
John ∈ **Londoner** ⇔ *John livesIn* London

Another variation is the *cardinality restriction* (or more precisely qualified cardinality restriction). In this case a necessary and sufficient membership condition is that there is a more precisely defined number of property values to other individuals or data values. Some examples are:

* Minimum cardinality restriction (≥)

**Parent** ≡ ≥ **1 hasChild.Human**

Note that the existential restriction is the special case of cardinality restriction at least one.

* Maximum cardinality restriction (≤)

LowBuilding ≡ ≤ 3 hasFloor.Floor

* Exact cardinality restriction (=)

**Human** ≡ **=2 biologicalParents.Human**

Negating the existential condition we are inevitably led to the *universal restriction* (coming from the universal quantifier ∀, which reads as *"for all"*). The membership criterion for the universal restriction is that all (possibly *zero!*) values from a property **P** are members of a class **C**. For example,

**Sober** ≡ ∀**drinks.NonAlcoholicDrink**
John ∈ **Sober** ⇔
$$\forall y (John \textbf{ drinks } y \Rightarrow y \in \textbf{NonAlcoholicDrink})$$

Note that *John* is **Sober** if he does not drink at all! The existential and universal restrictions can be combined in more complex definitions. For example, a **Vegetarian** is someone who eats **VegetarianFood** and only eats **VegetarianFood**.

115

$$Vegetarian \equiv \exists\, eats.VegetarianFood \cap$$
$$\forall\, eats.VegetarianFood$$

## More on Properties

The only way we will define properties is by introducing them axiomatically. Like classes, properties can be more or less specific which leads to *property hierarchies*. A property $R$ is a *subproperty* of a property $P$, denoted $R \subseteq P$, if $R$ implies $P$. It follows that each asserted triple $x$ $R$ $y$, implies a triple $x$ $P$ $y$. For example, if *John* has a daughter, then in particular, *John* has a child (Figure 5).

$$(hasDaughter \subseteq hasChild) \wedge (John\ hasDaughter$$
$$Mary) \Rightarrow John\ hasChild\ Mary$$

There are other useful ways that one asserted triple implies other triples if the properties we consider are special. If $R$ is the *inverse* of a property $P$ then it is the same predicate but with the order of subject and object reversed. For example, (see Figure 6), if *isDaughterOf* is the inverse of *hasDaughter* then

$$John\ \textbf{hasDaughter}\ Mary \Leftrightarrow$$
$$Mary\ \textbf{isDaughterOf}\ John$$

A property is *symmetric* if it is its own inverse, that is, $x\ P\ y \Rightarrow y\ P\ x$

For example, the property **bordersWith** is symmetric (Figure 7).

A *functional property* is a property that is at most single-valued. Thus if $P$ a functional property then $(x\ P\ a) \wedge (x\ P\ b) \Rightarrow a = b$. An example of a functional property is given in Figure 8.

Likewise, for an *inverse functional property* the inverse property is functional so that $(x\ P\ a) \wedge (y\ P\ a) \Rightarrow x = y$. Such properties are often used to *identify* an individual. In the example in Figure 9 **hasEmail** is an inverse functional property and is used to identify a person.

*Figure 5. Triple implied by a subproperty*

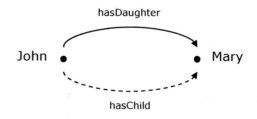

*Figure 6. Triple implied by an inverse property*

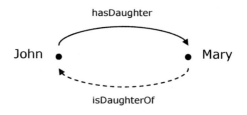

*Figure 7. Triple implied by a symmetric property*

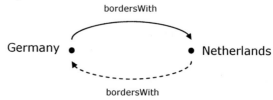

*Figure 8. Triple implied by a functional property*

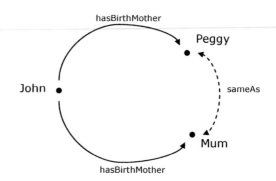

A property **P** is *transitive* if $(x \, \boldsymbol{P} \, y) \wedge (y \, \boldsymbol{P} \, z)$ $\Rightarrow x \, \boldsymbol{P} \, z$. For example, if **hasAncestor** is transitive then

$$(\textit{Mary \textbf{hasAncestor} John}) \wedge (\textit{John \textbf{hasAncestor}}$$
$$\textit{Peggy}) \Rightarrow \textit{Mary \textbf{hasAncestor} Peggy}$$

A property P is *reflexive* on a domain **D** if $x \in \boldsymbol{D} \Rightarrow x \, \boldsymbol{P} \, x$. For example, $\leq$ defined on the integers is reflexive.

## DIFFERENT REASONING TASKS

As we have seen, the formal definitions of classes, properties and individuals allow inferring new knowledge from knowledge that is already present. The basic inferences can be combined, and allow us to do more complex reasoning. It is useful to distinguish *property-*, *class-* and *individual-level* reasoning.

*Property-level reasoning* means inferring implied triples from the stated ones. This is a closure process that constructs the implied (dotted) triples. For example, for a transitive property we have to create the transitive closure of the graph defined by the triples with the transitive property as predicate.

*Class-level reasoning* means checking whether a class **B** is a subclass of class **A**. This reasoning task is called a *subsumption check*. In other words, subsumption is checking if the criteria for being member of class **B** imply the criteria for being member of class **A**. If **A** and **B** subsume each other they are *equivalent* and in particular have the same members. Checking class *satisfiablity* is a special case of subsumption reasoning. A class **C** is called unsatisfiable if $\boldsymbol{C} \subseteq \boldsymbol{Nothing}$, hence (since **Nothing** $\subseteq \boldsymbol{C}$ by definition), **C** is equivalent to **Nothing**, and cannot have any members. Conversely, we can check the subsumption $\boldsymbol{B} \subseteq \boldsymbol{A}$ by checking that the class $\boldsymbol{B} \cap \neg \boldsymbol{A}$ is unsatisfiable. If we construct the full subsumption graph of all classes in

*Figure 9. Triple implied by an inverse functional property*

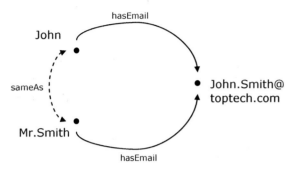

*Figure 10. Triple implied by a transitive property*

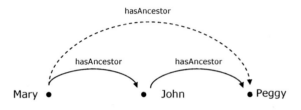

an ontology, we construct a *class hierarchy*. This reasoning task is called *classification*.

*Individual-level reasoning* means checking if an individual can exist in some model (called a *consistency check*) In particular if a class is unsatisfiable it cannot have a individual as a member. Thus to check if the class **C** is satisfiable, it suffices to check that there is no model with a member $x \in \boldsymbol{C}$.

A related task is to find the classes of which an individual is a member (called *realization*). Since the classes are partially ordered by subsumption we can in particular find the most specific class(es) to which an individual belongs which is *classification*. If we do this for only one class (which is a membership criterion !) and find all the known instances that provably belong to the class we say we *retrieve* its instances. Instance retrieval is of great practical importance because it allows a logical model to be used as a database. People have designed query languages to help formulating the membership criterion in convenient ways.

In the case study we will see some applications of the different reasoning tasks.

## Exercises

1.  Define **Man ≡ Human ∩ Male** as the intersection of **Human** and **Male**.

    (a) Suppose that **Boy ⊆ Human, Boy ⊆ Male** is a subclass of both **Human** and **Male**. Show that

    $$Boy \subseteq Man$$

    (b) Show that a necessary and sufficient condition for individuals to be of class **Man** is to be Human and Male:

    $$x \in Human \text{ and } x \in Male \Leftrightarrow$$
    $$x \in Man$$

    (c) Show that **Man** and **Woman** are disjoint classes if and only if

    **Man ∩ Woman ≡ Nothing**

2.  Define **Human ≡ Man ∪ Woman** as the union of **Man** and **Woman**.

    (a) Suppose that **Man ⊆ IntelligentBeing** and **Woman ⊆ IntelligentBeing**. Show that

    **Human ⊆ IntelligentBeing**

    (b) Show that a necessary and sufficient condition to be human is to be a **Man** or a **Woman**

    **(x ∈ Man) or (x ∈ Woman) ⇔ x ∈ Human**

3.  This exercise serves as a mild warning for the unintuitive way that the complement operator can work.

    (a) Define **Outdoor ≡ ¬ Indoor** as the complement of **Indoor**. Suppose that **Animal** and **Indoor** are disjoint. Show that

    **Animal ⊆ Outdoor**

    (b) Now redefine **Indoor ⊆ Space,** and **Outdoor ≡ ¬ Indoor ∩ Space** (i.e. the complement of Indoor in the class of Spaces). Assume that **Animal** is disjoint from **Space**. Show that **Animal** is disjoint from **Indoor** and **Outdoor**.

4.  Let **C** be a class and **p** a property. Show that

    $$\neg (\forall p.C) \equiv \exists p.(\neg C)$$

    Likewise show that

    $$\neg (\exists p.C) \equiv \forall p.(\neg C)$$

5.  Suppose **p** has domain **D**, and $C_1 \equiv \exists p.C_2$. Show that $C_1 \subseteq D$.

6.  Suppose the property **hasAncestor** is transitive. Suppose that we are given a number of triples with **hasAncestor** as predicate and a number of **People** $a_1 \dots a_n$ as subject and object. Consider the oriented graph on $a_1 \dots a_n$ with an arrow (oriented edge) from $a_i$ to $a_j$ if there is stated triple $a_i$ **hasAncestor** $a_j$. Show that the stated and implied triples span the transitive closure of the graph, that is the smallest oriented graph containing the original graph such that if two arrows lie head to tail, there is an arrow from the tail of the first to the head of the second.

## REASONING AS A PROCESS

To find the implications of a set of given logical statements we have to perform a process using an algorithm on a computer. We are thus immediately facing the core computer science problem of finding algorithms with low complexity in space and runtime. It is known that first order logic is in generally undecidable. Description logics have better decidability properties, and can be decided in polynomial time and space (Horrocks, & Patel-Schneider, 1999) and have some working reasoning implementations (see the section on reasoners). This seems to be one of the main reasons why description logic was chosen as a basis for the semantic Web (Horrocks, Patel-Schneider, & Harmelen, 2003), although this choice is certainly not uncontroversial even among its designers (Harmelen, 2002). One should not forget that while a provable complexity class is a good thing, it comes at the cost of expressivity and conceptual complexity.

Others have argued that description logic (and even first order logic) is insufficiently expressive for people to model their business logic, so that they will end up writing transformation rules in a language like the semantic Web rule language (Horrocks, Patel-Schneider, Boley, Tabet, Grosof, & Dean 2004). Since those have few decidability properties this defeats some of the purpose of basing on logic in the first place. Also note that very few computer programs in use are even provably terminating. There is something to be said to have a decidable declarative *data* model, even if the *information* model build on top of that data model undecidable. Rules of the type

condition(?x, ?y, ?z) $\Rightarrow$ consequence(?x, ?y, ?z),

are easier to understand for many people, even though the information model becomes effectively computational rather than declarative.

## The Tableau Algorithm

The tableau algorithm is a method to compute a model for a finite collection of description logic clauses or prove that such a model does not exist. As we have seen above, if we can compute a model we can check satisfiability, and therefore subsumption. An overview of techniques is given in (Baader Sattler, 2001). Here we explain only the simplest version, where we only have individuals, classes, membership ($x \in C$), property assertions ($x\,p\,y$), negation ($\neg$) conjunction ($\cap$), disjunction ($\cup$) existential restriction ($\exists p.C$) and universal restriction ($\forall p.C$). Using exercise 4 above (de Morgan's law) we can and will assume that assertion of negated classes only occurs before named classes.

Let $A_0$ be the original set of membership and property assertions (called the A-box). We can consider the A-box quite concretely as an oriented graph with two types of nodes individuals and classes, which include those defined as restrictions intersections unions or negations. The graph has oriented edges labeled with properties if they link individuals or the symbol $\in$ if they link an individual to a class.

Starting from $A_0$, the algorithm now recursively defines a tree of A-boxes with at most binary branches such that each branch has the same models in set theory or no model at all, and at each step the complexity in terms of the maximal number of conjunctions disjunctions and restrictions decreases to zero as we go down the tree.

To be precise the rules of the algorithm are to apply the following rules in any order

1.  If $A_n$ contains $x \in C_1 \cap C_2$ then let $A_{n+1} := A_n$ with $x \in C_1$ and $x \in C_2$ added provided the membership assertion does not exist already.
2.  If $A_n$ contains $x \in C_1 \cup C_2$ then let $A_{n+1}' := A_n$ with $x \in C_1$ added and $A_{n+1}''$ with $x \in C_2$ added provided the membership assertion does not exist already.
3.  If $A_n$ contains $x \in \exists p.C$ let $A_{n+1} := A_n$ with $x$ $p\,y$ and $y \in C$ for some new node $y$ added

provided the triple and the membership assertion do not exist already.

4. If $A_n$ contains $x \in \forall p.C$ and $x \ p \ y$ for some node $y$ then let $A_{n+1} := A_n$ with $y \in C$ added provided the membership assertion does not exist already.

If the application of each of the rules gives $A_{n+1} = A_n$ (or $A_{n+1}' = A_{n+1}'' = A_n$) the algorithm is terminated. The algorithm always terminates because the new nodes we introduce in the third $\exists$ rule has a membership to a class build up with strictly less quantifiers. It can therefore be applied only a finite number of times, after that we work with a fixed number of individuals to which we can apply rule 1, 2, 4 only a finite number of times.

The end result of the algorithm is that each leaf A-box of the tree is one of the following two types.

- Either the A-box contains both $x \in C$ and $x \in \neg C$ for some individual $x$ and it does not have an interpretation (i.e. we have a contradiction), or
- the set of individuals of the A-box (which we think of as a graph) including those constructed during the algorithm form a canonical domain for an interpretation, that is is a concrete set of "things" that satisfies the axioms. The interpretation of a class $C$ is the subset of individual nodes that have a membership link $x \in C$, the interpretation of a property $p$ is the subset of pairs of individual nodes $(x, y)$ connected by a link labeled by $p$.

The algorithm as presented may need exponential space an time. However refinements can be made to prune the tree and terminate the algorithm sooner that make the algorithm polynomial in space and time (Baader Sattler, 2001; Horrocks & Patel-Schneider, 1999).

## Reasoners

Unfortunately polynomial time does not mean it is easy to make a fast algorithm (Haarslev & Möller, 2004; Haarslev, Möller & Wessel, 2005; Horrocks, 2003). Practical reasoners implement variations and optimalisations of the above tableaux algorithm. An incomplete list of reasoners are the Fact/Fact++,[5] Pellet,[6] SWI prolog OWL library,[7] and the racer engine.[8] Most support DIG[9] (Bechhover, 2003), an interface to communicate between the reasoner and an application. A more complete list is maintained by Sattler[10] In addition to dedicated reasoners, triple databases such as Sesame[11] support some form of reasoning especially to satisfy queries that take an OWL (light) ontology into account (Kiryakov, Ognyanov, & Manov, 2005).

## CASE STUDY "RESOURCE DISCOVERY IN A BUILDING"

In this section we give an example of the use of OWL and description logic to represent the constraints in the subject domain model of an application, and show how reasoning is used to make use of these constraints. To do this, we typically define vocabularies grouped in an ontology to have a vocabulary for a particular domain and a knowledge base of "facts" to model a more specific situation. Together, the vocabularies and the knowledge base describe a formal model which may or may not be formally consistent. The more precise we model, the stricter the condition of consistency becomes. In practice, formal consistency is a very good thing, but it does *not* automatically mean the model is "correct," that is, captures reality sufficiently precise according to the consensus of the people who have to work with it. Formal *in*consistency however, strongly suggests that there is a misunderstanding, an improper modeling or that the model is pushed over its domain of applicability. The latter means that the underlying assumptions of the model are not valid for the case you want to apply it too. Thus the "correctness" here is like the correctness in the sense of the models used in physics or economics, while consistency is like the mathematical correctness of those physical or economical models. In practice this means that the designer of the vocabularies should have examples in mind to test his abstractions against, and that it is a good idea to document or specify the underlying assumptions. Also bear in mind that to illustrate various points we have made relatively complex constructions. More often than not, the main modeling problem is finding the right set of abstractions to describe the problem at hand.

## Scenario

We now consider a simple scenario. Suppose we want to create an application that supports users in discovering resources in a building (e.g., printers, beamers or coffee machines) and their own location for example to direct them to the closest printer.

What we need is a way to represent physical resources, and locations in buildings and being able to express where these resources are located. We also need to express that a resource is reachable from another location in a building. For this we set up several ontologies with the proper vocabulary that can be used generically, and a knowledge base for a particular building. For example, we could have

- An ontology with a vocabulary for physical entities and spatial temporal extension,
- An ontology with a vocabulary for representing spaces in buildings, locating physical resources in space, accessibility of spaces and various constraints that reflect the way spaces in buildings work,
- An ontology with a vocabulary for representing the physical resources (at least the ones we are interested in),

- A knowledge base with facts (or claims) describing the building we are interested in, the concrete physical resources in the building and where they are located. In a realistic scenario such a knowledge base might well be split up and maintained by different people.

The first ontology is a (basically trivial) foundational vocabulary for space and physical extension of physical entities. It provides names for the concept of space, and physical entity in the resource- and building ontology. The vocabulary for spaces in buildings names corridors, rooms, stairs, doors and floors and introduces the notion of accessibility. It allows us to make a schematic combinatorial description of a building similar to the schematic map of a subway system. If we wanted to, we could be more precise: we might want to introduce vocabulary for saying that rooms are adjacent on a corridor allowing us to define more elaborate combinatorial models of room. One could even introduce vocabulary for defining the precise shape of the room, or to link it to particular part of a drawing or a cad-cam model. However this is not needed for a textbook example. Given a vocabulary we need to make a model of a particular building, in this case a hypothetical and very simple one. Stating facts about a particular building has a different status then defining a vocabulary, so we call it, for lack of a better name, a knowledge base rather than an ontology. The resource vocabulary introduces vocabulary to describe physical resources, for example the class of beamers, printers and wireless access points. If we want to, we can introduce properties like the brand, serial id, or resolution for printers and beamers and access range for access points but we only introduce what we use for our modest purposes. Finally we need a knowledge base for resources that exist in our hypothetical building.

We now make some concrete OWL ontologies. One would normally use a tool such as Protégé[12] or Triple20[13] for such a task, but this not suitable for a book. Because it is close to the logical notation used in the previous section, much easier to understand, much shorter than the XML notation and actually useful in practice, we use the OWL/turtle notation (Beckett, 2004), a subset of N3 (Berners & Lee, 2000) equivalent to the XML notation. If convenient we will also use the logical language in the previous section. We first introduce four (invented) namespaces

```
@prefix space:
<http://www.example.org/ontologies/space#>.

@prefix building:
<http://www.example.org/ontologies/building#>.

@prefix resource:
<http://www.example.org/ontologies/resource#>.

@prefix our:
<http://www.example.org/knowledgebase/weRus#>.
```

We also use the conventional abbreviations of the system namespaces for the RDF/RDFS/OWL language.

```
@prefix rdfs:
<http://www.w3.org/2000/01/rdf-schema#>.

@prefix rdf:
<http://www.w3.org/1999/02/22-rdf-syntax-ns#>.

@prefix owl:
<http://www.w3.org/2002/07/owl#>.

@prefix owlx:
<http://www.w3.lab/work-in-progress/owl/1.1#>.
```

Note that OWL1.1[14] will support reflexive properties.

## The Space and Physical Entity Ontology

Physics has a lot of interesting things to say about space-time and physical entities, but we are not trying to tread in Albert Einstein's step here. We introduce space:Space and space:PhyicalEntity as classes, defined axiomatically. We do not know *a priori* which instances these classes have, although of course, we have an intent with them, informally suggested by the name.

```
space:Space a owl:Class.
space:PhysicalEntity a owl:Class.

space:hasExtension a owl:ObjectProperty;
 owl:inverseOf space:IsExtensionOf;
 rdfs:domain space:PhysicalEntity;
 rdfs:range space:Space.
```

We also want to able to say that a space X is contained in another space Y. Probably the most important fact about the "contained" relation is that it is a transitive relation: if X is contained in Y and Y is contained in Z then X is contained in Z. It is also a reflexive relation: each space X is contained in itself. Containment is not the only relation of geometric importance. For example, two spaces X and Y can meet, which means there is a space Z contained in both X and Y. In a realistic foundational geometric ontology it might also be useful to introduce more special notions such as distances or (more special still) coordinates, but we will not need them. We model the notion of spaces being contained in each other as a transitive, reflexive property space:contains.

```
space:contains a owl:TransitiveProperty,
                owlx:ReflexiveProperty;
 owl:inverseOf space:isContainedIn;
 rdfs:domain space:Space;
 rdfs:range space:Space.
space:sameSpaceAs rdfs:subPropertyOf space:contains,
space:isContainedIn.

space:sameSpaceAs a owl:SymmetricProperty,
                owl:TransitiveProperty,
                owlx:ReflexiveProperty;
 rdfs:subPropertyOf owl:sameAs;
 rdfs:domain Space;
 rdfs:range Space.

space:Space rdfs:subClassOf [ a owl:Restriction;
        owl:onProperty space:sameSpaceAs;
        owl:cardinality 1].
```

## Exercise

7. Following (Mindswap 2003,[15] example 9), show that

space:sameSpaceAs a owlx:ReflexiveProperty.
space:contains a owlx:ReflexiveProperty.

are redundant, that is the rest of the axioms force space:contains and space:sameSpaceAs to be reflexive.

## The Building Ontology

The building ontology is less abstract. To have something to play with we define concrete spaces like rooms and corridors contained in a building. To express "being indoor" we define the class building:Indoor as an abstract restriction defined by the condition of being contained in a building.

***Indoor*** $\equiv \exists$ ***isContainedIn.Building***

Note (cf. exercise 5) that necessarily ***Indoor*** $\subseteq$ ***Space*** because the domain of space:isContainedIn is space:Space.

We use the subclass mechanism to ensure that every room corridor, etc is an indoor space.

building:Building a owl:Class;
 rdfs:subClassOf space:Space.

building:Indoor a owl:Restriction;
 owl:onProperty space:isContainedIn;
 owl:someValueFrom building:Building.

building:Corridor a owl:Class;
 rdfs:subClassOf space:Space, building:Indoor.

building:Stair a owl:Class;
 rdfs:subClassOf space:Space, building:Indoor.

building:Room a owl:Class;
 rdfs:subClassOf space:Space, building:Indoor.

# Something we want to play with
building:PrinterRoom a owl:Class;
 rdfs:subClassOf building:Room, building:PrinterInside.

We can give building:PrinterInside a formal definition that captures the intent: something (in fact a space) that contains the spatial extension of a Printer.

***PrinterInside*** $\equiv$
 $\exists$ ***contains*** . $\exists$ ***isExtensionOf*** . ***Printer***

In OWL/turtle this becomes

building:PrinterInside a owl:Restriction;
 owl:onProperty space:contains;
 owl:someValueFrom [a owl:Restriction;
     owl:onProperty space:isExtensionOf;
     owl:someValueFrom resource:Printer ].

## Accessibility

For our purposes it suffices that we can say that a corridor gives access to rooms and a flight of stairs, we only express accessibility of rooms and other indoor spaces. Although not quite true, we will assume for simplicity that accessibility is symmetric: if room A is accessible from corridor B, then corridor B is accessible from room A (lock yourself out and see why this is only an approximation). Moreover we distinguish two kinds of accessibility: direct physical accessibility where, for example, a room is on a corridor, and logical accessibility where you have to go from a room to a directly accessible corridor and from the corridor to the directly accessible stairs and so forth until you can finally have physical access to another room. Direct accessibility implies logical accessibility, and logical accessibility is transitive: if we can get from A to B and from B to C, we can get from A to C. Note that unlike logical accessibility, direct accessibility is readily observable for somebody walking through the building.

building:accessTo a owl:TransitiveProperty,
                owl:SymmetricProperty;
 rdfs:domain building:Indoor;
 rdfs:range building:Indoor.

building:directAccessTo a owl:SymmetricProperty;
rdfs:subPropertyOf accessTo;
rdfs:domain building:Indoor;
rdfs:range building:Indoor.

## The Resource Ontology

Our resource ontology is simple, because we only have printers and wireless access points, and we do not want to say much about them. A wireless access point has an access range (which we model as a space) where we have a good signal. In practice we need to be more precise by what we mean with "good", for example, by specifying the average signal strength, but we just assume that we are either in or out of the access range. Given the access point, this range is unique so resource:hasAccessRange is at most single valued that is it is a functional property. Conversely, we assume that the access range can be used to find the unique wireless access point it belongs to. In practice this is true because access points broadcast a unique identifier of themselves (their SSID) so that, effectively, an access range is not just a space but a space that comes labeled with the name of the access point. Therefore we define resource:hasAccessRange as an owl:InverseFunction-

alProperty, which we recall means by definition that its inverse, resource:isAccessRangeOf, is a functional property.

resource:Printer a owl:Class;
rdfs:subClassOf space:PhysicalEntity.

resource:WirelessAccesPoint a Class;
rdfs:subClassOf space:PhysicalEntity.

resource:AccessRange rdfs:subClassOf space:Space.

resource:hasAccessRange a owl:ObjectProperty,
                        owl:FunctionalProperty,
                        owl:inverseFunctionalProperty;
owl:inverseOf isAccessRangeOf;
rdfs:domain WirelessAccessPoint;
rdfs:range resource:AccessRange.

## The Knowledge Base (Open World Version)

We create a straight forward knowledge base for a hypothetical building containing a printer and two wireless access points.

We will see later that for some applications it is useful to strengthen the knowledge base for reasons that have to do with the difference between the *open* and *the closed world assumption*. Our first version is subject to the open world

*Figure 11. Ground plan of the hypothetical building*

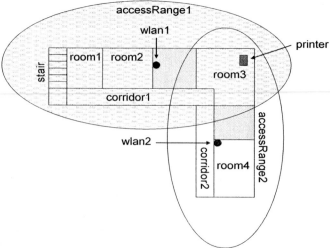
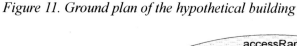

assumption, which here means the following. In the knowledge base we state the existence of a building, our:building. This is a building we *know* of and will be our domain of discourse. Of course we do not want to claim that this is the only building that exists, will ever exist or could exist. We also state the existence of certain rooms and corridors. Actually we will make an exhaustive list of public spaces in our building, but *in the open world version, it is not made explicit that the list is exhaustive.*

```
our:Corridor a owl:Class;
  rdfs:subClassOf building:Corridor.

our:Stair a owl:Class;
  rdfs:subClassOf building:Stair.

our:Room a owl:Class;
  rdfs:subClassOf building:Room.

our:PublicSpace a owl:Class;
  owl:oneOf(our:Corridor our:Stair our:Room).

our:building a building:Building;
 space:contains
  our:corridor1, our:corridor2, our:stair,
  our:room1,our:room2,our:room3,our:room4.

our:corridor1 a our:Corridor.
...

our:room4 a our:Room;
```

We also state facts about accessibility. These are the facts that *we know of,* or at least bothered to state. The reader is advised to check with Figure 11. Other accessibilities may also exist, in conformance with the open world assumption:

```
our:corridor1 building:directAccessTo
  our:room1, our:room2, our:room3, our:stairs,
  our:corridor2.

our:corridor2 building:directAccessTo
  our:room4.
```

Finally we introduce some equipment and a few facts about these bits of equipment. Again these are facts that we know of.

*Figure 12. Graph for the symmetric directAccessTo property*

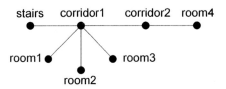

```
our:prn a resource:Printer;
  space:hasExtension our:prnExtension.

our:prnExtension a space:Space;
  space:isContainedIn our:room3.

our:wlan1 a resource:WirelessAccessPoint;
  resource:hasAccessRange our:accessRange1

our:wlan2 a resource:WirelessAccessPoint;
  resource:hasAccessRange our:accessRange2.

# We will make this more precise later !
our:accessRange1 a space:Space;
  space:contains our:corridor1, our:room1, our:room2,
our:room3.

our:accessRange2 a space:Space;
  space:contains our:corridor2, our:room3, our:room4.
```

## REASONING ABOUT THE KNOWLEDGE BASE AND THE ONTOLOGIES

As we have seen, the vocabularies we have defined encode some of the physical properties of buildings, printers and access points. We are now in a position to argue about these properties for our particular building, and we will see that they reflect reality.

### Consistency

The first question is whether our ontologies and the knowledge base are consistent with each other. We have only put one non trivial restriction in our vocabulary. For example because

$$Indoor \equiv \exists\ isContainedIn.Building$$
$$Room \subseteq Indoor$$

every room that we define must be contained in a resource:Building. Indeed for all the defined rooms corridors and stairs in the Knowledge base there is a triple asserting that they are contained in our: building , and our:building is a building:Building.

## Accessibility

The properties we have defined allow us to reason about the accessibility of spaces inside the building. Remember that we have stated accessibility from a physical point of view, in fact by stating which rooms are accessible from which corridors. On the other hand consider an application that informs a user of the status of a printer. We might then want to show the user the printers that are logically accessible from the user's terminal only. The data we have available, allow us to determine the logical accessibility from a given room to say our:room2. More precisely, we can find the rooms that are *known* to contain a printer and that are *known* to be accessible from our:room2. If there happens to be another printer but the system administrator did not make this knowledge available, then there is nothing we can do about it. The above is a retrieval task that we can formulate as follows: find all *known* instances ?prn, ?prnRoom such that

1.  ?prn a resource:Printer.
2.  ?prn space:hasExtension ?prnExtension.
3.  ?prnRoom a our:Room.
4.  ?prnRoom space:contains ?prnExtension.
5.  ?prnRoom building:accessTo our:room2.

for some (space) ?prnExtension. Let us analyse the query line by line

Line 1: This line states that the free variable ?prn is a resource:Printer. There are the following ways an instance can be implicitly declared a resource: Printer

There is an instance declared a resource:Printer,
There is an instance declared a *X* , where *X* is declared a subclass or an equivalent class of resource:Printer
There is an instance declared a *Y*, where *Y* is declared a subclass or an equivalent class of *X*
…..
There is a triple with a property that has domain or range a subclass of resource:Printer

In fact strictly speaking we also have to keep track of all the subproperties of rdf:type, and rdfs: subClassOf, but we will not have these here. We can check these conditions immediately from the knowledge base. For a reasoner checking the condition means that we have to walk an oriented graph of rdfs:subClassOf and owl:equivalentClass relations, and check all the triples involving a property with one of those subclasses as domain or range. Here we are lucky: the class resource: Printer does not have a subclass and there is no known property with domain or range resource: Printer. Thus we only find the explicitly declared instance our:prn:

```
?prn →
 our:prn # possibilities after line 1
```

Line 2: This line states that in the dots and arrows diagram there exists an implicit or explicit space: hasExtension arrow (predicate) from ?prn (subject), to a to be determined instance ?prnExtension (object). We find one explicit triple involving space: hasExtension with our:prn as a subject:

```
our:prn space:hasExtension our:prnExtension
```

To also find all the implicit statements we also have to check:

all statements involving the inverse space:isExtensionOf of space:hasExtension

all statements involving a subproperty *P* of space: hasExtension or space:isExtensionOf

all statements involving a subproperty **R** of **P**
.........

There are no subproperties of space:hasExtension and space:isExtensionOf. We already know the possibilities for ?prn. We check that there is no other statement with space:isExtensionOf as predicate and our:prn as object. Thus after line 2 the only possibility is:

(?prn ?prnExtension ) →
 (our:prn our:prnExtension)

Line3: Arguing just like we did for line 1 we come to the conclusion that the possibilities are:

(?prn ?prnExtension ?prnRoom ) →
 (our:prn our:prnExtension our:room1)
 (our:prn our:prnExtension our:room2)
 (our:prn our:prnExtension our:room3)
 (our:prn our:prnExtension our:room4)

Note that this example is a bit degenerate because the first two entries are always the same. In general, in listing possibilities we have to take combinations into account because only certain combinations may be possible.

Line 4: Here we demand the existence of an implicit or explicit statement with the property space:contains with a possibility for ?prnRoom as subject and a possibility for ?prnExtension as object. Like in line 2 we also have to take into account:

The inverse property space:isContainedIn of space:contains.
The (recursive) subproperties of space:contains and space:isContainedIn

The only such subproperty is space:sameSpaceAs. The only triples with sameSpaceAs are implied triples from a space to itself forced by reflexiveness, but there is no statement making a possibility for ?prnroom space:sameSpaceAs

with a possibility for **?prnExtension**. Checking the possibilities we do find a statement:

our:prnExtension space:isContainedIn our:room3.

Thus we conclude after line 4 we have the possibilities:

(?prn ?prnExtension ?prnRoom) →
 (our:prn our:prnExtension our:room3)

Line 5: Finally we have to check in the dots and arrow diagram the existence of an implicit or explicit building:accessTo property arrow between a candidate for ?prnRoom (i.e. our:room3) and our:room2. Since the property building:accessTo is declared a transitive property we have to check that there is a path of building:accessTo property arrows starting at our:room3 and ending at our:room2. Each of those arrows in the path can be either explicit or implicit. Since building:accessTo is symmetric it is its own inverse so we have to check

The explicit or implicit (recursive) subproperties of building:accessTo

We find a symmetric subproperty building:directAccessTo with no further subproperties. In our knowledge base (or for us humans in Figure 11 or Figure 12) we find a path of building:directAccessTo, hence of building:AccessTo, arrows between our:room3 and our:room2 and we conclude that:

(?prn ?prnExtension ?prnRoom) →
 (our:prn our:prnExtension our:room3)

This is the final answer.

What we learn from this example is that satisfying a simple query can involve a considerable amount of computation. However the cost of that computation is set off by the possibility of having a concise, yet precise, formulation of our model. In particular, while it would be easy in practice for a human to set up a direct accessibility database, it would be non trivial to fill the database for logical accessibility. Thus if we would have used say a relational database with direct accessibility data, we would need a program to compute logical accessibility to satisfy the same query. Therefore we would have to pay a computational price as well (a well written special purpose program may of course well be more efficient). However the main benefit is that we have now made the notion of logical accessibility, which is close to the problem domain, an explicit part of the information model and abstracted it from an implementation. This makes it a lot easier to reuse and maintain for other purposes.

## Signal Strength and Location

Another task is to reason about our possible whereabouts. Suppose we are carrying a device that can access wireless LAN. Suppose we know the device is in the access range from both the our:wlan1 and the our:wlan2 access points (or more precisely the physical devices corresponding to these logical entities). What can we say about our location? The naive approach would be to formulate the problem as a query, in the same way as we did before.

```
?here a space:Space,
?here space:isContainedIn ?AR1, ?AR2,
our:wlan1 resource:hasAccessRange ?AR1,
our:wlan2 resource:hasAccessRange ?AR2 .
```

However, such formulation assumes that we have spaces in our database that *exactly* match the query. We have a limited number of spaces (rooms corridors accessranges) in the database, and a portable device is much smaller than a room or a corridor. Thus the way we set up or knowledge base, there is no chance that we find the exact space taken up by the device. What we can do is formulate our whereabouts as class of possibilities and see if we can restrict this class properly. Our data has a precision of whole rooms.

Thus from the data we have, we can tell *at best* in which room we are located. More generally we may hope to tell that we are located in a subset of rooms. Instead of formulating a query for the possible public spaces we could be in, let us this time formulate the problem in terms of classes that we "temporarily" add to the knowledge base, and that we want to reason about. In fact our knowledge has indeed grown by the use of our device. Let us suppose in addition to the above that we know *a priori* that we are inside a PublicSpace in the building. What we can now do is formulate the conditions we have as restrictions.

*PossiblePublicSpace* ≡ *PublicSpace* ∩
$\qquad$ ∃*contains.PossibleHere*
*PossibleHere* ≡ *Space* ∩ ∃*isContainedIn.*(
∋*isAccessRangeOf.wlan1*) ∩ ∃*isContainedIn*
(∋*isAccessRangeOf.wlan2*)

Actually, we can use the knowledge base to simplify the notation a bit. Since isAccessRangeOf is an inverse functional property (its inverse hasAccessRange is a functional property) we see that

∋*isAccessRangeOf.wlan1* ≡ {*accessRange1*}

So we can reformulate

*PossibleHere* ≡ *Space* ∩ ∋*isContainedIn.acess-Range1* ∩ ∋*isContainedIn.acessRange2*

In the somewhat unwieldy OWL/turtle we introduce some names for the conditions corresponding to the restrictions. It then becomes

```
:PossibleHere a owl:Class;
owl:intersection(:Space :FullyInAccessRange1 FullyInAccessRange2).

:PossiblePublicSpace a owl:Class;
  owl:intersectionOf(:PublicSpace :ContainsPossibleHere).
```

```
:FullyinAccessRange1 a owl:Restriction;
  owl:onProperty space:isContainedIn;
  owl:someValue our:accessRange1.

:FullyInAccessRange2 a owl:Restriction;
  owl:onProperty space:isContainedIn;
  owl:someValue our:accessRange2.

:ContainsPossibleHere a owl:Restriction;
  owl:onProperty space:contains;
  owl:someValueFrom :PossibleHere.
```

Now we have *defined* our possible whereabouts and the possible public spaces.

We finally add one fact (as we know from the device): the *existence* of a space

```
device:here a :Space;
  space:isContainedIn our:AccessRange1;
  space:isContainedIn our:AccessRange2.
```

We can now query for the *known* possible public spaces

```
?pub a :PossiblePublicSpace.
```

If we unravel the definition of the restrictions we see that it means finding the *known* instances that are satisfying the following conditions

1.  ?pub a our:PublicSpace;
2.  ?pub space:contains ?x.
3.  ?x a space:Space;
4.  ?x space:isContainedIn our:AccessRange1;
5.  ?x space:isContainedIn our:AccessRange2.

What we really have been doing is change our original query in a definition! Note that the facts about here are added to the knowledge base by the device.

The *known* public spaces are

```
?pub →
 ( our:stairs our:room1 our:room2
   our:room3 our:room4 our:corridor1
   our:corridor2
 )
```

The spaces they contain are themselves (from reflexivity) and the printer extension for room3

```
(?pub ?x)  →
 (our:stairs our:stairs)
 (our:room1 our:room1)
 (our:room2 our:room2)
 (our:room3 our:room3)
 (our:room3 our:prnExtension)
 (our:room4 our:room4)
 (our:corridor1 our:corridor1)
 (our:corridor2 our:corridor2)
```

Using transitivity and the inverse isContainedIn of contains we check from the knowledge base that if ?x is contained in accessRange1 we are left with

```
(?pub ?x)  →
  (our:stairs our:stairs)
  (our:room1 our:room1)
  (our:room2 our:room2)
  (our:room3 our:room3)
  (our:room3 our:prnExtension)
  (our:corridor1 our:corridor1)
```

And if ?x is also contained in accessRange2 this leaves

```
(?pub ?x)  →
 (our:room3 our:room3)
 (our:room3 our:prnExtension)
```

Thus the only *known* public space that *we can check* satisfies our query is our:room3.

It is true that we can *we can check* that our: room3 satisfies the query, what is not true is that our:room3 is the *only logically possible* such public space. In fact, it is not logically *impossible* that our:stairs is contained in accessrange2, it is just *unknown*. If we look at the ground plan (Figure 11), we see that it is not contained, but, we have not stated this in the knowledge base, it is also *unknown*. In fact, a further glimpse at the ground plan shows that part of corridor1 and corridor2 are also contained in accessrange1 and accessrange2. We also note grey areas that are not mentioned in the knowledge base. Thus they are not known to be public spaces or off limits. Finally it is not *known* (or at least not asserted) that our device is contained in accessrange1 and accessrange2 and no other accessranges (this would be especially important in case the device would be in only one access range).

## A Tightened Knowledge Base (Closed World Assumption)

If we want to strengthen our conclusions we must state stronger facts in our knowledge base, namely that the public spaces contained in accessRange1 are *exactly* room2, room3, corridor1. Note that this extra information would be readily available in practice by walking around with a wireless device. Thus we give a characterization as a definition and as an explicit enumeration:

*PublicSpaceFullyInAccessRange1*
$\equiv$ *PublicSpace* $\cap$
$\ni isContainedIn$.*accessRange1*
$\equiv$ {*room2, room3, corridor1*}

Moreover we have noticed that we also need information about public spaces that overlap with accessranges. Every space contained in an access range contains a space contained in the access range, namely itself (by reflexivity of space:contains), we only need to add the extra spaces. For example, for access range2:

*PublicSpaceSomePartInAccessRange2*
$\equiv$ *PublicSpace* $\cap \exists contains.\ni isContainedIn.$
*accessRange1*
$\equiv$ *PublicSpaceFullyInAccessRange2* $\cup$
{*corridor1, corridor2*}

Finally, we want to say which access ranges a device is in

*AccessRangeContainingDevice* $\equiv$ *AccessRange*
$\cap \ni contains.here$
$\equiv$ {*accessRange1, accessRange2*}

In OWL/turtle this becomes:

```
our:PublicSpaceFullyInAccessRange1 a owl:Class;
 owl:intersectionOf(our:PublicSpace
 :FullyInAccessRange1);
 owl:oneOf(our:room2 our:room3 our:corridor1).

:SomePartInAccessRange1 a owl:Restriction;
 owl:onProperty space:contains;
 owl:someValueFrom :FullyInAccessRange1.
# Similar for AccessRange2

# Provide an explicit and implicit definition of public
spaces
# partly in range
our:PublicSpaceSomePartInAccessRange1 a owl:
Class;
 owl:intersectionOf( our:PublicSpace  :SomePartInAc-
cessRange1);
 owl:unionOf(owl:PublicSpaceFullyInAccessRange1
   [a owl:Class; owl:oneOf(corridor2)])

our:PublicSpaceSomePartInAccessRange2 a owl:
Class;
 owl:intersectionOf( our:PublicSpace  :SomePartInAc-
cessRange2);
 owl:unionOf(:PublicSpaceFullyInAccessRange2
   [a owl:Class; owl:oneOf(corridor1)]).

our:AccessRange a owl:Class;
 rdfs:subClassOf resource:AccessRange;
 owl:oneOf(our:accessRange1 our:accessRange2).

device:AccessRangeContainingDevice a owl:Class
 owl:intersection(resource:AccessRange
   [a owl:Restriction;
    owl:onProperty space:contains;
    owl:someValue device:here ]);
owl:oneOf(our:accessRange1 our:accessRange2)). #fact
from device
```

## Stronger Results from Stronger Assumptions

With the additional information available we can pin down the set unknown public space much better. We claim that:

*PossiblePublicSpace*
$\equiv$ {*room3, corridor1, corridor2*}

Indeed as we have seen on the ground plan this is the "correct" answer, because in each of these public spaces there is part where we have access to both wireless access points..

Let us do the formal argument. From the definition of **PossiblePublicSpace** we see that:

**PossiblePublicSpace**
   ⊆ (**PublicSpace** ∩
   ∃**contains**.∋**isContainedIn**.*accessRange1*)
   ≡   **PublicSpaceSomePartInAccess-**
**Range1**

with a similar statement for accessRange2. We conclude that:

**PossiblePublicSpace**
   ⊆ **PublicSpaceSomePartInAccessRange1**
   ∩   **PublicSpaceSomePartInAccess-**
**Range2**

We now just enumerate both classes on the right hand side and take the intersection. We conclude that:

**PossiblePublicSpace**
   ⊆ {*room3, corridor1, corridor2*}

On the other hand each of our:room3, our:corridor1 and our:corridor2 can be classified as an our:PossiblePublicSpace.

What we learn from this example is the usefulness of stating a formal definition of a class in terms of the conditions that members must satisfy, independent of whether we know such individuals exist, but that it is also useful to have precise information available about a full list of possibilities, that is what is true and what is *not* true.

## Exercise

8. Show that given the tightened Knowledge base if a device is in a PublicSpace and in access-range1 only, we can conclude that the (extension of) the device is contained in the stairs, room1 or room2.

## CONCLUSION

Description logic is a knowledge representation that has well understood algorithms for reasoning with them and existing implementations. Expressive description logics have been used as the basis for the OWL Ontology Web Language that has been accepted as a W3C recommendation. However the last word on the viability of description logic as a practical tool has not been said. In particular rule languages such as the SWRL (Semantic Web Rule Language) have been defined that are solving some reasonably obvious reasoning problems at the cost of decidability.

A good reason for using a logic language to represent an information model is to make explicit various assumptions by explicitly building them into a formal declarative model rather than as part of a procedural computer program that uses data. This sometimes requires some thinking but often we merely want to define a model with dots and arrows that is close to what things are, rather than how one would represent them in a computer. It is then useful to be able to define classes and properties from other classes and properties and more generally define the relationship between them. However this requires an algorithm to compute the implications that are implicit in the logical model. Practical reasoners to determine these implications vary from extensions to (triple) databases that efficiently deal with a limited set of reasoning tasks, to reasoners that can deal with more complex inferences at the cost of efficiency.

While using reasoners we find the important distinction between the open and closed world assumption. This reflects the important distinction between knowing all things with a certain property, and knowing the existence of things with a certain property. We gave an extensive example that emphasized the importance of proper modeling next to proper reasoning and showed how the difference between the open and closed world assumption can drastically change the results.

# REFERENCES

Baader, F., & Sattler, U. (2001). An overview of tableau algorithms. *Studia Logica, 69*(1). Springer. Retrieved October 18, 2001, from http://www.cs.man.ac.uk/~franconi/dl/course/articles/baader-tableaux.ps.gz

Bechhofer, S. (2003). The DIG Description Logic Interface: DIG/1.1. In *Proceedings of DL2003 Workshop,* Rome, Italy. Retrieved October 18, 2006, from http://dl-Web.man.ac.uk/dig/2003/02/interface.pdf

Beckett, D. (2004). *Turtle - Terse RDF triple language.* Retrieved October 18, 2006, from http://www.dajobe.org/2004/01/turtle/

Berners Lee, T. (2000) *Primer: Getting into RDF & Semantic Web using N3.* Retrieved October 18, 2006, from http://www.w3.org/2000/10/swap/Primer

Calvanese, D., McGuinness, D., Nardi, D., & Patel-Schneider, P. (2003). *The description logic handbook: Theory, implementation and applications.* Cambridge University Press. Retrieved October 18, 2006, from http://www.cambridge.org/uk/catalogue/catalogue.asp?isbn=0521781760

Dean, M., Schreiber, G. (Eds.), Bechhofer, S., van Harmelen, F., Hendler, J., Horrocks, I., McGuinness, D.L., Patel-Schneider, P.F., & Stein, L.A. (2004). *OWL Web Ontology Language Reference*, W3C Recommendation 10 February 2004. Retrieved October 18, 2006, from http://www.w3.org/TR/owl-ref/

Franconi, E. (2002). *Description logics tutorial course description.* Retrieved October 18, 2006, from http://www.inf.unibz.it/~franconi/dl/course/

Haarslev, V. & Möller, R. (2004, June 2-4). Optimization techniques for retrieving resources described in OWL/RDF documents: First results. In *Proceedings of the Ninth International Conference on Knowledge Representation and Reasoning*, Whistler, Canada. Retrieved October 18, 2006, from http://www.cs.concordia.ca/~haarslev/publications/KR2004.pdf

Haarslev, V., Möller, R., & Wessel, M. (2005). On the scalability of description logic instance retrieval. Retrieved October 18, 2006, from http://www.sts.tu-harburg.de/~r.f.moeller/racer/HaMW05.pdf

Harmelen, F. (2002, March-April). *The complexity of the Web ontology language.* IEEE Intelligent Systems, 17. Retrieved October 18, 2006, from http://www.cs.vu.nl/~frankh/postscript/IEEE-IS02.pdf

Horridge, M., Knublauch, H., Rector, A., Stevens, R., & Wroe, C. (2004, August 27). *A practical guide to building OWL ontologies using the Protégé-OWL Plugin and CO-ODE Tools Edition 1.0*, Manchester University. Retrieved October 18, 2006, from http://www.co-ode.org/resources/tutorials/ProtegeOWLTutorial.pdf

Horrocks, I. (2003). *Description Logic reasoning.* Tutorial given in Innsbruck. Retrieved October 18, 2006, from http://www.cs.man.ac.uk/~horrocks/Slides/Innsbruck-tutorial/pt3-dlreasoning.pdf

Horrocks, I., & Patel-Schneider, P.F. (1999). Optimising Description Logic Subsumption. *Journal of Logic and Computation, 9*(3), 267-293. Retrieved October 18, 2006, from http://www.cs.man.ac.uk/~horrocks/Publications/download/1999/090267.pdf

Horrocks, I., Patel-Schneider, P.F., Boley, H., Tabet, S. Grosof, B., & Dean, M. (2004). *SWRL: A semantic Web Rule Language Combining OWL and RuleML.* Submission to W3C. Retrieved October 18, 2006, from http://www.w3.org/Submission/SWRL/

Horrocks, I., Patel-Schneider, P.F., & Harmelen, F. (2003). From SHIQ and RDF to OWL: The making of a Web ontology language. *Journal of*

*Websemantics*. Retrieved October 18, 2006, from http://www.cs.man.ac.uk/~horrocks/Publications/download/2003/HoPH03a.pdf

Kiryakov, A., Ognyanov, D., & Manov, D. (2005, November). *OWLIM–a Pragmatic Semantic Repository for OWL*. Paper presented at the International Workshop on Scalable Semantic Web Knowledge Base Systems, New York. Retrieved October 18, 2006, from http://dip.semanticWeb.org/documents/Kiryakov-OWLIM-a-Pragmatic-Semantic-Repository-for-OWL.pdf

Mindswap. (2003). *Pellet demo*. Retrieved October 18, 2006, from http://www.mindswap.org/2003/pellet/demo.shtml

## ENDNOTES

[1]    http://www.w3.org/RDF/

[2]    http://www.inf.unibz.it/~franconi/dl/course/

[3]    http://protege.stanford.edu/

[4]    http://www.swi-prolog.org/packages/Triple20/

[5]    http://owl.man.ac.uk/factplusplus/

[6]    http://www.mindswap.org/2003/pellet/

[7]    http://www.swi-prolog.org/packages/semWeb.html see also http://www.semanticWeb.gr/TheaOWLLib/

[8]    http://www.sts.tu-harburg.de/~r.f.moeller/racer/

[9]    http://dig.sourceforge.net/

[10]    http://www.cs.man.ac.uk/~sattler/reasoners.html

[11]    http://www.openrdf.org/

[12]    http://protege.stanford.edu/

[13]    http://www.swi-prolog.org/packages/Triple20/

[14]    http://owl1_1.cs.manchester.ac.uk/

[15]    http://www.mindswap.org/2003/pellet/demo.shtml

# Chapter VII
# Introduction to Web Services

**Cary Pennington**
*University of Georgia, USA*

**Jorge Cardoso**
*University of Madeira, Portugal*

**John A. Miller**
*University of Georgia, USA*

**Richard Scott Patterson**
*University of Georgia, USA*

**Ivan Vasquez**
*University of Georgia, USA*

## ABSTRACT

*This chapter introduces the theory and design principles behind Web Service technology. It explains the models, specifications, and uses of this technology as a means to allow heterogeneous systems to work together to achieve a task. Furthermore, the authors hope that this chapter will provide sufficient background information along with information about current areas of research in the area of Web Services that readers will come away with an understanding of how this technology works and ways that it could be implemented and used.*

## INTRODUCTION

As the World-Wide Web (WWW) exploded into the lives of the public in the 1990s, people suddenly had vast amounts of information placed at their fingertips. The system was developed to allow information sharing within internationally dispersed working groups. The original WWW consisted of documents (i.e., Web pages) and links between documents. The initial idea of the WWW was to develop a universal information database to publish information that could be accessed in a reliable and simple way by consumers. The information would not only be accessible to users around the world, but information would be linked so that it could be easily browsed and quickly found by users. Organizations soon realized the importance of this technology to manage, organize, and distribute their internal data and information to customers and partners.

As organizations started to implement business-to-customer and e-commerce solutions, they realized that the initial technologies associated with the WWW were not sufficient to sell products over the Internet. Additional functionality was required to guarantee that transactions were conducted in a secure way. To this end, SSL (Secure Sockets Layer), a protocol defined by Netscape, was developed for transmitting private documents via the Internet. Using SSL, organizations were able to implement a solution to obtain confidential user information, such as credit card numbers.

With globalization, organizations were progressively undertaking mergers and acquisitions. This has created organizations with an IT environment composed of disparate legacy systems, applications, processes, and data sources. In order to meet increasing customer and business partner expectations for real-time information, organizations were required to link their heterogeneous, autonomous and distributed systems to improve productivity and efficiency. This important requirement led to the development and deployment of EAI (enterprise application integration)

solutions. EAI platforms were used for integrating incompatible and distributed systems such as ERP (enterprise resource planning), CRM (customer relationship management), SCM (supply chain management), databases, data sources, data warehouses, and other important internal systems across the corporate enterprise. While useful, most EAI frameworks required costly and proprietary protocols and formats, which presented many technical difficulties when it was needed to integrate internal systems with external systems running on partners' computers.

The limitations of EAI solutions made most organizations realize that integrating internal systems with external systems to business supply chain members was a key to staying competitive, since the majority of business processes spanned across several organizations. Internal and external systems needed to communicate over networks to allow businesses to complete a transaction or part of a transaction. To achieve this level of integration, business-to-business (B2B) solutions were developed. B2B infrastructures were directed to help organizations to streamline their processes so they could carry out business transactions more efficiently with their business partners (such as resellers and suppliers). To reach a higher level of integration, most B2B solutions have relied on the use of XML as the language to represent data. XML allows one to model data at any level of complexity since it is extensible with the addition of new tags. Data can be published in multiple

*Figure 1. The evolution of business usage on the WWW*

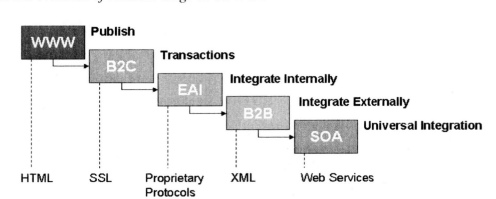

formats. In contrast to the proprietary protocols used by EAI platforms, XML is vendor and platform independent allowing standard commercial software to process any conforming document.

Many organizations have already seen and experience the advantages in using XML to represent data for Web-based information exchanges (such as B2B communications). Nevertheless, organizations realized that their B2B strategies have lead the development of architectural solutions that often exhibited a tight-coupling among interacting software applications which limited the flexibility and dynamic adaptation of IT systems. As a result and to overcome these limitations, the concept of service-oriented architecture (SOA) was introduced and defined a method of designing, developing, deploying and managing discrete pieces of computer logic (i.e., services) within the WWW. The SOA goals are to achieve structuring, loose coupling, and standardization of business functionality among interacting software applications. Applications invoke a series of discrete services in order to perform a certain task. A service is carried out by a service provider in response to the request of a service consumer. The most prominent implementation of the SOA principle uses XML and Web services as its technological backbone.

Web services are based on distributed computing technology and provide a standard means of interoperating between different software applications across, and within, organizational boundaries, using XML protocols and formats. Web Services comply with several WWW standards, such as Web Services Definition Language (WSDL) and Simple Object Access Protocol (SOAP). These standards enable interoperability by using XML-based communications protocols and service definitions. The use of standard XML protocols makes Web services platform, language, and vendor independent, and an ideal candidate for use in SOA implementations.

This chapter will introduce SOA, Web service technology and its standards. It begins in the second section, with a brief history of distributed computing, which serves as the backdrop for the development of today's Web service technology. The guiding principle behind the development of Web service technology is SOA which is described in the third section. The fourth section gives an overview of the role of Web services in the context of SOA. This section gives a description of today's standards and technologies for Web services. The fifth section introduces the second-generation of Web Services Protocols. It looks in detail at the threats and standards relevant to the Web Services Security landscape and examines problems and solutions in reliability and transactions of Web Services. Clearly, these areas must be addressed before Web service technology will be widely adopted. The sixth section explains how to develop Web services starting from the initial design and continuing until deployment and publication. A summary and conclusions can be found in the last section of this chapter.

## A BRIEF HISTORY OF DISTRIBUTED COMPUTING

Once networking became widespread across academia and industry, it became necessary to share data and resources. In the early years of distributed computing, message passing (e.g., using for example sockets developed in the early 1980s) was the prevailing method for communication. This involved encoding the data into a message format (i.e., how a structured piece of information is encoded prior to transmission) and sending the encoded data over the wire. The socket interface allowed message passing using send and receive primitives on transmission control protocol (TCP) or user datagram protocol (UDP) transport protocols for low-level messaging over Internet protocol (IP) networks. Applications communicated by sending and receiving text messages. In most cases, the messages exchanged conformed to an application-level protocol defined by programmers. This worked well but was cumbersome in the fact that the data had to be coded and then decoded. Using this approach, two programmers developing a distributed application must have knowledge of what the other is doing to the data. Programmers had to spend a significant amount of time specifying a messaging protocol and mapping the various data structures to and from the common transmission format.

As the development of distributed computing applications increased, new mechanisms and approaches became necessary to facilitate the construction of distributed applications. The first distributed computing technology to gain widespread use was remote procedure call (RPC). RPC technology was made popular in the 1980s by Sun Microsystems. RPC uses the client/server model and extends the capabilities of traditional procedure calls across a network. Remote procedure calls are designed to be similar to making local procedure calls. While in a traditional local procedure call paradigm the code segments of an application and the procedure it calls are in the same address space, in a remote procedure call the called procedure runs in another process and address space across the network on another processor.

RPC (Birrell, 1995) proved to be an adequate solution for the development of two-tier client/ server architectures. As distributed computing became more widespread, the need to develop, for example, N-tier applications emerged and RPC could not provide the flexibility and functionality required.

With such applications, multiple machines may need to operate simultaneously on the same set of data. Therefore, the state of that data became of great concern. Research in the area of distributed objects allowed overcoming this problem with the specification of two competing technologies: common object request broker architecture (CORBA) and distributed common object model (DCOM). Later, Java remote method invocation (RMI) was developed and also became a competitor.

The CORBA [4, 5] standard was developed by the Object Management Group (OMG) starting in the 1990's and defines an architecture that specifies interoperability between distributed objects on a network. With CORBA, distributed objects can communicate regardless of the operating system they are running on (for example, Linux, Solaris, Microsoft Windows, or MacOS). Another primary feature of CORBA is its interoperability between various programming languages. Distributed objects can be written in various languages (such as Java, C++, C, Ada, etc.). The main component of CORBA is the ORB (object request broker). Objects residing in a client make remote requests using an interface to the ORB running on the local machine. The local ORB sends the request to the remote ORB, which locates the appropriate object residing in a server and passes back an object reference to the requester. An object residing in a client can then make the remote method invocation of a remote object. When this happens the ORB marshals the arguments and sends the invocation over the network to the remote object's ORB which invokes the method locally and sends the results back to the client.

DCOM (Brown & Kindel, 1996) is a protocol, developed by Microsoft, which enables communication between two applications running on distributed computers in a reliable, secure, and efficient manner. DCOM is an extension of the Component Object Model (COM). COM is an object-based programming model and defines how components and their clients interact. COM allows the development of software components using a variety of languages and platforms to be easily deployed and integrated. The distributed COM protocol extends the programming model introduced by COM to work across the network by using proxies and stubs. Proxies and stubs allow remote objects to appear to be in the same address space as the requesting object. When a client instantiates a component that resides outside its address space, DCOM creates a proxy to marshal methods calls and route them across the network. On the server-side, DCOM creates a stub, which unmarshals method calls and routes them to an instance of the component.

Java RMI (Dwoning, 1998) is a package for writing and executing distributed Java programs by facilitating object method calls between different Java Virtual Machines (JVM) across a network. Java RMI hides most of the aspects of the distribution and provides a conceptually uniform way by which local and distributed objects can be accessed. An RMI application consists of a server interface, a server implementation, a server skeleton, a client stub, and a client implementation. The server implementation creates remote objects that conform to the server interface. These objects are available for method invocation to clients. When a client wishes to make a remote method invocation it invokes a method on the local stub, which is responsible for carrying out the method call on the remote object. The stub acts as a local proxy. A server skeleton exists for each remote object and is responsible to handle incoming invocations from clients.

CORBA, DCOM, and Java RMI enjoyed considerable success, but they present a set of shortcoming and limitations when used in Web environments. For example, they tend to create tightly-coupled distributed systems, some are vendor and platform specific (e.g., COM/DCOM only runs on Windows), the distributed systems developed run on closely administered environment, some use complex and proprietary protocols, and specific message formats and data representation. With the growth of the Web, the search soon started for a Web compliant replace-

ment for this technology. In the next sections, we will see that Web services are currently the most natural solution to develop distributed systems in the Web.

## SERVICE-ORIENTED ARCHITECTURE

As we have seen, in the 1980s distributed computing was introduced. This research led to the development of distributed objects architectures through the 1990's. The distributed platforms developed, such as Java RMI and DCOM, had several restrictions. For example, RMI was limited to Java, while DCOM was limited to Microsoft platforms. Moreover, distributed applications developed using different platforms were difficult to integrate. Integration was and is still one of the major concerns for Chief Information Officers. Figure 2 gives us a very good indication that application integration tops the priority list of high ranking business people.

To cope with the restrictions of more traditional distributed objects architectures, in the early 2000's, the concept of service-oriented architecture (SOA) was introduced (or reintroduced, since

*Figure 2. Priority list of CIOs (Channabasavaiah & Tuggle, 2003)*

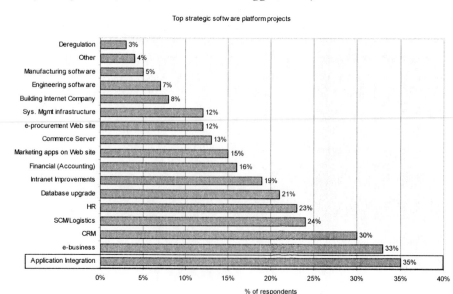

Top strategic software platform projects

% of respondents

in reality, the concept SOA was defined by Sun in the late 1990's to describe Jini (Waldo, 1999)). SOA describes an approach which facilitates the development and composition of modular services that can be easily integrated and reused to create distributed applications. It promises the development of truly flexible and adaptable IT infrastructures. According to the W3C, a Service-Oriented Architecture is a set of components which can be invoked, and whose interface descriptions can be published and discovered. Components are made available as independent services that are accessed in a standardized way.

In order for SOA to enjoy greater success than it predecessors, it should consider the following attributes:

- **Scalable:** The past solutions were not designed with the scale of the Web in mind. SOA should work in a variety of settings, such as within an organization, between business partners and across the world.
- **Loosely-coupled:** SOA is an evolution from tightly coupled systems to loosely coupled ones. Senders and receivers of a SOA should be independent of each other; the source can send the message independently of the target. Tight coupling is not suitable for SOA since it leads to monolithic and brittle distributed applications. Even trivial changes in one component lead to catastrophic breaks in function. Small changes in one application require matching changes in partner applications (Channabasavaiah & Tuggle, 2003).
- **Interoperability:** One party should be able to communicate with another party regardless of the machine they are running on.
- **Discovery:** One party should be able to communicate with a second party selected from a set of competent candidates. Services need to be dynamically discoverable. This is accomplished through services such as a directory of service descriptions.
- **Abstraction:** A SOA abstracts the underlying technology. Developers can concentrate on building services for business users rather than connecting systems and applications.
- **Standards:** Interaction protocols must be standardized to ensure the widest interoperability among unrelated institutions. Contracts should also be standardized. Explicit contracts define what may be changed in an application without breaking the interaction. Furthermore, standards are the basis of interoperable contract selection and execution.

When comparing SOA with previous approaches we can find the following major differences. Traditional Middleware, such as distributed object systems, are based on the client-server paradigm, have heavily asymmetric interaction model, are biased towards synchronous protocols, assign public interfaces to network accessible objects, and support "name-oriented" object discovery. On the other hand, service-oriented Middleware are based on a peer-to-peer paradigm, have symmetric interaction models, mixes synchronous and asynchronous protocols, assigns public contracts to network accessible objects, and supports capability based service discovery (Cardoso, Curbera, Sheth, 2004).

## Service Oriented Architecture and Web Services

Most distributed computing technologies have the concept of services and are defined by interfaces. While there are many different possibilities for developing an SOA (e.g., Web services, Java RMI, DCOM, and CORBA), Web services is currently the most desirable solution since it eliminates many of the interoperability problems between applications and services. Web services provide many of the necessary standards that are crucial for making a distributed system work. It should be noticed that using Web services does not necessarily mean that there is an SOA. Also, it is possible to have a service-oriented architecture without Web services.

There are three common actions associated with a service in SOA—discovery, request, and response. Discovery is the process of finding the service that provides the functionality that is required. A request provides the input to the service. The response yields the output from the service. It follows easily that this architecture must have three primary actors: requestor, provider, and registry.

The beginning of this figure (step 1) shows the process that two participants would become aware of one another. This is accomplished as the service provider publishes the Web Service Description (WSD) and Semantics (Sem.) to a registry after which the service requestor would discover that service. In step 2, the semantics and description are agreed upon so that there will be no misunderstanding about the data that is being exchanged during this communication. Once the WSD and semantics are accepted by and loaded into both the participants (step 3) then they can interact to carry out the operation that was needed.

A service provider may develop and deploy one or more Web services. Each service must contain at least one operation. Operations are also referred to as endpoints because they are the part of the service that actually does the processing.

## What are Web Services?

Web services are modular, self-describing, self-contained applications that are accessible over the Internet (Curbera & Nagy, 2001). They are the most popular realization of the service-oriented architecture. A Web service is a software component invokable over the Web via an XML (XML, 2005) message that follows the SOAP (SOAP, 2003) standard. The component provides one or more operations for performing useful actions on behalf of the invoking client. These operations and the formats of the input and output messages are described using WSDL (Christensen & Curbera, 2001). Being based on these Web standards makes Web services both implementation language and platform independent. Description of services in a language neutral manner is vital for the widespread use of Web services. For general usability, a service must be described and advertised. WSDL takes

*Figure 3. Process of discovery (Booth, 2004)*

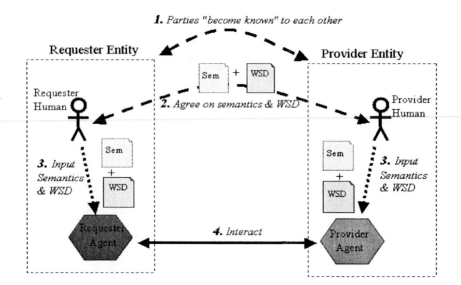

care of the description by providing a language to describe a service in enough detail to invoke any of its operations. Service providers describe their Web services and advertise them in a universal registry called UDDI (UDDI, 2002). This enables service requestors to search the registry and find services, which match their requirements. UDDI allows for the creation of registries that are accessible over the Web. A registry contains content from the WSDL descriptions as well as additional information such as data about the provider. Clients may use one or more registries to discover relevant services.

To describe Web services further, let us look at an example scenario. A company called Moon Company is a product distributor. They keep track of their clients, goods, and orders through a system that they have in-house. They do not want to provide unlimited access to this system to their customers, but they would like their customers to be able to place orders easier. Using Web services, the Moon Company can create an interface to their interior system so that a customer can be looked up, and once authenticated, order products. With these services in place, Moon needs only provide the WSDL definitions of the services to their clients and the clients will be able to compose any system on their side to handle ordering in any way they see fit. Since Moon does not know what type of system their customers are using, other remote technologies would be more difficult to implement.

## SOA and Web Service Standards

The use of standard protocols is one of the aspects that allow SOA to deploy technically compatible services. Currently, Web service standards are the preferred solution to develop SOA-based products. Web services technology has gained a suitable degree of maturity and is being used to easily publish business functions to an intranet or the Internet for remote execution. Business functions can reside in popular applications such as ERP (enterprise resource planning), CRM (customer relationship management), and SCM (supply chain management) systems.

Some of the standards associated with Web services are indispensable to developing SOA-based solutions as illustrated in Figure 4.

The most well-known protocols will be presented and discussed in this section, while the second-generation Web services standards, such as WS-Security, WS-Coordination, WS-Transaction, and WS-Policy will be discussed in the next section.

*Figure 4. Web Services and list standards (Cardoso, Curbera, & Sheth, 2004)*

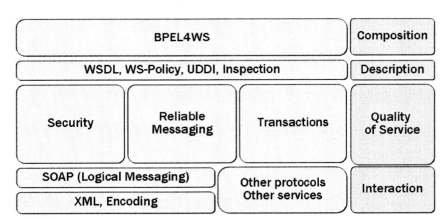

141

*Figure 5. The relationship between XML/SOAP/ WSDL/UDDI*

## Basic Web Service Standards

XML, SOAP, WSDL and UDDI (Graham & Simenov, 2002) are the fundamental elements to deploy SOA infrastructures based on Web services (see Figure 5). XML is the standard for data representation; SOAP specifies the transport layer to send messages between consumers and providers; WSDL describes Web services; and UDDI is used to register and lookup for Web services.

XML, the emerging standard for data representation, has been chosen as the language for describing Web services. XML is accepted as a standard for data interchange on the Web allowing the structuring of data on the Web. It is a language for semi-structured data and has been proposed as a solution for data integration problems, because it allows a flexible coding and display of data, by using metadata to describe the structure of data (using DTD or XSD). A well-formed XML document creates a balanced tree of nested sets of open and closed tags, each of which can include several attribute-value pairs.

Simple object access protocol (SOAP). This standard defines the types and formats of XML messages that may be exchanged between peers in a decentralized, distributed environment. One of the main objectives of SOAP is to be a communication protocol that can be used by distinct applications developed using different programming languages, operating systems, and platforms. Many software vendors are producing an implementation of SOAP into their systems. Examples of major vendors include Sun, Microsoft, and IBM. The latest version of the standard is SOAP 1.2 (http://www.w3.org/TR/soap). SOAP specification is not completed yet and as it goes through the W3C standardization process some minor changes will certainly occur.

The current specification defines a skeleton that looks like the listing below. The envelope defines the namespace of the SOAP specification and the encoding style that was used to create this message. The Header section is optional and contains additional information about the mes-

*Figure 6. SOAP skeleton listing (SOAP, 2002)*

```
<?xml version="1.0"?>
<soap:Envelope
xmlns:soap="http://www.w3.org/2001/12/soap-envelope"
soap:encodingStyle="http://www.w3.org/2001/12/soap-encoding">
<soap:Header>

...
</soap:Header>
<soap:Body>

...
 <soap:Fault>

 ...
 </soap:Fault>
</soap:Body>
</soap:Envelope>
```

sage. The Body section contains the data that is being transferred.

Web Service Description Language (WSDL). WSDL is the major language that provides a model and an XML format to describe the syntactical information about Web services. It is a W3C standard XML language for specifying the interface of a Web service. This standard enables the separation of the description of the abstract functionality offered by a service from concrete details of a service implementation by defining the interface that Web services provide to requesters. The definition of the interface (called a port type in version 1.x and called interface in version 2.0) gives the signatures for all the operations provided including operation name, inputs, outputs and faults. Beyond the interface, information about the service itself and allowed bindings is included in WSDL documents. The latest version of the standard is WSDL 1.1 (http://www.w3.org/TR/wsdl), although WSDL 2.0 has become a candidate recommendation (http://www.w3.org/TR/wsdl20). WSDL 1.1 uses XML Schema Definition (XSD) which provides constructs for creating complex types (http://www.w3.org/XML/Schema).

The following is brief and incomplete copy of a WSDL file. Notice how it defines the type of data to be used, the operations that exist in the service and the type of inputs and outputs that those operations require. With this information, a call to invoke any operation in this service can be made and carried out successfully.

UDDI (universal description, discovery, and integration). Currently, the industry standards available to register and discover Web services are based on the UDDI specification (UDDI, 2002). Once a Web service is developed, it has to be advertised to enable discovery. The UDDI registry is

*Figure 7. Partial WSDL listing (Semantic Web Services Challenge, 2006)*

```
<wsdl:definitions
targetNamespace="mooncompany"
xmlns:wsdl="http://schemas.xmlsoap.org/wsdl/" xmlns:wsdlsoap="http://schemas.xmlsoap.org/
wsdl/soap/" xmlns:xsd="http://www.w3.org/2001/XMLSchema">
<wsdl:message name="SearchCustomerResponseMessage">
 <wsdl:part element="impl:SearchCustomerResponse"
  name="SearchCustomerResponse"/>
 </wsdl:message>
 <wsdl:portType name="SearchCustomer">
             <wsdl:operation name="search">
  <wsdl:input message="impl:SearchCustomerRequestMessage"/>
             <wsdl:output message="impl:SearchCustomerResponseMessage"/>
             </wsdl:operation>
             </wsdl:portType>
             <wsdl:binding name="CRMServiceSoapBinding"
      type="impl: SearchCustomer ">
             <wsdlsoap:binding style="document"
      transport="http://schemas.xmlsoap.org/soap/http"/>
             <wsdl:operation name="search">
                     <wsdlsoap:operation soapAction="search"/>
                     </wsdl:operation>
             </wsdl:binding>
 <wsdl:service name="CRMService">
             <wsdl:port binding="impl:CRMServiceSoapBinding" name="CRMService">
             <wsdlsoap:address
      location="http://138.232.65.158/moon/services/CRMService"/>
                     </wsdl:port>
 </wsdl:service>
 </wsdl:definitions>
```

supposed to open doors for the success of service oriented computing, leveraging the power of the Internet. Hence the discovery mechanism supported should be scaled to the magnitude of the Web by efficiently discovering relevant services among tens and thousands (or millions according to industry expectations) of Web services. UDDI standard defines a SOAP-based Web service for locating WSDL descriptions of Web services. This standard defines the information content and the type of access provided by service registries. These registries provide the advertisement of the services that can be invoked by a client. UDDI can store descriptions about internal Web services across an organization and public Web services located in the Internet.

## OTHER WEB SERVICES STANDARDS AND PROTOCOLS: WS-*

Besides the core standards discussed in section 4, there are several other standards needed for Web services to be used in practice. This section gives a quick tour of some of these standards.

### Web Service Policy

In the process of discovering a service, there is an inherent problem. We might write a query that yields ten services that match our keyword, or meet our input and output specifications. Yet, at this point, we do not know what these services require of the messages that will be exchanged. Policy in Web services adds this information to the description. It allows the provider of the service to give all the information they see fit about the service; requirements, capabilities, and quality. With this information, the best service can be chosen from the discovered services based on much more complete information than just functional requirements and keywords. (Verma, Akkiraju, & Goodwin, 2005).

### WS-Policy

WS-Policy is a specification of a framework for defining the requirements and capabilities of a service. In this since, a policy is nothing more that a set of assertions that express the capabilities and requirements of a service. The specification WS-Policy (http://www-128.ibm.com/developer-works/library/specification/ws-polfram/) defines terms that can be used to organize a policy. Once a provider has a policy defined in XML, then he must publish that information by referencing it in the description of the service.

### WS-PolicyAttachment

This defines the method for attaching a policy to a WSDL file so that it can be published to the UDDI and thus used in deciding on services. There are several mechanisms defined for accomplishing this task. The simplest method is to write the policy directly into the WSDL file. A more complex, and more powerful method is to construct the policy as a stand alone file that is referenced in the WSDL file as a URI. These references can exist at any element of the WSDL. WS-Policy and WS-PolicyAttachment together give us hierarchy based on to which element the policy is attached and direction for merging policies together to create an effective policy for an element (WS-PolicyAttachment, 2005).

Both WS-Policy and WS-PolicyAttachment have recently been submitted to W3C for standardization.

### Web Service Security

In this section, we examine some of the concepts, theories, and practices in securing Web services at an introductory level. Our aim is for you to become familiar with these as well as the terms used. Security is a constantly changing arena driven by the changes in associated technologies.

The World Wide Web, or Web, has in some way touched the lives of most people living in an economically developed country. Unfortunately, it has not always been in a positive way. This is because once a computer is connected to the Web; it becomes part of a system that was not designed with security and privacy in mind. Computers hold information, sometimes sensitive information, for much longer than most users realize. Even during the simple event of entering information into a Web browser, information is stored onto disk. This may take place in a temporary file. Although once the information is sent to a Web server and the file is deleted, the information is still present on the disk; even though the file reference is gone. Many unsavory characters have learned how to glean this information off of remote systems through vulnerabilities of the operating system.

A basic definition of security can be thought of as "keeping unauthorized access minimal." This is true not only on the Web but also in our daily lives. We lock our doors when we leave our houses in an effort to keep unauthorized visitors out. This definition is simple, but it is clear. A more complete definition may become too convoluted. Let us consider a definition for privacy, "not making public what may be considered personal." Not a fancy definition, rather straight to the point. We all have different ideas of what is personal to us, and what being made public means. However, I think we can all agree that having our Social Security Number and checking account information sold to the highest bidder is a violation of our privacy.

Now that security and privacy are defined, let us consider how this fits into the Web. Suppose you would like to purchase a book online. Once you have found the book and placed it in your "Cart" it is time to checkout. In order to checkout you must pass through some security. Typically, you will be asked for your credit card information and billing address. This is the first security checkpoint and this information is verified with your bank; as well as making sure the card has not been reported stolen. The next checkpoint is physical possession of the card, which is verified by a security code on the back of your card. So, you the consumer trust this Web site to send the

book, or you would not have placed the order, and the Web site trusts you for payment since it has verified all your information. Trust is a key component of security and privacy as we shall see. As a consumer using sensitive personal information to make a purchase, have you considered privacy of your information? Somewhere in the information exchange between you and the Web site an agreement has been made; whereas, the Web site has promised not to sell your personal information. However, how well is it protected? Your credit card information, billing address, and security code are now stored in two places, the Web sites server and on your PC. More than likely one of those unsavory characters will not spend the time and effort to get one credit card number off a PC when with a little more work they could have access to thousands of entries. So this brings us back to security. This time that of the Web site server. As you can see, security and privacy go hand and hand, with mutual trust holding them together.

The above scenario is a simple client-server process, much like those that currently encompasses the Web. However, Web services extend the client-server model and are distributed as discussed in earlier sections. Although this combination is what gives Web services such promises in the SOA, it is also an area of concern for security and privacy. The more doors and windows a home has, the more opportunities a thief has, the more vigilant the home owner must be. This can be applied to Web services as well. Web services increases the number of access points to data and ultimately machines. Furthermore, because the access to data is increased, the sharing of information is increased. This in itself is opens the possibility of privacy invasion.

Now that the stage has been set, let us look at the specific security and privacy considerations. Web services are a distributed cross-domain environment. Therefore, it is difficult to determine the identity of the actors; in this case who is the service *requester* and who is the service *provider*. Message level security and privacy is important since these invocations may cross un-trusted intermediaries. It is necessary for the requester and provider to have a protocol for discovering each others policies and negotiating constraints at run-time, prior to interaction. Privacy rights and agreements should be explicitly described and agreed upon. We will look more closely at these considerations in the following paragraphs.

Message level security involves securing all aspects of the SOAP message. Encryption plays a large role in providing integrity of messages between the requester and the provider while traversing intermediaries. In addition, the requester and the provider can not always be trusted.

Man-In-The-Middle attack is when an attacker is able to compromise a SOAP message in transit. An attacker may gain access to confidential information contained in the message or may alter the message.

Unauthorized Access attack takes place when an attacker is able to gain access to a Web service which they do not have permissions to use. This can happen through brute-force or by compromising a SOAP message thereby gaining a username and token. An attacker may also pose as a legitimate Web service in order to gain an authentication mechanism, this is known as Spoofing.

The above threats can be alleviated using proper authentication and encryption techniques. However, there are other attacks that can only be alleviated through good programming habits and proper verification of parameters.

SQL injection attack is the insertion of malicious SQL statements. This requires preprocessing of any parameters passed to an operation which queries a SQL database to alleviate this threat. Command injection attacks are similar to SQL injection attacks in that malicious system commands are injected into the SOAP in an effort to exploit the systems vulnerabilities. This threat can be alleviated by proper configuration permissions and preprocessing.

Proper authentication and encryption schemes can alleviate threats which compromise message integrity. Point-to-Point schemes which are implemented at the transport layer, such as VPN, SSL, or IPSec, provide a "secure tunnel" for data to flow, however, they can not guarantee the integrity of the message. End-to-End schemes, which are implemented at the application layer, can guarantee the confidential integrity of the message and that the message has not been altered. This is because the message is encrypted and digitally signed with a key. End-to-End schemes also offer the granularity necessary for Web services such that sections of the SOAP message may be encrypted while other sections are not.

## WS-Security Framework

The WS-Security specification provides a framework and vocabulary for requesters and providers to secure messaging as well as communicate information regarding security and privacy. There are other security related specifications worth mentioning. XML-Encryption specifies the process of encrypting data and messages. XML-Signature provides a mechanism for messages integrity and authentication, and signer authentication. XACML is an XML representation of the Role-Based Access Control standard (RBAC). XACML will likely play an important function in Web services authorization. Security Assertion Markup Language, or SAML, is an OASIS framework for conveying user authentication and attribute information through XML assertions. There are many specifications and standards for Web services security. We would like to encourage you to investigate these on your own as an exercise.

## WS-SecurityPolicy

Policies for Web services that describe the access permissions as well as actions which a requester or provider are required to perform. For example, a policy may indicate that requesters must have an active account with the service and that messages be encrypted using a PKI scheme from a trusted certificate authority. A requester may also have a policy indicating which encryption schemes it accepts.

## WS-Trust

Before two parties are going to exchange sensitive information, they must establish a secure communication. This can be done by the exchange of security credentials. However, one problem remains, how one party can trust the credentials of the other. The Web Service Trust Language (WS-Trust) was developed to deal with this problem. It offers extensions to the WS-Security elements to exchange security tokens and establishing trust relationships (WS-Trust, 2005).

## WS-SecureConversation

The Web services protocol stack is designed to be a series of building blocks. WS-SecureConversation is one of those blocks. WS-Security provides message level authentication, but is vulnerable to some types of attacks. WS-SecureConversation uses SOAP extensions to define key exchange and key derivation from security context so that a secure communication can be ensured (WS-SecureConversation, 2005).

## WS-Authorization

Authorization for Web services still remains an area of research at the time of this publication. The difficulty of authorization is the inability to dynamically determine authorization for a requester whom a Web service has just been introduced. Some authorization frameworks being suggested include assertion based, role based, context based and a hybrid approach.

Assertion based authorization uses assertions about the requester to decided on the level of authorization. In a role based approach, requesters are given "user" labels and these labels are associated with roles, which in turn have permissions assigned to them. Context based authorization examines the context in which a requester is acting. For instance: proximity to the resource, on behalf of a partnership, or even the time of day. Obviously a hybrid approach is some combination of two or more approaches.

## WS-Privacy

Privacy is in the context of data and can be associated with the requester or the provider. The requester may be concerned that the information given to a provider will be propagated to other entities. Such information could be a credit card number, address, or phone number. A provider may be concerned with the proliferation of information which they have sold to a requester. In this case the provider does not want the requester to resell this information without proper compensation.

## Transaction Processing

The perceived success of composite applications in a service-oriented architecture depends on the reliability of participants that are often beyond corporate boundaries. In addition to already frequent errors and glitches in application code, distributed applications must cope with external factors such as network connectivity, unavailability of participants and even mistakes in service configuration. Web services transaction management enables participating services to have a greater degree of confidence in that the actions among them will progress successfully, and that in the worst case, such transactions can be cancelled or compensated as necessary.

## WS-Transaction

To date, probably the most comprehensive effort to define transaction context management resides in the WS-Coordination (WS-C) (Microsoft, BEA, IBM,`Web Service Coodination', 2005), WS-AtomicTransaction (WS-AT) (Microsoft, BEA, IBM, `Web Service Atomic Transaction', 2005) and WS-BusinessActivity (WS-BA) (Microsoft, BEA, IBM,`Web Service Business Activity', 2005) specifications. WS-C defines a coordination context, which represents an instance of coordinated effort, allowing participant services to share a common view. WS-AT targets existing transactional systems with short interactions and full ACID properties. WS-BA, on the other hand, is intended for applications involved in business processes of long duration, whose relaxed properties increase concurrency and suit a wider range of applications.

Neither the Web services architecture nor any specifications prescribe explicit ways to implement transactional capabilities, although it is clear that delivering such features should minimally impact existing applications. Some propose approaching the problem of transaction monitoring and support by means of intermediary (proxy) services (Mikalsen, 2002), while others by providing a lightweight programming interface requiring minimal application code changes (Vasquez, Miller, Verma, & Sheth, 2005). Whichever the case, protocol-specific messages should also be embedded in exchanged messages and propagated though all participants.

## WS-Composite Application Framework

Reliability and management are aspects highly dependent on particular Web service implementations and therefore no specification mandates or comments on them. However, just like the J2EE Enterprise JavaBeans (EBJ) technology has made available container-managed transactions (CMT) for some time, a way to procure increased Web service reliability could be through their deployment in *managed* environments, in which the hosting application server becomes responsible for support activities such as event logging and system recovery. These additional guarantees could potentially improve many aspects of Web services reliability, taking part of the burden away from their creators with regards to security, auditing, reliable messaging, transactional logging and fault-tolerance, to cite just a few. Some implementations leading this direction are already available from enterprise software companies such as Arjuna Transaction Service (Arjuna Transaction Service, 2005), IBM Transactional Attitudes (IBM Transactional Attitudes, 2005), and from open source projects like Apache

Kandula (Apache Kandula Project, 2005) and the academic community (Trainotti, Pistore, Pistore, et al., 2005; Vasquez et al., 2005).

## Messaging

### WS-ReliableMessaging

Communication over a public network such as the Internet imposes physical limitations to the reliability of exchanged messages. Even though failures are inevitable and unpredictable, certain techniques increase message reliability and traceability even in the worst cases.

At a minimum, senders are interested in determining whether the message has been received by the partner, that it was received exactly once and in the correct order. Additionally, it may be necessary to determine the validity of the received message: Has the message been altered on its way to the receiver? Does it conform to standard formats? Does it agree with the business rules expected by the receiver?

WS-Reliability and WS-ReliableMessaging have rules that dictate how and when services must respond to other services concerning the receipt of a message and its validity.

### WS-Eventing

Web services eventing (WS-Eventing) is a specification that defines a list of operations that should be in a Web service interface to allow for asynchronous messaging. WS-Eventing is based on WS-Notification that was submitted to OASIS for standardization.

### WS-Notification

Web service notification (WS-Notification) is a family of specifications that provide several capabilities.

- Standard message exchanges for clients
- Standard message exchanges for a notification broker service provider

- Required operations for services that wish to participate in notifications
- An XML model that describes topics.

WS-Notification is a top layer for the following specifications: WS-BaseNotification, WS-BrokeredNotification, and WS-Topics.

WS-BaseNotification defines the operations and message exchanges that must take place between the two parties. WS-BrokeredNotification defines messages and operations required of a Notification Broker Service and those that wish to use it. WS-Topics define the "topics" that are used to organize the elements in a notification message. It also defines XML to describe the metadata associated with different topics.

## DEVELOPING WEB SERVICES

The starting point of using Web service technology is to create Web services. Although it is similar to developing other software, there are some differences in that early focus on interfaces and tool support is of even greater importance. One can start by creating a WSDL specification, or alternatively, by creating, for example, a Java interface or abstract class. Since tools such as Axis (Apache Axis Documentation, 2006) or Radiant (2005) can convert one form to the other, it is a matter of preference where to start. In this chapter we will give a guide to developing Web services starting by designing the Java classes.

We will do this by following fundamental software engineering techniques to create the Web services. Start by creating a UML Class Diagram to define the requirements of the system. To illustrate the ideas in this section, we will use an example from the Semantic Web Services Challenge 2006 (Semantic Web Services Challenge, 2006). The Challenge scenario is to create a process to create a purchase order. The first step in this process is to confirm that a given business is a customer of the fictitious "Moon Company." Our example implements this service. Below are the eight steps to create this service:

1. **Create a UML Class Diagram:** Following software engineering practices, the initial step is to create a UML Class Diagram to define the classes that will be needed for the service. UML provides a succinct representation of modeling classes. The following is an example of a UML class diagram for a service that will take as input the name of a business and search a database to return the profile for this business if they are a partner of the Moon Company.

2. **Generate Java Code:** Using a UML tool such as Poseidon, the UML Class Diagram can easily converted into a Java class skeleton. It is important to note that while you are developing objects to be used for Web services that you must follow the Java bean programming conventions, for example, implementing "getters" and "setters" for every member variable. Fortunately, this is exactly the code that will be generated thanks to the UML tool based on the diagram that we have created in step one. For simplicity, we have generated our Web service as an abstract class.

3. **Adding in Web Services Annotations:** Java 6 includes annotations so that the compiler will know that the program code is a Web service. A partial list of available annotations is as follows:

- javax.jws.WebService
- javax.jws.WebMethod
- javax.jws.WebParam
- javax.jws.WebResult
- javax.jws.HandlerChain
- javax.jws.soap.SOAPBinding

Figure 9 illustrates an example of a Java service which has been annotated. Note that in the example the @WebService and @WebMethod are the annotations. The complier will recognize these tags and create the WSDL document.

*Figure 8. UML class diagram*

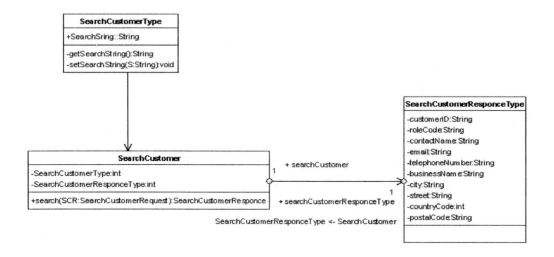

*Figure 9. Annotated Java example*

```
import javax.jws.WebService;
import javax.soap.SOAPinding;

@WebService
public class SearchCustomer
{

   @WebMethod
   public SearchCustomerResponce search (SearchCustomerRequest)
      //call to backend to verify Customer
      if(! verifyCustomer(SearchCustomerRequest))
      {
               return err;
               }

EarchCustomerResponce SCR = new SearchCustomerResponce;
SCR. setcustomerID(CustomerInfo.getcustomerID(SearchCustomerRequest)
SCR. setroleCode(CustomerInfor. getcustomerRole(SearchCustomerRequest)
   ...
   ...
   ...

      return SCR;
   }//WebMethod
}//SearchCustomer
```

Refer to the following link to see more information on annotations (https://mustang.dev.java.net/).

4. **Generate WSDL:** The annotations from the previous step indicate to the Annotation Processing Tool or the Java compiler that a WSDL is to be generated at compile-time. This description of the service is used in two ways. One, the description acts as an advertisement when it is published on the Web. The information gleaned from the WSDL file is published in UDDI registries so that queries can be executed to discover the service that is needed. Second, it provides all the information needed to invoke this service remotely.

5. **Implement Methods:** At this point in development, we want to create an implementation class that extends our abstract class. The difference that the developer must deal with is writing the code to the proper conventions. Any class that is created must have getters and setters for all member variables. These are used during invocation by the SOAP engine to serialize and deserialize the data that is in the SOAP messages into Java objects and back to SOAP.

6. **Deploy Service:** Deploying a service is accomplished using a Web application server and a SOAP engine, like Tomcat and Axis2 respectively. If using Axis2, deploying a service is as simple as dropping the .aar files, which are .jar files with a different extension, into the \WEB-INF\services directory. Directions on deployment in Axis2 can be found on the Web at http://ws.apache.org/axis2 .

7. **Test Service:** A simple Java program can be sufficient to test a service. In others it may require a more complex client. Either way the fundamentals for writing a client are the End Point Reference, which is a URL to the service, a call setting the target, and setting the transport information. All of this information is put into a call object that exists in the org.apace.soap package. The setup of this object is in Figure 10.

This code creates a call to a service named "CMRService" with an operation name "search". This operation takes a SearchCustomerType as input, thus you see an instance of this class is created and added as a parameter to the call object.

```
Response resp = call.invoke(url, "");
```

This calls the invoke method on the call object to execute the operation in the service. The results of the service are put into the Response object and can be accessed from there.

*Figure 10. Partial listing of Web service client*

```
Call call = new Call();
call.setSOAPMappingRegistry(smr); call.setTargetObjectURI("http://138.232.65.158/moon/services/CRMService");
call.setMethodName("search");
call.setEncodingStyleURI(Constants.NS_URI_SOAP_ENC);
Vector params = new Vector();
SearchCustomerType sct = new SearchCustomerType();
sct.setSearchString(name);
params.addElement(new Parameter("request", SearchCustomerType.class, sct, null));
call.setParams(params);
```

8. **Publish Service:** Publishing a service requires the use of UDDI registries. Setting up a registry varies based on which registry is chosen. For our example, we used the jUDDI registry on a Tomcat server. The action of publishing a service is similar to advertising a business. After deployment and testing, the service is open to the world and ready to accept request, but until it is published, it is unlikely that anyone will know about your service. Tools that simplify this process are Radiant and Lumina (Li, 2005), both from the METEOR-S tool suite.

## CONCLUSION

The service oriented architecture (SOA) is currently a "hot" topic. It is an evolution of the distributed systems technology of the 1990s, such as DCOM, CORBA, and Java RMI. This type of architecture requires the existence of main components and concepts such as services, service descriptions, service security parameters and constraints, advertising and discovery, and service contracts in order to implement distributed systems. In contrast to the Event-Driven Architecture, in which the services are independent, the SOA-based approach requires services to be loosely coupled.

SOA are often associated with Web services and sometimes, SOA are even confused with Web services, but, SOA does not specifically mean Web services. Instead, Web services can be seen as a specialized SOA implementation that embodies the core aspects of a service-oriented approach to architecture. Web service technology has come a long way toward achieving the goal of the SOA. With Web services, developers do not need to know how a remote program works, only the input that it requires, the output it provides and how to invoke it for execution. Web services provide standards and specifications that create an environment where services can be designed,

executed, and composed into processes to achieve very complicated tasks.

For some years now, Web services define a set of standards (such as WSDL, SOAP, and UDDI) to allow the interoperation and interoperability of services on the Internet. Recently, security and transactional stability have become priority areas of research to make Web services more accepted in the world of industry. The work done has lead to the development of a set of new specifications (such as WS-Security, WS-Policy, WS-Trust, WS-Privacy, WS-Transaction, etc.) that describe how Web services can establish secure communications, define policies services' interactions, and define rules of trust between services.

## REFERENCES

Arjuna Technologies Limited (2005). Arjuna transaction service suite. Retrieved October 18, 2006, from http://www.arjuna.com/products/arjunats/index.html

Axis Development Team (2006) . *Webservices – Axis.* Retrieved October 18, 2006, from http://ws.apache.org/axis/

Bellwood, T. (2002) *UDDI Version 2.04 Api specification.* Retrieved February 20, 2007 from http://uddi.org/pubs/ProgrammersAPI-V2.04-Published-20020719.htm

Birrell, A.D. & Nelson, B.J. (1984). Implementing remote procedure calls. *ACM Transactions on Computer Systems, 2*(1), 39-54.

Booth, D., Hass, H., McCabe, F., Newcomer, E., Champion, M., Ferris, C., & Orchard, D. (2004) *Web services architecture*, W3C Working Group Note. Retrieved October 18, 2006, from http://www.w3.org/TR/ws-arch/

Brewer, D., LSDIS Lab, University of Georgia (2005). Radiant. Retrieved October 18, 2006, from http://lsdis.cs.uga.edu/projects/meteor-s/downloads/index.php?page=1

Brown, N., & Kindel. C. (1996). *Distributed component object model protocol*, DCOM/1.0. Redmond, WA: Microsoft Corporation.

Cabrera, L. F., Copeland, G., Feingold, M., Freund, T., Johnson, J., & Joyce, S., et al. (2005) *Web services atomic transaction (WS-Atomic Transaction)*. retrieved February 20, 2007 from http://www128.ibm.com/developerworks/library specification/ws-tx/#atom

Cabrera, L. F., Copeland, G., Feingold, M., Freund R. W., Freund, T., & Joyce, S., et al. (2005). *Web services business activity framework (WS-BusinessActivity)*. Retrieved February 20, 2006 from http://schemas.xmlsoap.org/ws/2004/10/wsba/

Cabrera, L. F., Copeland, G., Feingold, M., Freund, T., Freund, R. W., Johnson, J. (2005) *Web service coordination (WS-Coordination)*. Retrieved February 20, 2006 from http://specs.xmlsoap.org/ws/2004/10/wscoor/wscoor.pdf

Cardoso, J., Curbera, F., & Sheth, A. (2004, May 17-22). Tutorial: Service oriented architectures and Semantic Web processes. In *Proceedings of the Thirteenth International World Wide Web Conference (WWW2004)*, New York.

Channabasavaiah, K., Holley, K., & Tuggle, E. (2003) Migrating to a service-oriented architecture, Part 1. Retrieved October 18, 2006, from http://www128.ibm.com/developerworks/Webservices/library/ws-migratesoa/

Christensen, E., Curbera, F., Meredith, G., Weerawarana, S. (2001) *W3C Web Services Description Language (WSDL)*. Retrieved October 18, 2006, from http://www.w3.org/TR/wsdl

Curbera, F., Nagy, W., Weerawarana, S. (2001). *Web services: Why and how*. Paper presented at the Workshop on Object-Oriented Web Services - OOPSLA 2001, Tampa, Florida.

Dwoning, T. (1998). *Java RMI*. Boston: IDG Books Worldwide.

Graham, S., Simenov, S., Davis, D., Daniels, G., Brittenham, P., Nakamura, Y., Fremantle, P., Koeing, D., & Zentner, C. (2002). *Building Web services with Java: Making sense of XML, SOAP, WSDL, and UDDI, SAMS*. Indianapolis, Indiana.

IBM, BEA Systems, Microsoft, SAP AG, Sonic Software, VeriSign (2006).

Web service policy attachment. Retrieved October 18, 2006, from http://www-128.ibm.com/developerworks/library/specification/ws-polatt/index.html

IBM, BEA Systems, Microsoft, Layer 7 Technologies, Oblix, VeriSign, Actional, Computer Associates, OpenNetwork Technologies, Ping Identity, Reactivity, RSA Security (2005). Web services trust language. Retrieved October 18, 2006, from http://www-128.ibm.com/developerworks/library/specification/ws-trust/

IBM, BEA Systems, Microsoft, Computer Associates, Actional, VeriSign, Layer 7 Technologies, Oblix, OpenNetwork Technologies, Ping Identity, Reactivity, RSA Security (2005). Web service secure conversation language specification. Retrieved October 18, 2006 from http://www-128.ibm.com/developerworks/library/specification/ws-secon/

Li, K. (2005). *Lumina: Using WSDL-S for Web service discovery*. Masters Thesis, University of Georgia.

Microsoft, BEA & IBM. (2005). *Web Services Atomic Transaction*

Microsoft, BEA & IBM. (2005). *Web Services Business Activity*

Microsoft, BEA & IBM. (2005). *Web Services Coordination*.

Mikalsen, T., Rouvellou, I., & Tai. S. (2003). *Advanced enterprise middleware: Transaction processing.* Retrieved October 18, 2006, from http://www.research.ibm.com/AEM/txa.html

Mikalsen, T., Tai, S., & Rouvellou, I. (2002). *Transactional attitudes. Reliable composition of autonomous Web services.* Paper presented at the International Conference on Dependable Systems and Networks.

Object Management Group. (1995, July). *CORBA: The Common Object Request: Architecture and Specification*, Release 2.0. Retrieved February 20, 2007 from http://www.omg.org/cgi-bin/apps/doc?formal/99-10-07.pdf

Orfali, R., & Herkey, D. (1998). *Client/Server programming with Java and CORBA* (2nd ed.). Hoboken NJ: John Wiley & Sons.

Semantic Web Services Challenge (2006). Main page. Retrieved October 18, 2006, from http://www.sws-challenge.org/

SOAP (2003). *Simple object access protocol 1.2.* Retrieved October 18, 2006, from http://www.w3.org/TR/soap/

Trainotti, M., Pistore, M., Calabrese, G., Zacco, G., Lucchese, G., Barbon F., Bertoli, P., Traverso P., & ASTRO. (2005). *Supporting composition and execution of Web services.* Paper presented at the International Conference on Service Oriented Computing.

UDDI (2002). *Universal Description, Discovery, and Integration.*

Vasquez, I., Miller, J., Verma, A., & Sheth, A. (2005). *OpenWS-Transaction: Enabling reliable Web service transactions.* Paper presented at the International Conference on Service Oriented Computing.

Verma, K., Akkiraju, R., Goodwin, R. (2005). *Semantic matching of Web service policies.* Paper presented at the Second International Workshop on Semantic and Dynamic Web Processes (SDWP 2005), Part of the 3rd International Conference on Web Services (ICWS'05).

Waldo, J. (1999, October). The Jini architecture for network-centric computing. *Communications of the ACM, 42*(10), 76-82.

Weeratunge, D., Weerawarana, S., & Gunarathne, T. (2004) *Kandula - Apache Kandula.* Retrieved October 18, 2006, from http://ws.apache.org/kandula/

XML (2005). Extensible Markup Language (XML) 1.0 (3rd ed.). W3C Recommendation 04 February 2004. Retrieved October 18, 2006, from http://www.w3.org/TR/REC-xml/

# Chapter VIII
# Service-Oriented Processes:
## An Introduction to BPEL

**Chun Ouyang**
*Queensland University of Technology, Australia*

**Wil M.P. van der Aalst**
*Eindhoven University of Technology, The Netherlands and Queensland University of Technology, Australia*

**Marlon Dumas**
*Queensland University of Technology, Australia*

**Arthur H.M. ter Hofstede**
*Queensland University of Technology, Australia*

**Marcello La Rosa**
*Queensland University of Technology, Australia*

## ABSTRACT

*The Business Process Execution Language for Web Services (BPEL) is an emerging standard for specifying the behaviour of Web services at different levels of details using business process modeling constructs. It represents a convergence between Web services and business process technology. This chapter introduces the main concepts and constructs of BPEL and illustrates them by means of a comprehensive example. In addition, the chapter reviews some perceived limitations of BPEL and discusses proposals to address these limitations. The chapter also considers the possibility of applying formal methods and Semantic Web technology to support the rigorous development of service-oriented processes using BPEL.*

## INTRODUCTION

Web services are a standardised technology for building and integrating distributed software systems. Web services are an incarnation of a software development paradigm known as service-oriented architectures (SOAs). Although there is no broad consensus around the definition of SOAs, it can be said that SOAs revolve around at least three major principles: (1) software systems are functionally decomposed into independently developed and maintained software entities (known as "services"); (2) services interact through the exchange of messages containing meta-data; and (3) the interactions in which services can or should engage are explicitly described in the form of interfaces.

At present, the first generation of Web service technology has reached a certain level of maturity and is experiencing increasing levels of adoption, especially in the context of business applications. This first generation relies on XML, SOAP and a number of so-called WS-* specifications for message exchange (Curbera, Duftler, Khalaf, Nagy, Mukhi, & Weerawarana, 2002), and on XML Schema and WSDL for interface description. In the meantime, a second generation of Web services, based on richer service descriptions is gestating. Whereas in first-generation Web services, interface descriptions are usually equated to sets of operations and message types, in the second generation the description of behavioural dependencies between service interactions (e.g., the order in which messages must be exchanged) plays a central role.

The Business Process Execution Language for Web Services (BEA Systems, Microsoft, IBM, & SAP, 2003), known as BPEL4WS or BPEL for short, is emerging as a standard for describing the behaviour of Web services at different levels of abstraction. BPEL is essentially a layer on top of WSDL and XML Schema, with WSDL and XML Schema defining the structural aspects of service interactions, and BPEL defining the be-haviioural aspects. To capture service behaviour, BPEL adopts principles from business process modeling. Indeed, the central idea of BPEL is to capture the business logic and behavioural interface of services in terms of process models. These models may be expressed at different levels of abstraction, down to the executable level. At the executable level, BPEL can be used to describe the entire behaviour of a new Web service that relies on several other services to deliver its functionality. This practice is known as service composition (Casati & Shan, 2001). An example of a composite service is a travel booking system integrating flight booking, accommodation booking, travel insurance, and car rental Web services.

In this chapter, we introduce BPEL by illustrating its key concepts and the usage of its constructs to define service-oriented processes and to model business protocols between interacting Web services. We also discuss some perceived limitations of BPEL and extensions that have been proposed by industry vendors to address these limitations. Finally, we review some research related to BPEL and conclude with a note on future directions.

## WHY BPEL?

BPEL supports the specification of service-oriented processes, that is, processes in which each elementary step is either an internal action performed by a Web service or a communication action performed by a Web service (sending and/or receiving a message). They can be executed to implement a new Web service as a concrete aggregation of existing services to deliver its functionality (i.e., composite Web service). For example, a service-oriented process may specify that when a "Sales" Web service receives a "purchase order" from the "Procurement" Web service of a customer, the Sales service engages in a number of interactions with the "Procurement" Web service as well as several other Web services related to invoicing, stock control, and logistics, in order to fulfil the order.

BPEL draws upon concepts and constructs from imperative programming languages including: (1) lexically scoped variables; (2) variable assignment; (3) sequential execution; (4) conditional branching; (5) structured loops; and (6) exception handling (try-catch blocks). However, BPEL extends this basic set of constructs with other constructs related to Web services and business process management, to address the following aspects:

- **Messaging:** BPEL provides primitive constructs for message exchange (i.e., send, receive, send/receive).
- **Concurrency:** To deal with concurrency between messages sent and received, BPEL incorporates constructs such as block-structured parallel execution, race conditions, and event-action rules.
- **XML typing:** To deal with the XML-intensive nature of Web services, BPEL variables have XML types described in WSDL and XML Schema. In addition, expressions may be written in XML-specific languages such as XPath or XSLT.

BPEL process definitions can be either fully executable or they can be left underspecified. Executable BPEL process definitions are intended to be deployed into an execution engine. This deployment results in a new Web service being exposed, which usually relies upon and coordinates several other Web services. This is why BPEL is sometimes referred to as a language for "Web service composition." Meanwhile, underspecified BPEL definitions (called *abstract processes*) capture a non-executable set of interactions between a given (Web) service and several other services. One possible usage of abstract BPEL processes is as a means for specifying the order in which the interactions (or "operations") that a given service supports should occur for the service to deliver its

functionality. Such specification of dependencies between interactions is usually called a *business protocol*. Coming back to the above purchase order process, one may capture the fact that an interaction "request for quote" must precede a related interaction "place order." A business protocol can be used for process monitoring, conformance checking and analysis of service compatibility. Importantly, a Web service whose business protocol is described as an abstract BPEL process does not need to be implemented as an executable BPEL process: it may very well be implemented using any other technology (e.g., standard J2EE or .Net libraries and extensions for Web service development). Another usage of an abstract process is as a template of a BPEL process that needs to be refined into an executable implementation. The use of BPEL abstract processes as business protocols or as templates is still the subject of ongoing research as discussed in the Section "BPEL-Related Research Efforts". At present, commercial BPEL technology is mainly focused on fully executable BPEL processes.

To further understand the reason for the emergence of BPEL, it is interesting to view it from a historical perspective. Since 2000 there has been a growing interest in Web services. This resulted in a stack of Internet standards (HTTP, XML, SOAP, WSDL, and UDDI) which needed to be complemented by a process layer. Several vendors proposed competing languages, for example, IBM proposed WSFL (Web Services Flow Language) (Leymann, 2001) building on FlowMark/MQ-Series and Microsoft proposed XLANG (Web Services for Business Process Design) (Thatte, 2001) building on Biztalk. BPEL emerged as a compromise between both languages, superseding the corresponding specifications. It combines accordingly the features of a block-structured language inherited from XLANG with those for directed graphs originating from WSFL. The first version of BPEL (1.0) has been published in August 2002, and the second version (1.1) has been released in May 2003 as input for the standardization within OASIS. The appropriate technical committee (OASIS Web Services Business Process Execution Language TC, 2006) is working since the time of submission and is in the process of finalizing the appropriate standard specification, namely Web Services Business Process Execution Language (WS-BPEL) version 2.0 (OASIS, 2005).

Currently BPEL is implemented in a variety of tools (see http://en.wikipedia.org/wiki/ BPEL for a compendium). Systems such as BEA WebLogic, IBM WebSphere, Microsoft BizTalk, SAP XI and Oracle BPEL Process Manager support BPEL to various degrees, thus illustrating the practical relevance of this language. Also, there is a relatively complete open-source implementation of BPEL, namely ActiveBPEL.

## OVERVIEW OF BPEL

BPEL defines a model and a grammar for describing the behaviour of a business process based on interactions between the process and its partners. A BPEL process is composed of activities that can be combined through structured operators and related through so-called control links. In addition to the main process flow, BPEL provides event handling, fault handling and compensation (i.e., "undo") capabilities. In the long-running business processes, BPEL applies correlation mechanism to route messages to the correct process instance.

BPEL is layered on top of several XML specifications: WSDL, XML Schema and XPath. WSDL message types and XML Schema type definitions provide the data model used in BPEL processes. XPath provides support for data manipulation. All external resources and partners are represented as WSDL services.

### Partners and Partner Links

Business processes that involve Web services often interact with different *partners*. The interaction with each partner occurs through Web service interfaces called *port types*, and the structure of the relationship at the interface level is identified by a *partner link*. A partner link specifies which port type must be supported by each of the partners it connects, and which port type it offers to each partner. A partner link is an instance of a typed connector, known as a *partner link type*, which specifies a set of *roles* and the port type provided by each role.

Consider a simple purchase order process which interacts with two partners: the client and the invoicing service. Each interaction involves one of the parties (i.e., the process or partner) exposing the required functionality via a port type, and the other party making use of that functionality. Figure 1 briefly depicts this process and the interactions between the process and each of its two partners.

For the above process, two partner links are created, namely "purchasing" and "invoicing". Figure 2 shows the XML code snippets defining these two partner links and their link types "purchasingPLT" and "invoicingPLT." The link type "purchasingPLT" includes the definition of a role "purchaseService" (played by the purchase order process) referring to port type "purchasePT" where a "purchase order" is received by the process. Similarly, the link type "invoicingPLT" is defined featuring two roles: "invoiceService" (played by the invoicing service) referring to port type "computerPricePT" where the operation of a "request for price calculation" is called, and "invoiceRequester" (played by the purchase order process) referring to port type "invoiceCallbackPT" where the invoice is received by the process. Following common practice, we define the partner link types in the WSDL document to which the BPEL process definition refers. Meanwhile, the partner links themselves are defined in the BPEL process definition.

*Figure 1. A purchase order process interacting with two partners: the client and the invoicing service*

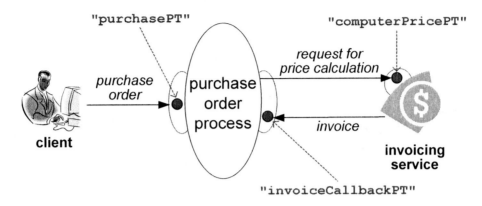

## Activities

A BPEL process definition relates a number of *activities*. Activities are split into two categories: basic and structured activities. *Basic activities* are also called *primitive activities*. They correspond to atomic actions and stand for work being performed within a process. *Structured activities* impose behavioural and execution constraints on a set of activities contained within them. Structured activities can be nested and combined in arbitrary ways, thus enabling the presentation of complex structures.

**Basic activities.** These contain: *invoke*, invoking an operation on some Web service; *receive*, waiting for a message from an external partner; *reply*, replying to an external partner; *wait*, pausing for a certain period of time; *assign*, copying data from one place to another; *throw*, indicating errors in the execution; *compensate*, undoing the effects of already completed activities; *exit*, terminating the entire service instance; and *empty*, doing nothing. Below, we look closer into three activities: *invoke*, *receive*, and *reply*.

*Invoke*, *receive*, and *reply* activities are three types of interaction activities defined in BPEL. Interaction activities must specify the partner link through which the interaction occurs, the operation involved, the port type in the partner

*Figure 2. Definition of the "purchasing" and "invoicing" partner links and their types*

```
WSDL snippet:
  ...
  <partnerLinkType name="purchasingPLT">
    <role name="purchaseService">
      <portType name="purchasePT"/>
    </role>
  </partnerLinkType>

  <partnerLinkType name="invoicingPLT">
    <role name="invoiceService">
      <portType name="computePricePT"/>
    </role>
    <role name="invoiceRequester">
      <portType name="invoiceCallbackPT"/>
    </role>
  </partnerLinkType>
  ...

BPEL snippet:
  ...
  <partnerLinks>
    <partnerLink name="purchasing"
          partnerLinkType="purchasingPLT"
          myRole="purchaseService"/>
    <partnerLink name="invoicing"
          partnerLinkType="invoicingPLT"
          myRole="invoiceRequester"
          partnerRole="invoiceService"/>
  </partnerLinks>
  ...
```

link that is being used, and the input and/or output variables that will be read from or written to. Note that variables are used to carry data (see Subsection on "Data Handling") and are required only in executable processes.

For an *invoke* activity, the operation and port type that are specified are that of the service being invoked. Such an operation can be a synchronous "request-response" or an asynchronous "one-way" operation. An *invoke* activity blocks to wait for a response if it is calling a request-response operation, whereas in the case of a one-way operation, *invoke* can be viewed as a "send" action. A synchronous invocation requires both an input variable and an output variable. An asynchronous invocation requires only the input variable of the operation because it does not expect a response as part of the operation. For example, in the purchase order process shown in Figure 1, the process initiates a price calculation service by sending a purchase order to the invoicing service. Figure 3 provides the XML definition of this *invoke* activity, which calls a one-way operation "initiatePriceCalculation".

A business process provides services to its partners through *receive* activities and corresponding *reply* activities. A *receive* activity allows the process to block and wait for a matching message to arrive, while a *reply* activity is used to send a response to a request that was previously accepted via a *receive* activity. Such responses are only meaningful for synchronous interactions. Therefore, a pair of *receive* and *reply* activities

*Figure 3. An invoke activity for initiating a price calculation service*

```
<invoke partnerLink="invoicing"
        portType="computePricePT"
        operation="initiatePriceCalculation"
        inputVariable="PurchaseOrder"/>
```

must map to a request-response operation. In such case, any control flow between these two activities is effectively the implementation of that operation. A *receive* with no corresponding *reply* must map to a one-way operation, and the asynchronous response is always sent by invoking the same one-way operation on the same partner link.

A *receive* activity specifies the partner link it expects to receive from, and the port type and operation that it expects the partner to invoke. In addition, it may specify a variable used to receive the message data being expected. A *receive* activity also plays a key role in the lifecycle of a business process. It is always associated with a specific attribute called *createInstance* with a value of "yes" or "no". The default value of this attribute is "no". A *receive* activity with the *createInstance* attribute set to "yes" must be an initial activity in a business process, which provides the only way to instantiate the process in BPEL (see structured activity *pick* for a variant). A *reply* activity shares the same partner link, port type and operation as the corresponding *receive* activity, but may specify a variable that contains the message data to be sent as the response.

Let's revisit the purchase order process in Figure 1. A process instance is instantiated upon receiving a purchase order from the client, and may be completed by replying to the client with an invoice listing the price for that purchase order. Figure 4 provides the XML definition of the corresponding pair of *receive* and *reply* activities over a request-response operation named "sendPurchaseOrder". In the same process, there is another *receive* activity referring to a one-way operation "sendInvoice". It is used for receiving the invoice produced by the invoicing service. The process defines this activity as the response to the price calculation request sent by the process before (see the *invoke* activity defined in Figure 3). Figure 5 gives the XML definition of this *receive* activity.

Before moving onto structured activities, it is worth mentioning the following two restrictions

*Figure 4. An initial receive activity for receiving a purchase order from the client and the corresponding reply activity for replying with an invoice for the order*

```
<receive partnerLink="purchasing"
      portType="purchasePT"
      operation="sendPurchaseOrder"
      variable="PurchaseOrder"
      createInstance="yes"/>

...

<reply partnerLink="purchasing"
      portType="purchasePT"
      operation="sendPurchaseOrder"
      variable="Invoice"/>
```

*Figure 5. A receive activity for receiving an invoice from the invoicing service*

```
<receive partnerLink="invoicing"
      portType="invoiceCallbackPT"
      operation="sendInvoice"
      variable="Invoice"/>
```

that BPEL applies on the above three interaction activities:

- First, BPEL does *not* allow two *receive* activities to be active (i.e., ready to consume messages) at the same time if they have the same partner link, port type, operation, and *correlation set* which is used for routing messages to process instances (see Subsection on "Correlation"). If this happens, a built-in fault named "conflictingReceive" will be raised at runtime.

- Second, BPEL does *not* allow a request to call a request-response operation if an active *receive* is found to consume that request, but a *reply* has not yet been sent to a previous request with the same operation, partner link, and correlation set. If this happens, a built-in fault named "conflictingRequest" will be thrown.

*Figure 6. A sequence of activities performed in the purchase order process in Figure 1*

```
begin sequence
   receive PurchaseOrder from client;
   invoke PriceCalculation on invoicing service;
   receive Invoice from invoicing service;
   reply Invoice to client
end sequence
```

**Structured activities.** BPEL defines six structured activities: *sequence, switch, pick, while, flow,* and *scope.* The use of these activities and their combinations enable BPEL to support most of the workflow patterns described in (Aalst, van der, Hofstede, ter, Kiepuszewski, & Barros, 2003).

A *sequence* activity contains one or more activities that are performed sequentially. It starts once the first activity in the sequence starts, and completes if the last activity in the sequence completes. For example, Figure 6 defines a sequence of activities performed within the purchase order process shown in Figure 1. To improve readability, this and the following code snippets do not use XML syntax. Instead, BPEL element names are written in bold while the level of nestings of elements is captured through indentation.

A *switch* activity supports conditional routing between activities. It contains an ordered list of one or more conditional branches called *case* branches. The conditions of branches are evaluated in order. Only the activity of the first branch whose condition holds true will be taken. There is also a default branch called *otherwise* branch, which follows the list of *case* branches. The *otherwise* branch will be selected if no *case* branch is taken. This ensures that there is always one branch taken in a switch activity. The switch activity completes when the activity of the selected branch completes. For example, consider a supply-chain process which interacts with a buyer and a seller. Assume that the buyer has ordered a volume of 100 items of a certain product. The process needs to check the stock inventory before fulfilment. If the result shows more than 100 items of the product in stock, the process performs the fulfilment work (which may contain a number of activities); if the result shows less than 100 items in stock, a fault is thrown indicating the product is out of stock; otherwise (i.e., no items are in stock), another fault is thrown signalling the product is discontinued. Figure 7 shows how to use a *switch* construct to model these activities.

A *pick* activity captures race conditions based on timing or external triggers. It has a set of branches in the form of an event followed by an activity, and exactly one of the branches is selected upon the occurrence of the event associated with it. If more than one of the events occurs, the selection of the activity to perform depends on which event occurred first. If the events occur almost simultaneously, there is a race and the choice of activity to be performed depends on both timing and implementation. There are two types of events: message events (*onMessage*) which occur upon the arrival of an external message, and alarm events (*onAlarm*) which occur upon a system timeout.

Note that *onMessage* is a *receive*-like construct and is thereby treated in much the same manner as a *receive* activity, for example,, both are used for process instantiation, share the same attributes, and should not violate the constraint on "conflictingReceive." A *pick* activity completes when one of the branches is triggered by the occurrence of its associated event and the corresponding activity completes. Figure 8 shows an example of a typical usage of *pick* for modeling the order entry/completion within a supply-chain process. There are three events: a line item message event whose occurrence will trigger an order entry action; a completion message event whose occurrence will trigger an order completion action; and an alarm event which will occur after a period of 3 days and 10 hours and thus trigger a timeout action.

*Figure 7. A switch activity modeling stock inventory check in a supply-chain process*

```
begin switch
    case StockResult >100 : perform fulfillment work
    case StockResult > 0 : throw OutOfStock fault
    otherwise : throw ItemDiscoutinued fault
end switch
```

*Figure 8. A pick activity modeling order entry/completion in a supply-chain process*

```
begin pick
    onMessage LineItem : add line item to order
    onMessage CompletionDetail : perform order completion
    onAlarm for 'P3DT10H' : handle timeout for order completion
end pick
```

*Figure 9. A while activity modeling a loop of the pick activity defined in Figure 8*

```
While MoreOrderEntriesExpected = true
    begin pick
        onMessage LineItem : add line item to order
        onMessage CompletionDetail :
            begin sequence
                perform order completion;
                MoreOrderEntriesExpected := false
            end sequence
        onAlarm for 'P3DT10H' :
            begin sequence
                handle timeout for order completion;
                MoreOrderEntriesExpected := false
            end sequence
    end pick
```

A *while* activity supports repeated performance of an activity in a structured loop, that is, a loop with one entry point and one exit point. The iterative activity is performed until the specified *while condition* (a boolean expression) no longer holds true. For example, the *pick* activity defined in Figure 8 can occur in a loop where the seller is accepting line items for a large order from the buyer. Figure 9 shows how this loop can be specified using a *while* activity. The *pick* activity nested within *while* can be repeated until no more order entries are expected.

A *flow* activity provides parallel execution and synchronization of activities. It also supports the usage of *control links* for imposing further control dependencies between the activities nested within it. Control links are non-structural constructs in BPEL and will be covered in more detail in the next subsection. Figure 10 shows an example of the simple usage of *flow* construct as equivalent to a nested concurrency construct. In this example, a supply-chain process sends questionnaires to the buyer and seller in parallel, and then blocks to wait for their responses. After both have replied, the process continues to next task (e.g., to generate an evaluation report). In Figure 10, the two *invoke* activities are enabled to start concurrently as soon as the *flow* starts. Assume that both *invoke* activities refer to synchronous request-response operations. The *flow* is completed after the buyer and the seller have both responded.

A *scope* is a special type of structured activity. It is used for grouping activities into blocks, and each block is treated as a unit to which the same event and exception handling can be applied. A *scope* has a primary activity (i.e. main activity) that defines its normal behaviour, and can provide *event handlers*, *fault handlers*, and also a *compensation handler*. Like other structured activities, scopes can be nested to arbitrary depth, and the whole process is implicitly regarded as

the top level scope. The usage of *scope* will be discussed in detail further on in Subsections on "Event Handlers", "Fault Handling" and "Compensation".

## Control Links

The *sequence, flow, switch, pick,* and *while* described in the previous subsection provide a means of expressing structured flow dependencies. In addition to these constructs, BPEL provides another construct known as *control links* which, together with the associated notions of *join condition* and *transition condition*, support the definition of precedence, synchronization and conditional dependencies on top of those captured by the structured activities.

A *control link* denotes a conditional transition between two activities. A *join condition*, which is associated to an activity, is a boolean expression in terms of the tokens carried by incoming control links to this activity. Each token, which represents the status of the corresponding control link, may take either a positive (true) or a negative (false) value. For example, a control link between activities A and B indicates that B cannot start before A has either completed or has been skipped (e.g., A is part of an unselected branch of a *switch* or *pick*). Moreover, activity B can only be executed if its associated join condition evaluates to true, otherwise B will not run. A *transition condition*, which is associated to a control link, is a boolean expression over the process variables (just like

*Figure 10. A flow activity modeling two concurrent questionnaire interactions in a supply-chain process*

```
begin flow
    invoke FillQuestionnaire (request-response) operation on the buyer
    invoke FillQuestionnaire (request-response) operation on the seller
end flow

    ...
```

the conditions in a *switch* activity). For example, an activity X propagates a token with a positive value along an outgoing control link L, if and only if X was executed (as opposed to being skipped) and the transition condition associated to L evaluates to true.

As mentioned above, if an activity has incoming control links, one of the enabling conditions for this activity to run is that its associated join condition evaluates to true. Otherwise, a fault called *join failure* occurs. When a join failure occurs at an activity, it can be handled in two different ways as determined by the *suppressJoinFailure* attribute associated with the activity. This attribute can be set to a value of "yes" or "no". If "yes," it instructs to suppress the join failure. In this case, the activity will be skipped, and the tokens carried by all its outgoing links will take a negative value. The process by which positive and negative tokens are propagated along control links, causing activities to be executed or skipped, is called *dead path elimination*. Otherwise, if the *suppressJoinFailure* is set to "no," the join failure is thrown, which triggers the standard fault handling procedure (see Subsection on "Fault Handling").

Control links are non-structural constructs defined in BPEL, and allow the definition of directed graphs. However, it is important to mention two link restrictions. First, control links must not create cyclic graphs. Second, control links must not cross the boundary of a loop (i.e., a *while* activity) as that would lead to an inconsistent state.

We revisit the example of the stock inventory check within a supply-chain process. This has been previously specified by a *switch* activity shown in Figure 7. We use control links to replace the *switch* construct for the modeling. For completeness, we add two activities: one is that the process inquires the stock result from the seller before the inventory check *switch* activity, and the other is that the process informs the seller about the updated stock result after the *switch* activity. Using structured constructs, the above two activities, together with the previous *switch* activity for stock inventory check, can be specified in a *sequence* construct. Using control link constructs, we obtain a directed graph representation shown in Figure 11. Figure 12 sketches the definition of the corresponding abstract BPEL specification.

*Figure 11. A directed graph representing the stock inventory check procedure within a supply-chain process*

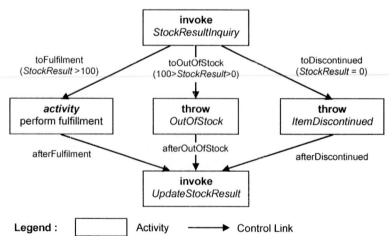

From the above example, it can be observed that any control link leaving an unexecuted activity or whose transition condition evaluates to false will have its link status set to false. As a result, each control link will propagate either a true or a false token so that the activities downstream which have a control dependency on the link do not end up waiting for ever. This is the mechanism of dead path elimination that we have mentioned before. Also note that, as a syntactical restriction in BPEL, control links must be used within a *flow* construct.

## Event Handlers

The purpose of *event handlers* is to specify logic to deal with events that take place concurrently while the process is running. An event handler is an event-action rule associated with a scope, and is in the form of an event followed by an activity.

*Figure 12. Using control links to model the stock inventory check procedure sketched in Figure 11*

```
begin flow (suppressJoinFailure ="yes")
   begin link declaration
      link "toFulfillment"
      link "toOutOfStock"
      link "toDiscontinued"
      link "afterFulfillment"
      link "afterOutOfStock"
      link "afterDiscontinued"
   end link declaration
   invoke StockResultQuery (request-response) operation on the seller
      source of link "toFulfillment" with
         transitionCondition (StockResult >100)
      source of link "toOutOfStock" with
         transitionCondition (StockResult > 0 and StockResult <100)
      source of link "toDiscontinued" with
         transitionCondition (StockResult = 0)
   activity : performing fulfillment work
      joinCondition LinkStatus("toFulfillment")
      target of link "toFulfillment"
      source of link "afterFulfillment"
         transitionCondition (true)
   throw OutOfStock fault
      joinCondition LinkStatus("toOutOfStock")
      target of link "toOutOfStock"
      source of link "afterOutOfStock"
         transitionCondition (true)
   throw ItemDiscoutinued fault
      joinCondition LinkStatus("toDiscontinued")
      target of link "toDiscontinued"
      source of link "afterDiscontinued"
         transitionCondition (true)
   invoke StockResultUpdate (one-way) operation on the seller
      joinCondition LinkStatus("afterFulfillment") or
                     LinkStatus("afterOutOfStock") or
                     LinkStatus("afterDiscontinued")
      target of link "afterFulfillment"
      target of link "afterOutOfStock"
      target of link "afterDiscontinued"
end flow
```

An event handler is enabled when its associated scope is under execution and may execute concurrently with the main activity of the scope. When an occurrence of the event associated with an enabled event handler is registered, the activity within the handler is executed while the scope's main activity continues its execution. Also, the activity within an event handler is invoked concurrently when the corresponding event occurs. For this reason, control links are not allowed to cross the boundary of an event handler.

It is important to emphasize that event handlers are part of the normal behaviour of a scope, unlike fault and compensation handlers (see Subsections on "Fault Handling" and "Compensation"). The event handlers associated with a scope are enabled when that scope commences, and are disabled when the normal processing of the scope is complete. Any event handler that has already started is allowed to finish its execution. An entire scope is not considered to complete until all event handlers associated with the scope have finished their executions.

BPEL allows any type of activity, except the *compensate* activity, to handle events. There are two types of events. One is the message events (*onEvent*) triggered by the arrival of an external message, the other is the alarm events (*onAlarm*) triggered by an alarm which goes off after a user-specified time.

**Message event handlers**. The semantics of *onEvent* message events is very similar to *receive* activities, except that these message events cannot create process instances. An event handler is not enabled prior to the creation of a process instance, and is capable of processing events only if an instance has been created. The message that triggers an event is identified by the partner link from which the message arrives, the appropriate port type, operation and optional variable and correlation set. This message can be part of either an asynchronous (one-way) or a synchronous (request-response) operation. In the latter case, the event handling logic is expected to have a

*reply* activity, in order to fulfil the requirements of the operation.

When a message event is triggered, the activity specified within the corresponding message event handler is carried out. Message event handlers remain active as long as the scope to which they are attached is active. An active message event handler can be triggered multiple times, even simultaneously, if the expected message events occur multiple times. However, it should be noted that simultaneously active instances of a message event handler is permitted, while the semantics of simultaneous *onEvent* from the same partner, port type, operation and with the same correlation set are undefined. The reader may recall that *receive* activities have a similar constraint.

**Alarm event handlers**. An *onAlarm* event marks a system timeout. It has two alternative attributes: *for* and *until*, and exactly one of them must be specified. These two attributes determine two forms of alarm events. The first specifies duration within *for* attribute. In this form, a timer for calculating the duration is started when the associated scope is activated. As soon as the specified duration is reached, the activity in the corresponding event handler is executed. In the second form, *until* attribute details a specific point in time when the alarm will be fired. As soon as this specific point in time is reached, the alarm event is triggered and the corresponding event handler is executed. It should be noted that, unlike message events, alarm events can be processed at most once while the associate scope is active.

Let's revisit the purchase order process shown in Figure 1. The process may terminate its execution if either a cancel message is received from the client or the process has been running already for two days in processing a purchase order from the client. In the latter case, the process will reply to the client with a cancel message (instead of an invoice). The two event handlers defined in Figure 13 are used to implement the above two scenarios when the sequence activity defined in Figure 6 is running.

*Figure 13. Examples of the message and alarm event handlers used for terminating the purchase order process shown in Figure 1*

```
begin scope
    onEvent Cancel from client : exit
    onAlarm for 'P2DT' :
        begin sequence
            reply Cancel to client;
            exit
        end sequence
    (* sequence activity defined in Figure 6 *)
end scope
```

## Fault Handling

Fault handling in a business process enables the process to recover locally from possible anticipated faults that may arise during its execution. For example, consider a fault caused by insufficient funds in the client's account for payment during a purchase order process. The fault may be handled by requesting the information of another available account from the client, without having to restart the entire process.

BPEL considers three types of faults. These are: *application faults* (or *service faults*), which are generated by services invoked by the process, such as communication failures; *process-defined faults*, which are explicitly generated by the process using the *throw* activity; and *system faults*, which are generated by the process engine, such as "conflictingReceive," "conflictingRequest" and join failures introduced before. Note that the first two types of faults are usually user-defined, while the last one consists of built-in faults defined in BPEL.

Fault handlers specify reactions to internal or external faults that occur during the execution of a scope, and are defined for a scope using *catch* activities. Unlike event handlers, fault handlers do not execute concurrently with the scope's main activity. Instead, this main activity is interrupted before the body of the fault handler is executed. In more detail, if a fault occurs during the normal process of a scope, it will be caught by one of the fault handlers defined for the scope. The scope switches from the normal processing mode to the fault handling mode. Note that it is never possible to run more than one fault handler for the same scope under any circumstances.

A fault handler is defined either explicitly or implicitly. An implicit fault handler is also known as a default fault handler. It is created, using a *catch*-all activity, to catch any fault that is not caught by all explicit fault handlers within the scope. Therefore, one can assume that each scope has at least one (default) fault handler. If a fault handler cannot handle a fault being caught or another fault occurs during the fault handling, both faults need to be re-thrown to the (parent) scope that directly encloses the current scope. A scope in which a fault has occurred is considered to have ended abnormally and thus cannot be compensated, no matter whether or not the fault can be handled successfully (without being re-thrown) by the corresponding fault handler.

Finally, control links may cross the boundary of fault handlers. However, a control link is only allowed to *leave* the boundary of a fault handler, and the converse is not true. Also, if a fault occurred within a scope has been handled successfully, any control link leaving from that scope will be evaluated normally.

Let's refer back to the stock inventory check specified in Figure 7. Figure 14 shows two fault handlers used to catch the two faults that may occur during the inventory check. If a fault occurs indicating the product is out of stock, the process invokes the order pending operation on the buyer. Otherwise, if a fault occurs indicating the product discontinued, the process invokes the order rejection operation on the buyer.

*Figure 14. Examples of the fault handlers for catching the corresponding faults occurred during the stock inventory check defined in Figure 7*

```
begin scope
    catch OutOfStock fault :
        invoke OrderPending operation on the buyer
    catch ItemDiscontinued fault :
        invoke OrderRejection operation on the buyer
    (* switch activity defined in Figure 7 *)
end scope
```

## Compensation

As part of the exception handling, compensation refers to application-specific activities that attempt to undo the already completed actions. For example, consider a client requests to cancel the air ticket reservation with a ticket order process. The process will need to carry out the following compensation actions, which involve the cancellation of the reservation with the airline, and optionally the conduction of fee charges to the client if there are fees applied for the cancellation of a reservation.

In BPEL, compensation actions are specified within a compensation handler. Each scope, except the top level scope (i.e. process scope), provides one compensation handler that is defined either explicitly or implicitly. Similarly to a default fault handler, an implicit (or default) compensation handler is created for a scope, if the scope is asked for compensation but an explicit compensation handler is missing for that scope. A fault handler or the compensation handler of a given scope, may perform a *compensate* activity to invoke the compensation of one of the sub-scopes nested within the given scope. Similarly to the control link restrictions applied to event handlers, control links are not allowed to cross the boundary of compensation handlers.

It is important to mention that whether the compensation handler of a scope is available for invocation depends on the current local state of the scope. For example, it is not possible to conduct the compensation of a scope that has never been executed. BPEL uses a term "*scope snapshot*" to refer to the preserved state of a successfully completed uncompensated scope. In such state, the data to which the scope has access is snapshotted for use when the associated compensation handler is running. Thus, the compensation handler of a scope is available for invocation only if the scope has a scope snapshot. Otherwise, invoking a compensation handler that is unavailable is equivalent to performing an empty activity. Since the compensation of already completed activities is a complex procedure, we decide not to include an example here and the interested reader may refer to (BEA Systems, Microsoft, IBM, & SAP, 2003) for more details.

## Data Handling

In the previous subsections, we mainly focus on the control logic of a BPEL process. Careful readers may already notice that the process data is necessary for the process logic to make data-driven decisions (e.g., in a *switch* activity). In the following, we introduce how data is represented and manipulated in BPEL.

**Messages.** Business protocols specified in BPEL prescribe exchange of *messages* between interacting Web services. These messages are WSDL messages defined in the appropriate WSDL definitions. Briefly, a message consists of a set of named *parts*, and each of these parts is typed generally using XML Schema. For example, in Figure 15 below, the *orderMsg* is shown with three message parts: an *orderNumber* of an integer type, an *orderDetails* of a string type, and a *timeStamp* of a dateTime type. Note that the integer, string and dateTime are all simple XML Schema types. If a complex XML Schema type is needed, it needs to be defined in the corresponding XML Schema file (see Section on "BPEL At Work").

*Figure 15. Example of a WSDL message definition*

```
<message name="orderMsg"/>
  <part name="orderNumber"
type="integer"/>
  <part name="orderDetails"
type="string"/>
  <part name="timeStamp"
type="dateTime"/>
</message>
```

*Figure 16. Examples of variable definitions in BPEL*

```
<variables>
  <variable name="order"
messageType="orderMsg"/>
  <variable name="order_backup"
messageType="orderMsg"/>
  <variable name="number"
type="integer"/>
</variables>
```

**Variables**. In a BPEL process definition, variables are used to hold messages exchanged between the process and its partners as well as internal data that is private to the process. Variables are typed, using WSDL message types, XML Schema simple types or XML Schema elements. Note that if a variable is of WSDL message type, it also consists of a set of named parts (each of which as specified in a *part* attribute). For example, in Figure 16 both *order* and *order_backup* variables are defined as of the *orderMsg* type above, and the *number* variable is defined as of an integer type.

Each variable is declared within a scope and is said to belong to that scope. Variables that belong to the global process scope are called *global variables*, while others are called *local variables*. BPEL follows the same rules as those in imperative programming languages with lexical scoping of variables. A variable is visible in the scope (e.g., namely Q) to which it belongs and all scopes that are nested within Q. Thus, a global variable is visible in the entire process. Also, it is possible to hide a variable in a scope (Q) by defining a variable with the same name in one of the scopes nested in Q.

**Expressions**. BPEL supports four types of expressions: (1) *boolean-valued* expressions for specifying transition conditions, join conditions, and conditions in *switch* or *while* activities; (2) *deadline-valued* expressions for specifying *until* attribute of *onAlarm* or a *wait* activity; (3)

*Figure 17. Examples of expressions used in BPEL*

```
... bpws:getLinkStatus('linkL2') ...
... bpws:getVariableData('order','orderNumber')>50
...
... until="'2006-01-31T18:00'" ...
... for="'P40D'" ...
```

*duration-valued* expressions for specifying *for* attribute of *onAlarm* or a *wait* activity; and (4) general expressions for assignments (see next). BPEL provides an extensible mechanism for specifying the language used to define expressions. This language must have facilities such as to query data from variables, to query the status of control links, and so forth XPath 1.0 is the default language for specifying expressions. Another language that can be used is XSLT. Figure 17 gives four examples of expressions used in BPEL. The first two are both boolean-valued expressions: one indicating the status of a control link, the other indicating whether the *orderNumber* of an *order* message is greater than a given number (e.g. 50). The third one is a deadline-valued expression, and the last one is a duration-based expression.

**Assignments**. Data can be copied from one variable to another using the *assign* activity. An assign activity may consist of a number of assignments, each of which being defined by a *copy* element with *from* and *to* attributes. The source of the copy (specified by *from* attribute) and the target (specified by *to* attribute) must be type-compatible. BPEL provides a complete set of possible types of assignments. For example, within common uses of assignment, the source of the copy can be a variable, a part of a variable, an XPath expression, and the target of the copy can be a variable or a part of a variable. Figure 18 illustrates copying data from one variable (*order*) to another (*order_backup*) as well as copying data from a variable part (*orderNumber* part of *order*) to a variable of compatible type (*number*), and both assignments are defined within one *assign* activity.

## Correlation

Business processes may in practice occur over a long period of time, possibly days or months. In long-running business processes, it is necessary to route messages to the correct process instance. For example, when a request is issued from a partner, it is necessary to identify whether a new business process should be instantiated or the request should be directed to an existing process instance. Instead of using the concept of instance ID as often used in distributed object system, BPEL reuses the information that can be identified from the specifically marked parts in incoming messages, such as *order number* or *client id*, to route messages to existing instances of a business process. This mechanism is known as *correlation*. The concept of *correlation set* is then defined by naming specific combinations of certain parts in the messages within a process. This set can be used in *receive*, *reply* and *invoke* activities, the *onMessage* branch of *pick* activities, and the *onEvent* handlers.

Similarly to variables, each correlation set is defined within a scope. Global correlation sets are declared in the process scope, and local correlation sets are declared in the scopes nested within a process. Correlation sets are only visible for the scope (Q) in which they are declared and all scopes nested in Q. Also, correlation set can

*Figure 18. Examples of assignments used in BPEL*

```
<assign>
 <copy>
  <from variable="order"/>
  <to variable="order_backup"/>
 </copy>
 <copy>
  <from variable="order"
part="orderNumber"/>
  <to variable="number"/>
 </copy>
</assign>
```

only be initiated once during the lifetime of the scope to which it belongs. How to define and use correlation sets will be illustrated through the example in the next section.

## BPEL AT WORK

This section describes the example of a BPEL process which provides sales service. This process, namely salesBP, interacts with a customer process (customerBP) by means of asynchronous messages. The process salesBP enacts the role of service provider, whilst the customer is the service requester.

### Process Description

Figure 19 depicts the behaviour of the process salesBP. The process is instantiated upon receiving a request for quote (*rfQ*), which includes the *description* and the *amount* of the goods needed, a unique identifier of the request (*rfQId*), and a deadline (*tO*). Next, the process checks the availability of the amount of the goods being requested. If not available, a *rejectRfQ* is sent back to the customer, providing the *reason* of the rejection. Otherwise, the process prepares a *quote* with the *cost* of the offer and then sends it back to the customer. After

*Figure 19. Flow diagram of the salesBP process*

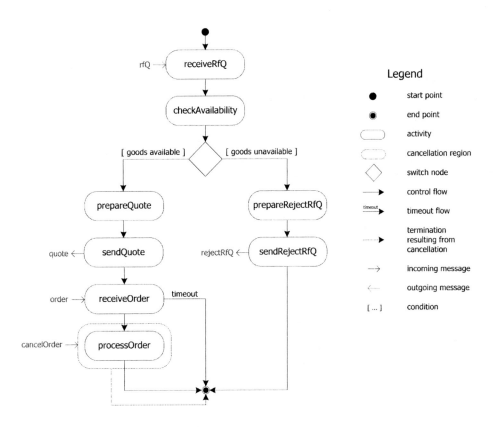

sending the *quote*, the process waits for an *order* until time-limit *tO* is reached. If the *order* is not received by that time, no more activities will be performed. Otherwise, if the order is returned before the deadline *tO*, it will be processed. After the order has been processed successfully, the entire process instance will complete. However, the processing of the order may be cancelled at any time upon receiving a *cancelOrder* message from the customer, and as a result, the process will be forced to terminate.

## XML Schema Definition

Figure 20 shows the XML Schema file "saleX. xsd" for the process salesBP. It defines the complex XML Schema types for messages *rfQ*, *quote*, *or-*

*der*, *rejectRfQ* and *cancelOrder* that are involved in salesBP (lines 7-26). In particular, messages *order* and *cancelOrder* have the same structure as message *quote* (lines 3-5). Besides, each message includes an element named *rfQId* (lines 9, 17, 23), through whose value a BPEL-compliant execution engine is able to identify the proper process instance. In this example, this value, which is initially set by the requester (i.e., customerBP) and then propagated to the provider, is supposed to be unique.

## WSDL Document

The BPEL process salesBP is layered on top of the WSDL document "sales.wsdl" shown in Figure 21. In particular, the first part of the code concerns the description of the messages exchanged by the service, and their mapping with the related elements in the salesX.xsd schema (lines 2-16). In the second part, two port types called "providerPT" and "requesterPT" are defined: the former groups all the input messages of the salesBP process, that is, *rfQ, order* and *cancelOrder* (lines 17-27), the latter groups all its output messages, that is, *quote* and *rejectRfQ* (lines 28-35). Each message is enclosed in a corresponding operation featuring the same name; each operation is asynchronous (i.e., one-way operation) since it contains only one input message.

BPEL requires the port types involved in an interaction to be included in a partner link type construct together with their corresponding roles. Therefore the partner link type "salesPLT" has been defined, featuring two roles: provider (played by salesBP) and requester (played by custom-

erBP), assigned to port types "providerPT" and "requesterPT," respectively (lines 36-43).

## BPEL Process Definition

Figure 22 shows an excerpt from the BPEL code that defines an executable salesBP process. A BPEL process basically consists of a header, regarding the general process definition, and the process flow, which will be concretely executed by the BPEL engine.

In the initial part, a partner link named "salesPL" is defined (lines 2-5): it refers to the partner link type "salesPLT" previously declared in the WSDL file and is used to allow the process to interact with its partner (customerBP). salesPL has two roles: provider, played by the process itself (line 3), and requester, played by the customer (line 4). A list of variables is also declared,

*Figure 20. XML Schema definition - salesX.xsd*

```
01: <schema ...>
02:   <element name="rfQ" type="rfQMsgType"/>
03:   <element name="quote" type="quoteMsgType"/>
04:   <element name="order" type="quoteMsgType"/>
05:   <element name="cancelOrder" type="quoteMsgType"/>
06:   <element name="rejectRfQ" type="rejectRfQMsgType"/>
07:   <complexType name="rfQMsgType">
08:     <sequence>
09:       <element name="rfQId" type="string"/>
10:       <element name="description" type="string"/>
11:       <element name="amount" type="integer"/>
12:       <element name="tO" type="dateTime"/>
13:     </sequence>
14:   </complexType>
15:   <complexType name="quoteMsgType">
16:     <sequence>
17:       <element name="rfQId" type="string"/>
18:       <element name="cost" type="double"/>
19:     </sequence>
20:   </complexType>
21:   <complexType name="rejectRfQMsgType">
22:     <sequence>
23:       <element name="rfQId" type="string"/>
24:       <element name="reason" type="string"/>
25:     </sequence>
26:   </complexType>
27: </schema>
```

which corresponds to the messages handled by the process (lines 6-13), and a correlation set called "salesCS", where *rfQId* (set as a value of the so-called *properties* attribute) contains the information for routing messages to the correct process instance (lines 14-16).

The process flow (lines 17-105) is basically a sequence of three activities: a *receive*, a check on some data and a *switch*, corresponding to the main flow depicted in Figure 15. Through the first activity, receiveRfQ, a new process instance is created once the initial message *rfQ* is received (line 20). This is then copied into variable *rfQ* (line 19), and the current instance is tagged with the value read from the correlation set "salesCS" (lines 21-23). The second activity, checkAvailability (not shown in the code for simplicity), sets the boolean variable *goodsAvailable* to "true" if the amount of the goods being requested is available, otherwise to "false".

Next, the *switch* activity checks the value of *goodsAvailable* to determine whether or not to continue processing the request for quote. This corresponds to take one of the two branches in the *switch* activity.

If the goods are available, the *case* branch (Lines 28-79) will be executed leading to a sequence of four sub-activities, as shown in Figure 15 under the [goods available] branch. The first activity is the *assign* prepareQuote (lines 30-39), through which salesBP can generate the *quote* message to be sent to the customer copying into variable *quote* the value of *rfQId* taken out from variable *rfQ* and setting the amount of the offer to *120* (in a real scenario, this value can be read from a proper database). Then the quote is sent by means of the following *invoke* activity, sendQuote (lines 40-46), using the same correlation set "salesCS" (lines 43-45). Now the process should be able to receive an *order* within a given time-limit: if this happens the order can be processed, otherwise the process must end. Accordingly, receiveOrder is realised with a *pick* activity (lines 47-77) specified to wait for the *order* to arrive (*onMessage*

*Figure 21. WSDL interface document - sales. wsdl*

```
01: <definitions name="sales".../>
02:   <message name="rfQMsg">
03:     <part name="payload" element="rfQ"/>
04:   </message>
05:   <message name="orderMsg">
06:     <part name="payload" element="order"/>
07:   </message>
08:   <message name="quoteMsg">
09:     <part name="payload" element="quote"/>
10:   </message>
11:   <message name="cancelOrderMsg">
12:     <part name="payload" element="cancelOrder"/>
13:   </message>
14:   <message name="rejectRfQMsg">
15:     <part name="payload" element="rejectRfQ"/>
16:   </message>
17:   <portType name="providerPT">
18:     <operation name="rfQ">
19:       <input message="rfQMsg"/>
20:     </operation>
21:     <operation name="order">
22:       <input message="orderMsg"/>
23:     </operation>
24:     <operation name="cancelOrder">
25:       <input message="cancelOrderMsg"/>
26:     </operation>
27:   </portType>
28:   <portType name="requesterPT">
29:     <operation name="quote">
30:       <input message="quoteMsg"/>
31:     </operation>
32:     <operation name="rejectRfQ">
33:       <input message="rejectRfQMsg"/>
34:     </operation>
35:   </portType>
36:   <partnerLinkType name="salesPLT">
37:     <role name="provider">
38:       <portType name="providerPT"/>
39:     </role>
40:     <role name="requester">
41:       <portType name="requesterPT"/>
42:     </role>
43:   </partnerLinkType>
44:   . . .
45: </definitions>
```

*Figure 22. BPEL executable process salesBP.bpel*

```
001: <process name="salesBP"...>
002:  <partnerLinks>
003:   <partnerLink name="salesPL" myRole="provider"
004:    partnerRole="requester" partnerLinkType="salesPLT"/>
005:  </partnerLinks>
006:  <variables>
007:   <variable name="rfQ" messageType="rfQMsg"/>
008:   <variable name="quote" messageType="quoteMsg"/>
009:   <variable name="order" messageType="orderMsg"/>
010:   <variable name="cancelOrder" messageType="cancelOrderMsg"/>
011:   <variable name="rejectRfQ" messageType="rejectRfQMsg"/>
012:   <variable name="goodsAvailable" type="boolean"/>
013:  </variables>
014:  <correlationSets>
015:   <correlationSet name="salesCS" properties="rfQId"/>
016:  </correlationSets>
017:  <sequence>
018:   <receive name="receiveRfQ" partnerLink="salesPL"
019:    portType="providerPT" operation="rfQ" variable="rfQ"
020:    createInstance="yes">
021:    <correlations>
022:     <correlation set="salesCS" initiate="yes"/>
023:    </correlations>
024:   </receive>
025:   ...checkAvailability: set variable "goodsAvailable" to true
026:    or false...
027:   <switch>
028:    <case condition="getVariableData('goodsAvailable')">
029:     <sequence>
030:      <assign name="prepareQuote">
031:       <copy>
032:        <from variable="rfQ" part="payload" query="/rfQ/rfQId"/>
033:        <to variable="quote" part="payload" query="/quote/rfQId"/>
034:       </copy>
035:       <copy>
036:        <from expression="120"/>
037:        <to variable="quote" part="payload" query="/quote/cost"/>
038:       </copy>
039:      </assign>
040:      <invoke name="sendQuote" partnerLink="salesPL"
041:       portType="requesterPT" operation="quote"
042:       inputVariable="quote">
043:       <correlations>
044:        <correlation set="salesCS" initiate="no".../>
045:       </correlations>
046:      </invoke>
047:      <pick name="receiveOrder">
048:       <onMessage partnerLink="salesPL" portType="providerPT"
049:        operation="order" variable="order">
050:        <correlations>
051:         <correlation set="salesCS" initiate="no"/>
052:        </correlations>
```

*continued on following page*

*Figure 22. continued*

```
053:          <scope name="processOrder_s">
054:           <faultHandlers>
055:            <catch faultName="forcedTermination">
056:             <exit/>
057:            </catch>
058:           </faultHandlers>
059:           <eventHandlers>
060:            <onMessage portType="sales:providerPT"
061:             operation="cancelOrder" variable="cancelOrder"
062:             partnerLink="salesPL">
063:             <correlations>
064:              <correlation set="salesCS" initiate="no"/>
065:             </correlations>
066:             <throw name="forcedTermination"
067:              faultName="forcedTermination"/>
068:            </onMessage>
069:           </eventHandlers>
070:           ...processOrder...
071:          </scope>
072:         </onMessage>
073:         <onAlarm
074:          until="getVariableData('rfQ','payload','/rfQ/tO')">
075:          <empty/>
076:         </onAlarm>
077:        </pick>
078:       </sequence>
079:      </case>
080:      <otherwise>
081:       <sequence>
082:         <assign name="prepareRejectRfQ">
083:          <copy>
084:           <from variable="rfQ" part="payload"
085:            query="/rfQ/rfQId"/>
086:           <to variable="rejectRfQ" part="payload"
087:            query="/rejectRfQ/rfQId"/>
088:          </copy>
089:          <copy>
090:           <from expression="'goods unavailable'"/>
091:           <to variable="rejectRfQ" part="payload"...
092:            query="/rejectRfQ/reason"/>
093:          </copy>
094:         </assign>
095:         <invoke name="sendRejectRfQ" partnerLink="salesPL"
096:          portType="requesterPT" operation="rejectRfQ"
097:          inputVariable="rejectRfQ">
098:          <correlations>
099:           <correlation set="salesCS" initiate="no".../>
100:          </correlations>
101:         </invoke>
102:       </sequence>
103:      </otherwise>
104:     </switch>
105:   </sequence>
106: </process>
```

branch—lines 48-72) or for the corresponding timeout alarm to go off (*onAlarm* branch – lines 73-76). In more detail, if the *order* arrives before the timeout expires, it will be processed by the system; otherwise, the process will terminate doing nothing (specified by an *empty* activity – line 75). Assume that the *onMessage* branch is taken. The execution of the activity processOrder may be interrupted when a *cancelOrder* message arrives. For this reason, a scope activity, processOrder_s, is defined (lines 53-71), featuring a fault handler, an event handler and having processOrder as its main activity.

In particular, the event handler (lines 59-69) captures the receipt of a *cancelOrder* message during the processing of the order, and then throws a "forcedTermination" fault, which interrupts the above order processing (lines 66-67). This fault will be immediately caught by the fault handler attached to the scope (lines 54-58), and as a result, the process will be forced terminate. Note that the *exit* activity (within the fault handler – line 56) models the explicit termination, since a BPEL process automatically ends when there is nothing left to do. The timeout value which triggers the *onAlarm* branch is extrapolated from the field *tO* of variable *rfQ* (line 74).

On the other hand, if the goods are unavailable, the otherwise branch of the *switch* is executed incorporating two activities (lines 80-103), as illustrated in Figure 15 under the [goods unavailable] branch. With the first one, prepareRejectRfQ, salesBP copies into variable *rejectRfQ* the value of *rfQId* taken out from variable *rfQ*, and sets the *reason* of the rejection with the string "goods unavailable" (lines 82-94). The second activity, sendRejectRfQ allows the process to send the message *rejectRfQ* back to the customer, reporting the rejection (lines 95-101).

Now, we take closer look into the correlation mechanism used in this example. When the *rfQ* is sent by an instance of customerBP, the BPEL run-time system performs the following tasks step by step. It generates a new instance of the receiving process salesBP (line 20), reads the value of *rfQId* from the input message, initiates the corresponding correlation set "salesCS," and associates a tag with that value to the newly generated instance (lines 21-23). Next, if the amount in the request is available (line 28), the *quote* is sent back to the customer with the same correlation set as *rfQ* (lines 40-46), and hence it will be delivered to the requester process instance that previously sent the *rfQ*. When an *order* is sent by the customer, since it has the same correlation set as the *quote* and *rfQ*, it will be delivered to the process instance of salesBP that previously sent the *quote* (lines 48-52). Analogously, messages *rejectRfQ* and *cancelOrder* are sent to the correct instances of customerBP (lines 95-101) and salesBP (lines 60-65, for the corresponding receipt). Therefore in this example, from a global point of view, customerBP is the initiator for the correlation set salesCS, whilst salesBP is the follower.

## BPEL Process Execution

We use Oracle BPEL Process Manager platform 10.1.2 (see http://www.oracle.com/technology/products/ias/bpel) to edit and execute the salesBP process. Figure 23 provides a graphical view of the BPEL process definition of salesBP in Oracle JDeveloper, a BPEL editor integrated in the Oracle platform. In JDeveloper, both the code and graphical perspectives are available to the user. After compiling the source files (including "salesBP.bpel," "sales.wsdl" and "salesX.xsd"), a BPEL process can be exposed as a Web Service deployed in a compliant run-time environment. A screenshot showing a running instance of salesBP on top of the Oracle BPEL engine is depicted in Figure 24. In the running instance, the amount of the goods being requested by the customer is available and the process salesBP is waiting for an order from the customer.

Note that in the salesBP process pictured in Figures 23 and 24, activity checkAvailability has been implemented by means of a scope (checkAvailability_s) which encloses the necessary activities to interact with another partner link representing an internal Web Service. This service is responsible to check the availability of the goods and to send the result back to salesBP.

## BPEL EXTENSIONS

The BPEL specification defines only the kernel of BPEL, which mainly involves the control logic of BPEL, limited definitions on the data handling and even less in the communication aspect. Given the fact that BPEL is already a very complicated language, a complete BPEL specification covering full definitions of BPEL will make the specification less maintainable and the corresponding implementation will become less manageable. For this reason, the OASIS technical committee on WS-BPEL decides to keep the scope of the current specification and allows future extensions to be made in separate documentations. So far, there have been three extensions proposed to BPEL.

**BPEL-SPE**. BPEL currently does not support the modularization and reuse of "fragments" of a business process. This has driven the publication of a joint proposal of *WS-BPEL Extension for Sub-Processes, known as BPEL-SPE (*Kloppmann, Koenig, Leymann, Pfau, Rickayzen, Riegen, et al., 2005 September*),* by two major companies involved in Web services standards: IBM and SAP. *BPEL-SPE* proposes an extension to BPEL that allows for the definition of *sub-processes* which are fragments of BPEL code that can be reused within the same or across multiple BPEL processes.

**BPEL4People**. In practice, many business process scenarios require human user interactions. For example, it may be desirable to define which people are eligible to start a certain business process; a process may be stuck because no one has been assigned to perform a particular task;

or it is not clear who should perform the task in hand. BPEL currently does not cover human user interactions. To fill in this blank, IBM and SAP have recently proposed an extension to BPEL, namely *BPEL4People* (Kloppmann, Koenig, Leymann, Pfau, Richayzen, Riegen, et al., 2005 July). *BPEL4People* mainly defines how human tasks can be implemented in a process. This can be viewed as to add (human) resource and resource allocation considerations to BPEL. In parallel, another tool vendor, Oracle, has implemented its own extension to BPEL for handling human tasks into its BPEL engine.

**BPELJ**. In BPEL, everything is seen as a service. A BPEL executable process is an implementation of a service that relies on other services. To express that a given service uses certain resources, such as a database, a file or a legacy application, it is necessary to expose the database system, the file system or the legacy application as services. Since BPEL needs to be used in environments where not all resources are exposed as services, it is sometimes handy to be able to break the "all-service" paradigm of BPEL. Driven by this imperative, an extension of BPEL allowing for Java code to be inserted at specific points has been defined, namely *BPELJ* (Blow, Goland, Kloppmann, Leymann, Pfau, Roller, & Rowley, 2004 March). This is similar to how Java code can be embedded into HTML code in the context of Java Server Pages (JSPs). As BPEL gains more adoption both in the .Net and the Java platforms, one can expect other similar dialects of BPEL to emerge. Also, as a competing product to BPELJ, Oracle has implemented its own Java Snippet for embedding Java program into a BPEL process.

## BPEL-RELATED RESEARCH EFFORTS

There has been a number of research activities conducted on BPEL. These include: systemati-

*Figure 23. Oracle JDeveloper 10.1.2: Graphical view of the BPEL process salesBP*

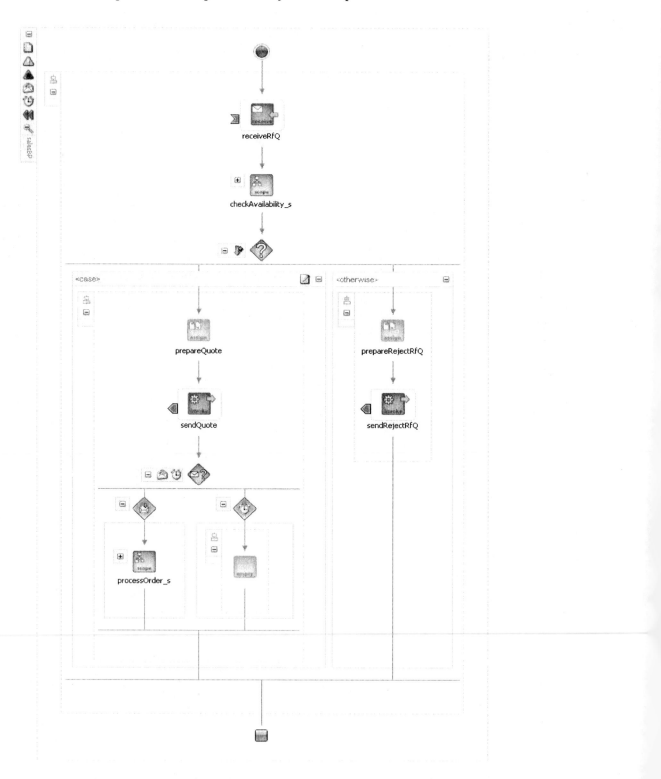

*Figure 24. OracleBPEL Process Manager Console 10.1.2: Execution flow of a running instance of the BPEL process salesBP*

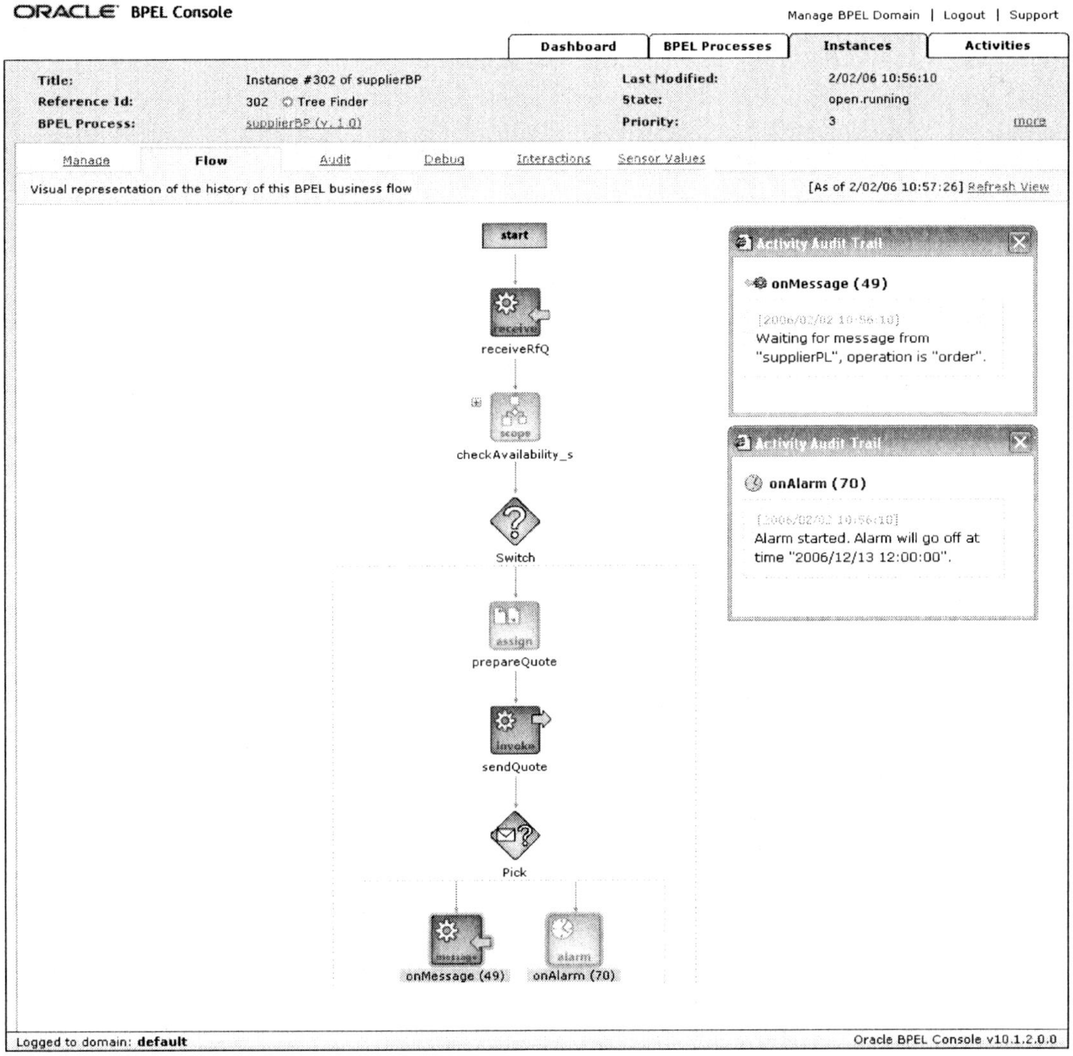

cal evaluation of BPEL based on the so-called workflow patterns (van der Aalst, ter Hofstede, Kiepuszewski, & Barros, 2003), analysis of BPEL process models, generating BPEL code from a "high-level" notations, and choreography conformance checking based on BPEL.

## Pattern-Based Analysis of BPEL

There are 20 control-flow patterns (van der Aalst, ter Hofstede, Kiepuszewski, & Barros, 2003) and

40 data patterns (Russell, ter Hofstede, Edmond, & van der Aalst, 2005), and accordingly the evaluation has been performed from control-flow perspective (Wohed, van der Aalst, Dumas, & ter Hofstede, 2003) as well as from data perspective (Russel, ter Hofstede, Edmond, & van der Aalst, 2005). The results of the pattern-based evaluation of BPEL show that BPEL is more powerful than most traditional process languages. The control-flow part of BPEL inherits almost all constructs of the block-structured language XLANG and

the directed graphs of WSFL. Therefore, it is no surprise that BPEL indeed supports the union of patterns supported by XLANG and WSFL. In particular, the BPEL *pick* construct (namely "deferred choice" in workflow control-flow patterns) is not supported in many existing workflow languages. From the data perspective, BPEL is one of the few languages that fully support the notion of "scope data" elements (one of the workflow data patterns). It provides support for a scope construct which allows related activities, variables and exception handlers to be logically grouped together. The default binding for data elements in BPEL is at process instance level and they are visible to all of the components in a process. In addition to the above evaluation of BPEL, work that has been conducted on the pattern-based evaluation of Oracle BPEL Process Manager (Mulyar, 2005) also involves the evaluation based on a set of 43 workflow resource patterns (Russell, van der Aalst, ter Hofstede, & Edmond, 2005).

## Generating and Analyzing BPEL Models

Since BPEL is increasingly supported by various engines, it becomes interesting to link it to other types of models. In this respect, it is insightful to consider the following: (1) BPEL more closely resembles a programming language than a modeling language and (2) BPEL supports the specification of service-oriented processes at various levels of details, down to executable specifications, but it is not designed to support any form of analysis (e.g., behaviour verification, performance analysis, etc.). In other words, BPEL definitions are somewhere in-between the higher-level process models that analysts and designers manipulate in the early phases of the development lifecycle, and fully-functional code. Hence, there are two interesting translations relating to BPEL: (1) a translation from a higher-level notation to BPEL and (2) a translation from BPEL to a model for

which established analysis techniques can be applied.

Until now, attention has focused on the second translation. Several attempts have been made to capture the behaviour of BPEL in a formal way. A comparative summary of mappings from BPEL to formal languages can be found in (van der Aalst, Dumas, ter Hofstede, Russell, Verbeek, and Wohed, 2005). The result of comparison shows that the work in Ouyang, van der Aalst, Breutel, Dumas, ter Hofstede, and Verbeek (2005) presents the first full formalization of control flow in BPEL that has led to a translation tool called BPEL2PNML and a verification tool called WofBPEL. Both tools are publicly available at http://www.bpm. fit.qut.edu.au/projects/babel/tools. WofBPEL is capable of performing useful and non-syntactic analysis, for example, detection of unreachable activities and detection of potentially "conflictingReceive" faults in a BPEL process. With respect to the verification issues related communication aspects, the work in Fu, Bultan, and Su (2004) discusses how to verify the correctness of collection of inter-communicating BPEL processes, and similarly, the work in (Martens, 2005) shows how to check the compatibility of two services with respect to communication.

In industry, various tools and mappings are being developed to generate BPEL code from a graphical representation. Tools such as the IBM WebSphere Choreographer and the Oracle BPEL Process Manager offer a graphical notation for BPEL. However, this notation directly reflects the code and there is no intelligent mapping. This implies that users have to think in terms of BPEL constructs (e.g., blocks, syntactical restrictions on control links, etc.). More interesting is the work of White (2005) that discusses the mapping of Business Process Modelling Notations (BPMN) to BPEL, the work of Mantell (2005) on the mapping from UML activity diagrams to BPEL, and the work by Koehler and Hauser (2004) on removing loops in the context of BPEL. However, none of these publications provides a mapping of some (graphical) process modeling language onto BPEL: White (2005) and Mantell (2005) merely present the problem and discusses some issues using examples and Koehler and Hauser (2004) focuses on only one piece of the puzzle. This then motivated the recent work on develop mappings from Workflow nets to BPEL (van der Aalst & Lassen, 2005) and from a core subset of BPMN to BPEL (Ouyang, van der Aalst, Dumas, & ter Hofstede, 2006).

## Choreography Conformance Checking Based on BPEL

To coordinate a collection of inter-communicating Web services, the concept of "choreography" defines collaborations between interacting parties, that is,, the coordination process of interconnected Web services that all partners need to agree on. A choreography specification is used to describe the desired behaviour of interacting parties. Language such as BPEL and the Web Services Choreography Description Language (WS-CDL) (Kavantzas, Burdett, Ritzinger, Fletcher, & Lafon, 2004 December) can be used to define a desired choreography specification.

Assuming that there is a running process and a choreography specification, it is interesting to check whether each partner (exposed as Web service) is well behaved. Note that partners have no control over each other's services. Moreover, partners will not expose the internal structure and state of their services. This triggers the question of conformance: "Do all parties involved operate as described?" The term "choreography conformance checking" is then used to refer to this question. To address the question, one can assume the existence of both a process model which describes the desired choreography and an event log which records the actual observed behaviour, that is, an actual choreography.

Choreography conformance checking benefits from the coexistence of event logs and process models and may be viewed from two angles. First

of all, the model may be assumed to be "correct" because it represents the way partners should work, and the question is whether the events in the log are consistent with the process model. For example, the log may contain "incorrect" event sequences which are not possible according to the definition of the model. This may indicate violations of choreography that all parties previously agreed upon. Second, the event log may be assumed to be "correct" because it is what really happened. In the latter case the question is whether the choreography that has been agreed upon is no longer valid and should be modified.

The work in van der Aalst, Dumas, Ouyang, Rozinat, and Verbeek (2005) presents an approach for choreography conformance checking based on BPEL and Petri nets (Murata, 1989). Based on a process model described in terms of BPEL abstract processes, a Petri net description of the intended choreography can be created by using the translation defined in (Ouyang, van der Aalst, Dumas, & ter Hofstede, 2006) and implemented in the tool BPEL2PNML. The conformance checking is then performed by comparing a Petri net and an event log (transformed from SOAP messages under monitoring). To actually measure conformance, a tool called *Conformance Checker* has been developed in the context of the *ProM framework* (see http://www.processmining.org, which offers a wide range of tools related to process mining.

## BPEL and Semantic Web Technology

Researchers in the field of Semantic Web have put forward approaches to enhance BPEL process definitions with additional information in order to enable automated reasoning for a variety of purposes. One area in which Semantic Web technology can add value to service-oriented processes is that of *dynamic binding*. The idea of dynamic binding is that rather than hard-coding in the BPEL process definition (or in an associated deployment descriptor) the identities and/or locations of the "partner services" with which the BPEL process interacts, these partner services are determined based on information that is only available at runtime. For example, Verma, Akkiraju, Goodwin, Doshi, and Lee (2004) present an approach to achieve dynamic binding of Web services to service-oriented processes described in BPEL by considering inter-service dependencies and constraints. They present a prototype that can handle BPEL process definitions extended with such dependencies and constraints and can exploit this additional information for runtime discovery of suitable Web services. The paper also discusses another area where Semantic Web technology complements service-oriented process technology: that of semi-automated refinement of process templates described as BPEL abstract processes (see Introduction section) into fully executable processes. An example of a tool that implements such refinement techniques is presented in (Berardi, Calvanese, De Giacomo, Hull, & Mecella, 2005).

Mandell and McIlraith (2003) present another approach to dynamic binding of Web services to BPEL processes. Their approach is based on the DAML Web service ontology (DAML-S) (Ankolekar, Burstein, Hobbs, Lasilla, Martin, McDermott, McIlraith, Narayanan, Paolucci, Payne, & Sycara, 2002), the DAML Query Language (DQL) (Fikes, Hayes, & Horrocks, 2002), and the Java Theorem Prover (JTP) (Frank, 1999) which implements DQL. Other approaches to capture Web service semantics include WSDL-S (Akkiraju, Farrell, Miller, Nagarajan, Schmidt, Sheth, & Verma, 2005) and OWL-S (Martin et al., 2005).

While the potential outcomes of these and similar research efforts are appealing, the scalability of the proposed techniques is still unproven and the involved tradeoffs restrict their applicability. Several questions remain open such as: "which languages or approaches to describe service semantics provide the best tradeoffs between expressiveness and computational complexity?" or "How much can a user trust the decisions made by an automated Web service discovery engine, especially at runtime?"

## CONCLUSION

In this chapter, we have presented the core concepts of BPEL and the usage of its constructs to describe executable service-oriented processes. We have also discussed extensions to BPEL that have been proposed by tool vendors to address some of its perceived limitations, as well as long-term challenges related to the use of BPEL in the context of rigorous system development methodologies.

Currently, BPEL is being used primarily as a language for implementing Web services using a process-oriented paradigm. In this respect, BPEL is competing with existing enhancements to mainstream programming environments such as WSE and WCF (which enhance the Microsoft .Net framework with functionality for Web service development), or Apache Axis and Beehive (which do the same for the Java platform). Certainly, BPEL is making inroads in this area, and there is little doubt that it will occupy at least a niche position in the space of service implementation approaches. Several case studies related to the use of BPEL in system development projects have been reported in the trade press. These include a report of BPEL use at the European Space Agency and in an outsourcing project conducted by Policy Systems for a state health care service (http://tinyurl.com/zrcje and http://tinyurl.com/krg3o).

However, it must not be forgotten that BPEL can also be used to describe the behaviour of services at a more abstract level. Unfortunately, up to now, tool vendors have given little attention to exploring the possibilities opened by the description of BPEL abstract processes. BPEL abstract processes can be used to represent "service behaviour" at different levels of details. In particular, they enable the representation of temporal, casual and exclusion dependencies between message exchanges. In this respect, BPEL abstract processes can be viewed as adding "behaviour semantics" on top of the basic structural definitions of service interactions provided by WSDL interfaces. Two open questions at the moment are: (1) how to best exploit this additional behaviour semantics in order to support the analysis, testing, operation and maintenance of service-oriented systems; (2) what level of automated support can be realistically provided to aid in refinement of abstract BPEL processes into executable ones. These and the other research directions reviewed in this chapter are only the tip of the iceberg of what can be achieved when richer semantic descriptions of Web services covering behavioural aspects are available.

## REFERENCES

Akkiraju, R., Farrell, J., Miller, J., Nagarajan, M., Schmidt, M., Sheth, A., & Verma, V. (2005, April). *Web Service Semantics – WSDL-S* (Technical note). University of Georgia and IBM. Retrieved October 18, 2006, from http://lsdis.cs.uga.edu/library/download/WSDL-S-V1.html

Ankolekar, A., Burstein, M., Hobbs, J., Lasilla, O., Martin, D., McDermott, D., McIlraith, S., Narayanan, S., Paolucci, M., Payne, T., & Sycara, K. (2002). DAML-S: Web service description for the Semantic Web. In *Proceedings of the 1st International Semantic Web Conference* (pp. 348-363).

BEA Systems, Microsoft, IBM & SAP (2003, May). Business process execution language for Web services (BPEL4WS). Retrieved October 18, 2006, from ftp://www6.software.ibm.com/software/developer/library/ws-bpel.pdf

Berardi, D., Calvanese, D., De Giacomo, G., Hull, R., & Mecella, M. (2005). Automatic composition of transition-based Semantic Web services with messaging. In *Proceedings of the 31st International Conference on Very Large Data Bases* (pp. 613-624).

Blow, M., Goland, Y., Kloppmann, M., Leymann, F., Pfau, G., Roller, D., & Rowley, M. (2004, March). *BPELJ: BPEL for Java* (White paper). BEA and IBM.

Casati, F., & Shan, M.-C. (2001). Dynamic and adaptive composition of e-services. *Information Systems, 26*(3), 143-162.

Curbera, F., Duftler, M., Khalaf, R., Nagy, W., Mukhi, N., & Weerawarana, S. (2002). Unraveling the Web services Web: An introduction to SOAP, WSDL, and UDDI. *IEEE Internet Computing, 6*(2), 86-93.

Fikes, R., Hayes, P., & Horrocks, I. (2002). *DAML Query Language, Abstract Specification*. Retrieved October 18, 2006, from http://www.daml.org/2002/08/dql/dql.

Frank, G. (1999) A general interface for interaction of special-purpose reasoners within a modular reasoning system. In *Proceedings of the 1999 AAAI Fall Symposium on Question Answering Systems* (pp. 57-62).

Fu, X., Bultan, T., & Su, J. (2004). Analysis of interacting BPEL Web services. In *Proceedings of the 13th International Conference on World Wide Web* (pp. 621-630). New York: ACM Press.

Kavantzas, N., Burdett, D., Ritzinger, G., Fletcher, T., & Lafon, Y. (2004, December). *Web services choreography description language version 1.0* (W3C Working Draft 17). Retrieved October 18, 2006, from http://www.w3.org/TR/2004/WD-ws-cdl-10-20041217/

Kloppmann, M., Koenig, D., Leymann, F., Pfau, G., Richayzen, A., Riegen, von, C., Schmidt, P., & Trickovic, I. (2005, July). *WS-BPEL extension for people: BPEL4People*. A Joint White Paper by IBM and SAP.

Kloppmann, M., Koenig, D., Leymann, F., Pfau, G., Rickayzen, A., von Riegen, C., Schmidt, P., & Trickovic, I. (2005, September). WS-BPEL extension for sub-processes: BPEL-SPE. A Joint White Paper by IBM and SAP.

Koehler, J., & Hauser, R. (2004). Untangling unstructured cyclic flows: A solution based on continuations. In *Proceedings of OTM Confederated International Conferences, CoopIS, DOA, and ODBASE 2004* (pp. 121-138). Berlin: Springer-Verlag.

Leymann, F. (2001). *Web services flow language, version 1.0*. Retrieved October 18, 2006, from http://www-306.ibm.com/software/solutions/Webservices/pdf/WSFL.pdf

Mandel, D., & McIlraith S. (2003). Adapting BPEL4WS for the semantic Web: The bottom up approach to Web service interoperation. In *Proceedings of the 2nd International Semantic Web Conference* (pp. 227-241).

Mantell, K. (2005). *From UML to BPEL*. Retrieved October, 18, 2006, from http://www.ibm.com/developerworks/Webservices/library/ws-uml2bpel

Martens, A. (2005). Analyzing Web service based business processes. In *Proceedings of the 8th International Conference on Fundamental Approaches to Software Engineering* (pp. 19-33). Berlin: Springer-Verlag.

Martin, D., Burstein, M., Hobbs, J., Lassila, O., McDermott, D., McIlraith, S., Narayanan, S., Paolucci, M., Parsia, B., Payne, T., Sirin, E., Srinivasan, N., & Sycara, K. (2005, November). OWL-S: Semantic markup for Web services, W3C Member Submission. Retrieved October 18, 2006, from http://www.w3.org/Submission/OWL-S

Mulyar, N. (2005). *Pattern-based evaluation of Oracle-BPEL* (BPM Center Report BPM-05-24). BPMcenter.org.

Murata, T. (1989). Petri nets: Properties, analysis and applications. *Proceedings of the IEEE, 77*(4), 541-580.

OASIS (2005, December 21). Web Services Business Process Execution Language version 2.0 (Committee Draft). Retrieved October 18, 2006, from http://www.oasis-open.org/committees/download.php/16024/wsbpel-specification-draft-Dec-22-2005.htm

OASIS Web Services Business Process Execution Language TC (2006). Retrieved October 18, 2006, from http://www.oasis-open.org/committees/tc_home.php?wg_abbrev=wsbpel

Ouyang, C., van der Aalst, W.M.P., Breutel, S., Dumas, M., ter Hofstede, A.H.M., & Verbeek, H.M.W. (2005). *Formal semantics and analysis of control flow in WS-BPEL* (BPM Center Report BPM-05-15). BPMcenter.org.

Ouyang, C., van der Aalst, W.M.P., Dumas, M., & ter Hofstede, A.H.M. (2006). *Translating BPMN to BPEL* (BPM Center Report BPM-06-02). BPMcenter.org.

Russell, N., ter Hofstede, A.H.M., Edmond, D., & van der Aalst, W.M.P. (2005). Workflow data patterns: Identification, representation and tool support. In *Proceedings of the 24th International Conference on Conceptual Modeling* (pp. 353-368). Berlin: Springer-Verlag.

Russell, N., van der Aalst, W.M.P., ter Hofstede, A.H.M., & Edmond, D. (2005). Workflow resource patterns: Identification, representation and tool support. In *Proceedings of the 17th International Conference on Advanced Information Systems Engineering* (pp. 216-232). Berlin: Springer-Verlag.

Thatte, S. (2001). XLANG Web services for business process design. Retrieved October 18, 2006, from http://www.gotdotnet.com/team/xml_wsspecs/xlang-c/default.htm

van der Aalst, W.M.P., Dumas, M., Ouyang, C., Rozinat, A., & Verbeek, H.M.W. (2005). *Choreography conformance checking: An approach based on BPEL and Petri nets* (BPM Center Report BPM-05-25). BPMcenter.org. To appear in ACM TOIT.

van der Aalst, W.M.P., Dumas, M., ter Hofstede, A.H.M., Russell, N., Verbeek, H.M.W., & Wohed, P. (2005). Life after BPEL? In *Proceedings of European Performance Engineering Workshop and International Workshop on Web Services and Formal Methods* (pp. 35-50). Berlin: Springer-Verlag.

van der Aalst, W.M.P., & Lassen, K.B. (2005). *Translating workflow nets to BPEL* (BETA Working Paper Series). Eindhoven, The Netherlands: Eindhoven University of Technology. To appear in Information and Software Technology.

van der Aalst, W.M.P., ter Hofstede, A.H.M., Kiepuszewski, B., & Barros, A.P. (2003). Workflow patterns. *Distributed and Parallel Databases, 14*(1), 5-51.

Verma, K., Akkiraju, R., Goodwin, R., Doshi, P., & Lee, J. (2004). On accommodating inter-service dependencies in Web process flow composition. In *Proceedings of the American Association for Artificial Intelligence (AAAI) 2004 Spring Symposium* (pp. 37-43). Stanford, CA: AAAI.

White, S. (2005). Using BPMN to model a BPEL process. *BPTrends, 3*(3), 1-18. Retrieved October, 2006, from http://www.bptrends.com/

Wohed, P., van der Aalst, W.M.P., Dumas, M., & ter Hofstede, A.H.M. (2003). Analysis of Web services composition languages: The case of BPEL4WS. In *Proceedings of the 22nd International Conference on Conceptual Modelling* (pp. 200-215). Chicago: Springer-Verlag.

## APPENDIX 1

### Exercises

1. Describe two different ways supported by BPEL for describing business processes. What are the differences between them? What are the usages of them?

2. Describe how BPEL uses WSDL, XML Schema, and XPath.

3. Define the partner link between a purchase order process and the external shipping service, and the corresponding partner link type. In this relationship, the purchase order process plays the role of the service requester, and the shipping service plays the role of the service provider. The requester role is defined by a single port type called "shippingCallbackPT". The provider role is defined by a single port type called "shippingPT".

4. Consider the following fragments of a BPEL process definition:

```
<flow>
  <sequence>
   <invoke name="inv1" partnerLink="pl1"
        portType="pt1" operation="op1"
        inputVariable="var1"/>
   <receive name="rcv1" partnerLink="pl2"
        portType="pt2" operation="op2"
        variable="var2"/>
  </sequence>
  <sequence>
   <receive name="rcv2" partnerLink="pl1"
        portType="pt2" operation="op2"
        variable="var3"/>
   <receive name="rcv3" partnerLink="pl3"
        portType="pt3" operation="op2"
        variable="var4"/>
  </sequence>
</flow>
```

(a) Write down all possible execution sequences of activities in the above definition.

(b) Can we add the following *pick* activity in parallel to the two existing *sequence* activities in the above *flow*? If yes, write down all possible execution sequences of activities in this updated process definition, otherwise explain why not.

```
<pick>
 <onMessage partnerLink="pl3" portType="pt3"
        operation="op2" variable="var5"/>
  <invoke name="inv2" partnerLink="pl1"
        portType="pt4" operation="op4"/>
 </onMessage>
 <onAlarm for='P1DT12H'>
```

## APPENDIX 1. CONTINUED

```
<exit/>
 </onAlarm>
</pick>
```

5.  This exercise involves two interacting BPEL processes P1 and P2. P1 consists of a sequence of activities starting with a *receive* activity and ends with a *reply* activity. The pair of *receive* and *reply* defines an interaction with process P2. In P2, there is an *invoke* activity calls a request-response operation on P1, which triggers the executions of the above pair of *receive* and *reply* activities in P1.

    (a)  Define an appropriate partner link between P1 and P2 (Assume that P1 plays *myRole*, and P2 plays *partnerRole*).

    (b)  Define the pair of *receive* and *reply* activities in P1.

    (c)  Define the *invoke* activity in P2.

6.  Describe the difference between *switch* and *pick* constructs. Given the four scenarios described below, which of them can be defined using *switch* and which of them can be defined using *pick*?

    (a)  After a survey is sent to a customer, the process starts to wait for a reply. If the customer returns the survey in two weeks, the survey is processed; otherwise the result of the survey is discarded.

    (b)  Based on the client's credit rating, the client's loan application is either approved or requires further financial capability analysis.

    (c)  After an insurance claim is evaluated, based on the findings the insurance service either starts to organize the payment for the claimed damage, or contacts the customer for further details.

    (d)  The escalation service of a call centre may receive a storm alert from a weather service which triggers a storm alert escalation, or it may receive a long waiting time alert from the queue management service which triggers a queue alert escalation.

7.  The diagram above sketches a process with five activities A0, A1, A2, A3 and A4. A multi-choice node splits one incoming control flow into multiple outgoing flows. Based on the conditions associated with these outgoing flows, one or more of them may be chosen. A sync-merge node synchronises all active incoming control flows into one outgoing flow. Based on the above, sketch two possible BPEL definitions for this process using *sequence*, *flow* and *switch* constructs. Also, sketch another BPEL definition of the process using only control link constructs (within a *flow*).

## APPENDIX 1. CONTINUED

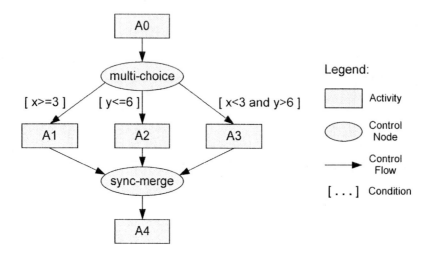

8.    The definition below specifies the execution order of the activities within a BPEL process:

```
begin flow
   begin switch
      case conditionC1: activityA1
      case conditionC2: activityA2
   end switch
   while conditionC3
      activityA3
   begin sequence
      activityA4
      activityA5
   end sequence
end flow
```

(a)   Can we create the following two control links? Justify your answer.
      i)    a control link leading from "activityA1" to "activityA3"
      ii)   a control link leading from "activityA3" to "activityA5"

(b)   Can we re-define the original process using only control links within the *flow* activity? If so, re-write the process definition, otherwise explain why not.

(c)   Assume that there exist two control links: one leading from "activityA1" to "activityA4", the other from "activityA2" to "activityA4". Both links have a default transition condition, that is, a transition condition that always evaluates to true if the source of the link is executed. Consider the following two scenarios:
      i)    "activityA4" has a join condition that is a *disjunction* of all incoming links.
      ii)   "activityA4" has a join condition that is a *conjunction* of all incoming links.
            In both scenarios, "activityA4" has its *suppressJoinFailure* attribute set to "yes". Determine whether "activityA4" will be performed in each scenario? Justify your

## APPENDIX 1. CONTINUED

      answer and provide a possible execution sequence for each scenario.

   (d)   What could verification do when analysing a syntactically correct BPEL process? Argue why automated verification of a BPEL specification is useful.

9.    Sketch the control logic of a BPEL process for requesting quotes from an *a priori* known set of N suppliers. The process is instantiated upon receiving a *QuoteServiceRequest* from the Client, and then a *QuoteRequest* is sent in parallel to each of the N suppliers (Supplier1, Supplier2, ..., SupplierN). Next, the process waits for *QuoteResponse* from these suppliers. Assume that (a) each supplier replies with at most one response and (b) only M out of N responses are required (M<=N), which means that after receiving the responses from M suppliers, the process can continue without waiting for the responses from the remaining N-M suppliers. To provide the ability to define how many responses are required, a loop is created that repeats until the required number of responses are received. The responses are collected in the order in which they are received. For each response received, the number of responses received (*NofResponse*) is incremented, and the variable containing the result (*Result*) so far is updated. Also, to provide the ability to stop collecting responses after some period of time (e.g., 2 hours), the above loop is contained within a scope activity that has an alarm event handler. If the alarm is triggered, an exception (*TimeOutFault*) is thrown to be caught in the outer scope, thus allowing the process to exit the loop before it finishes. If the exception is thrown, then all that needs to be done is to incorporate a "Timed Out" indication to the *Result*. Finally, the process completes by sending the *Result* to the Client.

10.   Below is the BPEL code for the definition of a Supplier abstract process. Since it is an abstract BPEL process, not all elements are fully specified. In particular, you may note that the condition in each *while* loop is omitted, which means that the loop may execute for an arbitrary number of times.

```xml
<process name="Supplier">
 <partnerLinks>
  <partnerLink name="client"
        partnerLinkType="clientPLT">
        myRole="supplierProvider"
        partnerRole="supplierRequestor"/>
 </partnerLinks>
  <variables>
  <variable name="inputVariable"
        messageType="supplierRequestMessage"/>
  <variable name="outputVariable"
        messageType="supplierResponseMessage"/>
 </variables>
 <sequence>
  <receive name="order"
      partnerLink="client" portType="servicePT"
      operation="order" variable="inputVariable"
      createInstance="yes"/>
  <invoke name="orderResponse"
      partnerLink="client"
      portType="serviceCallbackPT"
      operation="orderResponse"
      inputVariable="outputVariable"/>
  <scope name="cancellationScope">
```

## APPENDIX 1. CONTINUED

```
<faultHandlers>
  <catch faultName="orderChange">
    <sequence>
      <invoke name="orderChangeResponse"
          partnerLink="client"
          portType="serviceCallbackPT"
          operation="orderChangeResponse"
          inputVariable="outputVariable"/>
      <while>
        <invoke name="orderChangeResponse"
            partnerLink="client"
            portType="serviceCallbackPT"
            operation="orderChangeResponse"
            inputVariable="outputVariable"/>
      </while>
    </sequence>
  </catch>
</faultHandlers>
<eventHandlers>
  <onMessage partnerLink="client"
        portType="servicePT"
        operation="change"
        variable="outputVariable"/>
    <throw name="throwFault" faultName="orderChange"/>
  </onMessage>
</eventHandlers>
<while>
  <invoke name="orderResponse"
      partnerLink="client"
      portType="serviceCallbackPT"
      operation="orderResponse"
      inputVariable="outputVariable"/>
</while>
    </scope>
  </sequence>
</process>
```

(a)    Given the following sequences of executions, indicate which of them are possible and which of them are not possible based on the above definition. Justify your answer.

    i)     receive *order*;

    ii)    receive *order*, send *orderResponse*;

    iii)   receive *order*, send *orderResponse*, receive *change*;

    iv)   receive *order*, send *orderResponse*, send *orderResponse*, receive *change*, send *order-ChangeResponse*;

    v)    receive *order*, send *orderResponse*, receive *change*, send *orderResponse*, send *order-ChangeResponse*.

(b)    In the current process definition, the execution sequence "receive *order*, receive *change*, send *orderChangeResponse*" is not possible. Indicate what minimal changes need to be made to the current process definition, so that this execution sequence becomes possible and all the previous valid execution sequences are preserved.

# Chapter IX
# Semantic Web Services

**Rama Akkiraju**
*IBM T. J. Watson Research Center, USA*

## ABSTRACT

*The promise of dynamic selection and automatic integration of software components written to Web services standards is yet to be realized. This is partially attributable to the lack of semantics in the current Web service standards. To address this, the Semantic Web community has introduced semantic Web services. By encoding the requirements and capabilities of Web services in an unambiguous and machine-interpretable form, semantics make the automatic discovery, composition and integration of software components possible. This chapter introduces Semantic Web services as a means to achieve this vision. It presents an overview of Semantic Web services, their representation mechanisms, related work and use cases.*

## INTRODUCTION

Web services show promise to address the needs of application integration by providing a standards-based framework for exchanging information dynamically between applications. Industry efforts to standardize Web service description, discovery and invocation have led to standards such as WSDL (2001), UDDI (2002), and SOAP (2000) respectively. These industry standards, in their current form, are designed to represent information about the *interfaces of services, how they are deployed*, and *how to invoke them*, but are limited in their ability to express *what* the *capabilities* and *requirements* of services are. This lack of semantic representation capabilities leaves the promise of automatic integration of applications written to Web services standards unfulfilled. If all service providers in all industry domains agree upon a standardized format for representing their services, there would not be a need for semantics. However, it would be presumptuous to assume that all applications and their corresponding services that can be imagined can be standardized. This leads to disparities in service specifications by service providers and requesters for similar services in a given industry. Therefore, in the absence of standardized interfaces for all imaginable services, describing *how* the services may integrate alone is not sufficient. If no semantics are specified, a service requester may not be able to find a service provider due to the superficial differences in interface specifications even if it were a suitable match. A first step toward solving this service location problem is to "rise above these superficial differences in the representation of interfaces of services and to identify the semantic similarities between them" (Paolucci, Kawamura, Payne, & Sycara, 2002b). Adding semantics to represent the requirements and capabilities of Web services is essential for achieving automation in service discovery and execution. This need for semantics in Web services has led to the convergence of concepts from Web services and the Semantic Web community. These efforts have resulted in "Semantic Web services."

Semantic Web services are Web services whose "properties, capabilities, interfaces, and effects are encoded in an unambiguous, and machine-interpretable form" (McIlraith, Son, & Zeng, 2001a). Grosof (2003) states semantic Web services includes both the infrastructural and the application-specific services and that the term "Semantic Web services" can be parsed as "{Semantic Web} Services" (e.g., for relatively broad-purpose knowledge translation and inferencing) or as "Semantic {Web Services}" (e.g., knowledge based service descriptions dealing with discovery, composition, invocation, monitoring, etc.). Sheth (2003) argues that semantics play an important role in the complete lifecycle of Web services. This role of semantics in the lifecycle of Web services is presented in Figure 1. Broadly, the activities in the lifecycle of Web services can be categorized as modeling activities, build-time activities and deployment and run-time activities. During modeling activities, the service provider can explicate the intended semantics by annotating the appropriate parts of the Web service with concepts from a richer semantic model. Since se-

mantic models provide agreement on the meaning and intended use of terms, and may provide formal and informal definitions of the entities, there will be less ambiguity in the intended semantics of the provider. These semantic Web services can then be published in a registry. During discovery, the service requester can describe the service requirements using terms from the semantic model. Reasoning techniques can be used to find the semantic similarity between the service description and the request. In cases where no direct matches are found, the functionality of multiple services can be composed. During composition, the functional aspect of the annotations can be used to aggregate the functionality of multiple services to create useful service compositions while the semantics of nonfunctional aspects of services help determine whether these compositions are legal and valid. During deployment, semantics can be used again to find specific service instances to bind to the service interfaces. During invocation, semantics can be used to represent data transformations. In case of failure of a service during run time, semantics come to rescue to enable automatic service discovery and binding to find suitable substitutable services. This is shown as the "Runtime adaptation" loop in Figure 1. Therefore, once represented, semantics can be leveraged by tools to automate service discovery, mediation, composition, execution and monitoring.

In this chapter, we present an overview of Semantic Web services. The rest of the chapter is organized as follows. First, we motivate the need for semantics in Web services. Next, we present an overview and a comparison of the mechanisms for representing Semantic Web services. Third, we discuss the related work in the area of automatic Web service discovery and composition. Fourth, Semantic Web services use cases are discussed followed by their potential benefits. Finally, we present our conclusions.

*Figure 1. The role of semantics in the lifecycle of Web services*

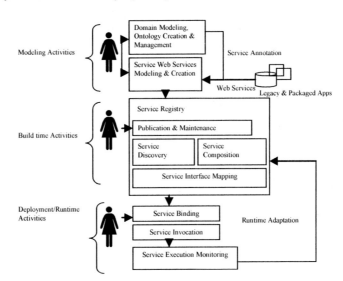

## MOTIVATING THE NEED FOR SEMANTICS IN WEB SERVICES

Identifying similarity between services is a difficult problem because the terminology used to describe Web services may not be identical to the one used in a request. In addition, the structure and type information present in service descriptions will have to be taken into account. Explicit semantics can play an important role in resolving terminology ambiguities. Below we examine the need for semantics in Web services in the context of automatic service discovery, composition, invocation and monitoring with a few examples.

### Service Discovery

Automatically discovering services involves finding a service that matches a given set of requirements (functional as well as nonfunctional) from among a repository (either central or distributed) of services. A match could be syntactic (based on type and structure matching) and/or semantic (based on lexical or other name similarities and ontology matching). In a business-to-consumer (B2C) setting, this would mean, finding a service

provider that can offer a service whose capabilities match the specified requirements, for example, finding an airline ticket booking Web service given a source, destination and payment method. On the other hand, in a business-to-business (B2B) setting, finding service providers on demand and invoking their services without formal agreements is rare. Therefore, a more suitable example would be in a software or asset reuse setting where the objective is to reuse as much of the existing functionality as possible when implementing new functionality. Service discovery in this context would mean finding suitable asset/software components that can be reused to implement full or part of new functionality. Semantics can play an important role in accomplishing discovery in both settings. We consider a few scenarios to examine the semantic issues in matching of services during discovery process.

### Syntactically Similar and Semantically Different Services

In the absence of standardization, multiple service providers could offer similar Web services with different interfaces. For example, two services that take a parameter of type "xsd:string" and return an "xsd:float" can perform completely different functions. One could be a *getStockQuote() service* that takes the name of the company (string) as input and returns stock price (float) and the other could be an *itemAvailabilityCheck() service* that takes an XML document as a string consisting of many parameters such as *partNum, date, quantity* and so forth, and return the quantity (float) that is available for the requested date and *partNum*. Syntactically, that is, by looking at the type of input and output parameters in this example, the interfaces seem like a match even if the service names do not match exactly. So, a syntactic matching engine could still consider this a match—if not a good one. But clearly, these two services are meant to perform very different functionality. This could lead to false positives in matching.

## Syntactically Different and Semantically Similar Services

Contrary to the previous scenario two syntactically dissimilar services can perform the same function semantically. For example, two services both of which provide item availability check interfaces can have syntactically different looking interfaces. Say, one service by the name *itemAvailabilityCheck()* could take an *ItemInfo* input in string form (containing information about the *partNum, dateOfDelivery, requestedQuantity* and so forth, in XML document represented as string) and return the available quantity as float while another service by the name *verifyInventoryAvailability()* could expose the individual parameters separately instead of packaging them in an XML document. Structurally these two services look different even though they perform same function of checking the availability of an item. Therefore, a syntactic matching engine may not consider these two services as good matches. This leads to false negatives. A semantic matcher based on lexical and name similarity may find the services

to be partial match depending on how similar the terms used in the two services are.

## Syntactically Different and Seemingly Semantically Different Services

Adding further complexity to the disparateness in the previous example, different service providers may choose different terminology to express same concepts. What one service provider may refer to as a *itemCode* may be referred to by another as an *SKU (Stock Keeping Unit)*. Sample WSDL snippets for these two cases are shown below. In the absence of domain semantics indicating that *SKU* is a *subClassOf itemCode* and that both are different ways of uniquely identifying an item, these two terms may be considered as unrelated terms. This leads to false negatives. These kinds of superficial differences may stand in the way of identifying suitable services if domain semantics are not explicitly specified.

```
........
<complexType name="ItemInfo">
 <all>
  <element name="itemCode" type="xsd:string"/>
  <element name="dueDate" type="xsd:dateTime" />
  <element name="qty" type="xsd:float" />
 </all>
</complexType>

<message name="request ">
 <part name="itemInfo_in" type="xsd:ItemInfo" />
 <part name="requesterID_in" type="xsd:string" />

</message>

<message name="response ">
 <part name="quantity_out" type="xsd:float"/>
</message>

<portType name="ItemAvailabilityCheck">
 <operation name="itemCheck" >
  <input message="tns:request" name="request"/>
     <output  message="tns:response"
name="response"/>
 </operation>
</portType>
........
```

Sample WSDL snippet for item availability service

```
........
<message name="request ">
 <part name="SKU_in" type="xsd:string" />
 <part name="reqAmt_in" type="xsd:float" />
 <part name="reqDate_in" type="xsd:string" />
 <part name="acctId_in" type="xsd:string" />

</message>

<message name="response ">
 <part name="quantity_out" type="xsd:float"/>
</message>

<portType name="verifyInventoryAvailability">
 <operation name="inventoryAvailability" >
  <input message="tns:request" name="request"/>
     <output message="tns:response"
name="response"/>
 </operation>
 </portType>
........
```

Sample WSDL snippet for inventory verification service

## Syntactically Similar and Seemingly Semantically Similar

In some scenarios the interfaces of services may look similar both syntactically and semantically at a first glance but indeed represent very different things. To illustrate this, we look at two Web services: (1) getChipQuote() service and (2) checkChipPrice() service – whose WSDL snippets are shown below. Both services take a parameter of type "xsd:string" and return an "xsd:float." The names of the parameters are similar as well. However, it these services perform completely different functions. One is a *getChipQuote() service* from semiconductor domain that takes the specification of the chip as an XML document (string) as input and returns price (float) and the other is an *checkChipPrice() service* from online gambling domain that takes the type of chip as a string and returns the bid price (float). If a syntactic matching is performed on these two services based on the number of parameters, and their types, they could incorrectly be considered a match because of type and structural similarity. If semantic matching based on lexical and name-similarity is performed

without considering the domain and context of these two services they could be considered a match. So overall, these two services could be misconstrued as very good match. This leads to false positives. In this example, the real intended semantics are revealed through domain context. Formally this domain context can be modeled using automatically inferenceable markup languages such as OWL (OWL) and WSMO (WSMO).

```
........
<message name="request ">
 <part name="chip_info" type="xsd:string" />
 </message>

<message name="response ">
 <part name="price_out" type="xsd:float"/>
 </message>

<portType name="ChipQuote">
 <operation name="getChipQuote" >
  <input message="tns:request" name="request"/>
     <output message="tns:response"
name="response"/>
 </operation>
 </portType>
........
```

Sample WSDL snippet for chipQuote service from semiconductor domain

```
........
<message name="request ">
 <part name="chip_in" type="xsd:string" />
 </message>

<message name="response ">
 <part name="price_out" type="xsd:float"/>
 </message>

<portType name="ChipPrice">
 <operation name="checkChipPrice" >
  <input message="tns:request" name="request"/>
     <output message="tns:response"
name="response"/>
 </operation>
 </portType>
........
```

Sample WSDL snippet for checking chip price in online gambling domain

Figure 2 summarizes the mishits that might occur with syntactic matching (structure and type matching) and even some types of semantic matching (lexical, name similarity matching). As we have seen in the four scenarios presented

*Figure 2. Pitfalls in syntactic matching and semantic matching based on lexical and name similarity matching*

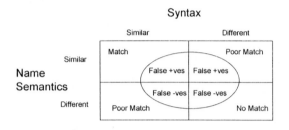

above there is possibility for falsely identifying some services as matches when they are not – leading to false positives (as in scenarios (a) and (d)) – and incorrectly identifying some services as poor or no matches when they could indeed be good matches – leading to false negatives (as in scenarios (b) and (c)). The vision of Semantic Web services is to enable better automatic matching of services based on semantic context so that these types of false positives and negatives can be minimized as much as possible. In the Representation Mechanisms for Semantic Web Services section, we present some approaches to capture semantics of Web services that can help resolve the semantic differences between terms such as "*SKU*" and "*itemCode*" in the above example. In the Related Work section of the chapter, we examine various techniques used to perform automatic service discovery.

## Service Invocation

Service discovery can help identify a suitable service at a semantic level. For example, it can help identify an inventory checking service that fits in within the general parameters specified in the request. However, in order for the application on the requester's side to invoke the chosen service automatically, a more detailed level of matching may be required to identify the actual interface mappings. For example, a service that

takes a "UPC code" as input can be matched at semantic level with a service that can provide "SKU code" since both concepts help uniquely identify items. However, this match may not be executable because of differences in the syntactic representation of these two codes (e.g., UPC may be a 14 digit code while SKU is a 12 digit code). A conversion service (that can convert a "UPC Code" to "SKU Code") may be required before the service invocation can occur. Web service invocation involves creating these interface mappings from the request service to the chosen service. Often this may involve deeper semantic analysis than what was done during service discovery. For example, in some services, the *firstname* and *lastname* parameters from one service need to be concatenated to match with the *fullname* parameter on another service. These kinds of associations can be derived from a semantic model and mappings can be generated and stored to facilitate invocation. Currently, users pour over the documentation to manually generate these mappings and then use tools or write code to get the services ready for invocations. The vision of semantic Web services for service invocation is that tools built using semantics can help reduce this burden on the user.

## Service Composition

Composing existing Web services to deliver new functionality is a requirement in many business domains. Service composition extends the notion of service discovery by enabling automatic composition of services to meet the requirements of a given a high-level task description. For example, to fulfill a high level task such as "place my purchase order with a supplier that can supply n number of parts of type x by a date y," one may require composing services that can perform digital signing and encryption if the supplier requires the information to be secure. Figure 3 shows such a composition. Currently, if such transformations are required to connect up services, a user must select these services manually, and specify the compositions. With semantic markup of services, on the other hand, the information necessary to select and compose services is available via the semantic descriptions of the requirements and capabilities of services. This enables automatic composition.

## Service Execution Monitoring

Semantics can play an important role in service execution monitoring. When services become unavailable new substitutable services can be discovered and bound to a task in place of the failed service. This could make systems built using Semantic Web services robust.

As illustrated in this section, domain semantics can play an important role in resolving ambiguities in the intent of Web services. Significant efforts have been underway by the semantic Web community to help represent such semantics. In the next section, we examine some approaches proposed for capturing semantics in Web services.

## REPRESENTATION MECHANISMS FOR SEMANTIC WEB SERVICES

Web services can be broadly classified as simple and complex services. Semantic Web community defines a simple or atomic Web service as a Web service where "a single Web-accessible computer program, sensor, or device is invoked by a request message, performs its task and perhaps produces a single response to the requester. With atomic services there is no ongoing interaction between the user and the service" (OWL-S, 2005). A simple Web service is typically considered stateless. In contrast a complex or composite service is defined as one that is "composed of multiple more primitive services, and may require an extended interaction or conversation between the requester and the set of services that are being utilized" (OWL-S, 2005). A complex Web service typically involves data flow from one step to another, possibly carrying state information. For example, a purchase order process can contain checking the availability of an item and then placing the purchase order with the same supplier with whom item availability has been verified. This process requires information to

*Figure 3. Illustration of Semantic Web service composition*

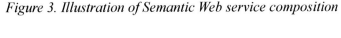

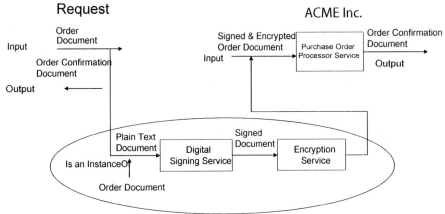

be passed from *check availability* task (represented as a Web service) to *place purchase order* task. Such a collection of related, structured activities that produce a specific service can be defined as a Web process or a complex Web service. Defining semantics for such a complex service could be complicated. Below we examine the representation mechanisms for both simple Web services and complex Web services (alternatively referred to as Web processes).

Semantic Web services representation languages have a significant body of work to draw upon from the fields of computer science and specifically from artificial intelligence. Description logics (Baader, Calvaneese, McGuinness, Nardi, & Patel-Schneider, 2003), frame logics (Kifer, Lausen, & Wu, 1995) and logic programming (Baral & Gelfond, 1994) lay the foundations for formal representations for ontologies. Theory on Finite State Machine (FSM) (Gill, 1962) and its variants such as Petri nets (Reisig, 1985) lay the foundations for distributed interacting systems upon which Web processes or complex Web services are modeled. Theories such as process algebra (Fokkink, 2000), situation calculus (Levesque, Pirri, & Reiter, 1998) and Pi Calculus (Sangiorgi & Walker, 2001) that help represent the state of the universe form the basis for languages such as PSL from which advanced languages for representing Semantic Web services such as FLOWs have emerged.

Below we examine some of the recent efforts to bring semantics to Web services. Example proposals include initiatives, projects and languages such as OWL-S (2001), WSMO (2005), WSDL-S (2005), and SWSA/SWSL (SWSA, 2005; SWSL, 2005). We look at some of them below.

## OWL-S

OWL-S defines an upper ontology (please refer to end notes section of a definition of the term upper ontology) for describing the properties and capabilities of Web services in OWL (OWL, 2004). It is intended to enable users and software agents to automatically discover, invoke, compose, and monitor Web resources offering services, under specified constraints. It defines high level constructs such as a *service profile*: to represent the interfaces of services including inputs, outputs, preconditions and effects, a *service (process) model* to represent the details of inner working of a service, and a *service grounding* to provide information about how to use a service. Whereas OWL-S profile model views a service as an *atomic* process, OWL-S service (process) model captures the state of a service as a *complex* interaction process. While OWL-S profile defines a model for describing the functional properties of a service via constructs such as inputs, outputs, preconditions and effects (sometimes referred to as IOPEs), OWL-S service model uses workflow constructs such as sequence, if-then-else, fork, repeat-until and so forth, to define a composite processes. OWL-S grounding model defines the necessary links to Web service industry standard WSDL to use its invocation model. OWL-S, the result of a DARPA funded project, is among the first efforts to define a formal model for Semantic Web services. This work helped trigger many research efforts both in the academic and industrial research communities. OWL-S is one of the submissions to W3C for defining a framework for semantics in Web services.

The following OWL-S snippets illustrate how *checkInventory()* service discussed in the Motivation section can be represented in OWL-S. The profile, process and grounding models together with a corresponding ontology define a semantic Web service.

```
<profileHierarchy:CheckInv rdf:ID="Profile_CheckIn-
ventory_Service">
   <profile:serviceName>CheckInventoryService_
Agent</profile:serviceName>
   ....
   <profile:hasInput rdf:resource="http://www.daml.org/
services/owl-s/1.0/CheckInvProcess.owl#UPC"/>
   <profile:hasInput rdf:resource="http://www.daml.org/
services/owl-s/1.0/CheckInvProcess.owl#DueDate"/>
   <profile:hasInput rdf:resource="http://www.daml.org/
```

services/owl-s/1.0/CheckInvProcess.owl#Qty"/>

```
    <profile:hasOutput rdf:resource="http://www.daml.
org/services/owl-s/1.0/CheckInvProcess.owl#ItemAvail
Confirmation"/>
    </profileHierarchy: CheckInv >
    OWL-S profile model snippet for CheckInventory()
service

    <process:AtomicProcess rdf:ID="CheckInv">
      <process:hasInput>
      <process:Input rdf:ID="UPC">
      <process:parameterType rdf:resource="http://www.
w3.org/2001/XMLSchema#string"/>
      </process:Input>
      </process:hasInput>
      <process:hasInput>
        <process:Input rdf:ID="dueDate">
      <process:parameterType rdf:resource="http://www.
w3.org/2001/XMLSchema#dateTime"/>
      </process:Input>
       </process:hasInput>
      <process:hasInput>
        <process:Input rdf:ID="numItems">
      <process:parameterType rdf:resource="http://www.
w3.org/2001/XMLSchema#float"/>
      </process:Input>
       </process:hasInput>
      </process:AtomicProcess>
    OWL-S process model snippet for CheckInventory()
service

    <message name="CheckInv_Input">
      <part name="UPC" owl-s-wsdl:owl-s-parameter="
CheckInv:#UPC"/>
      <part name="dueDate" owl-s-wsdl:owl-s-paramete
r="CheckInv:#DueDate"/>
      <part name="numItems" owl-s-wsdl:owl-s-paramete
r="CheckInv:#Qty"/>
      </message>
    OWL-S grounding model for CheckInventory() ser-
vice
```

A visual representation of CheckInvProcess. owl is given below in Figure 4. It can be noted, based on these relationships, that a UPC Code can be passed in place of EAN Code and that EAN scanners can parse UPC Code fine since UPC is a subset of EANCode. This type of information is very useful in trying to match two service interfaces where one refers to a UPC code while the other to an EAN Code. If a domain model such as the one below did not exist, the service interfaces would go unmatched due to the superficial terminology differences.

## WSMO

Web Service Modeling Ontology (WSMO, 2004), a European Union funded project, proposes "four main elements: (1) *ontologies*, which provide the terminology used by other WSMO elements, (2) *Web service* descriptions, which describe the functional and behavioral aspects of a Web service, (3) *goals* that represent user desires, and (4) *mediators*, which aim at automatically handling interoperability problems between different WSMO elements" (WSMO, 2004).

Just as OWL-S relies on OWL ontology language for defining its upper ontology, WSMO framework relies on Web Service Modeling Language (WSML) (Bruijn, Fensel, Keller, Kifer, Lausen, Krummenacher, Polleres, & Predoiu, 2005) for language constructs. Just as OWL defines multiple flavors namely OWL-DL, OWL-Lite, OWL-Full, WSML has variants such as WSML-Core, WSML-DL, WSML-Rule, and WSML-Flight. The conceptual difference between OWL and WSML is primarily in the formal logic languages that they rely on. While OWL relies on Description Logics (DL), WSML is based on different logical formalisms, namely,

*Figure 4. A visual representation of a partNumber ontology*

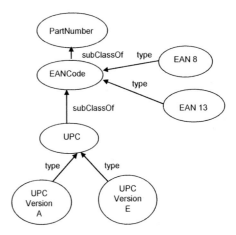

Description Logics, First-Order Logic and Logic Programming, which are useful for the modeling of semantic Web services.

WSMO shares with OWL-S the vision that ontologies are essential to support automatic discovery, composition and interoperation of Web services. But despite sharing a unifying vision, OWL-S and WSMO differ greatly in the details and the approach to achieve these results. Whereas OWL-S explicitly defines a set of ontologies that support reasoning about Web services, WSMO defines a conceptual framework within which these ontologies will have to be created. Another difference between OWL-S and WSMO is that while OWL-S does not make any distinction between types of Web services, WSMO places a lot of stress in the specification of mediators: mapping programs that solve the interoperation problems between Web services. (OWL-S, 2004b)

The following WSML snippet illustrates how *checkInventory()* service discussed in the Motivation section can be represented in WSML.

```
................
/*******************************
 * ONTOLOGY
 ******************************/

ontology_"http://www.example.org/ontologies/exam-
ple"
.......

  concept Item
   nonFunctionalProperties
    dc#description hasValue "concept of an Item"
   endNonFunctionalProperties

  hasUPC ofType xsd#string
  hasDate ofType xsd:dateTime
  hasQty ofType xsd:float

  concept AvailabilityResponse
   nonFunctionalProperties
    dc#description hasValue "concept of an Availabili-
tyResponse"
   endNonFunctionalProperties

  hasConfirmation ofType xsd:string
.....

/*******************************
 * WEBSERVICE
 ******************************/
```

```
webService _"http://example.org/CheckInv"
.........

 capability
 sharedVariables ?item
 precondition
   nonFunctionalProperties
   dc#description hasValue "The input has to contain
a UPC, due date and qty."
   endNonFunctionalProperties

 definedBy
 ?item memberOf Item.

 effect
   nonFunctionalProperties
   dc#description hasValue "After the item availability
check confirmation is sent"
   endNonFunctionalProperties

 definedBy
 ?conf memberOf AvailabilityResponse
 [forItem hasValue ?item].

 interface
  choreography _"http://example.org/exChoreogra-
phy"

  orchestration _http://example.org/exOrchestration
```

## WSDL-S

Keeping upward compatibility of WSDL, semantic support for XML schema and industry adoption issues in view WSDL-S (2005) proposes an incremental approach to add semantic annotations to WSDL documents. In WSDL-S, users can add semantic annotations to WSDL documents using the extensibility framework defined in the WSDL specification. The semantic annotations could be references to concepts defined in an external ontology. WSDL-S as such does not prescribe any particular ontology language and is defined to be agnostic to the semantic representation language. Users can use OWL or WSMO or any other modeling language of their choice. WSDL-S work came out of METEOR-S (2003) project from University of Georgia which was later significantly revised jointly by IBM and METEOR-S team. Figure 5 captures the essence of WSDL-S. It highlights how the domain model is kept external to a Web service model and how the associations between WSDL concepts and their corresponding semantic annotations are maintained using (URI) references.

The following WSDL 1.1 excerpt shows how message parts of *checkInventoryService()* have been semantically annotated with OWL ontology concepts.

*Figure 5. WSDL-S: Externalized representation and association of semantics to WSDL elements ( WSDL-S, 2005)*

**WSDL**           **Domain Model**

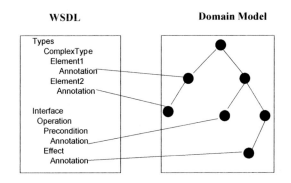

```
.........
  xmlns:wssem=" http://www.myschema.com/sche-
mas/2004/wssem"
  xmlns:ElectronicsOnt="http://www.standards.com/
ontologies/ElectronicsDomain.owl" >

   <message name="CheckInventoryServiceReque
st">
     <part name="UPC_in" type="xsd:string" wssem:
modelReference="ElectronicsOnt#UPC"/>
     <part name="dueDate_in" type="xsd:dateTime" ws-
sem:modelReference="ElectronicsOnt#DeliveryDate"/>
        <part name="numberOfItems_in" type="xsd:float"
wssem:modelReference="ElectronicsOnt#Quantity"/>
     </message>

   <message name="CheckInventoryServiceRespo
nse">
       <part name="itemAvailConfNum_out" type="xsd:
string" wssem:modelReference="ElectronicsOnt#Conf
irmation"/>
     </message>

  <portType name="CheckInventoryService">
  <operation name="checkInventoryService" >
     <input message="tns:CheckInventoryServiceRe-
quest" name="checkInventoryServiceRequest"/>
     <output message="tns:CheckInventoryServiceRe-
sponse" name="checkInventoryServiceResponse"/>
     </operation>
     </portType>
.........
```

Representing CheckInventory Service in WSML

*Table 1. Comparative analysis of languages for providing semantics in Web services*

| Proposal | Comment | Semantic Language | Formalism | Relation with WSDL |
|---|---|---|---|---|
| OWL-S Profile Model | An OWL based upper ontology for Web services. | OWL | Description Logics | Defines connectivity to WSDL via Grounding Model but overlaps in defining inputs, outputs and operations exist. |
| WSDL-S | Uses extensibility elements in WSDL to annotate elements with terms in externalized ontologies. | Agnostic to ontology language (can work with OWL, WSMO, UML, XML or any other modeling language) | Agnostic to ontology language. Therefore, users are at will to pick a formalism of their choice | Specifies annotations directly in WSDL as extensibility elements. |
| WSMO | A Web Service Modeling Ontology expressed using WSML. | WSML | Description Logics, First-Order Logic and Logic Programming (F-Logic) | Defines connectivity to WSDL via Grounding Model but overlaps in defining inputs, outputs and operations exist. |

## Discussion

Table 1 summarizes the Semantic Web service representation language submissions to W3C. This is a modified version of the table given by Sheth (Sheth, Verma, & Gomadam, 2006).

OWL-S, WSMO and WSDL-S all three have been submitted to W3C as alternate proposals to define a framework for semantics in Web services. While in principle, all three proposals use similar conceptual underpinnings, the difference is primarily in the scope. As has been discussed OWL-S proposal presents a framework for simple (atomic) as well as complex (process) services. WSMO proposal includes frameworks for Web service choreography, orchestration in the scope. WSDL-S, on the other hand, proposes an approach to add semantics to Web services specifically aligning itself with industry standard WSDL while excluding the process specification models from the scope. In addition, while OWL-S and WSML services are closely tied with OWL and WSMO ontology languages respectively, WSDL-S is agnostic to ontology languages. It can work with any ontology language because the annotations are externalized. WSDL-S on the other hand does not have anything to say about semantic Web processes as it only deals with adding semantic annotations to simple Web services represented as WSDLs.

At the time of writing of this chapter, a new working group has been initiated by W3C organization to help define semantic annotations for Web services. The working group is called "Semantic Annotations for Web Services" (SAWSDL, http://www.w3.org/2002/ws/sawsdl/). The charter for the working group (http://www.w3.org/2005/10/sa-ws-charter) indicates that "A Member Submission, WSDL-S, related to this work, has been acknowledged by W3C and should be used as one input to the Working Group."

Apart from these, efforts to create architectures and language requirements for Semantic Web services were started under the Semantic Web Services Initiative (SWSI). These include Semantic Web Services Architecture (SWSA) (SWSA, 2005) and Semantic Web Services Language Requirements (SWSL, 2005). SWSL puts forth the following as functional requirements for any Semantic Web services language: *advertising and matchmaking, negotiation and contracting, process modeling* and *process enactment*. It also intends to identify formalisms that can adequately support these functional requirements. The architecture working group (SWSA, 2005) intended to develop architectural and protocol abstractions thereby resulting in the development of a reference architecture to support Semantic Web service technologies. Some work was done toward achieving these objectives. A related effort by the WSMO community to create a reference implementation of WSMO led to Web Service Modeling eXecution environment (WSMX, 2004) framework. It is an execution environment for business application integration where semantically enhanced Web services are integrated for various business applications.

## Representation Mechanisms for Semantic Web Processes

In this section, we examine the issues involved in representing the semantics for complex services or Web processes and the efforts in this space.

As mentioned, OWL-S relies on the expressivity of OWL for representing Semantic Web services. Although OWL language has considerable expressive power to describe semantic models of Web services, it has certain limitations that become more apparent when modeling complex Web services or Web processes. OWL has rich set of constructs for expressing classes but the expressiveness of the language has limitations in describing properties. Also, OWL does not provide for the use of variables, especially when defining related classes in an ontology. This restriction poses limitations in relating the inputs and outputs of composite processes with those of other processes. In addition, "there is no composition constructor, so, it is impossible to capture relationship between a composite property and another (possible composite) property. The standard example here is the obvious relationship between the composition of the 'parent' and the 'brother' properties with the 'uncle' property" (Horrocks & Schneider, 2004). Other process modeling languages such as Finite State Machines, Pi-Calculus, and Petrinets are good at expressing the aspects of a process but are not good at expressing things such as conditional effects, and nonfunctional constraints (Gruninger et al., 2005). To overcome these limitations, SWSL committee had developed a new more expressive language called FLOWs: A first-order logic ontology for Web services. FLOWs builds on the ISO standard (ISO 18629) Process Specification Language (PSL) (PSL, 2003). FLOWs adds extensions to PSL for expressing control, ordering, occurrence, state and exception constraints. These constructs make primitive and complex processes first class objects in FLOWs. With these extensions, it is relatively easy for a trained programmer to express the semantics of complex Web processes. The limitation of FLOWs is that the syntax is unsuitable for an average programmer. Additional surface languages and tools have

to be developed to make it more accessible to an average programmer.

The following table summarizes the semantic languages for representing Web processes that were submitted to W3C. This is a modified version of the table given by Sheth (Sheth et al., 2006).

## RELATED WORK ON SEMANTIC WEB SERVICES

Significant amount of work has been done in the area of Web service discovery and composition. Below we examine some of the related work.

### Service Discovery

Many approaches such as information retrieval, AI, database schema matching, software engineering and so forth. have been applied to accomplish syntactic and semantic matching of service requirements with capabilities.

One of the earliest works on matchmaking engines put in the context of semantic Web services is presented by Sycara et al. (1999). An updated system that uses OWL-S based semantics for match making is given by Paolucci (2002a). In addition to utilizing a capability-based semantic

*Table 2. Comparative analysis of languages for representing semantics in Web processes*

| Proposal | Comment | Ontology Language | Formalism |
|----------|---------|-------------------|-----------|
| OWL-S Process Model | An OWL based upper ontology for representing Web processes. | OWL | Description Logics |
| FLOWs | A combination of First Order Logic and rules to represent Web services. Based on Process Specification Language (PSL). FLOWs rectifies the problems with OWL-S process model. | SWSO (FLOWs + ROWs) | First-Order Logic |
| WSMO Orchestration | The orchestration model in WSMO refers to complex services with states. | WSML | Description Logics, First-Order Logic and Logic Programming (F-Logic) |

match, this engine uses various IR-based filters such as namespace comparison, word frequency comparison, ontology similarity matching, ontology subsumption matching, and constraint matching, thereby reducing the number of false positives. Li and Horrocks (2003) in their work present a software system for matchmaking based on DL subsumption reasoning. They use Racer reasoner (Haarslev & Moller, 2003) to compute semantic matching between service requirements and service advertisements. These works introduce the concept of a degree of match in performing semantic matching using the notions of exact, plug-in, subsumption, intersection and disjoint. Much of the rest of the work in semantic matching of Web services that followed is inspired by these approaches.

The problem of automatically finding semantic relationships between schemas has also been addressed by a number of database researchers lately (Madhavan, Bernstein, & Rahm, 2001; Melnik, Garcia-Molina, & Rahm, 2002; Popa et al., 2002). The notion of elemental and structural level schema matching has been present in the METEOR-S project (Patil, Oundhakar, Sheth, & Verma, 2004), where the engine can perform both element and structure level schema matching for Web services. The element level matching is based on a combination of Porter Stemmer (Porter, 1980) for root word selection, WordNet dictionary (Miller, 1983) for synonyms, abbreviation dictionary to handle acronyms and NGram algorithm for linguistic similarity of the names of the two concepts. The schema matching examines the structural similarity between two concepts. Both element match score and schema match score are then used to determine the final match score. In a related work Syeda-Mahmood et al. (2005) explore the use of domain-independent and domain-specific ontologies to find matching service descriptions. The domain-independent relationships are derived using an English thesaurus after tokenization and part-of-speech tagging. The domain-specific ontological similarity is derived

by inferencing the semantic annotations associated with Web service descriptions. Matches due to the two cues are combined to determine an overall semantic similarity score. They demonstrate that by combining multiple cues, we show that better relevancy results can be obtained for service matches from a large repository, than could be obtained using any one cue alone.

Recently, clustering and classification techniques from machine learning are being applied to the problem of Web service matching and classification at either the whole Web service level (Hess & Kushmerick, 2003) or at the operation level (Dong, Halevy, Madhavan, Nemes, & Zhang., 2004). In Hess and Kushmerick (2003), for example, all terms from portTypes, operations and messages in a WSDL document are treated as a bag of words and multidimensional vectors created from these bag of words are used for Web service classification. Although this type of classification retrieves matches with higher precision than full-text indexed search, the overall matches produced, however, do not guarantee a match of operations to operations, messages to messages, and so forth. The paper by Madhavan and colleagues (2001) addresses this aspect by focusing on matching of operations in Web services. Specifically, it clusters parameters present in inputs and outputs of operations (i.e., messages) based on their co-occurrence into parameter concept clusters. This information is exploited at the parameter, the inputs and output, and operation levels to determine similarity of operations in Web services.

## Semantic Matching in Web Services Registries

There has been a flurry of activity in the area of business service registries to which semantic matching has been applied. This work ranges from assuming centralized public or private business service registries (such as the one proposed by the UDDI consortium) to a decentralized notion of services where each company makes its own services available on its Web site. Several approaches have been suggested to enable semantic matching of Web service capabilities in the context of these registries.

In their follow-up work to DAML-S specification, a precursor to OWL-S, Paolucci et al. (2002b) tie the semantic representation of Web services work with Web service directories/registries such as UDDI. In their approach, they propose to enhance search in UDDI by intercepting the search calls to a UDDI registry and performing semantic matching outside of the UDDI registry. The functionality of UDDI registry itself is untouched in this approach. While this approach is a good start, it has an inherent disadvantage. Every user of UDDI registry has to have the infrastructure developed by Paolucci and colleagues (2002b), for the semantic matching to take place. To address this limitation in a follow up work, Akkiraju, Goodwin, Doshi, and Roeder (2003) present a design mechanism for a tighter integration of semantic matching with UDDI registry by directly extending UDDI's inquiry application programming interface (API) (find_service()) and its implementation. This approach incorporates semantic matching directly in UDDI registry by altering the find_service() API that users of UDDI registry are familiar with. While this is a workable solution, it proposes embedding matching capability into UDDI registry implementation. This makes UDDI matching specific to a particular service description language – in their case, DAML-S. To address this, Colgrave and colleagues, in their work (Colgrave, Akkiraju, & Goodwin, 2004), present an approach in which a UDDI registry can select a matchmaking engine dynamically based on the service requirements and find suitable service advertisements whose capabilities are described in the language that the requester can understand. In this approach, the matchmaking engines themselves are advertised as Web services in the registry.

All of these approaches discussed so far assume a centralized repository of Web services that offers search functions. Some work has also been done to investigate how semantic matching could work in a decentralized service environment.

Peer-to-peer networks have been investigated as an alternative to centralized Web services registries such as UDDI. A discussion on Semantic Web and peer-to-peer issues is presented by works such as Armugam, Sheth, and Arpinar (2001) and Schlosser et al. (2002). Verma et al. (2005) present a scalable peer-to-peer infrastructure of registries for semantic publication and discovery of Web services. This work proposes an ontology-based approach to organize registries by enabling semantic classification of Web services to be published and the use of peer-to-peer networking as a scalable infrastructure for registries.

Some work is also done to automatically suggest annotations for Web services. Hess and Kushmerick (2003) suggest the use of machine learning to generate suggestions for annotating Web services. In a related effort, Patil and colleagues have developed MWSAF, a Web service annotation framework (Patil et al., 2004). In their work, they generate recommendations for automatically annotating WSDL documents. To accomplish this they match XML schema used by the WSDL files with ontologies by creating canonical schema graphs. A survey of semantic annotations platforms is presented by Reeve and Han (2005).

## Service Composition

The literature on Web services matching and composition has focused on two main directions. One body of work explored the application of AI planning or logic-based algorithms to achieve composition while the other investigated the application of information retrieval techniques for searching and composing of suitable services in the presence of semantic ambiguity from large repositories.

First, we consider work that is done on composing Web services using planning based on some notion of semantic annotations. A general survey of planning based approaches for Web services composition can be found in (Peer, 2005). SWORD (Ponnekanti & Fox, 2002) was one of the initial attempts to use planning to compose Web services. It does not model service capabilities in an ontology but uses rule chaining to composes Web services. In McIlraith et al. (2001), a method is presented to compose Web services by applying logical inferencing techniques on predefined plan templates. The service capabilities are annotated in DAML-S/RDF and then manually translated into Prolog. Given a goal description, the logic programming language of Golog (which is implemented over Prolog) is used to instantiate the appropriate plan for composing the Web services. In Traverso and Pistore (2004), executable BPELs are automatically composed from goal specification by casting the planning problem as a model checking problem on the message specification of partners. The approach is promising but presently restricted to logical goals and small number of partner services. Sirin and colleagues (2003) use contextual information to find matching services at each step of service composition. They further filter the set of matching services by using ontological reasoning on the semantic description of the services as well as by using user input. Synthy (Agarwal, Chafle, & Dasgupta, 2005) takes an end-to-end view of composition of Web services and combines semantic matching with domain ontologies with planning.

While these bodies of work use the notion of domain annotations and semantic reasoning with planning, none of them use domain-independent cues such as thesaurus. Moreover, they do not consider text analysis techniques such as tokenization, abbreviation expansions, and stop word filtering and so forth. in drawing the semantic relationships among the terms referenced in Web services. Shivashanmugam and colleagues (2003) propose semantic process templates to capture the semantic requirements of Web process in their work on MWSCF. The semantic information about services in the templates can be used to dynamically discover suitable services and generate executable BPEL documents. Compositions are enabled via user interactions.

The second body of work looked at composition of Web services using domain independent cues alone. Syeda-Mahmood (2004) models Web service composition as bipartite graph and solves a maximum matching problem while resolving the semantic ambiguities using domain-independent ontologies and text analysis approaches. This work takes its roots in schema matching. However, this work does not use domain-dependent ontologies which are crucial to resolving the differences between domain-specific contextual terms.

Bringing both approaches together, a recent work by Akkiraju (Akkiraju, Srivastava, Ivan, Syeda-Mahmood, & Goodwin, 2006) presents a new technique to combine domain-independent semantic cues (e.g., thesaurus) with domain-dependent ones (represented as domain ontologies) with planning approaches for achieving composition. In addition, this approach applies text analysis techniques such as tokenization, abbreviation expansion and stop word filtering to do fine granular semantic matching of terms used in Web services descriptions.

Composing Web services based on nonfunctional properties by modeling the quality of service properties as constraints in mathematical programming has also been looked into. Among some of the works in this space include Zeng (Zeng et al., 2003) and Agarwal (Agarwal et al., 2004). Claro and colleagues (Claro, Daniela, Albers, Patrick, Hao, & Jin-Kao, 2005) present a multi-objective evolutionary algorithm for composing Web services.

## Semantic Matching of Nonfunctional Properties of Web Services

Much of the discussion so far centered on the matching of functional properties of Web services represented by their interfaces. Matching nonfunctional properties (such as security, policy, privacy, transactional requirements and capabilities) of Web services is just as important in determining a good match. Below we examine some work that has been done in the area of matching non-functional properties of Web services that are typically represented as Web services policies using languages such as WS-Policy.

Among the matching efforts that are based on syntax alone include Wohlstadter et al. (2004) and Mukhi and Plebani (2004). Wohlstadter and colleagues (2004) extend the grammar of WS-Policy to add qualifying conditions and numerical predicates, but is still based on syntactical domain models. Having XML based models limits the expressivity of the assertions and also limits the matching to syntactical matching. Yang et al. (2003) address syntactical heterogeneity of homogeneous assertions from a mathematical point of view.

There has also been some work in matching policies using Semantic Web technologies. Uszok et al. (2004) have developed the KAOS system for representing policies using OWL. Kagal and colleagues (2004a) use a rule based engine for handling trust and privacy of Web services. In another paper (Kagal et al., 2004b), the authors have discussed the interaction of OWL ontologies and SWRL rules as an open problem. Li and Horrocks (2004) provide an approach for matching nonfunctional attributes using semantics, but their framework is restricted as they rely solely on subsumption for the matching and their expressivity is limited by description logics. In a follow-on work, Verma et al. (2005b) present a more flexible approach to match Web service policies while accounting for the intra and inter domain relationships by using SWRL (Horrocks & Schneider, 2004) type of rules.

Table 3 summarizes some characteristics of semantic Web services in which research has been conducted.

*Table 3. Summary of Semantic Web service discovery and composition approaches*

| Topic | Kinds/Approaches |
| --- | --- |
| Type of Semantic Web services | Simple, Complex |
| Properties of Semantic Web services | Functional, Nonfunctional |
| Sources of semantic information | Domain models (such as ontologies), Domain-independent models (such as dictionaries) and combinations |
| Service discovery methods | Information retrieval (such as text analysis, vector space, probabilistic models), AI techniques (such as machine learning, semantic reasoning), Mathematical modeling techniques (such as linear programming) and combinations |
| Service composition methods | Information retrieval (such as text analysis, vector space, probabilistic models), AI techniques (such as machine learning, semantic reasoning, planning), Mathematical modeling techniques (such as linear programming) and combinations |
| Service registry approaches | Centralized (such as UDDI), Decentralized/Peer-to-Peer |
| Service registry types | Public, Private |

## MAKING A BUSINESS CASE FOR SEMANTIC WEB SERVICES

While the work on standards for representing semantics in Web services is evolving, both the academic and industry communities have recognized the need to make a business case for articulating the value of semantics in Web services. Efforts to define business scenarios that can benefit from the use of semantic Web services are underway. Semantic Web service Architecture (SWSA, 2005) had outlined the following areas among the consumers of Semantic Web services technology: business-to-business (B2B) enterprise integration systems, business-to-consumer (B2C) Web-based commercial and informational systems, scientific grid computing, ubiquitous computing powered by wireless devices, and agent-based systems for control and coordination tasks (SWSA use cases, 2005). Below, we examine a few scenarios where automatic Web service discovery and composition powered by semantics could be useful.

### Use Case for Service Discovery in B2B Enterprise Systems

Automatic discovery of new business applications, represented as Web services, offered by new service providers has been presented as a standard scenario in B2B enterprise integration systems. However, informal studies reveal that in a business setting dynamically finding new service providers is not desirable. Typically, businesses prefer to have well defined agreements and procedures in place before they can start invoking each others' services. A more credible scenario that is emerging is that of software asset reuse (a software asset could be software code, documentation, best practices, templates, frameworks and so forth. In its simplest form, a software asset could be a Web service wrapper to a legacy application). While building new business applications or changing the existing ones, often it is desirable to use as much of the existing functionality as possible while only building what is needed incrementally on top of the existing functionality. In a large enterprise that is formed via mergers and acquisitions, there could be many applications that are developed over time. In such a situation, finding suitable existing functionality from among a large collection could be time consuming. Simple category-based and keyword-based search functions offered by current repository software are insufficient to make software reuse decisions. Business applications whose functionality is semantically described can be found and integrated with more easily than those without semantic descriptions. This presents opportunities for Semantic Web services in integrating enterprise systems. An example use case for this would be: "find me an RFID checkout service for retail industry that can take RFID and coupon codes and produce total basket price and new coupons for next purchase." In this example, if a company has several services that it has implemented over time for retail industry solutions, a particular service that can perform RFID (Radio Frequency Identification) tag based checkout is what needs to be retrieved. There may be other checkout services that are available in the repository that may not use RFID as input and these should not be a match. So, in this asset reuse use case, automatic service discovery involves carefully matching the requirements to extract only those services that are relevant from among a large repository of services.

### Use Case for Service Composition in B2B Enterprise Systems

Automatic service composition in B2B enterprise integration could play an important role. A commonly occurring situation is that systems that are built overtime typically use old formats and standards and often need to be transformed into the current state-of-the-art format to be integrated with newer systems. For example, newer systems may require documents to be digitally signed and encrypted before they can be processed. So, transforming a given plain text document into a secure document requires some transformation services. This problem can be framed as a semantic composition problem. For example, a semantic description such as: "given a digital signing service, encryption service and a purchase order service from service provider XYZ that requires purchase orders to be digitally signed and encrypted, place my plain text purchase order with service provider XYZ. Also, note a constraint that documents have to be digitally signed before they can be encrypted" could be handed off to an automatic semantic composition system to achieve the required transformation. In this example, automatic service composition system would transform "my plain text purchase order" into a digitally signed and encrypted document by composing a digital signing service and an encryption service (note that due to the constraint, this order is important) and then invokes the service of service provider XYZ.

## Use Case for Service Discovery in B2C Domain

Examples in B2C domain include consumer oriented online shipping services such as travel reservation, book buying, financial service services and so forth. Examples articulated by semantic Web community include: "Find me an airline service that enables me to reserve a flight before providing a credit card number" (Gruninger et al., 2005). "Find me a florist that enables me to pay with PayPal" (Gruninger et al., 2005)

## Use Case for Service Composition in B2C Domain

*Given a workshop registration service, a flight booking service, a car rental service, a taxi reservation service, a hotel reservation service, Ima's home address and a Ima's online schedule, please book Ima's Cheapstake trip to the W3C Workshop on Web Services.* (Gruninger et al., 2005)

Semantics are gaining increasing popularity and attention in life sciences and health care domains. Realizing this interest, W3C has formed a new semantic Web life sciences and health care interest group. More scenarios and working systems are discussed on the Web site of that interest group (HCLSIG, 2005).

Having looked at some use cases for semantic Web services, we now discuss their potential benefits.

## POTENTIAL BENEFITS OF SEMANTIC WEB SERVICES

Below we examine some of the potential benefits Semantic Web services as applied to business process integration when the vision of semantic Web services is realized.

## Reduced Development Costs and Time

Web services provide a foundation for easier system integration by providing a standards-based approach. Usage of Web services is continuing to grow with Web services forming the basis of integration solutions in many industries. However, integration and process automation projects are often expensive and time consuming even with Web services, and may not result in solutions that are as flexible and reconfigurable as needed to best react to today's dynamic business environment. Semantic Web services offer the promise of automating integration tasks. This automation facilitated by semantic Web services could potentially save development time and reduce implementation costs. Technologically this seems credible. However, these claims are yet to be verified in rigorous benchmarking exercises by applying the technology on real-world scenarios.

Given that semantic Web services are still early in adoption stage, proving its value may still take some time.

## Facilitates the Development of Flexible and Robust Systems

Semantics can help not only in automating development tasks but also in runtime activities. Runtime environments in business contexts are dynamic: services that were available a moment ago may suddenly become unavailable. Process changes sometimes would have to be executed at runtime without disrupting the existing environment, new and multiple instances of services may have to be managed based on load requirements and so on. Techniques used for service discovery and interface mapping can be reused at runtime to dynamically find new or substitutable services. This makes software systems less brittle, more robust, flexible and maintainable.

## Formal Models Promote Better Software System Maintenance

The semantic approach put forth by semantic Web services aids in instituting the discipline of formally documenting the concepts and the domain during the application integration process. This disciplined process offers an added intangible benefit of making it easy to maintain the software systems as they change hands.

## CONCLUSION

Web services are becoming an important technological component in the application integration domain. Large enterprises are deploying as many as several hundred Web services, a situation that brings into focus the need for tools to discover and integrate these services with each other and with the other applications in use. Semantics can play a crucial role in the development of these tools

as they enable dynamic discovery, composition and execution of Web services. In fact, multiple factors are pointing toward the need for a shift in focus from syntax only to syntax and semantics based integration solutions. First, ever growing market pressures for implementing IT projects at breakneck speeds while designing solutions that are flexible, reusable, easy to maintain and update are exerting great strains on the existing architectures and are necessitating new flexible and standards-based architectural paradigms. Second, as the business community's integration requirements have evolved from data integration to application connectivity to business process management, integration requirements are increasingly demanding better solutions (Figure 6). Finally, pressures to keep IT implementation costs in check are demanding increased developer productivity via automation tools. To support these integration needs, modeling languages are evolving from syntax oriented, human consumption focus to more semantics and machine interpretability focus (Figure 7). With the emergence of semantic modeling languages such as Resource Description Framework (RDF) and Web Ontology Language (OWL), the required foundations for semantics-based integration are laid. Semantic Web services supported by modeling languages such as OWL, and WSMO are emerging as potential candidates to address this gap. By providing machine-interpretable and inferenceable meaning to data, functional and execution aspects of Web services, semantics can help in automating the process integration. This confluence of business needs and technology evolution now make it possible to build better integration solutions powered by semantic Web services.

On the other hand, it is important to note that a large segment of developer community views semantics powered by ontology languages such as OWL as complex and an area of research not ready for prime time. Therefore, the onus is on the semantic Web community to build small and incremental proof points to demonstrate the

*Figure 6. Integration trends are driving the need for semantics*

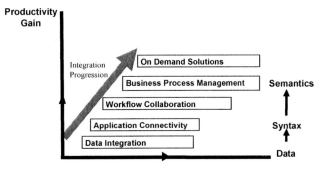

*Figure 7. Web standards: From presentation to semantics*

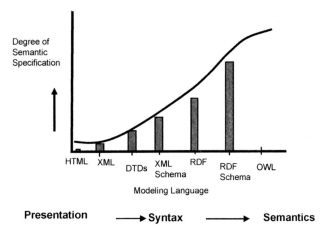

value of semantics by applying them to credible, real-world scenarios by working closely with the industry and customers. Efforts are already underway to encourage sharing of business scenarios and real-world experiences via forums such as academic and industry sponsored conferences, and challenges and so forth. This flurry of activity is likely to further invigorate research in this area.

## ACKNOWLEDGMENTS

The author would like to thank her collaborators Richard Goodwin, Tanveer Syeda-Mahmood, Anca-Andreea Ivan, Biplav Srivastava, Juhnyoung Lee, Prashant Doshi, Kunal Verma, Amit Sheth, Joel Farrell and John Miller for the stimulating and constructive discussions throughout her work on Semantic Web services.

## REFERENCES

Agarwal, V., Chafle, G., Dasgupta, K., et al. (2004). Synthy. A system for end to end composition of Web services. *Journal of Web Semantics, 3*(4).

Akkiraju, R., Goodwin, R., Doshi, P., & Roeder, S. (2003). A method for semantically enhancing the service discovery capabilities of UDDI. In *Proceedings of the Eighteenth International Joint Conference on Artificial Intelligence: Information Integration on the Web, WEB-1* (pp. 87-92).

Akkiraju, R., Srivastava, B., Ivan, A., Syeda-Mahmood, T., & Goodwin, R. (2006). SEMAPLAN: Combining planning with semantic reasoning to achieve Web services composition. Accepted at *IEEE International Conference on Web Services (ICWS) 2006*.

Armugam, M., Sheth, A., & Arpinar, I.B. (2001). Towards peer-to-peer Semantic Web: A distributed environment for sharing semantic knowledge on the Web. In *Proceedings of the International World Wide Web Conference 2002*. Retrieved October 25, 2006, from http://webster.cs.uga.edu/~budak/papers/workshop02.pdf

Baader, F., Calvaneese, D., McGuinness, D., Nardi, D., & Patel-Schneider, P. (Ed). (2003). *The description logics handbook. Theory, implementation and tools*. Cambridge University Press.

Baral, C. & Gelfond, M. (1994). Logic programming and knowledge representation. *Journal of Logic Programming, 19*(20), 73-148.

Bruijn, J., Fensel, D., Keller, U., Kifer, M., Lausen, H., Krummenacher, R., Polleres, A., & Predoiu, L. (2005). *Web service modeling language (WSML)*. A W3C submission. Retrieved October 25, 2006, from http://www.w3.org/Submission/WSML/

Cabral, L., Domingue, J., Motta, E., Payne, T., & Hakimpor, F. (2004). *Approaches to Semantic Web services: An overview and comparisons*. Retrieved October 25, 2006 from http://kmi.open.ac.uk/projects/irs/cabralESWS04.pdf

Claro, D.B., Albers, P., Hao, & Jin-Kao. (2005, July). Selecting Web services for optimal composition. In Proceedings of the *ICWS 2005 Second International Workshop on Semantic and Dynamic Web Processes* (Vol. 140), Orlando, Florida.

Colgrave, J., Akkiraju, R., & Goodwin, R. (2004).

External matching in UDDI. In *Proceedings of the IEEE International Conference on Web Services*. 226.

Dong, X., Halevy, A., Madhavan, J., Nemes, E., & Zhang, J. (2004). Similarity search for Web services. In *Proceedings of VLDB* (pp. 372-283), Toronto, Canada.

Fokkink, W. J. (2000). *Introduction to process algebra* (Texts in Theoretical Computer Science, an EATCS Series). Springer.

Gill, A. (1962). *Introduction to the theory of finite-state machines*. McGraw-Hill.

Grosof, B. (2003, May). *Intro to panel at WWW-2003: Semantic Web services: Obstacles and attractions*. Slides presented at the 12th International Conference on World Wide Web, Budapest, Hungary. Retrieved October 25, 2006, from http://ebusiness.mit.edu/bgrosof/paps/talk-sws-panel-intro-www2003.pdf

Gruninger, M., Hull, R., & McIlraith, S. (2005). *A first order logic ontology for Semantic Web services*. Paper presented at the Frameworks for Semantics in Web Services W3C Workshop, Innsbruck, Austria.

Gruninger, M., Hull, R., & McIlraith, S. (2005). *A first order logic ontology for Web services (FLOWs)*. Paper presented at the W3C Workshop on Frameworks for Semantics in Web Services, Innsbruck, Austria. Retrieved October 25, 2006, from http://www.w3.org/2005/04/FSWS/Submissions/59/Flows.pdf

Haarslev, V. & Moller, R. (2001). RACER system description. Retrieved October 25, 2006 from http://www.sts.tu-harburg.de/~r.f.moeller/racer/papers/2001/HaMo01a.pdf

HCLSIG. (2005). W3C semantic web health care and life sciences interest group. Retrieved October 25, 2006, from http://www.w3.org/2001/sw/hcls/

Hess, A. & Kushmerick, N. (2003). Learning to attach metadata to Web services. In *Proceedings of the International Semantic Web Conference (ISWC)*. Retrieved October 25, 2006, from http://www.few.vu.nl/~andreas/publications/hess-iswc03.pdf

Horrocks, I., & Schneider, P.P. (2004). A proposal for OWL rules language. In *Proceedings of the WWW 2004*. Retrieved October 25, 2006, from http://www2004.org/proceedings/docs/1p723.pdf

Kagal, L., Finin, T., & Joshi, A. (2004b). Declarative policies for describing Web service capabilities and constraints. In *Proceedings of the W3C Workshop on Constraints and Capabilities for Web Services*. Retrieved October 25, 2006, from http://www.w3.org/2004/08/ws-cc/umbc-20040904

Kagal, L., Paoucci, M., Srinivasan, N., Denker, G., Finin, T., & Sycara, K. (2004a). Authorization and privacy for semantic Web services. In *Proceedings of the AAAI Spring Symposium on Semantic Web Services*. Retrieved October 25, 2006, from http://www.daml.org/services/owls/pub-archive/AuthAndPrivForSWSIEEE.pdf

Kifer, M., Lausen, G., & Wu, J. (1995, July). *Logical foundations of object-oriented and frame-based languages. Journal of the ACM, 42*, 741-843.

Levesque, H., Pirri, F., & Reiter, R. (1998). Foundations for the situation calculus. *Electronic Transactions on Artificial Intelligence, 2*(3-4), 159-178.

Li, L., & Horrocks, I. (2003). A software framework for matchmaking based on Semantic Web terminology. In *Proceedings of the WWW Conference*. Retrieved October 25, 2006, from http://www.cs.man.ac.uk/~horrocks/Publications/download/2003/p815-li.pdf

Madhavan, J., Bernstein, P., & Rahm E. (2001). Generic schema matching with cupid. In *Proceedings of the 27th VLDB Conference*, Italy, Rome. Retrieved October 25, 2006, from http://research.microsoft.com/~philbe/CupidVLDB01.pdf

Mandel, D., & McIlraith, S. (2003). Adapting BPEL4WS for the Semantic Web: The bottom up approach to Web service interoperation. In *Proceedings of the Second International Semantic Web Conference (ISWC2003)*, Sanibel Island, Florida. Retrieved October 25, 2006, from http://www.ksl.stanford.edu/sds/iswc2003sam-djm-FINAL.pdf

McIlraith, S., Son, T.C., & Zeng H. (2001a, March/April). Semantic Web services. *IEEE Intelligent Systems, Special Issue on the Semantic Web, 16*(2), 46-53.

McIlraith, S., Son, T.C., & Zeng, H. (2001b). *Mobilizing the Semantic Web with DAML-enabled Web services*. Paper presented at the Semantic Web Workshop 2001, Hong Kong, China.

Melnik, S., Garcia-Molina, H., & Rahm E. (2002). Similarity flooding: A versatile graph matching algorithm and its application to schema matching. In *Proceedings of the 18th International Conference on Data Engineering (ICDE)*, San Jose, California.. Retrieved October 25, 2006, from http://research.microsoft.com/~melnik/pub/melnik_ICDE02.pdf

METEOR-S: Semantic Web Services and Processes. (2003). Large scale distributed information systems (LSDIS) lab. University of Georgia. Retrieved October 25, 2006, from http://lsdis.cs.uga.edu/projects/meteor-s/

Miller, G.A. (1983). WordNet: A lexical database for the english language, in Comm. ACM 1983.

Mukhi, N.K. & Plebani, P. (2004). Supporting policy-driven behaviors in Web services: Experiences and issues (2004). In *Proceedings of the*

*International Conference on Services Oriented Computing (ICSOC).* Retrieved October 25, 2006, from http://icsoc.dit.unitn.it/abstracts/A223.pdf

OWL Technical Committee (2004). OWL: Web ontology language. A W3C specification. Retrieved October 25, 2006, from http://www.w3.org/2004/OWL/

OWL-S Technical Committee (2004). OWL-S: Semantic markup for Web services. W3C member submission. Retrieved October 25, 2006, from http://www.w3.org/Submission/2004/SUBM-OWL-S-20041122/

OWL-S Technical Committee (2004b). OWL-S' relationship to selected other technologies. Retrieved October 25, 2006, from http://www.w3.org/Submission/2004/SUBM-OWL-S-related-20041122/#wsmo

Patil, A., Oundhakar, S., Sheth, A., & Verma, K. (2004). METEOR-S: Web service annotation framework. In *Proceedings of the WWW Conference* (pp. 553-562). Retrieved October 25, 2006, from http://www2004.org/proceedings/docs/1p553.pdf

Paolucci, M., Kawamura, T., Payne, T.R., & Sycara, K. (2002a, June) Semantic matching of Web services capabilities. In *Proceedings of the First International Semantic Web Conference (ISWC)*, Sardinia, Italy.

Paolucci, M., Kawamura, T., Payne, T.R., & Sycara, K. (2002b). Importing the Semantic Web in UDDI. In *Proceedings of the Web Services, E-Business and Semantic Web Workshop.*

Peer, J. (2005). Web service composition as a planning problem: A survey. Retrieved October 25, 2006, from http://elektra.mcm.unisg.ch/pbwsc/docs/pfwsc.pdf

Popa, L., Hernandez, M., Velegrakis, Y., & Miller, R.J. (2002). Mapping XML and relational schemas with clio. In *Proceedings of the 18th International Conference on Data Engineering (ICDE)*, San Jose, California.

Ponnekanti, S., & Fox, A. (2002). SWORD: A developer toolkit for Web service composition. In *Proceedings of the 11th International World Wide Web Conference.*

Porter, M.F. (1980, July). An algorithm for suffix stripping. *Proceedings of the Program, 14*(3), 130-137. Retrieved October 25, 2006, from http://www.tartarus.org/~martin/PorterStemmer/def.txt

PSL Technical Committee (2003). Process specification language (PSL). Retrieved October 25, 2006, from http://www.mel.nist.gov/psl/

Reeve, L., & Han, H. (2005). Survey of semantic annotation platforms. SA 2005, Santa Fe, New Mexico.

Reisig, W. (1985). Petri nets, an introduction. In W. Brauer, G. Rozenberg, & A. Salomaa (Eds.), *Monographs on theoretical computer science.* Berlin: Springer Verlag.

Sangiorgi, D., & Walker, D. (2001). *The Pi-calculus: A theory of mobile processes.* Cambridge University Press. ISBN 0521781779.

Schlosser, M., Sintek, M., Decker, S., & Nejdl, W. (2002). A scalable and ontology-based P2P infrastructure for Semantic Web services. In *Proceedings of the Second International Conference on Peer-to-Peer Computing (P2P'02)*, 104.

Sheth, A. (2003) Semantic Web process life cycle. Role of semantics in annotation, discovery, composition and execution. Invited talk at *WWW 2003 Workshop on e-Services and the Semantic Web*, Budapest, Hungary.

Sheth, A., Verma, K., & Gomadam, K. (2006). Semantics to energize the full services spectrum: Ontological approach to better exploit services at technical and business levels. Paper submitted to *Communications of the ACM (CACM).*

Sivashanmugam, K., Miller, J., Sheth, A., & Verma, K. (2003). Framework for Semantic Web process composition. *Special Issue of the International Journal of Electronic Commerce (IJEC)*.

Sirin, E., Hendler, J., & Parsia, B. (2003, April). Semi-automatic composition of Web services using semantic descriptions. In *Proceedings of* Web Services: *Modeling, Architecture and InfrastructureWworkshop in conjunction with ICEIS2003*.

Sivashanmugam, K., Verma, K., Sheth, A., & Miller, J. (2003, June 23-26). Adding semantics to Web services standards. In *Proceedings of the 2003 International Conference on Web Services (ICWS'03)* (pp. 395-401). Las Vegas, Nevada.

SOAP Technical Committee (2000). Simple object access protocol (A W3C Tech. Rep.). Retrieved October 25, 2006, from http://www.w3.org/TR/soap/

Sycara, K., Klusch, M., Widoff, S., & Lu, J. (1999, March). Dynamic service match making among agents in open information environments. In *Journal ACM SIGMOD Record, 28*(1), 47-53.

Syeda-Mahmood, T. (2004). *Minelink: Automatic composition of Web services through schema matching*. Poster paper at the World Wide Web Conference.

Syeda-Mahmood, T., Shah, G., Akkiraju, R., Ivan, A., & Goodwin, R. (2005). Searching service repositories by combining semantic and ontological matching. In *Proceedings of the Third International Conference on Web Services (ICWS)*, Florida.

SWSA Technical Committee (2005). Semantic Web services architecture (SWSA). Retrieved October 25, 2006, from http://www.daml.org/services/swsa/note/swsa-note_v5.html

SWSA (2005b). Semantic Web services architecture (SWSA) use cases. Retrieved October 25, 2006, from http://www.daml.org/services/usecases/architecture/

SWSL Technical Committee (2005). Semantic Web service language (SWSL). A W3C Member Submission. Retrieved October 25, 2006, from http://www.w3.org/Submission/SWSF-SWSL/

Traverso, P. & Pistore, M. (2004, November). Automated composition of semantic Web services into executable processes. In *Proceedings of the 3rd International Semantic Web Conference*.

UDDI Technical Committee (2002). Universal description discovery and integration. An OASIS technical specification. Retrieved October 25, 2006, from http://www.uddi.org/

Uszok, A., Bradshaw, J.M., Jeffers, R., Johnson, M., Tate, A., Dalton, J., & Aitken, S. (2004). Policy and contract management for Semantic Web services. In *Proceedings of the AAAI Spring Symposium on Semantic Web Services*.

Verma, K., Akkiraju, R., & Goodwin, R. (2005b). Semantic matching of Web service policies. In *Proceedings of the 2nd International Workshop on Semantic and Dynamic Web Processes (SDWP 2005)* (pp. 79-90). Orlando, Florida.

Verma, K., Akkiraju, R., Goodwin, R., Doshi, P., & Lee, J. (2004, March). On accommodating inter service dependencies in Web process flow composition. In *Proceedings of the AAAI Spring Symposium on Semantic Web Services* (pp. 37-43). Stanford, California.

Verma, K., Sivashanmugam, K., Sheth, A., Patil, A., Oundhakar, S., & Miller, J. (2005). METEOR-S WSDI: A scalable infrastructure of registries for semantic publication and discovery of Web services. *Journal of Information Technology and Management, Special Issue on Universal Global Integration, 6*(1), 17-39.

Wohlstadter, E., Tai, S., Mikalsen, T., Rouvello, I., & Devanbu, P. (2004). GlueQoS: Middleware to sweeten quality-of-service policy interactions.

In *Proceeding of the 26th International Conference on Software Engineering (ICSE 2004)* (pp. 189-199).

WSDL Technical Committee (2001). Web services definition language (WSDL) (A W3C Tech. Rep.). Retrieved October 25, 2006, from http://www.w3.org/TR/wsdl

WSDL-S Technical Committee (2005). WSDL-S Web services semantics – WSDL-S, W3C Member Submission. Retrieved October 25, 2006, from http://www.w3.org/Submission/WSDL-S/

WSMX Technical Committee (2004). Web service execution environment (WSMX). Retrieved October 25, 2006, from http://www.wsmx.org/

WSMO Technical Committee (2005). Web service modeling ontology (WSMO). A W3C Member Submission. Retrieved October 25, 2006, from http://www.w3.org/Submission/WSMO/

Zheng, L., Benatallah, B., Dumas, M., Kalagnanam, J., & Sheng, Q. (2003). Quality-driven Web services composition. In *Proceedings of the WWW 2003*, Budapest, Hungary.

## ENDNOTE

- **Upper Ontology:** "An upper ontology is limited to concepts that are meta, generic, abstract and philosophical, and therefore are general enough to address (at a high level) a broad range of domain areas. Concepts specific to given domains will not be included; however, it provides a structure and a set of general concepts upon which domain ontologies (e.g., medical, financial, engineering, etc.) could be constructed." - http://suo.ieee.org/

# Chapter X
# The Process of Semantic Annotation of Web Services

**Christoph Ringelstein**
*University of Koblenz-Landau, Germany*

**Thomas Franz**
*University of Koblenz-Landau, Germany*

**Steffen Staab**
*University of Koblenz-Landau, Germany*

## ABSTRACT

*Web services are software components that are—in general—distributed over multiple organizations. They provide functionality without showing implementation details for the purpose of abstracting from implementation as well as for the purpose of hiding private, that is, organization-internal, processes. Nevertheless, to use a Web service one must know some of its details, that is, what it does, what it requires, what it assumes, what it achieves, and to some extent, how it achieves its purpose. The different Web service standards, frequently summarized as WS\*, allow Web services to be specified with descriptions of such details. In this chapter, we argue that one should go beyond WS\* and that it is preferable to provide semantic descriptions, that is, specifications that can be understood and correctly interpreted by machines. Thereby, the particular focus of this contribution lies in analyzing the process of semantic annotation, that is, the process of deriving semantic descriptions from lower level specifications, implementations and contextual descriptions. Hence, the concern of this chapter is really orthogonal to most other work which equates Web service annotation with Web service specification. We illustrate here that this is not the case.*

## INTRODUCTION

Web services are software components that are accessible as Web resources in order to be reused by other Web services or software. Hence, they function as middleware connecting different parties such as companies or organizations distributed over the Web. Thereby, a party providing a service may not be interested in exhibiting their organization-internal processes to the outside world. A second party consuming such a service may not be interested in analyzing a given Web service in order to be able to use it. Therefore, an abstracting description of a Web service is necessary to allow for its effective provisioning and use.

The description of a Web service needs to include some bare technical information in order that it can be used. This includes:

1. *What* it does;
2. *How to invoke* the Web service (i.e., the used communication protocol);
3. *What parameters* to provide to the Web service (i.e., its signature);

To embed it into an organizational process it must also contain information about

4. *which protocol* should be followed when using the Web service (e.g., "register user; then, book journey!").

A Web service user may have some expectations about a service's

5. *properties*, concerning, for example, security means (e.g., "always use secure communication for my bank account information!").

This list is by no means complete. One may require further technical descriptions (e.g., transactions) or legal aspects (e.g., contractual issues). However, it indicates that two parties that plan to cooperate via a Web service need specifications of the service allowing them to share and exploit technical and nontechnical descriptions.

Such sharing of descriptions is extremely difficult if the means of sharing are not standardized and descriptions boil down to verbose textual documents. To simplify use of Web services, several properties of Web services are described following standardized XML documents (e.g., SOAP, UDDI, WSDL, WS-Security), for further properties standardization activities for XML descriptions are underway (e.g., WS-Transaction, WS-BPEL, WS-Policy) and for yet others there is a discussion whether standardization should be initiated.[1]

Exploitation of Web service descriptions may occur in various ways. Technical and nontechnical descriptions may be used (1) to select a service, (2) to compose it with other Web services, or (3) to derive relevant properties about a composition of Web services (e.g., combined cost or validity for a given specification).

In this chapter, we consider the process of provisioning data about a Web service to constitute a specification of the Web service. At this point, the question arises how a machine may attribute machine-understandable meaning to this metadata. The XML standards (WS*) listed above lack the formal semantics to achieve common interpretation and interoperability of Web service annotations. Therefore, we argue for the use of ontologies for giving a formal semantics to Web service annotations, that is, we argue in favor of semantic Web service annotations. A Web service ontology defines general concepts such as service or operation as well as relations that exist between such concepts. The metadata describing a Web service can instantiate concepts of the ontology (Patil, Oundhakar, Sheth, Verman, & Kunal, 2004). This connection supports Web service developers to understand and compare the metadata of different services described by the same or a similar ontology. Consequently, ontology-based Web service annotation leverages the use, reuse and verification of Web services.

The process of semantic Web service annotation in general requires input from multiple sources, that is, legacy descriptions, as well as a labor-intensive modeling effort. Information about a Web service can be gathered for example from the source code of a service (if annotation is done by a service provider), from the API documentation and description, from the overall textual documentation of a Web service or from descriptions in WS* standards. Depending on the structuredness of these sources, semantic annotations may (have to) be provided manually (e.g., if full text is the input), semi-automatically (e.g. for some WS* descriptions) or fully automatically (e.g., if Java interfaces constitute the input). Hence, a semantic description of the signature of a Web service may be provided by automatic means, while the functionality of Web service operations or pre- and postconditions of a Web service operation may only be modeled manually.

Benefits of semantic specifications of Web services include a common framework that integrates semantic descriptions of many relevant Web service properties. In contrast to WS* standards, such a semantic framework allows complex requirements to be queried for (e.g., "Give me all Web shop services that offer customer care facilities and use 128-bit encoding of all communication"; cf. (Oberle, 2006)). The benefits harvested from semantic specifications must be traded off against manual semantic modeling, that is, manual semantic annotation of Web services. While the benefits of semantic specifications, that is, the result of a semantic annotation process, are explored in many papers there are few papers that investigate the efforts that have to be carried out during modeling (cf. some very notable exceptions like Hess & Kushmerick, 2003; Patil et al., 2004; Sabou, Wroe, Goble, & Struckenschmidt, 2005; Zaremba, Kerrigan, Mocan, & Moran, 2006). It is the purpose of this chapter to explain the conceptual gap between legacy descriptions and semantic specifications and to indicate how this gap is to be bridged.

To clarify this point in even more detail: Merriam-Webster online defines "annotation" as:

*Function: noun*
*1: a note added by way of comment or explanation*
*2: the act of annotating*

Most proposals about semantic annotation, such as ones to W3C like (Akkiraju, Farrell, Miller, Nagarajan, Schmidt, Sheth, & Verma, 2005; Battle, Bernstein, Boley, Grosof, Gruninger, Hull, Kifer, Martin, McIlraith, McGuinness, Su, & Tabet, 2005) only consider "semantic annotation of Web services" according to the first meaning of "annotation," some others use "annotation" as a synonym to "specification" and do not intend to add to anything. The purpose of this contribution is to investigate the problem of "annotation" in the second sense. For ease of writing and understandability, we never use "(semantic) annotation" to refer to the first sense here, but use "(semantic) specification" or "(semantic) description" instead.

In the following, we start with an application example that functions as a run through example throughout this chapter. It demonstrates an application use case of building a Web shop. It also shows how semantic specifications resulting from semantic annotation may facilitate the development task of building the Web shop by providing a semantics-based development environment.

In the subsequent section, we analyze the purpose of Web service specifications in such a development scenario as well as the legacy sources of information about a Web service, including textual descriptions as well as the use of WS* documents. They help us to show (1) what semantic specifications we would like to provide and (2) how to represent them. Eventually, we use this illustration as input for requirements to support the semantic annotation process, as this process needs more and more sophisticated support than is currently offered by semantic environments.

## USE CASE

As use case scenario we consider the development of a Web shop. In order to save time, reduce costs, and improve maintainability, existing software should be reused to implement the shop. Web services are chosen for the implementation as they meet such requirements, among others, allowing for easy use of services provided by other companies, for example payment services. The Web shop should provide a Web based user interface, but should also be reusable. Hence, the Web shop will be a complex service composed of several other complex services. Ideally, the development process is supported by a Web service development environment that can be used to organize the Web services from which the Web shop is built.

## Architecture

Figure 1 shows parts of the Web shop architecture using other Web services.

The payment service is a central component of the Web shop. It is not an atomic service but an aggregation of several specialized services. The aggregated payment service provides a uniform interface partly independent of the interfaces of the underlying services. The specification of this general service has to merge the properties and conditions of all its subsidiary Web services' specifications. For instance, a credit card number is essential for credit card payment, but not for money order payment. Internally, the payment service delegates to an appropriate subsidiary Web service which can be part of the Web shop (like the Money Order Service in the example), or which are services offered by other providers such as the Credit Card Payment Services of provider A.

## Development Process

In order to build the Web shop, the developer proceeds as follows: When he needs a specific Web service, he queries a Web service registry by specifying the desired properties of that Web service. For instance, a query specifying the effect of a successful money transfer has as result a list of all payment services. A query with the condition that only credit card payment can be used will get as response all credit card payment services. In the ideal case, the query processor finds a service that matches all requirements, but in most cases it only finds services that fulfill some but not all requirements, so the engineer has to make some adjustments to use them.

*Figure 1. Web shop architecture example*

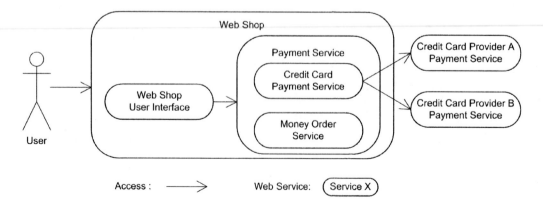

For the previously illustrated development process to work, the registry needs specific information about the services it manages. As an example of which information it is, we examine some relevant properties of the Payment Service. The Payment Service provides three operations. The first operation *MethodSupported* takes as input the kind of payment method and asks the service if a specific payment method (like credit card or money order) is supported. The output of this method is true or false depending on whether a service for the payment method exists and is reachable. The second operation *ValidityCheck* checks the validity of payment information. The inputs of the operation are the verifiable details of the payment (like the existence of accounts, the validity of credit cards, and so on) and the output is the validation of the information. The third one is the *Transaction*-operation that executes a specified transaction. For this purpose, it collects all details of the transaction to be executed and returns a transaction identification number. Since Web services are stateless, the *Transaction*-operation needs all information, even if the *ValidityCheck*-operation has been called before with the same information.

## The Up-and-Running Web Shop

In Figure 2, the workflow of the payment process is shown. The workflow starts at the user interface, where the first action is the user interface calling the *MethodSupported*-operation of the payment service using the interface description specified in the service specification of the payment service. The payment service returns an answer, which the user interface can interpret, because the answer format is also described in the specification. In the next step, the *ValidityCheck*-operation as specified in its interface description is called. The payment service itself calls the matching operation of the specific credit card payment service and passes response to the user interface. The payment service can successfully

call the operation, because the input and output interfaces of the credit card payment service are also specified. The final call of the user interface calls the *Transaction*-operation handing over the result of the validity check. Because the output of one operation is required by the second one, the possible sequences of Web service invocations are limited. The call of the *Transaction*-operation has the same invocation sequence as the call of the *ValidityCheck*-operation.

## ANNOTATING WEB SERVICES

We now analyze different aspects of annotating Web services by asking four questions relevant in this context:

- Which information sources containing information relevant to the specification of Web services exist?
- Which descriptions are needed to manage and reuse Web services?
- How should the metadata be represented?
- How can the description be exploited?

In the following, we give answers to these questions and illustrate central aspects by means of application example.

## Purpose of Web Service Annotation

The goal of the annotation of Web services is to simplify the management of services in the Web by partial automation of management tasks like composition or invocation of Web services. A challenge in automating Web service management is that most information about Web services is in formats only humans understand, for example documentations. Thus, a machine interpretable Web service description is needed that fills the semantic gap between existing information about Web services and the information needed. Semantic descriptions are a means to bridge this

*Figure 2. Payment workflow*

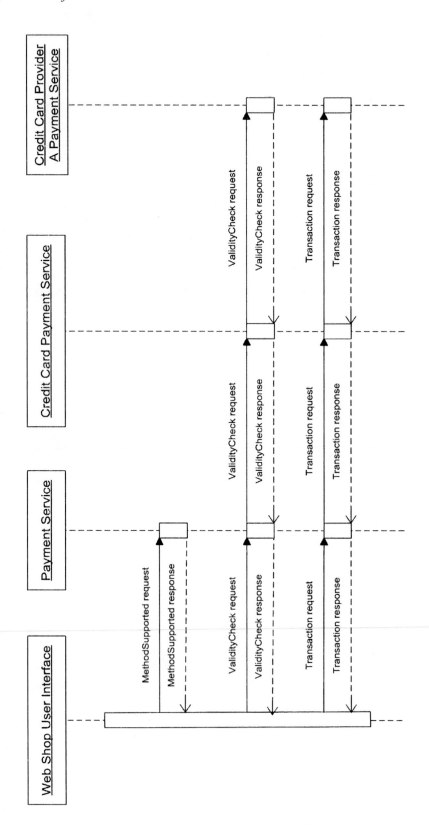

gap in the form of semantic metadata describing the semantics of an item of information in a machine interpretable format. As mentioned in the introduction, a Web service description specifies the properties of a Web service by metadata. A semantic description does it by semantic metadata that is ontology-based and connects a Web service property with the corresponding concept defined in an ontology.

## Sources of Information

Various information sources of different quality describing different Web service properties exist. In the following, we give a list of such sources and analyze the provided information:

- One of the most common information sources is the documentation of a Web service. The documentation contains selected information about a Web service. In most cases, the information given in the documentation is defined in natural language and thus not formalized and not in a machine-understandable form. Determining actual properties of a Web service from such text becomes difficult or even impossible for a machine.

- Source code contains all information about operations including all inputs and outputs. The extractable information differs between programming languages. For instance, a method signature in Java reveals type information about input and output parameters. Programming languages with less restrictive signatures do not contain such type information. Furthermore, source code defines programming logic which contains information about the Web service's functionality, the Web service's preconditions that must be fulfilled before the execution of an operation, and effects of the execution of an operation of the service.

- API descriptions consisting of interface declarations in source code and explanations in natural language are another common information source. In contrast to the documentation, API descriptions focus on particular operations of a Web service and not on the Web service as a whole. In contrast to source code, the API description can be more detailed and often is focused on the relevant methods. In principle the explanations are as expressive as the documentation and share the same disadvantages. Furthermore, API descriptions often contain signatures copied from the source code.

- Comments included in the source code denote another information source that can also be used to determine information about operations as well as about the functionality of the whole Web service. Comments, however, inherit the pros and cons of documentations and API-descriptions. If the source code is not accessible, the comments are also not accessible.

- Software specifications and UML-diagrams are information sources that provide the same kinds of information as API descriptions.

- Other information sources are contracts like end user license agreements (EULA). As they are written in natural language, interpreting them is as problematic as interpreting documentations or other sources written in natural language.

- Background knowledge is information that is usually not provided with a Web service. For instance, background knowledge is programming knowledge needed to understand technical aspects, knowledge about the application area (like payment), and about relevant laws that clarify domain specific properties. All such background knowledge could be useful for specifying properties of Web services.

## Nonsemantic Web Service Description

In the following subsections we examine the reuse of nonsemantically described Web services. We assume, the developer of the Web shop in our use case scenario wants to integrate a new credit card payment service. The information sources the developer has about the new service are the service's documentation and API descriptions. In the following, we analyze which information is provided and how it can be used.

## Description Example: Documentation and API-Description

Listing 1 shows a cutout of the documentation provided for the payment service as used in our example. The cutout describes the *Transaction*-operation and refers to the API-description, here called format description. The description of the operation is very short and does not contain very valuable information as it only inaccurately characterizes input parameters by stating that all transaction information including the payment service provider are submitted to the service. The specification of the output parameter, the transaction identification number, is more detailed because only one parameter exists and is mentioned in the description, but the exact format of it is also missing. While information about preconditions that must hold before the operation of a Web service can be executed and effects of the operation's execution are completely missing in the sample documentation, some of these can be derived from respective laws and the contracts, like the fact that specified accounts must be valid.

A cutout of an API description is depicted in Listing 2. It gives the names of the parameters and a detailed description of assigned values. For instance, the description states that the value of the *payerName*-parameter must be a combination of the payer's last name and first name separated by a comma. The *payerAccountID* is an optional parameter that is only needed for credit card payment and must then contain the payer's credit card number. In the case of the money order payment this parameter can be skipped or must be empty. Like the documentation, this API-description does not contain any statements about preconditions or effects relevant to the *Transaction*-operation. So if the Web shop developer does not have that knowledge himself, he has to gain the needed information from other sources as listed before.

Using only the documentation and the API-description, the Web shop engineer in our example would have to collect the information about the interfaces of the Web service's operations without tool support. Furthermore, the developer would have to make all decisions about which Web service to use for which task and how to use it, in advance and by the developer. If the preconditions and effects are not characterized in detail, the engineer needs domain knowledge to avoid mistakes and to correctly reuse the service.

*Listing 1. Example documentation of a Web service operation[2]*

> Transaction requests submit all transaction information to the Payment Service and receive in return a transaction identification number. The Transaction is executed by a specified payment service provider.
> A list of all needed and optional parameters of transaction requests are listed in the Transaction Request Format description.

*Listing 2. Cutout of an example API-Description*

```
Transaction Request Format
The following list shows all valid name-value pairs that must or can be
    used in a transaction request:


Name            Description
payerName       The name of the payer. The format is:
    "LastName, FirstName"
payerAccountID              If credit card payment is chosen, this must be
    the
    payer's credit card number. If money order payment is
    chosen this parameter must be empty or skipped.

...
```

## Description Example: Operation Interface Description

To enable reuse and discovery of Web services, information about a Web service's interface is needed. The interface is the property of a Web service which can be described very simply as it consists of all methods a Web service provides as an endpoint for machine-to-machine communication, and the messages which those methods accept and which they return. A method interface can be described with languages like the Web Services Description Language (WSDL), which is a XML based general-purpose language designed for the description of Web service interfaces (Christensen, Curbera, Meredith, & Weerawarana, 2001). WSDL is a widespread language adopted by many Web service supporting application servers which often facilitate the dynamic generation of WSDL files out of the source code or java class descriptions. Because WSDL is designed for the syntactical specification of Web service interfaces, a WSDL description does not include any semantic information about the service.

Listing 3 illustrates the use of WSDL to describe the operation interfaces of a simplified version of a credit card payment service. The first lines (lines 2-6) of the description declare used namespaces, which define the used XML-elements and XML-types, and facilitate readability. After the namespace specifications, new complex data types are declared from line 7 to line 23, for example the validity information type that holds all needed information for a validity check. WSDL describes operations of a Web service as network endpoints (Christensen et al., 2001) that communicate by retrieving and sending messages which contain the data delivered to or returned from the operation (lines 24-29). From line 31 to line 35 port types are defined and associated with corresponding operations, which are connected with the appropriate input and output messages. After the port types are defined the binding between the Web service's endpoints, their port types, and the kind of their supported invocation is specified (in line 38 to line 55). The last part of the listing (from line 56) describes the Web service and contains the locations (as URI) where the service's operations can be reached. Some further information can be gained from optional comments, but in general other information sources are needed to gain all knowledge needed to automate the reuse of a Web service described with WSDL.

Using WSDL, an engineer developing the Web shop gets detailed descriptions of Web services telling him how to invoke operations on Web

*Listing 3. Description of a simplified payment service in WSDL*

```
01 <?xml version="1.0"?>
02 <definitions name="SimplifiedCreditCardPayment"
03    targetNamespace="http://example.org/creditcardpayment.wsdl"
04    xmlns:tns="http://example.org/creditcardpayment.wsdl"
05    xmlns:soap="http://schemas.xmlsoap.org/wsdl/soap/"
06    xmlns="http://schemas.xmlsoap.org/wsdl/">
07 <types>
08  <schema targetNamespace="http://example.org/creditcardpayment.xsd">
09   <element name="ValidityInformation">
10    <complexType>
11     <all>
12      <element name="OwnerName" type=" xsd:string"/>
13      <element name="CreditCardID" type="xsd:string"/>
14      <element name="ValidityDate" type="tns:Date"/>
15      ...
16     </all>
17    </complexType>
18    <element name="Date">
19     ...
20    </element>
21    ...
22   </schema>
23 </types>
24 <message name="ValidityCheckInput">
25  <part name="body" type="tns:ValidityInformation"/>
26 </message>
27 <message name="ValidityCheckOutput">
28  <part name="body" type="string"/>
29 </message>
30 ...
31 <portType name="SimplifiedCreditCardPaymentPortType">
32  <operation name="ValidityCheck">
33   <input message="tns: ValidityCheckInput"/>
34   <output message="tns: ValidityCheckOutput"/>
35  </operation>
36  ...
37 </portType>
38 <binding name="SimplifiedCreditCardPaymentBinding"
39    type="tns:SimplifiedCreditCardPaymentPortType">
40  <soap:binding style="rpc"
41      transport="http://schemas.xmlsoap.org/soap/http"/>
42  <operation name="ValidityCheck">
43   <soap:operation
44    soapAction="http://example.org/creditcardpayment/ValidityCheck"/>
45   <input>
46    <soap:body use="encoded"/>
47   </input>
48   <output>
49    <soap:body use="encoded"
50       namespace="http://soapinterop.org/xsd/"
51       encodingStyle="http://schemas.xmlsoap.org/soap/encoding/"/>
52   </output>
53  </operation>
54  ...
```

*continued on following page*

*Listing 3. continued*

```
55 </binding>
56 <service name="SimplifiedCreditCardPaymentService">
57   <documentation> This is a ... </documentation>
58   <port name="SimplifiedCreditCardPaymentPort"
59     binding="tns:SimplifiedCreditCardPaymentBinding">
60     <soap:address location="http://example.org/creditcardpayment"/>
61   </port>
62 ...
63 </service>
64 </definitions>
```

services and which format the returned answers have. This information is detailed enough to allow tools to support the engineer adjusting interfaces to access the Web service, but the engineer still has to collect information about service functionality, execution and so on from other sources.

## Semantics of Descriptions

We previously analyzed descriptions of Web services. In the following, we inspect which kind of information serves which annotation purpose in connection with which kind of Web service semantics. We distinguish between four categories of semantics:

- The first category *data semantics* includes the semantics of all inputs and outputs of a Web service (Patil et al., 2004). For instance, the specification that the credit card payment service has a validity date parameter which has a specific format like "month/year".

- The category *protocol semantics* includes the semantics related to the protocol that defines dependencies between Web services and between their operations, for example the order of execution. In the Web shop example, the protocol defines that the payment information has to be validated before the transaction-operation can be called.

- The category *functional semantics* covers all semantics related to the functionality of a Web service (Patil et al., 2004). For example, a credit card payment service should be annotated with metadata that refers to an agreed terminology of tasks, describing e. g. that a money transfer takes place.

- The last category, *nonfunctional semantics*, bundles all semantics of nonfunctional properties of a service. All properties of a Web service that are not directly related to the Web service's functionality are nonfunctional properties. For example, the description of cost parameters, e. g. of the fee that must be paid to use the credit card payment service falls under this category. Further examples are special properties like security, quality of service, and so on.

The introduced categories of semantics are used to specify Web services semantically. A service description specifying all those semantics for a service is called semantic service specification. The semantic service specification contains all information needed for the service advertising and discovery. The combination of data semantics with the location of the service (specified by an URI) and semantics of the used middleware protocols is a special subset of the semantic service specification called semantic grounding specification. In other words, the grounding specification describes how to access a Web service.

## Semantic Web Service Description

WSDL has been designed to specify the endpoints of Web services, but lacks the ability to express any kind of semantics. Knowledge representation languages allow to give Web service descriptions a formal semantics since they enable the definition of concepts, classes, types, and relations to specify conceptualizations or ontologies, respectively. While many such description languages exist with varying expressivity, we here introduce the language Flora-2 (Yang, Kifer, Zhao, & Chowdhary, 2005). The purposes of Flora-2 are the definition of ontologies and the description of all metadata relevant to Web services discovery and invocation. Interoperability between Web service descriptions is achieved if they commit to the same ontology, that is, express a Web service by referencing concepts and relations defined in a particular ontology. Consequently, knowledge representation languages enable Web service descriptions including semantics.

There exist many other languages that can be used to annotate services. Some are specialized for the annotation of Web services (see related work section), but for many of these languages fundamental tools, for example reasoners, are not or only partially implemented. In the following we use Flora-2 as it is supported by a fully implemented reasoner[3] and is powerful in expressing schemata. A weakness of Flora-2 is its capability to depict processes. A—somewhat inelegant and not very powerful—workaround can be achieved by the means of reifications. The reification is implemented as a class that enables the manipulation and reasoning about its attribute's values. A term is reified by instantiating the reification class.

## Data and Protocol Semantics

To specify data semantics of a Web service operation, connections between ontology concepts and the corresponding input and output parameters, and the parameter types have to be build. The connections are made by instantiating appropriate ontology concepts for each parameter and Web service operation.

Protocol semantics describe the protocol to follow for accomplishing a specific task by means of Web services. The protocol defines the order of operations, including sequences, loops, forks, joins, and so on. In general the protocol semantics describe the workflow and the dataflow relevant for the Web service's execution. A protocol may be specified in different notations that are more or less intuitive for the developer. In the following, the protocol semantics are specified with the help of pre-conditions and postconditions, which are discussed in the following subsection.

## Functional Semantics

The functional semantics describe the functionality of a Web service operation. This can be expressed with the help of effects. Before the execution of an operation, certain pre-conditions have to be fulfilled. For instance, a money transfer from account A to account B can only take place if account A is solvent. Preconditions and effects can be used to express the protocol semantics and functional semantics of Web services. Before we continue to examine how information about them can support the Web service development process we want to analyze both in more detail.

We distinguish between internal preconditions which are checked (internally) by the application logic or ensured by type conditions of the programming language, and external, more general preconditions which must be fulfilled for a correct and successful execution of the Web service and can not be checked within a Web service implementation. Within the internal conditions, we further distinguish between implicit and explicit conditions. Implicit preconditions are conditions that are a consequence of standards, types and definitions. In the example of the credit card payment service, we assume that one of the parameters passed to the service is the validity date of the credit card number. An implicit internal precondition is that the date has to be in a specific format, for example has to contain a day, a month, and a year and has to be of a particular type used in the programming language to represent dates. Explicit preconditions are conditions that are specified for a specific operation. In our example, an explicit internal condition for the validity date parameter is that the value must denote a date in the future, which can only be checked programmatically by comparing the current date with the date represented by the parameter.

As an example of an external precondition, consider the validity check of a credit card. The validity of a credit card number may depend on several external facts that are not available within our payment Web service, for example the current balance of the bank account of the card owner. Thus, evaluation of a credit card number is only possible for the credit card provider which has access to the relevant facts that determine the validity of a credit card number. In order to enable validity checks by third parties, credit card providers usually offer a Web service that allows to retrieve the validity of a credit card. As the determination of validity of a credit card is out of the scope of our payment Web service since it is missing the necessary external background knowledge, the condition that a Web service must be reachable that is able to check credit card validity, is an external precondition.

Effects describe the output and the impact of a Web service's execution. While the term post-condition often focuses only on the description of the conditions regarding return values of the

Web service operations, we prefer the term effect to emphasize that the impacts of a Web service execution are also considered. In our example above, an impact of the execution would be the real money transfer from the credit card account to the destination account while the postcondition describes that no money got lost during the transfer. While it is possible to describe the money transaction by postconditions only, such a description would only focus on the fact that one account is decreased by a specific amount of money and another account is increased. The effect of a money transfer, however, can include more than changing account balances.

## Semantic Description Example: Functional Semantics

Before we exemplify the use of knowledge representation languages for Web service specifications, we briefly examine the definition of a Web service ontology that defines the concepts and relations used by the later specification. Listing 4 shows a snippet of a simplified service ontology written in Flora-2 that defines among others the concepts *semanticSpecification, groundingSpecification* and *service*. The *semanticSpecification* specifies the semantics related to the preconditions and effects of an operation. For this purpose the *semanticSpecification*-class has two attributes, *precondition* and *effects*, which are inheritable attributes (*) of the type (=> reification) defined by the reification class. The *paramPos* class specifies a type that is defined to connect parameter names with their position in a sequence of parameters. The *groundingSpecification* specifies the reference to the service implementation (*serviceImplRef*), the name of the described operation (*operationName*), and the sequences of input and output parameters (*inParamSequence* and *outParamSequence*). The *service*-class represents the concept that represents a service, including the grounding and the nonfunctional properties, of all operations of a service. For the following examination we skip nonfunctional properties since we examine them later.

Based on a general service ontology as described in Listing 4, a domain ontology can be build that defines domain specific concepts, types and relations. Listing 5 is a cutout of a domain ontology defining the types *validityInformation* and *date* as mentioned in the documentation of the credit card payment service. Besides the two types, the domain ontology additionally specifies the *isValid* relation that has two arguments of the type *validityInformation* and *date*.

The concrete credit card payment service is described by instantiating (:) concepts and utilizing relations of the ontologies sketched before. In Listing 6, *creditCardPayment* is defined as an instance of the *service*-class defined in the service ontology of Listing 4. Furthermore, it shows in detail the semantic specification part of the description of the *validityCheck*-operation. The instance *validityCheckSpec* of the *semanticSpecification*-class is an assigned value (->) of the semantic spec attribute of the *creditCardPayment*-instance of the *service*-class. The specified preconditions, which are specified by reifications ($\{...\}$), are that the *ValidityInfo* parameter of the operation is of the type *validityInformation*, and that *ActualDate* is

another parameter of the operation which is of type *date*. The described effects include that the output parameter *Valid* is of the type *boolean* and that the relation *isValid* must be true for the given *ValidityInfo* and *ActualDate*. In addition, Listing 6 depicts the grounding specification of the *validityCheck*-operation (the _# represents an unnamed instance).

As we have seen, if the description of a service is given in the above mentioned manner, the engineer reusing the Web service gets detailed information about the preconditions and parameters of a service.

Given a proper semantic Web service specification and its referenced ontologies, the annotated Web service can be reused with only a small amount of extra knowledge. In addition, if the language used to define the ontology is machine-interpretable, development tools can offer the developer semi-automatic support for the Web service integration process. The first kind of support that can be given is discovery support by finding a service that matches a given request. A request can be the result of a planning process or the description of desired behaviors and properties specified by the engineer. The request can then be translated into a query that represents a generic

*Listing 4. Definition of service related concepts in an example ontology[4]*

```
semanticSpecification[precondition *=> reification,
          effects   *=> reification].

paramPos[pos *=> ordinal,
    name *=> string].

groundingSpecification[serviceImplRef *=> string,
          operationName *=> string,
          inParamSequence *=>> paramPos,
          outParamSequence *=>> paramPos].

nonFunctionalProperties[...].
...

service[semanticSpec *=> semanticSpecification,
    groundingSpec *=> groundingSpecification,
    nfProp   *=> nonFunctionalProperties].
```

*Listing 5. Definition of classes and relations in a payment domain ontology*

```
validityInformation[ownerName *=> string,
        credidCardId *=> string,
        validityDate *=> date,
        ...].

date[day *=> ordinal,
 month *=> ordinal,
 year *=> ordinal].
...

isValid(validityInformation, date).
```

*Listing 6. Service specification of a simplified credit card payment service*

```
creditCardPayment:service[
 semanticSpec -> validityCheckSpec:semanticSpecification[
  precondition -> ${ValidityInfo:validityInformation, ValidityInfo:parameter,
        ActualDate:date, ActualDate:parameter},
   effects  -> ${Valid:boolean, Valid:parameter,
        isValid(ValidityInfo, ActualDate)}],
 groundingSpec -> validityCheckGround:groundingSpecification[
  serviceImplRef -> "http://example.org/creditcardpayment/":string,
  operationName  -> "ValidityCheck":string,
  inParamSequence ->> {_#:paramPos[pos -> 1, name -> "ValidityInfo":string],
        _#:paramPos[pos -> 2, name -> "ActualDate":string]},
  outParamSequence ->> {_#:paramPos[pos -> 1, name -> "Valid":string]}],
 nfProp  -> validityCheckNFP:nonFunctionalProperties[...],
 ...].
```

service specification which specifies the desired properties stated in the request. The support tool queries an appropriate registry which returns a list of matching service specifications. In the case of a suitably specified Web service, further assistance can be given in the form of semi-automatic Web service invocation and integration into an existing workflow.

## Nonfunctional Semantics

Many different nonfunctional properties exist. We provide a short list of common nonfunctional properties below:

- The *costs* of a Web service are a nonfunctional property that is relevant for the customer who wants to use the service.
- *Security* is a nonfunctional property that is (like costs) relevant to most Web services. Security enfolds aspects like communication and data encryption.
- The *quality of service* property is a bundle of different properties that all affects the quality of specific aspects of the service, its usage and its output. Examples for such properties are the response time of an operation call and the capacity of the service.
- The information about the *resource usage* of a Web service can be of importance, if

the Web service needs special resources or if using the service is billed with respect to its resource usage.

In order to achieve a correct interpretation of nonfunctional properties logical descriptions have to be found. For this purpose different sources exist, for instance standards and laws. If a standard defines that an encryption algorithm has to be used with at least a specific key length, this information can be interpreted as a property of a certain security level. Another source for nonfunctional property specifications are laws which sometimes also specify a minimum level of encryption for specific data transfers.

## Semantic Description Example: Non-functional Semantics

To enable the annotation with nonfunctional properties a concept defining nonfunctional properties is needed. In Listing 7 a refining of the *nonFunctionalProperties*-concept of the service ontology from Listing 4 is depicted that extends the concept by two simple nonfunctional properties, the service's name and the name of the provider.

The insertion of the concept of nonfunctional properties enables any domain ontology that is based on the service ontology to define domain specific nonfunctional properties and types needed by these. For the payment example in Listing 8, the cutout of Listing 5 is extended by the type *securityType*, which defines different levels of security. The different levels are defined as an inheritable instance of an array (->>) that contains a set of specified values ({…, …}). In this example the service engineer can choose between *none* and *norm_X. none* stands self-explanatory for no security support and *norm_X* for security as defined in the norm X. In addition, the *securityNFProps* is defined as a subclass (::) of the *nonFunctionalProperties*-concept that includes security.

In Listing 9, the service description of the concrete payment service of Listing 6 is refined. Since the security level should be specified, the *validityCheckNFP* is no longer an instance of the *nonFunctionalProperties*-concept but of the *securityNFProps*-concept. While the property values of *serviceName*, and *providerName* are set to string, the value of the *security* property must be chosen from the pre-defined ones. In the example, the *norm_X*-level is specified.

*Listing 7. Expansion to listing 4: Definition of service related concepts in an example ontology*

```
nonFunctionalProperties[serviceName *=> string,
                        providerName *=> string].
```

*Listing 8. Expansion to Listing 5: Definition of classes and relations in a payment domain ontology*

```
securityType::enumeration[values *->> {"none", "norm_X"}].

securityNFProps::nonFunctionalProperties[security *=> securityType].
```

*Listing 9. Expansion to Listing 6: Service specification of a simplified credit card payment service*

```
creditCardPayment:service[
 ...
 nfProp -> validityCheckNFP::securityNFProps[
   serviceName -> "SimplifiedCreditCardPaymentService":string,
   providerName -> "Credit Card Service Provider X":string,
   security  -> validityCheckSType::securityType[
   values ->> {"norm_X"}].
 ...].
```

*Listing 10. Querying an operation by precondition*

```
X:service[
 semanticSpec->Y:semanticSpecification[
   precondition-> (${_G:validityInformation}, ${_H:parameter} , _)]].
```

The annotation with nonfunctional properties supports the service engineer, even if they are often not machine-interpretable. For instance, the name of the provider, especially if extended to complete address information, can be used to contact the provider in order to gain more information. The reference to a particular security specification allows the engineer to find out about the standards to which a service conforms, and which standards need to be fulfilled to communicate with the service.

### Semantic Description Example: Exploiting Semantic Descriptions

As mentioned above, the annotation of a Web service with a knowledge representation language enables the discovery of Web services. For instance the Web shop developer of our application example wants to query a registry for a service by specifying a subset of desired preconditions. The preconditions may state that a parameter of the type *validityInformation* has to be assigned at the operation's call. Listing 10 shows such a query, which will return the matching service instance (in our example this will be at least the *creditCardPaymentService*) and the instance of the semantic specification of the operation (in our example this will be for the credit card payment service the *validityCheckSpec*). The query can be read in the following way: We want all X that are instances of the *service*-class and all Y that are instances of the *semanticSpecification*-class assigned to the *semanticSpec*-attribute of X. In addition, the *precondition*-attribute of Y must be a reification that contains at least two attribute-type pairs. One of these pairs specifies an attribute of the type *validitiyInformation* and the other one specifies an attribute of the *parameter*-type. The associated attributes (_G and _H) and additional pairs the reification may contain (, _) are ignored.

### The Annotation Process

We explained the representation of Web service descriptions and how these descriptions can be exploited, but have not yet outlined the annotation process. Thus, in this section we annotate the payment service of the application example step by step while introducing exemplary methods and tools that support the annotation process. Generally, we assume that descriptions are developed by the engineer who implements the Web service. In this case the source code is well known and the background knowledge of the engineer should be sufficient. Figure 3 depicts the process of annotation.

The first step is the nonsemantic annotation. The inputs of this step are gained from the different information sources introduced before and include the Web services documentation (see Listing 1), and the interface descriptions of the Web service's operations (see Listing 2). The outcomes of the nonsemantic annotation are WSDL files (see Listing 3) and other kinds of nonsemantically annotated API-descriptions and documents. The second step is the semantic annotation, which takes the same inputs as the first step in combination with relevant ontologies, such as Web service ontologies (see Listing 4) and different domain ontologies (see Listing 5). The outcome of the semantic annotation is a semantic service specification (see Listings 6 and 8).

Nonsemantic annotation is semi-automatically supported by different tools. For instance, for many programming languages tools exist that support the generation of WSDL. One framework that supports this is Axis, a SOAP (the Simple Object Access Protocol is the communication protocol to access Web services (Mitra, 2003)) engine that provides various tools to develop and use Web services (Apache, 2005). Axis provides a tool named Java2WSDL, a translator that generates complete WSDL files out of a Web service's Java code.

The process of semantic annotation consists of different steps. The first step is the classification of the Web service. The result of the classification is the assignment of the Web service to its domain. The service developer classifies services by decisions based on his background knowledge or with the help of classification tools, for example ASSAM (Hess, Johnston, & Kushmerick, 2004). ASSAM, a semi-automatic Web service classification tool, applies text classification algorithms to the WSDL description of a Web service to classify the service into a specific domain, for example banking. In advance, ASSAM can classify the functionality of operations and the types of input

*Figure 3. The annotation process*

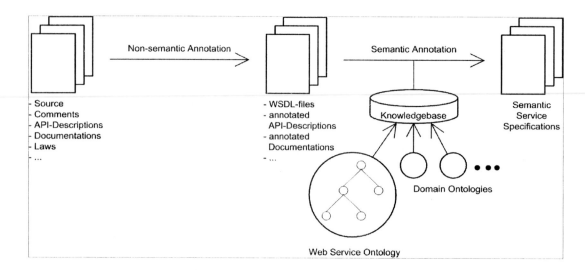

and output parameters. After the classification of the Web service's domain the developer has to select an appropriate domain ontology, or, if no suitable one exists, define a new one. For the development of domain ontologies tool support exists as well: For example, the method described in (Sabou et al., 2005) supports the service engineer by extracting terms from textual sources (e.g., documentation) using text processing methods like parts of speech (POS) and dependency relations (DEP). In a second step, corresponding concepts and relations are derived and arranged in a hierarchy. The engineer only has to filter the proposed concepts and relations and refine the derived hierarchy.

Once an ontology is selected the engineer has to connect the metadata describing the Web service functionalities with ontology concepts. This process can be separated into different subprocesses. Each subprocess addresses one kind of semantics. Even if no special order exists for the execution of the single subprocesses, it makes sense to start annotating the metadata with data semantics. For this purpose the first step is to specify the operation's interfaces. If a nonsemantic interface description exists, it can be translated into the knowledge description language used to notate the semantic specification. Dependent of the language used for the nonsemantic description the translation can

be automated to a certain degree. For instance, WSDL files can semi-automatically be translated, because of their machine-interpretable form. For the translation, the used types and the elements of the operation interfaces have to be mapped onto ontology concepts. For this task, tools like ASSAM or the deep annotation mechanism of the OntoMat-Service-Browser can be used (Agarwal, 2005). Using the OntoMat-Service-Browser, the engineer can build the connections between ontology concepts and the metadata using the drag and drop mechanism provided by the graphical user interface. The result of this step is the semantic grounding specification and the parts of preconditions and effects that specify input and output parameters (see highlighted parts of Listing 11).

The next step is the specification of the protocol and functional semantics. If the data semantics are specified, parts of the protocol and the functionality are already specified implicitly. The implicit specification of the protocol results from the specification of the input parameters. From this specification we can derive which information has to be gathered before an operation can be invoked. The implicit specification of the functionality is part of the parameter specifications. In other words: all parts of the protocol and the functionality that can be derived from the dataflow can be specified implicitly. The other parts

*Listing 11. Data semantics derived from WSDL*

```
creditCardPayment:service[
 semanticSpec -> validityCheckSpec:semanticSpecification[
  precondition -> ${ValidityInfo:validityInformation, ValidityInfo:parameter,
      ActualDate:date, ActualDate:parameter},
  effects   -> ${Valid:boolean, Valid:parameter,
      isValid(ValidityInfo, ActualDate)}],
 groundingSpec -> validityCheckGround:groundingSpecification[
  serviceImplRef -> "http://example.org/creditcardpayment/":string,
  operationName  -> "ValidityCheck":string,
  inParamSequence ->> {_#:paramPos[pos -> 1, name -> "ValidityInfo":string],
      _#:paramPos[pos -> 2, name -> "ActualDate":string]},
  outParamSequence ->> {_#:paramPos[pos -> 1, name -> "Valid":string]}],
 ...].
```

of the semantics require an explicit specification by means of relations. As input of this process step information from all sources mentioned in the section about information sources is imaginable. The explicit specifications of preconditions and effects are complex and have to be defined by the service developer manually. The highlighted parts of Listing 12 depict the parts of the service specification of the example service that specify the protocol and functional semantics of the Web service. The dataflow of the validity check is described by the parameters *Validity-Info, ActualDate* and *Valid*. To fully express the functionality of the *ValidityCheck*-operation the input and output parameters are not sufficient. A relation that describes the dependency between the validity information and the actual date is necessary. For this purpose the *isValid*-relation has to be specified.

The last step is the specification of the nonfunctional semantics of the Web service. Some of the simple nonfunctional properties like the name of the service can be extracted automatically from the WSDL file. More complex nonfunctional properties like the security property are described by the engineer. For this purpose he also can use information from all information sources introduced in the Sources of Information section. In our example, the engineer can choose between two levels of security defined in the payment domain ontology (see Listing 8). The highlighted parts of Listing 13 show the parts of the specification that specify the nonfunctional semantics of the *ValidityCheck*-operation. As result of the semantic annotation process the engineer gets a semantic description of the Web service.

A common aspect of the nonsemantic and semantic annotation processes is the effort of annotating. A description of a service containing all relevant properties leverages reuse and enables better tool support, but also requires much higher efforts from the engineer. A tradeoff between modeling efforts and management efforts has to be achieved (Oberle, 2006), where modeling efforts comprise the annotation and documentation process, while management efforts denote among

*Listing 12. Protocol and functional semantics*

```
creditCardPayment:service[
  semanticSpec -> validityCheckSpec:semanticSpecification[
    precondition -> ${ValidityInfo:validityInformation, ValidityInfo:parameter,
        ActualDate:date, ActualDate:parameter},
    effects  -> ${Valid:boolean, Valid:parameter,
        isValid(ValidityInfo, ActualDate)}],
  ...].
```

*Listing 13. Nonfunctional semantics*

```
creditCardPayment:service[
  ...
  nfProp -> validityCheckNFP::securityNFProps[
    serviceName -> "SimplifiedCreditCardPaymentService":string,
    providerName -> "Credit Card Service Provider X":string,
    security  -> validityCheckSType::securityType[
    values ->> {"norm_X"}].
  ...].
```

others the reuse of the service. To decrease annotation efforts one has to increase the management efforts and vice versa. A reasonable tradeoff is usually achieved when the combination of both is minimal; however, for different scenarios there are other factors influencing the optimal combination. For instance, a service provider may increase his modeling efforts to decrease his customers' management efforts to gain an advantage over his competitors. Thus, everyone annotating a Web service has to find his own tradeoff depending on his individual context.

## RELATED WORK

In this chapter we have shown how Web services can be annotated to ease Web service discovery, reuse, composition, and further Web service management tasks. The approach followed in this chapter uses existing resources to fulfill the task of Web service annotation. The techniques and methods presented here are independent of the used languages or tools. In addition, our approach uses one description language to specify all semantic descriptions. In this section we introduce some other approaches to describe Web services.

While we have shown what specifications of Web services are and how they can be achieved, different approaches exist for developing semantic descriptions of Web services:

- In Zaremba et al. (2006) the authors follow the same approach regarding the use of one description language to specify all semantics and the grounding. They introduce their own language, the Web Service Modeling Language (WSML), a description language they specifically developed for Web service description. They also introduce the Web Service Modeling Ontology (WSMO), which defines all concepts relevant to Web service descriptions. Their Web Service Execution Environment (WSMX) combines WSML and WSMO to support the description of Web services and the exploitation of Web service descriptions.

- In Akkiraju et al. (2005) the authors describe WSDL-S, an approach that adds semantics to the WSDL specification. Like the approach followed in this chapter, WSDL-S reuses already existing techniques and languages. In addition, WSDL-S is upward compatible to WSDL, because the description is an extension to existing document elements of WSDL. The descriptions can refer (by means of URI) to ontology concepts defined in external ontologies. These ontologies can be defined using any description language.

- The authors, Battle, Bernstein, Boley, Grosof, Gruninger, Hull, Kifer, Martin, McIlraith, McGuinness, Su, & Tabet (2005), also use one description language for all descriptions. For this purpose they introduce their own language, the Semantic Web Service Language (SWSL). SWSL consists of two components: a first-order logic language (SWSL-FOL) and a rule-based language (SWSL-Rules). By means of SWSL the Semantic Web Service Ontology (SWSO) is specified, which defines concepts required to describe semantics of Web services.

- Beside approaches dealing with the Web service description as a whole, many solutions for subproblems exist. For instance, many proposals for ontologies defining concepts related to the description of Web service properties exist. Such a proposal is the Web Ontology Language for Services[5] (OWL-S) that builds upon the DAML-S (Sycara, Paolucci, Ankolekar, & Srinivasan, 2003), and uses the Web Ontology Language (OWL) that is created as a language with the purpose of ontology definition (McGuinness & van Harmelen, 2004). OWL-S contains three interrelated sub-ontologies which define concepts for the profile, the process model, and the grounding of a Web service. With the help of the profile sub-ontology the functional semantics can be described, the process sub-ontology expresses the protocol semantics and the grounding sub-ontology the data semantics.

Different approaches exist in the field of semi-automatic annotation and reuse support:

- For instance, in Patil et al. (2004), the ME-TEOR-S Web Service Annotation Framework (MWSAF) is introduced that provides algorithms, which semi-automatically match items in WSDL files to ontology concepts by means of SchemaGraphs. SchemaGraphs are devised by the authors as graphs that are used to represent ontologies independent of the language the ontology is specified in.
- Another example is ODESWS (Gómez-Pérez, González-Cabero, & Lama, 2004), a tool suite that provides tools for semi-automatic annotation, design and composition of Web services. For this purpose ODESWS provides miscellaneous ontologies to support semantic specifications.

## CONCLUSION

In this chapter we have shown how the process of annotation leads to semantic specifications that leverages Web service use and eases Web service development. We examined different information sources, their information content, and potential exploitations of the content. Different aspects of Web service development have been addressed on the basis of an application example that illustrates the development of a Web shop by composing other Web services to a new one. Finally, the challenges of dealing with nonfunctional properties and the annotation process itself were analyzed.

The introduced techniques enable a semi-automatic reuse and management of Web services. We illustrated, that under the condition that Web services are semantically annotated using one language, for example Flora-2, Web service management can be accomplished over one common interface. Therefore, Web service development as well as management efforts are decreased, and Web service employment is leveraged. Flora-2 presents a running implementation of a description language that is applicable for semantic Web service description and its exploitations.

Besides partial automation of Web service management, automating Web service annotation is an underexplored research area. We conjecture that many annotation tasks can be automated so that semi-automatic annotation methods utilize the possible simplifications of automation and the power of manual annotation.

## ACKNOWLEDGMENTS

This work is conducted with respect to the Adaptive Services Grid (ASG) project and the project Knowledge Sharing and Reuse across Media (X-Media), both funded by the Information Society Technologies (IST) 6th Framework Programme.

## REFERENCES

Agarwal, S., Handschuh, S., & Staab, S. (2005). Annotation, composition and invocation of semantic Web services. *Journal of Web Semantics, 2*(1).

Akkiraju, R., Farrell, J., Miller, J., Nagarajan, M., Schmidt, M., Sheth, A., & Verma, K. (2005). Web service semantics - WSDL-S, W3C Member Submission 7 November 2005. Retrieved October 17, 2006, from http://www.w3.org/Submission/2005/SUBM-WSDL-S-20051107/

Apache, Software Foundation (2005). Axis user's guide. Retrieved October 17, 2006, from http://ws.apache.org/axis/java/user-guide.html

Battle, S., Bernstein, A., Boley, H., Grosof, B., Gruninger, M., Hull, R., Kifer, M., Martin, D., McIlraith, S., McGuinness, D., Su, J., & Tabet, S. (2005). Semantic Web Services Language (SWSL), W3C Member Submission 9 September 2005. Retrieved October 17, 2006, from http://www.w3.org/Submission/2005/SUBM-SWSF-SWSL-20050909/

Christensen, E., Curbera, F., Meredith, G. & Weerawarana, S. (2001). Web Services Description Language (WSDL) 1.1, 15 March 2001. Retrieved October 17, 2006, from http://www.w3.org/TR/2001/NOTE-wsdl-20010315

Gómez-Pérez, A., González-Cabero, R., & Lama, M. (2004). A framework for design and composition of Semantic Web services. In *Proceedings of the AAAI Spring Symposium on Semantic Web Services* (pp. 113-120). Stanford, California.

Hess, A., Johnston, E., & Kushmerick, N. (2004). ASSAM: A tool for semi-automatically annotating semantic Web services. In *Proceedings of the International Semantic Web Conference 2004* (pp. 320-334).

Hess, A., & Kushmerick, N. (2003). *Learning to attach semantic metadata to Web services.* Paper presented at the International Semantic Web Conference 2003.

McGuinness, D.L., & van Harmelen, F. (Ed.). (2004). OWL Web Ontology Language - Overview, W3C Recommendation 10 February 2004. Retrieved October 17, 2006, from http://www.w3.org/TR/2004/REC-owl-features-20040210/

Mitra, N. (Ed.). (2003). SOAP Version 1.2 Part 0: Primer, W3C Recommendation 24 June 2003. Retrieved October 17, 2006, from http://www.w3.org/TR/2003/REC-soap12-part0-20030624/

Oberle, D. (2006). *Semantic management of middleware.* New York: Springer.

Patil, A.A., Oundhakar, S.A., Sheth, A.P., & Verma, K. (2004). METEOR-S Web service annotation framework. In *Proceedings of WWW 2004* (pp. 553-562). ACM Press.

Sabou, M., Wroe, C., Goble, C., & Stuckenschmidt, H. (2005). Learning domain ontologies for semantic Web service descriptions. *Journal of Web Semantics, 3*(4).

Sycara, K.P., Paolucci, M., Ankolekar, A., & Srinivasan, N. (2003). Automated discovery, interaction and composition of Semantic Web services. *Journal of Web Semantics, 1*(1), 27-46.

Yang, G., Kifer, M., Zhao, C., & Chowdhary, V. (2005). Flora-2: User's manual. Retrieved October 17, 2006, from http://flora.sourceforge.net/docs/floraManual.pdf

Zaremba, M., Kerrigan, M., Mocan, A., & Moran, M. (2006). Web services modeling ontology. In J. Cardoso & A. Sheth (Eds.), *Semantic Web services, processes and applications.* Kluwer Academic Publishers.

## ENDNOTES

[1] Cf. http://www.oasis-open.org/committees/tc_cat.php?cat=ws and http://www.w3.org/2002/ws/

[2] This example follows the style of a Google API description. (http://www.google.com/apis/download.html)

[3] Download location for the XSB Flora-2 reasoner: http://flora.sourceforge.net/

[4] The Flora-2 examples follow the style of the ontology defined in the ASG-project, http://asg-platform.org ASG, Adaptive Services Grid, is an Integrated Project supported by the European Union

[5] http://www.daml.org/services/owl-s/1.0/

# Chapter XI
# Semantic Web Service Discovery:
## Methods, Algorithms, and Tools

**Vassileios Tsetsos**
*University of Athens, Greece*

**Christos Anagnostopoulos**
*University of Athens, Greece*

**Stathes Hadjiefthymiades**
*University of Athens, Greece*

## ABSTRACT

*This chapter surveys existing approaches to Semantic Web service discovery. Such semantic discovery will probably substitute existing keyword-based solutions in the near future, in order to overcome the limitations of the latter. First, the architectural components along with potential deployment scenarios are discussed. Subsequently, a wide range of algorithms and tools that have been proposed for the realization of Semantic Web service discovery are presented. Moreover, key challenges and open issues, not addressed by current systems, are identified. The purpose of this chapter is to update the reader on the current progress in this area of the distributed systems domain and to provide the required background knowledge and stimuli for further research and experimentation in semantics-based service discovery.*

## INTRODUCTION

Right after the Web infrastructure had matured enough, both academia and industry have recognized the necessity of enabling interactions between processes over the Web. The nature of the Web itself dictated that such enabling infrastructure should be loosely-coupled, based on open interfaces and, mostly, asynchronous communication. The outcome of the academic and industrial research in this field was the Web Services infrastructure, which has been standardized by W3C (World Wide Web Consortium). Web Services (WS) can be defined as "programmatic interfaces for applications (i.e., business logic), available over the WWW infrastructure and developed with XML technologies."

The lifecycle of WSs includes the following main steps (see Figure 1):

- **Advertisement:** The process of publishing the description and endpoints of a WS in a service registry.
- **Discovery:** The process of locating all WSs that match the requestor's functional requirements.
- **Selection:** The process of selecting the most suitable WS out of the discovered ones, usually based on application-dependent metrics (e.g., QoS).
- **Composition:** The process of integrating selected WSs into a complex process.
- **Invocation:** The process of invoking a single WS or complex process, by providing it with all the necessary inputs for its execution.

In practice, service discovery and selection are not always discrete processes, since the discovery algorithm may also rank the discovered services according to their relevance to the user inquiry. Out of all five steps, WS discovery is regarded the most important one, or, at least, it has attracted the major attention of the research community and industry. The main reason is that one cannot use a service unless she is aware of its existence or discovers it. Furthermore, the deviation of the provided service functionality from the requestor's desired functionality heavily depends on the ability to locate the best available services.

At this point, we would like to discriminate the concept "Web service discovery" from the more generic concept "service discovery." The first refers only to Web services while the latter can be applied to other types of services, too (e.g., printing services). Although both concepts are enabled by similar architectures, they use different protocols and technologies, and they apply to different application domains. Some indicative service discovery frameworks are Service Lo-

*Figure 1. Web services lifecycle*

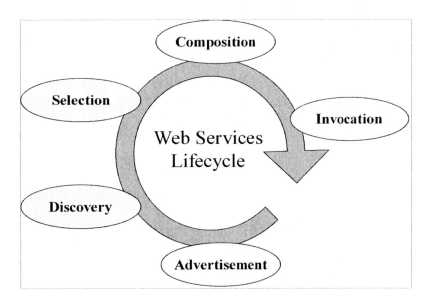

cation Protocol (SLP), Universal Plug and Play (UPnP) and Jini (Richard, 2002). However, in the rest of the book we will use the terms "Web service" and "service" interchangeably.

WS descriptions are usually expressed as simple key-value pairs, with service requests following the same pattern. Hence, the procedure of discovering a service involves a keyword-/syntax-based comparison between the registered service descriptions and the service request. In practice, this kind of discovery it does not constitute an "intelligent retrieval method" and is a somewhat naïve way of matchmaking.[1]

With the advent of Semantic Web (SW), new knowledge representation technologies that enable advanced reasoning functionality over the available data are at the disposal of application engineers. The representation power of SW is mainly due to the exploitation of ontologies as its core modeling method and technology. SW research has already experienced great progress and many SW technologies have already been standardized (e.g., RDF, OWL) or are in the final standardization process (Antoniou, 2004). As expected, SW had also its effect on WS technologies and theory. Thus, some service-oriented SW technologies have also appeared, such as DAML-S, OWL-S, WSDL-S, SWSO/SWSL, WSMO/WSML, and so forth. (Cardoso, 2005). The services developed with such technologies are called Semantic Web Services (SWS) (Lara, 2003; MacIlraith, Son, & Zeng, 2001; Nixon, 2005; Wang, 2004). These technologies provide means of describing in detail the service capabilities, execution flows, policies and other related information. Moreover, these technologies have given a new boost to service discovery and service composition research as new fields for experimentation have emerged.

The added value of semantics in the field of Web services is the improvement of their representation expressiveness (key-value pairs are no longer used) and the logic-based matchmaking that such representation facilitates. These enhancements should be creatively used by Web engineers so as to improve the effectiveness of current WS methods. And the better place to start such "method-shift" is the service discovery field, since it is crucial not only for productively using WS, but is also involved in other lifecycle steps such as service composition. Until today, many researchers have proposed service discovery techniques for Semantic Web Services. Some of them have been implemented in tools, while others still remain in the pages of scientific articles.

Three factors mainly affect service discovery: (a) the ability of service providers to describe their services, (b) the ability of service requestors to describe their requirements, and (c) the "intelligence" of the service matchmaking algorithm. Throughout the chapter, it will become evident that Semantic Web Services address all these factors, thus resulting in better discovery quality.

The main focus of the chapter will be on service discovery *algorithms and methods* and not on SWS description languages. Familiarity with such languages, as well as basic knowledge of WS and related technologies, is not a prerequisite, although it would help the reader in better comprehending the chapter. In general, we have tried to keep the descriptions of the various approaches as technology-agnostic as possible, in order to emphasize on their conceptual and algorithmic parts.

Since most approaches to SWS discovery exploit logic-based (especially Description Logics) matchmaking algorithms, some familiarity with basic Description Logics formalism and terminology is necessary. Unfamiliar readers can refer to Appendix II, which contains a very brief Description Logics primer.

This chapter aims at summarizing the existing techniques, algorithms and tools in order to provide a thorough overview of the basic approaches in the field of SWS discovery. The rest of the chapter is organized as follows. First, we discuss how service discovery is performed for conventional WSs. Hence, we describe a reference architecture and explain the interactions and functionality of its main components. The main algorithms used, as well as common tools and technologies, are also briefly mentioned. Subsequently, the limitations and drawbacks of conventional WS discovery are identified. Next, a survey of modern SWS discovery architectures and approaches is presented. The rationale and main characteristics of each approach are described and demonstrated with examples, where deemed necessary. Some of these approaches have been implemented as tools. The most known of these tools will be also described. The SWS discovery overview is followed by a discussion on current and future trends and challenges. The chapter concludes with a tutorial on a well-established service matchmaking tool, namely OWL-S/UDDI Matchmaker (Srinivasan, 2004), and a short introduction to Description Logics, which have been extensively used in SWS discovery.

## WEB SERVICE DISCOVERY

Before delving into the details of the discovery process for semantic WS, we will describe a reference architecture of conventional WS discovery systems. Subsequently, we will discuss how this architecture has been implemented in real world systems. Concluding the section we will identify the shortcomings of such systems and, thus, justify the necessity for the enhancement of the discovery process through semantics-based methods.

## Web Service Reference Architecture

Figure 2 depicts the components of a typical service discovery system. The main components and actors of this system, along with their interactions, are described in the following paragraphs.

A *service provider* is an entity that offers some services to other entities upon request. Each implemented service of a provider is called *service instance* and usually resides in the provider location. Each provider tries to promote/advertise its services to potential service users in order to maximize its profit (in any possible form). This advertisement is performed by publishing/registering appropriate *service advertisements* (or descriptions) in a site accessible and searchable by third-parties. This place is the *service registry*, a public or private directory of service advertisements. The entities that search for services, namely the *service requestors*, issue *service requests* against this registry. Depending on the application domain, service requestors may be enterprise systems, human users, mobile agents or any other systems that adopt the Web services paradigm. In general, the service requests are structurally

*Figure 2. Service discovery reference architecture*

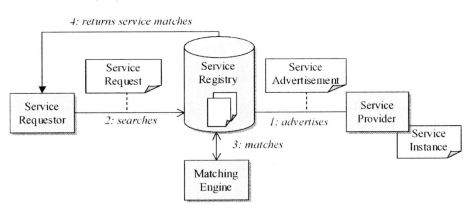

and conceptually similar to the service descriptions. Finally, the service requests are matched against the service descriptions with the aid of *matching algorithms* (implemented in a matching engine) in order the service requestor to discover the available services that are most relevant to its requirements. If the matching algorithm successfully discovers a service description, it provides the requestor with the service invocation details for the corresponding service instance.

- **Service Registry:** It is an implementation of a directory service (i.e., "yellow pages"). It indexes service advertisements in several ways. For example, it may classify them according to their application domain, service provider, and so forth. It is important to note that the service registry does not contain the actual service instances but only the bindings of service descriptions with the actual service instances.
- **Matching Algorithm:** Tightly coupled with the service registry is the algorithm for matching service requests with service descriptions. This algorithm significantly affects the overall discovery quality, that is, how effectively and efficiently will the service requestor be served.
- **Service Request:** A service request declares the intention of the service requestor regarding the desired service functionality. It is a formal or informal description of the functional and technical capabilities and/or constraints that should be satisfied by the discovered service.
- **Service Advertisement:** A service advertisement is analogous to a service request but from the provider's perspective. Hence, it describes the functionality, invocation details and execution flow of an offered service. Depending on the registry type, this specification may be more or less formal.

Both the service request and advertisement are specified in service description languages with certain expressiveness. Such expressiveness highly affects the quality of the discovery procedure. Moreover, the completeness of the descriptions is also affecting the matching process. Further discussions on these topics will be provided in following sections.

**Note:** Many different approaches have been proposed regarding the physical architectures of service discovery. For example, some researchers have deployed UDDI registries in distributed architectures or implemented similar registries over Peer-to-Peer networks (Banaei-Kashani, 2004). However, such variations of the reference architecture affect only the performance efficiency and scalability of the discovery subsystem and not its actual quality and accuracy. In general, issues on physical architectures are out of the scope of this chapter.

## Web Service Description Technologies

Web services are described through the Web Service Description Language (WSDL), which is currently in version 2.0 (Chinnici, 2006). Each WSDL file accompanying a WS contains the service name and a textual documentation of the overall service functionality. In addition, it contains a name and a description for each operation of the service and for each input/output operation parameter. All textual descriptions are expressed through natural language sentences.

As already mentioned, the WSDL descriptions are published/registered in service registries. The dominant standard for WS registries is the UDDI protocol (Universal Description, Discovery and Integration), which has recently reached its version 3.0 (Clément, 2004). The UDDI specifications describe:

- the UDDI data model used for describing businesses and Web services, and

- the UDDI API used for inquiring and publishing UDDI data

The UDDI data model is specified through XML Schema documents, which consist of four main elements:

- **businessEntity:** Information about the service provider (i.e., business). Such information includes the provider's name, description and contact details. Usually, each entity is described with reference to a business catalog (taxonomy)
- **businessService:** Information about a Web service or a group of services. Such information includes the service name, description and an optional list of bindingTemaplates
- **bindingTemplate:** Information about how and where to access a specific Web service
- **tModel (technical Model):** Usually a pointer to external technical specifications and service descriptions. One common type of such descriptions is WSDL documents. tModels include also a name and a description

In UDDI architectures, service discovery is performed either manually (through Web forms or browsing taxonomies in Web pages) or programmatically (through the UDDI API).

## Matching Methods

Standard UDDI registries allow for keyword-based search methods. Specifically, services can be searched by category, name, location, business, bindings or tModels. Such matching can be facilitated by the so-called "find qualifiers", which enable case-sensitive/insensitive search and approximate search through wildcards. Many researchers have proposed extensions to this querying mechanism. The most interesting approaches are based on information retrieval techniques. Their core idea is to represent the

service descriptions using Information Retrieval (IR) data models (e.g., document vectors) on which IR techniques can be applied (e.g., similarity measures, clustering, latent semantic indexing). Since a detailed description of such approaches is out of the scope of the chapter, the reader is referred to Dong (2004) and Sajjanhar (2004) for more details.

## Shortcomings and Limitations of Conventional Web Services Discovery

The aforementioned service discovery approaches suffer from some shortcomings, primarily caused by the service description technologies and secondarily by the matching algorithms. These shortcomings, discussed in the following paragraphs, prevent WS discovery methods from retrieving the most relevant services.

*Informal description of service functionality/capabilities*: The high-level functionality of the services is described in an unstructured or semi-structured format. Most service descriptions are provided in natural language form. In addition, inference cannot be performed on UDDI business and service catalogs. This further hinders the matching process, if the provider and requestor do not use common vocabulary. For example, a service belonging to the NAICS[2] category "Dating Services" cannot be matched with a user request for "Personal Relationships Services."

*Incomplete description of service functionality/capabilities*: The level of detail for the service descriptions is determined by each provider. Since no predefined and mandatory fields exist, providers are free to describe their services in arbitrary detail.

*Syntactic relevance vs. intentional relevance*: The pure syntax-based matching of service capabilities cannot give quality results, because a service request matches an advertisement only if their keywords match. This prevents what is known as *inexact matching* (i.e., the matching between two services even if they are described with different keywords). The real problem with exact matching methods is that they cannot fully capture the intentional semantics of services or service requests. Moreover, phenomena such as linguistic polysemy (i.e., the property of a word having many meanings) and ambiguity undermine the matching performance. Furthermore, keyword-based descriptions cannot describe internal service structure (e.g., data and execution flows), which may be of use during service discovery or composition.

*Lack of constraint specifications*: Apart from the specification of service capabilities, a provider should also specify which preconditions or other constraints should hold for each service in order to be successfully executed. Such constraints, although may not significantly affect the initial discovery phase, should be taken into account upon invocation of the selected service.

*Limited expressiveness of domain classification schemes*: Two of the most popular classification schemes used for describing service functionality in UDDI-based methods are NAICS and UNSPSC,[3] which constitute standard category vocabularies. Hence, the service classification is considerably restricted, and not very flexible.

*No support for indirect matching*: The search methods of UDDI cannot produce chains (or more complex graph structures) of services when no single service matches a request, that is, support indirect matching. This may be a serious limitation, especially if there are only primitive and very simple services available in a registry.

## SEMANTIC WEB SERVICE DISCOVERY

Semantic service annotations were introduced in order to automate the whole service lifecycle, from advertisement to invocation and execution. Their role in service discovery is very crucial and affects the architectures, algorithms, tools,

effectiveness of service retrieval and every other aspect of the discovery process. In the following paragraphs we survey some of the existing approaches for SWS discovery.

## SWS Discovery Architectures and Components

In a SWS discovery architecture, the components of the WS discovery reference architecture (shown in Figure 2) are maintained, but implemented differently in order to provide enhanced functionality. In addition, several new components are introduced, namely *Service Annotation Ontologies* and *Domain Ontologies*. In the following paragraphs, we describe the enhancements of each component and present several architecture variations that have been proposed in the SWS literature in order to support more effective and "intelligent" service discovery.

### Service Advertisement

Service advertisements are not described through the WSDL parameters or operation/service names anymore, but according to specific *Service Annotation Ontologies*. Such ontologies define semantic models for describing various different perspectives of WS (functionality, execution flow, invocation details). The actual annotation terms used in the service advertisements are expressed through shared vocabularies, defined by *Domain Ontologies*. Hence, service advertisements are documents that comply to specific models and refer to description terms from external terminologies.

### Service Annotation Ontologies

Service annotation ontologies can be regarded as service description models, which aim to explicitly capture the semantics of service functionality, process structure/workflow and invocation/implementation details of WS. Such ontologies define a set of service capability attributes, with the most interesting being the *IOPE (Inputs, Outputs, Preconditions and Effects),*[4] defined as:

- **Inputs:** Specify the information that the service requires for its execution
- **Outputs:** Specify the information produced after service execution
- **Preconditions:** Specify all conditions that must be satisfied in order for the service to execute successfully
- **Effects:** Specify side-effects of the service execution, that is, changes in the state of the world after the service has been executed, either successfully or unsuccessfully

The values of the IOPE attributes are usually terms (i.e., atomic or complex concepts) specified in domain ontologies (see subsequent paragraph).

Several upper (i.e., application-independent) ontologies have been already proposed for service description. The first one was DAML-S (MacIlraith & Martin, 2003), based on the DAML+OIL ontology definition language. However, with the wide acceptance of the Web Ontology Language (OWL) family of languages, DAML-S was replaced by OWL-S (Martin, 2005). At the same time, other academic and industry groups were working on similar specifications, resulting in the WSDL-S (Li, 2006), WSMO (Roman, 2005) and SWSO (SWSL Committee, 2005) ontologies.[5] All these specifications, although sharing many modeling elements, differ in terms of expressiveness, complexity and tool support.

Most service annotation ontologies are divided in three *logical parts*, which, according to the popular OWL-S terminology, are:

- **Service profile:** Service profile is divided into three main parts: (1) a textual service description and provider's contact information (intended for human users), (2) a functional description of the service, which contains semantic information related to the aforementioned IOPE tuple, and (3) a list of additional parameters used to describe other features of the service, for example, relevant to QoS or to the duration of service execution. Most matching algorithms used in the discovery and selection of SWS, focus on the service profile.
- **Service model:** Service model gives a detailed description of the operation of a service. Such operation is described in terms of a process model, which details both the control and data flow structure required to execute a service.
- **Service grounding:** Service grounding specifies the details of how to access the service through messages (e.g., communication protocol, message formats, addressing). This part involves linking the service operations to WSDL descriptions.

## Domain Ontologies

The semantic service annotations, as specified by the Service Annotation Ontologies, are no more expressed through unstructured text, but rather refer to concepts in Domain Ontologies. Such ontologies describe the terminology and term relationships in specific application domains. For instance, when describing services about wines, a Wine Domain Ontology describes the various kinds of wine, by also defining their special characteristics. Domain ontologies may be written in various ontology languages (e.g., OWL, DAML+OIL or RDF(S)). For an overview of such languages the reader is referred to (Antoniou, 2004; Gomez-Perez, 2004). Such languages, in general, have different expressive power. However, all of them can at least model hierarchies of concepts and concept roles (i.e., properties, attributes or relationships). As discussed in subsequent paragraphs, such hierarchies are at the core of most logic-based service matching algorithms.

## Service Request

Depending on the system implementation, the service request may vary from natural language text to documents compliant to the service annotation ontologies. Irrespectively of the adopted format, a request should contain information relevant to that specified by the used service annotation ontology (e.g., IOPE values). In general, possibly after appropriate mediation, the request is transformed to a document that structurally resembles the service advertisement. The use of the same Domain Ontologies by both the service requestors and providers, although not mandatory, significantly simplifies the matching process by eliminating the need for mediation layers. However, this is a rather optimistic scenario, not suitable for open information environments like the Web.

## Service Registry

The traditional WS registries (e.g., UDDI) are still used by most SWS discovery architectures. However, besides the traditional WS descriptions (e.g., tModel entries, WSDL documents), they also store, or contain references to, semantics information annotating the advertised services. Several methods have been proposed for linking semantic service annotations to UDDI registry entries (e.g., tModels). Some of these will be briefly discussed in the following paragraphs.

## Matching Algorithm

The semantic matching algorithms are, in general, more complex and "intelligent" than their syntax-based counterparts. They are designed so as to exploit the explicit functionality semantics of the provided service descriptions and requests. Many matchmaking algorithms have

been proposed with different characteristics. In this section we examine in more detail the basic principles of the most important and influential SWS matchmaking algorithms.

The aforementioned components can be deployed in several variations of the reference architecture shown in Figure 2. What differentiates these architecture variations is, primarily, the implementation and integration of the semantic matching engine with the service registry, and, consequently, the imposed deviation from established discovery standards (e.g., extensions to UDDI API). We should note, however, that the service discovery interaction steps remain the same as for traditional Web services:

- **Step 1:** the service provider advertises services
- **Step 2:** the requestor searches for services fulfilling its functional requirements
- **Step 3:** the registry/matching engine locates (and selects) suitable services
- **Step 4:** the best matches are returned to the requestor

We categorize the SWS discovery architectures to: (1) those exploiting *a centralized service registry*, and (2) those performing discovery according to the *peer-to-peer paradigm*.

## Centralized Discovery Architectures

In this architecture category, several possible deployments of the SWS discovery components have been proposed. We briefly describe two indicative examples, in order to exemplify potential variations.

### Architecture I: Importing Semantics to UDDI

The authors in (Paolucci, 2002b; Srinivasan, 2004) discussed an extension to the UDDI registry so that they take advantage of the semantic service annotations, while using the popular and standardized UDDI infrastructure. The authors proposed the idea of semantically extending UDDI by mapping semantic annotations (e.g., DAML-S service profiles) to standard UDDI entries (e.g., tModels). Such translation of the semantic service advertisement or request to a UDDI-compliant representation combines the popularity and support of the UDDI standard and the semantically-grounded descriptions of services. In addition, an *external* matching engine is introduced that performs semantic matching on service capabilities. Specifically, the Semantic UDDI registry receives service advertisements and requests with embedded descriptions in a service annotation ontology. The Translator component constructs the UDDI tModel entry for each advertised service. When a semantic

service request arrives, its description is passed to the matching engine, and the latter performs the service capability matching, with respect to the available domain ontologies. Thus, such architecture (see Figure 3) provides two ways of service discovery: one using the standard UDDI keyword-based matching (applied also to the extended tModel fields and invoked through the standard UDDI Inquiry API) and one exploiting service semantics (invoked through a custom API). A similar approach is also adopted by authors in (Akkiraju, 2003), which further expand this architecture by specifying an extension to the UDDI Inquiry API, thus wrapping all requests under a common interface. In conclusion, Architecture I represents a tight integration of semantic matching engines with UDDI registries, but deviates from the UDDI specification.

*Figure 3. Centralized discovery architecture I*

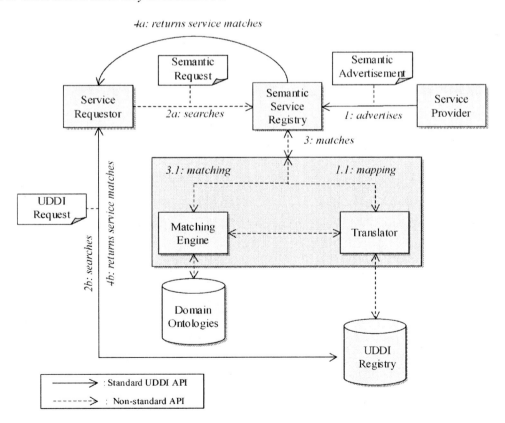

## Architecture II:
## External Matching Services

A more seamless integration of semantic matching mechanism with UDDI registry can be seen in Figure 4, where the matching algorithms are published as WS in the UDDI. Thus, UDDI can detect and select the most suitable matching service for each service request, and then invoke it for the actual semantic matching. Moreover, the UDDI registry may offer the possibility to use multiple matchmaking services to fulfill a given service request. For instance, there may be *matching service providers* that offer diverse semantic matching mechanisms (e.g., implementing different algorithms or supporting different service annotation ontologies).

In order to support such functionality, UDDI is extended with two processes. The first determines whether a request is due for external matching and not for a literal match based on the tModel key. Such information is explicitly indicated by the requestor along with the description format of the request (e.g., OWL-S). The request description format is used for filtering out incompatible advertisements. In addition, a compatible matching service is selected with respect to this format. In case there are many such services, the selection should be based on some policy. Subsequently, the compatible matching service is invoked taking as inputs the compatible advertisements and the service request. Finally, the discovered services are returned to the requestor.

This architecture eliminates the need for installing the matchmaking infrastructure either on the registry side, or the requestor's side. Instead, it allows independent matching service providers to offer their matchmaking mechanisms, thus

*Figure 4. Centralized discovery architecture II*

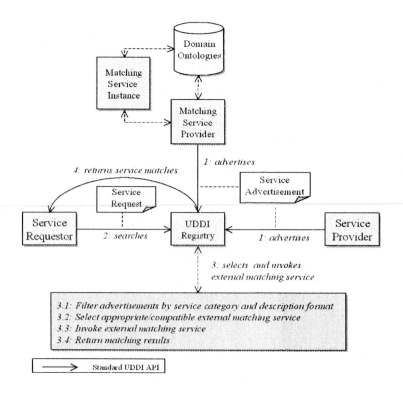

allowing for many and flexible WS business models. Moreover, the limitations of the previous architecture do not apply in this setting, since minor UDDI API modification is needed (method find_tModel()) and no UDDI data structure extension is required. On the other hand, such approach does not provide the coordination required for creating ad hoc services through the composition of existing services. This is due to the fact that matching service providers use their own semantic matching algorithm, leading to diverse service matches. The authors in (Colgrave, 2004) describe an architecture similar to Architecture II.

## Peer-to-Peer Service Discovery Architecture

During the last years, the convergence of WS, SW and peer-to-peer (P2P) networks has attracted much attention from the research community (Maedche, 2003). This can be attributed to the suitability of P2P architectures for open and distributed environments like the Web. P2P architectures are scalable and work quite efficiently. In a P2P service-oriented architecture, each peer is a service provider, a service requestor or both. Accordingly, every peer should contain semantic

descriptions of its offered services, links to domain ontologies, as well as, a P2P discovery component, where the matching engine resides (see Figure 5). A service requestor queries other peers in its network (or a specific network domain) in order to locate the required WS. When it obtains the semantic service advertisements it performs the matching process locally.

The lack of a central repository implies more complexity (in terms of protocol interactions) in identifying matching services, but, on the other hand, more reliability and distribution of the organizational effort. Furthermore, in such architecture, service advertisements are always up to date, while a registry could contain stale information. This is attributed to the fact that the service advertisements are co-located with service instances, and implementation updates can instantly trigger advertisement updates. Another advantage of this approach is the fact that a service requestor is free to use its "own" matching algorithm and not bound to the implementation of a central registry. This way, custom discovery policies and constraints can be easily embedded in the matching engine. Alternatively, each service provider can also provide its matching services. In general, such architectures allow for

*Figure 5. P2P SWS discovery architecture*

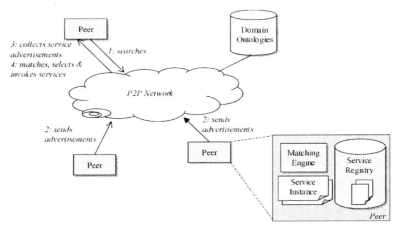

high flexibility, which can be reflected in a wide range of business models for WS. In (Langley, 2001; Paolucci, 2003; Verma, 2005), the authors discuss in more detail such P2P architectures for discovering SWS.

## Algorithmic Approaches to Matchmaking

Most service matchmaking approaches exploit the service profile of a SWS. This is expected, since, during discovery, the requestor is more interested in whether a service can fulfill the posed requirements than in how it works or how it can be invoked. Moreover, most approaches exploit the IOPE attributes, described in the service profile. This is also intuitively correct, since two services that have similar IOPE attributes are generally considered similar.

However, no matter on which elements the matching algorithm is applied, the most important problem in matchmaking is that it is unrealistic to expect advertisements and requests to be in perfect match. Hence, adopting a hard-decision logic, would result in ignoring services that partially match a service request. The problem is becoming worse if we take into account that the service request may not fully capture the requestor's intention. In that case, one can observe the paradox where a service advertisement that partially matches the issued service request might perfectly match the requestor's intention. The concept of the *"Degree of Match" (DoM)* has to be introduced for dealing with these problems. DoM can be informally defined as a value from an ordered set of values that expresses how similar two entities are, with respect to some similarity metric(s). Such entities may be services, IOPE attributes or specific service operations. A service matchmaking algorithm calculating the DoM can, thus, be used for ranking the discovered services according to their relevance to the issued request.

We can categorize matchmaking approaches, according to various criteria. One possible classification is the following:

- **Direct:** A service request is matched against single service advertisements
- **Indirect:** A service request is matched against composite services, constructed from simple or complex workflows of single service advertisements.

In essence, indirect matchmaking involves service composition techniques. These may vary from naïve ones that produce simple sequential "service chains" to more advanced techniques. In the context of this chapter, we will only deal with direct and simple indirect matching methods. Complex service composition theory and tools are out of the scope of the chapter.

Moreover, one could also classify matchmaking as: supporting DoM or not, using only service profile or other service information as well, assessing service similarity through logic-based reasoning or other techniques. In the following paragraphs we describe some typical algorithms that belong to these categories and discuss their main concepts and differentiating characteristics. The selection of the discussed approaches has been based on factors such as practicality and tool support, novelty, and impact in the related literature. Only approaches that are directly addressing SWS have been considered. Each approach may not be completely different from the others in terms of its underlying mechanism, but has to include some design decisions that affect the service discovery process. In general, the approaches are presented in ascending degree of effectiveness and/or sophistication.

Most approaches are based on service annotation ontologies expressed in Description Logics (DLs) and, thus, perform DL-based matching. DLs are knowledge representation languages with less expressiveness than First Order Logic

(FOL), but with much more efficient reasoning algorithms. In Appendix II, a DL primer can be found, that describes all DL-specific terminology and knowledge required for the understanding of some matchmaking algorithms. A more comprehensive reading on DLs is (Baader, 2003).

Before proceeding with the description of the different approaches, we should note the following assumptions:

- The semantic annotations in advertisements and requests adhere to the same domain ontologies.
- The algorithm descriptions are not bound to any specific service annotation ontologies or domain ontology languages. We try to capture and present in a unified way the basic ideas of the various approaches.
- The notation in Table 1 is used for the description of the matching algorithms.
- All matching approaches, unless stated otherwise, perform direct service matching.
- The domain ontology used in some of the examples can be found in Appendix I (Figure 16).

## Approach I: Semantic Capabilities Matching

One of the first, and probably most influential, works in the field of SWS discovery is that described in (Paolucci, 2002a). The basic idea behind this approach is that "an advertisement matches a request when all the outputs of the request are matched by the outputs of the advertisement, and all the inputs of the advertisement are matched by the inputs of the request" (p. 338). Thus, this method takes into account only the inputs and outputs of the service profiles during matchmaking. The degree of match between two outputs or two inputs depends on the relationship between the domain ontology concepts associated with those inputs and outputs. Four degrees of match have been specified in Paolucci (2002a), as shown in Table 2 (in decreasing significance order). The DoM in this table is computed per output. For service inputs, req.o and adv.o should be substituted by adv.i and req.i, respectively (such inversion is dictated by the approach). The DoM between a service advertisement and a service request is the minimum DoM of all inputs and outputs.

*Table 1. Useful notation*

| req | The service request |
|---|---|
| A | The set of all service advertisements in a service registry |
| adv | A single advertisement in A |
| req.O | The set of desired service outputs as specified in req |
| adv.O | The set of outputs for advertisement adv |
| req.I | The set of inputs given by req |
| adv.I | The set of required service inputs for advertisement adv |
| X.o | A single output of the set X.O (X=adv or req) |
| X.i | A single input of the set X.I |
| X.SC | A description of the service category of X |
| X.par | Other "user-defined" parameters of X |

The matching algorithm is outlined in Figure 6. The function *degreeOfMatch* implements the rules of Table 2. This algorithm returns an ordered list of matching service advertisements. How many of them are really relevant to the request is decided by the requestor, who should define a threshold for the minimum acceptable DoM. This approach is based on a logic-based interpretation of matching, in particular *subsumption matching*. We say that a concept subsumes another if the first is more general than the latter (i.e., it is higher in the conceptual hierarchy). The definitions of the terms "equivalent" and "subsumes" in Table 2 are given in Appendix II. Subsumption matching has gained great popularity in the knowledge discovery community, because items (e.g., concepts, services) more abstract or more specific than a given item are regarded relevant to it. However, the direction of the subsumption relation between two service attributes implies different meaning and different consequences for the whole matching process. Such consequences are listed in Table 3. In addition, the output matching is regarded more significant than the input matching during service discovery, since the requestor usually searches services by their outputs and is ready to provide any required service input upon the actual negotiation and invocation of the service.

## Approach II:
## Multilevel Matching

A variant of the Approach I is presented in (Jaeger, 2004). The key differentiator in this work is the

*Table 3. Implications of subsumption relations between service inputs/outputs*

| Degree of Match | Matching conditions |
|---|---|
| EXACT | If req.o is *equivalent* to adv.o, or<br>If req.o is a direct subclass of adv.o |
| PLUGIN[6] | If adv.o *subsumes* req.o |
| SUBSUMES | If req.o *subsumes* adv.o |
| FAIL | If there is no subsumption relationship between req.o and adv.o |

*Table 2. Degrees of match (per output)*

| Subsumption relation | Meaning/Potential problems |
|---|---|
| req.i subsumes adv.i | More specific input information might be required for the proper execution of the service described by *adv* |
| adv.i subsumes req.i | The request contains all input information required for the proper execution of the service described by *adv* |
| req.o subsumes adv.o | The output is valid for the requestor, though it may contain only a fraction of the desired results. The requestor may need a set or composition of such services in order to fulfill its requirements |
| adv.o subsumes req.o | The service may not be able to produce the required outputs. In extreme cases, the service execution results may be totally irrelevant to the request. However, we usually make the assumption that the service provider provides more specific services, too |

*Figure 6. Outline of algorithm I*

```
Main algorithm: match(req, A)
1: matchedServices = {}
2: For all adv in A do
3: If((DoMI=Imatch(req, adv)) !=FAIL AND (DoMO = O match(req,
adv)) !=FAIL)
4:     adv.DoM=min (DoMI, DoMO)
5:     matchedServices=matchedServicesÈ{adv}
6: Return sortByDoM(matchedServices)

Function: Omatch (req, adv)
7: DoM={}
8: For all req.o in req.O do
9: For all adv.o in adv.O do
10:   DoM=DoMÈ{degreeOfMatch(req.o, adv.o}
11: Return min(DoM)

Function: Imatch(req, adv)
12: DoM={}
13: For all adv.i in adv.I do
14:   For all req.i in req.I do
15:   DoM=DoMÈ{degreeOfMatch(adv.i, req.i)}
16: Return min(DoM)
```

fact that the matchmaking process is performed at many levels, that is, between inputs/outputs, service categories and other custom service parameters (e.g., related to QoS issues). Such approach, reflects the intuition that ideal service discovery should exploit as much of the available functional and nonfunctional service information as possible. In addition, it introduces the concept of *DoM aggregation*. As a result, a more fine-grained and effective ranking of matched services can be provided, by assigning different weights to the different matching stages. The stages of the system, which for the particular work are four, are outlined in Figure 7. In this figure, the function *aggregate()* can implement any arbitrary aggregation (e.g., weighted sum) of the four DoMs. The main problem of this approach is that, in general, it is difficult to find an optimal aggregate function, since it depends on many factors (e.g., application domain, requestor's and provider's ability to describe the exact service functionality). The *Xmatch()* functions in this algorithm are similar to the functions of Algorithm I.

## Approach III: DL Matchmaking with Service Profile Ontologies

The Approach I, as already discussed, is based on subsumption matching of service capabilities. Particularly, the various capabilities (i.e., inputs and outputs) of service advertisements are matched against the corresponding request capabilities. The actual degree of match is evaluated according to the subsumption relations between the domain ontology concepts that describe these capabilities. In (Gonzales-Castillo, 2001; Li, 2004) another logic-based approach is presented, where the matchmaking of services is performed through a *service profile ontology*. In this ontology, each service is represented by a complex DL concept expression, which describes all the service constraints (inputs, outputs, etc.). For the Dating Services domain, a part of such ontology would resemble that shown in Figure 8(a). In fact, such ontology can be considered as a logic-based registry for service advertisements.

*Figure 7. Outline of algorithm II*

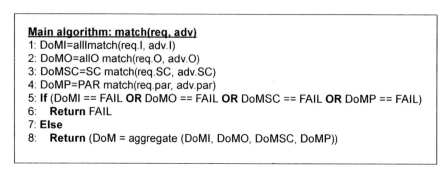

```
Main algorithm: match(req, adv)
1: DoMI=allImatch(req.I, adv.I)
2: DoMO=allO match(req.O, adv.O)
3: DoMSC=SC match(req.SC, adv.SC)
4: DoMP=PAR match(req.par, adv.par)
5: If (DoMI == FAIL OR DoMO == FAIL OR DoMSC == FAIL OR DoMP == FAIL)
6:    Return FAIL
7: Else
8:    Return (DoM = aggregate (DoMI, DoMO, DoMSC, DoMP))
```

*Figure 8. A service profile ontology before (a) and after (b) the insertion/classification of the service request Q*

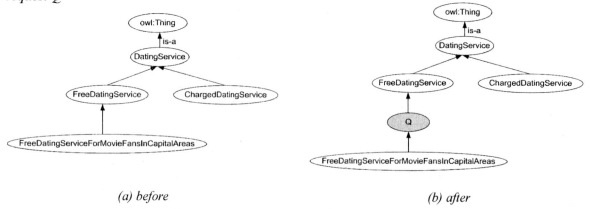

*(a) before*                    *(b) after*

Once such ontology is defined and contains all the available service advertisements, service requests can be expressed through DL concepts and inserted to it. Then a DL reasoner can be used in order to classify the request-concept into the ontology. The final DoM is evaluated according to a ranking similar to Table 2, with the difference that the various degrees and their conditions refer to service profile descriptions and not single service outputs.

**Example**. Figure 9 depicts two service advertisements in DL syntax. Specifically, *FreeDating-Service* is described by its service profile through the *hasServiceProfile* role (we assume that this role and the concept *ServiceProfile* are specified in a service annotation ontology, while all other

roles and concepts referenced in this example are specified in the domain ontology of Figure 16 in Appendix I). Moreover, it describes information about the payment mode of that service, which in this case is free of charge (service *FreeOfCharge*). *FreeDatingServiceForMovieFansInCapitalAreas* is subsumed by the previous service, since it involves a more specific personal profile. Similarly, the service request *Q* describes a service that is free of charge, and refers to persons located in Urban Areas, who are interested in Entertainment topics. We add this concept to the ontology of Figure 8(a) and classify it with a DL reasoner like Racer (Haarslev, 2003). The inferred concept hierarchy is shown in Figure 8(b). The concept *Q* subsumes the *FreeDatingServiceForMovieFansInCapitalAreas* concept, since, according to

*Figure 9. The service descriptions of the example in DL syntax*

---

**FreeDatingService**≡DatingService⊓∃hasServiceProfile.9ServiceProfile
⊓∃requiresPayment.FreeOfCharge)

**FreeDatingSErviceForMovieFansInCapitalAreas**≡DatingService
⊓∃hasServiceProfile.(ServiceProfile⊓∃requiresPayment.FreeOfCharge
⊓∃hasPersonalProfile.(ContactProfile⊓∃hasLocation.CapitalArea)
⊓∃has InterestProfile.(InterestProfile⊓∃hasInterest.Movies))

**Q**≡DatingService⊓∃hasServiceProfile (ServiceProfile⊓∃requiresPaymentFreeOfCharge
⊓∃hasPersonalProfile (ContactProfile⊓∃hasLocation.UrbanArea)
⊓∃hasInterstProfile (InterestProfile⊓∃hasInterest.Entertainment))

---

the ontology in Figure 16 (see Appendix I), it is constructed by concepts more specific than those involved in the latter concept (i.e., *UrbanArea* subsumes *CapitalArea*). Similarly, *Q* is subsumed by *FreeDatingService*.

By applying the algorithm of Approach I (properly adapted for service profile matching instead of output matching), we see that there is no EXACT match and that the best matching advertisement is that of *FreeDatingService* (i.e., PLUGIN match). Note also that *FreeDatingServiceForMovieFansInCapitalAreas* and *Q* are associated with the SUBSUMES degree, which by definition is weaker than PLUGIN.

Another contribution of this approach is the definition of an additional matching condition. Specifically, a service request *req* matches with advertisements *adv* that: (1) their service profiles (described as concepts) are subconcepts of any direct superconcepts of the *req*'s service profile, and (2) the logical intersection of *adv* and *req* is satisfiable. We remind that, an intersection of concepts, which is also a concept, is regarded satisfiable in DLs, if there can be some individuals belonging to this concept. This condition states that subsumption matching (involving only direct and indirect super/subconcepts of the *req* concept) alone is not sufficient, since candidate matching concepts may also be found in paths of the terminological hierarchy which do not include the

*req* concept. This observation forms a basis for the following approach.

## Approach IV:
## Similarity Measures and Information Retrieval Techniques

All the variants of the aforementioned logic-based approaches have the drawback of exploiting only the subsumption relations in various ontologies (domain or service profile) in order to assess similarity of services, service capabilities, and so forth. However, this is not sufficient as shown in the following example.

**Example**. A requestor of a dating service searches for services that take as input the concept {InterestProfile ⊓ ∃hasInterest.SciFiMovies}, which is a subconcept of InterestProfile, and return as output the concept ContactProfile (i.e., the service finds contact details for persons that are interested in SciFi movies). In the service registry there are only two services whose inputs match (as defined in Approach I) with the concept InterestProfile:

```
Find_Interests_Of_Female_MSN_Us-
    ers: input={Person⊓∃hasGender.Male}
    output={InterestProfile, ChatID}
Find_Person_by_Interest: input={InterestProfile}
    output={ContactProfile}
```

If we adopt the Approach I, the DoM between the request outputs and the first service's outputs is FAIL, because the concepts ContactProfile, ChatID and InterestProfile are terminologically disjoint siblings (see Figure 16 in Appendix I). Hence, only the second service would be discovered. Such system behavior, however, may not be desirable, since once we have the ChatID of a person we are able to contact it and retrieve any other contact details.

A way to overcome such limitations during service discovery is to use the implicit semantics of the services, besides the explicit semantics that are described by the domain ontologies. This can be achieved by borrowing techniques from other information processing fields such as Information Retrieval (IR). The core idea in this approach is that IR similarity measures could be applied when logic-based (subsumption) matching fails. Hence, we modify the range of DoM in Table 2 as follows:

- Substitute FAIL by LOGICAL-FAIL
- Add a new degree, called $SIM_{IR}$ with lower significance than LOGICAL-FAIL. This degree holds true when the inputs/outputs of the request and the advertisement are similar with respect to the used IR similarity measure
- Add a new degree, called FAIL, which holds true when none of the rest degrees applies

A generic algorithm for this approach is shown in Figure 10. The functions *Imatch()* and *Omatch()* are similar to those described in Figure 6, and the variable *threshold* is a numeric value that denotes the minimum acceptable value of the similarity measure, in order to achieve a request-advertisement match. Such threshold usually depends on many factors (e.g., application domain, structure and characteristics of domain ontology, type of similarity measure) and is, in general, difficult to optimally define. A realization of this algorithm can be found in (Klusch, 2005).

Among the most effective and popular IR techniques are those assessing similarity by exploiting the linguistic semantics of textual descriptions or using TFIDF (Term Frequency/Inverse Document Frequency) term weighting schemes (Cohen, 2003). The objective of such measures is to evaluate the semantic distance/closeness between concepts, words or documents. This distance, which is an abstract concept, is inferred through measurable characteristics of the compared data,

*Figure 10. Outline of algorithm IV*

```
Main algorithm: match(req, adv)
1: DoM=logicalMatch(req, adv)
2: If DoM == LOGICAL-FAIL
3:     If sim(req, adv) threshold
4:         Return FAIL
5:     Else
6:         Return SIM_IR
7: Else
8:     Return DoM

Function: logicalMatch(req, adv)
9: Return min(Omatch(req, adv), Imatch(req, adv))

Function sim(req, adv)
10: Any similarity measure
```

such as edit distance, term frequency, and so forth. Among the most popular similarity measures are those that exploit lexical databases such as Word-Net (Richardson, 1994). Such techniques have also been extensively used in other information integration tasks, for example, database schema matching (Rahm, 2001), ontology mapping (Kalfoglou, 2003; Rodriguez, 2003).

The presented approach can be extended in many ways. One option would be to incorporate more effective similarity metrics (possibly identified through experimental evaluations). However, there always remains the problem of determining to which extend the (semantically vague) value of each metric should affect the final ranking of the discovered services. In fact, this is a combinatorial optimization problem. Another extension point would be to define more degrees of match, corresponding to values of the similarity metrics. Furthermore, such metrics could be applied to different service description elements, such as IOPE attributes, full text of service description, and so forth. Finally, more knowledge engineering-based techniques can be used like those proposed in (Borgida, 2005) for measuring semantic similarity in DL knowledge bases.

## Approach V: A Graph-Based Approach

In Trastour (2001) a semantic graph matching approach is proposed. A service description (request or advertisement) is represented as a directed graph (RDF-graph), whose nodes are instances of concepts (i.e., individuals) and arcs are properties (i.e., concept roles) relating such instances. The root node of each graph is the individual representing the service advertisement/request itself. The other nodes refer to concepts borrowed from domain ontologies. Such concepts describe the service functionality (capabilities, constraints, etc.). An example graph for a dating service is shown in Figure 11. The actual nodes of the service graph are those written in lowercase letters and having outgoing "io" arcs. The matchmaking between two graphs, one representing a service request and another representing a service advertisement, is performed with the recursive algorithm shown in Figure 12.

This approach, as described in Figure 12, exploits standard subsumption matching through the "subsumes" operator. However, other operators could be used as well. For instance, one could replace the "subsumes" operator

*Figure 11. Graph representing the service S (io:instance-of, dashed line:concept role)*

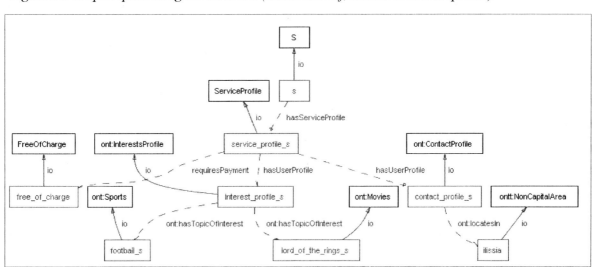

by a concept similarity measure "is-similar". Thus, the novelty of the approach is not on the actual matching/comparison method, but on the fact that we compare two graph structures. In addition, this approach examines all the properties of the concepts (i.e., graph arcs) in order to identify service matches and does not rely only on specific properties of a service annotation ontology (e.g., IOPE attributes). An important drawback of such approach is that it does not support degrees of match, at least as presented in Figure 12; two service graphs either match or not. However, if we adopt such a graph-based perspective towards matchmaking, established graph-based algorithms and methods from the schema-matching domain (Rahm, 2001) can be reused, after proper adaptation.

## Approach VI: Indirect Graph-Based Matching

As already mentioned, indirect matching refers to the identification of the service compositions that are most relevant to the user request. In case of simple compositions, we can think of them as graph-like workflows (see Figure 13), which can be reduced to "service chains" (i.e., acyclic paths in the workflow graph) in the simplest cases.

An approach for performing indirect match-making is presented in (Giv, 2004). This is a hybrid approach, which exploits both semantic matching techniques (e.g., subsumption-based matching of input/output parameters) and graph searching algorithms. The main idea behind constructing simple composite services (i.e., service chains) is based on the following two guidelines:

1. The inputs of each service involved in the composition should match the inputs given either by the service request or the outputs of the previous service in the chain.
2. Each output of the service request should be matched against an output of the last service in the chain.

The first step is to construct a *service graph* according to these guidelines. The elements of such graph are defined as follows:

$n_i$: *a node corresponding to the service description* $d_i$

*Figure 12. Algorithm VI*

```
Main algorithm
1: N1 = root(graph1)
2: N2 = root(graph2)
3: Result = match(n1, n2)

Function match (n1, n2)
4: If (n1 subsumes n2 OR n2 subsumes n1)
5:      matching = TRUE
6:      For each property p1 or n1 do
7:         For each property p2 of n2 do
8:            If NOT [(p1 equivalent-to p2 OR p1 subproperty-of p2 OR  p2  subproperty-of p1) AND
                match(target(p1), target (p2))]
9:               matching = FALSE
10:     Return matching
11: Else
12:     Return FALSE
```

*(n<sub>i</sub>, n<sub>j</sub>): a directed arc originating from n<sub>i</sub>, created only when all the inputs of the service n<sub>j</sub> can be matched against: a) the outputs of the service n<sub>i</sub>, or, b) the data provided by the requestor.*

According to this definition, the nodes represent services and the arcs represent data flows. For example, a service graph for the services of Table 4 is shown in Figure 13, under the assumption that the Service Request has the inputs A. B, C, D and the outputs Z, Y.

By definition, two nodes are linked with an arc if the inputs of the one *match* with the outputs of the other. This matching can be performed with any of the direct matching algorithms presented earlier in this section that involves Input/Output matching. Once the graph is in place, we can execute typical graph searching algorithms in order to compute the paths (i.e., service chains) that provide the requested service functionality. These paths should start at nodes with zero in-degree (S1 and S2 in Figure 13) and end at nodes with zero out-degree (S5 and S7). According to the abovementioned guidelines, the set of outputs of all serviced participating in a path should be a superset of the requested outputs in order for the path to be valid. The possible, and valid, paths in our example service graph are:

Service Chain 1: S1, S3, S4, S6, S7
Service Chain 2: S1, S3, S4, S5
Service Chain 3: S2, S4, S6, S7
Service Chain 4: S2, S4, S5

If we impose further restrictions on the discovery process, for example, always prefer the shortest service chains, then a shortest path algorithm could be used (e.g., Dijkstra). In our example, this would result in selecting the Service Chain 4. Such matchmaking method can be further extended and become more flexible. One extension point is the introduction of weighted arcs, possibly depending on the degree of match between the inputs/outputs of two successive services. Moreover, one could define arcs as follows, resulting in more refined service composition:

*(n<sub>i</sub>, n<sub>j</sub>): a directed arc originating from n<sub>i</sub>, created only when there is at least one match between an input of n<sub>j</sub> and an output of n<sub>i</sub>*

*Table 4. Example service descriptions*

| Service Name | Inputs | Outputs |
|---|---|---|
| S1 | A, B | E |
| S2 | A, B, C | F, N |
| S3 | E, C | F |
| S4 | F | K, M |
| S5 | K, D | Z, Y |
| S6 | K | D, Z |
| S7 | D | Y |

*Figure 13. A service graph for the services in Table 4*

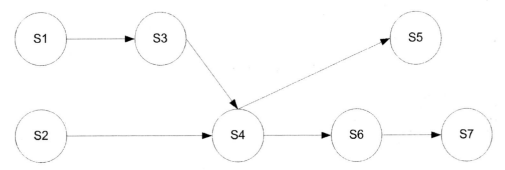

Such definition leads to more complex graph creation and service composition algorithms, as well as to more complex composite services, which are represented by directed graphs and not just by sequences of nodes (i.e., service chains). The topic of service composition is very relevant to service discovery and could be the subject of an entire book. In the area of SWS, most service annotation languages and ontologies support the description of composite services while some algorithms and tools have already been proposed (McIlraith, 2002; Narayanan, 2002). Such tools can automatically orchestrate and compose individual services and produce service-based workflows that fulfill the requestor's requirements. For a survey of service composition algorithms the reader is referred to (Rao, 2004).

## Approach VII:
## Indirect Backward Chaining Matching

Another, more logic-based, approach for indirect service matching is based on the backward chaining inference method. Backward chaining is a goal-driven reasoning procedure (see Figure 14) similar to the way the Prolog language works. The main idea behind this approach is that, starting from services that match the service request outputs but not its inputs, we recursively try to link them with other services until we find a service with all its inputs matched to the inputs given by the service request.

Applying this backward chaining algorithm to the same example would lead to the following indicative execution description:

```
Execution step 1: S=S5, G={K}, SC=[S5]
Execution step 2: S'=S4, G={F}, SC=[S5, S4]
Execution step 3: S'=S3, G={E}, SC=[S5, S4, S3]
Execution step 4: S'=S1, G={}, SC=[S5, S4, S3, S1]
Execution step 5: Exit
Discovered Service Chain: SC=[S1, S3, S4, S5]
```

The above algorithm is quite simplistic and just demonstrates the core idea. Hence, it always returns *one arbitrary* service chain. With appropriate extensions it can return all four possible chains. More information on backward chaining inference can be found in (Brachman, 2004). Finally, as the reader may observe, Approach VII resembles Approach VI. Indeed, Approach VI can be regarded as a way of implementing backward chaining. However, we have presented both approaches in order to provide two different perspectives for the discovery mechanism to the reader: Approach VI treats such mechanism as a graph searching algorithm, while Approach VII treats it as a logic program (i.e., Horn rules) "executed" by a resolution procedure. Each perspective represents service data in a different way, thus, exploiting the representational (and reasoning) power of the respective formalism.

*Figure 14. Outline of algorithm VIII*

```
Main algorithm
1: find a service S whose outputs of the service request R
2: G = {all inputs of S except those matched by the inputs of R}
3: List SC = Null
4: Insert S to SC
5: Repeat infinitely
6:   If G== ∅
7:     Return SC
8:   Else
9:     Find a service S' with its outputs matching all elements of G
10:    G = {all inputs of S' except those matched by the inputs of R}

11:    Insert S' to SC
```

## Synopsis

In Table 5, we present a synopsis of the previously described matchmaking approaches. The columns of this table reflect the following characteristics:

- **Matching Elements:** The elements of the service advertisement and service request, on which actual matching is performed. Possible options are "service profile" (used to build service profile ontologies), "IOPE" (all or a subset of the IOPE attributes), "custom parameters" (other functional and nonfunctional service parameters), "service category" (according to some classification scheme, such as NAICS), and "textual descriptions" (describing any element of a service description).
- **Support for DoM:** Indicates whether the approach enables ranking of the matching results
- **Indirect Matching:** Indicates whether the approach enables simple composition of service chains
- **Algorithm Type:** The type of matchmaking algorithm. The possible options are "logic" (i.e., subsumption-/logic-based), "hybrid-s"

(i.e., logic- and similarity-based), and "hybrid-g" (i.e., logic- and graph-based).

## Other Approaches

The approaches described above, are only a portion of the approaches that have been proposed in the relevant literature. The area of SWS discovery is still in its initial phase (i.e., no standards have gained wide adoption yet) and, thus, there is much experimentation from researchers worldwide. One of the most important approaches, which is also pursuing standardization, is WSMO, which is the cornerstone for WSMO Discovery (Keller, 2004). This involves a quite mature suite of modeling specifications and tools and has been developed by the Digital Enterprise Research Institute (DERI) in the general context of the Web Services Modeling Framework—WSMF (Fensel, 2002). This approach focuses on a very flexible SWS architecture suitable for commercial and industrial use scenarios. The researchers have developed a suite of languages, ontologies and execution environments (WSML, WSMO, and WSMX, respectively) that can support practical SWS provision. The discovery in this framework is supported by the WSMO service annotation ontology. This approach focuses on a more re-

*Table 5. Synopsis of matchmaking approaches*

| Approach | Characteristics | | | |
|---|---|---|---|---|
| | **Matching elements** | **Support for DoM** | **Indirect matching** | **Algorithm type** |
| I | IO | Yes | No | Logic |
| II | IO, service category, custom parameters | Yes | No | Logic |
| III | Service profile | Yes | No | Logic |
| IV | Textual descriptions, IOPE | Yes | No | Hybrid-s |
| V | Service profile | No | No | Hybrid-g |
| VI | IO | No | Yes | Hybrid-g |
| VII | IO | No | Yes | Logic |

fined logic-based analysis of the matchmaking procedure, in the sense that the user intention is also taken into account. This results in a more detailed scale of degrees of match. In addition, the WSML language, which is a First-Order Logic language, enables more expressive service descriptions. In the present chapter, we do not describe in detail this approach, since it has been addressed elsewhere in this book. This approach shares many concepts with the approach presented in Grimm (2004).

Another interesting approach is described in (Benatallah, 2003). The main idea behind this approach is that "we want a matching algorithm that enables to compute the best combination of Web services that satisfies as much as possible the outputs of the query Q and that requires as less as possible of inputs that are not provided in Q" (p. 243). The authors exploit DL reasoning and advanced graph algorithms in order to compute such combination. In (Benatallah, 2003) all the technical and algorithmic details can be found, along with a comprehensive example. A main drawback of this approach is that special extensions to the expressiveness of common Semantic Web ontology languages (e.g., RDF, OWL, DAML) are required.

Other approaches like that proposed in Bernstein (2002), give more significance to the structural relevance of services during the discovery process. Thus, they mainly exploit the service model in order to assess matching, in combination with domain knowledge (i.e., ontologies). We remind that a service model contains information about the various subprocesses (or activities) that compose a service, the data flows between those activities, and so forth. Hence, one can increase the accuracy of the service discovery process.

## SWS Matchmaking Tools

As expected, the variety in matching algorithms for SWS discovery is followed by variance in relevant tools. In this section, we survey some

of the most known tools for SWS discovery and selection, highlighting their special features and differences. Note that this is not an exhaustive list of such tools. Their selection was mainly based on their maturity and popularity in SWS research community.

Prior to the tool description, we discuss on the key features that characterize them:

- **Service Annotation Ontology:** This feature refers to the upper ontologies used for the semantic annotation of the services.
- **Implemented algorithm:** This feature refers to the matchmaking algorithm that is being implemented by the tool (see Table 5). Through such information, we can deduce other features of the tool (e.g., if it performs IO matching, if it ranks the discovered services according to their degree of match).
- **Domain Ontology Languages:** This feature refers to the languages supported by the tool for expressing domain ontologies, whose concepts are used as annotations in the service descriptions. The expressiveness of those ontology languages affects the discovery procedure. For instance, RDF does not support the axiom of disjointness between concept definitions, as OWL-DL does.
- **Technical Details:** This feature refers to other technical details.

The tools and their specific features are summarized in Table 6.

## OWL-S/UDDI Matchmaker (OWL-S/UDDIM)

This is one of the first tools supporting semantic service matching. It adopts and implements the matchmaking Approach I, a subsumption-based matching of OWL-S service requests and advertisements. The tool also allows users to build their OWL-S descriptions, either advertisements or requests. The domain ontologies are described in the OWL language. This tool is available in two versions, a Web-based and a standalone version. The Web-based version is demonstrated in the tutorial included in Appendix I. The standalone version, provides a matching engine and a client API for invoking this engine. All the tools come in the form of open source software. For the execution of the tool, a UDDI implementation and a DL reasoner are also required. OWL-S/UDDIM is written in Java and is available from (OWL-S/UDDIM, 2005).

## IBM Semantic Tools for Web Services (STWS)

This tool is developed by the IBM alphaWorks team and is part of the Emerging Technologies Toolkit (ETTK). In STWS, if a single service cannot be found to meet the requestor's requirements, its engine uses backward chaining inferences and other Artificial Intelligence planning algorithms over service descriptions, in order to find an appropriate composition of services. This semantic matching and composition of SWS results in a set of weighted matches that can be further filtered by the developer. In order to assist in this task, STWS includes a tool that allows the relationships between the request and the matched services to be analyzed and mediation work to begin. The SWS descriptions adhere to the WSDL-S specification. Finally, the domain ontologies are expressed through the OWL notation, which is the de facto standard in SW ontology representation. The tool is implemented as a set of Eclipse plug-ins (Holzner, 2004), and also exploits the WordNet lexical database (Fellbaum, 1998). STWS is available from (STWS, 2006).

## Hybrid OWL-S Web Service Matchmaker (OWLS-MX)

The hybrid matchmaking tool OWLS-MX (Klusch, 2005) has been developed in the context of the project SCALLOPS led by the German Research Center for Artificial Intelligence, DFKI Saarbruecken. This tool adopts and implements the matchmaking Approach IV, that is, performs service IO-matching by combining logic-based semantic matching with syntactic token-based similarity metrics in order to determine the degree of match. Several different similarity measures have been already implemented. OWLS-MX supports OWL-S service descriptions and domain knowledge described in OWL. The developers have also formulated a service retrieval test collection for enabling further experimentation with the tool. The tool is implemented in Java and is available as open source software from (OWLS-MX, 2005).

## METEOR-S Web Service Discovery Infrastructure (MWSDI) and Lumina

The METEOR-S Project, founded by the Large Scale Distributed Information Systems (LSDIS) Lab at University of Georgia, attempts to add semantics to the complete Web process lifecycle by providing constructs for adding semantics to current industry standards. The MWSDI framework (Verma, 2005) is developed for semi-automatically marking up Web service descriptions with domain ontologies, publishing and discovering them in P2P architectures. The WSDL-S service annotation language is used for service annotation. In addition, in the context of METEOR-S the Lumina semantic discovery tool (Li, 2006) has been also developed. This graphical tool is implemented as Eclipse plug-in and is based on the METEOR-S discovery API. It supports both standard UDDI discovery (e.g., based on Business Service or tModel) and semantic discovery of SWS. In the latter case, the WSDL-S service descriptions (including IOPE values) are mapped to UDDI structures through other tools of the METEOR-S framework. The domain ontologies are described in the OWL ontology language.

The tool is open-source and is available from (MWSDI, 2005).

## The TUB OWL-S Matcher (OWLSM)

The OWL-S Matcher, developed by the Technical University of Berlin (TUB), is a tool that adopts and implements the matchmaking Approach II for OWL-S service descriptions. The technical details of its matchmaking engine are described in Jaeger (2004). The domain ontologies are expressed through the OWL language. The previous version of this tool (DAML-S Matcher) used the DAML-S service ontology, while the domain ontologies were written in DAML+OIL. The tool is available from (OWLSM, 2005).

## WSMX Discovery Component (WSMX)

The WSMX working group, part of the European Semantic Systems cluster initiative, has designed and implemented a reference implementation of a discovery engine, in the context of the WSMO reference implementation (i.e., WSMX). The WSMX Discovery Component performs a hybrid keyword-based and semantic matchmaking algorithm for matching user requests with WSMO service advertisements stored in a WSMX service registry. The domain knowledge can be expressed in the WSML variants with reasoning support (i.e., WSML-DL and WSML-Rule). For the semantic matchmaking the respective reasoners are used. The tool is open source software, implemented in Java and available from (WSMX, 2006). It should be also noted that efforts towards aligning the WSMO service annotation ontology with OWL-S and WSDL-S have already commenced, and similar mappings between WSML and the OWL, XML and RDF languages have been specified.

## DISCUSSION ON OPEN ISSUES

### Discovery Evaluation

In the previous section, numerous approaches for SWS discovery have been discussed. Such approaches are, more or less, similar to each other. Moreover, their high-level qualitative comparison can be intuitively performed. For instance, a more sophisticated algorithm that fully exploits a service profile is expected to perform better than an algorithm that simply exploits IOPE parameters. Moreover, many researchers have performed extensive performance evaluation tests measuring *retrieval times* and *scalability* of their

*Table 6. Synopsis of SWS discovery tools*

| Tool | Feature | | |
|---|---|---|---|
| | *Service Annotation* | *Algorithmic Approach* | *Domain Ontology Language* |
| OWL-S/UDDIM | OWL-S | Approach I | OWL |
| STWS | WSDL-S | N/A | OWL |
| OWLS-MX | OWL-S | Approach IV | OWL |
| MWSDI-Lumina | WSDL-S | N/A | OWL |
| OWLSM | OWL-S 1.0 | Approach II | OWL |
| WSMX | WSMO | WSMO Discovery | WSML (OWL, XML, RDF through mappings) |

tools. However, what is still missing from the current literature is a quantitative analysis and comparison of the *retrieval effectiveness* of the discussed approaches. To our knowledge, only a few researchers have contacted such experimental evaluations (Bernstein, 2002; Klusch, 2005; Stroulia, 2005). There are several reasons for this situation, with the main being:

- Lack of service test sets and SWS testbeds. Most researchers use minimal service sets just to implement a proof of concept. Hence, even if they want to compare their results with others' they cannot because there is no service set large enough and commonly adopted. We should, however, mention that the authors in (Klusch, 2005) recently have published a service retrieval test collection of OWL-S advertisements, test queries and the relevant ontologies, under the name OWLS-TC2.

- Lack of established evaluation metrics. Most evaluation efforts try to apply, possibly adapted, well known IR evaluation metrics to service discovery evaluation. The most popular are *precision* and *recall,* along with their combinations, for example, the F-measure (Buckland, 1994). Such metrics have been widely used in other fields where matchmaking is involved, such as schema matching (Do, 2002). However, unless in-depth analysis is performed, one cannot be sure that they apply in the same way to service discovery, as well. For example, the authors in Klusch (2005) state that "for discovery of semantic Web services, precision may be more important to the user than recall, since the set of relevant services is subject to continuous change in practice." Such analysis should define, for instance, how can the various service discovery objectives be expressed through precision/recall metrics and how do they

relate to the concepts of false positives and false negatives.

## Semantic Interoperability and Mediation

Until now, we have made some assumptions, mainly for presentation simplicity reasons. A certain assumption is that the service requestors and service providers use the same domain ontologies and vocabularies for describing their requests and advertisements, respectively. Obviously this is a weak assumption for an open information environment like the Web. In practice, it is expected that service requestors use local ontologies, different from those used by service providers. However, such diversity in service descriptions should be eliminated in order to successfully apply matchmaking algorithms. This can be achieved through what is termed a *mediation layer,* where mediators, potentially implemented as intelligent agents, appropriately translate the service descriptions in common formats. Mediation between ontologies can be performed in several ways. Two common approaches are:

a. By directly matching and aligning the concepts of the requestor's ontology to those of the provider's ontology, possibly through the use of similarity measures
b. By linking the top-level concepts of each domain ontology to a common standard upper (i.e., abstract) ontology, like Standard Upper Ontology (Niles, 2001).

Another reason for mediation is the inherent difficulty in describing services with knowledge engineering techniques (e.g., DL ontologies, rules). Neither SWS providers, nor requestors are expected to be knowledge engineering experts. Furthermore, the service annotation, publishing and discovery tasks should be as easy as possible. This vision can only be realized through proper mediation. The trend for service mediation is gaining attention in academia and industry. Among the leaders of this effort is the WSMO working group (Roman, 2005), who introduce mediators as key business actors in the service discovery architectures of the previous section. Finally, one should note that the necessity of mediation is also dependent upon the adopted architecture. For example, in a P2P discovery scenario we expect a wider diversity in domain ontologies than in a centralized scenario, since service providers are more inclined to the use of "local" ontologies.

## Maturity and Interoperability of Tools

Besides semantic level interoperability, successful and flexible SWS discovery dictates interoperability in tools, too. The term "tools" refers not only to discovery tools and frameworks, but also on service annotation tools, registries and ontology editors (SemWebCentral, 2006). Although, many qualitative tools have been developed, migrating from one to another is still a very demanding task. This can be mainly attributed to the lack of dominant standards in service description ontologies and languages. Many developers try to bridge such gap by developing custom translator plug-ins to existing tools. This approach, however, does not scale well and is not adequate for providing a rich service development and discovery framework for commercial SWS services.

## Fuzzy and Approximate Service Discovery

In case the service requestors are human users, they would expect to interface with the system through an intuitive and user-friendly way, such as natural language interfaces. However, such requests may contain imprecise and vague information, not represented by domain knowledge terms. Such imprecision could be handled by approximate discovery techniques. The authors in Chao (2005) discuss a fuzzy matchmaking

framework, which abstractly represents the underlying context of WS using fuzzy logic and semantic Web technologies. Specifically, such framework exploits fuzzy logic in order to abstract and express the domain data through fuzzy terms and rules. Consider, for instance, a car rental Web service, which manages cars with rent prices ranging from 85 to 205 Euros per day. Let us also consider an imprecise service request including the phrase: "find car rental companies with cheap rental prices." In order to enable such matchmaking, explicit semantics should be given to the term "cheap," possibly in terms of a range of prices. The open issues regarding such approaches are that current logic-based reasoning engines do not (fully) support reasoning on concrete domains (e.g., numbers, strings). For example, a DL reasoner could not infer that a person with age 15 years old is subsumed by a person with age between 10 and 30 years old. Furthermore, the semantic interoperability problem, mentioned earlier, is also relevant, since it is difficult to develop shared fuzzy representations of domain knowledge, yet (e.g., to commonly agree on what is a cheap car rental company). Such imprecise matchmaking constitutes a great challenge for the research community and we anticipate more efforts towards this direction in the future.

## ACKNOWLEDGMENT

This work was performed in the context of the "PENED" Programme, co-funded by the European Union and the Hellenic Ministry of Development, General Secretariat for Research and Technology (research grant 03ED173).

## REFERENCES

Akkiraju, R., Goodwin, R., Dishi, P., & Roeder, S. (2003, August). *A method for semantically enhancing the service discovery capabilities of UDDI.* Paper presented at the IJCAI-03 Workshop on Information Integration on the Web (IIWeb), Acapulco.

Antoniou, G. & van Harmelen, F. (2004). *A semantic Web primer*. Boston: The MIT Press.

Baader, F., Calvanese, D., McGiuness, D., Nardi, D., & Patel-Schneider, P. (2003). *The description logic handbook: Theory, implementation, and applications*. Cambridge: Cambridge University Press.

Banaei-Kashani, F., Chen, C.-C., & Shahabi, C. (2004). WSPDS: Web services peer-to-peer discovery service. In H.R. Arabnia & O. Droegehorn (Eds.), *International Conference on Internet Computing* (pp. 733-743),. Las Vegas, Nevada: CSREA Press.

Benatallah, B., Hacid, M-S., Rey, C., & Toumani, F. (2003). Request rewriting-based Web service discovery. In D. Fensel, K. Sycara, J. Mylopoulos (Ed.), *The Semantic Web - ISWC 2003* (pp. 242-257). Berlin: Springer-Verlag.

Bernstein, A., & Klein, M., (2002). Towards high-precision service retrieval. In I. Horrocks & J. Hendler (Eds.), *First International Semantic Web Conference on the Semantic Web,* Sardinia (*LNCS* 2342, pp. 84-101). Springer-Verlag.

Borgida, A.,Walsh, T., & Hirsh, H. (2005). Towards measuring similarity in description logics. In I. Horrocks, U. Sattler, & F. Wolter (Eds.), *International Workshop on Description Logics (DL): Vol. 147*, Edinburgh. CEUR.

Brachman, R., & Levesque, H. (2004). *Knowledge representation and reasoning*. San Francisco: Morgan Kaufmann.

Buckland, M. & Gey, F. (1994). The relationship between recall and precision. *Journal of the American Society for Information Science, 45*(1), 12-19.

Cardoso, J. & Sheth, A. (2005). Introduction to semantic Web services and Web process composition. In J. Cardoso & A. Sheth (Eds.), *A Semantic Web process: powering next generation of processes with semantics and Web services* (*LNCS* 3387, pp. 1-13). Heidelberg: Springer-Verlag.

Chao, K., Younas, M., Lo, C., & Tan, T. (2005). Fuzzy matchmaking for Web services. In *Proceedings of the 19th International Conference on Advanced Information Networking and Applications (AINA'05),* Taipei, Taiwan, (pp. 721-726). IEEE Computer Society Press.

Chinnici, R., Moreau, J.-J., Ryman, A., & Weerawarana, S. (Eds.). (2006). Web services description language (WSDL) Version 2.0 Part 1: Core language. World Wide Web Consortium (W3C). Retrieved October 24, 2006, from http://www.w3.org/TR/wsdl20/

Clément, L., Hately, A., van Riegen, C., & Rogers, T. (2004). UDDI Version 3.0.2. Retrieved October 24, 2006, from http://uddi.org/pubs/uddi_v3.htm

Cohen, W., Ravikumar, P., & Fienberg, S. (2003, August). *A comparison of string distance metrics for name-matching tasks*. Paper presented at the IJCAI-03 Workshop on Information Integration on the Web (IIWeb), Acapulco.

Colgrave, J., Akkiraju, R., & Goodwin, R. (2004). External matching in UDDI. In *Proceedings of the International Conference of Web Services (ICWS),* San Diego, California (pp. 226-233). IEEE Computer Society.

Do, H., Melnik, S., & Rahm, E. (2002, October). *Comparison of schema matching evaluations*. Paper presented at 2nd Annual International Workshop of the Working Group "Web and Databases" of the German Informatics Society (GI), Erfurt, Thuringia, Germany.

Dong, X., Halevy, A.Y., Madhavan, J., Nemes, E., & Zhang, J. (2004). Similarity search for Web services. In M.A. Nascimento, M.T. Özsu, D. Kossmann, R.J. Miller, J.A. Blakeley, & K.B.

Schiefer (Eds.), *Proceedings of the Thirtieth International Conference on Very Large Data Bases (VLDB),* Toronto, Canada (pp. 372-383). Morgan Kaufmann.

Fellbaum, C. (Ed.). (1998). *WordNet: An electronic lexical database.* Cambridge, MA: The MIT Press.

Fensel, D. & Bussler, C. (2002). The Web service modeling framework WSMF. *Electronic Commerce Research and Applications, 1(2),* 113-137.

Giv, R.D., Kalali, B., Zhang, S., & Zhong, N. (2004). *Algorithms for direct and indirect dynamic matching of Web services* (Tech. Rep.). Waterloo, Ontario, Canada: University of Waterloo, School of Computer Science.

Gomez-Perez, A., Fernandez-Lopez, M., & Corcho, M. (2004). *Ontological engineering: With examples from the areas of knowledge management, e-commerce and the Semantic Web.* London: Springer-Verlag.

Gonzales-Castillo, J., Trastour, D., & Bartolini, C. (2001). Description logics for matchmaking of services. In G. Görz (Ed.), *Proceedings of the KI-2001 Workshop on Applications of Description Logics* (pp. 74-85). Vienna: CEUR.

Grimm, S., Motik, B., & Preist, C. (2004, November). *Variance in e-business service discovery.* Paper presented at the Semantic Web Services: Preparing to Meet the World of Business Applications, Hiroshima, Japan.

Haarslev, V. & Möller, R. (2003, October). *Racer: A core inference engine for the Semantic Web.* Paper presented at the 2nd International Workshop on Evaluation of Ontology-based Tools (EON2003), located at the 2nd International Semantic Web Conference ISWC 2003, Florida.

Holzner, S. (2004). *Eclipse.* Sebastopol, CA: O'Reilly & Associates.

Jaeger, M.C. & Tang, S. (2004). Ranked matching for service descriptions using DAML-S. In J. Grundspenkis & M. Kirikova (Eds.), *CAiSE'04 Workshops* (pp. 217-228). Riga, Latvia. Faculty of Computer Science and Information Technology, Riga Technical University.

Kalfoglou, Y. & Schorlemmer, M. (2003). Ontology mapping: The state of the art. *The Knowledge Engineering Review, 18*(1), 1-31.

Keller, U., Lara, R., Polleres, A., Toma, I., Kifer, M., & Fensel, D. (2004), *WSMO Web service discovery* (WSML Deliverable D5.1v0.1). Retrieved October 24, 2006, from http://www.wsmo.org/TR/

Klusch, M., Fries, B., Khalid, M., & Sycara, K. (2005). OWLS-MX: Hybrid semantic Web service retrieval. In *Proceedings of the 1st International AAAI Fall Symposium on Agents and the Semantic Web,* Arlington, Virginia. AAAI Press.

Langley, B., Paolucci, M., & Sycara, K. (2001, May). *Discovery of infrastructure in multi-agent systems.* Paper presented at Agents 2001 Workshop on Infrastructure for Agents, MAS, and Scalable MAS, Montreal, Canada.

Lara, R., Lausen, H., Arroyo, S., de Bruijn, J., & Fensel, D. (2003, June). *Semantic Web services: Description requirements and current technologies.* Paper presented at the Semantic Web Services for Enterprise Application Integration and e-Commerce Workshop (SWSEE03), in conjunction with ICEC 2003, Pittsburgh, Pennsylvania.

Li, L., & Horrocks, I. (2004). A software framework for matchmaking based on Semantic Web technology. *International Journal of Electronic Commerce, 6(4),* 39-60.

Li, K., Verma, K., Mulye, R., Rabbani, R., Miller, J., & Sheth, A. (2006). Designing Semantic Web processes: The WSDL-S approach. In J. Cardoso & A. Sheth (Eds.), *Semantic Web services, pro-*

*cesses and applications* (pp. 163-198). Springer-Verlag.

Maedche, A., & Staab, S. (2003, January). *Services on the move – towards P2P-enabled Semantic Web services.* Paper presented at the 10th International Conference on Information Technology and Travel & Tourism, ENTER 2003, Helsinki, Finland.

Martin, D., Paolucci, M., McIlraith, S., Burstein, M., McDermott, D., McGuinness, D., Parsia, B., Payne, T., Sabou, M., Solanki, M., Srinivasan, N., & Sycara, K. (2005). Bringing semantics to Web services: The OWL-S approach. In J. Cardoso & A. Sheth (Eds.), *A Semantic Web Process: Powering Next Generation of Processes with Semantics and Web Services* (pp. 26-42). Heidelberg, Germany. Lecture Notes in Computer Science 3387. Springer-Verlag.

McIlraith, S., & Martin, D. (2003). Bringing semantics to Web services. *IEEE Intelligent Systems, 18*(1), 90-93.

McIlraith, S., & Son, T. (2002, April). *Adapting golog for composition of Semantic Web services.* Paper presented at the Conference on Knowledge Representation and Reasoning (KR2002), Toulouse, France.

McIlraith, S., Son, T.C., & Zeng, H. (2001). Semantic Web services. *IEEE Intelligent Systems, 16*(2), 46-53.

MWSDI. (2005). Lumina - Semantic Web Service Discovery. Retrieved October 24, 2006, from http://lsdis.cs.uga.edu/projects/meteor-s/illumina/

Narayanan, S. & McIlraith, S. (2002, May). *Simulation, verification and automated composition of Web services.* Paper presented at the Eleventh International World Wide Web Conference (WWW), Honolulu, Hawaii.

Niles, I. & Pease, A. (2001). Towards a standard upper ontology. In C. Welty & B. Smith (Eds.), *Proceedings of the 2nd International Conference on Formal Ontology in Information Systems (FOIS)* (pp. 2-9). Ogunquit, Maine. ACM.

Nixon, L., & Paslaru, E. (2005). *State of the art of current semantic Web services initiatives.* (Tech. Rep. No. D2.4.ID1). KnowledgeWeb Project.

OWLSM. (2005). The TUB OWL-S Matcher. Retrieved October 24, 2006, from http://kbs.cs.tu-berlin.de/ivs/Projekte/owlsmatcher/index.html

OWLS-MX. (2005). Hybrid OWL-S Web Service Matchmaker. Retrieved October 24, 2006, from http://www.dfki.de/~klusch/owls-mx/

OWL-S/UDDIM. (2005). OWL-S UDDI Matchmaker. Retrieved October 24, 2006, from http://projects.semwebcentral.org/projects/owl-s-uddi-mm/

Paolucci, M., Kawamura, T., Payne, T.R., & Sycara, K.P. (2002a). Semantic matching of Web services capabilities. In I. Horrocks & J. Hendler (Eds.), *First International Semantic Web Conference on the Semantic Web,* Sardinia, (LNCS 2342, pp. 333-347). Springer-Verlag.

Paolucci, M., Kawamura, T., Payne, T., & Sycara, K. (2002b). Importing the Semantic Web in UDDI. In C. Bussler, R. Hull, S. McIlraith, M.E. Orlowska, B. Pernici, & J. Yang (Eds.), *Web Services, E-Business and Semantic Web Workshop (WES 2002)* (pp. 225-236). Toronto, Ontario. Springer-Verlag.

Paolucci, M., Sycara, K., Nishimura, T., & Srinivasav, N. (2003) Using DAML-S for P2P discovery. In L.J. Zhang (Ed.), *International Conference on Web Services (ICWS '03)* (pp. 203-207). Las Vegas, Nevada. CSREA Press.

Rahm, E. & Bernstein, P.A. (2001). A survey of approaches to automatic schema matching. *VLDB Journal, 10(4),* 334-350.

Rao, J. & Su, X. (2004, July). *A survey of automated Web service composition methods.* Paper presented at the Semantic Web Services and Web

Process Composition: First International Workshop (SWSWPC), San Diego, California.

Richard, G.G. (2002). *Service and device discovery: Protocols and programming.* New York: McGraw-Hill Professional.

Richardson, R., Smeaton, A.F., & Murphy, J. (1994). *Using WordNet as a knowledge base for measuring semantic similarity between words* (Working paper CA-1294). Dublin, Ireland: Dublin City University, School of Computer Applications.

Rodriguez, M.A. & Egenhofer, M.J. (2003). Determining semantic similarity among entity classes from different ontologies. *Transactions on Knowledge and Data Engineering, 15*(2), 442-456.

Roman, D., Keller, U., Lausen, H., de Bruijn, J., Lara, R., Stollberg, M., Polleres, A., Feier, C., Bussler, C., & Fensel, D. (2005). Web service modeling ontology. *Applied Ontology, 1*(1), 77-106.

Sajjanhar, A., Hou, J., & Zhang, Y. (2004). Algorithm for Web services matching. In J.X. Yu, X. Lin, H. Lu, & Y. Zhang (Eds.), *Advanced Web Technologies and Applications: 6th Asia-Pacific Web Conference (APWeb)* (pp. 665-670). Hangzhou. Springer-Verlag.

SemWebCentral. (2006). Open source tools for the Semantic Web. Retrieved October 24, 2006, from http://www.semwebcentral.org

Srinivasan, N., Paolucci, M., & Sycara, K. (2004, July). *An efficient algorithm for OWL-S based semantic search in UDDI.* Paper presented at the Semantic Web Services and Web Process Composition: First International Workshop (SWSWPC), San Diego, California.

Stroulia, E. & Wang, Y. (2005). Structural and semantic matching for accessing Web service similarity. *International Journal of Cooperative Information Systems, 14*(4), 407-437.

STWS (2006). IBM semantic tools for Web services. Retrieved October 24, 2006, from http://www.alphaworks.ibm.com/tech/wssem

SWSL Committee. (2005). Semantic Web services framework (SWSF). Retrieved October 24, 2006, from http://www.daml.org/services/swsf

Trastour, D., Bartolini, C., & Gonzalez-Castillo, J. (2001, July). *A Semantic Web approach to service description for matchmaking of services.* Paper presented at the Semantic Web Working Symposium, Stanford, California.

Verma, K., Sivashanmugam, K., Sheth, A., Patil, A., Oundhakar, S., & Miller, J. (2005). METEOR-S WSDI: A scalable P2P infrastructure of registries for semantic publication and discovery of Web services. *Information Technology and Management, 6*(1), 17-39.

Wang, H., Huang, J.Z., Qu, Y., & Xie, J. (2004) Web services: Problems and future directions. *Journal of Web Semantics, 1*(3), 309-320.

WSMX. (2006). Web service execution environment. Retrieved October 25, 2006, from http://www.wsmx.org/

Zaremski, A.M. & Wing, J.M. (1997). Specification matching of software components. *ACM Transactions on Software Engineering and Methodology, 6*(4), 335-369.

## ENDNOTES

[1] In the rest of the chapter, the terms "matching," "discovery" and "matchmaking" will be used interchangeably.

[2] NAICS: North American Industry Classification System.

[3] UNSPSC: Universal Standard Products and Services Classification.

[4] IOPE attributes are not the only way to describe service functionality, although they are regarded as necessary service description elements. Depending on the actual Service Annotation Ontology, other description elements may be available.

[5] WSDL-S is not actually an ontology but an extension of the WSDL language.

[6] The term "Plug-in match" originates from the software engineering domain (Zaremski, 1997).

[7] Not shown in this figure, due to size limitations.

## APPENDIX I. SHORT TUTORIAL ON OWL-S/UDDI MATCHMAKER

In this Appendix we demonstrate how the steps involved in SWS discovery, from creating and semantically annotating WS to retrieving the most relevant ones, can be performed with a popular tool, namely OWL-S/UDDI Matchmaker. The online version of this tool can be found in (OWL-S/UDDIM, 2005). Specifically, in this appendix we deal with:

1.  Creating an OWL Ontology describing the context for the offered services, like person profile, ChatIDs, location, and interests,
2.  Semantically annotating the service advertisements according to the IO parameters of the OWL-S service profile,
3.  Semantically annotating the requestor's service requests describing the preferred IO attributes, also expressed in OWL-S,
4.  Discovering the most relevant matching SWSs.

### Step 1: Creation of the Domain Ontology and the Service Definitions (in OWL)

We introduce an OWL representation of the domain knowledge used by the advertised services. Such ontology (Ont) consists of concepts and roles among them. Ont defines the concept Person, which is associated with a Location, a Gender (male or female) and a PersonalProfile. Moreover, the concept PersonalProfile subsumes the ChatID, the ContactProfile, and the InterestProfile concepts. The first denotes the specific chat identifier given by Instant Messaging providers, while the other two contain information related to contact information (e-mail, mobile phone number) and user interests (entertainment, movies, sport), respectively. The complete taxonomy and the basic roles of this ontology are shown in Figure 16. In practice, one would use a different spatial ontology for the spatial concepts, and so forth. We have merged all domain concepts into Ont for simplicity reasons.

Let us consider the example service S1 (see Figure 15). Such service takes as inputs the person's gender, the person's location (any city area) and the person's interests (movies). It returns the person's ChatID and the person's contact information. Service S2 is expressed similarly (see Figure 15). The two service advertisements are those that will be matched against any request description in the OWL-S/UDDI Matchmaker.

## Step 2: Semantic Annotation of Service Advertisements (in OWL-S)

Every service provider has not only to describe the service profile, as discussed in Step 1, but also to annotate its functional parameters (e.g., inputs, outputs) according to the OWL-S specification. Actu-

*Figure 15. Service advertisements S1 and S2 (written in DL notation). The concept ServiceProfile and the roles hasInput, hasOutput and presents are OWL-S terminology.*

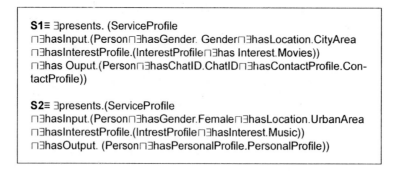

**S1**≡ ∃presents. (ServiceProfile
⊓∃hasInput.(Person⊓∃hasGender. Gender⊓∃hasLocation.CityArea
⊓∃hasInterestProfile.(InterestProfile⊓∃has Interest.Movies))
⊓∃has Ouput.(Person⊓∃hasChatID.ChatID⊓∃hasContactProfile.Con-
tactProfile))

**S2**≡ ∃presents.(ServiceProfile
⊓∃hasInput.(Person⊓∃hasGender.Female⊓∃hasLocation.UrbanArea
⊓∃hasInterestProfile.(IntrestProfile⊓∃hasInterest.Music))
⊓∃hasOutput. (Person⊓∃hasPersonalProfile.PersonalProfile))

*Figure 16. The domain ontology "Ont"*

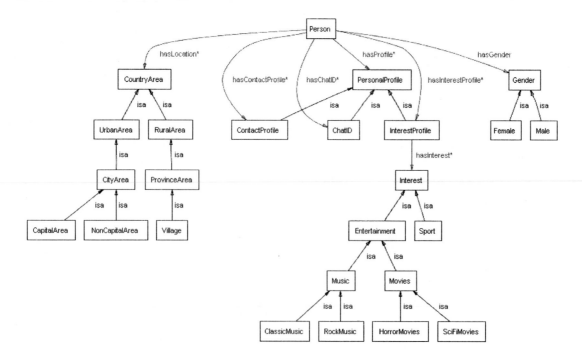

ally, the service provider has to explicitly define: (1) the corresponding domain ontology, (2) the inputs and outputs, and (3) other service parameters, using the OWL-S notation. Figure 17 depicts a part of the advertisement S1 in OWL-S syntax. Note that the hasInput and hasOutput tags refer to Ont concepts.

Figure 19 shows how such specifications can be loaded in the Matchmaker registry. Specifically, the provider sets a service name and a text description.[7] Furthermore, the service provider defines the two inputs and the two outputs through their corresponding concepts. In the service category field,[7] the provider can define one or more service category classes referring to some well-known service classification schemes, like NAICS and UNSPSC. Once the provider has successfully annotated the advertisement, she submits it to the OWL-S/UDDI registry, and an advertisement ID is returned. We repeat Step 2 for service S2.

*Figure 17. Advertisement S1 in OWL-S syntax*

```
<profile:Profile>
  <profile:serviceName>S1</profile:serviceName>
  <profile:textDescription>
    Service that takes the user gernder and intrerests and location as inputs
    and returens the user chat ID and its contact profile
  </profile:testDescription>
  <profile:hasInput>
    <process:Input rdf:ID="in_1">
      <process:parameterType>
      http://p-comp.di.uoa.gr/ont#Gender
      </process:Input>
  </profile:hasInput>

  …
  </profile:hasOutput>
    <profile:hasOutput>
      <process:UnConditionalOutput rdf:ID="out_1">
        <process:parameterType>
        http://p-comp.di.uoa.gr/ont#ChatID
        </process:parameterType>
    </profile:hasOutput>
    …
```

*Figure 18. Service requests Q1 and Q2*

```
Q1≡ ∃presents.(ServiceProfile
⊓∃hasInput.(Person⊓∃hasGernder.Female⊓∃hasLocation.CapitionArea
⊓∃hasInterestProfile.(InterestProfile⊓∃hasInterest.ClassicMusic))
⊓∃hasOutput.(person⊓∃hasChatID.ChatID))

Q2≡ ∃presents.(ServiceProfile
⊓∃hasInput.(Person⊓∃hasGender.Male⊓∃hasLocation.RuralArea
⊓∃hasInterestProfile.(InterestProfile⊓∃hasInterest.Sport))
⊓∃hasOutput.(Person⊓∃hasChatID.ChatID⊓∃hasContactProfile.ContactProfile))
```

## Step 3: Semantic Annotation of Service Requests

Consider that a requestor wants to find services that return the ChatIDs of female persons, who are interested in ClassicMusic, and reside in a CapitalArea. Figure 18 presents this request (query Q1) in DL notation. We specify this request using the OWL-S/UDDI Web interface, similarly to Step 2.

## Step 4: Ranked Matchmaker Results

The response of the semantic OWL-S/UDDI Matchmaker to the Q1 query and the S1, S2 service advertisements include the degree of match (i.e., rank or score) for each matched service. Actually, the Q1 query inputs are matched against S1 service inputs as follows: Q1 gender type is Female, which is subsumed by the S1 Gender type. In addition, Q1 location refers to CapitalArea, which is a sub-concept of the CityArea, defined in S1. The Q1 interest referring to classical music cannot be matched with the S1 interest referring to movies, since they have been defined as disjoint in Ont. As far as the outputs are concerned, the first output of Q1, which refers to ChatID, is exactly matched with the S1 first output. On the other hand, there is another output in Q1, which does not match, with any output of S1. Hence, the matchmaker returns the score 5 (see Table 7). In the matching between Q1 and S2 service, we observe that Q1 input parameters are matched better with those of S2. Specifically, Q1 gender type is exactly

*Figure 19. The Web interface of OWL-S/UDDI matchmaker*

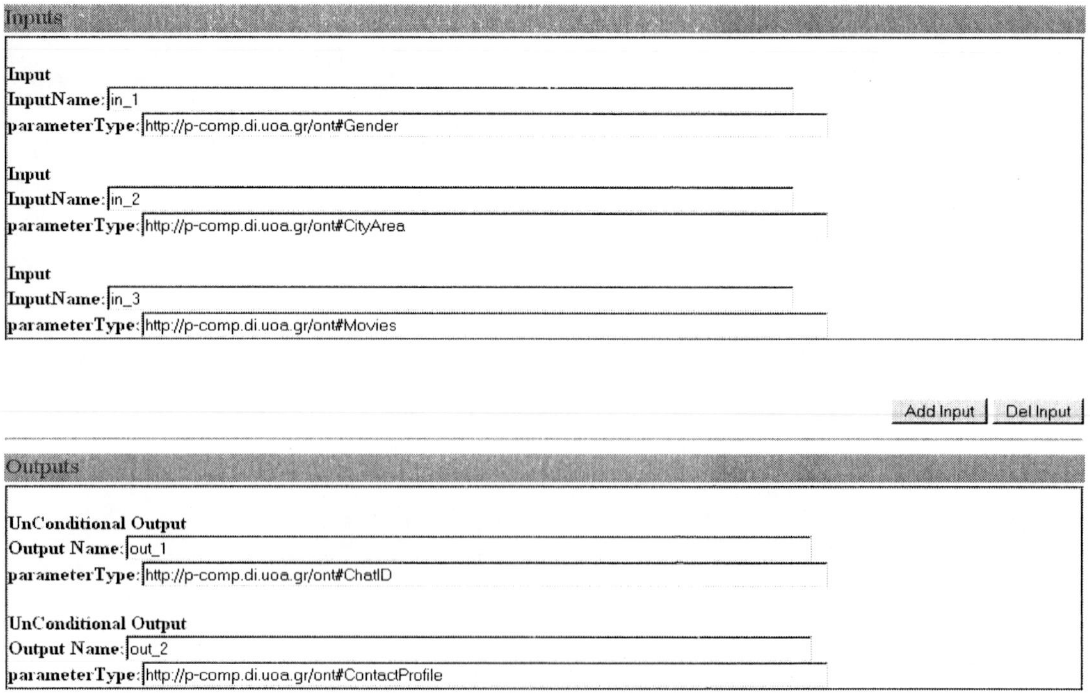

**Inputs**

Input
InputName: in_1
parameterType: http://p-comp.di.uoa.gr/ont#Gender

Input
InputName: in_2
parameterType: http://p-comp.di.uoa.gr/ont#CityArea

Input
InputName: in_3
parameterType: http://p-comp.di.uoa.gr/ont#Movies

Add Input    Del Input

**Outputs**

UnConditional Output
Output Name: out_1
parameterType: http://p-comp.di.uoa.gr/ont#ChatID

UnConditional Output
Output Name: out_2
parameterType: http://p-comp.di.uoa.gr/ont#ContactProfile

matched with S2 gender type (both are of type Female). Additionally, Q1 interest type is subsumed by S2 interest type, something that not applied for S1. Finally, the Q1 location type (CapitalArea) is sub-concept of the S2 UrbanArea. Thus, all of the S2 inputs subsume the inputs of Q1. Moreover, Q1 output type is a ChatID, which is more specific than the S2 output type (PersonalProfile). Hence, the S2 is selected with the same score as S1, and the Matchmaker returns it with a score of 5.

More interesting is the semantic matching between Q2, as defined in Table 7, with the two service advertisements. Moreover, Q2 inputs are partially subsumed by the S1 and S2 inputs, but Q2 outputs are exactly matched with those of S1, something that does not hold for the outputs of S2 (Personal Profile is super-concept of both Q2 output types). Hence, the Matchmaker assigns a score 7 to S1 and a score 2 to S2.

## APPENDIX II : A DESCRIPTION LOGICS PRIMER

Description Logics (DLs), also known as terminological logics, describe knowledge in terms of concepts and (restrictions on) their roles. DLs provide a means of describing structured knowledge in a way that one can reason about it efficiently (i.e., infer new knowledge). DLs are subsets of the First-Order Logic, thus, providing decidability and computationally feasible reasoning at the cost of expressiveness. Knowledge bases expressed in DLs are decomposed to two components, the TBox (Terminological base) and the ABox (Assertional base). The former constitutes the vocabulary of an application domain, that is, the terminology, while the latter contains real world assertions of individuals (instances) in terms of that vocabulary. A terminology consists of concepts and roles. Concepts denote sets of asserted individuals. Roles denote binary relationships between individuals. The key characteristic of DL terminologies is the inclusion axiom (subsumption relations) between their concepts, which is used for building IS-A hierarchies (i.e., taxonomies) from concepts. The elementary DL descriptions are atomic concepts and atomic roles. Complex descriptions can be built inductively from them through concept constructors

*Table 7. Synopsis of request/advertisement matches*

| Description | Input Type | Output Type | Score out of 10 |
|---|---|---|---|
| Q1 | In_1: Female<br>In_2: CapitalArea<br>In_3: ClassicMusic | Out_1: ChatID | Q1 with S1: 5<br>Q1 with S2: 5 |
| Q2 | In_1: Male<br>In_2: Sport<br>In_3: RuralArea | Out_1: ChatID<br>Out_2: ContactProfile | Q2 with S1: 7<br>Q2 with S2: 2 |
| S1 | In_1: Gender<br>In_2: CityArea<br>In_3: Movies | Out_1: ChatID<br>Out_2: ContactProfile | |
| S2 | In_1: Female<br>In_2: Music<br>In_3: UrbanArea | Out_1: PersonalProfile | |

(see Table 8). Moreover, DLs have terminological axioms, which make statements about how concepts or roles are related to each other (see Table 9).

The concepts of a terminology may be either *primitive* (described through necessary conditions, i.e., inclusion axioms) or *defined* (described through necessary and sufficient conditions, i.e., equality axioms).

**Example**: The following DL description illustrates the primitive concept of those young males (C) that are interested in sports and dislike all kinds of movies. Hence, in DL syntax:

C ⊑ Young ⊓ Male ⊓ ∃hasInterest.(Interest ⊓ Sports) ⊓ ∀dislikes.(Movies)

Through this description it is implied that if a person is a kind of C, then she is interested in sports and dislikes all kinds of movies. The inverse does not hold. If, on the other hand, we define C as:

C ≡ Young ⊓ Male ⊓ ∃hasInterest.(Interest ⊓ Sports) ⊓ ∀dislikes.(Movies)

we additionally imply that if a young male person is interested in sports and dislikes all kinds of movies, then it definitely is a kind of C, which may not be the case in general. Thus, one should be sure that the defined concepts are well defined, or else she may receive false inferences.

The popularity of DL-based ontologies is based on the fact that DL reasoning engines (a.k.a. reasoners) offer efficient services over the TBox and ABox assertions (i.e., concepts, roles and individuals).

*Table 8. Main DL constructors (C, D: concepts - R: role)*

| Constructor | DL syntax | Example | Meaning |
|---|---|---|---|
| Intersection | C⊓D | Young ⊓ Male | All individuals that are Young and Male |
| Union | C⊔D | Young ⊔ Male | Any individual that is either Young or Male |
| Value restriction | ∀R.C | ∀ hasInterest.Movies | All individuals that are interested only in Movies |
| Existential role quantification | ∃R.C | ∃ hasInterest.Sports | All individuals that are interested, at least, in Sports |
| Atomic negation | ¬C | ¬Male | Any individual that is not Male |

*Table 9. DL axioms (they also apply to roles)*

| Axiom | DL syntax | Example | Meaning |
|---|---|---|---|
| Inclusion (subsumption) | C⊑D | Young ⊑ Person | An individual of type Young is also of type Person |
| Equality | C≡D | Young ≡ Teenager | Every Young is also a Teenager and vice versa |
| Disjoint | C⊑¬D | Teenager⊑¬Adult | Someone cannot be Teenager and Adult at the same time |

The most important services are *concept satisfiability* (i.e., if a concept can be populated with instances and, thus, the TBox knowledge is consistent), and determination of *concept subsumption* (i.e., whether a concept C is more general than a concept D, or, otherwise stated, C *subsumes* D). Another service that is provided by a DL reasoner is the decision on whether a set of ABox assertions is *consistent*, that is, the *instances* do not have contradicting implications. Satisfiability and consistency checking are useful to determine whether a knowledge base is meaningful at all. The following example illustrates the concept of *concept satisfiability*.

**Example**: There could never exist a person P who has an interest I which is both Sports and Movies, that is, I ⊑ (Interest ⊓ Movies ⊓ Sports), since the latter two concepts are disjoint. Hence, the TBox containing a concept P such that:

P ⊑ Person ⊓ ∃ hasInterest.(Interest ⊓ Movies ⊓ Sports)

is considered inconsistent (i.e., the concept P is not satisfiable). Instead, concept P':

P' ⊑ Person ⊓ ∃ hasInterest.(Interest ⊓ Movies) ⊓ ∃ hasInterest.(Interest ⊓ Sports)

is satisfiable, since it describes a person interested, at least, one interest in Movies and at least another interest in Sports.

DL reasoners also perform *classification* in a TBox. This is the task of placing a new concept expression in the proper position in a hierarchy of concepts. An example of classification is the following:

**Example**: A young person, who is interested in SciFiMovies (concept C), is subsumed by another young person, who is interested in Movies (concept D). On the other hand, a young person who is interested in Sports (concept E) does not subsume C, since Movies (and consequently SciFiMovies) are considered as disjoint with Sports. Hence, the following TBox statements, could only infer that C ⊑ D:

C ⊑ Young ⊓ ∃ hasInterest.(Interest ⊓ SciFiMovies)
D ⊑ Young ⊓ ∃ hasInterest.(Interest ⊓ Movies)
E ⊑ Young ⊓ ∃ hasInterest.(Interest ⊓ Sports)
SciFiMovies ⊑ Movies ⊑ Interest
Sports ⊑ Interest
Sports ⊑ ¬Movies.

The reader is referred to (Baader, 2003) for further information on DL theory and applications.

# APPENDIX III: ABBREVIATIONS

| | |
|---|---|
| API | Application Programming Interface |
| DAML | DARPA Agent Markup Language |
| DL | Description Logic |
| DoM | Degree of Match |
| FOL | First Order Logic |
| IOPE | Inputs, Outputs, Preconditions, Effects |
| IR | Information Retrieval |
| OWL | Web Ontology Language |
| P2P | Peer-to-Peer |
| RDF | Resource Description Framework |
| SLP | Service Location Protocol |
| SW | Semantic Web |
| SWS | Semantic Web Service |
| SWSL | Semantic Web Services Language |
| SWSO | Semantic Web Services Ontology |
| TFIDF | Term Frequency / Inverse Document Frequency |
| UDDI | Universal Description, Discovery and Integration |
| UPnP | Universal Plug and Play |
| W3C | World Wide Web Consortium |
| WS | Web Service |
| WSDL | Web Service Description Language |
| WSML | Web Service Modeling Language |
| WSMO | Web Service Modeling Ontology |

# Chapter XII
# Semantic Web Service Discovery in the WSMO Framework

**Uwe Keller**
*Leopold-Franzens-Universität Innsbruck, Austria*

**Rubén Lara**
*Grupo Analistas, Tecnología, Información y Finanzas, Spain*

**Holger Lausen**
*Leopold-Franzens-Universität Innsbruck, Austria*

**Dieter Fensel**
*Leopold-Franzens-Universität Innsbruck, Austria*

## ABSTRACT

*The Web service modeling ontology (WSMO) provides a conceptual framework for semantically describing Web services and their specific properties. In this chapter we discuss how WSMO can be applied for service discovery. We provide a proper conceptual grounding by strictly distinguishing between service and Web service discovery and then present different techniques for realizing Web service discovery. In order to cover the complete range of scenarios that can appear in practical applications, several approaches to achieve the automation of Web service discovery are presented and discussed. They require different levels of semantics in the description of Web services and requests, and have different complexity and precision.*

## INTRODUCTION

The Web is a tremendous success story. Starting as an in-house solution for exchanging scientific information, it has become, in slightly more than a decade, a world-wide used media for information dissemination and access. In many respects, it has become the major means for publishing and accessing information. Its scalability and the comfort and speed in disseminating information have no precedent. However, it is solely a Web for humans. Computers cannot "understand" the provided information and in return do not provide any support in processing this information. Two complementary trends are about to transform the Web, from being for humans only, into a Web that connects computers to provide support for human interactions at a much higher level than is available with current Web technology.

- The Semantic Web is about adding machine-processable semantics to data. The computer can "understand" the information and therefore process it on behalf of the human user (cf. Fensel, 2003).
- Web services try to employ the Web as a global infrastructure for distributed computation, for integrating various applications, and for the automation of business processes (cf. Alonso, Casati, Kuno, & Machiraju, 2003). The Web will not only be the place where human readable information is published but the place where global computing is realized.

The Semantic Web promises to make information understandable to a computer and Web services promise to provide smooth and painless integration of disparate applications. Web services offer a new level of automation in eWork and eCommerce, where fully open and flexible cooperation can be achieved, on-the-fly, with low programming costs. However, the current implementations of Web service technology are still far from reaching these goals, as integrating heterogeneous and dynamically changing applications is still a tremendous task.

Eventually, Semantic Web services promise the combination of Semantic Web with Web service technology in order to overcome the limitations of current Web services by adding explicit semantics to them. The exploitation of such semantics can enable a fully mechanized Web for computer interaction, which would become a new infrastructure on which humans organize their cooperations and business relationships (cf. Fensel & Bussler, 2002). OWL-S (The OWL Services Coalition, 2004) and WSMO (Roman, Lausen, & Keller, 2005) are the major proposals for providing semantic annotations on top of a Web service infrastructure.

An important step for fully open and flexible e-commerce would be the mechanization of service discovery. As long as human intervention is required in service discovery the potential costs of establishing a new eCommerce link may outrange the potential savings and advantages. Open, flexible, on-the-fly creation of new supply chains is essentially based on full or nearly full automation of this process. Therefore, it is not surprising that automatic Web service discovery is a popular research topic and many papers are published on it (cf. Akkiraju, Goodwin, Doshi, & Roeder, 2003; Benatallah, Hacid, Rey, & Toumani, 2003; Gonzlez-Castillo, Trastour, & Bartolini, 2001; Li & Horrocks, 2003; Paolucci, Kawamura, Payne, & Sycara, 2002; Sycara, Widoff, Klusch, & Lu, 2002; Verma, Sivashanmugam, Sheth, & Patil, 2004; Zein & Kermarrec, 2004). Still, many of these papers discuss discovery in the setting of multi-agent systems or in the setting of description logic based reasoning and none of them really seems to take a look at the actual conceptual and pragmatic issues that are involved in service discovery by using Web services.

Therefore, we provide an in-depth analysis of the major conceptual issues that are involved in service discovery via Web services:

- First, we strictly distinguish between service and Web service discovery, identifying three major steps in service discovery where only one of them is about Web service discovery.
- Second, we discuss different techniques for Web service discovery using this as a means for achieving a better understanding of the dialectic relationship between discovery and mediation. In this context, we discuss the mediation support needed for different approaches to Web service discovery.
- Third, we discuss in detail semantic-based discovery of Web services. Stepwise we will enrich the scenario we are able to support. In this chapter, we focus on the essential *principles* underlying semantic-based discovery based on a simple formal model, that is independent of any particular knowledge representation language. For a discussion of an implementation of these principles in particular logics, we refer to Keller, Lara, and Polleres (2004).

In conclusion, we provide a conceptual model for service discovery and different approaches to one of the steps of such model, Web service discovery, which can be realized by WSMO and related efforts.

This chapter is organized as follows: we first provide some the necessary background on the Web Service Modeling Ontology (WSMO) framework and the relevant notions for discovery therein. Then we identify three major conceptual phases in service discovery. Next, we discuss in detail the issues around semantic-based discovery of Web services. Finally, we give some conclusions about the WSMO discovery framework at the end of the chapter.

# BASICS

In the following, we briefly overview the Web service modeling ontology (WSMO) (Roman et al., 2005) and discuss the notions that are relevant for discovery. In particular, WSMO distinguishes the notions of *Web service* and *service* in the context of discovery. Furthermore, we summarize what WSMO eventually aims at in regard of Web service discovery.

## The Web Service Modeling Ontology

Taking the Web Service Modeling Framework (WSMF) as its conceptual basis (Fensel & Bussler, 2002), the WSMO project is an ongoing research and development initiative[1] for defining a capacious framework for Semantic Web services.

### Design Principles and Approach

Semantic Web services aim at realizing the vision of the Semantic Web. Therefore, WSMO is based on the following design principles that integrate Web design principles, Semantic Web design principles, as well as design principles for distributed, service-oriented computing for the Web:

- **Web Compliance:** WSMO inherits the concept of Internationalized Resource Identifiers (IRIs) for unique identification of resources as the essential design principle of the Web. Moreover, WSMO adopts the concept of Namespaces for denoting consistent information spaces, and supports XML as well as other W3C Web technology recommendations.
- **Ontology-Based:** Ontologies are used as the data model throughout WSMO, meaning that all resource descriptions as well as all data interchanged during service usage are

based on ontologies. Following the idea of the Semantic Web, this allows semantically enhanced information processing as well as support for semantic interoperability.

- **Goal-driven Architecture:** User requests are formulated as goals independently of available Web services. Thereby, the underlying epistemology of WSMO differentiates between the desires of clients and available Web services.

- **Strict Decoupling:** Each WSMO resource is specified independently, without regard to possible usage or interactions with other resources. This complies with the open and distributed nature of the Web.

- **Centrality of Mediation:** Mediation addresses the handling of heterogeneities that naturally arise in open environments like the Web. As a complementary design principle to strict decoupling, WSMO recognizes the importance of mediation for the successful deployment of Web services by making mediation a first class component of the framework.

- **Description versus Implementation:** WSMO differentiates between the *description* and the *implementation* of Web services. The former denotes the unambiguous description of Web services that is needed for automated usage of Web services; the latter is concerned with the internal implementation of the Web service which is not of interest for Semantic Web service technologies.

The design principles are reflected in the four WSMO top level elements shown in Figure 1. Ontologies provide the formal terminology definitions that are used as the data model throughout WSMO; goals are formal specifications of objectives that a client aims to achieve by using Web services, realizing a goal-driven approach that ontologically decouples requesters and providers; WSMO Web services are formal descriptions needed for automated service handling and usage,

whereby the internal implementation of a Web service is not of interest; finally, mediators are the top level element for handling heterogeneity.

While referring to the WSMO specification (Roman et al., 2005) for detailed definitions, the following explains the WSMO elements with regard to their purpose and constitutive description elements.

## Top Level Elements

### Ontologies

In compliance to the vision of the Semantic Web, WSMO uses ontologies as the underlying data model for Semantic Web services. This means that all resource descriptions and all information interchanged during collaboration execution is based on ontologies, thereby providing the basis for semantically enhanced information processing and ensuring semantic interoperability between Semantic Web services.

In accordance to the AI-theory of ontologies (Staab & Studer, 2004), WSMO ontologies consist of the following elements: *concepts* describe the entities of a domain that are characterized by *attributes*; *relations* describe associations between concepts, whereby subsumption and membership relationships define the taxonomic structure of an ontology. An *instance* is a concrete individual of a concept, and *axioms* define constraints and complex aspects of the domain

*Figure 1. WSMO top level elements*

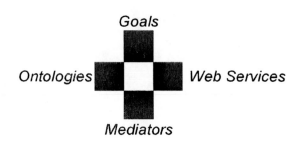

in terms of logical expressions. Regarding engineering methodologies developed for the Semantic Web (Fensel, 2003), ontology design in WSMO demands and supports *modularization*, that is, small-sized and concise ontologies, *decoupling*, that is, distributed and multi-party ontology development, and *ontology mediation* for resolving possibly occurring mismatches between loosely coupled ontologies for a specific usage scenario.

## Web Services

WSMO defines a description model that encompasses the information needed for automatically determining the usability of a Web service. As shown in Figure 2, a WSMO Web service description is comprised of four elements: (1) *nonfunctional properties*, (2) a *capability* as the functional description of the service, summarized as service interfaces, (3) a *choreography* that describes the interface for service consumption by a client (i.e., how to interact with the Web service), and (4) an *orchestration* that describes how the functionality of the service is achieved by aggregating other Web services. These notions describe the *functionality* and *behavior* of a Web service, while its internal implementation is not of interest.

While the nonfunctional properties contain descriptions like quality of service, financial information, and versioning information, the functional service description elements are the *capability* and the *service interfaces*. The former describes the functionality of a Web services from a black box perspective for supporting automated functional discovery, meaning to determine whether a Web service can be used to satisfy a user request on basis of its capability. The service interfaces describe the interaction behavior of the Web service for consuming, respectively achieving its functionality: a client that wants to utilize the Web service needs to comply with its choreography interface; similar, a Web service that realizes it functionality by aggregating other Web services in its orchestration—which is a main objective of Web service technology—needs to consume these via their respective choreography interfaces.

As outlined above, WSMO differentiates two service interfaces that are concerned with the interaction behavior of the Web service. The choreography interface describes the behavior of the Web service for consuming its functionality in terms of the information interchange expected, and the orchestration describes how the Web service interacts with other Web services in order to achieve its functionality.

*Figure 2. WSMO Web service description*

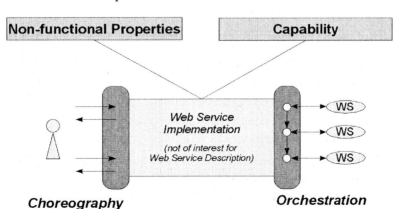

In contrast to several existing Web service technologies that focus on describing the interaction execution in detail—like WSDL, BPEL4WS, and WS-CDL (see Barros, Dumas, & Oaks, 2005 for an extensive discussion)—the aim of WSMO service interface descriptions is to provide the foundation for determining automatically whether the interactions between a Web service, its clients, and other aggregated Web services that need to be performed for achieving its functionality. Therefore, WSMO defines a formal model for service interface descriptions that supports ontologies as the underlying data model as is based on the Abstract State Machine (ASM) framework, a high-level, abstract technique for validating complex systems or programs and provide a highly expressive, flexible, and formally sound means for representing dynamics (Boerger & Staerk, 2003).

In the remainder of the chapter we will focus on the functional description contained in the capability and will not further consider behavioral aspects due to space limitations.

## Goals

In order to facilitate automated Web service usage and support ontological separation of user desires, service usage requests, and Web service descriptions, goals in WSMO allow specifying objectives that clients—which can be humans or machines—wish to achieve.

The general structure of WSMO goal descriptions is similar to Web service descriptions. The client can specify the functionality expected in a *requested capability*. Also, a goal can carry information on the expected behavior of an acceptable Web service in so-called *requested interfaces* that can define the excepted communication behavior for consuming a Web service with respect to its choreography interface as well as restrictions on other Web services aggregated in the orchestration of an acceptable Web service (e.g., only Web services are accepted that utilize a trusted payment facility). It is important to remark that goal descriptions are defined from the client perspective, thereby decoupled from Web service descriptions.

## Mediators

Mediation is concerned with handling heterogeneity, that is, resolving possibly occurring mismatches between resources that ought to be interoperable. Heterogeneity naturally arises in open and distributed environments, and thus in the application areas of Semantic Web services. Hence, WSMO defines the concept of mediators as a top level notion.

Mediator-orientated architectures as introduced in (Wiederhold, 1994) specify a mediator as an entity for establishing interoperability of resources that are not compatible a priori by resolving mismatches between them at runtime. The aspired approach for mediation relies on declarative description of resources whereupon mechanisms for resolving mismatches work on a structural and a semantic level, in order to allow generic, domain independent mediation facilities as well as reuse of mediators. Concerning the needs for mediation within Semantic Web services, WSMO distinguishes three levels of mediation:

1. **Data Level Mediation:** mediation between heterogeneous data sources; within ontology-based frameworks like WSMO, this is mainly concerned with ontology integration.

2. **Protocol Level Mediation:** mediation between heterogeneous communication protocols; in WSMO, this mainly relates to choreographies of Web services that ought to interact.

3. **Process Level Mediation:** mediation between heterogeneous business processes; this is concerned with mismatch handling on the business logic level of Web services

(related to the orchestration of Web services).

## Web Service vs. Service

A workable approach to automating service discovery must precisely define its conceptual model and the particular assumptions underlying the proposed solution. For this purpose, we start by providing a common understanding of what a service is and the levels of abstraction in its description based on (Preist, 2004), as well as our assumptions on the elements involved in the process of locating suitable services for service requesters.

### What is a Service?

It has been pointed out in Preist (2004) that the notion of *service* is semantically overloaded. Several communities have different interpretations which make it difficult to understand and relate single approaches and exchange ideas and results. In order to reach a common understanding of the problem we address here, we need to precisely define the term *service* and, therefore, what kind of entities we aim at locating in principle.

In this chapter, we use the following interpretation for the term *service*, as described in the conceptual architecture for Semantic Web services presented in Preist (2004): *Service as provision of value in some domain.* This definition regards a service as a *provision of value* (not necessarily monetary value) in some given domain, independently of how the supplier and the provider interact. Examples of services in this sense are the provision of information about flight tickets or the booking of a trip with certain characteristics by a tourism service provider.

### Abstract Services and Web Services

Usually, a service provider *P* does not only provide one particular service *S*, but a set of coherent and logically related services. For instance, a hotel usually does not only provide the possibility to book a particular room at a particular date for a given number of nights, but instead it will offer the general service of booking rooms. Thus, a provider will be interested in advertising *all the services* it is able to provide, that is, a set $A_p$ of services. Following the terminology from Preist (2004), we call this *collection of services* an *abstract service* offered by a provider. The smallest unit of advertisement is considered to be an abstract service.

In order to deliver a service, a service provider *P* usually needs certain information from the requester. For instance, a hotel might require the name of the person booking the room, the requested room features, and a valid credit card number as input information in order to book a room. This input data $i_1, ..., i_n$ will determine what *concrete service* (Preist, 2004) $S \in A_p$ has to be provided by *P*.

Finally, *Web services* are computational entities using standardized interfaces that allow clients to interact with a provider *P* to access, explore and consume concrete services $S \in A_p$. A service requester technically needs to interact with the Web service to get what he actually aims for: a concrete service or more generally, a set of concrete services that fulfill the requesters goal, that is, an abstract service. Hence, we will not distinguish between Web services and abstract services of a provider throughout this document and treat both notions as synonyms. Moreover, we can observe that a concrete service $S \in A_p$ is being delivered in the course of or as a result of a particular *execution* of the Web service by invocation with specific data $i_1, ..., i_n$ for the required input parameters.

### Dynamics of Abstract Services Over Time

In the real-world, we have a further complication of matters in regard of discovery and Web service description: in general, an abstract service $A_p$ offered by some provider $P$ does not stay the same, but changes over time. For instance, a hotel will not be able to book a room with a single bed on a specific date if all such rooms in the hotel are already booked on this date.

Since clients are basically interested in finding abstract services which actually can solve their problem at hand (as specified in a WSMO goal), discovery in general needs to take into account this dynamics in order to create accurate results. This basically means, that purely static descriptions of Web services are not sufficient in the general case. In applications where highly accurate results are requested, Web service descriptions will have to consist of a dynamic component as well.

On a description level there are various options to achieve the proper representation of dynamically changing abstract services of a provider: (1) Use a purely static description of the abstract service and change the description in its entirety every time the abstract service changes or (2) use a static description where some parts refer to a well-defined resource that reflects that currently valid information of the dynamic part (for instance a database table with all available rooms of a hotel at a certain point in time). Clearly, the first approach is not really scalable since constant changes of a stored abstract service description are needed, whereas the second approach is a viable one, as we can see with dynamically generated Web pages of online stores like Amazon.com that give an up-to-date perspective on prices of single books. In the latter case, we simply externalize the details of the changing aspects of an abstract service and provide a reference in the remaining part of the Web service description. Hence, the abstract service description including the reference does not need to change over time when the abstract service of the provider changes and Web service descriptions get more compact.

Nonetheless, the latter approach requires *communication* with the provider of an abstract service (in some way, for instance via a Web service that accesses a certain database table) and thus can potentially be a costly step in terms of computation time. Hence, there is a clear trade-off between accuracy of discovery results and efficiency of the discovery process that has to be considered for any specific application that leverages Web service discovery.

## Knowledge Representation Languages in the Framework

Before we explain in more detail the model of our framework, we want to stress that the framework, as it is presented in the following is language-independent in the first place and stresses the essential aspects of Web services, matchmaking and Web service discovery on the basis of a mathematical model. The choice of a particular knowledge representation language for the model is in *no way essential* for the WSMO Discovery Framework; however, when giving the examples of Web service descriptions for the various levels of our model in the following, we use a *specific* description (or knowledge representation language) for illustration purposes: the WSML language[2] (de Bruijn, 2005).

In general we want to note the following observation, since it embodies distinct feature as well as a clear and essential contribution of the WSMO working group to the Semantic Web service community in regard of Semantic Web service description and discovery: traditionally,[3] people in various communities, especially the Semantic Web community as well as the Description Logic community had a heavily language-centered perspective when studying the semantic description of Web services as well as matchmaking. Because of this over-emphasized (and rather narrow) language focus[4] the community unfortunately overlooked until recently the most essential aspect of any proper description framework: A clear understanding of *what* the object actually is, that one needs to describe (i.e., Web service). In a sense, a fundamental principles underlying formal logics have been ignored, namely that a language is tailored towards the domain its applied in and that the semantics of a description language usually is defined in model-theoretic terms. The latter requires that one needs some proper mathematical model of Web services and enables a clear understanding of the matter. Subsequently, matching of Web service advertisements and requests (and thus service discovery) can then be considered in a proper way with respect to this mathematical model in a *completely language independent* manner. One can focus on the essential aspects rather than a concrete language (which only is of secondary importance) and get a far better understanding of the overall matters.

During the work on the WSMO discovery framework this prevalent misconception has been understood and properly addressed (see in particular Lausen, 2005 and Keller et al., 2004): discovery in the first place is not a matter of using a specific language, but understanding a mathematical model and developing matching based on the model. Later on, one can address the problem of deriving a suitable formalization in a concrete language. Eventually, there might be many different languages that one can use for this purpose. That is one of the definite strengths of the WSMO discovery framework. In the following, we use therefore the universal framework of set theory to describe and discuss Web services as well as Web service discovery.

## Web Services at Various Levels of Abstraction

The descriptions of Web services as published by service providers and the goals of service requesters need to be compared to each other during the discovery process in order to identify matching Web services and goals. In essence, matching in the discovery process is about finding common elements of these descriptions.

In the model that we discussed above, an abstract service $A$ of a provider essentially is a set of elements that we call services. Services themselves are abstract entities in this model. Depending on how detailed we consider these entities, we end up with a model of Web services on different levels of abstraction that is depicted in Figure 3.

On the most fine-grained level, we can consider services as concrete state-transitions $(s,s')$ from a state $s$ to another state $s'$ in the world. The notion of *state* here refers to an abstract

*Figure 3. Web services considered at different levels of abstraction*

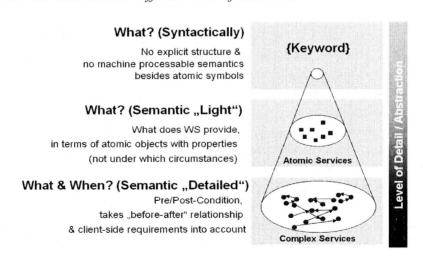

object that describes all the *relevant* properties of the world at some specific moment in time.[5] The states *s* and *s'* precisely determine, how the world looks like before and after the service has been provided. One a more abstract level, we can ignore the detailed structure of services (i.e., the respective states, their interdependency, and the respective state-transition) and understand them purely as abstract objects and characterize their specific properties. The objects themselves have no longer an elaborate structure. Relevant information about the single services is captured by simple properties. In terms of ontologies we would then consider services (epistemologically) as instances and abstract services or Web services as (complex) concepts. Eventually, we can abstract even more in the description of abstract services by ignoring the description of the possible elements of the set. On this level, we would simply use a term or keyword for describing the abstract service and neglect any information about fine-grained structure. Web services on this level are merely considered as atomic objects without any explicit structure (i.e., as symbols). Essentially, we consider keyword-based descriptions here. In the simplest case, one can use free text (sets of words or keywords) here to describe the advertised or requested set of services. In this case, no explicit machine-processable semantics of the description is available for agents performing matching between requests and advertisements; natural language processing techniques can be used to (heuristically) guess the correct meaning of the description. Instead of free text, one could use simple keywords from *controlled vocabularies* as well to still have a representation with very shallow (i.e., non-explicit), but yet machine-processable semantics. Such a representation is necessarily based on very strong agreements between service requesters and service providers on how to describe and model Web services and goals.

To illustrate the different levels of abstractions in our model, we consider a simple example of a Web service of the financial domain and see how

it could be described at the single levels. Consider the following scenario:

ABank is a specialized German bank that offers domestic wire transfers to arbitrary branches of other Austrian Banks, whereby money can only be transferred in European currencies, and a transfer may not exceed 100.000 Euros for private customers and may not exceed 2.000.000 Euros for companies. For the successful execution of the transfer, a (customer-specific) minimum balance of the customer's account is required. The minimum balance is computed as follows: (...). The respective business service is provided as a Web service.

How can we describe this scenario on the single levels identified in Figure 3, that is, how does a description *A* of the respective Web service look like?

## Syntactic Level

In case of a natural language free text, we could literally use the scenario description given above, that is,

A = {ABank is a specialized German bank that offers international wire transfers to arbitrary branches of Austrian Banks, whereby money can only be transferred in European currencies, and a transfer may not exceed 100.000 Euros for private customers and may not exceed 2.000.000 Euros for companies. For the successful execution of the transfer, a (customer-specific) minimum balance of the customer's account is required. The minimum balance is computed as follows: (...)}

or a more condensed description based on a list of keywords, for example,

A = {Bank Wire Transfer, ABank, in Germany, to Branch of Austrian Bank, European Currencies only, not more than 100.000 Euros for private customers, no more than 2.000.000 Euros for companies, suitable minimum balance needed}.

Such descriptions are easily processable for humans (with respective domain knowledge), however they are hard to deal with for computers: natural language processing techniques must be applied to heuristically find out relevant relations between the single information chunks, for instance that "100.000" refers to an upper limit of the transfer and not the transferred amount itself, that this is only applies to the case of private customers but not to companies (where the limit is significantly higher), that Austrian branch refers to the target accounts of the wire transfer (and not the source account) and so forth.

Finally, one could use a term of an agreed upon shared vocabulary to regain machine-processability, for example, a term from the eClass[6] system that denotes "Account Management":

A = { 25 - 15 - 13 - 04 [AJZ69300201]}

However, in the last case, much relevant information about the Web service that one might want to specify can not be expressed in such simple representation frameworks as controlled vocabularies because of the expressivity of the vocabulary. The quality of the results that are computed in a discovery process are thus of limited quality, and strong agreement between service providers and service requesters are absolutely necessary.

## Light Semantic Level

Here, the set of (atomic) objects which represent the Web service under consideration could be captured by a formula $\Phi(?t)$ formally representing the definition of an unary predicate (and thus a set of objects in some domain). In particular, the formula $\Phi(?t)$ is based on a suitable ontologies describing concepts that are relevant in the finan-

cial domain (such as bank transfer, wire transfer, branch, account, currency, private customer etc.) or geographic ontologies (defining elements like Germany, Austria). Hence, as the description $A$ we could use the following formula $\Phi(?t)$ (with free variable $?t$ representing the objects under investigation, i.e., transfers with specific properties):

```
Φ(?t) = (
?t memberOf BankTransfer and
?t memberOf WireTransfer and
exists ?F, ?T,?A,?C(
?t[ fromAcc hasValue ?F,
   toAcc hasValue ?T,
   amount hasValue ?A,
   currency hasValue ?C ]
and ( ?F.owner memberOf PrivateCustomer implies
   ?A < convertCurrency(100000, ?C, Euro)
and ( ?F.owner memberOf CompanyCustomer implies
   ?A < convertCurrency(2000000, ?C, Euro)
and ?F.bank = ABank
and ?F.branch. locatedIn = Germany
and ?T.branch.locatedIn = Austria
and isEuropeanCurrency(?C)
and ?F.balance >= requiredMinBalance(?F, ?F.owner) )
```

Because of the use of a simple, yet formal language and the use of domain ontologies, such descriptions allow machines to exploit the explicit representation of semantics without any "guessing" based on natural language processing and similar heuristic techniques.

The symbols used to construct such formulas (such as requiredMinBalance, isEuropeanCurrency, convertCurrency, <) are defined in ontologies representing domain-specific (or even entitiy-specific) knowledge.

One can observe that on this level, we can not really represent, what actually happens to the world (i.e. the actual state-changes that one can observe when the executing the Web service: what happens to the balances of accounts ?F and ?T ?) or what the obligations of the requester really are, in terms of the input that is to be provided. For instance, the expression specifies that for any suitable tuple of values *(?F,?T,?A,?C)*, a respective transfer *?t* can be delivered by the service, neglecting the dependency on the input of the invoker. It is not clear from the description above, that ?F.balance in the very last part of $\Phi(?t)$ refers to the balance of account ?F before the execution of the Web service (i.e., in the pre-state) and not to the balance of the account afterwards. Such things can thoroughly be represented within a state-based framework, such as the one underlying the most-detailed level of Web services in our model.

## Detailed Semantic Level

On this level, we exploit a state-based perspective on the world and Web services acting therein, and consequently are really able to distinguish between properties of the pre-state of the Web service execution and properties of the respective final state. Furthermore, we can thus clearly point out the obligations of the requester when invoking the Web service (in terms of the inputs that needs to be provided).

To represent our example on this level, one could use a description $A$ similar to the following pair of formulae $\Phi$-pre (?F, ?T, ?A, ?C) and $\Phi$-post (?F, ?T, ?A, ?C) where $\Phi$-pre (?F, ?T, ?A, ?C) describes the state of the world as well as the requirements on the input values before the execution of the Web service, $\Phi$-post (?F, ?T, ?A, ?C) describes the state of the world after the execution of the Web service as well as the output, and the variables (?F, ?T, ?A, ?C) represent the inputs that must be provided by the user, when invoking the Web service, namely the account ?F from which the transfer is initiated, the target account ?T, the amount ?A to be transferred and the currency ?C to which the amount refers:

```
Φ-pre (?F, ?T, ?A, ?C)=
  (?F.owner memberOf PrivateCustomer implies
?A < convertCurrency(100000, ?C, Euro)
and ( ?F.owner instanceOf CompanyCustomer implies
  ?A < convertCurrency(2000000, ?C, Euro)
and ?F.bank = ABank
and ?F.branch. locatedIn = Germany
and ?T.branch.locatedIn = Austria
and isEuropeanCurrency(?C)
and ?F.balance >= requiredMinBalance(?F, ?F.owner)
```

```
Φ-post (?F, ?T, ?A, ?C)=
exists ?t (
 ?t memberOf BankTransfer and
 ?t memberOf WireTransfer and
 ?t[ fromAcc hasValue ?F,
  toAcc hasValue ?T,
  amount hasValue ?A,
  currency hasValue ?C ]
and
 ?F.balance = ?F.balance@pre - convertCurrency(?A,
?C, ?F.currency)
and
 ?T.balance = ?T.balance@pre + convertCurrency(?A,
?C, ?T.currency))
```

In particular, the last part of $\Phi$-post (?F, ?T, ?A, ?C) describes in detail what happens to the respective account balances after the execution (?F.balance) in regard of their values before the execution (?F.balance@pre) and the specifically provided input (?F, ?T, ?A, ?C).

In contrast to the last example, we will use a little different and more specific way to model Web service on this most fine-grained level of abstraction in the context of this chapter which is a little closer to the level of light semantic descriptions and eventually allows us to establish a mathematically well-defined relationship between the the level of rich semantic descriptions and the next higher level of abstraction. Eventually, this enables semantic interoperability between descriptions on different levels of abstraction (e.g., a description on the detailed semantic level and one at the level of light semantic descriptions). A deeper and more general discussion of the level of detailed semantic descriptions can be found in Lausen (2005).

Each of these levels of abstraction imposes different descriptions of Web services, ranging from detailed characterizations of possible state-transition, less detailed descriptions as (complex) concepts in an ontology to simple unstructured keywords. Consequently, the achievable accuracy of result in the discovery process varies significantly, since more or less structure is actually reflected in the descriptions. On the other hand, the ease of providing the descriptions varies on the single levels as well drastically: Whereas simple keywords are easy to provide, the descriptions of concepts is still not hard but requires more effort. The provision of detailed state-based descriptions definitely requires more elaborate skills of the people creating the formal descriptions. Eventually, the more fine-grained information the descriptions reveal, the more complex algorithms are needed to deal with these descriptions.

Therefore, there is an interesting trade-off between the possible achievable accuracy and the ease of creating the descriptions as well as the potential computational efficiency of the discovery process.

## Goal of the WSMO Discovery Framework

During the design of the WSMO discovery framework the following aspects were desired goals that we aimed to achieve:

- It should be a general framework that supports a wide variety of application scenarios. Among the supported scenarios should be applications for which efficiency is far more important than very accurate results,[7] as well as applications that require highly accurate results of the discovery process, for instance when aiming at full automation of processes where suitable Web services need to be integrated on the fly.
- The framework should put specific focus on pragmatic aspects that allow workable and scalable solutions for discovery in industrial and end-user applications.
- It should provide an understanding of the trade-offs between ease of use and simplicity of description, efficiency of computation and accuracy of the results and try to balance these aspects of a discovery framework.
- Following the spirit of the WSMO framework in general, it should facilitate interoperation between various communities

and user groups rather than defining only a specific solution that is suitable for a particular application scenario.

## Scope of the Chapter

For the sake of space we do not consider the WSMO framework in its entirety in this chapter. In the following, we focus instead on a specific aspect of the overall model of Web service and goal descriptions, which can be seen as the most fundamental aspect of such descriptions, namely, the capability description of goals and Web services.

In particular, that we do not explore the behavioral part of descriptions (i.e., the service interface) as well as the non-functional properties, which clearly are important and interesting aspects in the context of discovery as well. The techniques that are need to address these aspects can be very different to the ones that are used when considering capabilities. However, the aspects themselves are orthogonal to each other, thus, the solutions to the single problems can be combined in a modular way.

## A CONCEPTUAL MODEL FOR SERVICE DISCOVERY

Approaches to automating discovery of suitable Web services must precisely analyze what kind of descriptions can be used for capturing the static and dynamic aspects of a given Web service, and how such descriptions can be exploited for efficiently and accurately locating a requested service. While a number of proposals are available in our area of interest (e.g., Benatallah et al., 2003; Gonzlez-Castillo et al., 2001; Li & Horrocks, 2003; Paolucci et al., 2002; Sycara et al., 2002), none of them has precisely discussed these aspects, but they mainly focused on some specific description languages and frameworks, partly neglecting overall needs. Therefore, we will first define a model that takes into account pragmatic considerations and defines the border line between different steps involved in the process of locating services, namely: goal discovery, goal refinement, Web service discovery, and service discovery.

In this section, we will first briefly introduce the gist of the matter of heuristic classification. Then we show how this model is applied in WSMO to structure the service discovery process as the underlying conceptual pattern.

### Heuristic Classification

Clancey (1985) provided a land marking analysis in the area of experts systems. Based on an analysis of numerous rule-based systems for classification and diagnosis he extracted a pattern of three inference steps that helped to understand the various production rules implemented in the various systems.[8] The problem-solving method he called *heuristic classification* separates abstraction, matching, and refinement as the three major activities in any classification and diagnosis task (see Figure 4).

### Abstraction

Abstraction is the process of translating concrete description of a case into features that can be used for classifying the case. For example, the name of a patient can be ignored when making a diagnosis, his precise age may be translated into an age class, and his precise body temperature may be translated into the finding "low fever." The process is about extracting classification relevant features from a concrete case description.

### Matching

Matching is the process of inferring potential explanation, diagnoses, or classifications from the extracted features. It matches the abstracted case description with abstract categories describing potential solutions.

### Refinement

Refinement is the process of inferring a final diagnosis explaining the given findings. This pro-

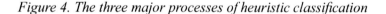

*Figure 4. The three major processes of heuristic classification*

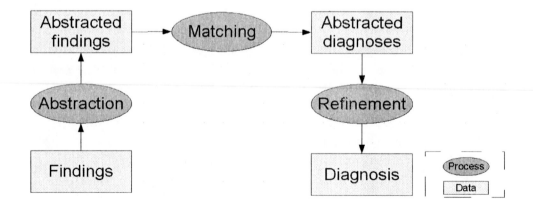

cess may include the acquisition of new features describing the given case. However, it is now the potential solution that guides the acquisition process of these features.

As the latest step indicates, the entire process can be executed in an iterative fashion. Instead of acquiring all potential findings an initial set can be used to derive intermediate potential explanation that can be further used to guide the next iteration of the process.

## Service Discovery

Now, what has this to do with Web service or service discovery? We strongly believe that a scalable and workable service discovery approach should follow the same pattern (see Figure 5).

### Abstracting Goals from User Desires

Users may describe their desires in a very individual and specific way that makes immediate mapping with service descriptions very complicated. Therefore, each service discovery attempt requires a process where user expectations are mapped on more generic goal descriptions.

Notice that this can be hidden by the fact that a discovery engine allows the user only to select from predefined goals. However, then it is simply the user who has to provide this mapping that is, who has to translate his specific requirements and expectations into more generic goal descriptions. This step can be called *goal discovery*, that is, the user or the discovery engine has to find a goal that describes (with different levels of accuracy) his requirements and desires. In the current literature on service and Web service discovery this step is mostly neglected.

An example of such a user desire would be to buy a train ticket from Innsbruck to Venice, on December 12, 2004, and leaving Innsbruck between 15:00 and 17:00. It can be seen that this is a very concrete and detailed desire, while goals typically are intended to be *generic and reusable*, for example, buy train tickets or buy train tickets in Europe. Therefore, a mapping from the user desire to generic goals becomes necessary.

In order to fully understand the difference between matching and refinement in the service discovery context we distinguish between services and Web services (cf. Preist, 2004) and, in consequence, between service and Web service

*Figure 5. The three major processes in service discovery*

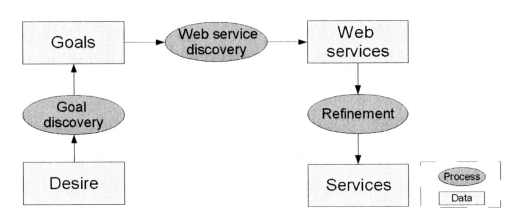

discovery. Let us take again a traveling scenario as a means to illustrate the difference. A customer may want to travel from Innsbruck to Venice and he is looking for a service that provides this to him. The service may be provided by an airline or a train company. This is the service he is looking for. In order to find (and buy) the service he is accessing a Web service, that is, a software artifact. This software artifact will not provide him the service to travel from Innsbruck to Venice (for this he needs a plane or a train) but it may help him to find this service. He will find a suitable Web service based on the semantic annotations of available Web services.

Actually, Web services are means to find (and buy) services, that is, they are to a large extent service discovery engines and a discovery engine should not try to replace or duplicate this functionality.[9] Using the previous traveling example, when somebody wants to travel from Innsbruck to Venice on a given date and with some time constraints, he looks for a Web service which is offering traveling services, based on the semantic annotations of the Web service, and then he consults the Web service to check whether this trip can be done by train or plane, on the given date, and with the given time constraints. Taking the analogy with databases as illustration, Web service discovery is about searching for databases that may contain instance data we are looking for, while service discovery is about finding the proper instance data by querying the discovered databases. The same analogy can be extended to consider services that imply some effects in the real world. Web service discovery is about searching for Web services that can be used to for example, buy tickets. service discovery is about checking whether the ticket sellers offering such Web services can really provide the concrete requested ticket.

Unfortunately, most approaches around service and Web service discovery neglect this distinction leading to nonpragmatically assumptions and nonworkable proposals for the discovery process,

for example, Li and Horrocks (2003). Assuming to find services based on the semantic annotation of Web services requires complete and correct meta descriptions of all the services offered by a Web service for example, a train ticket seller has to include in the Web service description information about all the available departures and destinations, on what dates and at what times, with what price, and so forth. This would imply that the semantic annotation and the discovery process duplicate most of the actual service of the Web service. It is no longer necessary to execute a Web service to find a service, rather the semantic annotation and the related reasoning provide this support.

We do not think that complete and correct descriptions of all the services offered by a Web service are a realistic assumption; it would make Web services no longer necessary (at least for the discovery process); and we wonder whether logical reasoning would scale under this conditions where the execution of an efficient program accessed via the Web service is simulated by reasoning over its semantic annotation.

Alternatively one could assume to directly query the Web service during the Web service discovery process. However, this may lead to network and server overload and it makes a very strong assumption: in addition to data mediation, protocol and process mediation for the Web service must be in place before the discovery process even starts. We do not think that this is a realistic assumption in the general case as we will further discuss in a later section. In consequence we think it is essential to distinguish between Web service and service discovery for coming up with a workable approach that scales and makes realistic assumptions in a pragmatic environment.

## Web Service Discovery

Web service discovery is based on matching abstracted goal descriptions with semantic annotations of Web services. This discovery process can only happen on an ontological level, that is, it can only rely on conceptual and (widely) reusable elements. For this, two processes are required: (a) the concrete user input has to be generalized to more abstract goal descriptions, and (b) concrete services and their descriptions have to be abstracted to the classes of services a Web service can provide. We believe that this twofold abstraction is essential for lifting Web service discovery on an ontological level that is the prerequisite for a scalable and workable solution for it. In the following sections, different approaches to Web service discovery will be discussed in more detail.

## Service Discovery

Service discovery is based on the usage of Web services for discovering actual services. Web service technology provides automated interfaces to the information provided by software artifacts that is needed to find, select, and eventually buy a real-world service or simply find the piece of information somebody is looking for. service discovery requires strong mediation and wrapping, since the specific needs of a choreography of a Web service have to be met in order to interoperate with it. Notice that automation of service discovery defines significant higher requirements on mediation than Web service discovery, as it also requires protocol and process mediation. In a sense, the role of Web service discovery can be compared with the role of an internet search engine like GOOGLE,[10] and service discovery with the process of extracting the actual information from the retrieved Web sites.

## Relation between Discovery and Mediation

In a distributed environment, different users and Web services can use different terminologies, which leads to the need for mediation in order to allow heterogeneous parties to communicate.

In this section we analyze the relation between discovery and mediation, identifying what kind of mediation is required in different scenarios.

## Assumptions on Mediation

One could assume that Web services and goals are described by the same terminology. Then no data mediation problem exists during the discovery process. However, it is unlikely that a potentially huge number of distributed and autonomous parties will agree beforehand in a common terminology.

Alternatively, one could assume that goals and Web services are described by completely independent vocabularies. Although this case might happen in a real setting, discovery would be impossible to achieve. In consequence, only an intermediate approach can lead to a scenario where neither unrealistic assumptions nor complete failure of discovery has to occur. Such an scenario relies in three main assumptions:

- Goals and Web services most likely use different vocabularies, or in other words, we do not restrict our approach to the case where both need to use the same vocabulary.
- Goals and Web services use controlled vocabularies or ontologies to describe requested and provided services.
- There is some mediation service in place. Given the previous assumption, we can optimistically assume that a mapping has already been established between the used terminologies, not to facilitate our specific discovery problem but rather to support the general information exchange process between these terminologies.

Under these assumptions, we do not simply neglect the mapping problem by assuming that it does not exist and, at the same time, we do not simply declare discovery as a failure. We rather look for the minimal assumed mediation support that is a pre-requisite for successful discovery.

Notice that this has also been the approach taken in IBROW (cf. Benjamins, Plaza, Motta, Fensel, Studer, Wielinga, Schreiber, Zdrahal, & Decker, 1998), a project in the area of internet-based matchmaking of task descriptions and competence definitions of problem-solving methods. Both tasks and methods used different ontologies to describe their requests and services. However, both description ontologies were grounded in a common basic ontology that allowed theorem proving to rewrite the terms until equality could be proven.

## WEB SERVICE DISCOVERY

In this section, we discuss different approaches to Web service discovery in the WSMO framework which require different effort in annotation and description of both goals and services and deliver discovery results of different accuracy. Each approach addresses a different level of abstraction in Web service descriptions as discussed in the Section *Conceptual Model for service Discovery*. Our interest in this document is primarily on semantic-based approaches to Web service discovery. We believe that the different techniques altogether help to create a workable solution to the problem of Web service discovery which addresses practical requirements and is based on realistic assumptions; our final goal here is thus ensure that the WSMO framework and a respective discovery component is adequate for a wide range of application scenarios with rather different requirements.

### Keyword-Based Discovery

The keyword-based discovery is a basic ingredient in a complete framework for Semantic Web service discovery. By performing a keyword-based search the huge amount of available services can be fil-

tered or ranked rather quickly. The focus of WSMO Web service discovery is not in keyword-based discovery but we consider this kind of discovery a useful technique in a complete Semantic Web service discovery framework.

In a typical keyword-based scenario a keyword-based query engine is used to discover Web services. A query, which is basically a list of keywords, is provided as input to the query engine. The query engine match the keywords from to query against the keywords used to describe the Web service. A query with the same meaning can be formulated by using a synonyms dictionary, like WordNet[11] (Fellbaum, 1998). The meaning of the query remains "the same" but because of the different keywords used, synonyms of previous ones, more services that possible fulfill user request are found. Moreover, by using dictionaries like WordNet as well as natural language processing techniques an increase of the semantic relevance of search results (wrt. to the search request) can principally be achieved (Richardson & Smeaton, 1995); nonetheless, such techniques are inherently restricted by the ambiguities of natural language and the lack of semantic understanding of natural language descriptions by algorithmic systems.

Web service descriptions on this level at least consist of a dedicated list of keywords for categorization and indexing. Furthermore, they additionally could include richer, semantic-based elements.

### Discovery Based on Simple Semantic Descriptions

Although keyword-based search is a widely used technique for information retrieval, it does not use explicit, well-defined semantics. The keywords used to retrieve relevant information do not have an explicit formalization and, therefore, do not allow inferencing to improve the search results.

For these reasons, as a second approach we consider the use of controlled vocabularies with explicit, formal semantics. Ontologies, which offer a formal, explicit specification of a shared conceptualization of some problem domain (Gruber, 1993), are excellent and prominent conceptual means for this purpose. They provide an explicit and shared terminology, explicate interdependencies between single concepts and thus are well-suited for the description of Web services and requester goals. Moreover, Ontologies can be formalized in logics which enables the use of inference services for exploiting knowledge about the problem domain during matchmaking and discovery.

In this section, we discuss the description of Web services on the intermediary level of abstraction, where they are understood as sets of (unstructured) elements (that are called services), that is, as concepts from an ontological perspective. A capability of an abstract service on this level of abstraction is a description which does not depend on dynamic factors, that is, the current state of the world as well as the requester input needed by the provider. The capability describes only what an advertised abstract service $A$ can potentially deliver but not under which circumstances (that means preconditions) the single services $S \in A$ can be actually provided.

The presentation that we use here provides a formal yet comprehensive model of the description of service capabilities and goals. In particular, it is independent from specific knowledge representation languages such as logics. To achieve this, we chose a set-based approach for the description of abstract services and goals. How to ground this modeling and discovery approach eventually in some specific logic is demonstrated in (Keller et al., 2004).

## Abstracting from the Basic Formal Model

On the most detailed level of abstraction, a (concrete) service $S \in A$ corresponds to a state transformation on the state space $U$: when starting in a specific state $w \in U$ we end up in a state $w' \in U$ where the world has changed (some effects are observable) and some output has been provided to the user. Both effects $eff_S(w, i_1, ..., i_n)$ and outputs $out_S(w, i_1, ..., i_n)$ can be seen as sets of objects depending on the initial state $w$ and the input information $i_1, ..., i_n$ which has been provided to the service provider by the service requester in $w$. The circumstances under which a service $S$ can be delivered by the provider are represented by $w$ and $i_1, ..., i_n$. For example, the description of a concrete service provided by a European airline could be that a business-class flight is booked for the male passenger James Joyce on January 5th, 2005 from Dublin to Innsbruck, and 420 Euros are charged on a MasterCard with number #120127933.

If we abstract the description of an abstract service $A$ from the dependency of the contained concrete services on the provided inputs $i_1, ..., i_n$ and on the particular initial states $w \in dom(A(i_1, ..., i_n))$, the description will only specify which objects we can expect from the abstract service as effects $eff_A$ and as outputs $out_A$. For example, an abstract description of a European airline could state that the airline provides information about flights within Europe as well as reservations for these flights, but not what input has to be provided and how this input will determine the results of the service provision. In general, we expect completeness but not necessarily correctness of the abstract capability: every concrete service provided by an abstract service should be covered by the capability (on this intermediate level of abstraction), but there might be services which are models of capability but can actually not be delivered as part of the abstract service $A$ by the provider (since we abstract from the circumstances under which a service can be provided). More formally, we assume:

$$\bigcup_{i_1, ..., i_n} \bigcup_{w \in dom(A(i_1, ..., i_n))} eff_S(w, i_1, ..., i_n) \subseteq eff_A$$

and

$$\bigcup_{i_1,\ldots,i_n} \bigcup_{w \in dom(A(i_1,\ldots,i_n))} out_S(w,i_1,\ldots,i_n) \subseteq out_A$$

Abstracting further beyond the unions over sets for the single initial states $w$ and input values $i_1$, ..., $i_n$ might in particular be helpful for a provider to simplify the description of abstract capabilities further, since it allows to skip some details on specific constraints of the delivered objects. For instance an online book store like amazon.com could just advertise to sell any book, that is, use the concept "BookSale" to (incorrectly, but completely) specify its provided set of services. However, the more abstraction is used beyond these unions (e.g., the airline only specifies to provide tickets for flights all over the world), the less accurate the descriptions of what the service provider is actually able to provide become. Goals specify the desire of a client that he wants to have resolved after consuming a service. They describe the information the client wants to receive as output of the service as well as the effects on the state of the world that the client intends to achieve by using the service. This desire can be represented as sets of elements which are relevant to the client as the outputs and the effects of a service provision. According to the WSMO model (Lausen, Roman, & Keller, 2004), goals refer to the state which is desired to be reached by service execution.

According to this view, abstract services and goals are both represented as sets of objects during the Web service discovery step. The single descriptions of these sets refer to ontologies that capture general knowledge about the problem domains under consideration. Hence, the objects described in some abstract service description and the objects used in some goal description can or might be interrelated in some way by ontologies. Eventually, such interrelation is needed to establish a match between goals and services.

This way, abstract service and goal descriptions become largely decoupled and modelers have reasonable flexibility when describing Web services and goals. In particular, they do not have to know in detail about how the corresponding matching elements (i.e., services or goals) have precisely been described to actually ensure that a match can formally be established between compatible goals and Web services but instead they only refer to domain ontologies which are not specific to a particular goal or a particular Web service. Ontologies and ontology mediation provide a reasonable framework for decoupling of Web service and goal descriptions as well as a flexible semantic-based matching which are considered as major desiderata for matching engines in Paolucci et al. (2002).

An important observation[12] in our approach is that the description of a set of objects for representing a goal or a capability can be interpreted in different ways and, thus, the description by means of a set is not semantically unique: A modeler might want to express that either all of the elements that are contained in the set are requested (goal) or can be delivered (abstract capability), or that only some of these elements are requested (or can be delivered). For this reason, a modeler has to explicitly specify his intention when describing the set of relevant objects for a goal or abstract capability. This intention will strongly affect if we consider two descriptions to match. Therefore, goals as well as abstract capabilities are pairs $D = (R_D, I_D)$ where $R_D$ is the set of objects which are considered as relevant for the description (e.g. a specific set of flights in the travel scenario) and $I_D \in \{\forall,\exists\}$ is the respective (universal or existential) intention.

**Example.** Consider the following goal and Web service:

- **G:** I want to know about some flights from Innsbruck (Austria) to some place in Ireland (the client does not necessarily care which one).
- **W:** offers information about all flights for any place in Europe to any place in Europe.

*Table 1.*

| Goal / WS | Set $R$ of relevant Objects | Intention of $R$ |
|---|---|---|
| $G$ | {$f$\|$f$ is a flight starting at Innsbruck in Austria and ending at any city $c$ located in Ireland} | Existential ($\exists$) |
| $W$ | {$f$\|$f$ is a flight starting at city $s$ and ending at city $e$, $s$ any city in Europe, $e$ any city in Europe} | Universal ($\forall$) |

For the set-based specification, we refer to an appropriate set of ontologies for geographical data and traveling are in place. Hence, we can use the following definitions for the set of relevant objects as well as the respective intentions(see Table 1).

For the sake of simplicity, we will consider in the following only outputs of a service and do not treat effects explicitly. The separation of effects and outputs is conceptual and effects can be dealt with in the very same way. Nonetheless, it is useful to distinguish both since they are conceptually different and we believe that it is beneficial for users to have the ability to apply different criteria for matching outputs and effects in a service discovery request. Augmenting the model discussed here accordingly is a straightforward endeavor.

## Semantic Matching

In order to consider a goal $G$ and an abstract service $A$ to match on a semantic level, the sets $R_G$ and $R_A$ describing these elements have to be interrelated; precisely spoken, we expect that some set-theoretic relationship between $R_G$ and $R_A$ exists. The most basic set-theoretic relationships that might be considered are the following: $R_G = R_A$, $R_G \subseteq R_A$, $R_G \supseteq R_A$, $R_G \cap R_A \neq \emptyset$, $R_G \cap R_A = \emptyset$.

These set-theoretic relationships provide the basic means for formalizing our intuitive understanding of a match between goals and abstract services. For this reason, they have been considered to some extent already in the literature, for instance, in Li and Horrocks (2003) or Paolucci et al. (2002), in the context of Description Log-ics-based service matchmaking.

On the other hand, we have to keep in mind that in our model these sets only capture part of the semantics of goal and service descriptions $D$, namely the relevant objects for the service requester or service provider. The intentions of these sets in the semantic descriptions $D$ is not considered but clearly affects whether a certain existing set-theoretic relationship between $R_G$ and $R_A$ is considered to actually correspond to (or formalize) our intuitive understanding of a match in the real-world. Therefore, we have to consider the intentions of the respective sets as well. Figure 6 gives an overview of the single set-theoretical relations as well as their interpretation[13] as matches when considering the request and provider intentions. In the table we distinguish several forms of matches: A match (Match) means that $A$ completely satisfies $G$, a partial match (ParMatch) means that $A$ partially satisfies $G$ and additional abstract services would be required to completely satisfy the request, a possible match (PossMatch) means that there might be an actual match given a more detailed description (at service discovery time, when actually interacting with the Web service) of the abstract service, a possible partial match (PossParMatch) means that there might be a partial match given more detailed description (at service discovery time when interacting with the provider) of the abstract service or a non-match (NoMatch). Due to space restrictions, we only briefly discuss some entries from the table. A detailed discussion can be found in Keller et al. (2004) (Figure 6).

*Figure 6. Interaction between set-theoretic criteria, intentions and our intuitive understanding of matching*

| Intention of $\mathcal{G}/\mathcal{A}$ | $I_A = \forall$ | | $I_A = \exists$ | |
|---|---|---|---|---|
| $I_G = \forall$ | $R_G = R_A$ | Match | $R_G = R_A$ | PossMatch |
| | $R_G \subseteq R_A$ | Match | $R_G \subseteq R_A$ | PossMatch |
| | $R_G \supseteq R_A$ | ParMatch | $R_G \supseteq R_A$ | ParMatch |
| | $R_G \cap R_A \neq \emptyset$ | ParMatch | $R_G \cap R_A \neq \emptyset$ | PossParMatch |
| | $R_G \cap R_A = \emptyset$ | No Match | $R_G \cap R_A = \emptyset$ | NoMatch |
| $I_G = \exists$ | $R_G = R_A$ | Match | $R_G = R_A$ | Match |
| | $R_G \subseteq R_A$ | Match | $R_G \subseteq R_A$ | PossMatch |
| | $R_G \supseteq R_A$ | Match | $R_G \supseteq R_A$ | Match |
| | $R_G \cap R_A \neq \emptyset$ | Match | $R_G \cap R_A \neq \emptyset$ | PossMatch |
| | $R_G \cap R_A = \emptyset$ | No Match | $R_G \cap R_A = \emptyset$ | NoMatch |

*Table 2.*

| Goal / WS | Set *R* of relevant Objects | Intention of *R* |
|---|---|---|
| G | {*f*|*f* is a flight starting at Innsbruck in Austria and ending at any city *c* located in Ireland} | Existential ($\exists$) |
| W | {*f*|*f* is a flight starting at city *s* and ending at city *e*, *s* any city in Europe, *e* any city in Europe} | Universal ($\forall$) |

Match $-I_G = \forall$, $I_A = \forall$, $R_G \in R_A$:

The requester wants to get all the objects specified as relevant ($I_G = \forall,$), whereas the provider claims that he is able to deliver all the objects specified in $R_A$ ($I_A = \forall$). In this case, the requester needs are fully covered by the abstract service since all the requested objects $R_G$ can be delivered by the abstract service according to its abstract capability $A$.

**Example.**

• **G:** I want to know about all flights from Innsbruck (Austria) to some place in Ireland (the client does not necessarily care which one).

• **W:** offers information about all flights from any place in Europe to any place in Europe (see Table 2).

ParMatch $-I_G = \forall$, $I_A = \forall$, $R_G \cap R_A \neq \emptyset$:

The requester wants to get all the objects that he has specified as relevant, whereas the provider claims that the abstract service is able to deliver all the objects specified in $R_A$. However, the two sets of reference objects do only overlap. In this case, the requester needs cannot be fully satisfied by the abstract service. At best, the service can contribute to resolve the desire of the client. Thus, we consider this case as a partial match.

**Example.**

*Table 3.*

| Goal / WS | Set *R* of relevant Objects | Intention of *R* |
|---|---|---|
| *G* | {*f*\|*f* is a flight starting at Innsbruck in Austria and ending at any city *c* located in any country of the world} | Existential (∃) |
| *W* | {*f*\|*f* is a flight starting at city *s* and ending at city *e*, *s* any city in Europe, *e* any city in Europe} | Universal (∀) |

*Table 4.*

| Goal / WS | Set *R* of relevant Objects | Intention of *R* |
|---|---|---|
| *G* | {*f*\|*f* is a flight starting at Innsbruck in Austria and ending at any city *c* located in Ireland} | Universal (∀) |
| *W* | {*f*\|*f* is a flight starting at city *s* and ending at city *e*, *s* any city in Europe, *e* any city in Europe} | Existential (∃) |

- **G:** I want to know about all flights from Innsbruck (Austria) to some place in the world (the client does not necessarily care which one).
- **W:** offers information about all flights from any place in Europe to any place in Europe (see Table 3).

PossMatch – $I_G = \forall$, $I_A = \exists$, $R_G \subseteq R_A$:

The requester wants to get all the objects that he has specified as relevant, whereas the provider claims he is only able to deliver some of the objects specified in $R_A$. Finally, the set of relevant objects to the service requester is a subset of the set of reference objects advertised by the service provider. In this case, we cannot determine from the given descriptions whether there is a match or not, since we don't know which (non-empty) subset of $R_A$ the provider actually can deliver. However, it might turn out when examining a more detailed description (or interacting with the provider at service discovery time) that there is a match. Such detailed description is considered during service discovery. Hence, we consider this as a possible match.

**Example.**

- **G:** I want to know about all flights from Innsbruck (Austria) to some place in Ireland (the client does not necessarily care which one).
- **W:** offers information about some flights from any place in Europe to any place in Europe (see Table 4).

PossParMatch – $I_G = \forall$, $I_A = \exists$, $R_G \cap R_A \neq \varnothing$:

The requester wants to get all the objects that he has specified as relevant, whereas the provider claims that the abstract service is able to deliver only some of the objects specified in $R_A$. Additionally, the two sets of reference objects do only overlap (and this is the strongest applicable set-theoretic relation between $R_G$ and $R_A$). In this case, the requester needs cannot be fully satisfied by the abstract service, but at best only partially. However, we cannot determine from the given descriptions whether there is such a partial match or not, since we don't know which (non-empty) subset of $R_A$ the provider actually can deliver. When examining a more detailed description (or

*Table 5.*

| Goal / WS | Set *R* of relevant Objects | Intention of *R* |
|---|---|---|
| *G* | {*f*\|*f* is a flight starting at Innsbruck in Austria and ending at any city *c* located in any country of the world} | Universal (∀) |
| *W* | {*f*\|*f* is a flight starting at city *s* and ending at city *e*, *s* any city in Europe, *e* any city in Europe} | Existential (∃) |

*Table 6.*

| Goal / WS | Set *R* of relevant Objects | Intention of *R* |
|---|---|---|
| *G* | {*f*\|*f* is a flight starting at Innsbruck in Austria and ending at any city *c* located in any country of the world} | Existential (∃) |
| *W* | {*f*\|*f* is a train connection starting at city *s* and ending at city *e*, *s* any city in Europe, *e* any city in Europe} | Universal (∀) |

interacting with the provider at service discovery time) it might turn out that there is a partial match. Such detailed description is considered during service discovery. Hence, we consider this as a possible partial match.

**Example.**

- **G:** I want to know about all flights from Innsbruck (Austria) to some place in the world (the client does not necessarily care which one).
- **W:** offers information about all flights from any place in Europe to any place in Europe (see Table 5).

NoMatch – $I_G = ∃$, $I_A = ∀$, $R_G ∩ R_A ≠ ∅$:

The requester wants to get some of the objects that he has specified as relevant, whereas the provider claims that the abstract service is able to deliver all the objects specified in $R_A$. However, the two sets of reference objects have no common elements. In this case, the requester needs clearly cannot be satisfied by the abstract service and we consider this case as a non-match.

**Example.**

- **G:** I want to know about some flights from Innsbruck (Austria) to some place in the world (the client does not necessarily care which one).
- **W:** offers information about all train connections from any place in Europe to any place in Europe (see Table 6).

## Further Discussion of the Set-Theoretic Criteria

As shown in Figure 6, we basically have for each pair of intentions for a goal and a Web service several formal criteria that capture actual matches, partial matches as well as non-matches. The question arises whether this is needed or what we gain from distinguishing the single notions. In case that indeed such a distinction is not useful or needed, we have to find out which of the several candidate criteria is the "right" one. In this paragraph we want to investigate and answer this question.

According to most elementary set theory the single criteria we considered above are not completely separated, but the following interdependencies hold:

For any descriptions $R_G, R_W \subseteq U$:

$R_G = R_W \Rightarrow R_G \subseteq R_W$

$R_G = R_W \Rightarrow R_G \supseteq R_W$

$R_G \subseteq R_W, R_G \neq \varnothing \Rightarrow R_G \cap R_W \neq \varnothing$

$R_G \supseteq R_W, R_W \neq \varnothing \Rightarrow R_G \cap R_W \neq \varnothing$

$R_G \cap R_W = \varnothing, R_W \neq \varnothing, R_G \neq \varnothing \Rightarrow R_G \not\subseteq R_W, R_W \not\subseteq$

$R_G, R_W \neq R_G$

That means that certain formal set-theoretic criteria that we consider here are logically stronger notions than others: if the stronger relationship holds than the weaker relationship must holds as well. Using these properties, we can partially order the set-theoretic criteria: $C_1 \leq C_2$ iff $C_2$ is logically weaker (or equivalent) than $C_1$, that is:

$$(R_G = R_W) \leq (R_G \subseteq R_W), (R_G \subseteq R_W) \leq (R_G \cap R_W \neq \varnothing)$$

This partial order actually represents a lattice structure. Given two particular intentions for a goal and a service description, let be $C_1$ a criterion which captures an actual match wrt. the given intentions and $C_2$ be a logically weaker criterion (i.e. $C_1 \leq C_2$), then $C_2$ denotes a match as well. Clearly, there is always a weakest criterion which denotes an actual match (wrt. $\leq$), if there is a criterion which denotes an actual match at all. But the weakest criterion for an actual match (wrt. given intentions $I_G$ and $I_W$) does not have to be the only criterion denoting an actual match.

Thus, if $C_1 \leq C_2$ and $C_2$ denotes a match, $C_1$ represents more semantic information about the match than $C_2$, in other words it provides additional knowledge about the specific kind of relationship between matching goal and Web service descriptions (besides mere matching in the sense of $C_2$). If a specific criterion $C_1$ is used during the matching phase which is not the weakest criterion for an actual match and a match can be detected, then additional properties on the kind of interrelation besides the mere fact that there match.

By requesting the use of a particular criterion for the matching between goal and Web service descriptions, a service requester basically could exploit this property during a discovery process in order to ensure certain convenient properties from the discovered Web services. We will investigate this aspect briefly:

- The Intersection-Criterion ($\boldsymbol{R_G} \cap \boldsymbol{R_W} \neq \varnothing$)

reflects no special additional information for the search request (beyond what is given in the goal description $R_G$ and its corresponding intention $I_G$). In particular, in case that this criterion denotes an actual match (wrt. the given intentions) there is no weaker criterion which denotes a match as well.

- The Subsumes-Criterion ($\boldsymbol{R_G} \subseteq \boldsymbol{R_W}$)

reflects the additional property that only relevant elements will be delivered. This holds regardless of the intention which applies to a Web service description. Thus, if the user insists on getting only Web services which do not deliver items that are not of interest for resolving his goal then he should request explicitly that for matching a criterion is used which represents an actual match and is $\leq$-smaller than the Subsumes-match.

- The Plugin-Criterion ($\boldsymbol{R_G} \supseteq \boldsymbol{R_W}$)

on the other hand reflects the additional property that all relevant elements can be delivered by an abstract service (in case of universal intention of a Web service Description) or (in case of an existential intention a lot weaker) that all elements that are relevant for the requester are relevant for the service as well. There might be objects which are relevant for the Web service description but not for the service requestor.

If the service request has existential intention then obviously this property is not interesting for the requester, since otherwise he would have chosen a universal intention. In the case of a universal intention of the service request, this property is automatically guaranteed, since the weakest criterion for an actual match is the Plugin-Match.

Hence, it does not make any sense for the user to use this criterion for detecting matches if a weaker criterion (wrt. given intentions) applies as well.

- Finally, the Identity-Criterion ($R_G = R_W$)

precisely combines the Subsumes- and the Plugin-criterion and thus specifies that objects the Web service description refers to and the objects the requester refers to precisely match; In particular, it holds (independent of the intention of the Web service description) that irrelevant objects will not be delivered by the Web service. For the property that is represented by the Plugin-Match part, the same argument as for the Plugin-Match holds. Hence, the corresponding semantic property is irrelevant and the Exact-Match basically coincides (in the context of our discussion in this paragraph) with the Subsumes match.

To sum up, we have seen that there are cases where a client could benefit from exploiting the additional semantics captured by matching criteria that are stronger (i.e., $\leq$-smaller) than the weakest (i.e., $\leq$-maximal) criterion which represents an actual match. Hence, it makes sense to not only allow the use of the weakest (i.e., $\leq$-maximal) criterion that actually denotes a match (for the respective intentions of the goal and the Web service) to be applied for matching but to allow the user to manually "raise" the semantic requirements that are captured by the criterion to apply and thus to reflect his interest faithfully.

We have seen as well that in our general framework there is only one such additional property that actually can be considered as useful, namely the property of a Web service to not deliver objects that are irrelevant to the user.

In order to ensure that this property is satisfied when matching, the discovery component has to apply a $\leq$-maximal criterion, which is $\leq$-smaller than the Subsumes criterion $R_G \supseteq R_W$ (that means either $R_G \supseteq R_W$ itself or $R_G = R_W$) and represents an actual match (wrt. the given intentions of the goal and the Web service).

In case that the requester does not want to have this specific property reflected in the discovery result, the appropriate criterion to apply for matching clearly is one which is $\leq$-maximal among the criteria that represent an actual match, since it is the weakest that formalizes our intuition understanding of a real-world match and thus does not restrict the set of possible matches unnecessarily.

Basically the same holds if we want to check whether a Web service partially matches, possibly matches or possibly partially matches a given goal: we have to apply the criterion which is $\leq$-maximal among the criteria that represent a partial match.

Finally, for detecting nonmatches we simply check for matches, partial or possible matches. If neither criterions is satisfied, we have established a nonmatch.

Figure 7 represents the result of the discussion in case that the requester just gives a goal description, whereas Figure 8 describes the situation when additionally the requester wants to avoid Web services that might deliver irrelevant objects.

## Discovery Scenario

During the discovery process the scenario for matching between goal and Web service descriptions in general can be considered as follows: A requester specifies his goal by means of a set of relevant objects and the respective intention. Moreover, he might additionally specify that he is interested in Web services which deliver objects that are relevant for his goal only (and such raise the semantic requirement for matches). Furthermore, the requester can indicate in his request whether

*Figure 7. Which formal criteria should be used for checking different degrees of matching?*

| Intention of $G/A$ | | $I_w = \forall$ | | $I_w = \exists$ | |
|---|---|---|---|---|---|
| $I_G = \forall$ | Match | $R_G \subseteq R_W$ | Match | — | |
| | ParMatch | $R_G \cap R_W \neq \emptyset$ | ParMatch | $R_G \supseteq R_W$ | |
| | PossMatch | — | PossMatch | $R_G \subseteq R_W$ | |
| | PossParMatch | — | PossParMatch | $R_G \cap R_W \neq \emptyset$ | |
| | No Match | $R_G \cap R_W = \emptyset$ | No Match | $R_G \cap R_W = \emptyset$ | |
| $I_G = \exists$ | Match | $R_G \cap R_W \neq \emptyset$ | Match | $R_G \supseteq R_W$ | |
| | ParMatch | — | ParMatch | — | |
| | PossMatch | — | PossMatch | $R_G \cap R_W \neq \emptyset$ | |
| | PossParMatch | — | PossParMatch | — | |
| | No Match | $R_G \cap R_W = \emptyset$ | No Match | $R_G \cap R_W = \emptyset$ | |

he is interested in partial matches, in case that no actual matches can be detected. A similar option can be used for possible matches.

If the discovery request of the client contains only a goal description $(R_G, I_G)$ (without the requirement on returning relevant objects only), then we check for a match using the respective criterion for matching under intentions $(I_G, I_w)$ from Figure 7. In case of a detected match, we store the Web service in a list with actual matches. On the other hand, if a match has not been detected and the discovery request indicates that the user is interested in partial matches, we check for a partial match using the corresponding criterion from the same table. If a partial match has been detected we store the Web service in a list with partial matches. Similarly, we proceed for possible and possible partial matches. Eventually, we return the list of actual matches and (if the request indicates that) the lists of partial, possible and possible partial matches.

If the discovery request of the client specifies besides $(R_G, I_G)$ that only Web services are requested that deliver relevant objects only, then proceed in the very same way, but apply the criterions with respect to Figure 8 instead.

The discussion shows that during discovery and matching intentions can be dealt with on a meta-level (in comparison to the set-theoretic notions), that is, they do not directly affect single set-theoretic criterions and the respective checks themselves, but rather their interpretation as some sort of match. Hence, we just need an implementation of the different set-theoretic criteria in order to realize a system for matchmaking.

## Discussion

The proposed modeling approach is based on set theory and ontologies for capturing domain knowledge. By abstracting from dynamic aspects of abstract services, we provide static and general abstract capability descriptions. All the information necessary for checking a match is already available when abstract service descriptions are published, and no interaction with any of the involved parties (requester and provider) is needed for this discovery step. On the other hand, the accuracy we can achieve when is limited. Hence, this discovery step based on such simple descriptions allows an efficient identification of candidate abstract services, but does not guarantee that a

*Figure 8. Which formal criteria should be used for checking different degrees of matching when a requester insists on services delivering relevant objects only?*

| Intention of $G/A$ | $I_w = \forall$ | | $I_w = \exists$ | |
|---|---|---|---|---|
| $I_g = \forall$ | Match | $R_g = R_w$ | Match | — |
| | ParMatch | $R_g \supseteq R_w$ | ParMatch | $R_g \supseteq R_w$ |
| | PossMatch | --- | PossMatch | $R_g = R_w$ |
| | PossParMatch | — | PossParMatch | $R_g \cap R_w \neq \emptyset$ |
| | No Match | $R_g \not\supseteq R_w$ | No Match | $R_g \cap R_w = \emptyset$ |
| $I_g = \exists$ | Match | $R_g \supseteq R_w$ | Match | $R_g = R_w$ |
| | ParMatch | — | ParMatch | — |
| | PossMatch | — | PossMatch | — |
| | PossParMatch | — | PossParMatch | — |
| | No Match | $R_g \not\supseteq R_w$ | No Match | $R_g \neq R_w$ |

matched abstract service will deliver a concrete service fulfilling the requester goal. Abstraction can be used as a means to simplify the description of abstract services by the provider. The overall model is simple, comprehensive and can be implemented in a logical framework (Keller et al., 2004). However, the model itself is not based on a specific logical language. The concept of intentions in set-based capability and goal descriptions has not been considered in the literature so far and gives the modeler additional freedom in modeling. Eventually, the use of a set-based model for abstract capabilities can enable the use of Description Logics for classifying and efficiently discovering abstract services to be considered for service discovery. This idea is further elaborated in Lara, Binder, Constantinescu, Fensel, Keller, Pan, et. al. (2004).

## Discovery Based on Detailed Semantic Descriptions

Using simple semantic annotations for a service as it described in the previous section basically adds machine-processable semantic information to service descriptions which allows a discovery mechanism to exploit this semantics during the discovery process and deliver results with high precision and recall.

Nonetheless, the kind of semantic information that can be expressed in that approach is limited wrt. the details of the service characteristics that can be captured. Therefore, the precision that can be achieved by a discovery component is limited as well, if the user could already state more detailed information in the discovery request (and wants to do so). For certain applications and users, in particular, if you aim at a high-degree of automation in a dynamic service-based software system, definitely an approach is needed which allows to model nuances of meaning of the functionality of Web services and the goal that a client wants to have resolved.

An elaborate description of the single main entities which are involved in the discovery process, namely service capabilities and goals, can be achieved by refining the pure conceptual level (where services and goals are basically concepts) as described before. This requires at least a rich modeling language which allows to talk about objects in a world and hence variables, constant symbols and perhaps function symbols. That means, on this level we definitely want to use a First-order language (or possibly some restricted subset of such a language).

However, this is not enough. At this level of description we are interested to describe how outputs and effects created by a service execution actually depend on the concrete input provided by the user when invoking a Web service. That means to consider an abstract service as a relation on an abstract state-space and to capture the functionality provided by a service in these terms. Here, we would consider for services input, output, preconditions, assumptions, postconditions and effects of an abstract service, whereas for goals we consider the state of the world that is reached after the execution of a Web service and hence postconditions and effects.

In this section we show how to extend the set-based modeling to capture the actual relation implemented by the service as well. That means, we skip the abstraction step that we have decided to take in the previous section and consider service executions explicitly. Thus, we increase the level of detail of our service model.

## The Informal Service Model Revisited

According to our discussion in the beginning of this chapter, a Web service can be seen as computational object which can be invoked by a client. At invocation time, the client provides all the information needed by the Web service to identify and deliver the concrete service that has been requested. The resulting execution of the Web service generates (wrt. a set of input values) certain information as an output and achieves certain effects on the state of the world. An output and an effect can be considered as objects which can be embedded in some domain ontology.

So far we ignored inputs and their relations to outputs and effects of the Web service execution and considered a Web service as delivering a single

set of objects. In fact, when considering actual executions of a Web service, the sets describing the outputs and effects of the execution actually depend on the provided input values. Hence, a Web service execution can be described by a set of outputs and a set of effects (for the specific values for input parameters), whereas a Web service is seen as a collection of possible executions and thus should be modeled by a collection of sets of outputs and effects: one pair of such sets for each service execution (or concrete values for the input parameters of the Web service).

When invoking a Web service $ws$ with some specific input values $i_1, ..., i_n$ in some state of the world (pre-state), the execution of the service results in a (different) state of the world (post-state) where the service delivers a set of elements as its output ($ws^{out}(i_1, ..., i_n)$) as well as a set of effects ($ws^{eff}(i_1, ..., i_n)$).

In the WSMO framework the client specifies his desire as a goal. More precisely, the goal description consists of the specification of a set of desired information ($goal^{out}$) as well as a set of desired effects ($goal^{eff}$).

As before, matching mainly is based on checking certain set-theoretic relationships between the sets related to the output ($ws^{out}(i_1, ..., i_n)$ and $goal^{out}$) as well as the sets related to effects ($ws^{eff}(i_1, ..., i_n)$ and $goal^{eff}$). The interpretation of the various relationships between those sets has already been discussed. Intentions for goal and Web service descriptions are independent of the discussion here, and thus can be dealt with in the very same way as in our model for simple semantic annotations. Since intentions do not affect the logical representation of our set-theoretic relationship and are basically during matching considered on a metalevel on top of the set-theoretic criteria, we do not explain them explicitly here again.

Additionally, we can enrich our set of matching notions given in the previous section by an orthogonal dimension[14]: We can express that we can satisfy a particular matching notion wrt. a single execution of a Web service as well as wrt.

an arbitrary number of Web service executions. This results in additional matching notions that capture additional semantics in a given discovery request.

We want to illustrate the difference of the two new option by means of a simple example:

Imagine the following goal a user:

*I want to know about all sports events in Tyrol today*

and a Web service with the following capability

*The service delivers all events for a given city in Austria for today.*

Given appropriate domain knowledge about Austria and events the service can not deliver the requested information by a single execution of the Web service, but instead it can actually deliver all requested information, if it is invoked several times (i.e., for each city in the region "Tyrol").

As the examples shows, there might be situations, where such relaxed notions of matching actually can be useful for a user. Thus, we will discuss them here as well.

In the following paragraphs we will show how to formalize the extended Web service model and discuss how to extend the matching notions to cover service executions. For the sake of simplicity, we will only mention one set of objects in the descriptions of goals and services. Handling the set of outputs and effects separately can be achieved in the very same way.

## Adapting the Formal Matching Notions

Since we adapted the way we describe Web services, we have to adapt the formal criteria for our matching criteria as well. In the following we will show how to adapt the single notions ($\equiv, \subseteq, \supseteq, \cap$) accordingly and give a definition for the case in which we only consider single executions as well as the case of considering multiple executions.

This way, in principle we end up with (almost) eight different notions of matching which potentially could be used by a client to specify his desire in a service request.

- Exact-Match ($W \equiv^{1} G$, $W \equiv^{+} G$).

If we consider Exact-match under the assumption that the Web service is executed only once, we have to formalize the following statement: there are input values $i_{1}, ..., i_{n}$ such that the sets of objects $R_{W}(i_{1}, ..., i_{n})$ that the Web service claims to deliver[15] when being invoked with input values $i_{1}, ..., i_{n}$ coincides with the set $R_{G}$ of objects which are relevant for the requester. In this case we write $W \equiv^{1} G$ to indicate this particular kind of match.

If we instead want to consider multiple executions we use the following condition: For each object $x$ it holds that $x$ can be delivered by Web service execution on some input values $i_{1}, ..., i_{n}$ iff $x$ is relevant for the client. In this case we write $W \equiv+ G$ to indicate this particular kind of match.

- Subsumes-Match ($W \subseteq^{1} G$, $W \subseteq^{+} G$).

If we consider Subsumes-match under the assumption that the Web service is executed only once, we have to formalize the following statement: there are input values $i_{1}, ..., i_{n}$ such that the sets of objects $R_{W}(i_{1}, ..., i_{n})$ that the Web service claims to deliver when being invoked with input values $i_{1}, ..., i_{n}$ is a subset of the set $R_{G}$ of objects which are relevant for the requester. In this case we write $W \subseteq^{1} G$ to indicate this particular kind of match.

If we instead want to consider multiple executions we would have formalize the following statement: For each object $x$ in the universe it holds that if $x$ can be delivered by Web service execution on some input values $i_{1}, ..., i_{n}$ then $x$ is relevant for the client. In this case we write $W \subseteq^{+} G$ to indicate this particular kind of match.

- Plugin-Match ($W \supseteq^{1} G$, $W \supseteq^{+} G$).

If we consider Plugin-match under the assumption that the Web service is executed only once, we have to formalize the following statement: there are input values $i_1, ..., i_n$ such that the sets of objects $R_W(i_1, ..., i_n)$ that the Web service claims to deliver when being invoked with input values $i_1, ..., i_n$ is a superset of the set of objects $R_G$ which are relevant for the requester. In this case we write $W \supseteq^1 G$ to indicate this particular kind of match.

If we instead want to consider multiple executions we would have formalize the following statement: For each object $x$ in the universe it holds that $x$ can be delivered by Web service execution on some input values $i_1, ..., i_n$ if $x$ is relevant for the client. In this case we write $W \supseteq^+ G$ to indicate this particular kind of match.

- Intersection-Match($W \cap^1 G$, $W \cap^+ G$).

If we consider Intersection-match under the assumption that the Web service is executed only once, we have to formalize the following statement: there are input values $i_1, ..., i_n$ such that the sets of objects $R_W(i_1, ..., i_n)$ that the Web service claims to deliver when being invoked with input values $i_1, ..., i_n$ has a common element with the set of objects $R_G$ which are relevant for the requester. In this case we write $W \cap^1 G$ to indicate this particular kind of match.

If we instead want to consider multiple executions we would have formalize the following statement: There is an object $x$ in the universe such that $x$ that can be delivered by Web service execution on some input values $i_1, ..., i_n$ and $x$ is relevant for the client. In this case we write $W \cap^+ G$ to indicate this particular kind of match.

Obviously, the both criteria $\cap^1$ and $\cap^+$ are logically equivalent and thus are the very same criteria. Thus, we do not have to distinguish between the two cases.

## Relation of the Extended Model to the Simple One

To conclude the discussion of the multiple notions we want to mention the following: The multiple execution notions actually check a set-theoretic relationship between the goal and the union of the sets of delivered objects over all possible (valid) inputs. Indeed, this can be considered as some sort of abstraction from concrete executions of a Web service when checking a match and thus is very close to what we have discussed previously. The main difference is there we do not consider explicit input parameters of a Web service and do not refer to valid inputs only (i.e. refer explicitly to a precondition). Hence, we can consider the matching notions of this type as special cases of the ones discussed previously.

## RELATED WORK

By defining a mathematical model for Web services, goals and the notion of matchmaking we provide a basis for applications like Semantic Web service repositories and discovery engines. Work in this area has previously leveraged a different (less detailed) formal view on the concept of a Web service: Web services there have been formally mostly considered as sets of objects (describing input, outputs). On a description (language) these sets allow for a natural representation by means of concept expressions in Description Logics. Matching then has been reduced to standard reasoning tasks in the language (Li & Horrocks, 2003; Paolucci et al., 2002), however the dynamics associated with a detailed (state-based) perspective on Web services, can not be represented in such a setting.

Until recently, it seemed to be a common practice in the Semantic Web Community when considering semantic descriptions of Web service, to strictly focus on languages (e.g., Description

Logics) rather than an adequate (language-independent) mathematical model of the objects of investigation that underlies such descriptions. The latter question is conceptually interesting and compatible with various concrete representation languages. We consider it as feature and not a drawback to be able to not make commitments on the language levels, but to leave this to the concrete needs of particular implementations.

In the area of software specification, functional descriptions (i.e., the detailed state based perspective) are a well studied phenomena. Hoare (1969) introduced the approach describing a component by its pre- and postconditions. Numerous systems have been developed since then (Jones, 1990; Meyer, 1992; Spivey, 1992) that follow the same line of description. They have commonalities with the detailed state based perspective of our framework. However our framework is different in two dimensions: (1) we do not fix the underlying language and therefore address the current situation in the Semantic Web with various different languages used in various formalisms, and (2) we explicitly take the existence of background knowledge (represented by some Ontology) and the notion of side effect in the real world modeled into account.

Furthermore there exist several formalisms to specify dynamics such as Transaction Logic (Bonner & Kifer, 1998) or Situation Calculus (McCarthy, 1963), which also can be used as a model for specification and discovery, however compared to those rather generic approaches we take a minimal approach with respect to the Web service domain, that is, we only define those aspects in our model that are essential to our domain and do not make unnecessary assumptions on the formalism used. For example, Transaction Logics present a minimal approach in the sense that it allows describing constraints over any number of states, but does not have specific means for relevant phenomena like input bindings. On the other hand, situation calculi require a certain encoding of states but

requires to keep the history of all intermediate states that appears to be too prescriptive in order to serve as a general model.

It is interesting to note, that recently there has been work in the Description Logic Community (Baader, Lutz, Milicic, Sattler, & Wolter, 2005a; Baader, Lutz, Milicic, Sattler, & Wolter, 2005b) which extends Description Logic with elements of the Situation Calculi (in a decidable manner) and can be seen as work that tries to move decidable languages (Description Logics) that typically can be used for describing Web service on the intermediate level of abstraction in our model a closer to the lowest level in this model.

## CONCLUSION

In this chapter we have presented a conceptual model for service discovery which avoids unrealistic assumptions and is suitable for a wide range of applications. One of the key features of this model is the explicit distinction between the notions of Web services and services. Moreover, the model does not neglect one of the core problems one has to face in order to make discovery work in a real-world setting, namely the heterogeneity of descriptions of requestors and providers and the required mediation between heterogeneous representations. As discussed in the conceptual model for service discovery, the discussed approaches are based on using terminologies, controlled vocabularies or rich descriptions which are based on ontologies. For each of them, a working solution to the mediation problem is possible or not unrealistic.

We have outlined various approaches on discovery of Web services with different requirements on the description of Web services and the discovery request itself. Our main focus has been on semantic-based approaches to Web service discovery.

For further details, we refer the interested reader to related documents of the WSMO and

WSML working groups (cf. http://www.wsmo.org/TR), in particular the documents (Keller et al., 2004) and (Lausen, 2005).

## ACKNOWLEDGMENTS

The work summarized in this chapter was carried out in the context of the WSMO and WSML working groups, and various academic projects. We want to express our special thanks to Michael Stollberg, Cristina Feier and Dumitru Roman for contributing to the first section. Numerous people have been involved in the discussions and in generating ideas. We especially would like to thank Axel Polleres (Universidad Rey Juan Carlos, University of Madrid, Spain) and Michael Kifer (State University of New York (SUNY) at Stony Brook, USA) for their continuous critique and advice. Finally, we would like to thank to all the members of the WSMO, WSML and WSMX working groups for their input and fruitful discussions about the work presented in this chapter.

The presented work has been funded by the European Commission under the projects DIP, Knowledge Web, InfraWebs, SEKT, SWWS, ASG and Esperonto; by Science Foundation Ireland under Grant No. SFI/02/CE1/I131 and the Austrian Federal Ministry for Transport, Innovation, and Technology under the project RW$^2$ (FIT-IT contract FFG 809250).

## REFERENCES

Akkiraju, R., Goodwin, R., Doshi, P., & Roeder, S. (2003). A method for semantically enhancing the service discovery capabilities of UDDI. In S. Kambhampati & C.A. Knoblock (Eds.), *Proceedings of the IJCAI-03 Workshop on Information Integration on the Web (IIWeb 03)* (pp. 87-92). Acapulco, Mexico.

Alonso, G., Casati, F., Kuno, H., & Machiraju, V. (2003). *Web services.* Springer.

Baader, F., Lutz, C., Milicic, M., Sattler, U., & Wolter, F. (2005a). A description logic based approach to reasoning about Web services. In *Proceedings of the WWW 2005 Workshop on Web Service Semantics (WSS2005),* Chiba City, Japan. Retrieved February 20, 2007, from http://citeseer.ist.psu.edu/735340.html

Baader, F., Lutz, C., Milicic, M., Sattler, U., & Wolter., F. (2005b). Integrating description logics and action formalisms: First results. In *Proceedings of the 20th National Conference on Artificial Intelligence (AAAI 05).* Retrieved February 20, 2007, from http://sunsite.informatik.rwth-aachen.de/Publications/CEUR-WS/Vol-147/

Barros, A., Dumas, M., & Oaks, P. (2005). Standards for Web service choreography and orchestration: Status and perspectives. In *Proceedings of the 1st International Workshop on Web Service Choreography and Orchestration for Business Process Management at the BPM 2005* (pp. 61-74). Nancy, France.

Benatallah, B., Hacid, M.-S., Rey, C., & Toumani, F. (2003). Request rewriting-based Web service discovery. In *Proceedings of the Semantic Web - ISWC 2003* (pp. 242-257).

Benjamins, V.R., Plaza, E., Motta, E., Fensel, D., Studer, R., Wielinga, B., Schreiber, G., Zdrahal, Z., & Decker, S. (1998). Ibrow3: An intelligent brokering service for knowledge-component reuse on the World-Wide Web. In *Proceedings of the 11th Banff Knowledge Acquisition for Knowledge-Based System Workshop (KAW98),* Banff, Canada. Retrieved February 20, 2007, from http://ksi.cpsc.ucalgary.co/KAW/KAW98/KAW98Proc.html

Boerger, E. & Staerk, R. (2003). *Abstract state machines. A method for high-level system design and analysis.* Springer.

Bonner, A. & Kifer, M. (1998). A logic for programming database transactions. In J. Chomicki & G. Saake (Eds.), *Logics for databases and information systems* (Chapter 5, pp. 17-66). Kluwer Academic Publishers.

Clancey, W.J. (1985). Heuristic classification. *Artificial Intelligence, 27*(3), 289-350.

de Bruijn, J. (2005). The WSML specification. Working draft, Digital Enterprise Research Insitute (DERI). Retrieved October 25, 2006, from http://www.wsmo.org/TR/d16/

Fellbaum, C. (Ed.). (1998). *WordNet: An electronic lexical database.* MIT Press.

Fensel, D. (2003). Ontologies: Silver bullet for knowledge management and electronic commerce (2nd ed.). Berlin: Springer-Verlag.

Fensel, D. & Bussler, C. (2002). The Web service modeling framework (WSMF). *Electronic Commerce Research and Applications, 1*(2), 113-137.

Gonzlez-Castillo, J., Trastour, D., & Bartolini, C. (2001). Description logics for matchmaking of services. In *Proceedings of the KI-2001 Workshop on Applications of Description Logics.*

Gruber, T.R. (1993). A translation approach to portable ontology specification. *Knowledge Acquisition, 5*(2), 199-220.

Hoare, C.A.R. (1969). An axiomatic basis for computer programming. *Communications of the ACM, 12*(10), 576-580.

Jones, C.B. (1990). *Systematic software development using VDM.* Upper Saddle River, NJ: Prentice Hall.

Keller, U., Lara, R., & Polleres, A. (2004). WSMO Web service discovery. Deliverable D5.1, WSMO Working Group. Retrieved October 25, 2006, from http://www.wsmo.org/TR/d5/d5.1/

Lara, R., Binder, W., Constantinescu, I., Fensel, D.,

Keller, U., Pan, J., Pistore, M., Polleres, A., Toma, I., Traverso, P., & Zaremba, M. (2004). *Semantics for Web service discovery and composition* (Tech. Rep.). Knowledge Web.

Lausen, H. (2005). Functional description of Web services. Deliverable D28.1, WSMO Working Group. Retrieved October 25, 2006, from http://www.wsmo.org/TR/d28/d28.1/

Lausen, H., Roman, D., & Keller, U. (Eds.). (2004). Web service modeling ontology -standard (WSMO-Standard), version 1.0. Working draft, WSMO Working Group. Retrieved October 25, 2006, from http://www.wsmo.org/2004/d2/v1.0/

Li, L. & Horrocks, I. (2003). A software framework for matchmaking based on semantic web technology. In *Proceedings of the 12th International Conference on the World Wide Web,* Budapest, Hungary.

McCarthy, J. (1963). *Situations, actions and causal laws* (Tech. Rep.). Stanford University.

Meyer, B. (1992). *Eiffel: The language.* Prentice Hall PTR.

Paolucci, M., Kawamura, T., Payne, T., & Sycara, K. (2002). Semantic matching of Web services capabilities. In *Proceeding of the First International Semantic Web Conference (ISWC2002),* Sardinia, Italy.

Preist, C. (2004). A conceptual architecture for Semantic Web services. In *Proceedings of the International Semantic Web Conference 2004 (ISWC 2004).*

Richardson, R. & Smeaton, A.F. (1995). Using wordNet in a knowledge-based approach to information retrieval (Tech. Rep. No. CA-0395). Dublin, Ireland.

Roman, D., Lausen, H., & Keller, U. (2005). Web service modeling ontology (WSMO). Deliverable D2, final version v1.2. Retrieved October 25, 2006, from http://www.wsmo.org/TR/d2/

Spivey, J. (1992). *The Z notation, a reference manual* (2nd ed.). Prentice Hall International.

Staab, S. & Studer, R. (Eds.). (2004). *Handbook on ontologies in information systems* (International Handbooks on Information Systems). Springer.

Sycara, K., Widoff, S., Klusch, M., & Lu, J. (2002). Larks: Dynamic matchmaking among heterogeneous software agents in cyberspace. In *Proceedings of Autonomous Agents and Multi-Agent Systems* (pp. 173–203).

The OWL Services Coalition (2004). OWL-S 1.1, beta release. Retrieved October 25, 2006, from http://www.daml.org/services/owl-s/1.1B/

Verma, K., Sivashanmugam, K., Sheth, A., & Patil, A. (2004). Meteor-s wsdi: A scalable p2p infrastructure of registries for semantic publication and discovery of Web services. *Journal of Information Technology and Management, 6*(1) 17-39.

Wiederhold, G. (1994). Mediators in the architecture of the future information systems. *Computer, 25*(3), 38-49.

Zein, O. & Kermarrec, Y. (2004). An approach for describing/discovering services and for adapting them to the needs of users in distributed systems. In *Proceedings of the AAAI Spring Symposium on Semantic Web Services.*

## ENDNOTES

[1] WSMO is a working group of the European Semantic Systems Initiative, a joint initiative of European research and development efforts around the Semantic Web and Web services (http://www.essi-cluster.org). All specifications and related information are available at the website of the WSMO working group at http://www.wsmo.org.

[2] WSML (Web Service Modeling Language) is a formal language that implements the WSMO ontology in a particular representation language with formal semantics. In particular, WSML can be used to describe ontologies and supports various widely-used knowledge representation principles in a single family of languages: Description Logic-based, Rule-based, Object-oriented as well First-order-based Modelling.

[3] Before the appearance of WSMO Working Group

[4] For instance, the almost religious use of OWL ontology language (as well as underlying Description Logics) despite any consideration of adequacy of the language for the purpose.

[5] For our purposes, it is not really relevant what a state actually is. It is only relevant, what kind of information we can attach to (and read off) a specific state and that it represents the world at some moment in time. For instance, this could be a interpretation of a non-logical signature in the context of some logic. It can be more than this as well. For instance, see Lausen (2005) for some discussion.

[6] eClass is a standardized classification system for product groups and product properties that is commonly used in Germany. See http://www.eclass.de/ for further information.

[7] Following the principle of a "good-enough" answer

[8] In Omelayenko and Fensel (2001) we already used heuristic classification as a model for improving the translation process between different XML schema dialects.

[9] Spoken more precisely, Web Services are the interface to a software artifact that may help to find and buy services (cf. Preist, 2004), however, we neglect this distinction here and try the Web Service interface and the accessed software artifact identically.

10   http://www.google.com

11   The WordNet homepage: http://www.cogsci.
princeton.edu/wn/

12   Again, this observation has not been made
by the Semantic Web community before,
because of a strict language focus.

13   Please note, that when assigning the intuitive
notions we assume that the listed set-theoretic properties between $R_G$ and $R_A$ are the
strongest ones that actually hold between
$R_G$ and $R_A$.

14   This dimension precisely corresponds to the
feature that we added when refining service
model from previous section: we can now
talk about Web service executions instead
of a single abstract Web service concept.

15   Of course, this depends on the respective
intention used in the Web service description.

# Chapter XIII
# Semantic Search Engines
# Based on Data Integration Systems

**Domenico Beneventano**
*Università degli Studi di Modena e Reggio Emilia, Italy*

**Sonia Bergamaschi**
*Università degli Studi di Modena e Reggio Emilia, Italy*

## ABSTRACT

*As the use of the World Wide Web has become increasingly widespread, the business of commercial search engines has become a vital and lucrative part of the Web. Search engines are common place tools for virtually every user of the Internet; and companies, such as Google and Yahoo!, have become household names. Semantic search engines try to augment and improve traditional Web Search Engines by using not just words, but concepts and logical relationships. In this chapter a relevant class of semantic search engines, based on a peer-to-peer, data integration mediator-based architecture is described. The architectural and functional features are presented with respect to two projects, SEWASIE and WISDOM, involving the authors. The methodology to create a two level ontology and query processing in the SEWASIE project are fully described.*

## INTRODUCTION

Commercial search engines are mainly based upon human-directed search. The human directed search engine technology utilizes a database of keyword, concepts, and references. The keyword searches are used to rank pages, but this simplistic method often leads to voluminous irrelevant and spurious results. Google with its 400 million hits per day, and over 4 billion indexed Web pages, is undeniably the most popular commercial search engine used today, but even with Google, there are problems. For example, how can you find just the right bit of data that you need out of the ocean of irrelevant results provided? A well-know problem is that traditional Web search engines use keywords that are subject to the two well-known linguistic phenomena that strongly degrade a query's precision and recall:

- Polysemy (one word might have several meanings) and
- Synonymy (several words or phrases, might designate the same concept).

Precision and recall are classical information retrieval evaluation metrics. Precision is the fraction of a search output that is relevant for a particular query, that is, is the ratio of the number of relevant Web pages retrieved to the total number of irrelevant and relevant Web pages retrieved. The recall is the ability system to obtain all or most of the relevant pages, that is, is the ratio of the number of relevant Web pages retrieved to the total number of relevant pages in the Web.

As Artificial Intelligence (AI) technologies become more powerful, it is reasonable to ask for better search capabilities which can truly respond to detailed requests. This is the intent of semantic-based search engines and agents. A semantic search engine seeks to find documents that have similar concepts not just similar words. In order for the Web to become a semantic network, it must provide more meaningful meta-data about its content, through the use of Resource Description Framework (RDF) (www.w3.org/RDF/) and Web Ontology Language (OWL) (www.w3.org/2004/OWL/) tags which will help to form the Web into a semantic network. In a semantic network, the meaning of content is better represented and logical connections are formed between related information.

Semantic search methods augment and improve traditional search results by using not just words, but concepts and logical relationships (Alesso, 2002; Boley, 2002).

Several systems have been built based on the idea of annotating Web pages with Resource De-

scription Framework (RDF) and Web Ontology Language (OWL) tags to represent semantics (see Related Work). However, the limitation of these systems is that they can only process Web pages that are already manually annotated with semantic tags and it seems unfeasible to annotate the enormous amount of Web pages. Furthermore, most semantic-based search engines suffer performance problems because of the scale of the very large semantic network. In order for the semantic search to be effective in finding responsive results, the network must contain a great deal of relevant information. At the same time, a large network creates difficulties in processing the many possible paths to a relevant solution.

The requirements for an intelligent search engine are given by a special class of users, small and medium-sized enterprises (SMEs) which are threatened by globalization. One of the keys to sustainability and success is being able to access information. This could be a cheaper supplier, an innovative working method, a new market, potential clients, partners, sponsors, and so on. Current Internet search tools are inadequate because even if they are not difficult to use, the search results are often of little use with their pages and pages of hits. Suppose an SME needs to find out about a topic -a product, a supplier, a fashion trend, a standard, and so forth. For example, a search is made for fabric dyeing processes for the purpose of finding out about the disposal of the dyeing waste material. A query to www.google.com for fabric dyeing listed 44.600 hits at the time of writing, which related not only manufacturers of fabric dyeing equipment, but also the history of dyeing, the dyeing technology, and so on. Eventually, a useful contact may be found, and the search can continue for relevant laws and standards concerning waste disposal. But is it law or the interpretation of the law? What if the laws are of a different country where the practices and terminologies are different? Thus, intelligent tools to support the business of SMEs in the Internet age are necessary.

We believe that *data integration systems, domain ontologies* and *peer-to-peer architectures* are good ingredients for developing Semantic Search Engines with good performance. In the following, we will provide empirical evidence for our hypothesis. More precisely, we will describe two projects, SEWASIE and WISDOM, which rely on these architectural features and developed key semantic search functionalities. They both exploit the MOMIS (Mediator EnvirOnment for Multiple Information Sources) data integration system (Beneventano, Bergamaschi, Guerra, & Vincini, 2003; Bergamaschi, Castano, Vincini, & Beneventano, 2001).

## Data Integration Systems

Data integration is the problem of combining data residing at different autonomous sources, and providing the user with a unified view of these data. The problem of designing Data Integration Systems is important in current real world applications, and is characterized by a number of issues that are interesting from a theoretical point of view (Lenzerini, 2002).

Integration Systems are usually characterized by a classical wrapper/mediator architecture (Wiederhold, 1993) based on a Global Virtual Schema (*Global Virtual View - GVV*) and a set of data sources. The data sources contain the real data, while the *GVV* provides a reconciled, integrated, and virtual view of the underlying sources. Modeling the mappings among sources and the *GVV* is a crucial aspect. Two basic approaches for specifying the mapping in a Data Integration System have been proposed in the literature: *Local-As-View* (*LAV*), and *Global-As-View* (*GAV*), respectively (Halevy, 2001; Ullman, 1997).

The LAV approach is based on the idea that the content of each source should be characterized in terms of a view over the *GVV*. This idea is effective only whenever the data integration system is based on a *GVV* that is stable and well-established in the organization; this constitutes the main limitation of the LAV approach; another negative issue is the complexity of query processing which needs reasoning techniques. On the other hand, as a positive aspect, the LAV approach favours the extensibility of the system: adding a new source simply means enriching the mapping with a new assertion, without other changes.

The GAV approach is based on the idea that the content of each class of the *GVV* should be characterized in terms of a view over the sources. GAV favours the system in carrying out query processing, because it tells the system how to use the sources to retrieve data (unfolding). However, extending the system with a new source is now more difficult: the new source may indeed have an impact on the definition of various classes of the *GVV*, whose associated views need to be redefined.

MOMIS is a Data Integration System which performs information extraction and integration from both structured and semi-structured data sources. An object-oriented language, with an underlying Description Logic, called $ODL_{I3}$ (Bergamaschi et al., 2001), is introduced for information extraction. Information integration is then performed in a semi-automatic way, by exploiting the knowledge in a Common Thesaurus (defined by the framework) and $ODL_{I3}$ descriptions of source schemas with a combination of clustering techniques and Description Logics. This integration process gives rise to a virtual integrated view of the underlying sources for which mapping rules and integrity constraints are specified to handle heterogeneity. Given a set of data sources related to a domain it is thus possible to synthesize a *basic domain ontology* (the *GVV*). MOMIS is based on a conventional wrapper/mediator architecture, and provides methods and open tools for data management in Internet-based information systems. MOMIS follows a GAV approach where the *GVV* and the mappings among the local sources and the *GVV* are defined in a semi-automatic way. We faced the problem of extending the *GVV* after the insertion of a new source in a semi-automatic way. In Beneventano et al. (2003), we proposed a method to extend a *GVV*, avoiding starting from scratch the integration process.

## Schema Based Peer-to-Peer Networks

A new class of P2P networks, so called schema based P2P networks have emerged recently (Aberer, Cudrè-Mauroux, & Hauswirth, 2003; Bernstein, Giunchiglia, Kementsietsidis, Mylopoulos, Serafini, & Zaihrayeu, 2002; Halevy, Ives, Madhavan, Mork, Suciu, & Tatarinov, 2004; Löser, Siberski, Wolpers, & Nejdl, 2003b), combining approaches from P2P as well as from the data integration and semantic Web research areas. Such networks build upon peers that use metadata (ontologies) to describe their contents and semantic mappings among concepts of different peers' ontologies. In particular, in Peer Data Management Systems (PDMS) (Halevy et al., 2004) each node can be a data source, a mediator system, or both; a mediator node performs the semantic integration of a set of information sources to derive a global schema of the acquired information.

As stated in a recent survey (Androutsellis-Theotokis & Spinellis, 2004), the topic of semantic grouping and organization of content and information within P2P networks has attracted considerable research attention lately (Castano, Ferrara, Montanelli, Pagani, & Rossi, 2003; Tempich, Harmelen, Broekstra, Ehrig, Sabou, Haase, Siebes, & Staab, 2003). In super-peer networks (Yang & Garcia-Molina, 2003), metadata for a small group of peers is centralized onto a single super-peer; a super-peer is a node that acts as a centralized server to a subset of clients. Clients submit queries to their super-peer and receive results from it; moreover, super-peers are also connected to each other, routing messages over this overlay network, and submitting and answering queries on behalf of their clients and themselves.

The semantic overlay clustering approach, based on partially-centralized (super-peer) networks (Löser, Naumann, Siberski, Nejdl, & Thaden, 2003a) aims at creating logical layers above the physical network topology, by matching semantic information provided by peers to clusters of nodes based on super-peers.

## The SEWASIE and WISDOM Projects

SEWASIE and WISDOM are Semantic Search Engines which follow a super-peer mediator-based approach and try to face and solve the problems of: *Ontology creation, semi-automatic annotation and efficient query processing.*

The first, SEWASIE (www.sewasie.org), rely on a two-level ontology architecture: the low level, called the peer level contains a mediator-based data integration system; the second one, called super-peer level integrates peers with semantically related content (i.e., related to the same domain). A novel approach for defining the ontology of the super-peer and querying the peer network is introduced. The search engine has been fully implemented in the SEWASIE project prototype exploiting agent technology, that is the individual components of the system are implemented as agents (Gong, 2001).

The second, WISDOM (www.dbgroup.unimo.it/wisdom/), is based on an overlay network of semantic peers: each contains a mediator-based data integration system. The cardinal idea of the project is to develop a framework that supports a flexible yet efficient integration of the semantic content. Key feature is a distributed architecture based on (1) the P2P paradigm and (2) the adoption of domain ontologies. By means of these ingredients the integration of information sources is separated in two levels: at the lower level a strong integration, which involves the information content of a bunch of sources to form a semantic peer; an ontology describes the (integrated) information offer of a semantic peer. At the upper level, a loose integration among the information offered by a set of semantic peers is provided; namely a network of peers is built by means of semantic mappings among the ontologies of a set of semantic peer. When a query is posed against one given semantic peer, it is suitably propagated towards other peers among the network of mappings.

The rest of the chapter is organized as follows. In section "The SEWASIE project" the architecture of a semantic search engines, SEWASIE, is described. In the Building the SEWASIE System Ontology section, a two-level data integration system and the methodology to build a two-level ontology are described. In the Querying the SEWASIE System section, we briefly introduce the query tool interface and fully describe the query reformulation techniques for the two-level data integration system. Moreover, the agent-based prototype for query processing implemented in the SEWASIE system is presented. In The Wisdom Project section, a semantic search engine which represents an architectural evolution of SEWASIE is described. A section on related work briefly synthesizes other research efforts. Conclusions and an Appendix on the ontology language of MOMIS, $ODL_{I3}$, conclude the chapter.

## THE SEWASIE PROJECT

SEWASIE (SEmantic Web and AgentS in Integrated Economies) implemented an advanced search engine that provides intelligent access to heterogeneous data sources on the Web via semantic enrichment to provide the basis of structured Web-based communication. The prototype provides users with a search client that has an easy-to-use query interface to define semantic queries. The query is executed by a sophisticated query engine that takes into account the semantic mappings between ontologies and data sources, and extracts the required information from heterogeneous sources. Finally, the result is visualized in a useful and user-friendly format, which allows identifying semantically related clusters in the documents found. From an architectural point of view, the prototype is based on agent technology, that is the individual components of the system are implemented as agents, which are distributed over the network and communicate with each other using a standardized agent protocol (FIPA).

## SEWASIE Architecture

Figure 1 gives an overview of the architecture of SEWASIE. A user is able to access the system through a central user interface where the user is provided with tools for query composition, for visualizing and monitoring query results, and for communicating with other business partners about search results, for example, in electronic negotiations. SEWASIE Information Nodes (*SINodes*) are mediator-based systems, providing a virtual view of the information sources managed within a SINode. The system may contain multiple SINodes, each integrating several data sources of an organization. Within a SINode, wrappers are used to extract the data and metadata (local schemas) from the sources. The Ontology Builder, based on the MOMIS framework, is a semi-automatic tool which creates a bootstrap domain ontology by extracting and integrating the local schemata of the sources into a *GVV*. The *GVV* is annotated w.r.t. a lexical ontology (Wordnet) (Miller, 1995). The annotated *GVV* and the mappings to the data source schemas are stored in a metadata repository (*SINode* ontology in Figure 1) and queries expressed in terms of the *GVV* can be processed by the Query Manager of a SINode.

Brokering agents (*BA*) integrate several *GVVs* from different SINodes into a *BA* Ontology, that is of central importance to the SEWASIE system. On the one hand, the user formulates the queries using this ontology. On the other hand, it is used to guide the Query Agents to select the useful SINodes to solve a query.

The SEWASIE network may have multiple *BAs*, each one representing a collection of SINodes

*Figure 1. SEWASIE architecture*

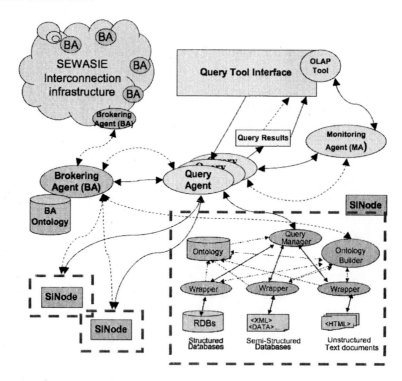

for a specific domain. Mappings between different *BAs* may be established. A Query Agent receives a query (expressed in terms of a specific *BA* Ontology) from the user interface, rewrites the query, in cooperation with the *BA*, in terms of the *GVVs* of the useful SINodes; sends the rewritten subqueries to the involved SINodes. The result integrates the answers of the subqueries of the SINodes and is stored in a result repository, so that it can be used by the various end-user components.

For example, Monitoring Agents can be used to store a query result in a permanent repository. The monitoring agent will then execute the query repeatedly, and compare the new results with previous results. The user will be notified if a document that fits his monitoring profile has changed. Furthermore, the Monitoring Agent can link multidimensional OLAP reports with ontology-based information by maintaining a mapping between OLAP models and ontologies. Finally, the Communication Tool provides the means for

ontology-based negotiations. It uses query results, the ontologies of the *BAs*, and specific negotiation ontologies as the basis for a negotiation about a business contract.

## BUILDING THE SEWASIE SYSTEM ONTOLOGY

We describe a two-level ontology architecture: the low level, called the *peer level* integrates data sources with semantically close content, the upper level, called *super-peer level* integrates peers with semantically close content. The architecture is shown in Figure 2:

- A *peer* (called *SINode*) contains a mediator-based data integration system, which integrates heterogeneous data sources into an *ontology* composed of: an annotated *GVV*,

*Figure 2. The brokering agent/SINodes architecture*

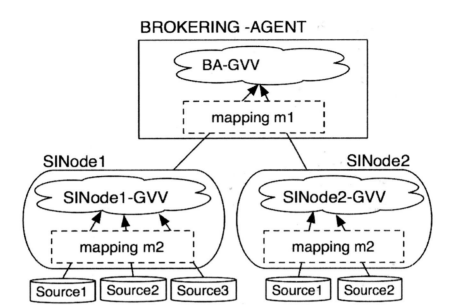

denoted by *SINode-GVV*, and *Mappings* to the data source schemas.

- A *super-peer* (called *BA -Brokering Agent*) contains a mediator-based data integration system, which integrates the *GVV* of its peers into an *ontology* composed of: an annotated *GVV*, denoted by *BA-GVV*, and Mappings to the *GVVs* of its SINodes.

The BA/SINodes architecture is realized with a two-level data integration system. From an organizational point of view, with a two-level architecture we have a greater flexibility as we can integrate both data sources and data integration systems, already developed in an independent way (on the basis, for example, of sectorial or regional objectives). From a theoretical point of view, our architecture based on two different levels of mappings (Figure 2) represents a nontraditional setting in data integration and an interesting case of mapping composition. In fact, Madhavan and Halevy (2003) show that, in general, the mapping from the sources to the *BA-GVV* is not simply the

composition of *m1* and *m2*; in our case *m1* and *m2* are GAV mappings and was proved that the mapping is indeed the composition of m1 and m2 (see section "Query Reformulation").

## A Two-Level Integration System

An integration system *IS = (GVV, N, M)* is constituted by:

- A *GVV*, which is a schema expressed in $ODL_{I3}$ (Bergamaschi et al., 2001); a short description of the $ODL_{I3}$ language is in APPENDIX I.
- A set *N* of *local sources*; each local source has a *schema* also expressed in $ODL_{I3}$.
- A set *M* of GAV mapping assertions between the *GVV* and *N*, where each assertion associates to an element *g* in *GVV* a query $Q_N$ over the schemas of a set of local sources in *N*.

More precisely, for each global class *C* of the *GVV* we define:

- A (possibly empty) set of local classes, denoted by $L(C)$, belonging to the local sources in $N$.
- A conjunctive query $Q_N$ over $L(C)$.

Intuitively, the *GVV* is the intensional representation of the information provided by the Integration System, whereas the mapping assertions specify how such an intensional representation relates to the local sources managed by the Integration System. The semantics of an Integration System, and then of the SEWASIE system, is defined in Beneventano and Lenzerini (2005) and Calì, Calvanese, Di Giacomo, and Lenzerini (2004).

SINodes and the BA are defined as integration systems:

- An *SINode* is an Integration System *SINode = (GVV, N, M)* where the local sources $N$ are *data sources*.
- A *BA* is an Integration System *BA = (GVV, N, M)* where the local sources *N* are SINodes, that is, $N = \{$ *SINodes1, SINodes2, . . . , SINodesn}*.

## Ontology Creation with MOMIS

The *GVV* and the mapping assertions (mappings for short) have to be defined at design time by the Ontology Designer. This is done by using the Ontology Builder graphical interface, built upon the MOMIS framework.

The methodology to build the ontology of a *SINode* and of a *BA* is similar; we describe, first, the methodology for an *SINode* and then discuss the differences for a *BA* ontology.

The methodology is composed of two steps:

1. **Ontology generation:** The system detects semantic similarities among the involved source schemas, automatically generates a *GVV* and the mappings among the *GVV* and the local schemata;

2. **Mapping refinement:** The Ontology Designer interactively refines and completes the automatic integration result; in particular, the mappings, which have been automatically created by the system can be fine tuned and the query associated to each global class defined.

## An Example in the Textile Domain

We show our methodology applied on the integration of five Web sites, three Italians and two Americans, that describe enterprises and products in the textile domain. The Comitato Network Subfornitura Italian Web site (www. subfor.net) allows the users to query an online database where detailed information on Italian enterprises and their products are available. The second Italian Web site (www.ingromarket.it) describes products and information about one of the major center for wholesales. The third Italian website is www.prontocomune.com.

The American Apparel Producers' Network Web site (www.usawear.org) gives information about products, goods and services related to the textile business. Finally, we analyze a Web portal (www.fibre2fashion.com) where garment, textile, fashion products are presented.

## Ontology Generation

The Ontology generation process can be outlined as follows (see Figure 3):

1. *Extraction of Local Source Schemata:*

Wrappers acquire schemas of the involved local sources and convert them into $ODL_{I3}$. Schema description of structured sources (e.g., relational database and object-oriented database) can be directly translated, while the extraction of schemata from semistructured sources need suitable techniques as described in (Abiteboul, Buneman, & Suciu, 2000). To perform information extraction

*Figure 3. The ontology generation process for an SINode*

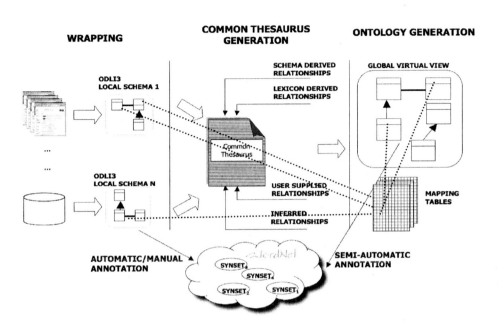

and integration from HTML pages (see paragraph *Automatic Data and Metadata Extraction* in The WISDOM Project section), research and commercial Web data extraction tools, such as ANDES (Myllymaki, 2002), Lixto (Baumgartner, Flesca, & Gottlob, 2001) and RoadRunner (Crescenzi, Mecca, & Merialdo, 2001), have been experimented and adopted.

## 2. *Local Source Annotation*:

Terms denoting schemas elements in data sources are semantically annotated. The Ontology Designer can manually choose the appropriate Wordnet meaning(s) for each term and/or perform an automatic annotation which associates to each term the *first meaning* of Wordnet.

## 3. *Common Thesaurus Generation*:

Starting from the annotated local schemata, MOMIS builds a Common Thesaurus that describes intra and inter-schema knowledge in the

form of: synonyms (*SYN*), broader terms/narrower terms (*BT/NT*), meronymy/holonymy (*RT*), equivalence (*SYNext*) and generalization (*BText*) relationships. The Common Thesaurus is incrementally built by adding *schema-derived relationships* (automatic extraction of intra schema relationships from each schema separately), *lexicon-derived relationships* (inter-schema lexical relationships derived by the annotated sources and Wordnet interaction), *designer-supplied relationships* (specific domain knowledge capture) and *inferred relationships* (via Description Logics equivalence and subsumption computation).

## 4. *GVV Generation*:

Starting from the Common Thesaurus and the local sources schemata, MOMIS generates a *GVV* consisting of a set of global classes, plus mappings to connect the global attributes of each global class with the local sources' attributes. Going into details, the *GVV* generation is a process where $ODL_{I3}$ classes describing the same or semantically related concepts in different sources are identified and clustered in the same global class. The Ontology Designer may interactively refine and complete the proposed integration results; in particular, the mappings which have been automatically created by the system can be fine tuned as discussed in the next section (Mapping Refinement).

5. *GVV Annotation*:

The *GVV* is semi-automatically annotated, that is each its element is associated to the meanings extracted from the annotated sources. *GVV* annotation will be exploited in the *BA* Ontology building process; moreover, the *GVV* annotation can be useful to make the domain ontology available to external users and applications (Beneventano et al., 2003).

## Mapping Refinement

The system automatically generates a *Mapping Table* (*MT*) for each global class *C* of a *GVV* , whose columns represent the local classes *L(C)* belonging to *C* and whose rows represent the global attributes of *C*. An element *MT [GA][LC]* represents the set of local attributes of *LC* which are mapped onto the global attribute *GA*. Figure

4 shows part of the *MT* of Enterprise that groups the classes *Company* of *usawear* and *Company* of *fibre2fashion*.

The query $Q_N$ associated to a global class *C* is implicitly defined by the Ontology Designer starting from the *MT* of *C*. The Ontology Designer can extend the *MT* by adding:

- *Data Conversion Functions* from local to global attributes
- *Join Conditions* among pairs of local classes belonging to *C*
- *Resolution Functions* for global attributes to solve data conflicts of local attribute values.

On the basis of the resulting *MT* the system automatically generates a query $Q_N$ associated to *C*, by extending the *Full Disjunction* operator (Galindo-Legaria, 1994) that has been recognized as providing a natural semantics for data merging queries (Rajaraman & Ullman, 1996).

## Data Conversion Functions

The Ontology Designer can define, for each not null element *MT[GA][L]*, a *Data Conversion Function*, denoted by *MTF[GA][L]*, which rep-

*Figure 4. Mapping table of enterprise*

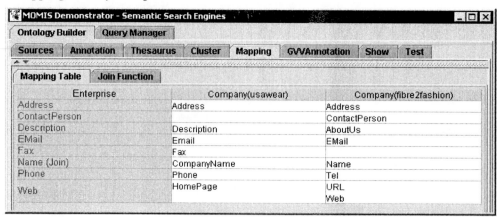

| Enterprise | Company(usawear) | Company(fibre2fashion) |
|---|---|---|
| Address | Address | Address |
| ContactPerson | | ContactPerson |
| Description | Description | AboutUs |
| EMail | Email | EMail |
| Fax | Fax | |
| Name (Join) | CompanyName | Name |
| Phone | Phone | Tel |
| Web | HomePage | URL |
| | | Web |

resents the mapping of local attributes of $L$ into the global attribute $GA$. $MTF[GA][L]$ is a function that must be *executable/supported* by the class $L$ local source. For example, for relational sources, $MTF[GA][L]$ is an SQL value expression. $T(L)$ denotes $L$ transformed by the *Data Conversion Functions*.

As an example, in Figure 4, the designer can define:

MTF[Web][ fibre2fashion.Company]: URL + Web

where '+' is the standard SQL operator for string concatenation.

## Join Conditions

Merging data from different sources requires different instantiations of the same real world object to be identified; this process is called *object identification* (Naumann & Haussler, 2002). The topic of *object identification* is currently a very active research area with significant contributions both from the artificial intelligence (Tejada, Knoblock, & Minton, 2001) and database communities (Ananthakrishna, Chaudhuri, & Ganti, 2002; Chaudhuri, Ganjam, Ganti, & Motwani, 2003).

To identify instances of the same object and fuse them we introduce *Join Conditions* among pairs of local classes belonging to the same global class. Given two local classes $L1$ and $L2$ belonging to $C$, a *Join Condition* between $L1$ and $L2$, denoted with $JC(L1,L2)$, is an expression over $L1.Ai$ and $L2.Aj$ where $Ai$ ($Aj$) are global attributes with a not null mapping in $L1$ ($L2$).

As an example, in Figure 4, the designer can define:

JC(L1, L2) : L1.CompanyName = L2. Name

where $L1=$ *usawear.Company* and $L2=fibre2fashion.Company$.

## Resolution Functions

The fusion of data coming from different sources taking into account the problem of inconsistent information among sources is a hot research topic (Bertossi & Chomicki, 2003; Di Giacomo, Lembo, Lenzerini, & Rosati, 2004; Greco, Greco, & Zumpano, 2003; Lin & Mendelzon, 1998; Naumann & Haussler, 2002). In MOMIS the approach proposed in Naumann and Haussler (2002) has been adopted: a *Resolution Function* for solving data conflicts may be defined for each global attribute mapping onto local attributes coming from more than one local source.

*Homogeneous Attributes* : If the designer knows that there are no data conflicts for a global attribute mapped onto more than one source (that is, the instances of the same real object in different local classes have the same value for this common attribute), he can define this attribute as an *Homogeneous Attribute*; this is the default in MOMIS. Of course, for homogeneous attributes resolution functions are not necessary. A global attribute mapped onto only one source is a particular case of an homogeneous attribute.

As an example, in *Enterprise* we defined all the global attributes as homogeneous attributes except for *Address* where we used a precedence function: *L1.Company.Address* has a higher precedence than *L2.Company.Address*.

## Full Disjunction

$Q_N$ is defined in such a way that it contains a unique tuple resulting from the merge of all the different tuples representing the same real world object. This problem is related to that of computing the natural outer-join of many relations in a way that preserves all possible connections among facts (Rajaraman & Ullman, 1996). Such a computation has been termed as *Full Disjunction* (FD) by Galindo Legaria (Galindo-Legaria, 1994).

In our context: given a global class $C$ composed of L1,L2, ..., Ln, we consider

FD(T (L1),T (L2),...,T (Ln)), computed on the basis of the *Join Conditions*.

The problem is how to compute *FD*. With two classes, *FD* corresponds to the full (outer) join: FD(T (L1),T (L2)) = T (L1) full join T (L2) on (JC(L1,L2)).

With more than 2 local classes, the computation of *FD* is performed as follows. We assume that: (1) each *L* contains a key, (2) all the *join conditions* are on key attributes, and (3) all the join attributes are mapped into the same set of global attribute, say *K*. Then, it can be proved that: (1) *K* is a key of *C*, and (2) *FD* can be computed by means of the following expression (called *FDExpr*):

```
(T(L1)   full   join   T(L2)   on   JC(L1,L2))
                fulljoinT(L3)on(JC(L1,L3)ORJC(L2,L3))
  . . .          full        join        T ( L n )
     on (JC(L1,Ln) OR JC(L2,Ln) OR ... OR JC(Ln-
     1,Ln))
```

Finally, $Q_N$ is obtained by applying Resolution Functions to the attributes resulting from *FDExpr*: for a global attribute *GA* we apply the related Resolution Function to *T (L1).GA, T (L2).GA, . . ., T (Lk).GA*; this query $Q_N$ is called *FDQuery*.

## The Brokering Agent Ontology

We suppose that the American Web sites have been integrated into *SINode1*; the obtained *GVV* (Figure 5a) contains three global classes. The Italian Web sites have been integrated into another SINode (SINode2); the obtained *GVV* (Figure 5.b) cont

A first version of the *BA* ontology is bootstrapped using the same techniques applied for an *SINode*. The *BA-GVV* generation process is performed starting step 3 (extraction and annotation of the local schemata has not to be done (see Figure 3)): in this case we integrate *SINode-GVVs* which are already annotated $ODL_{I3}$ schemata.

The *BA-GVV* has to be refined and enriched as it represents the interface of the *BA*: relationships with other *BAs* and other agents (see Figure 1) are built through the *BA* ontology; also, we foresee that users interact (i.e., query and browse information) with the system by means of the *BA* ontology. Therefore, a more sophisticated ontology design tool was developed, starting from the *i.com-tool* (Franconi & Ng, 2000); the tool provides the usual feature of ontology editors and, in addition, it is connected to a reasoner which enables consistency checks or the deduction of implicit relationships.

With references to our example, we can assume that the two *SINodes* of Figure 5 have been associated to the same *BA*, as they refer to the same domain ontology. The following semantic relationships:

*Figure 5.*

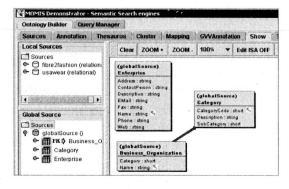

*(a) SINode1 GVV*

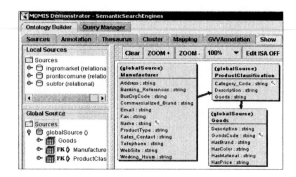

*(b) SINode2 GVV*

*Figure 6. The brokering agent ontology*

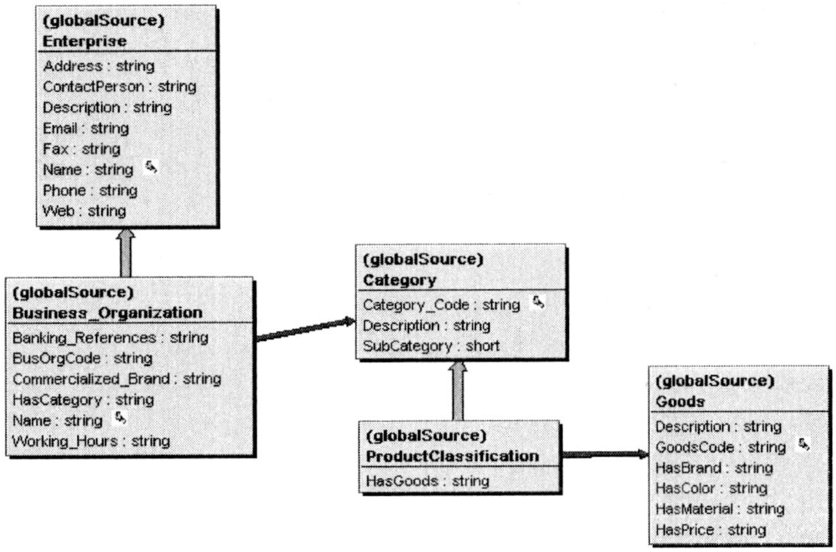

1. BusinessOrganization SYN Manufacturer
2. ProductClassification NT Category

are discovered by the system on the basis of the meanings stated in the annotated *SINode-GVVs*. The obtained *BA-GVV* contains five global classes: *Enterprise, BusinessOrganization (Manufacturer), Category, ProductClassification* and *Goods*. Then (see Figure 6) the Ontology Designer defines an *IS-A* relationship between *Enterprise* and *BusinessOrganization* and between *Category* and *ProductClassification*.

Finally, the translation of the *BA-GVV* into the Semantic Web standards for ontologies such as OWL, is a straightforward process (see Appendix I).

## QUERYING THE SEWASIE SYSTEM

In this section we briefly describe a query tool interface that supports the user in formulating a query; then, we define the query reformulation process for the two-level data integration system;

finally the agent-based prototype for query processing implemented in the SEWASIE system is briefly described.

## SEWASIE Query Interface

The SEWASIE Query Interface assists users in formulating queries. A query can be composed interactively by browsing the ontology in a tree-like structure and selecting relevant items for the query (Catarci, Dongilli, Mascio, Franconi, Santucci, & Tessaris, 2004). The query interface is intelligent as it contains an online reasoning functionality, that is, it allows only a combination of items which is consistent w.r.t. the ontology. The underpinning technologies and techniques enabling the query user interface are described in (Dongilli, Fillottrani, Franconi, & Tessaris, 2005).

### Query Formulation

Initially the user is presented with a choice of different query scenarios which provide a meaningful starting point for the query construction. The interface guides the user in the construction of a query by means of a diagrammatic interface, which enables the generation of precise and unambiguous query expressions.

The focus paradigm is central to the interface user experience: manipulation of the query is always restricted to a well defined, and visually delimited, subpart of the whole query (the focus). The compositional nature of the query language induces a natural navigation mechanism for moving the focus across the query expression (nodes of the corresponding tree). A constant feedback of the focus is provided on the interface by means of the kind of operations which are allowed. The system suggests only the operations which are compatible with the current query expression; that is, do not cause the query to be unsatisfiable. This is verified against the formal model (the ontology) describing the data sources.

The interface, accessible by any HTML browser, is shown in Figure 7; it is composed by three functional elements. The first one (top part) shows the tree structure of the query being composed, and the current focus. The second one is the query manipulation pane (bottom part) providing tools to specialise the query. The last one is a query result pane containing a table representing the result structure. The interface shows the user the meaning of the formulated query. This is performed in an automatic way by using the annotation of the ontology (*BA-GVV*), which associates classes and properties with a meaning expressed in a natural language fashion.

The query tool is built around the concept of classes and their properties, so we consider conjunctive queries composed by unary (classes) and binary (attribute and associations) terms.

For example, the following query composed with the query interface (see Figure 7)

Name, Address and Web address of the Enterprises having a category, a contact person and a Web address which ends with ".com" is translated into the following conjunctive query:

$$Q = \{ (X1, X2, X3) \mid \text{Enterprise}(X), \ \text{Name}(X, X1),$$
$$\text{Address}(X, X2), \ \text{Web}(X, X3), \ \text{Like}(X3, '*.com'),$$

*Figure 7. Query formulation interface*

```
ContactPerson(X,X4), EqualTo(X4,'yes'),
BusinessOrganization(X),HasCategory(X,X5),
Category(X5)}
```

where

- *Enterprise, BusinessOrganization* and *Category* are classes
- *Name, Address, Web, ContactPerson* and *HasCategory* are attributes
- *Like* and *EqualTo* are standard comparison predicates.

## Query Reformulation

Query reformulation takes into account the two different levels of mappings (Figure 2): in Calì et al. (2004) and Beneventano and Lenzerini (2005), it is proved that if *m1* and *m2* are GAV mappings, the mapping is indeed the composition of *m1* and *m2*; this implies that query answering can be carried out in terms of two reformulation steps: (1) Reformulation w.r.t. the BA Ontology and (2) Reformulation w.r.t. the SINode Ontology.

These two reformulation steps are similar and are:

1. **Query Expansion:** The query posed in terms of the *GVV* is expanded to take into account the explicit and implicit constraints: all constraints in the *GVV* are compiled in the expansion, so that the expanded query can be processed by ignoring constraints. Then, the atoms (i.e., subqueries referring to a single global class) are extracted from the expanded query.
2. **Query Unfolding**: The atoms in the expanded query are unfolded by taking into account the mappings *M* between the *GVV* and the local sources in *N*.

In the following, we show an example of query expansion (the algorithm for query expansion is reported in Calvanese, Di Giacomo, Lembo, Lenzerini, and Rosati (2004) and we discuss the unfolding process of an *atom* by taking into account the query $Q_N$ introduced before.

## Query Expansion Example

The output of the query expansion process is an expanded query (called *EXPQuery*) and its atoms (called *EXPAtoms*); *EXPQuery* is a union of conjunctive queries on the *GVV*; an *EXPAtom* is a *Single Class Query* on a Global Class of the *GVV*.

As an example, the query expansion process for the previous query Q, produces:

- EXPQuery = Q1 ∨ Q2

where *Q1 = Q* and

```
Q2={(X1,X2,X3)|
    Enterprise(X),Name(X,X1), Address(X,X2),
    Web(X,X3),   Like(X3,'*.com'),
    ContactPerson(X,X4), EqualTo(X4,'yes'),
    BusinessOrganization(X),HasCategory(X,X5),
    ProductClassification (X5)      }
```

that is, *Q2* takes into account the constraint *ProductClassification IS-A Category.*

- A set of *EXPAtoms*:

```
ExpAtom1 = { (X1,X2,X3) | Enterprise(X), Name(X,X1),
    Address(X,X2), Web(X,X3), Like(X3,'*.com'),Cont
    actPerson(X,X4), EqualTo(X4,'yes')}
ExpAtom2 = { X5 | BusinessOrganization(X),HasCateg
    ory(X,X5) }
ExpAtom3 = { X5 | ProductClassification (X5)}
```

## Query Unfolding

The query unfolding process is performed for each *EXPAtom* which is a *Single Global Query* Q over a global class C of the *GVV* (for sake of simplicity, we consider the query in an SQL-like format):

```
    Q = SELECT <Q_SELECT-list> from C where
<Q_condition>
```

where <Q_condition> is a Boolean expression of positive atomic constraints: (GA1 op value) or (GA1 op GA2), with GA1 and GA2 attributes of *C*. Let L1,L2, ... Ln *be* the *local* classes related to the *C*, that is, which are integrated into *C*.

Let us consider the SQL version of *Expatom1*:

```
S E L E C T    Name, Address, Web
    F R O M        Enterprise
    WHERE WEB LIKE '*.com' and ContactPerson
    = 'yes'
```

The (portion of) the Mapping Table of the class *Enterprise* involved in the query is:

| *Enterprise* | *SN1.Enterprise* | *SN2.Manufacturer* |
|---|---|---|
| *Name* | *Name* | *Name* |
| *Address* | *Address* | *Address* |
| *Web* | *Web* | *Website* |
| *ContactPerson* | *ContactPerson* | |

where

*   the Join Condition is *SN1.Enterprise. Name=SN2.Manufacturer.Name*
*   *Web* is an homogeneous attribute
*   *Address* is defined by a precedence function.

The query unfolding process is made up of the following three steps:

**Step 1)** Generation of Single Local Class Queries:

```
FDAtom = SELECT <SELECT-list> from L where <con-
    dition>
```

where *L* is a local class related to *C*.

The <SELECT-list> is computed by considering the union of:

*   the global attributes in <Q_SELECT-list> with a not null mapping in *L*,
*   the global attributes used to express the join conditions for *L*,
*   the global attributes in <Q_condition> with a not null mapping in *L*.

The set of global attributes is transformed in the corresponding set of local attributes on the basis of the Mapping Table.

The <condition> is computed by performing an *atomic constraint mapping*: each atomic constraint of <condition> is rewritten into one that is supported by the local source. The atomic constraint mapping is performed on the basis of the *Data Conversion Functions* and *Resolution Functions* defined in the Mapping Table. For example, if the numerical global attribute *GA* is mapped onto *L1* and *L2*, and we define *AVG* as resolution function, the constraint *(GA = value)* cannot be pushed at the local sources, because *AVG* has to be calculated at a global level. In this case, the constraint is mapped as true in both the local sources. On the other hand, if *GA* is an homogeneous attribute the constraint can be pushed at the local sources. For example, an atomic constraint *(GA op value)* is mapped onto the local class *L* as follows:

(MTF [GA][L] op value) if MT [GA][L] is not null and the *op* operator is supported into *L true*

**otherwise**

```
The set of FDAtoms for Expatom1 is:
FDAtom1: SELECT Name, Address, Web
FROM SN1.Enterprise
WHERE Web LIKE '*.com' AND ContactPerson = 'yes'

FDAtom2: SELECT Name, Address, Website
FROM SN2.Manufacturer
WHERE Website LIKE '*.com'
```

**Step 2)** Generation of FDQuery which computes the Full Disjunction of the FDAtoms:

In our example:

```
SELECT * FROM FDATOM1 full join FDATOM2
    on (FDATOM1.Name=FDATOM2.Name)
```

**Step 3)** Generation of the final query (application of *Resolution Functions*):

- for Homogeneous Attributes (e.g. *Web*) we can take one of the value (either FDATOM1. Web or FDATOM2.Website);
- for non Homogeneous Attributes (e.g. Address) we apply the associated Resolution Function (in this case the precedence function).

## An Agent-Based Prototype for Query Processing

We have just implemented in SEWASIE a "naive approach" of query processing in an agent-based prototype (see Figure 8).

The coordination of query processing is performed by the Query Agent, which accepts the query from the Query Tool Interface, interacts with a Brokering Agent and its underlying SINode Agents, and returns the result as a materialized view in the SEWASIE DB. Playmaker performs the reformulation of the query w.r.t. the *BA* ontology. It has two components: the Expander, which performs the query expansion, and the Unfolder, which performs the query unfolding. Once the execution of the PlayMaker is completed, the output of the Play Maker computation is sent from the BA to the QA with a single message.

**Query Agent:** it performs the following three steps:

**Step 1)** Execution: for each FDAtom (Parallel Execution):

- INPUT: FDAtom
- MESSAGES: from QA to an SINode Agent
- OUTPUT: a view storing the FDAtom result in the SEWASIE DB

*Figure 8. Query processing functional architecture*

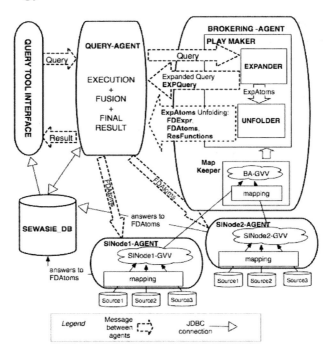

333

**Step 2)** Fusion: For each *EXPAtom* (Parallel Execution):

- INPUT: FDAtoms, FDQuery, Resolution Functions
  (a) Execution of FDQuery (Full Disjunction of the FDAtoms)
  (b) Application of the Resolution Functions on the result of (a)
- OUTPUT: a view storing the EXPAtom result in the SEWASIE DB

**Step 3)** Final result:

- INPUT: Output of the Fusion step
  (a) Execution of the Expanded Query
- OUTPUT: Final Query result view stored in the SEWASIE DB.

At this point, the query agent sends a message to the query tool interface with the name of the final query result.

**SINode Agent:** One of the modules of the SINode Agent, the SINode query manager, executes queries on the SINode GVV, with a query processing similar to the one explained at the BA level.

## THE WISDOM PROJECT

The WISDOM (Web intelligent search based on DOMain ontologies) project aims at studying, developing and experimenting methods and techniques for searching and querying information sources available on the Web. The main goal of the project is the definition of a software framework that allows computer applications to leverage the huge amount of information contents offered by Web sources (typically, as Web sites). In the project it is assumed that the number of sources of interest might be extremely large, and that sources are independent and autonomous one each other. These factors raise significant issues, in particular because such an information space implies heterogeneities at different levels of abstraction (format, logical, semantics). Providing

effective and efficient methods for answering queries in such a scenario is the challenging task of the project.

WISDOM represents an architectural evolution w.r.t. SEWASIE as:

- data extraction from large Web-sites will be automatically performed by generating wrappers (Crescenzi et al., 2001);
- a loose integration among the information offer of a network of semantic peers is provided;
- semantic mappings among the ontology of semantic peers will be discovered;
- peer-to-peer query processing will be performed on the basis of the inter-peer mappings which are enriched by content summaries which provide quantitative information;
- peer-to-peer query processing takes into account quantitative information to implement execution strategies able to quickly compute the "best" answers to a query.

## WISDOM Architecture

The WISDOM architecture follows a schema-based super-peer network architecture. An overlay network of semantic peer is built in order to allow to retrieve information of interest even outside the semantic peer that received the query. Figure 9 illustrates the main architectural elements that frame such a network. The overall idea is to associate with every semantic peer an ontology *Onti*, which describes the information offered by the semantic peer itself. A network of semantic peers is thus built by defining mappings between the ontologies of a set of semantic peers (we consider binary mappings).

### Semantic Peer

A semantic peer contains a data integration system, which integrates heterogeneous data sources into an ontology composed of an annotated *GVV* and Mappings to the data source schemas. In particular, in the context of the WISDOM project the problem of wrapping large Web sites is faced.

## Automatic Data and Metadata Extraction

A large number of Web sites contain highly structured regions. These sites represent rich and up-to-date information sources, which could be used to populate WISDOM semantic peers. However, since they mainly deliver data through intricate hypertext collections of HTML documents, it is not easy to access and compute over their data.

To overcome this issue, several researchers have recently developed techniques to automatically infer Web wrappers (Arasu & Garcia-Molina, 2003; Chang & Lui, 2001; Crescenzi et al., 2001; Wang & Lochovsky, 2002), that is, programs that extract data from HTML pages, and transform them into a machine processable format, typically in XML. The developed techniques are based on the observation that many Web sites contain large collections of structurally similar pages: taking as input a small set of sample pages exhibiting a common template, it is now possible to generate as output a wrapper to extract data

from any page sharing the same structure as the input samples.

These proposals represent an important step towards the automatic extraction of data from Web data sources. However, as argued in Arasu and Garcia-Molina (2003) and Crescenzi et al. (2001), intriguing issues arise when scaling up from the single collection of pages to whole sites. The main problems, which significantly affect the scalability of the wrapper approach, are how to identify the structured regions of the target site, and how to collect the sample pages to feed the wrapper generation process. Presently, these tasks are done manually. To overcome this limitation, techniques to addresses these issues, making it feasible to automatically extract data from large data intensive Web sites are investigated in the project.

Tijerino, Embley, Lonsdale, Ding, and Nagy (2005) introduces an approach to generating ontologies based on table analysis. Based on conceptual modeling extraction techniques, this approach attempts to (1) understand a table's structure and conceptual content; (2) discover the constraints that hold between concepts extracted from the table; (3) match the recognized concepts with ones from a more general specification of related concepts; and (4) merge the resulting structure with other similar knowledge representations.

*Figure 9. WISDOM semantic peer network*

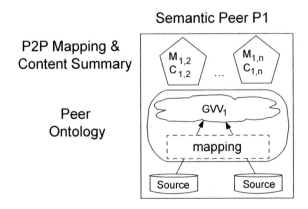
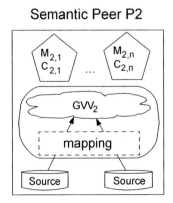

## Peer-to-Peer Mapping and Query Processing

To frame a network of semantic peers we adopt peer-to-peer mappings: a semantic peer-to-peer mapping, denoted $Mi,j$, is a relationship between the ontology $Onti$ of the semantic peer $Pi$, and the ontology $Ontj$ of the semantic peer $Pj$. Intuitively a mapping $Mi,j$ allows the rewriting of a query posed against the ontology $Onti$ into a query over the ontology $Ontj$. Mappings will be computed by extending the methodology for p2p semantic coordination presented in Bouquet, Serafini, and Zanobini (2005). The main idea is that discovering mappings across ontologies requires a combination of lexical knowledge, world knowledge and structural information (how concepts are arranged in a specific ontology). This information is used in a methodology called semantic elicitation, which builds a formal representation of the information represented by a concept in an ontology (or even more frequently in "light weight ontologies," like for example taxonomies of classification schemas). This formal representation is then used to infer relations with formal objects in other ontologies by automated reasoning systems (e.g., SAT solvers, description logic reasoners, and so on); the choice of the system depends on the expressiveness of the representation which is built during the elicitation phase.

By means of peer-to-peer mappings, a query received by a given peer can be ideally extended to every peer for which a mapping is defined. However, it is not always convenient to propagate a query to any peer for which a mapping exists. For example, it can be inefficient to include in the query processing peers having a limited extension of the concepts involved by the query. To overcome this issue, every peer-to-peer mapping has associated a content summary. *Content summaries* provides a "profile" of a data source by means of quantitative information; peer-to-peer query processing takes into account such quantitative information to implement execution strategies able to quickly compute the "best" answers to a query. Given a pair of semantic peers for which it exists a peer-to-peer mapping, the content summary associated with such a mapping provides quantitative information about the extension of the concepts in the source ontology that can be found through the mapping in the target semantic peer. A simple example of the information provided by a content summary is the cardinality, in the target peer, of the concepts of the source ontology.

In Bergamaschi, Bouquet, Ciaccia, and Merialdo (2005) more details about wrapping large Web sites, and optimizing the distribution of queries by providing content summaries are provided.

## Browsing the Results

Visualizing the results of a WISDOM query faces a common problem, that is, to guarantee a satisfactory compromise between expressivity and domain-independence when visualizing and navigating RDF-like graphs. Here expressivity is meant as the capability of delivering an intuitive representation of knowledge and some tailored navigation primitives to end-users working in a given application domain, while domain-independence aims to accomplish a high degree of reusability. Most existing tools, such as KAON (Volz, Oberle, Staab, & Motik, 2003) and WebOnto (Domingue, Motta, & Garcia, 1999), favour domain-independence and represent entities in a way that is closer to the abstract form used to formally define them. This is familiar to knowledge engineers but not to domain experts. Indeed, though domain-specific formalisms have a lower degree of reusability, they provide graphically richer constructs allowing for a representation that is closer to how entities appear in the application domain. The approach developed in WISDOM to address this issue is to build a flexible framework in which reusable components realize the domain-independent tasks in generating a friendly presentation of a piece of knowledge (Golfarelli, Proli, & Rizzi, 2006).

## RELATED WORK

Several projects have been developed in the area of Semantic Web and semantic search engines.

### Semantic Search Engines Exploiting Annotation of Web Pages

The SHOE (Simple HTML Ontology Extension) project, begun in 1995, was one of the first efforts to explore languages and tools that enable machine understandable Web pages (Heflin, Hendler, & Luke, 2003; Hendler & Heflin, 2000). In the SHOE framework, HTML pages are annotated via ontologies to support information retrieval based on semantic information; the annotated pages are gathered into a knowledge base by a Web-crawler; the knowledge base can be queried using the ontology as a schema for query forming.

The major challenge of this project is designing a query tool that can exploit the power of a Knowledge Base (SHOE uses description logics as its basic representation formalism) while still being simple enough for the casual user; when the query returns very few or no results, it provides a tool to automatically convert the formal query into a suitable query string for a Web search engine to find relevant pages. A major problem of the SHOE search tool is that it limits search within one class and it is hard to specify query conditions on multiple nodes at the same time. For example, a query such as "find people whose research group is in a specific department" cannot be specified.

OntoBroker (Decker, Erdmann, Fensel, & Studer, 1999) is in many ways similar to SHOE and allows the annotation of Web pages with ontological metadata. A broker architecture called Ontobroker with three core elements: a query interface for formulating queries, an inference engine used to derive answers, and a webcrawler used to collect the required knowledge from the Web has been implemented. It provides a more expressive framework for ontologies, using Frame-Logic for the specification of ontologies, annotation data and queries. OntoBroker includes a query interface and a hyperbolic viewer, which implements a visualization techniques to allow a quick navigation in a large ontology (Decker et al., 1999) but searching with complicated conditions is limited.

### P2P Architecture for Semantic Search Engines

Due to the scale of the ever-growing Web, classic centralized models and algorithms can no longer meet the requirements of a search system for the whole Web. Decentralization seems to be an attractive alternative. Consequently Web retrieval has received growing attention in the area of peer-to-peer systems. Decentralization of Web retrieval methods, in particular of text-based retrieval and link-based ranking as used in standard Web search engines have become subject of intensive research. This allows both to distribute the computational effort for more scalable solutions and to share different interpretations of the Web content to support personalized and context-dependent search. In Aberer and Wu (2005) a review of existing studies about the algorithmic feasibility of realizing peer-to-peer Web search using text and link-based retrieval methods is presented. A common framework consisting of architecture for peer-to-peer information retrieval and a logical framework for distributed ranking computation that enables interoperability of peers using different peer-to-peer search methods is described.

ALVIS (Buntine & Taylor, 2004) is an ongoing research project founded by the European Community under the IST programme. Its goal is the design, use and interoperability of topic-specific search engines with the goal of developing an open-source prototype of a peer-to-peer, semantic-based search engine. Existing search engines provide poor foundations for semantic-based Web operations, and are becoming monopolies, distorting the entire information landscape. Their approach is not the traditional Semantic Web approach with coded metadata, but rather an engine that can build on content through semi-automatic analysis.

## CONCLUSION

In this chapter we discussed some ingredients for developing Semantic Search Engines based on Data Integration Systems and peer-to-peer architectures.

With reference to Data Integration Systems, we refer to the list outlined in the invited tutorial on "Information Integration" by Lenzerini (2003) to point out the topics covered by the chapter.

First of all, the strength of the proposed approach is a solution to the problems of "How to construct the global schema (*GVV*)" and "How to model the mappings between the sources and the global schema." MOMIS follows a semantic approach to perform extraction and integration from both structured and semistructured data sources. Semantics means semantic annotation w.r.t. a lexicon ontology and Description Logics background. MOMIS follows a GAV approach where the *GVV* and the mappings among the local sources and the *GVV* are defined in a semi-automatic way.

Regarding the problem of "Data extraction, cleaning and reconciliation" we adopted some *ad-hoc* solutions, such as *Data Conversion Functions*, *Join Conditions* and *Resolution Functions*. For more general solutions and a deeper discussion, the reader may refer to the bibliography given in the Building the SEWASIE System Ontology section.

Regarding "The querying problem: How to answer queries expressed on the global schema" we overview the major aspects involved in querying the system, that is, the query building, the query reformulation and the query evaluation process, in the context of query reformulation for the two-level data integration system. For query evaluation we showed a "naive approach," implemented in an agent-based prototype.

As the proposed architecture is a distributed architecture distributed query processing techniques can be applied (Kossmann, 2000) for a state of the art. Moreover, query optimization algorithms and efficient query execution engines for data integration systems have been proposed (Ives, Florescu, Friedman, Levy, & Weld, 1999).

Regarding the problem of "(Automatic) source wrapping," we discussed *Extraction of Local structured Source* and we implemented wrappers for structured sources. In WISDOM, data extraction from large Web-sites will be automatically performed by generating wrappers (Crescenzi et al., 2001) will be performed.

Other open problems and issues not covered by this chapter are: "Limitations in accessing the sources" and "How to incorporate the notion of data quality (source reliability, accuracy, etc.)."

## REFERENCES

Aberer, K., Cudrè-Mauroux, P., & Hauswirth, M. (2003). The chatty Web: Emergent semantics through gossiping. In *Proceedings of the ACM-WWW Conference* (pp. 197-206).

Aberer, K. & Wu, J. (2005). Towards a common framework for peer-to-peer Web retrieval (LNCS 3379, 138-151). Springer.

Abiteboul, S., Buneman, P., & Suciu, D. (2000). *Data on the Web: From relations to semistructured data and XML*. Morgan Kaufmann.

Alesso, H.P. (2002). *Semantic search technology*. Retrieved October 24, 2006, from http://www.sigsemis.org/columns/swsearch/SSE1104

Ananthakrishna, R., Chaudhuri, S., & Ganti, V. (2002). Eliminating fuzzy duplicates in data warehouses. In *Proceedings of the VLDB Conference* (pp. 586-597).

Androutsellis-Theotokis, S. & Spinellis, D. (2004). A survey of peer-to-peer content distribution technologies. *ACM Computer Survey, 36*(4), 335-371.

Arasu, A. & Garcia-Molina, H. (2003). Extracting structured data from Web pages. In *Proceedings of the ACM SIGMOD Conference* (pp. 337- 348).

Baumgartner, R., Flesca, S., & Gottlob, G. (2001). Visual Web information extraction with lixto. In *Proceedings of the VLDB Conference* (pp. 119–128).

Beneventano, D., Bergamaschi, S., Guerra, F., & Vincini, M. (2003). Synthesizing an integrated ontology. *IEEE Internet Computing, 7*(5), 42-51.

Beneventano, D., Bergamaschi, S., Lodi, S., & Sartori, C. (1988). Consistency checking in complex object database schemata with integrity constraints. *IEEE Transactions on Knowledge and Data Engineering, 10*(4), 576-598.

Beneventano, D. & Lenzerini, M. (2005). *Final release of the system prototype for query management.* Sewasie, Deliverable D.3.5. Retrieved October 24, 2006, from http://www.dbgroup. unimo.it/prototipo/paper/D3.5 final.pdf

Bergamaschi, S., Bouquet, P., Ciaccia, P., & Merialdo, P. (2005). Speaking words of wisdom: Web intelligent search based on domain ontologies. In *Proceedings of the Italian Semantic Web Workshop.*

Bergamaschi, S., Castano, S., Vincini, M., & Beneventano, D. (2001). Semantic integration of heterogeneous information sources. *Data Knowledge Engineering, 36*(3), 215-249.

Bernstein, P.A., Giunchiglia, F., Kementsietsidis, A., Mylopoulos, J., Serafini, L., & Zaihrayeu, I. (2002). Data management for peer-to-peer computing: A vision. In *Proceedings of the WebDB Workshop* (pp. 89–94).

Bertossi, L.E. & Chomicki, J. (2003). Query answering in inconsistent databases. In J. Chomicki, R. van der Meyden, & G. Saake (Eds.), *Logics for emerging applications of databases* (pp. 43–83). Springer.

Boley, H. (2002). *The Semantic Web in ten passages.* Retrieved October 24, 2006, from http://www.dfki.uni-kl.de/~boley/sw10pass/sw10pass-en.htm

Bouquet, P., Serafini, L., & Zanobini, S. (2005). Peer-to-peer semantic coordination. *Journal of Web Semantics, 2*(1), 130-145.

Buntine, W.L. & Taylor, M.P. (2004). Alvis: Superpeer semantic search engine. In *Proceedings of the EWIMT Workshop* (pp. 49-58).

Calì, A., Calvanese, D., Di Giacomo, G.D., & Lenzerini, M. (2004). Data integration under integrity constraints. *Information Systems, 29*(2), 147-163.

Calvanese, D., Di Giacomo, G.D., Lembo, D., Lenzerini, M., & Rosati, R. (2004). What to ask to a peer: Ontolgoy-based query reformulation. In *Proceedings of the KR Conference* (pp. 469-478).

Castano, S., Ferrara, A., Montanelli, S., Pagani, E., & Rossi, G. (2003). Ontology-addressable contents in p2p networks. In *Proceedings of the Semantics in Peer-to-Peer and Grid Computing Workshop*, Budapest, Hungary.

Catarci, T., Dongilli, P., Mascio, T.D., Franconi, E., Santucci, G., & Tessaris, S. (2004). An ontology based visual tool for query formulation support. In *Proceedings of the ECAI Conference* (pp. 308-312).

Chang, C.-H. & Lui, S.-C. (2001). Iepad: Information extraction based on pattern discovery. In *Proceedings of the WWW Conference* (pp. 681–688).

Chaudhuri, S., Ganjam, K., Ganti, V., & Motwani, R. (2003). Robust and efficient fuzzy match for online data cleaning. In *Proceedings of the ACM Sigmod Conference* (pp. 313-324).

Crescenzi, V., Mecca, G., & Merialdo, P. (2001). RoadRunner: Towards automatic data extraction from large Web sites. In *Proceedings of the VLDB Conference* (pp. 109-118).

Decker, S., Erdmann, M., Fensel, D., & Studer, R. (1999). Ontobroker: Ontology based access to distributed and semi-structured information. In *Proceedings of the IFIP Conference* (pp. 351-369).

Domingue, J., Motta, E., & Garcia, O. (1999). *Knowledge modelling in webOnto and OCML: A user guide.* Milton Keynes, UK: Knowledge Media Institute.

Dongilli, P., Fillottrani, P.R., Franconi, E., & Tessaris, S. (2005). A multi-agent system for querying heterogeneous data sources with ontologies. In *Proceedings of the SEBD Italian Symposium* (pp. 75-86).

Franconi, E. & Ng, G. (2000). The i.com tool for intelligent conceptual modeling. In *Proceedings of the KRDB Workshop* (pp. 45-53).

Galindo-Legaria, C.A. (1994). Outerjoins as disjunctions. In *Proceedings of the ACM-SIGMOD Conference* (pp. 348-358).

Di Giacomo, G.D., Lembo, D., Lenzerini, M., & Rosati, R. (2004). Tackling inconsistencies in data integration through source preferences. In *Proceedings of the ACM IQIS Workshop* (pp. 27-34).

Greco, G., Greco, S., & Zumpano, E. (2003). A logical framework for querying and repairing inconsistent databases. *IEEE Transactions on Knowledge Data Engineering, 15*(6), 1389-1408.

Golfarelli, M., Proli, A., & Rizzi, S. (2006). M-FIRE: A metaphor-based framework for information representation and exploration. In *Proceedings of the WEBIST Conference* (pp. 332-340).

Gong, L. (2001). Industry report: JXTA: A network programming environment. *IEEE Internet Computing, 5*(3), 88-95.

Halevy, A.Y. (2001). Answering queries using views: A survey. *VLDB Journal, 10*(4), 270-294.

Halevy, A.Y., Ives, Z.G., Madhavan, J., Mork, P., Suciu, D., & Tatarinov, I. (2004). The piazza peer data management system. *IEEE Transactions on Knowledge Data Engineering, 16*(7), 787-798.

Heflin, J., Hendler, J.A., & Luke, S. (2003). Shoe: A blueprint for the semantic Web. In *Spinning the Semantic Web* (pp. 29-63). MIT Press.

Hendler, J. & Heflin, J. (2000). Searching the Web with SHOE. In *Proceedings of the AAAI Workshop - Artificial Intelligence for Web Search* (pp. 35-40).

Ives, Z.G., Florescu, D., Friedman, M., Levy, A.Y., & Weld, D.S. (1999). An adaptive query execution system for data integration. In *Proceedings of the ACM-SIGMOD Conference* (pp. 299-310).

Kossmann, D. (2000). The state of the art in distributed query processing. *ACM Computing Surveys, 32*(4), 422-469.

Lenzerini, M. (2002). Data integration: A theoretical perspective. In *Proceedings of the ACM-PODS Conference* (pp. 233-246).

Lenzerini, M. (2003). *Intelligent information integration.* Tutorial at the IJCAI Conference.

Lin, J. & Mendelzon, A.O. (1998). Merging databases under constraints. *International Journal of Cooperative Information Systems, 7*(1), 55-76.

Löser, A., Naumann, F., Siberski, W., Nejdl, W., & Thaden, U. (2003a). Semantic overlay clusters within super-peer networks (LNCS 2944, 33-47). Springer.

Löser, A., Siberski, W., Wolpers, M., & Nejdl, W. (2003b). *Information integration in schema-based peer-to-peer networks* (LNCS 2681, 258-272). Springer.

Madhavan, J. & Halevy, A.Y. (2003). Composing mappings among data sources. In *Proceedings of the VLDB Conference* (pp. 572-583).

Miller, A. (1995). WordNet: A lexical database for English. *Communications of the ACM, 38*(11), 39-41.

Myllymaki, J. (2002). Effective Web data extraction with standard XML technologies. *Computer Networks, 39*(5), 635-644.

Naumann, F. & Haussler, M. (2002). Declarative data merging with conflict resolution. In *Proceedings of the MIT-IQ Conference* (pp. 212-224).

Rajaraman, A. & Ullman, J.D. (1996). Integrating information by outerjoins and full disjunctions. In *Proceedings of the ACM-PODS Conference* (pp. 238-248).

Tijerino, Y., Embley, D., Lonsdale, D., Ding, Y., & Nagy, G. (2005). Towards ontology generation from tables. *WWW Journal, 7*(3), 261-285.

Tejada, S., Knoblock, C.A., & Minton, S. (2001). Learning object identification rules for information integration. *Information Systems, 26*(8), 607-633.

Tempich, C., Harmelen, F.V., Broekstra, J., Ehrig, M., Sabou, M., Haase, P., Siebes, R., & Staab, S. (2003). A metadata model for semantics-based peer-to-peer systems. In *Proceedings of the SemPGRID Workshop.*

Ullman, J.D. (1997). Information integration using logical views. In *Proceedings of the ICDT Conference* (pp. 19-40).

Volz, R., Oberle, D., Staab, S., & Motik, B. (2003). KAON SERVER: A Semantic Web management system. In *Proceedings of the WWW Conference.*

Wang, J. & Lochovsky, F. (2002). Data-rich section extraction from html pages. In *Proceedings of the WISE Conference* (pp. 313-322).

Wiederhold, G. (1993). Intelligent integration of information. In *Proceedings of the ACM SIGMOD Conference* (pp. 434-437).

Yang, B. & Garcia-Molina, H. (2003). Designing a super-peer network. In U. Dayal, K. Ramamritham, & T.M. Vijayaraman (Eds.), *Proceedings of the IEEE ICDE Conference* (pp. 49-56).

## ENDNOTE

[1] The Object Database Management Group (ODMG) is a consortium of companies defining standards for object databases (www.odmg.org).

# APPENDIX I: THE ODLI3 LANGUAGE

ODLI3 is an extension of the object-oriented language ODL (Object Definition Language) (www. service- ODLI3 architecture.com/database/articles/odmg_3_0.html) which is a specification language used to define the interfaces to object types that conforms to the ODMG object model is introduced for information extraction. ODLI3 extends ODL with constructors, rules and relationships useful in the integration process both to handle the heterogeneity of the sources and to represent the GVV. In particular, ODLI3 extends ODL with the following relationships that express intra- and inter-schema knowledge for source schemas:

Intensional relationships. They are terminological relationships defined between classes and attributes, and are specified by considering class/attribute names, called terms:

- Synonym of (SYN) relationships are defined between two terms ti and tj that are synonyms;
- Broader terms (BT) relationships are defined between two terms ti and tj, where ti has a broader, more general meaning than tj. BT relationships are not symmetric.
- Narrower terms (NT) relationships are the opposite of BT relationships.
- Related terms (RT) relationships are defined between two terms ti and tj that are generally used together in the same context in the considered sources.

An intensional relationship is only a terminological relationship, with no implications on the extension/compatibility of the structure (domain) of the two involved classes (attributes).

Extensional relationships. Intensional relationships SYN, BT (NT) between two class names and may be "strengthened" by establishing that they are also extensional relationships:

- Ci SYNext Cj: this means that the instances of Ci are the same of Cj;
- Ci BText Cj: this means that the instances of Ci are a superset of the instances of Cj;

The standard IS-A relationship Ci IS-A Cj of object-oriented languages implies the extensional relationship Cj BText Ci .

ODLI3 also extends ODL with the addition of integrity-constraint rules, which declaratively express if-then rules at both the intra- and inter-source level. ODLI3 descriptions are translated into the Description Logic OLCD - Object Language with Complements allowing Descriptive cycles - (Beneventano, Bergamaschi, Lodi, and Sartori, 1988), in order to perform inferences that will be useful for semantic integration.

Because the ontology is composed of concepts (represented as global classes in ODLI3) and simple binary relationships, translating ODLI3 into a Semantic Web standard such as RDF, DAML+OIL, or OWL is a straightforward process. In fact, from a general perspective, an ODLI3 concept corresponds to a class of the Semantic Web standards, and ODLI3 attributes are translated into properties. In particular, the IS-A ODLI3 relationships are equivalent to subclass-of in the considered Semantic Web standards. Analyzing the syntax and semantics of each standard, further specific correspondences might be established. For example, there is a correlation between ODLI3's simple domain attributes and the DAML+OIL DataTypeProperty concept. Complex domain attributes further correspond to the DAML+OIL ObjectProperty concept (www.w3.org/TR/daml+oil-reference).

# About the Authors

**Jorge Cardoso** joined the University of Madeira (Portugal) in 2003. He previously gave lectures at University of Georgia (USA) and at the Instituto Politécnico de Leiria (Portugal). Dr. Cardoso received his PhD in computer science from the University of Georgia (2002). In 1999, he worked at the Boeing Company on enterprise application integration. Dr. Cardoso was the co-organizer and co-chair of the first, second, and third International Workshop on Semantic and Dynamic Web Processes. He has published over 60 refereed papers in the areas of workflow management systems, Semantic Web, and related fields. He has also edited three books on Semantic Web and Web services. Prior to joining the University of Georgia, he worked for two years at CCG, Zentrum für Graphische Datenverarbeitung, where he did research on computer supported cooperative work.

\* \* \*

**Wil M. van der Aalst** is a full professor of information systems at the Technische Universiteit Eindhoven (TU/e) having a position in both the Mathematics and Computer Science Department and the Technology Management Department. Currently he is also an adjunct professor at Queensland University of Technology (QUT) working within the BPM group. His research interests include workflow management, process mining, Petri nets, business process management, process modeling, and process analysis.

**Rama Akkiraju** is a senior technical staff member at the IBM T.J. Watson Research Center in New York. She holds a master's degree in computer science and an MBA from New York University, Stern School of Business. Since joining IBM Research in 1995, she has worked on agent-based decision support systems, electronic market places and business process integration technologies. She is interested in applying artificial intelligence techniques to solving business problems. Her current focus is on Semantic Web services and its applications to services science.

**Christos Anagnostopoulos** received his BSc (2002) in informatics from the informatics and tele-communications department at the University of Athens, Greece, and his MSc (2004) in the division of advanced information systems from the same department. He is currently a PhD student in the same department and member of the Pervasive Computing Research Group. He has been involved as software designer and developer in several national and European R&D projects (E2R, PoLoS). His research interests are in the areas of knowledge representation, context awareness, pervasive computing, and Semantic Web.

**Grigoris Antoniou** is a professor of computer science at the University of Crete, and head of the Information Systems Laboratory at FORTH, Greece. Previously he held professorial appointments at Griffith University, Australia, and the University of Bremen, Germany. His research interests lie in knowledge representation and reasoning, and their applications to the Semantic Web, e-commerce and ubiquitous computing. He is author of over 150 technical papers, and co-author of three books, among them *A Semantic Web Primer*, MIT Press 2004. In 2006 he was elected ECCAI Fellow by the European Coordinating Committee for Artificial Intelligence.

**Domenico Beneventano**, PhD, is an associate professor at the Faculty of Engineering of the University of Modena e Reggio Emilia (Italy). His research activity has been mainly devoted to the application of Description Logics reasoning techniques to databases for knowledge representation and query optimiza-tion. His current research interests are in the area of intelligent information integration and Semantic Web and are devoted to the development of techniques for building a common ontology, that is, an integrated view of the information in the separate sources, and for query processing and optimization.

**Sonia Bergamaschi** is a full professor at the Information Engineering Department at the University of Modena and Reggio Emilia (Italy). She leads the database research group (DBGROUP). Her research activity has been mainly devoted to the application of description logics techniques to databases for consistency check and query optimization. Her current research efforts are devoted to intelligent infor-mation integration and Semantic Web. She has published about 90 international journal and conference papers and was the coordinator of research projects founded by the European Community and Italian MURST, CNR, ASI institutions. She has served on the committees of international and national data-base and AI conferences.

**Jos de Bruijn** received his master's degree in technical informatics from the Delft, University of Technology, The Netherlands (2003). Since 2003 he has been employed as a researcher at the Digital Enterprise Research Institute (DERI), at the University of Innsbruck, Austria. His research interests include Semantic Web (services, languages), logical languages, logic programming and nonmonotonic reasoning. He is the author of over 15 peer-reviewed publications in the area of Semantic Web (Services) languages, including several journal publications. He has been actively involved in European funded projects COG, SEKT, DIP, and Knowledge Web, and has been the project lead for SEKT at DERI. He is a member of the WSMO and WSML working groups and of the W3C RIF working group.

**Rogier Brussee** is a researcher at the Telematica Institute in Enschede The Netherlands since 2000. He is working on multimedia content management, information extraction, and applications to knowledge management. He received a PhD in mathematics at Leiden university and subsequently held positions at the universities of Oxford, Bayreuth, and Bielefeld.

**Oscar Corcho** is working as a Marie Curie fellow at the Information Management Group of the University of Manchester. His research activities include the semantic grid, the Semantic Web and ontology engineering. He participates at the EU FP6 IST project OntoGrid (FP6-511513). He has participated in the HALO project (funded by Vulcan, Inc.), and in the following EU IST projects from FP5 and FP6: Esperonto (IST-2001-34373), DIP (FP6-507483), HOPS (IST-2002-507967), SWWS (IST-2001-37134), Knowledge Web (IST-2003-507482), and OntoWeb (IST-2000-25056). He has published the books *Ontological Engineering* and *A layered declarative approach to ontology translation with knowledge preservation* and over 30 journal and conference/workshop papers.

**Martin Doerr** has studied mathematics and physics from 1972-1978 and holds a PhD in experimental physics from the University of Karlsruhe, Germany. Since 1990 he has been principle researcher at FORTH. He is leading the development of systems for knowledge representation and terminology management. He has actively participated in a series of national and international projects for cultural information systems. He is chair of the working group of ICOM/CIDOC, which is currently finalizing ISO/DIS 21127, a standard for the semantic interoperability of digital cultural information. His research interests are ontology engineering, ontology-driven systems, and terminology management.

**Marlon Dumas** is senior lecturer at Queensland University of Technology and fellow of the Queensland Government ("Smart State" Fellow). He received a PhD (2000) from University of Grenoble (France). His research interests are in the areas of business process management, application integration and e-commerce technology.

**Ana Lisete Nunes Escórcio** is a teacher at the Exact Science and Technology Department of Carmo's School in Câmara de Lobos, Madeira. She teaches TIC (Tecnologias de Informação e Comunicação) and AIB (Aplicações Informáticas B). She graduated in language and knowledge engineering (2002) at the University of Lisbon, science faculty. She is doing her MS in software engineering at Madeira's University. Her current research interests include ontology building in general, Semantic Web, ontology reuse, methodologies for building ontologies and knowledge engineering. She is developing an ontology for e-tourism following a methodology that she will present on her thesis.

**Dieter Fensel** was awarded a doctoral degree in economic science from the University of Karlsruhe (1993) and he received his Habilitation in Applied Computer Science (1998). Throughout his doctoral and postdoctoral career, he has held positions at the University of Karlsruhe, the University of Amsterdam, and the Vrije Universiteit Amsterdam. In 2002, he took a chair at the Institute for Computer Science, Leopold Franzens University of Innsbruck, Austria. In 2003, he became the scientific director of the Digital Enterprise Research Institute (DERI) at the National University of Ireland, Galway, and in 2006 he became the director of the Digital Enterprise Research Institute (DERI) at the Leopold Franzens University of Innsbruck, Austria. His current research interests are centered around the usage of semantics in 21st century computer science. He has published over 200 papers via scientific books and journals, conferences, and workshop contributions. He has co-organized over 200 academic workshops and conferences. He is an associate editor of various scientific journals and publications. He has been an executive member in various international research project such as the IST projects ASG,

Asia-Link Eastweb, COG, DIP, enIRaF, Esperonto, eSwan, h-TechSight, IBROW, InfraWebs, Knowledge Web, Multiple, MUSING, Ontoknowledge, Ontoweb, SALERO, SEEMP, SEKT, SemanticGov, SUPER, SWAP, SWING, SWWS, SystemOne, TransIT, TripCom, and Wonderweb, the SFI funded project DERI-Lion—as well as the Austrian projects DSSE, Grisino, LBSCult, RW2, SemBiz, Sense, Semantic Web Fred, SemNetMan, and TSC. He has supervised over 50 master theses and PhDs and is a recipient of the Carl-Adam-Petri-Award of the faculty of economic sciences from the University of Karlsruhe (2000).

**Mariano Fernández-López** is director of the Software and Knowledge Engineering Department at the Technical School of Universidad San Pablo CEU, and he belongs to the Ontological Engineering Group at Universidad Politécnica de Madrid. His current research activities include, among others: methodologies for ontology development, ontological foundations and ontology mappings.

**Thomas Franz** is a doctoral student in the Computer Science Department at the University of Koblenz-Landau, Germany. His research interests include knowledge representation, personal information management, and the Semantic Web. He received his MSc in computer science from the University of Freiburg.

**Asunción Gómez-Pérez** (BA) is associate professor at the Computer Science School at Universidad Politécnica de Madrid, Spain. She has been the director of the Ontological Engineering Group since 1995. The most representative projects she is participating in are: SEEMP (FP6-23747), NeOn (FP6-027595), OntoGrid (FP&-511513) as project coordinator, Knowledge Web NoE (Fp6-507482) acting as scientific vice-director, Esperonto (IST-2001-34373), the OntoWeb (IST-2000-25056) thematic network, and also the MKBEEM (IST-1999-10589) project. She has published more than 25 papers on the above issues. She is author of one book on ontological engineering and co-author of a book on knowledge engineering. She has been codirector of the summer school on ontological engineering and the Semantic Web in 2003, 2004, 2005. She is program chair of ESWC'05 and was of EKAW'02.

**Stathes Hadjiefthymiades** received his BSc, MSc, PhD degrees (in computer science) from the University of Athens (UoA), Athens, Greece and a joint engineering-economics MSc from the National Technical University of Athens. Since 1992, he was with the consulting firm Advanced Services Group. He has been a member of the Communication Networks Laboratory of the UoA. He has participated in numerous EU-funded and national projects. He served as visiting assistant professor at the University of Aegean,in the information and communication systems engineering department. He joined the faculty of Hellenic Open University (Patras, Greece) as an assistant professor. Since December 2003 he has belonged to the faculty of the informatics and telecommunications department, UoA, where he is an assistant professor. His research interests are in the areas of mobile/pervasive computing and networked multimedia applications. He is the author of over 100 publications in the above areas.

**Arthur H.M. ter Hofstede** received his PhD in computer science from the University of Nijmegen in The Netherlands (1993). Currently he works as an associate professor at the School of Information Systems of the Faculty of Information Technology of Queensland University of Technology in Brisbane, Australia. He is co-leader of the BPM group in the faculty. His main research interests are in the conceptual and formal foundations of workflow. He is committed to the Workflow Patterns Initiative and the Yet Another Workflow Language (YAWL) Initiative.

**Uwe Keller** is a researcher in semantic technologies and their applications at the Digital Enterprise Research Institute (DERI), Leopold Franzens University, Innsbruck, Austria. He joined DERI in 2004. His current research interests include logics and automated reasoning with specific focus on Semantic Web applications, semantic description of Web services and the exploitation of such descriptions in applications, knowledge-based applications, formal methods and semantically-enriched service-oriented architectures. He has been involved in various European and national research projects, such as DIP, Knowledge Web, ASG, RW2 and SENSE. At DERI, he is responsible for the Semantic Engineering Support Environment (SEnSE) project. Uwe holds a diploma degree in computer science which he attained at the University of Karlsruhe (TH), Germany. He has been awarded with a scholarship by the Studienstiftung des deutschen Volkes in 1996.

**Marcello La Rosa** received his MS in computer engineering from Politecnico di Torino, Italy (2005). His thesis focused on model-based development based on collaborative business processes. As part of his degree, he also investigated the areas of Service Oriented Design and Web Services standards. He is currently a PhD candidate within the Business Process Management Group of the faculty of IT, at the Queensland University of Technology, Australia. His PhD research concerns the tool-based design and configuration of reference process models, with the aim of facilitating their workflow-based execution.

**Rubén Lara** is R&D director at Tecnología, Información y Finanzas (TIF). He is an active researcher in the area of Semantic Web services and service-oriented architectures. Before joining TIF, he has worked as a researcher in the area of Semantic Web services at the Digital Enterprise Institute (DERI), where he has also been the managing director of the EU Network of Excellence Knowledge Web. Rubén obtained his MS in computer science at Universidad Autónoma de Madrid in 2001, and received the First National Award in computer science by the Spanish Ministry of Culture and Science, as well as the Special Award in computer science at Universidad Autónoma de Madrid.

**Holger Lausen** obtained his diploma in computer science at Flensburg University of Applied Science in 2003. His diploma thesis discussed the integration of Semantic Web technologies and document management systems. Before he joined the Digital Enterprise Research Institute (DERI) as researcher in April 2003, he carried out various software development projects in Germany and abroad. Within DERI, he has been project coordinator for the Semantic Web Enabled Web Services (SWWS) project, a European research project pioneering in the field of Web services and is coordinating the Austrian funded project Reasoning with Web services (RW2). Continuing his engagement in semantic portal technologies, he currently is active in the field of ontology and language design for the annotation of services.

**Miltiadis Lytras** holds a PhD from the management science and technology department of the Athens University of Economics and Business (AUEB), Greece. His research focuses on e-learning, knowledge management and Semantic Web with more than 35 publications in these areas. He is guest co-editing a special issue in *International Journal of Distance Education Technologies* with the special theme

*Knowledge Management Technologies for E-learning* as well as one in *IEEE Educational Technology and Society Journal* with the theme *Ontologies and the Semantic Web for E-learning*.

**John A. Miller** is a professor of computer science at the University of Georgia. Dr. Miller received a BS (1980) in applied mathematics from Northwestern University and an MS (1982) and PhD (1986) in information and computer science from the Georgia Institute of Technology. Dr. Miller is the author of over 100 technical papers in the areas of database, simulation, bioinformatics and Web services. He has been active in the organizational structures of research conferences in all these areas. He has served in positions from track coordinator to publications chair to general chair of the following conferences: Annual Simulation Symposium (ANSS), Winter Simulation Conference (WSC), Workshop on Research Issues in Data Engineering (RIDE), NSF Workshop on Workflow and Process Automation in Information Systems, and Conference on Industrial & Engineering Applications of Artificial Intelligence and Expert Systems (IEA/AIE). He is an associate editor for *ACM Transactions on Modeling and Computer Simulation* and *IEEE Transactions on Systems, Man and Cybernetics* as well as a guest editor for the *International Journal in Computer Simulation and IEEE Potentials*.

**Chun Ouyang** received her PhD in computer systems engineering from the University of South Australia (2004). She currently works as a postdoctoral research fellow at the faculty of information technology in Queensland University of Technology, Australia. Her research interests are in the areas of business process management, process modeling and analysis, Petri nets, and formal specification and verification.

**Richard Scott Patterson** is a master's candidate of computer science at the University of Georgia. His research interests include Web services, Semantic Web, security, and access control. Patterson received his BBA in economics form the University of Georgia (1998). Patterson worked for five years in IT architecture and security consulting before returning to pursue his master's degree.

**Cary Pennington** has worked in the computer science field for eight years. He received his undergraduate degree in computer science from Furman University (under Dr. Ken Abernethy), where he focused on software engineering. He is currently completing the master's program in computer science at the University of Georgia (with Dr. John Miller) focusing on Semantic Web services. His work was on the automatic deployment time binding of Web services into a composite business process. This should aid nontechnical personnel in using the advances that are being made by researchers to develop efficient and accurate processes. He is committed to making the world of information technology easier to understand and use for the people it will benefit the most. Before continuing his education at UGA, Cary worked at Ipswitch Inc., a leading internet software company, on the WS-FTP product and IMail Server.

**Stanislav Pokraev** is member of the scientific staff at Telematica Instituut, the Netherlands since 2001 and PhD candidate in the computer science department of the University of Twente, the Netherlands since 2003. Previously he was employed as Scientific Researcher at KPN Research, the Netherlands. Stanislav holds a MSc (Eng) degree from the Technical University of Sofia, Bulgaria. His main expertise is in the area of information modeling and service-oriented business integration.

**Christoph Ringelstein** is a doctoral student in the Computer Science Department at the University of Koblenz-Landau. His research interests include Web service annotation, knowledge representation, ontology engineering, and the Semantic Web. He received his diploma in computer science form the University of Koblenz-Landau.

**Steffen Staab** is professor for databases and information systems in the computer science department at the University of Koblenz-Landau and heads the research group on information systems and the Semantic Web (ISWeb). His research interests range from ontology management and ontology learning to the application of Semantic Web technologies in areas such as multimedia, personal information management, peer-to-peer and Web services. In particular, he is interested in combining sound and diligent ontology engineering with real world concerns and applications. His research activities have led to over 100 refereed publications and 7 books as well as to the foundation of Ontoprise GmbH, a company focusing on the exploitation of Semantic Web technology.

**Vassileios Tsetsos** received his BSc in informatics from the Informatics and Telecommunications Department at the University of Athens, Greece, in 2003, and his MSc in the division of communication systems and data networks from the same department in 2005. He is currently a PhD student in the same department and member of the Pervasive Computing Research Group. He has been involved as software designer and developer in several national and European R&D projects (PoLoS, PASO, PENED). His research interests are in the areas of mobile and pervasive computing, Semantic Web, ontological engineering, and Web applications.

**Ivan Vasquez** is an MSc candidate at the LSDIS Lab (University of Georgia), working under the direction of Dr. John Miller. He joined the program in Fall 2002, while working at the Information Technology Outreach Services (ITOS) of the University of Georgia. Given his industry experience with relational databases and middleware, his research has been focused on conducting transactions on service oriented computing environments. The product of his research resulted in OpenWS-Transaction, a METEOR-S module that can be easily adopted by existing applications to deliver reliable Web service transactions.

# Index